SMYTH'S

LECTURES ON THE FRENCH REVOLUTION.

VOL. I.

AMS PRESS
NEW YORK

LECTURES

ON

THE HISTORY

OF

THE FRENCH REVOLUTION.

BY

WILLIAM SMYTH,

PROFESSOR OF MODERN HISTORY IN THE UNIVERSITY OF CAMBRIDGE.

NEW EDITION.

WITH THE AUTHOR'S LAST CORRECTIONS, AND AN ADDITIONAL LECTURE.

IN TWO VOLUMES.

VOL. I.

O 3180

LONDON:

HENRY G. BOHN, YORK STREET, COVENT GARDEN.

MDCCCLV.

Reprinted from the edition of 1855: London

First AMS edition published in 1971

Manufactured in the United States of America

International Standard Book Number:
Complete Set: 0-404-06145-1
Volume I: 0-404-06146-X

Library of Congress Catalog Card Number: 71-175988

AMS PRESS INC.
NEW YORK, N.Y. 10003

CONTENTS.

VOL. I.

UNPUBLISHED LECTURE,

Found among the papers of Professor Smyth, apparently intended to follow Lecture XIV.

GENERAL REFLECTIONS ON THE CAUSES OF THE FRENCH REVOLUTION.

WE may now consider ourselves as having passed through one portion of the History of the French Revolution.

It may not perhaps be amiss to turn round, and at this point survey once more the main events to which we have adverted, consider the various statements we have made, and see whether there are any general conclusions at which we can finally arrive.

I should accomplish a great object if by any recapitulation of this kind I could furnish you with materials for future reflection ; above all, if I could present to you certain land-marks, as it were, to direct your future progress through this great subject.

The opinions of men on the whole, and on every part of it, are various. Are there any which we may venture to adopt as sufficiently reasonable ? I have exhibited before you the views and testimonies of every description of writer and reasoner that I could find. They are often opposed to each other. This could not but be the case. The understandings of men are different ; and so, too, their feelings, their associations, and their situations. We see enough of this on every occasion within our own experience in concerns the most trivial, as in affairs the most important—even to this hour the mighty passions and animosities that were excited by the breaking out and long continuance of the French revolution still agitate mankind. Yet from the beginning of this great convulsion we are now removed to a certain distance, it is possible that of this part of the commencement at least, we may be able to judge.

And it must be observed that if any lessons can be drawn from the earlier periods of these troubles it is these, that are of all others the most important—to prevent revolutions still more than to learn how to conduct them—to acquire timely habits of caution and forethought, of modesty and calmness—to obtain instruction from history, which we do not purchase by our own suffering—to have our existing passions and prejudices, our selfishness and our unreasonableness, awed into silence and subdued and transformed into practical wisdom by meditation on the past.

Now the first observation that I have to offer, or to remind you of, as far as we have hitherto considered the French Revolution, is this—that the lesson for a long part of this period, from the accession, is to be drawn from the faults of the privileged orders, and that it is in the latter part only of this period that it begins to turn, and that it is then to be drawn from the conduct of the patriots.

What did we open with? The very amiable nature and benevolent exertions of the young King.—He was grave, decorous, sensible, modest, pious, virtuous, and deeply interested in the happiness of his people. Such he originally was—such he never ceased to be; no wrongs, no sufferings, no misfortunes ever made him otherwise. He called to his assistance the experience of the Count de Maurepas, and the philosopher the celebrated Turgot. The finances were the great point to be considered. There could be no repose for the monarch, and no reform in the other parts of the administration, till some happy alteration could be effected in this department. And what was the great object that was to be accomplished?—it was this, that the privileged orders should contribute their share to the general expenditure. Now could they ever be persuaded to do so? They never could, never at least till it was too late. And this is the great lesson to be deduced from the early parts of the French Revolution. A lesson, most obvious, most simple, most impressive, from the fatal consequences with which it was attended, but still a lesson, which it is very doubtful whether it will ever have a proper influence upon men of this description; and this, from the prevalence of a particular notion which they convert into a maxim, that if they once begin to concede, they can never afterwards stop; in other words, that there is no advantage in improving their case. Now this is not the conclusion to be drawn from the French Revolution. The king and his ministers had no difficulty but this—the difficulty of obtaining from the privileged orders this concession. While they were endeavouring to obtain it, years the most precious, years within which the revolution might have been prevented, passed away; and when the States General were once called, the concession was too late.

The general reasonings on this subject, of timely concession, of early reform, are very conclusive; they are stated by no one so well as by Mr. Burke, in some of his speeches prior to the French Revolution and not connected with it. But meditate this early part of the French Revolution for yourselves—see what is here the fact; see what experience says. It may indeed be affirmed by some, that nothing could stop the French Revolution. Now there is no subject of human discussion on which something may not be affirmed, and a reasoner of a paradoxical or perverse nature, after having made his affirmation, may move away contented to have said what is agreeable to his fancy or his feelings, and leaving his position to its fate ; but on this occasion it may at least be replied that the best chance of averting the French Revolution was the timely concession we speak of ; that the minds of men got gradually inflamed from year to year ; that the necessity of some change grew more and more urgent ; that the embarrassment of the finances was the great evil to be remedied ; the concession of the privileged orders the only means ; that if men persevere in injustice their opponents will naturally become violent, and may become unjust in their turn ; that if concessions were refused, it was evident the States General might at last be convened ; that they actually had been called for, by one of the members of parliament, twelve years before they were demanded effectively ; and that there could be no wisdom, so far as the privileged orders were concerned, in driving the king and his ministers, or the public, to so dangerous an experiment. But now for the history. The young king summons Turgot to his counsels—very well ; but what does he also do ? by the advice of Maurepas, he recalls the parliaments. These bodies were of a judicial nature, and consisted very much of the privileged orders ; and whatever might be the motives of the old courtier, the measure was a mistake in the king.

But the king was young, and could little suspect the situation in which he and his kingdom were placed ; Turgot, however, the philosophic minister, does what alone was possible, he produces six edicts, in the last of which only the privileged orders are approached ; and how approached ?

The suppression of the horrible *corvées* was attempted ; the roads were to be repaired, and the expenses defrayed by a contribution, from which the privileged orders were not to be exempt ; and this was, it seems, not to be endured.

A clamour arose among the privileged orders, as if every right of property was endangered, and all the marks and distinctions of the ancient monarchy obliterated. The minister was dismissed, and the nobles, the parliaments, and the clergy were triumphant. But how triumphant ? Now certainly this is a part of the subject which, in my second Lecture, I endeavoured to impress upon the attention of my hearers, and which I cannot but now finally leave to your meditation. It belongs to the first part of the subject I have mentioned, the faults of the privileged orders. Another subject of meditation which I would offer to you, is the conduct of the king. I repeatedly propose to my hearers in the course of these lectures to consider, what is the king now to do—in the unhappy circumstances in which he is placed, what measure is he now to attempt ?

You will see him fail, no doubt, from want of decision, from want of character, from want of taking a part in securing the advantages belonging to one mode of conduct, and foregoing the advantages that belong to its opposite. Public men must do this, as indeed must private. We may pass between advantages, as the king too often did, and take hold of neither; but if we seize those on the right, we cannot also have those on the left; and we must make our choice. In the last instance, the king had countenanced Turgot; had committed himself completely, and when the minister's sixth edict only required from the privileged orders what was just and right, young as he was, he should have seen that he was not to give way, and that no minister of intelligence and spirit could hope to serve him if he did. But he did give way, and Turgot was dismissed.

M. Necker was next called into administration, and the selection of him was reasonable. He was considered as a man of integrity, and of great skill in matters of finance; but our American War immediately followed, and an interference in it was surely a mistake in the French king and Court, and in all concerned. It is understood indeed, that the king did not make this mistake—but he suffered it to be made. His want of character was here once more fatal; but again, it may be said, he was young.

The influence of the new debt that was contracted in consequence of the war, and the new spirit of liberty that was caught by the officers and the people of France, you will easily see, may be fairly stated as highly contributing to make the nation revolutionary; indisposed to those counsels of moderation, forgetful of those ancient feelings of loyalty and attachment to the person of their monarch, which were so particularly necessary to Necker and to Louis at this critical juncture.

Publicity of accounts, and representation of the people, were in truth the expedients of Necker to remedy the miseries of France. The publicity of the accounts he effected, and was never forgiven for it by the Court. He had hoped thus to persuade, or morally to oblige, the privileged orders to contribute to the public burdens; and with respect to the representations of the country, he endeavoured to avail himself of ancient institutions; he revived the idea of Turgot, and formed a scheme of provincial administrations of a less popular nature than his predecessors; less objectionable, therefore, and very well fitted to have warded off the measure of calling together the States General.

But the parliaments saw that their influence would be affected —the privileged orders, their immunities and prerogatives; the old minister, Maurepas, united with them, the king once more wanted character, once more gave way, and Necker was dismissed. These are the great and more early faults of the king. You are now then to consider, how far Necker is to be blamed for all the evils of the French Revolution, and how far the court and the privileged orders themselves. The privileged orders of a country and the reasoners that are attached to them, expect that a patriot opposition, or a patriotic minister, is to have no sympathy with the public; no interest in the present or future improvement of the community; to be as torpid and indifferent as themselves; and when he is otherwise, and when he states his complaints and offers his remedies, he is met by them with every resistance, every accusation and suspicion, that can irritate him; every perverseness, that has a tendency to render his plans either doubtful or dangerous, by forcing him to seek for other assistance; and when the people get inflamed, when bolder spirits naturally interfere and take the business out of his hands, and out of the hands of the first reformers, it is he and these first reformers that are criminated and never forgiven; though the first and great criminality has been all along with the privileged orders themselves, and though the first patriots are, of all concerned, those in whose characters sense and virtue are most to be found.

I should hope, that when you come to consider this part of the general subject of the History of the French Revolution, you will think with me, that if Necker had succeeded in his first administration, the Revolution might have been adjourned, and probably would have been prevented; and that if he had continued to succeed, the king's mind might have been gradually opened, and even the minds of the privileged orders, to the crisis in which they were placed. But in his first administration, Necker did not succeed. He fell a victim to the privileged orders, and with Necker departed in the year 1781, as I must still contend, all real hope for any peaceful alterations in the objectionable institutions, inconvenient usages, and unfortunate opinions of the inhabitants of this great country.

The fault, however, was the fault of the privileged orders, and I really must add, the fault too of those who are considered by many as the patriots of the country, the members of the parliament of Paris. Calonne followed—a doubtful character, it must be confessed, as a man and as a minister. But in justice I must add, and you will yourselves, I think, agree with me hereafter, that his efforts were directed to the right point—that of obtaining in the first place assistance for the finances from the privileged orders. But with all his skill, his management, his address, his courtierlike qualities, this could not be done—all were vain. The parliament, the intriguing Bishop of Toulouse, the clergy, the people of consequence, even the queen, were against him; at last he seemed to have no friend, and he was obliged to fly. No doubt this minister was too sanguine; but to whom is the fault, is the guilt of the calamities that followed, to be imputed? to the minister, who has depended too confidently on the disinterestedness, the sense of justice, the reasonableness of the privileged orders; or to those privileged orders themselves, who in a great crisis of public affairs, have been wanting to their country in such necessary qualities?

I must here repeat the two conclusions which I before offered to your consideration—they follow from the fate and fortunes of Calonne—1st, that *no* minister is to collect bodies of men together, with no other dependence than the reasonableness of his own views —2nd, that bodies of men show an adherence to their prejudices and selfish interests, and are often perfectly infatuated and blind; which in situations of a critical nature is generally fatal to them.

And now you will observe that another most precious year was lost—and you must ask yourselves, what could possibly be the meaning of the parliaments and the privileged orders in thus thwarting every measure that the king could propose; in doing everything to offend him; everything to force him to a measure so unexampled, and so perilous, as the call of the States General?

The privileged orders have no right to complain of the revolution; the fault was not Necker's or the king's, but theirs, that it took place at all. The king wanted character, no doubt, but what could he do?—how was he to manage these privileged orders? Of the parliaments indeed, the conduct is totally inexplicable; it was they themselves that called for the States General —it was they themselves that said to their monarch in July 1787, that they wished to see the whole nation assembled. Here then the lesson begins to alter. This call for the States General must surely have been made by men of patriotic feelings—by D'Espremenil and others, and, therefore, the lesson is not one directed to the privileged orders, but to their opponents; it is that lesson, of all the most common, yet which has been for ever repeated in vain—namely, that though men are not to stand by indifferent, and see their country miserable, they are to proceed step by step; they are not to depend upon vague, general, sanguine estimates, but to be precise, cautious, and practical; above all, to fly from everything that tends to revolution; because revolutions are not favourable to civil freedom; they break up society, and then the violent alone bear sway.

These parliaments and their early patriots, instead of giving up their own immunities from taxation, favouring the provincial assemblies, and uniting themselves to the king in every measure that he and his minister proposed, for the gradual improvement of the system of government and the situation of the country, called aloud for the States General.

Now this was not proceeding in the manner of rational reformers and intelligent statesmen; it was to go on, without considering where. Not weighing consequences—but satisfied with taking a measure, rather than estimating what might be the result; like the youthful, the giddy, the inexperienced, who, caught by some splendid generality, adopt it and take their chance.

This was very unworthy of the grave and probably good men of which these bodies were composed, and this must, I think, be considered, and I therefore mention it, as one of the warnings of the French Revolution—the warning, remember, that is held out by the inconsiderate and sanguine, or perverse and factious conduct of the parliaments in the period between the two administrations of Necker in '81 and '88.

You will next direct your attention to the conduct of the minister who succeeded Calonne. The observations of the Baron de Grimm, who resided in Paris at the time, are very remarkable. I quoted them to you, they were very unfavourable to the minister M. de Brienne, the Archbishop of Toulouse. This minister, like the rest, totally failed, and he at last thought it prudent to retire; the consequence was, that Necker returned in August 1788. Fifteen months had been lost during the administration of Brienne. This loss of time was always a subject of great lamentation to Necker: I confess I think, justly. The minds of men had been left to inflame, the government had in the interval lost character more and more. This loss of character was from the first the secret and greatest evil of all, even more than the disorders of the finances, for hence arose from time to time the growing prevalence of the new opinions—and these new opinions, during the absence of Necker, had an opportunity afforded them of becoming more universal and more violent.

And it is now that begin what were probably the faults of Necker. He seems to have been quite overpowered by the force of public opinion; to have had no object but to ascertain it; no plan but to submit to it.

Of the intentions of M. Necker there can be no doubt. He wished for the happiness of France, was anxious to establish its civil and religious liberties, yet was certainly faithful to the king and to the monarchy; but he must have seen that the Court would do nothing but under the operation of fear, and it must have been his secret meaning to put them under a moral coercion, to a certain extent, as far as the cause of liberty required, and as far as the safety of the monarchy permitted. This moral coercion he thought necessary, yet at the same time he meant well to the king and the monarchy. These being conjointly his views, it seems to have been clearly a mistake to summon the Notables together, as he did, to desire them to deliberate on such questions as these, "How the States General that had been called were to be composed," "the form of convocations," "the order of elections," "the manner in which were to be held the different assemblies, which were to give instructions to their deputies;" in short, to abandon to the consequences of a public discussion, to surrender up to others, formally and voluntarily, the regulation of those important points, which it was the natural office of the king to decide himself. Necker chose (he thought it necessary) to be fortified by public opinion in everything he did. I conceive that all regular statesmen will hold him to have wanted on this occasion, not merely political courage, but common prudence.

Not only should Necker never have called the Notables together to give their opinion, but he should have settled the two great points, as of course, by the king's authority—they should have appeared in the king's declaration—first, whether the number of the Tiers Etat should equal the number of the other two conjointly; secondly, whether these orders were to vote in different houses or in one, by orders or by head. These points he should have settled (as if by the king's authority) as he thought expedient, not necessarily as the popular party might at the time wish. He himself and the king and the privileged orders, the clergy, and the nobility, standing upon the broad ground of the king's authority, would have maintained the contest against the new opinions with more advantage than they were ever likely afterwards to do upon any other; and whether they had succeeded or not, this was the only chance for any temperate movement in favour of the happiness of France, for any real improvement to be effected by the progress of the revolution.

This is a great question in the history of the revolution. M. Necker has defended himself; his celebrated daughter has in part done the same; but I consider the general apprehension on the subject to be right, and I conceive the general conclusion from the experience of the facts of this part of the history to be this, that the only chance which the rulers of mankind have, is to settle points of a delicate or doubtful nature before popular bodies meet, particularly bodies called, as it were, for the first time, unused to the exercise of power, and uncertain in their composition; that any subsequent discussion, from the inflammable nature of all public bodies, and the sympathy of the public, must otherwise turn against them.

This again, as in other instances before, seems a very obvious conclusion, one that might be derived from mere reasoning, without any experience. Yet must such conclusions be mentioned to you, as now to be deduced from the testimony of events; politics being a science that has to do with human beings and their nature and probable conduct, and therefore a science of all others the most uncertain.

I have dwelt at considerable length in my Lectures on this point of the History of the Revolution. I exhibited to you the topics of M. Necker's defence. The whole is very deserving of your study, for it is always, as I cannot too often repeat, worthy of study, how revolutions might have been prevented, how efforts for the advancement of liberty may be made, and the public peace not sacrificed. The violent can easily make a commotion and thus endanger civil liberty, rather than promote it—it is only for the wisest, as well as the best of men, to succeed in enterprises of this most noble, but difficult nature.

Necker, as you know, granted the double representation, *i. e.* that the Tiers État should equal in number both the clergy and the nobility together. There can be little doubt that he depended on the influence he should himself have on the States General, when assembled ; that he conceived it would be sufficient if he showed them, as he was satisfied he could, what it was just and right and wise for them to do. But in this he was deplorably mistaken ; and in subsequent instances again mistaken. I apprehend that Necker, in his retirement (in Switzerland), at the close of his career and of his life, would have warned any young statesman not to depend, for the management of mankind, on the cogency of reason, or the prevailing nature of truth, of right, and of justice. Such considerations have their weight ; sooner or later they may be expected to prevail, when the discussions have passed from one generation to another ; but Necker, I think, would have been taught by what he had himself experienced, to warn any practical statesman, that reason, the love of truth, a sense of propriety, of right, and of justice, were but *part* of the constitution of human nature, and not the *whole* of it—were but elements to be taken into account in the consideration of any given case, but not of force *alone* to decide it.

There were three great leading descriptions of public men about the time of Necker's first recall, the close of the year 1788—parties that long continued : first, the most violent adherents of the Court, and the advocates of the old opinions ; again, the more violent supporters and propagators of the new opinions—the ultras on each side ; and again, between the two, the first reformers, the first friends of freedom—those who wished well to France and to liberty, but to its monarchy also and its king.

Now the great question, you will easily see, was, how were these last to succeed, how were these (the intermediate patriots) to overpower the Court on the right, and not be themselves overpowered by the more violent on the left.

In mixed questions of this kind, people will think differently ; but the patriots who are interesting, the men who are above all respectable, the men of virtue and talents, are these *first* patriots ; and it is *their* failure, it is *their* fall, that disheartens those who wish well to the best interests of mankind ; that affects those who know not how to be wise, if these men were not so ; who know not how they are to stand respectable in the eyes of their country, so as to awe the presumption of demagogues and to stay the headlong passions of the populace, if these could not ; nor know how, on the other hand, by the general weight of their abilities and characters, to attract the confidence of the higher orders, and be protected from suspicion, obloquy, and opposition, if these could not.

All that can be done is, that the mistakes of these men must be noted, that no such mistakes may again be committed by men respectable and virtuous and intelligent as these. The French Revolution has failed, and it is the great calamity of Modern History. Its lessons, therefore, must be observed.

Of these men, Mounier is one of the most distinguished—he has written on the French Revolution, as well as Necker, who is another, and Lally Tolendal.

Now you will consider their views and conduct. It must be confessed that the difficulties of these first patriots were very great. These difficulties you will see the more you consider the nature and character of their opponents. But one thing was certain : it was an intuition of reason, it was a matter of historic experience, that if their differences with the Court were not brought to an amicable conclusion soon after the meeting of the States General, other men would rush forward and throw everything into confusion. In the English history, as they had seen, first came the Falklands and the Hydes, and then Cromwell. We will now observe their conduct. You will remember the unfavourable circumstances under which the States General assembled in May, 1789 ; these circumstances remained for a long time the same, and were in truth most embarrassing ; they were these—the king was indecisive, was amiable, but not fitted to command ; the Court too bigoted to the old opinions ; the populace tumultuous and ferocious.

Now what do the Tiers Etat, the *Patriots*, do? The Tiers Etat began with usurpation ; this must, I think, be confessed. They were determined that the three orders should vote in *one* assembly ; that the vote should be by head, not by order. They called upon the two orders to unite with them, in fact for that purpose only.

But this was usurpation ; themselves to require the other orders to come and verify their powers in *their* particular chamber, and for the ultimate purpose of voting hereafter by head. This was usurpation ; and was this usurpation justified? Men will think differently. They might at the time think it was ; but they may now, perhaps, perceive that it was not. The Court was insincere no doubt, and meant no alteration in the constitution of France that could have satisfied the patriots. No doubt ; but this was not the case with Necker, nor with the king. How then were either of them (the king or Necker) to maintain the cause, whether of freedom or improvement, against the Court, unless the patriots were reasonable and conciliatory ; unless they assisted and justified the efforts and views of Necker and the king by the nature of their conduct? The revolution, it is true, would not have gone on at the expected rate on the supposition of voting by orders ; but much improvement might have been effected in the first place, and most of the best doctrines laid down by the supporters of the new opinions might have obtained admission in the second. Ultimately the leaders of the Tiers Etat, the patriots among the clergy and the nobility, could not but have been willing, and could not but have been able, to provide for future calls of the States General. What was wanting to France but a regular return of constituent bodies? What else, to save the country from the former abuses of the monarchy?

But the king, it may be said, had they once been regularly dissolved, would never have suffered them to appear again. Supposing, however, that they had not usurped power in the way they did, and given their opponents a case against them, could the growing consequence of the middle and lower orders, could the widely increasing prevalence of the new opinions, could the real advancement made in intelligence and knowledge, taking into account also the undoubted benevolence and patriotism of the king—could all these have been really set aside in this manner, so as to produce no subsequent effect for the improvement of the constitution? Can this be fairly supposed?

We must bring candour and temper to the appreciation of these questions of probability, or it will be in vain to read history.

The great lesson of revolutionary periods is, in the first place, that which is addressed to the constituted authorities to concede in time; but to the popular party afterwards the lesson is, not to push their victories too far, to leave their opponents sufficiently in good humour, so situated that they may acquiesce without degradation in any new arrangements or diminutions of their power that may have been introduced.

The Tiers Etat not only assumed the appellation of National Assembly, that is, voted themselves *alone* the proper representatives of the community, but possessed of the authority of it, they actually proceeded to exercise its powers, without the concurrence of the other two orders; and without waiting for the approbation of the king, they issued a decree to declare, that they consented, *provisionally* for the nation, that the taxes and contributions, though now illegally established and levied, should continue to be levied till the day of the separation of the Assembly; after which they were to cease, if not regranted by the Assembly.

This was on the 17th of June. Now you are to consider what had the Court,—above all, what had the king done,—to render such an act necessary.

Was there any fair, open, generous, or even grateful feeling to the king and his ministers displayed by the Assembly on this occasion? If they, the members of the Assembly, once committed themselves, and assumed thus (or so nearly assumed) the sovereignty of the State, how could they afterwards retreat? Where was then the wisdom of such an assumption? Was this, or was it not, the direct way to bring everything to the issue of a civil war?

Certainly it was not for measures like these that they were called together by the king, nor for measures like these that they were sent to the States General by their constituents.

These acts of usurpation in the Tiers Etat you will, therefore, make the subject of your meditation. They are very important circumstances in the history of the revolution. I consider them as fatal mistakes.

In return for these measures, some counter-measure from the ministers of the king was now to be expected. This counter-measure was attempted by Necker. He formed his measure of the 23rd of June, but upon a system of prudence and forbearance; and now you are to observe that we have here another great crisis in the history of the revolution—Necker's measure of the 23rd of June. For myself I lay great stress upon it, and I hope you will consider it. The Court, you will find on this occasion, were once more unable to resist the temptations of their situation, for, at a second sitting of the cabinet, they altered the declaration, which Necker at the first sitting had proposed, and to which the king would have acceded. Necker had made the king's declaration sufficiently favourable to the interests of the crown, for by this declaration the sovereignty assumed by the Assembly would have been silently nullified; but this was not enough to satisfy what, no doubt, were the natural, though then very unseasonable, feelings of the Court; and therefore the king was made by the declaration, as altered by the Court openly, to produce his authority, and by that authority openly nullify and pronounce illegal the former decrees of the Assembly. This was harsh and irritating, and, on the whole, most unwise. But though I admit this, I still contend that the declaration was left such that the Assembly should have received it, and on the basis of it proceeded heartily and earnestly with the king to the general settlement of the concerns of the kingdom, and the improvement and adjustment of the constitution of the State.

The declaration was, on the whole, a great outline of a system of government; it was an offer of the Court and the king to the patriots—the extent of the concessions that could be admitted by the retainers of the old opinions to the patrons of the new.

This, I must repeat, is a great crisis in the history of the revolution—one of the greatest; I must leave it to your consideration. What I contend for is, that the main points were, even by this Court declaration, secured, and that therefore the Assembly should have closed with the king, and taken its chance of making hereafter any smaller improvements that might appear desirable; the main points, I must affirm, were secured, because no new tax was to be levied, no old one prolonged, without the consent of the representatives of the nation. When the right of the purse and a new meeting of the States were thus secured, what further concession was necessary? The public finances were to be submitted to the examination of the States. The clergy and the nobility were to be sanctioned by the king in the renunciation of their pecuniary privileges, which they had already promised. These were the main points; but there were others determined fairly enough, existing circumstances considered, in favour of the people; and these were quite sufficient for the Assembly to have proceeded upon, in a spirit of union and conciliation with the king; that he would on his part have acted with sincerity, and perfectly in the spirit and to the effect of his declaration, they could not possibly have doubted. Such are the remarks that I have before made, that I now repeat, and that I must finally leave to your consideration. The declaration to which I thus refer you, as one to which the National Assembly should have acceded, was thought of so lightly by the leaders of the popular party at the time, that it does not seem to have been entertained by them at all, the terms of it not for a moment considered, and the authoritative parts of it, where the king retained the ancient and accustomed language and feelings of a king of France, were alone adverted to both in and out of the kingdom, and adverted to only to be reprehended. Such was the inflammation of the minds of men at that particular season, so ardent and unlimited their hopes, in the supposed happy progress of the new opinions, and the expected labours of the many enlightened men of which the Assembly was composed; and so deep and universal the unfavourable opinion entertained of the ancient institutions and existing government of France. This declaration, then, of the 23rd totally failed—failed, as I conceive, unhappily for the interests of France and of all mankind. To whom, then, is the blame to be imputed? On the whole, the main blame must, on this most important occasion, be imputed to the Tiers Etat, after deducting the blame that rests with the Court, first, for altering Necker's original declaration; and secondly, for making no preparatory efforts with the patriotic leaders for its reception; finally, for a great want of management in the detail, and in the antecedent circumstances of this royal sitting of the 23rd. You will now see that the parties were at issue. The declaration having failed, and such terms as the king and the Court thought they could grant being rejected, nothing remained to the king and Court but to effect, if possible, the dissolution of the Assembly; and this, if it was a possible measure at all, was only so on the supposition of a new one being at the same time called, the declaration published as the case of the king, and troops brought up; but this opportunity was lost, for, instead of any attempt to dissolve the Assembly, the king positively and personally interfered in the dispute between the Assembly and the privileged orders. The king himself was the immediate reason why the union of the remaining part of the clergy, and more particularly of the nobility, was completed—why the Assembly, when thus composed, seemed at last to deserve the title which they had assumed, the title of National Assembly ; but this was an overture of peace on the part of the king, and after this measure it was no longer possible for him to alter his policy, and bring up troops to dissolve the Assembly, unless their conduct gave him some *new* cause of alarm or offence. Nothing, however, of the kind was done by the Assembly, and yet they perceived that the troops were approaching, and the metropolis and their own existence evidently menaced. That the experiment of force was resolved upon, they could not but conclude was the fact. And, on the whole, it appears that, on whatever account and for whatever representations or deceptions to the king, the decision might arise, still, that the fact was, that the trial of force was determined upon. This seems to me the only explanation of the phenomena that now appeared, and this explanation is confirmed by the representations of writers and reasoners whose opinions are decisive.

The Court, however, should have taken it for granted that, if they brought up troops, the Assembly would resist. The Assembly did so. Their part of the contest was executed with great calmness and spirit ; the Court, on the contrary, managed their part with a want of skill that cannot well be explained.

And now it must be observed that, however we may consider the National Assembly as guilty of the first assumptions of power, the first usurpations, and however we may think, that they are answerable for all the calamities that followed, still we find ourselves under the necessity of considering *their* cause as the cause of civil liberty ; still are we obliged to suppose, that the best interests of mankind were brought at last to depend on their being able to maintain their existence in the presence of their country and of Europe. This was, indeed, one of the great objections originally to their usurpations, that, when advanced, they could not well retreat ; that they would provoke the exertions of force against them ; and that, if force once prevailed, their downfall would be probably complete, and no terms be made with them. This seemed the issue to which matters were now brought. Troops were drawn round the Assembly, troops hovered about Paris ; to what purpose, but, on the mildest supposition, to awe the one and eventually to dissolve the other. What chance for liberty, were this once effected ? How was the king to be prevailed upon to call again the States General ? Who was ever again to resist the Court, if the experiment had already failed when made under the most promising circumstances ? Right or wrong, the National Assembly had the wishes and the prayers of the friends of liberty, particularly out of France ; and it is not too much to say, that when the Bastile was taken, Paris armed, the troops drawn off, and seen to be uniting with the people, and when the Court was left alone, helpless and disappointed, the exultation was loud and general ;—it was despotism that was supposed to have fallen, and the acknowledged rights and liberties of mankind to have prevailed.

And now, at a distance of time and place, it is impossible for the historian, while he meditates upon these transactions, to wish that this experiment of force on the part of the Court, about the middle of July, 1789, should have succeeded, and I submit the following three positions to your inquiry and reflection—1st, that it cannot be supposed that the military force under Broglio was only meant to preserve the peace of Paris and leave the deliberations of the Assembly free, as was pretended, and as is even now supposed by Sir Walter Scott in his late publication, a publication that is very able, and that I have no doubt will live ;—2ndly, that, though the Tiers Etat had been guilty of acts of usurpation, such as justified the king in any regular attempts to dissolve them (calling, for instance, another assembly at the same time, and issuing the declaration as his case), still, the opportunity had been lost and a system of peace adopted—and not only this, but the attempt was made by the Court without pledging the king to the cause of freedom in any way whatever, made by open military force, and the cause of the Assembly was thus rendered at once the cause of the liberties of France and of mankind ;—and 3rdly, that the rising of Paris on the 14th of July to save themselves, and prevent their capital from being entered by Marshal Broglio and the troops, was an impulse in itself virtuous, and a measure in itself necessary, and a case perfectly analogous to that of a nation honourably and wisely contending for its independence, and at all events, right or wrong, beating off invasion ; in a word and on the whole, that the language of the Court (I do not say of the king) was insincere, that the triumph of the Assembly was desirable, and that the insurrection of the City was defensive.—These I consider as strong positions, but they are those to which I conceive you will find yourselves obliged to accede, notwithstanding all the subsequent calamities of the French Revolution, if you mean to do justice to all parties, situated as they really were at that most extraordinary crisis.

After these general conclusions, we must advert to another consideration, that of the incapacity of the king's ministers. This must be remembered as a part of the case. No doubt their difficulties were great, as they were to use force, and yet be subject to the interference of the king, who could not bear that force, if likely to be attended with bloodshed, should be used. It was impossible to conceal this tenderness in the character of the monarch from the knowledge of the Assembly, or even of the mob —it was impossible to prevent them from presuming upon it, though it could not be known to what extent it would be carried ; these were difficulties of an intolerable nature to ministers and commanders of the old régime; they were, indeed, not a little irremediable. Still, neither the ministers nor commanders showed any foresight of events, or made proper provision or exertion to direct them; it was evidently their business so to manage, by the unexpected rapidity and decisive energy of their movements, as to put all resistance out of the question; and, if this could not be done, nothing was to be attempted at all.

The character of the king was to be taken into account; they were not to wait to see the Hotel des Invalides emptied of its arms and artillery, the Paris populace provided with weapons, the Bastile stormed, and an insurrection regularly prepared and organized; they were not to remain all this time inactive. This was a crisis which they could not for a moment suppose the king would encounter; he was sure to give way on the slightest appearance of an approaching civil war. And here is another observation, which I have already made and must again repeat, and which I must finally leave with you. It is this, that the great fault and criminality of the Tiers Etat consisted in this, that they had originally usurped power, while the king was a patriot; they had thus reduced everything to an issue of force, though their king was all the time a man of benevolence. They had been hurrying on, inflamed with their new opinions to set aside the old opinions, though their king, who had been the offspring, and was the representative, of those old opinions, had been the very king who had called them together. Had he told them, in the bitterness of a wronged and generous spirit, that they were unprincipled, unfeeling, and ungrateful, what answer could have been made him?

You remember the testimony of Bailly, the philosophic Mayor of Paris; how complete and how unobjectionable; he concludes it with observing, "A king less of a good man, and ministers more skilful, and we should have had no revolution." Nor is it on the character of the king merely as an object of historical curiosity that I thus endeavour to fix your attention; it is for the purpose also of showing you the inflammable nature of political opinions, particularly of new political opinions.

A new constitution was to be given, France was to be regenerated: such was the language of the most enlightened and virtuous men of France, and indeed of Europe, at the time; the king was to go along with the stream, he was to ride upon the surface; this indeed was hoped and was intended, but, sink or swim, he was to go along with it. Such were the feelings of the followers of the new opinions, and to have desired men of this mind, at the time, to be more doubtful of human nature than they were, to be more modest in their estimates of themselves, and more respectful of those who had gone before them, would have been then, as it will be hereafter on similar occasions, to offer music to the deaf and pictures to the blind. I must again refer you to Bailly, uniting, as he did, in all the measures of the Constituent Assembly (in those I have taken upon me to blame.) He confesses, when he comes afterwards to write, to meditate on the past, and to afford instruction to others : " However," says he, " the men of loftier minds, who vote themselves the only children of liberty, may look down upon, as spurious, those who condescend to consider and to calculate, a little more of this sort of philosophic reasoning, would have done us no harm in the Constituent Assembly."

Memoirs, too, have been written by the Marquis de Ferrieres, a nobleman of the old school ; but his representations are quite clear and decisive.

From what you have already understood of the history of the Revolution, you will have already seen how dangerous, how fatal in every respect, it is, to suffer the people visibly and personally to express their opinion on what is going on in the debates of any legislative Assembly. This might have been expected before experience had proved the fact, and you will have hereafter but too abundant reason to come to the same conclusion, from what you are yet to see ; but I mention it now, because I am endeavouring to exhibit to you such general conclusions as the annals of the Revolution in its earlier stages offer down to the 14th of July and a little after, and because all vindications, by facts and experience of theoretic conclusions, should be mentioned. Indeed the more reasonable and respectable leaders were, from the first, aware how dangerous was the liberty allowed to spectators of applauding the speeches and motions made in the Assembly ; but they considered themselves as only supported, and even defended, from the violence of the Court, by the sympathy of the public, which was in this manner announced and made clear to the Court, as well as to themselves.

I mentioned an anecdote in my lecture the other day, told by Bailly, which will, in a few words, for ever keep present to your minds the two great opposite and obvious lessons of the French Revolution—lessons which I have repeated, and shall for ever have to repeat, a thousand and a thousand times. " Why are you not satisfied," said one of the ministers to Bailly, " with this declaration of the king (the declaration of the 23rd June)—Had the king made one like this ten years ago, would it not have been received with enthusiasm ?" " Oh, yes," replied Bailly, " no doubt—ten years ago." " Why, what then does the Assembly want or wish ?" " To do everything itself," returned Bailly ; " not for you to do it." What is the conclusion from this anecdote ? It is evidently this—concessions are put off by the rulers, till the reformers take the management into their own hands ; the former are unreasonable, till the latter become so too, and both perish, certainly the former.

But the question is, whether resistance could have been made to the Revolution. If by resistance be meant entire resistance, such as would have satisfied the Court, or men of their high opinions, without a civil war, whoever had been the monarch and whatever had been his qualities, surely not. And the great question of the whole is, whether even the patrons of the old regimé (I say nothing of the cause of liberty or the interests of mankind) should not even for the sake of maintaining to a sufficient degree their own privileges and consequence, have conceded in time; made their cause more agreeable to the obvious notions of benevolence and justice, and more fit to be respected, at least tolerated, by the advancing intelligence and importance of the rest of the community.

There is one peculiarity about the French people, which exists more in them than in other nations, and which affected their Revolution. It is mentioned very distinctly by the Marquis de Ferrieres and by Madame de Stael, that in Paris, that is France, the direction of public affairs depends not so much on any of the constituted authorities as on what is called fashion. A cry for the States General became the fashion ; they were therefore to be called. The Revolution was the fashion : there was, therefore, to be a revolution. Anything old was out of fashion; there was a call, therefore, for everything that was new. Nothing but the new opinions could be tolerated; and therefore, the king, the Court, the old regime, the nobility, and the clergy, were to be voted out of the world in this great kingdom, and on this great occasion, by a twirl of the features and a shrug of the shoulders. No doubt the sentiment lay deeper in minds more respectable ; the government had lost all character but for the sort of frivolity just mentioned ; it was not easy to find a remedy, and, ridiculous as the cause may seem, it must be borne always in the minds of my hearers as one that contributed to the misfortunes of France and of Europe. Again, I believe that no sane mind can in the slightest degree conceive the fermentation that existed in the minds of the people of Paris from the time of the meeting of the States General. Men are not employed in Paris as they are in London. It is observed by foreigners that every one in London has an air of business and occupation ; every one seems, as they call it, to be on full trot ; and with the exception of the West End of the town, where the helpless, loitering children of fashion and frivolity are to be found, this is certainly the case ; everything in London is bustle and business ; but each man is intent upon his own, and he who gives out that he is intent upon that of the public, is at first more likely to be received by the suspicion or sneer of sensible people than by their sympathy. Paris, on the contrary, seems everywhere the resort and rendezvous of the idle. No difficulty there to find an audience, to create a group at least, and, from the theatrical nature of every Frenchman, fury and violence in the gestures, the language, the opinion, and the measure proposed, were quite matters of course.

The theatrical and excitable nature of the French people will be, therefore, a point that you will bear away as one belonging to this great drama of the French Revolution, and, though one as not peculiarly, yet as very particularly, belonging to it. You will remember, too, that the representations of the Marquis de Ferrieres, one of the old school, are quite clear and decisive on all the main points connected with the 14th of July. For instance, that the dissolution of the Assembly was intended; that force was to be employed; that the language of the Court and the advisers of the king was insincere; and finally, that all Frenchmen looked upon the cause of the National Assembly as their own, as the cause of freedom and all the best interests of the country.

Again, from his account, and from the account of others, the existence of the Orleans faction, as it is called, must be admitted, and considered as one of the most effective causes of the failure of the Revolution. There are men not only of designing, desperate characters, but men who delight in mischief, mischief for its own sake; and such men must be taken into calculation, by all those patriots on the one side, and all those rulers on the other, who really mean well.

These men, and all men like these, were certainly very different from those who were the first patriots and movers of the French Revolution; but the failure of the Revolution, and the crimes and calamities by which it was attended, have enabled those who love not liberty to confound them together, have indisposed even the wise and the good to all projects of reform. This, however, is to run into an extreme on the other side; and this observation, though so very obvious, has so little effect on our conduct that I have taken every pains to illustrate the more early portion of the Revolution, those periods where the characters of distinguished men are at issue; and I have done this to a degree perhaps of tediousness, anxious to produce an impression on the minds of my hearers of a sound and rational nature, deduced from a careful consideration of the faults on each side—the first unfeeling resistance of the privileged orders, which caused the impatience of the patriots; and the intemperance of the patriots which caused the violence of the Court and privileged orders. Virtuous and moderate men certainly sometimes prompted and sometimes countenanced those measures which led to the destruction of the ancient monarchy. How this could happen is the great subject for your inquiry and meditation, and the more honourably you are animated with the love of your own country, and the love of mankind, the more interesting will the subject become. The political faults and mistakes of rulers and governors are easily seen—original selfishness, and, if necessary, cruelty; but it is not so easy to observe with accuracy the faults and mistakes of the patriots of a country. The great fault, in the instance of the French patriots, was that of not acting in a spirit of conciliation with the Court.

This is always the fault of patriots, and this, therefore, is an observation which I must leave to your consideration. Patriots should do anything rather than suffer the question to become a question of force. If the appeal be once made to violence, the violent must bear sway.

In the instance before us, it cannot be properly said that it was the Court that hurried anything to an issue of force by bringing up the soldiers, for, on the contrary, it was the Tiers Etat, that, by a system of encroachment and usurpation from the first moment of their meeting, began the attack on the Court. No doubt they thought this was necessary to the establishment of liberty; we contend that it was not; that, on the contrary, it was fatal to all reasonable hopes of it, and this is the question for the student to consider hereafter.

The unfortunate Louis, it is understood, was often reading the history of the great struggle in our own country, the history of the times of Charles I. It does not appear to me that this was sufficiently done by the virtuous patriots of the Tiers Etat. With us, the love of civil liberty, by the assistance of the religious principle, became the most violent enthusiasm; in France, the same love of civil liberty, assisted by the hope and ardour of the new opinions, became the most violent enthusiasm also;—but the leaders neither observed the frightful nature of all enthusiasm, nor the different character of the two monarchs—their own temptations to violent counsels—their real security while Louis was their king in his personal character.

It is very true that the faults and mistakes of the popular leaders may be explained, may be understood, may be even excused, but they must be for ever lamented, and they must not be concealed that they may not be repeated; their situation was novel, the times were very extraordinary, the new opinions were very intoxicating, the proceedings of the Court were, even after the meeting of the States General, very injudicious and exasperating, the power of the Court was naturally overrated, the applauses of the people and of the country were very animating; vanity was easily mistaken for patriotism, and rashness for wisdom.

There seemed no apprehension on the one side (the part of the Court) of what the progress of the human mind and the influence of the new opinions required; and on the other part (of the patriots) no sense of the lessons of caution that were to be drawn from the experience of the past.

Such are the general observations which I would now finally leave to the consideration of my hearers; they are those general conclusions which, whether many of them might appear obvious to the human understanding before or not, is of no consequence, if they are those which are supported now by the facts of the French Revolution, as far down as the crisis that took place in July, 1789. If they are those that grow out of the events down to that period, then they are the proper lessons of history, and, as such, worthy your attention. Scenes like these are in their incidents deeply interesting and affecting; the minds and the feelings of every one will be sufficiently eloquent while perusing them; they need not be presented to the view by any particular description, or recommended by any variety or strength of colouring. The historian or the lecturer may consider himself as having accomplished every object if he can but offer, in the course of his statements, remarks that may tend to save society hereafter from similar failures of the good, from similar atrocities of the bad. Neither those who rule, nor those who would reform, have, on the occasion of the French Revolution, the slightest reason to plume themselves on their particular merit or success; the whole is a lesson of moderation, the necessity of mutual sacrifices, the folly of expecting forbearance and magnanimity, wisdom and virtue, in our opponents, while we exhibit none in ourselves.

I now conclude: I have endeavoured to present to you in this lecture the main events of the French Revolution down to the end of July, 1789. I have recapitulated such general conclusions as I had made in the preceding lectures, such as I thought might reasonably be drawn from these events. The middle of the month of July, 1789, I consider as an epoch in this memorable history, by the proceedings that then took place; the king and the ancient monarchy and ancient constitution of France were, in fact, surrendered to the National Assembly, and not to the National Assembly only, but to the National Assembly in conjunction with the armed inhabitants of Paris. It now remained to be seen what was to be the fate of that king and ancient monarchy and constitution, what were to be the views of that National Assembly, what sort of constitution they would form, and how far they were or were not to be themselves controlled by that power of the people to which they so much owed their triumph.

LECTURES

ON THE

FRENCH REVOLUTION.

LECTURE I.

LOUIS XIV.

*The two following Lectures were originally delivered immediately after
the Lectures on the Revolution of 1668.*

1810.

WE have been now long engaged in the history of England,
which it was impossible to leave, while the civil and at last the
religious liberties of the country were at issue.

But we may at length turn to the continent, and inquire what
had been in the mean time the history of France.

We are supposed to have left the French history at the death
of Henry IV. The monarchy of France grew up from small beginnings, from the constant accession of one province after another, to the central province, of which Paris was the capital;
in this manner it swelled out at last into that great kingdom,
which of all others has had the most influence on the affairs of
Europe. Of this monarchy it was Henry IV. that must be
considered as amongst the most distinguished founders; it was
he who combined and compressed its discordant parts into a
whole; who first harmonised to a sufficient degree its jarring
civil and religious interests by the mildness of his counsels and
the vigour of his administration. He appeared at the precise
period when the want of such a man was most urgent; and with
serious faults in his private, and such defects in his public
character, as we have noticed, he has always been (and not very
unnaturally) the idol of the French people.

The next interval is from that event to the death of Mazarin,
when Louis XIV. assumed the reins of government himself, and
became his own minister. This was an interval of about half a
century, from the middle of the reign of James I. in our own
history to the Restoration. During this time, in England, the

VOL. I.

B

constitution had been struggling through its difficulties in the strange manner we have seen ; and it might have been hoped that the constitution of France would have made some similar advance to regularity and amelioration. But this was not the case ; and so forgotten were all the best interests, so dissipated and misdirected were all the energies of this great nation, that it is difficult for any one, not a native, even to read the narratives of their historians.

Louis XIII. came to the crown at the age of nine, and, though the son of the great Henry, remained through life only a fit object of tutelage. Louis XIV. became king when only five years old. So that it is the history of the first favourites, and it is the reigns of Richelieu and Mazarin that we are to read, not of the kings of France.

The whole, therefore, as might be expected, is a tissue of inexplicable intrigue, which no patience can well unravel, and which it were not worth the labour to unravel, if the attempt were practicable. Whoever succeeded, or whoever failed, the queen consort or the queen mother, the minister or the nobility, the Italian favourite or the prince of the blood, the intriguer in the court or the intriguer in the parliament and in the mob of Paris, the people were equally forgotten, and the constitution of the kingdom equally neglected. The authority of the crown, the grandeur of France, and her weight in the politics of Europe, are the only objects deserving of attention which the annals of France have now to offer, even when the objects are of the most dignified nature ; the public good, in every rational sense of the word, seems never to have been within the comprehension of any functionary, or any one description of men in the state.

In reading the history of France, the Abbé de Mably, an author of strong democratic feelings, may perhaps have accustomed us to expect too much ; but, with the story of England fresh in the memory, it is impossible not to be impatient on the subject of the civil liberties of France ; impatient to observe, that by no prince or minister, at any period or in any shape, any proper representative body, or any fair approach to it, could be created or suffered to exist ; even the great Henry, though he called the States General together, in his conversation with his courtiers made light of their authority.

The first surprise that an English student meets with, on turning to consider this period, is to find that there is no history of the ministers, Richelieu and Mazarin, not even of Richelieu, that has obtained any literary reputation. The lives that are quoted are those by Aubery, which are represented by Voltaire as very fit for the purposes of information; but it will not, I think, be found an easy task to read them. There is a life of Richelieu by Le Clerc, which is considered as very accurate, and may therefore, like the former, be consulted: but this work is not esteemed in France the work of a good writer, or of a man capable of forming political views.

With regard to Mazarin, it is quite a specimen of the times, of the minister, and of the people, that a sort of history of him has been manufactured out of the different satires, epigrams, and occasional pieces of pleasantry which appeared in the course of his administration, arranged in the order of the events to which they refer.

The memoirs of these times that have been drawn up and published with and without names are innumerable. Of original works, the best are those of M. De Motteville, M. De Montpensier, Cardinal De Retz, Guy Joly, Rochefoucault, M. De la Fayette, La Faire, Gourville, and St. Simon; these are read, particularly the Memoirs of De Retz. From original works like these, the following histories have been drawn up: L'Intrigue du Cabinet, Louis XIV. sa Cour et le Régent, par D'Anquetil; L'Esprit de la Fronde, not by D'Anquetil, as supposed; these last are the books to which I think it best to refer you.

The memoirs of De Retz are always read; but, notwithstanding their general liveliness, and the sagacity of the maxims with which they abound, the reader will do well to choose out of the pages such as promise well. For a continued scene of intrigue, which cannot be supposed fairly represented by one who was himself the soul of it, which from its complexity it is impossible to understand, and of which the object seems only to have been whether an Italian favourite, a man of like subtlety and intrigue with the author himself, should or should not be the minister of the country; a picture like this, whatever be the ability of the artist, soon loses its attraction; and the work, even while entertaining and instructive, for the reasons I have mentioned, seldom rises to the merit of historical instruction.

The better to judge of this period, and of what may be expected from the accounts given of it by the French writers, the English reader may, in the first place, look at the history as given in different chapters in Russell's Modern History; he may next find an account sufficiently detailed in the Modern Universal History, with all the French Works referred to in the margin; and lastly, he may consider all that Voltaire, no incompetent judge when the history of France is concerned, has thought it necessary to say on this part of his subject, in the one hundred and seventy-fifth and one hundred and seventy-sixth chapters of his Essay on the Manners and Spirit of Nations; when to all these have been added the animated observations of the Abbé de Mably, the reader will be able, I expect, without further research, to form an estimate of the whole sufficient for all the purposes of real instruction.   The chapters in Russell, then, and those in the Modern Universal History and in Voltaire, with the Abbé de Mably, may be sufficient; or, finally, the French work L'Intrigue du Cabinet presents a narrative which an English reader may go through with considerable interest in many parts, and on the whole without fatigue, and it is quite circumstantial enough for the most regular reader of history.

But while these sheets are going to press, I perceive that new assistance has been offered to the English reader, and I have had an opportunity of reading the late work of Mr. James on the Life and Times of Louis XIV.; the two first volumes are dedicated to that part of the history which preceded his formal accession to the throne; great diligence seems to have been employed by the author, and I know not how the student can so readily find, as in these pages, all that he need wish to know of the intrigues of Cardinal De Retz, the war of the Fronde, the efforts made to remove Cardinal Mazarin from the administration of the government, and the struggles of the minister, with the assistance of Anne of Austria, the queen mother, to retain it. Condé and Turenne give some dignity to the scene, by their appearance in it; but it is still a miserable scene, tedious and perplexing from its petty intrigues and the total want of any elevated views or patriotic objects in those who were the principal actors in it. We may be grateful to Mr. James for having, notwithstanding, made an interesting work, and for having endeavoured to enable us to understand their movements, and having on this account consulted all the memoirs that relate to them, and compared and judged of their results with candour and ability.   His general conclusion may be adopted, that during the wars of the Fronde, neither De Retz, nor Condé, nor Turenne, nor Bouillon, nor La Rochefoucault, nor Beaufort, nor the Duke of Orleans had any other design but to serve their vanity, their interest, their pride, or their resentment;—that, on the contrary, there really did exist with the court party a great and permanent object, the maintenance of the royal authority; for this the queen and all her partisans struggled throughout the whole of the contest, and without securing it Mazarin could not rule with any effect; and this unanimity with regard to their object gave ultimate predominance to the royal party.

The work that is most known and quoted, more particularly by English readers, is La Vassor; it must be consulted, especially when any decision is to be formed about the conduct of the Huguenots or Louis XIV., but it is too long and tedious, and embraces too wide a range. La Vassor was a French refugee, and is not liked by the French critics and writers, chiefly, I suspect, on account of the freedom and propriety of his remarks. The description of his work by Voltaire, in his account of the writers of the age of Louis XIV., will, to an English ear, sound rather like praise, than the censure which seems intended.

In England, during the period we are now considering, the public disturbances were connected with the public interests; so, on the continent, the religious interests every where, but in France, had a reference to the civil interests of the contending parties. In France, on the contrary, the constitution of the country seemed little concerned in the public disputes; and when the great Henry and Sully were removed, this unfortunate country was doomed to feel how wide is the difference between a good king or minister and a good constitution of government. These men, great and good as they were, and patriotic as they might think themselves, had left no public assembly to represent the nation. The States General had been suffered to fall into disuse, or when summoned, only appeared an unwieldy mass, torn asunder by internal jealousies, and partial interests, and without any public views. The parliament, in the mean time, could not exercise the authority of the community without evident usurpation. There remained, therefore, on the stage of public affairs, the sovereign, the princes of the blood, and the nobles, the Huguenots, the intriguers in and out of Paris, and the court and court favourites. The intriguers and the court contending with the princes of the blood, and the nobles for the plunder of the public; the nobles, when foiled, ready to set up for sovereign-princes in their own domains, or join the arms of Spain; the Huguenots always feeling or apprehending infractions of the edict of Nantes, and therefore exposed to be driven or led aside into new civil and religious wars by every enemy of the court or state; and the power of the crown, the object of the general veneration and regard, converted by force, or by fraud, to serve the private purposes of all parties in their turn; an afflicting spectacle this, and a striking proof of the value of the representative assemblies of a nation in every era of society, from the rudest to the most refined. Of this period, as I have mentioned, the two distinguished men are Richelieu and Mazarin.

Richelieu, who first appears, is evidently fitted for a scene like this in many most important respects; but he either did not comprehend the whole of his high office, or did not live to perform it. The first supposition seems nearest the truth; his objects were the grandeur of France and the force of the monarchy. The permanent happiness of the great mass of the community was only secondary, if indeed it occurred at all. His great merit was that power of genius, which rules every thing around it apparently with or without the necessary means; his great fault, the want of real patriotism and enlightened benevolence. He, however, surveyed the situation of his country, had his objects, and accomplished them. He could be at no loss to perceive that abroad the great power opposed to France was the house of Austria; that at home the executive authority was constantly thwarted or controlled, and would always continue to be so, if the princes of the blood and the nobles were not broken down and subdued. And to Richelieu it must have appeared, that neither the house of Austria nor the nobles could be reduced to any tolerable state of inferiority, unless the Huguenots were first crushed; a powerful body, who could be practised upon by both, and between whom and the court there was a never-failing source of mutual jealousy and hostility in the difference of their religious tenets. Such must have been the views and reasonings of Richelieu, and therefore, without troubling himself about principles or rights, and with no other means but the resources of his own genius, and the authority which belonged to him as the representative of the crown, no leader of armies or military conqueror, he performed the achievements of those who are. He supported the Protestants in Germany, while he subdued the Protestants in France; he broke the force of the house of Austria abroad, and of the nobles at home; awed the legislative bodies, the parliaments, and all the functionaries of the state; dissipated, terrified, and subjected to his will the intriguers, the courtiers, the generals, the princes of the blood, the nobility, the queen consort, the queen mother, and the very king he served; imprisoned, ruined, proscribed, or brought to the scaffold every person of authority or respect who could be opposed to him; and, on the whole, must be considered as the greatest example of the controlling powers of a single mind in the history of any civilized country.

Peter the Great, when he visited France, embraced his statue in a transport of admiration. We may understand this in the Tamer of Russians; but it is difficult, after all, to consider Richelieu as a patriot, or the enlightened benefactor of France; he cleared away the ground, and this was no doubt a great achievement, for any edifice to be hereafter erected for the happiness of his country, but he erected none himself: he left nothing behind him but the royal authority. It may be said, indeed, by his admirers, that amidst the violence of friends and foes, it may not be easy to appreciate his character, proper reference being had to the times in which he lived. "Il a fait trop du mal," says the French epigram, "pour en dire du bien; il a fait trop du bon pour en dire du mal." He is favourably dismissed with a distich like this.

Had another minister succeeded with powers of genius like his own, and animated with a generous patriotism, it is possible that during the feebleness of Louis XIII. and the minority of Louis XIV. some provisions might have been made for the proper management of the powers and principles of the constitution, for the States General, the parliaments, and the various acknowledged authorities of that great kingdom, and that England might not have been the only country in the world where the civil and religious liberties of mankind were to be found successfully established, amid the ruins of the papal power and of the feudal system, at the close of the seventeenth century. But no such happiness awaited France or Europe, for it was Mazarin who succeeded; a minister who assisted to build up the national grandeur of France (according to the general notions of national grandeur), and that with more skill and success than were at the time acknowledged, but not a minister with a genius like Richelieu, still less with a benevolence that could meditate upon the political situation of a great people; still less with the understanding that could revive the energies of a free constitution.

The nation, in the mean time, thought as little of its best interests as did Mazarin. Compare it with England: instead of the Hampdens and Falklands of our own country, the debates of the long parliament, the battle of Naseby, the exile of James, the election of William, and the enactment of the Bill of Rights, —we have the Cardinal De Retz and the Counsellor Broussel, the intrigues of the town house of Paris, the parliament, and the court, the war of the Fronde, and the alternate fortunes of the Italian favourite; while the issue of the whole is, the settlement of all differences and disputes, and the final extinction of all hope for the liberties of France, in the rising talents and popularity of Louis XIV.

Louis finished the work which Richelieu had so powerfully begun; he stepped at once, while yet a youth of fourteen, into the place which that extraordinary man had so prepared for his reception; and this great nation, most unfortunately for itself and for the world, seems from that moment to have identified its own dignity and happiness with the personal authority and aggrandisement of the monarch on the throne.

The great object on which the eyes of Europe were turned, for nearly half a century, was Louis XIV.: and on this account, not only the political but even the personal character of the monarch has become a subject of history, and as such must be studied.

In like manner, a very great interest belongs to the lives and characters, the qualities and talents, of the statesmen, the generals, the men of science and literature, who adorned this remarkable age.

The subject, therefore, in all its relations, is very copious. It has attracted the genius of the celebrated Voltaire, and has given occasion to one of his most agreeable and admired productions. If in the general subject, of the reign of Louis, the literature connected with it be included, it may occupy your attention to any possible extent; and it becomes my province, as usual, to mention such works, not as *may*, but as *must* be read; and to attempt, at the same time, to give some faint description of the general importance that belongs to the whole.

But there is another reason which induces me to recommend this part of history to your consideration. It is this: the European forms of government, though originally founded on principles more or less popular, have in general lost their public assemblies, and degenerated into arbitrary monarchies; monarchies, no doubt, very easily to be distinguished from the monarchies of the east; but to be distinguished also from that particular monarchy established in our own island. Now to me it appears, that Louis XIV. and his court, the French monarchy and its establishments, the king, the courtiers, and the nobles, the fleets and the armies, the laws and the police, public edifices and institutions, the arts, the sciences, the literature of France, at this renowned period, form altogether, not indeed a fair general specimen, but the most favourable specimen that can be well conceived of an arbitrary government founded upon the European model, but existing without any proper representative bodies of the people.

What I wish, therefore, the student to do, is to consider well this the most favourable specimen before him ; what are its merits, what its demerits, what on the whole its value, and continually to compare it with our own.

The whole subject, thus considered, comprises a multiplicity of facts, and has relation to many different principles, but is still, I think, intelligible, and within the limit of an estimate : and to form such an estimate is, as I conceive, a task worthy of any student's best powers of investigation and reflection.

The form of government established in this island will materially facilitate the progress and increase the importance of an inquiry like this. The histories and constitutions of the two kingdoms have always served to illustrate each other ; and this relation of contrast and comparison by no means ceases at the period now before us. It rather increases and seems brought to a sort of close. Survey the whole of society in each kingdom ; in France, for instance, the character of the monarch, the statesman, the courtier, the nobleman, the lawyer, the merchant, and the citizen ; survey the military, the aristocratic, the national character. These may, and should be, all compared with the corresponding characters that exist in our own country. The peculiar faults and merits of each of these should be traced up, as in general they may, to the single circumstance of certain differences in the forms of government established in the two countries, particularly to the presence or absence of the legislative assembly ; and still more particularly to the presence or absence of that assembly which represents the people. Certain merits and benefits are compatible with either form : some are found more in the one than in the other ; some, for instance, more under an arbitrary or purely monarchical government, like that of Louis XIV., than under a mixed and free form like our own.

But as all human good is but the result of a favourable balance struck between contending advantages and disadvantages, the question is, on which side does this favourable balance lie : in favour of the arbitrary or the mixed form ? and to what degree does it preponderate ?

Were a subject like this, which I have now mentioned, thoroughly investigated, many important mistakes and unfortunate delusions might be avoided, especially by those who live under a mixed government like our own. Such men are continually expecting to enjoy the blessings of a free form of government without any of its concomitant evils ; the greatest good, without any of the disadvantages by which it must be purchased ; they would have liberty, for instance, without ever being exposed to any popular excesses; but this is not the manner in which Nature dispenses her benefits; it is to require impossibilities.

Again, the euthanasia of the British constitution has been said to be an arbitrary monarchy; an arbitrary monarchy is certainly the point to which it has a great tendency to converge in any ordinary state of the world. Let, therefore, the arbitrary monarchy of Louis XIV. be considered; it is, as I have already mentioned, the most favourable specimen that can be offered for our reflection. Let it then be considered, and it will be seen what is the very best result that can possibly take place, if ever the democratic part of our mixed form of constitution, on whatever account, should fall into decay.

It is for these reasons that I would recommend a more diligent and extensive perusal of the private memoirs and literary works belonging to the age of Louis XIV. than on other occasions I should be disposed to think necessary. An historian, that is, a writer or reader of history, as distinguished from other writers or readers, must no doubt be distinguished by a more intimate knowledge of the private memoirs and literary productions connected with the courts and different kingdoms of Europe. But this is a species of reading which, though very attractive in itself, approaches not a little to a sort of novel reading; it is apt to occupy too large a portion of time, and rather fitted to render a man entertaining in society than instructive in a senate, or intelligent in a cabinet. It is a species of reading which, if long dwelt upon, is not likely to form the mind to those commanding views and general conclusions which constitute the great interest of history, and which, when they are just and can fairly be drawn, distinguish the statesman from the courtier, and the philosopher from the man of letters. With respect, however, to the age of Louis XIV., for the reasons I have mentioned, more of this species of reading may be indulged in than would in general be advisable; and I shall proceed to state such works as I think may be properly recommended to your attention.

The great magazine from which subsequent writers of history and compilers of anecdotes have drawn their materials is the Memoirs of the Duc de St. Simon.

On the breaking out of the late French Revolution, a complete edition of this work seems then, for the first time, to have been given to the world. Before that event it seems not to have been allowed to appear, except in a mutilated state. The freedom, that is the propriety, of remark, which the duke had occasionally exercised, was too great to be exposed to the consideration of the public while the system of government remained the same : but this is only an additional recommendation to a philosophic inquirer. Of the thirteen volumes, the first six belong to the reign of Louis XIV., the two next to the regency of the Duke of Orleans, four others to the history of distinguished individuals, and the concluding one to the researches of the duke into the nature and prerogatives of the French peerage, the political constitution of Spain, and matters of a similar nature.

To render these memoirs properly interesting, or even intelligible, the general detail of the events of the reign must be first known, and must be learnt elsewhere ; and I should therefore propose that some concise account should be read, like that of Hanault, for instance, or Millot, or the late history of D'Anquetil ; when this has been done, the allusions and passing remarks and descriptions of St. Simon will be properly felt and understood. Amidst a variety of other matter, particulars of the following nature may be found : the extent of the king's natural genius and talents ; his ignorance of history, laws, persons, and events, to a degree that led him into occasional mistakes of the grossest nature ; his hatred of birth and talents ; his rage for flattery ; his extreme egotism ; his taste for details ; the manner in which his ministers made him suppose that he directed everything, while he was in fact himself directed ; his contrivances to keep every one anxious only for his favour, and dependent on that favour for all personal consequence ; his system of espionage, extended even to the opening of letters. The very arbitrary and violent nature of his selfishness, rendering every one around him (his children, mistresses, and courtiers) entirely subservient to his own whims and amusements, in defiance of all considerations of their convenience, and even of their health ; his exterior advantages, his fêtes, his gallantries, his mistresses, his splendour ; the remarkable history of Madame de Maintenon, her management of the king and his ministers ; these are the topics of the work, interspersed with many curious anecdotes and descriptions of the king's children, legitimate and illegitimate, with some account of Fénélon ; of the Duke of Burgundy, the hope of the nation, and of his duchess, the delight of the court.

The revocation of the edict of Nantz, and some of the leading events of the reign are also discussed ; and among the lives of distinguished persons, some may be readily selected as of more particular consequence, Fénélon, for instance, Heinsius, James II., William III.

That part which relates to military transactions seems imper-

fect and very partial, but may be consulted by those who wish
to see the manner in which the humiliation of France was surveyed by St. Simon, and probably by most Frenchmen at the
time. No proper testimony is paid to the genius of Marlborough,
and the English reader looks in vain for the hero and triumphs
of his nation.

On the whole, the greatest part of these six volumes is worth
reading. It is observable, however, that all the good sense, that
all the virtue, and even the almost cynical spirit of St. Simon,
never seem to have suggested to his mind the radical and fatal
defect of the whole system, and amidst all the misfortunes of his
country, the greatest misfortune of all, the want of a free constitution. The duke even declares to his reader, that he meddles
not with politics, and means only to describe what he has himself seen or learned from others of the scene that is more immediately around him. But this circumstance does not render the
work at all less important, in the way I have proposed this
subject of the reign of Louis XIV. to your consideration. You
have only, on this account, the picture of the court of an arbitrary monarch on the European model more faithfully given,
and the facility of comparing it with your own more complete.
And to this task I must therefore take this opportunity of again
exhorting you to direct your attention.

But before I proceed, I must add a word more on the subject
of these Memoirs of the Duc de St. Simon.

The lectures that I am now delivering, on the reign of Louis
XIV. and on the regency of the Duke of Orleans, were written
nearly twenty years ago, and I then naturally depended on the
edition of the Memoirs of the Duc de St. Simon which had just
been published; a new edition is now, at the close of 1829,
making its appearance, being the real Memoirs that were drawn
up by the *Duke* himself, and which are now given to the world
by the *Marquis* de St. Simon, from the original MS. in the
possession of the editors. The fact seems to have been that the
duke had put together eleven folio volumes of papers, manuscript
and printed, which he made the materials of his Memoirs; from
these eleven volumes, that were lodged in the Dépôt des Affaires
Etrangers, an extract was made by the Abbé de Voisenon, in
eight volumes quarto, and from this extract was made another
extract, in three volumes octavo, with four of supplement; but
these last seven volumes seem not to have satisfied the public,
and on the breaking out of the French Revolution, as I have
mentioned, a new work was formed out of the eleven volumes

folio, which is the work of which I have just described the contents, and on which I have hitherto relied.   Upon comparing it with the edition now given to the world by the Marquis de St. Simon, I find no occasion to make any alteration in what I have said in my prior lectures ; every thing that is in the old edition will be found somewhere or other in the new ; but the expressions are sometimes a little modified, and slight omissions made ; the whole, however, is new arranged, and much is added by the duke, many new personages are brought forward, many new scenes described, additional anecdotes given ; on the whole, the work is now more than ever fitted to answer the purpose I have just mentioned, that of affording the reader a complete notion of the nature of the characters that are to be found under an absolute European monarchy.   It is not too much to say, that while reading these volumes, we are as much placed by the side of Louis and the regent, and passing our days in the midst of the court and courtiers by whom they were surrounded, as if we had lived at Versailles at the time.   We hear of the deaths and the marriages, the characters and views of the parties, the fêtes and balls, the intrigues, the gossip and scandal, the news, private and public, every subject, grave or gay, that has occurred, and all given by a very spirited observer, a man of sagacity and sense, and one the very child and creature of such scenes in every respect, except that he was a man of sincere religion and severe virtue.

It is true, that a description of this kind will differently affect men of different education and views ; men of republican character will turn away from it with impatience and contempt ; while, on the other hand, it will not be without its interest, or even its charm, to those who are fitted to take a part in such scenes by the elegance of their manners or the variety of their accomplishments ; and even the philosopher, while he cannot approve (though he may feel the necessity of monarchy) such an exhibition of human nature, as this must be thought, will, perhaps, be content to consider it as an unfortunate exaggeration of what is in itself neither without its grace nor without its use ; he will be ready to acknowledge, as the physical strength is always with the multitude, that ranks and distinctions, ceremonials and etiquettes (and therefore those of a court) are among the fences and safeguards of civilized society ; that they silently and peacefully undermine and weaken the empire and brute force among mankind, and call into play other influences of a more intellectual, and therefore more elevated nature ; and the only point of anxiety to such a philosopher will be, that the expense of the machinery be not too great, and the injury done to the natural feelings and affections of the heart not too deep and too extensive.

Certainly the court of Louis XIV. must always be considered as a very remarkable phenomenon in the history of the civilization of mankind ; such, we may say, were our fellow-creatures once, in the most distinguished portion, at the time of improving Europe, and what a curious spectacle, it may surely be added, is here displayed ! under what strange, and often whimsical forms, does our common nature here appear ! our vanities, our frailties, and our follies, our noble qualities, our heroism, and our virtues, our genius, our religious feelings, all that is great in our composition, and all that is little, under what extraordinary aspects are they here presented ! Who can wonder that the memoirs connected with these scenes should never want an interest, and to this hour should not want an interest to the readers in fashionable life ; and even, if a real speculator on human nature, to the philosopher in the shade. But with reference to this new edition of St. Simon, the great misfortune is, that it is now extended to twenty volumes, and I have therefore to observe to you with some satisfaction, that to each chapter there is a very good index, and by this means a selection of the topics that are most interesting may easily be made. The impression that was given me by the former work, has been now renewed and extremely strengthened. What my first impression was, you will see in the next lecture ; from the present work, what I have chiefly brought away is a more strong sense of the misery and ruin of France, produced by the victories of Marlborough and Eugene ; and of the terror and subdued state not only of Louis and his court, but still more of the common people of Paris, and, at the same time, of all intelligent men in the kingdom. Again, a very strong confirmation is afforded of the accuracy of the views of the Whig party in England. All this appears very strongly marked in the present production. And again, the minute and more endless detail of the new work makes more than ever striking the extraordinary system of etiquette that was established, and all the faults and prejudices not only of Louis, the monarch, but of St. Simon, the peer of France, himself.

The work, however, of St. Simon, it must be confessed, presents a task of considerable labour to the general reader, even though proper advantage is taken of the index, as I have already recommended ; and I proceed, therefore, to mention a book which may be proposed not only as a sort of substitute, but as one which, on account of its own merits and popularity, must, at all events, be perused. This is the work of Du Clos. There is a good preface, and the author acknowledges his obligations to the Duke of St. Simon, whose particular prejudices he states, and proposes to avoid. It is the history of men and manners, the spirit of the age which Du Clos hopes to give ; and the work is certainly very pleasing, the observations those of an acute and sensible writer. That part which relates to Louis XIV. is short ; the work begins, unfortunately, at too late a period ; it must be all read ; and the second book, which contains, more especially, the author's estimate of Louis, should be well weighed.

After Du Clos, may be consulted a work lately published by Lacretelle ; a history of France during the eighteenth century, to be connected with his late work on the French Revolution. Lacretelle is an author of reputation ; the first book relates to the close of the reign of Louis XIV., and is very well worth reading.

But the most agreeable work of all is that of D'Anquetil, entitled, " Louis le Quatorze, sa Cour et le Régent." It is a work compiled from all the most interesting performances that relate to the general subject. Every thing that concerns Louis XIV. is touched upon, and in a manner the most easy and agreeable. But no subject can be said properly to be discussed ; and with all the good sense of the author, it is entertainment, rather than philosophic instruction, that he affords. The work may be likened to a gallery of portraits, which a spectator is led along to look at, and when something interesting and appropriate has been said of each, he is left to depart. The work is prefaced by a valuable account of all the publications connected with the general subject, accompanied with a short critique on each. Both are, on every account, of great consequence to an English reader.

The student must, on the whole, remember that the kind of personal acquaintance which is desirable with all the more remarkable characters of this age, can only be acquired from this publication, which D'Anquetil seems to have devoted to that very purpose.

Among such characters must be numbered Madame de Maintenon, the mistress, or rather the wife of Louis. Such were her qualities, her talents, and her situation, that the particulars of her life form a part of the history of the times ; and her memoirs must be read to make you thoroughly acquainted with that monarch and that court, on whom, unfortunately, so much of the happiness of Europe at the time depended. Her memoirs, edited by Beaumelle (the book so decried by Voltaire), has been able to preserve its reputation, notwithstanding the censures and invectives of a writer so universally read and admired on the continent, as Voltaire. It is still considered by French scholars as giving an extremely good account of what it professes to describe, and as necessary to be read.

The reader must prepare himself to submit to the eternal praises of Madame de Maintenon, and he may contrast the unfavourable representations of St. Simon with the unlimited panegyrics of the writer of her memoirs.

There are several small volumes of her letters; some of the letters may be read. The student, after becoming acquainted with the history of the reign, will be at no loss to select a few for his perusal, judging of their contents from the persons to whom they are addressed. As parts of history, they are little interesting or instructive, but they are letters of a woman of taste and good natural sense, placed in an extraordinary situation, connected with the leading personages, and influencing the events of a remarkable period. The letter to the Duchess of Burgundy may be mentioned as a favourable specimen of the writer and of the publication. Other letters have lately been published. You will see an account of them in the eighty-eighth number of the Edinburgh Review, by Sir James Mackintosh, and several curious and important historical notices which he has been able to select from them.

The work of Voltaire, the Age of Louis XIV., is well known, and has long been universally admired; as it is not very long, and is every where written with liveliness and ease, it may be read with advantage twice; that is, after, as well as before the works I have alluded to. The great praise of Voltaire as an historian is, that he was the first who directed the attention of mankind to the more proper subjects of history—the arts, manners, and laws of every country, the progress of society, the history of human happiness; that he was the first who gave those general results, those comprehensive estimates which are the great lessons of statesmen.

Had he been born and educated under a free government, the great subjects of history would, in all probability, have been all of them regularly and gravely discussed; and much of what may now be objected to him in the way of defect or fault, would then, as I conceive, not have appeared. In writing the Age of

Louis XIV. he had every possible advantage; he was about twenty-one when Louis died; he had all the information, oral and written, within his reach, and he lived at a distance of time when he could investigate the truth, and estimate the importance of every thing before him.

Voltaire is a writer whose expressions always convey his thoughts very clearly to his reader, and he treats particular subjects separately; yet it still appears to me very difficult to draw any distinct results from those of his chapters, more particularly, which are connected with subjects of political economy and ecclesiastical affairs; and if this observation be just, it is an important fault in this celebrated performance.

The work has been noticed in a general manner by Lacretelle in his third volume. Lacretelle considers it as an effort of Voltaire in the cause of all that heroism, elevation of character, and good taste, which Voltaire conceived to be on the decline when he drew up his work. Lacretelle supposes him to have been desirous to display, at the same time, the striking influence of letters and the arts, and to have hoped to animate his countrymen to the imitation of the virtues of Turenne, Catinat, and Fénélon, and the splendid qualities of Louis XIV. The work, when it appeared, was received with enthusiasm; the situation of Louis XV. and of the court at the time, gave a new interest, and secured a ready reception and applause for whatever could revive the remembrance of the brilliant scenes and imposing character of his predecessor.

In later times it has been thought not quite to satisfy the French scholars, as being, after all, rather a general view and outline of this interesting era, than a complete and well-digested history; but it is possible that on the subject of their *grand monarque*, nothing that was not intolerably minute and tedious would have satisfied such critics. An English student may rest contented when he finds that its general merits are acknowledged, and when he hears it confessed that no better work on the subject has ever yet been produced.

The constant merit of Voltaire is the ease and beauty of his narrative, the agreeable and often valuable observations with which it is accompanied; above all, that he never trifles with the time of his reader.

The great objections to the work will be sufficiently apparent to all but Frenchmen, and are not such as Frenchmen at any former period would have discovered.

But of late, when a new order of things was beginning to

appear, the celebrated Condorcet, while writing the life of Voltaire, thought it necessary to declare, that this renowned author, in his Age of Louis XIV., had certainly sacrificed too much to the prejudices of his youth.

But a far greater and more constant fault of Voltaire, in his historical writings, is a never-ceasing disposition to place every thing in a lively point of view.

To the production of this species of dramatic effect it cannot but happen that the dull precision of facts must be sometimes sacrificed—characters and events must be strained into an antithesis; they must be huddled up together into a general estimate; they must be disposed of by a stroke of satire or a witticism; they must "point a moral, or adorn a tale." All this may be entertaining: it always is; but it is not always history; the representation and remarks of Voltaire must be therefore received at all times with hesitation and distrust. It must be confessed, however, that the reader will be surprised to find, on further examination, as Dr. Robertson appears to have been, how often this most amusing of writers has authorities for his facts, and proper foundations on which to rest the liveliness of his sallies, and the instruction of his remarks.

On the whole, Voltaire's Age of Louis XIV. may be studied by an English reader, as conveying the most full and distinct impression that can be found of the nature of the French character; of the character of the government, the monarch, the nobles, the generals, the courtiers, and women of quality, and of the whole nation, when found in the state that is to them most natural and agreeable; in short, of the great edifice which was in the first place levelled to the earth by the French Revolution.

When works like these, the publications of the French nation, have been read, they must be afterwards compared with the writings of our own country. The whole picture will then be complete, and not before. With our own authors, the constant theme of reprobation is the ambition of Louis XIV., and the miseries it occasioned. It cannot be expected that this ambition will be very properly criticised by the French writers, or even the personal faults of the monarch very accurately estimated; yet more is said than could have been expected both by St. Simon and Du Clos. Voltaire is always ready to raise his voice against war and intolerance, and therefore occasionally against the leading faults of the monarch, but by no means in a tone sufficiently strong; and he must be considered, on the whole, as the panegyrist rather than the historian, both of his countrymen and of Louis. Lacretelle had the advantage of writing since the Revolution, and it was therefore more easy for him both to discover and to state the unfavourable as well as the favourable characteristics of the reign.

Through the whole, however, of these French publications, a jealousy, not to say hatred, of England, and a passion for their own nation, is manifest, sometimes to a degree that annihilates, always to a degree that obscures in them, the more regular suggestions of propriety and candour, not to say all due consideration of the general rights and interests of Europe.

But these rights and interests of mankind ought never to be forgotten by any reader, above all, by the readers of a free country. On the continent, the state whose liberties were more immediately in peril was Holland, but the power that could best be opposed to Louis, to preserve the balance of Europe, was the House of Austria. In conjunction, therefore, with the accounts of the French writers and those of our own country, some idea ought to be formed of the situation of that House, and of the empire; and the work of Mr. Coxe on this occasion very opportunely presents itself. As this part of it is very concise, and founded on the best authorities, I recommend it to be read at the same time with the works before mentioned. They will be found all to illustrate each other, and united, to be sufficient to give you, as I conceive, a very full view of the whole subject.

But I must now recommend to you a book, which you might not perhaps have expected me to mention as a portion of historic reading — the Adventures of Telemachus. The connexion, however, of this celebrated work with the general subject now before us, and its own separate importance, may be easily described to you.

One of the subjects which occupies the history and the memoirs of this period is the education and character of the Duke of Burgundy, the grandson of Louis, the presumptive heir to the crown.

The merits of the duke will be found to illustrate by contrast all the faults of Louis; to exhibit to the view in various ways all the objectionable parts of the king's character and administration.

The Duke of Burgundy, originally debased by every evil propensity, and distinguished by every unfortunate habit, that could have rendered him the disgrace and dread of his country, became, at last, by the happy influence of his own reflections and of wise and good men, who laboured for his improvement, the hope and promise of France, and indeed of Europe. This is a fact that may keep us from lightly despairing of ourselves or others; it may really be regarded as a problem whether, if the duke had lived and come to the throne, the late French Revolution would have occurred. Fénélon was his instructor, and the character of the prelate becomes on that account more than ever interesting. It is given at great length by St. Simon, and appears in all the books I have recommended.

The subsequent events, the late Revolution in France, may naturally awaken in us some curiosity to know what could have been the communications that passed between such a preceptor and such a pupil; what could have been the lessons of instruction that were offered by the virtuous prelate to the grandson of such a jealous and despotic prince as Louis XIV.

Some idea may be formed from the book I have mentioned—the Telemachus. This work, by a lucky accident, has reached us; it was not intended for the public eye.

We may have already perused it as an elevated sort of novel, as an inferior sort of epic poem; but, for the reasons I have mentioned, there are parts of it which fall within the province of historical reading. No doubt the general topics of instruction that are here supposed to be addressed to the son of Ulysses must have been insisted upon by the bishop in his private conferences with his illustrious pupil. It is to these I would wish you to advert. By looking over the arguments affixed to the different books, it will be easy to select particular topics of this nature, and to meditate them, without reading those descriptions and narratives which might once have appeared to us the more interesting portion of the work.

It cannot be expected that the lessons of the prelate should be other than of a very general nature; but the subjects chosen are the right subjects—the importance of the distribution of justice, of a sincere and active interest in the happiness of the community, the temptations to which all princes are exposed, their necessary defects, the great merit of candour and docility, the difficulty with which they can escape from flatterers, how seldom they search for men of wisdom and virtue; unless they do, how impossible it is that the wise and the virtuous should approach them; the importance of frugality in a state; of morality; of religion; and the lesson which the bishop seems to have had, above all others, at heart, is the invaluable nature of the blessings of peace, and how inseparable is the love of it from the character of every intelligent and virtuous ruler. On the whole, the maxims of government which the prelate presents to the reception of the duke, are all of a mild and enlightened cast, and well fitted to contribute to the happiness of the community. The most material omission seems, at first sight, to be, that no notice is taken of the value of representative assemblies, in all forms of government. The bishop must have known that they were a regular part of the constitution of his own country, and in our neighbouring island of England, he had seen a most desirable revolution effected by means of them without bloodshed or disorder. But he discusses neither their merits nor their defects; and, without entering into any specific exemplification of his own political principles, seems to think it sufficient to inculcate them in a general manner, to inspire his pupil, if possible, with the proper tone and sentiment, and to leave the application to his own discernment of fit seasons and circumstances.

And this was perhaps the best and only course. To have attempted more than this would have been most probably to have defeated his own intentions. What he wrote in his work was sufficiently strong to be considered, in many places, as a satire on Louis XIV., and many have supposed that Fénélon was nominated, or rather banished to a bishopric at Cambray, not so much because his religious heresies as because his political instructions were disrelished by the court. It is certain that the Duke of Burgundy was himself animated with the most lively interest in the welfare of the community; and there is a remarkable letter of Madame de Maintenon among those which have been given to the public, in which she tells the Duke of Bouvilliers that the king, on the death of the prince, the Duke of Burgundy, had looked over his papers, and had committed every thing that came from Fénélon to the flames; no slight testimony to the merit of the bishop.

But the Telemachus is to be considered on another account. It has been represented as containing the principles of that more improved system of political economy, which, under the auspices of Adam Smith, has been for some time slowly, and at last rapidly making its way not only into the deliberations of cabinets, but even into the understanding of the public. There is certainly merit of this kind in the work of Fénélon; merit which must be considered as very great, when we reflect that he was thinking on these subjects, and in general thinking reasonably, at the very time that the celebrated Colbert, the minister of France, was proceeding upon a more obvious, and then an established system directly the reverse. Colbert was marshalling from his desk, as he flattered himself, the industry of mankind by the powers of legislation, and supposing that he could move his pen, as a magician would his wand, and by bounties and drawbacks, and by the encouragement of the state (as he called it), raise up wealth and happiness at his pleasure.

The ideas of the good bishop were far more just and profound. On account of the importance of the subject of political economy, I will give an instance or two; and I do this the rather, I confess, to take the chance of attracting your thoughts to this great subject—the science of national prosperity, a subject that will hereafter often and deeply occupy your minds, if you come to be men of reflection and benevolence. I am at the close of my lecture, but one or two points may be mentioned; and I will take those that are among the most important in the science.

" Instruct me," says Telemachus in the third book, " how I may establish in Ithaca commerce like that of the Tyrians. The true way, replies Narbas, is to receive all strangers readily; let them find in your ports safety, accommodation, perfect freedom; above all, do not attempt to restrain commerce by directing it according to your own notions. Let the prince have no concern in it. He will be sufficiently enriched by the riches which commerce will bring into his dominions. It is with commerce as with some springs; attempt to change their course, and you dry them up." To write thus at the period when Fénélon wrote, was no doubt extraordinary merit.

It is not to be expected that, in the infancy of the science of political economy, Fénélon should be entirely accurate. Thus he says, " the true secret of gaining much is, not to wish to gain too much." Adam Smith could say nothing better— nothing that more completely opposes those custom-house statesmen who draw forth all the machinery of bounties and restrictions, and vainly hope to make their own nation rich by keeping every other nation poor; that is, to enrich the tradesman by impoverishing his customers. But the bishop immediately subjoins these words,—" and by knowing the proper moment when to lose." Here Fénélon seems not to be quite aware that if the intercourse is spontaneous, neither nation can ever lose; that the very existence of the traffic, if no laws have interfered, is of itself a sufficient indication that not only one, but that both parties more or less profit by it; that to suppose that the gain of the one is the loss of the other, is the great and important mistake of the whole subject.

The next striking feature of the system of Fénélon, is the

earnestness with which he lays down the paramount importance
of agriculture. " The reason of the happy change which you
see is that agriculture is had in honour, and that the lands are
well cultivated. The true force and the true riches of a community depend on the number of the people and the abundance of
provisions." But Fénélon next proceeds to lay down the fatal
evils of luxury ; and when he comes to the remedy of these
evils, he becomes a Colbert in his turn ; he makes, in the first
place, a distinction between those arts which are superfluous
and those which are liberal ; vainly proposing to expel the one
and retain the other. He then goes on to state, that in such a
case the taste and manners of a nation must be changed. But
how ? Why, says he, new laws must be established ; as if men
could be made moderate in their desires or reasonable in their
fancies by edicts and commands. This is little to understand
this important subject, the nature of the human mind, or the
principles on which the exertions of mankind, mental and cor-
poreal, i. e. their prosperity and their happiness, really depend.
A proper estimate of this particular subject of luxury, and the
more peculiar vices of civilization (a very curious and indeed
difficult subject), must be derived neither from the licentious
Mandeville, who undertook to prove with great powers of
lively, though coarse declamation, that private vices are public
benefits, nor the eloquent Rousseau, nor the pure and elevated
Fénélon, but from the essays of the reasoning Hume—those,
for instance, on commerce and on refinement in the arts.

Fénélon seems himself almost to abandon his confidence in
laws and edicts, and to modify in the next sentence the nature of
his political prescription. " Who," says he, " can undertake a
reformation like this, but some philosophic king ; one who
would by his own example shame the ostentatious prodigality
of others ; one who would encourage the wise by the sanction
of his authority in their honourable frugality ?"

It is instructive to see the mind of Fénélon labouring with the
difficulties of the great problem of rendering the people happy
by good government. His general notions I have already
alluded to ; they are stated with still greater regularity in his
twelfth book. He depends too much on the operation of laws ;
is too ready to interfere with regulations of this kind ; and his
plans, which could not be carried into effect in a small state, nor
attempted in a large one, are after all inconsistent with many of
the leading and vital principles of public prosperity and freedom. One important mistake seems to be this : he supposes

that the earth will always continue to produce sufficient food for the inhabitants, if properly cultivated, yet, in the progress of his speculations, we find him at last obliged to regulate the extent of ground which each family is to possess, and still pursued by difficulty, finally to propose that when the land of any particular society of men is insufficient for their proper support, colonies should be sent abroad; but this is only to adjourn the difficulty one stage more. What at length are the colonies to do?

This is to cut the knot, not untie it; and they who would learn the real nature of this great problem of human prosperity, the difficulties with which it has to struggle, and the kind of assistance which it may receive from the exertions of self-denial and virtue in individuals, and from the operation of wise counsels in the legislature, must meditate long and anxiously the works of Adam Smith and Mr. Malthus.

I may mention, as I am concluding my lecture, that there have been some books published by Mr. Butler on the subject of Fénélon, the Gallican church, and other topics connected with this and the subsequent reign.

They are highly deserving of your consideration, and they are a sort of literary curiosity, as it seems to have been the object of the author—I speak not of his controversial but his historic works—to give the greatest possible quantity of information in the least possible compass, a very novel idea, not likely to be very popular in Paternoster Row.

LECTURE II.

LOUIS XIV.

In my last lecture I endeavoured to give you an account of such histories and memoirs as might convey an adequate notion of a monarch so celebrated as Louis XIV., and an era so remarkable as that in which he flourished.

The subject will be found very extensive, even if contracted within the least possible limits; it is impossible now, in the slightest degree, to conceive the impression that was once made on Europe by this extraordinary king, of this extraordinary people; in times less interesting than our own, the subject might occupy, as I do not doubt it often has occupied, even a large portion of the life of men of literature and science.

I cannot advise this, in the present situation of human knowledge and human affairs; it is certainly fitted to afford you much entertainment and instruction, but when these have been derived, I would recommend you to hasten on to other characters and other periods, which have also a claim on your curiosity and diligence.

The reign of Louis was very long, and the history of the reign is the history of Europe.

In like manner, the particulars respecting the monarch himself are innumerable; no detail, therefore, either of the one or the other can be here attempted.

I will, however, select from the history two subjects for your reflection, which, whenever remembered, will always revive in your mind a very strong and proper impression of the real character of this celebrated prince, and always prevent you from being too much deceived by his showy qualities, and even his solid claims to your approbation.

The two subjects that I shall select from the history are,— first, the revocation of the edict of Nantz; second, the burning of the Palatinate.

The revocation of the edict of Nantz is a subject with which, as Protestants, as Englishmen, as readers of history, you cannot be too well acquainted. No event ever excited a greater sensation in Europe; as such it must be considered attentively by those who read history.

But it deserves also your meditation as a very striking specimen of the evils of intolerance. The evils which this great measure of national intolerance produced were very striking, and are acknowledged. And similar evils every measure of national intolerance has a tendency to produce.

We do not say that states are not to support or defend their establishments; but we say that it is the practice of men, even in the best of times, to defend them by harsh and unnecessary, and therefore by unjust and unwise expedients; that in concerns of this nature the members of the superior sect are always deplorably selfish or unreasonably timid.

The edict of Nantz was the final adjustment of the religious wars in France; the terms that were procured for the Huguenots by Henry IV. When Louis therefore revoked this edict, he in fact declared that he would keep terms with this part of his subjects no longer.

There is a very striking chapter on this subject of the revocation by the Duc de St. Simon, where he reprobates this measure with all the warmth of an enlightened statesman, and all the indignant feeling of a lover of truth and a man of humanity. His sentiments are, in part, transferred by D'Anquetil to his own work. This unjust and cruel revocation is likewise noticed in very proper terms by Beaumelle, in his Memoirs of Madame de Maintenon, and again briefly in Du Clos. Voltaire has also treated the subject in his chapter on Calvinism, in his Age of Louis XIV. His account of the more early conduct of the Huguenots seems not sufficiently favourable. He may indeed be always suspected of surveying the *comparative* merits of different sects with too much indifference to treat them with relative justice; and this indifference will operate unfavourably to the oppressed sect; yet the chapter, on the whole, does him honour, particularly if we consider the early period of life at which it was written, and the age and nation to which he belonged. The criminality of Louis is sufficiently apparent even from this representation of his biographer.

There is a regular and professed work on this subject—the History of the Edict of Nantz, printed in Holland, and published a few years after the revocation. These volumes must be considered as a statement of the whole of the case of the members of the reformed church, drawn up, probably, by one of themselves. The preface of this work should at least be read. At the end of the fifth volume will be found a collection of edicts, and other official documents, that sufficiently tell their own story.

From all these books and treatises however, I will content myself with giving you one extract only; it is from St. Simon. Observe his assertions, observe the manner in which he describes the effects of this revocation; he lived at the time. "In this way," says he, "without the slightest pretext, the slightest necessity, was one fourth of the kingdom to be depopulated; its trade to be ruined; the whole country to be abandoned to the public and avowed pillage of dragoons; the innocent of both sexes were to be devoted to punishment or torture, and that by thousands; families were to be stripped of their possessions; relations armed against each other; our manufactures to be transferred to strangers, and the world was to see crowds of their fellow-creatures proscribed, naked, fugitive, guilty of no crimes, and yet seeking asylum in foreign lands, not in their own country, which was in the mean time subjecting to the galleys and to the lash the noble, the affluent, and the aged, the delicate and the weak, and in many cases those who were

distinguished for their piety, their knowledge, and their virtue;
and all this on no other account than that of religion : and still
further to enhance the horrors of such proceedings, in this
manner was every province to be filled with sacrilegious or perjured men ; those who were forced, or those who pretended wil-
lingly to conform, and who sacrificed their consciences to their
worldly welfare and repose ; nay, such in the result were the
abominations thus produced by obsequiousness and by cruelty,
that the same space of twenty-four hours was sufficient not unfrequently to conduct men from tortures to abjuration, from abjuration to the holy communion ; and an unhappy sufferer found
a conductor, and a witness, on these occasions, often in the
person of the common hangman."

A melancholy history this ! of which St. Simon proceeds still
further to give the detail—a detail in which I need not follow
him.

The king, it seems, received from all quarters the most soothing accounts of the conversions that had been effected ; two thousand in one place ! six thousand in another ! congratulated himself on the wonders achieved by his piety and his power ; and
flattered himself, says St. Simon, that he had renewed the times,
and rivalled the glory of the first propagators of Christianity.

The revocation of the edict of Nantz is memorable in the history of mankind ; and, fortunately for the interests of humanity,
those who had to be exiles from their native land, and to fly for
refuge to strangers, were in general men of such industrious
habits and useful occupations, men so meritorious and so ingenious, that the impolicy of the measure was even more glaring
than might at the time, perhaps, appear its injustice.   As such
it has remained in the eyes of posterity.   Its impolicy has become a sort of by-word among the nations of Europe ; and the
most uninformed and unenlightened man has never, from this
period, wanted an instance sufficiently strong to strike his understanding, and to show him how great are the mistakes which
may be committed in this important subject of the management
of religious sects.

For some time the influence of this measure was favourable
to the world, though perhaps not so much in this as in another
respect.   It inspired every state in Europe with a hatred of
Louis, which materially assisted William III. not only in his
efforts to establish the freedom of England, but at all times in
his laudable ambition to resist the unlawful ambition of Louis;
but this revolution, in its more natural and immediate effect,

that of conveying an awful warning against intolerance, probably neither had at the time, nor ever will have, all the influence which it ought to have on the reflections of mankind.

Indeed the effect produced for a long time was rather of an opposite nature.

The two sects were but the more inflamed against each other. The Protestants naturally supposed that the bigotry of their Roman Catholic opponents had no limits, and that they were justified in defending themselves, and in establishing by any possible means their own predominancy. This could not be done without legal provisions and enactments of a very horrible nature in the first instance, and which were to remain on statute books long after the reasons which gave occasion to them had ceased to exist. Consequences like these could not be favourable to the general principles of toleration,—these principles were in many instances grossly violated; and mankind have been subsequently benefited by the example of the edict of Nantz, only in the way I have already described, in showing the impolicy of intolerance rather than the injustice of it. The impolicy at least was visible— for to England and other countries were driven in exile many of the most valuable and respectable artisans and families of France.

I now proceed to the second subject, which I propose to select as a specimen of the character of Louis,—the burning of the Palatinate.

The student will find, if he reads the history, that in order to distress the enemy for provisions this fine country was to be converted into a desert. In the midst of winter the whole population was to be driven by the military from their habitations; and while these hapless beings were to leave behind them their towns and villages in flames, they were to wander forward—the aged and the helpless—to seek food and shelter in whatever manner and in whatever country they thought best. A monster, says Lamontey, has been found to applaud the massacre of St. Bartholomew, but none ever to excuse the burning of the Palatinate.

It is sometimes said that Louis was not harsh in his nature, or intentionally cruel, though his minister was. It is indeed difficult to suppose that he was. There are anecdotes mentioned in different books of memoirs, one more particularly in St. Simon, which enable us to entertain more favourable ideas of his character. But the lesson to be derived from these outrages is only rendered more striking and instructive, if such be the fact.

These orders, which Attila might have issued from his camp, were dispatched by Louis from his palace at Versailles, from the midst of his fêtes and spectacles—while he was surrounded by every thing which could awaken his senses to pleasure, and harmonize his mind to happiness.

The imagination of the monarch, amid the various artifices of bliss which his situation afforded, was employed, it should seem, in a manner too agreeable to turn aside and survey all the repulsive spectacles of misery which his abominable orders could not fail to occasion.

Not referring, therefore, at this moment, as I naturally might, to the indignation and horror which such atrocious proceedings will necessarily excite in your minds, I shall make a remark rather of a collateral nature, on account of what I conceive to be its practical importance.

The remark is indeed familiar to you, but may strike you more when made to you on an occasion like the present.

It is—the unfortunate effect of affluence more or less upon every one of us; the manner in which we are made to participate, in a certain degree, the insensibility of Louis.

The delicacies of food and clothing, for instance, are enjoyed with little concern for those to whom the necessaries of life are scarcely attainable; and it has thus passed into a proverb, that one half of the world knows not what becomes of the other. One of our first moral writers has been pleased to speak in a manner somewhat disrespectful of those moralists and poets, like Thomson, who have noticed and lamented this disposition in the human mind, to enjoy its own blessings rather than disquiet itself with the calamities of others. I allude to Adam Smith—but was he well employed on this occasion? It is the province of sympathy to render us alive to the evils of those around us. This he would admit. So is it equally the province of reason and good sense to save the mind from too deep an interest in afflictions which we can neither prevent nor remedy. This we concede on our part. No doubt, therefore, it is the perfection of the human character to be at once equal to its own happiness, and yet sensible to those miseries of our fellow-creatures which its exertions can alleviate. But surely it remains to be remarked, that it is not in any deficiency of attention to *ourselves* that human nature offends. This is not the weakness of mankind, or the aspect under which they need be regarded by a moralist with any pain. If there be sometimes found those who are formed of a finer clay, so as really to have the comforts of their own existence diminished and interrupted by sympathizing too long and too quickly with the calamities of those around them, such may

surely be considered as exceptions to be set apart from their fel-
low-mortals, as those more amiable beings, who are not likely
by their example to injure the general cause of reasonable enjoyment in the world; and whom the more natural prevalence of
careless selfishness renders it not easy often to find, and surely
not very possible long to censure.

Having now presented to your remembrance two particular
subjects so necessary to a proper estimate of Louis XIV., I will
next endeavour to propose to you a system of arrangement which
may enable you the better to form a general notion of the vast
assemblage of events and circumstances which belong to the character of this renowned monarch and this most memorable era.

In reading, therefore, the various works to which I have referred, it will, I think, contribute to give you a clearer idea of
the whole, if you consider Louis XIV. under three different
aspects: 1st, His conduct with respect to those more immediately
around him—his personal character.   2ndly, His conduct to his
people—his character as the sovereign of France.   3rdly, His
conduct with respect to surrounding states—his character as one
of the great potentates of Europe.

All these subjects are necessarily connected with each other;
in strict propriety they cannot be well separated; and the discussion of the one immediately runs into references to some one
of the other.   But there may still be some advantage in keeping
them as much apart as the nature of things will allow; and, in
considering the whole subject as made up of these three parts,
to each of which the student may more immediately turn, as the
particular object of his studies at the time requires.

The personal character of Louis affords a striking specimen
of the virtues and vices that may result from an extreme sensibility to praise; his vanity, his pride, his love of applause and
his love of glory are continually presented to the reader.

As this sensibility to praise is found more or less in every man;
and though given us by our Creator for the wisest purposes,
liable like every other principle of our nature to be abused, it
may not be amiss briefly to state the three leading distinctions that belong to the subject.   These distinctions are often
neglected, or not seen; and as one of the uses of history is to
improve the moral character, as well as to enlighten the political
views of the student, I may perhaps be allowed to turn for a
moment from the one to the other, more particularly as I am
addressing myself to the young, to those whose dispositions may
be considered as now in the very act of assuming the tone and

direction, which may materially influence their subsequent happiness and usefulness to the community.

The highest merit is to learn and practise virtue for its own reward : not indeed to be insensible to the praise of others ; to receive it when reasonably offered, and even to enjoy it ; but to receive it and enjoy it rather as a good that is properly an *attendant* on the performance of meritorious actions, than as the original *object* to be attained by them—as an attendant on good actions, not the object of them.   In this manner the character is kept modest and reasonable, and is left susceptible of the highest motives which can be inspired by virtue and religion ; and yet it is not required from any man to make vain efforts to exclude from his feelings that co-incident pleasure which we are by nature formed to derive from the applause of our fellow-creatures: so to understand virtue and so to practise it seems the highest merit.

The next merit is to perform good actions from the love of true glory ; that is, from sensibility to praise, but to praise bestowed on actions that are themselves praiseworthy, that are really meritorious, and the proper objects of moral approbation. This, though not the highest merit of which human nature is capable, is still merit.

What I have now, in the third and last place, to mention, is sensibility to praise, *however* procured ; to praise when given to actions, whether meritorious or not ; when even given by *mistake* to supposed qualities or actions not really existing.   To this last description of sentiment belongs vanity, under all its whimsical, contemptible, and prevailing forms ; to the second (the love of true glory), belongs self-estimation ; to the first (the love of virtue), belongs the high consciousness of purity and right.

In certain respects, all these are connected with, and bordering upon each other ; and the confounding of them together, and the attributing indiscriminately to each, or to all, the praise or censure that belongs exclusively to some one of them, is the great fallacy of the licentious moralists, Rochefoucault and Mandeville for instance.

It is the fault too, or mistake, often of men of the world ; and of all who have more acuteness in their understandings, than kindness in their temperaments ; a fault very visible in their writings, and for ever in their conversation.

These three descriptions of sentiment, which I have thus adverted to, are, however all essentially different in themselves ; and it is no unprofitable amusement for a philosophic mind to observe, in its own instance, and in the instances of others, the various combinations and alternations of these different principles,—the love of virtue, the love of true glory, and the love of mere praise.

It is the last, the love of mere praise, which is the original and first rude impulse of nature.

By education and reflection this is gradually improved into the second, the love of true glory ; and at length elevated into the first, the love of virtue. But it may happen that this conversion of the one into the other, this happy improvement of the moral character, may never take place at all, or at least very imperfectly.

Of all mortals those who are the most unfortunately situated in this respect, and the *least* likely to receive this improvement, are the rulers of the earth, kings and princes, those who have a merit in the eyes of others, independent of their own personal good qualities ; in like manner all who belong to the privileged orders of society, the nobility of a country, its gentry and men of family and distinction.

The same observation may even descend, more or less, to every man, who from any advantage whatever, not only of birth or fortune, but even of personal appearance, of beauty, strength, or activity, possesses any merit in the eyes of others which is not properly his own, any merit which he does not strictly earn by the superiority of his understanding, or of his virtues.

But if such be the situation of all beings, and of whatever sex, whether privileged by society or favoured by nature, it was more particularly so of Louis XIV. ; and this is one of the lessons which his character affords. Louis was one of those rulers of the earth, who became a king while an infant, whose education was most defective, who was left ignorant, according to the account of St. Simon, to a degree that is quite astonishing ; who was surrounded, not only by courtiers and sycophants, but by a nation, whose character, if analyzed, seems never to ascend beyond the merit of the second degree I have mentioned, the love of true glory, not often so high ; whose character is much more generally moulded by the mere love of praise, of praise however procured.

As Louis was, unfortunately for the world, possessed also of a fine constitution and a handsome person, his moral improvement was rendered still more impossible ; and the result, as seen in St. Simon, was precisely all that a speculator on human nature would have expected.

Eternally uneasy, and in action, as every man will be, who (though on a smaller scale) thinks of nothing but praise ; eternally finding, or looking to find, an audience, before whom he might exhibit his performances ; eternally at his levees or on his terraces, a sort of posture-master; the very rising and going to bed was with Louis a sort of drama; through the whole of the royal day he had his exits and his entrances; and whether he rode or walked, or dined or dressed, the whole world was supposed to be present, and the hero of the piece was Louis. Even at the hour of prayer, it was the *grand monarque* that was at his devotions; and no ideas, however awful, however overwhelming, could sweep away from his mind, even for a moment, the tinsel trumpery of human grandeur.

But Louis not only desired to live upon applause, but was enabled to do so. The applause was always ready, he had only to look and to receive it; and in the total absence of all that moral discipline which other human beings more or less find in the looks and words of those around them, no wonder that he became ungovernably selfish, a ridiculous egotist, so as even to join in singing his own panegyrics; no wonder that he was a slave to his passions, and that he at last conceived not only that his own people, but that the world itself was intended merely to furnish out materials for what he was pleased to denominate, his glory.

It is remarkable how completely the French nation gave in to these delusions, how thoroughly they identified themselves with their monarch. They had lost their States General, they had no houses of representation to convey any worthier images of the nation, or to furnish them with the materials of more dignified reflection; they had just emerged from the horrors of religious wars and the miseries of domestic confusion and dispute. Independent of these political circumstances, their own merits and faults, their wisdom and their follies, were all those of the young king; their virtues the same, the same their vices. Praise is with them to be acquired; if by proper means, well, but at all events to be acquired. The cause, therefore, of both was common; their sympathies with their monarch, their excuses for his conduct were always ready; and their property, their lives, their talents, and their genius, all became the instruments of his power, and were wielded at his pleasure to the purposes of his own gratification and aggrandizement.

And this leads me to the second aspect under which he is to be viewed. What was he to his people? To them he has often been considered as a benefactor; at least it has been thought that France, as a great kingdom, is under lasting obligations to him. This may be admitted, but must then be understood in a certain limited sense.

For instance, the religious and civil wars, and long years of contest, hatred, and bloodshed, of private wrongs, and public executions, had left the French nation fierce and ferocious. Louis had the merit of civilizing them. This he did in the first place, as has been generally observed, by the arts and sciences which he encouraged and protected. But, again, he must have produced the same salutary effect in another way, one not so generally noticed. For instance, he constantly exhibited in his own person, and in the persons of his ministers and officers, the whole power of the state, regularly asserted, exercised, and diffused all over the community; maintaining, everywhere, order, tranquillity, and the due execution of the laws of civil and criminal justice. On both accounts, therefore, he contributed to civilize France. This is the most favourable point of view in which Louis can be surveyed. It is very creditable to Louis that, coming to the throne so young, and to a kingdom so situated as France then was, he was yet able to carry on the government without incurring any renewal of domestic confusion, or the apparent domination of any minister, by whose power or genius he was himself eclipsed. Again, under the influence of his personal qualities, the great feudatories of the state became no longer a dangerous description of men, ready to be themselves monarchs, but a mere court noblesse, dependent on the sovereign for their honours, distinctions, and often even their private fortunes. He could

> "Grace with a smile and ruin with a frown."

Louis, in this respect, followed up, and indeed carried to excess, the original achievement of the great Henry and the triumphs of Richelieu; even the manners of the people were affected; and, on the whole, the kingdom, in every respect, though not without some unfavourable collateral effects, was materially civilized. He had undoubtedly, at the same time, the very important merit of choosing able men for the various departments of the state. And this is not only at all times the best criterion of the merit of every prince, but it is more particularly so of Louis; from whose ignorance, vanity, pride, and impetuosity, no conduct so rational could have been expected.

It happened that during the reign of Louis the most celebrated men appeared that have ever adorned this great kingdom. And as they all seemed to move under the influence of his protection and encouragement, their glory has, in the general apprehension of mankind, been reflected on the monarch. Nor is this entirely unjust; however soberly we may estimate the influence of the great on the talents of those around them, and however powerful the effect, which we may ascribe, in affairs of this nature, to the mere operations of chance, merit, and even considerable merit, must still be left to Louis, when we consider all those very striking and successful exertions of genius and learning which are seen, under his auspices, to have illustrated his age and nation.

This, the great praise of Louis, has been seized upon by one of his panegyrists. "Turenne," says he, " Condé, Luxemburgh, were his generals; Colbert, Louvois, Tourcy, were his statesmen; Vauban, his engineer; Perault constructed his palaces—they were adorned by Le Poussin and Le Brun; Le Notre laid out his gardens; Corneille and Racine wrote his tragedies; Molière, his comedies; Boileau was his poet; Bossuet, Bourdaloue, Massillon, were his preachers. It is in this august assemblage of men, whose fame can never die, that this monarch, whom they acknowledged as their patron and protector, presents himself to the admiration of posterity."

There is certainly something here to arrest us in the career of our censure, after travelling through all the strange and disgraceful disorders of the former reign. We see, at length, a disciplined army, public order, authority everywhere vigilant and resistless; regular government duly administered through all its departments; habits of obedience and loyalty deeply engrafted, and thoroughly introduced into the national character. To these, the solid basis of this system, and of every system of government, must be added the more ornamental part—the paintings, the statues, the splendid vases, the libraries—all the rich and massy furniture, with which the great national edifice, the work of Louis XIV., was adorned; and we thus see, altogether presented to us, that magnificent whole, which so strongly impressed, which so entirely fascinated and overpowered not only the French people, but the people of all the kingdoms of Europe; and if no more remained to be told, the admiration of posterity might not only be demanded for Louis, but allowed. There is, however, much more to be told, and we must not, like the French people themselves at the time, be insensible to the serious faults which so obscured the merits of their *grand monarque*.

The great object of the administration of Louis was, from the first, to suffer nothing of weight or dignity to exist in the state, but what immediately emanated from the throne, or was visibly dependent on his pleasure. He wished himself to direct the marine, the army, and the finances; everywhere to be the spring and principle of every movement. The people were to have no other guardian of their happiness, the empire no other security; his ministers, his generals, no other patron or protector; above all, there was to appear no representative of the national consequence and will but himself. The ancient assemblies of the community, the States General, were, at all events, not to be summoned. " L'état, c'est moi" was his favourite phrase. He was in his own apprehension, as is very apparent from different passages in his works, a sort of divinity on earth, certainly the representative of the Divinity.

All this was but the result of his inordinate love of distinction, his total selfishness, and the contracted views which had resulted from an education originally defective. To accomplish this monopoly of all power and all consequence was the secret and entire labour of his life on every occasion—at the most frivolous entertainment as at the most important sitting of the cabinet. His ministers were therefore obliged to endeavour to direct his councils by contrivance and stratagem, and to deceive him into a belief that he was himself the origin of the plans which he only adopted. His nobility was to remain continually within the reach of his smiles or frowns, or they lost all their personal influence and weight. It was a sufficient accusation that he " never saw them," as he termed it.

Not only the nobility, but every person was to be kept in a state of constant subjection to his criticisms by an extensive system of espionage, which descended to the most disgraceful expedients, and entered into the detail of all the intrigues and silly adventures of the metropolis; he had a police that kept every person and every concern within his view; every being was to be fixed in his own exact station and office, and the movements of every mind and body that approached the court, or enjoyed any distinction there or elsewhere, were to be combined into a sort of harmony with those of the monarch, by the most widely extended and duly adjusted system of form and etiquette that was probably ever devised or executed: Louis, and the court which I have thus described, were to meet and parade in palaces, whose extent and magnificence were to rival the romances of the imagination; even Nature herself was to be insulted and overpowered, to achieve the wonders of Versailles; the sums expended are understood to have increased in so frightful a manner that the king at last threw the accounts into the fire; still, however, continuing them. They had reached more than sixty millions of our money; the very roofs of this palace

would cover a surface of twenty-five French acres; similar prodigality was exhibited at Marly, and his rage for expensive
buildings was quite a characteristic and a most criminal one of
his reign. All this was fitted to produce what it did produce,
the spectacle which I have already described, as so striking to
all Europe, and as so deserving of the curiosity and reflection of
every reader of history; the best specimen that can be shown of
the court and the administration of an arbitrary monarch, on the
European, not Asiatic model, but without any representative
bodies of the people, or indeed of the nobility; the spectacle of
a great kingdom advanced to a situation in some respects of an
enviable, and in most respects of a very imposing appearance;—
opulent cities, spacious roads, canals, and ports, and harbours,
arsenals and dockyards, every apparatus, naval and military, for
attack or defence;—academies, hospitals, public buildings and
palaces;—manufactures, arts and sciences;—statesmen, theo-
logians, philosophers, historians, and antiquarians, orators and
poets;—much of the accommodation, much of the embellish-
ment, all the outward magnificence of civilization. All this is
certainly to be found, and gave rise to what was called the Age
of Louis XIV.; and it seems at first sight too presumptuous to
say that all this is still insufficient, to say that civilization can
realize something still more valuable to the community, and
more dignified to the monarch; yet such is assuredly the truth;
and it is no improper indulgence of national pride to say, that
in consequence of our public assemblies, and more particularly
of our representative assembly, our House of Commons, more,
and even far more than all this, striking and splendid as it may
be, is undoubtedly to be found in this distinguished island of
our own.

It might perhaps be too much to have expected from Louis a
foresight of the danger as well as knowledge of the injustice of
his system; a consciousness that though the grandeur of his reign
could not be denied, the solidity was doubtful, that the bubble
might at any moment burst, that all was false and hollow, and
that no government was really safe which violated the common
feelings and reason of mankind. But the whole is a memorable
illustration of this great maxim in political science; a striking
spectacle for the instruction of posterity. The lesson may be
said to commence with the destruction of the free constitution
of France by Louis XI. and Richelieu, to have proceeded along
with the confirmation of arbitrary power, which was advanced
to an elaborate and perfect system by Louis XIV., and to have

terminated in the awful catastrophe that has happened in our own times.

An enlarged philosophy of this kind it might have been too much to have required from a prince so educated and so situated as Louis; but though he might not have discovered the true and best foundations of the security and grandeur of his monarchy, still he might have understood the obvious interests of his people, the ruinous nature of his passion for military glory and expense, and the more than ordinary wickedness of his unprincipled ambition.

On the contrary, to advert now to the third consideration, his relation to foreign states, Louis was long the terror of the civilized world; he was long considered as the tyrant that menaced the liberties of Holland and every kingdom that he could overpower; as the monarch who had entertained thoughts even of universal empire.

But what was to be the result? At home a system of taxation was to be urged on to the most oppressive expedients; peasants were to be hunted down and seized, to be forcibly enlisted in the armies: abroad, Holland, England, Europe were to be attacked or insulted; a succession of battles was to be fought, attended with the most frightful carnage; that is, the industrious were to be impoverished, the tender were to mourn, and the brave were to die, because Louis was to be called great, because Louis had chosen to be enrolled among the conquerors of the earth! It is surely difficult to love, it is surely strange to admire a monarch like this. Of the last forty-eight years of his reign, twenty-nine were years of war; more than a million of men were sacrificed; the state was so reduced that the very servants of the king, covered with his liveries, asked alms at the doors of his palace at Versailles.

He had scarcely begun to reign when he assumed those imperious and menacing airs which indicated but too clearly what Europe had to expect.

The invasion of the Franche Comptè followed in 1668, and of Holland in 1672; and so insolent was his conduct, so unreasonable and so unjust, that he enabled William, the great hero of the liberties of mankind, to form, in opposition to his designs, the celebrated league of Augsburg. Ten years of war, bloody and ruinous both to France and Europe, followed; and the character of Louis had been now so displayed, and its ambition so well understood, that the will of the king of Spain, which gave the Spanish crown to one of the younger princes of his family, was resisted by Europe, and gave occasion to the war of the Succession—the war which was so marked by the triumphs of Marlborough and Eugene, and which had almost reduced Louis to contend for his crown, and France for its independence, at the very gates of Paris.

These, the leading measures of his reign, form, united, a most dreadful indictment against him; and it is impossible to distinguish such a monarch from any other of those mistaken and guilty mortals who have so misused their power as to deserve every mark of disgust and reprobation which can be inflicted upon them by the historian and by the thinking part of mankind.

On his death-bed, when it was now indeed but too late, when, as one of our old divines expresses it, " the fantastic images of self-love are removed, and the gay remembrances of vain opinion and popular noises ;" at this awful period the monarch seems to have been conscious, if not entirely of his fault, at least that he had much mistaken the first duties of a sovereign. " My child," says he to the dauphin, " seek peace as the source of every good ; avoid war as the source of every evil. My example in this respect is not a good one; do not imitate it ; it is that part of my life and reign which I most repent."

But how strong must have been the reasons for repentance before they could have reached the infatuated mind of a monarch like Louis.

France is understood never to have recovered from the efforts which she made to gratify the pride and injustice of her sovereign.

The punishments of kings and nations are sometimes awful in their ultimate, though not immediate accomplishment.

Louis found himself and his empire advanced at one period of his reign to the highest point of what he conceived to be human glory. In a century afterwards his monarchy was at an end, and his descendant was expiring under the hand of the public executioner.—But I must now hasten to take leave of this celebrated age and its celebrated hero.

Madame de Genlis, in a preface to one of her beautiful compositions, the Memoirs of Madame de Valière, has endeavoured to assert the cause of this renowned monarch, and to present him to the love as well as the remembrance of mankind; but the character of her favourite has been already decided, and no new estimate, agreeable to her wishes, can now be procured. There is little (that I may briefly recapitulate what I have said), there is little in Louis to be loved, and not much that can properly be admired. He violated his most acknowledged duties; he was an adulterer, and even openly so; in the same carriage with him, and in presence of his armies, were seen his two mistresses and his queen. He found in Madame de Valière one whom he not only loved, but one who would have thought herself but too happy to have been loved by him; too happy, as he well knew, if she had been the object of his affection and choice in a private station, and had shared with him, and for his sake endured the obscurity of a cottage or the privations of the most laborious life; yet this mistress—his mistress in spite of all her sense of right and honourable feelings, this unfortunate lady, he saw consign herself to a living death in a cloister, only because he had abandoned her for another. What next ensued? This second object of his attachment he again abandoned for a third; an adulterer to his queen while she lived, and, at last, by his connexion with Madame de Maintenon, subsiding into an anomalous and mixed situation of right and wrong, licentiousness and duty; too proud to be supposed a husband, too devout (as he imagined) to be a keeper, and at last only taught to know himself by the defeats of his generals, and the overwhelming calamities which he had brought upon his people. What is there here to be loved? What is there in the man, as a husband, a father, or a master, to interest our affections? What is there that we would wish to be found in the character of our children, our friends, or ourselves? As a king, what are his praises? The reducing of his kingdom to order and civilization by the authority of his government; the selection of men of ability for his ministers; the protection of the fine arts; important merits these, no doubt; but these are all.

If the maxims of government which he confirmed and established—its revolting practices, his lettres de cachet, and his Bastile; if the spirit of ambition which he indulged and transmitted; if the habits of licentiousness and expense which he countenanced in his court; if the systems of taxation which he entailed on his people; if these could not fail immediately to produce the most severe calamities; if ultimately they produced the necessity, or at least gave occasion to the late dreadful revolution—if these points be admitted—and how are they to be contested?—it will be difficult to select from the whole course of history a single mortal whose follies have been so injurious, whose faults have been so fatal to his fellow-creatures as were those of Louis XIV.

The concluding scenes of the life of Louis are described with great minuteness by St. Simon. He died penitent, and was often observed joining his hands in prayer, and striking his breast while in the act of self-confession. I could wish you to turn to this particular portion of the Memoirs of the duke, not only because Louis is an example to show that after an ill-spent life the bitter hour of self-reproach must come, and this, whatever be the deceitful nature of the human heart (no man ever had one so deceitful as Louis), but because a youthful student can never be too strongly reminded of the transitory nature of everything human ; however he may value, and justly value, the proper enjoyments of this sublunary state, he must never forget that the pleasures, whether rational or not, of his existence and his existence itself, in this world at least, must pass away.

He has seen Louis XIV. the idol and the master of the most brilliant court that Europe has ever witnessed ; he has seen him surrounded by his mistresses, his ladies, and his courtiers, his statesmen and his generals, his artists and his bards, and he has now to see of all these things the awful and concluding lesson—

> " To what complexion they must come at last."

Louis is to undergo the same appalling change which is the law of our common nature—Louis is to die.

The physicians are assembled, and they can afford no succour ; the gens d'armerie are brought up, and at last they can no longer be reviewed, even from the window ; the musicians cannot now be listened to, " charm they never so wisely ;" the conversation of Madame de Maintenon and the ladies can interest no more ; the king sits drowsy or asleep, and wakes confused : the pulse fails, and he lies on his royal bed helpless and expiring, fallen from his high estate, and his kingdom departing from him ; a greater monarch than he has at last appeared, to whose dart, as he prepares to strike, his own earthly sceptre, if opposed, would be but a pigmy's straw ; and this terrific being now marshals him the way he is to go, the way to that vale and shadow, glimmering on the confines of the present world and the future, which he is now to enter, and which stands for ever open to receive the fleeting generations of mankind. It must be ever thus, and the poet, while musing in his churchyard path, repeats but the sentiment which might have been felt on the terraces of Versailles :—

> " The boast of heraldy, the pomp of power,
> And all that beauty, all that wealth e'er gave,
> Await alike the inevitable hour ;
> The paths of glory lead but to the grave."

I will make one observation more, not unconnected with the general subject of the reign, and conclude.

Literature and the arts flourished in the reign of Louis, as they did in that of Augustus. It has hence been made a question whether they flourish not under an arbitrary monarchy better than under a government that is free ; nor are there wanting reasons to show that this may be the case, and, at all events, it will be said, what reasoning like the fact ?

But when this is made a question, it should be considered what is included under the terms of literature and the arts.

Literature and the arts can flourish while they disturb not the arbitrary maxims, civil or religious, which are adopted by the government under which they appear—but no longer.

This measured licence, however, this contracted indulgence, can never be favourable to the common cause of the genius of the human mind, which kindles by mutual sympathy in every direction, and which can in this manner, and in this manner only, reach its full and natural perfection.

It is not considered how capricious and unjust may be the arbitrary monarch, even while he professes himself to be the patron of literature and the arts. Virgil could find a patron in Augustus, but Ovid experienced only a persecutor and a tyrant. The same despot who could give a donation to the Mantuan bard for the compliment to Marcellus, could tear away the author of the Metamorphoses from the splendours of Rome, and the delights of polished society, and cast him out upon the snows of Thrace amid the barbarians that surrounded the Euxine ; his complaints, the tender and elegant Tristia, that were written from the desolate wastes of these inhospitable regions, have never ceased to move every reader of sensibility and taste, but they could produce no impression on the master of an arbitrary government ; and the hapless poet, sickening under the sensations of hope deferred, at last despaired, and confessed that his genius had been his ruin.

" Ingenio perii Naso poeta meo."

Virgil, however, and Ovid might both have sung in courts and capitals, where Tacitus could not have thought ; and the pages of this philosophic historian will now for ever attest the connexion that subsists between the genius and the freedom of the human mind. The same great truth was again felt, even under all the patronage of a court, by Longinus. In every age and succeeding period of the world the conclusion is the same. Raphael and Michael Angelo might have adorned palaces and temples with all the forms of sublimity and beauty, in cities where Galileo could not have unveiled the science of the heavens, nor Luther laid open the book of life.   Under Louis XIV., in like manner (the celebrated patron of every muse), Boileau, and Poussin, and Bossuet, and other illustrious men, divines, and artists, and poets could find emoluments and distinctions; but Fénélon had to be removed to a distance and to disguise the effusions of his patriotism and wisdom.

In our own country, in like manner, the immortal Locke, under James II., was a student persecuted and silent; the world received no benefit from the labours of his thoughts. But the lapse of a few years and the renewal of a free form of government saw him cherished and admired; saw him give to mankind his Treatise on Government, his Reasonableness of Christianity, his Essay on Toleration, his Essay on the Human Mind, and contribute more, perhaps, than any individual who can be mentioned, to the best interests of his fellow-creatures, by contributing to remove obscurity from the mind, servility from the heart, and dogmatism from the understanding.

I need not continue this subject further.   The arts that adorn, and the literature that charms the polished leisure of society, may flourish under a Louis as they did under an Augustus, but not so the higher pursuits of the human understanding.   It is freedom alone which can conduct the genius of mankind to that sublimer perception of truth, to which the Almighty Master sometimes admits (as in his wisdom he sees best) the aspiring, though bounded faculties of his creatures.

LECTURE III.

LOUIS XV.

The two following Lectures were originally delivered after the Lectures on the American War, and were the conclusion of the second Course.   The character of the Regent is adverted to in the twenty-seventh Lecture of the same Course.

1811.

IT is impossible for us, who live at this period, not to turn to the reign of Louis XV. with an interest that those who lived before us can never have experienced.   To them it must have appeared (in this island at least) little more than the history of private and public profligacy, of an ambitious and licentious court, of a debauched king, and of his unprincipled mistresses; a scene, that by the virtuous and the good, under our own free government, would be only surveyed for a moment, and that with scorn and horror; of which the image would be banished from the memory, as a sort of pollution to the thoughts.

We approach it, now, with sentiments not of less repugnance, but of more curiosity, and indeed with a sort of awful anxiety. Most of us have seen, we all of us feel, (our children, to many a distant age, are destined to feel,) the effects of the most tremendous Revolution that Europe has ever known, since the decline of the Roman empire. Even in the reign of Louis XIV. we can now discern, as we read, the coming of this great event. What signs may we not expect to see in the long reign of his immediate successor, Louis XV.? Ignorant as men are, at the time, of the bearings and consequences not only of what they see passing around them, but often of what they are doing themselves,—it is still competent for us, after the event is known, to trace out the causes with which it appears to have been connected through many a distant year; and if men are ever, by any reading and meditation, to be improved in the great scale of their public relations, if they are ever to be formed, some into statesmen, others into intelligent citizens, it is not a little by retrospects like these.

After what I have now said of the interest that belongs to this period, you will be disappointed to hear from me that there is no very good account of the reign to which I can refer you. It has not yet been written as a portion of French history. It is indeed the misery of all those who have to read French history, to find on all occasions a crowd of memoirs offered to them, with and without names, instead of any regular history, delivered to the world by any author of reputation. But the history of Louis XV. probably appeared at the time to be only the history of his mistresses and their favourites. To have given any account of their proceedings, that would have been worthy of the name of history, might not at the moment have been very prudent. Perhaps no writer adequate to the task could have been found; and every thinking man in France, *after* the reign of Louis XV., amid the confusion and pressure of the events that succeeded it, was little at leisure to begin a history of the times that were past. Du Clos deserts us about the period at which we are now arrived. A few words about Cardinal Fleury, and a good account of the Seven Years' War, more particularly of the concern the French took in it, comprises the remainder of his work. We are therefore left to look out for some other guide, and I do not conceive that any can be found who would properly satisfy a French scholar;

but, perhaps, English students like yourselves may be more easily satisfied. Certain reasons exist why you may be. For instance, the great subjects of the reign, to which you will turn with interest, may be considered in a general manner; and therefore you may be satisfied when a native of the country may not—the foreign politics of the reign form the first subject of inquiry.

Now, these may be found in the histories of other countries, and are of the usual stamp; the politics of craft and ambition. They therefore may be estimated in a general manner. Next, you will observe, that the domestic politics, though of the most important nature, can also be estimated in a general manner. What were they?

1st, The disputes between the court and the parliaments; those of a financial and those of an ecclesiastical nature.

2nd, The effect, in the mean time, which the writings of different eminent authors were producing upon the public mind,—the progress of the new opinions.

These, together, constitute the great subject of domestic interest during the reign of Louis. And they, too, can be best comprehended by looking at them, as it were, from a distance, and throwing them, if possible, into large masses.

The detail, therefore, on the whole, I venture to conclude, though naturally sought for by French scholars, need not be required by those of this country.

We might find, as the French readers may find, and as they require us to find, memoirs of mistresses and favourites; of Madame de Pompadour, of La Comtesse Dubarri, or even of the Duc de Choiseul, the minister. But we should perceive that it was to little purpose we had occupied our time and run the chance of debasing our minds by accompanying such personages through their disgusting scenes of court intrigue or impudent profligacy.

It is known beforehand that it is by such means that states and empires, whatever be their apparent strength, may be brought to destruction; and, when this is known, what is there else to know? The more minute transactions of these disgraceful scenes we need not dwell on.

Again, we should find it very difficult to go through all the particulars of the struggle between the crown and the parliaments, even were they anywhere presented to our view. But I know not that they are. There is a work by Voltaire on the subject of the parliaments, but it is little to our present purpose; stops short and huddles up the subject, where we might have wished it to proceed fully and methodically; is rather a history

of them from the earliest epoch than a history of them during
this important period ; and it has been considered as a partial
representation, as a sacrifice to the court, made by this distinguished author, the better to dispose the court to favour, or to
tolerate his own designs against Christianity.

In like manner, it would not be very easy to read the detail of
the financial history of these times, though its *general* importance
is easily understood.   It seems enough for us to comprehend, as
we can readily do, that the court would not be economical ; would
neither be virtuous at home, nor abstain from wars abroad ; that
the clergy and nobility would not pay their shares to the general
contribution ; and that, therefore, different comptrollers-general,
who were to find supplies for the general expense, had only the
same impossibilities to perform, and lamentations to utter.

If then the detail of these subjects be not entirely necessary,
you may be more reconciled to the *apparently* inadequate information which can be offered to you, even on such a subject as
the reign of Louis XV. ; a reign which I have announced, and
must continue to announce, to you, as the prelude to the French
Revolution.

But I spoke of general information that might be offered to
you ; what then is it ?

Though no writer, as I have already observed, has made a
regular history of this period, something has been done.

In the first place, a sort of history of Louis XV. has been written by Voltaire.   The foreign politics of the reign may be collected from this work, and an idea of the principal events.

The same may be done from the short account supplied by D'Anquetil, in his late History (of fifteen octavo volumes), which, as a
short general history of France, drawn up at the instigation of
Buonaparte, I have already taken occasion to recommend.

But, finally, and on the whole, the work on which I depend,
both for the internal and external concerns of this reign, is the
work of Lacretelle.   I have already mentioned it.   It is intended
by him as an introduction to his estimate (his Précis) of the
French Revolution.   It embraces a view of the foreign politics
of the reign, and of the more domestic transactions ; the disputes
between the court and parliaments, and, lastly, an account of the
different authors, and writings, that influenced the subsequent
fortunes of the French monarchy.

Here then we have, as I conceive, what we want.   Lacretelle
is considered as having drawn up his account from such books
as are in the hands of men of letters in France, and from such

other sources of conversation and inquiry as are to us in this country inaccessible. The author may be thought, and I believe is thought, by those *French scholars* who are conversant with these times, to have passed over the transactions of them, with a sort of general, and sometimes even superficial elegance, which he interrupts not by any occasional display of very minute research. But I must here recall to your mind what I have just said. He may still present an English reader with an account that, for the reasons I have mentioned, will be sufficiently detailed and profound; nay, more, one that is only the fitter for our perusal, from being of a general nature. I do not think the matter of these volumes of Lacretelle well arranged, and it will easily be perceived that due deference is paid to the political views of the present ruler of France, Buonaparte; that the author's hatred also to England is unceasing: but in a literary point of view he is always a pleasing, and often a very beautiful writer; and with the exceptions I have mentioned, may be welcomed not only as a guide, but, on the whole, as a sufficient guide.

Since I wrote this paragraph, I have observed that Me. de Staël speaks favourably of this author, of Lacretelle.

We will now advert a little more particularly to the reign before us. Louis XV. reigned a considerable part of the last century, from 1715 to 1774, almost as long as he lived. In 1715 began the regency of the Duke of Orleans, who died in 1723. A short period of about two years and a-half comprehends the administration of the Duke of Bourbon, or rather of his mistress, la Marquise de Prie. Fleury then appears on the stage, and dies in 1743. He was, therefore, minister of France for seventeen years. On his death, the king (Louis XV.) undertook to be his own prime minister; an unpromising experiment for a country at any time. In this instance the result was only, that the king's mistress, Me. de Chateauroux, became the ruler of France, and soon after Me. de Pompadour, another mistress, whose reign was prolonged from 1745 to 1763. Different courtiers and prelates were seen to hold the first offices of the state during this apparent premiership of the monarch. The ladies seem to have chosen or tolerated Cardinal Tençin, Argençon, Orsy, Mauripaux, and Amelot, who, with the Dukes Noailles and Richelieu, succeeded to Fleury.

Afterwards, we have Argençon and Machault, and then come the most celebrated of the ministers or favourites of Me. de Pompadour, the Abbé de Bernis and the Duc de Choiseul. The last is the most distinguished minister after Fleury. He continued in favour from 1758, not only to 1763, when Me. de Pompadour died, but for a few years after. He was at length disgraced by la Comtesse Dubarri, who had become the king's mistress soon after the death of M^e. de Pompadour, and remained so, nearly to the death of the monarch himself, in 1774.

You will learn from Lacretelle more fully the names and characters of these mistresses and ministers by whom France was thus governed during this reign. Little or no information respecting them is to be derived from Voltaire. And his account, in many respects, particularly in this, appears to me but meagre and indifferent. He probably chose to be on good terms with the principal persons of the court and administration at the time he lived. Madame de Pompadour was a kind of patroness to him.

You will then, for the present, bear in mind, the better to understand what observations I can offer, that the regent, Duke of Orleans, of whom I have already spoken, is the first ruler of the kingdom, down to the year 1723 ; Cardinal Fleury soon follows, and continues minister seventeen years ; Madame de Pompadour succeeds for about seventeen years more, till the termination of the great war, in which Lord Chatham was our minister, in the year 1763 ; then comes la Comtesse Dubarri ; that the Duc de Choiseul, during the last five years of M^e. de Pompadour had been minister ; that he continued minister about thirteen years, till the end of the year 1770, when la Comtesse Dubarri was disgraced, and the chancellor Maupeou, and the Duc D'Aiguillon remained in power till 1774, the end of the reign.

The whole subject may be now divided into two parts ; the foreign politics and the domestic.

These are (necessarily perhaps) mixed up and intermingled in Lacretelle, but I would wish you to consider the train of each of them apart, referring, no doubt, each to the other, from time to time, but keeping each of them in the first place as much as possible apart, that you may afterwards be more aware of the folly of the whole course of the one, from observing, by a sort of side glance as you go along, the folly of the whole course of the other. For, to describe the whole, in one word, you will see in the foreign politics, for the most part, every readiness to embark in enterprises of war and expense, while, at home, in the meantime, you will observe every readiness on the part of the court to outrage the opinions of the public ; i. e., every means employed to increase the embarrassment of the finances, and yet every pains taken at the same time to render it impossible to tax the people and repair the evil.

We will now treat of these two subjects, the foreign and domestic concerns, each in their order: our notices can be but slight, but I will endeavour to direct your views to the principal points.

Of the foreign politics Voltaire gives the leading facts, still more Lacretelle; but Coxe's House of Austria must be read along with them; and these, with our own histories, will be sufficient.

Of the foreign politics of the reign, you will remember that the great features are, 1st, The peace maintained between France and England during the administration of the regent and Fleury. Then the war, in which Maria Theresa, the young empress queen of the house of Austria was attacked in the year 1741, in which France took a part, and to which war Fleury most disgracefully assented. Next a total change in the policy of France; an alliance with the house of Austria during the reign of Mᵉ. de Pompadour, and an interference in the Seven Years' War in 1756, in favour of Maria Theresa, and against the kings of Prussia and England.

These are the three great features. There are two events of a more detached nature, that may be kept apart from the rest : 1st, An interference in the affairs of Poland by Fleury, early in the year 1735, in consequence of which the Duchies of Lorraine and Bar were ceded to France; and, 2ndly, An interference in the affairs of Genoa and Corsica, by the Duc de Choiseul, in the year 1768, in consequence of which Corsica was annexed to the crown of France.

These seem to me the great features of the foreign politics of the reign : but we will allude a little more distinctly to them, and then to the ministers who conducted them. Of the administration of the regent we have spoken in a former lecture. A most fortunate union of interest, between France and England, then existed; fortunate even in the apprehension of the rulers of each country.

Cardinal Fleury, who succeeded the regent, was distinguished, like the sensible minister of England (Walpole), for his love of peace.

> "Peace is my dear delight, not Fleury's more."

This was again most fortunate for mankind; but it must be confessed that Fleury was quite undone by Walpole in this inestimable quality, the love of peace. Fleury suffered (however unwillingly), but he suffered France to interfere in the succession to the crown of Poland, and placed England in such a situation that Walpole must have been perplexed in the extreme.

It is with the greatest difficulty we can accede to the cautious politics of Walpole on this occasion, while he declined assisting the house of Austria.

The cardinal had no right to try the peaceful temper of England and her ministers so severely. The Duchies of Lorraine and Bar were annexed to France, and became the boasts of the administration of the pacific Fleury.

Accession of territory should form no part of the wishes of any such minister; it is not on such objects that he should rest his fame. The great accusation of Fleury is, that though fond of peace, he had not magnanimity enough to be consistent; to abstain from attempts to aggrandize France, and to depress the house of Austria; but without a magnanimity and consistency of this kind, how vain is it to pretend to the praise of a love of peace!

This affair of Poland you will see sufficiently detailed in Coxe, and it is interesting. The next transaction is the war of 1741, against Maria Theresa. Fleury seems to have had the merit of opposing those counsels in the French cabinet which produced and assisted the unjustifiable attack on the young queen. But, to oppose is not always sufficient. He ought assuredly to have retired from the cabinet, or insisted on directing it to the purposes of peace and justice. He did neither. He died in the midst of the first misfortunes of the war; misfortunes which justified, no doubt to his own mind, the pacific counsels he had offered, while the invasion of England, by the Pretender, must in like manner have sanctioned to the mind of Walpole, at the time when he also was dying, the pacific policy which *he* too had maintained through the whole of his administration.

The war which Fleury suffered his country to engage in against Maria Theresa, is the war to which Johnson alludes in his " Vanity of Human Wishes;" the poem, in which he continues, by a variety of instances, to imitate one of the finest compositions of ancient literature, till he produces one of the finest of modern; certainly of its kind, the finest:

"The bold Bavarian, in a luckless hour," &c.

On the character of Fleury, and on the character of his administration, there are good observations scattered through the work of Lacretelle. I depend upon your reading them, and do not undertake to afford you here the proper benefit of them. The character of this minister was that of wisdom, not of genius; and rather the wisdom of old age than of the understanding in its vigour. He might be distinguished among the rulers of France (he easily was) for disinterestedness and a love of economy. But he left nothing to live after him. No institution, no scheme of useful policy, no improvement of the constitution, or even laws of his country. Lorraine alone spoke his merits; an objectionable testimony, as his real merits were of a peaceful and a different kind.

His views, however, his intentions, his wishes, if these were in the minister of a great country sufficient, were of the proper nature; and, as far as the foreign politics of France were concerned, would not have tended, as did those of his successors, to accelerate the Revolution we have seen.

Descending then, thirdly, from the regent and Fleury, who died in 1743, we have to observe, that his death, during the war, produced no favourable effect on the councils of France; much the contrary: Louis XV. was rendered only more eager to rule, and more unfit. When the venerable governor of his youth was no more, he became more than ever devoted to his mistress and to his pleasures. And the energies of this great kingdom were directed by different ministers and generals, who acted but little in concert with each other, and therefore the French arms were not successful, and Maria Theresa was not subdued.

In 1744, England and France, that had been only auxiliaries, became principals, inflamed (as usual) by their most unfortunate spirit of rivalship, and the Duke of Cumberland was little able to renew the triumphs of Marlborough, circumstanced as Europe then was, and opposed as he was to Marshal Saxe. The war was at length brought to a conclusion by the peace of Aix-la-Chapelle in 1748; and the monarch and the ministers, of *France at least,* might have been asked for what intelligible reason they had embroiled instead of pacifying Europe, and why their country and England were to be seen as principals contending in every quarter of the world. Even England, that began with a war against Spain in Sir Robert Walpole's administration, made a peace that had no reference to the original grounds of her indignation and fury. In making, however, the peace of Aix-la-Chapelle, France seems to have deserved, for one passing interval, the applause of mankind. Her conduct was conciliatory, and her terms moderate.

Of this war and of the peace you will see an ample account in all the different histories.

We now come to the Seven Years' War.

It will no doubt surprise you, as you proceed in the history, to find France at length uniting herself to the House of Austria:—that Maria Theresa should be anxious to gain over or even neutralize France, is very intelligible; she might thus recover from the king of Prussia the province of Silesia; but that France should assist the House of Austria, her ancient rival,

to depress a new power, that of Prussia, whom it was more natural for her to convert into a new ally, was surely a system of
policy never to have been .expected. Such, however, was the
fact. You will see the account well given in Coxe.

This union gave occasion to the celebrated Seven Years'
War ; the war which Maria Theresa waged, to recover her possessions, and, if possible, destroy Prussia. England we see (as
usual) engaging with France in every quarter of the world, each
power appearing as a principal, for they found a subject of dispute even in the back settlements of America. Europe, Asia,
Africa, and America, all beheld their battles and their sieges ;
the diseases and the death that marked the presence of their
arms ; and even the far distant and lonely tracts of the ocean
were broken in upon by the sounds, and dyed by the carnage of
their bloody contentions. The same tragedies of guilt and
madness that had a few years before been brought to a conclusion, and even greater than these, were again renewed. The
continent in the meantime, which these arbiters of the world,
France and England, might have attempted (and successfully)
to rescue from its fate was abandoned to slaughter and devastation, while the king of Prussia defended by all the qualities of
an unconquerable hero, what he had acquired by all the arts of
an unprincipled politician.

These are melancholy scenes for you to witness ; you will
draw, I hope, the proper lessons from them. I have already
taken every opportunity to recommend them to your thoughts.
You will best understand the part that France took in the
Seven Years' War, and the mistakes which were committed, by
consulting Du Clos. By the extraordinary exertions of England,
and talents of the great war minister, Mr. Pitt, France was
obliged to sue for peace, and under the counsels of Lord Bute,
soon after the accession of his present majesty, it was granted to
her in the year 1763.

Of these enterprises of ambition and impolitic wars, I must
content myself with this general notice. The great characteristics of these foreign politics of France were a spirit of rivalship
to England, and an ambition to be the leading power on the
continent. But the observation that I think ought to be made
is not only the general injustice of these projects of France,
and therefore their general impolicy, but the peculiar impolicy,
the peculiar infatuation of the monarch and ministers of this
great country during the whole of the last half century, who
could all this time entirely turn away their eyes from all that

was passing more near them in their own country, and never condescend to consider how far their schemes of aggrandizement and hostility abroad ought to be checked and controlled by the state of the public opinion and public debt at home. It is an awful lesson to see the court, the ministers, the nobility of a great empire like this, all proceeding upon the established principles and prejudices of their respective situation, never for a moment casting a philosophic view on their real situation, and thus hurried along like the savage in his canoe, who sleeps upon the stream till the stream has become a torrent, and he is precipitated to his destruction.

Finally, I must add that the ill success of these wars, and some defeats that the French arms experienced, put the people of France (fond as they were, and have always been, of military glory) quite out of humour with their government, and in this way somewhat contributed, as it has been always understood, to produce the Revolution.

So much for the first part of our general subject—the foreign politics of France.

We now proceed to the consideration of the domestic concerns of France. These, as I have already observed, have now an interest which formerly they could not have been thought to deserve, for while you are considering these domestic concerns, you must bear in mind the Revolution you have lately witnessed, even more than while considering the foreign concerns to which we have just alluded. The foreign wars, it is true, contributed to the difficulties of the state, and placed the public debt more and more out of the reach of all management, by the financiers of France; but the domestic events, in the mean time, contributed still more to the late Revolution, and therefore are not only deserving your observation as parts of general history, but more particularly as parts of the history of that great event.

In these domestic transactions of the reign of Louis XV. the two principal points to which you are to look are the disputes of the crown with the parliaments, and the progress of the new opinions. It was by these means that at length such an alteration took place in the public sentiment, that the monarchy itself became unpopular, and the physical strength of the community was at length turned against this monarchy and its upholders, in the reign of Louis XVI.

You have already adverted to the foreign politics of France, and are aware of their effects on the public debt; you are now then to observe the history of the domestic concerns, and to consider how the disputes between the crown and the parliaments operated to alienate those constitutional bodies from the court; how the opinions and feelings of the people were continually outraged; while you are next to observe, that during all this period the most distinguished writers were sometimes enlightening, sometimes misleading, but at all events were continually agitating the public mind on subjects of religion and government.

Here, then, we have in a general point of view presented to us the great causes of the Revolution.

1st, The wars, the public debts, and distresses of the state; 2d, The crown and the court rendered unpopular by the disputes with the parliaments; and, 3dly, in the mean time writers of every description turning the attention of the public to the concerns of religion and government, and that in a manner totally hostile to her existing establishments.

The result of the whole was, the loss of all public opinion, the destruction of all the proper supports of government, and the consequence, an *unrestrained* Revolution—a Revolution of the most tremendous nature.

To begin, then, this subject of the domestic concerns of France. It may be distinguished, as I have mentioned, into two great divisions—the disputes of the crown with the parliaments, and the progress of the new opinions.

First, then, with respect to these disputes with the parliaments, and the resistance made by these bodies to the crown.

One might at first suppose that this resistance would have been always of a civil nature, respecting the finances, for instance: but not so; the resistance not only had a reference to the finances, but for a long time to points of a religious nature.

And in this manner is an interest given to many discussions and transactions, which could otherwise have no great attraction, for many of the readers of history.

I shall now proceed to allude, in the first place, to the history of these religious disputes, afterwards to those of a financial nature.

You will recollect, while I am alluding to them, that the continual effect of them was to alienate the minds of the public from the court, and even from the monarch himself, and thus to prepare the way for the Revolution.

These religious disputes then turned chiefly on the nature and operation of grace, and the freedom of the human will. The Jesuists and the Jansenists were the combatants on the different sides. The court sided with the former—the Jesuits; the parliaments with the latter—the Jansenists.

These topics of dispute (the nature and operation of grace, and the freedom of the human will) are represented by many as of a frivolous nature; but none ever less deserved the name. The points debated are among the most important questions, the most magnificent problems, that can be proposed to the human understanding.

The fact, however, is, that it does not appear that the great Creator of the human mind ever intended that such problems should be solved by any faculties which he has bestowed. And the mistake of mankind is, not *that* of originally endeavouring to comprehend them, and of being anxious about them, but that of peremptorily deciding upon them, as if they were subjects within our reach; not only deciding, but even converting them into doctrines which we call upon others to believe; which we even convert into marks, by which we distinguish communities and sects, and by which we actually proceed to determine their favourable or unfavourable acceptance with the Almighty. It is not that these topics are frivolous, but that they lead to discussions which become so. When men affect to instruct each other upon questions which they are not in reality permitted to understand: when they endeavour to reply to their opponents by distinctions without a difference: when they produce explanations that only offer one term instead of another: which speak to the ear, not the mind, and when in the result they surround themselves by a labyrinth, where it is impossible to find either a resting place or an exit. Controversies of this nature marked (you may remember) the first progress of the Reformation.

They were presented to you in the History of the Low Countries; Arminius and Gomar were (you may remember) the great leaders on the different sides. As you read the French history you may recollect them in the reign of Louis XIV.

This monarch was in truth a mere bigot, for such must every man be called who insists upon points of doctrine to a degree neither warranted by their importance nor the nature of their evidence, and insists upon them in a manner unfavourable to the interests of society at any time, still more so to the particular interests of the community at the period in which he lives.

A good account is given of our present subject by Belsham, in his eleventh book of the History of Great Britain; it is as concise as possible: a more lively and detailed account by Voltaire, in his chapter on Jansenism, in his Age of Louis XIV. Lacretelle must be read as giving the particulars in a less desultory and epigrammatic, and therefore more reasonable and intelligible manner than Voltaire, who has generally on these occasions the unpardonable fault of Gibbon—that of so telling his story that it cannot possibly be understood, unless the facts have been learned elsewhere.

From Voltaire, however, it may be collected that a doctor of Louvaine, named Baius, so early as 1552 had published on the subject of predestination and free-will, that his doctrines were resisted by the pope, and that the Spanish Jesuit, Molina, having also thought that he had made some discoveries on these points, set about explaining them to the world. His opinions to a certain degree prevailed, and they gave rise to the sect of the Molinists, who favoured the doctrines of free-will.

But some time after, the opposite tenets of Baius—the necessarian tenets—were revived by Cornelius Jansen, bishop of Ypres; and his writings were so successful that they were followed by the appearance of a sect called, after their founder, Jansenists.

The Jesuits and the court espoused the former system, that of free-will; the parliaments, and particularly the Parliament of Paris, the latter, that of necessity. These general terms will give you a sufficient idea of the nature of their systems. "Superstition (says Hume) is an enemy to civil liberty, enthusiasm a friend to it. The Molinists (says Hume), while conducted by the Jesuits, are great friends to superstition, rigid observers of external forms and ceremonies, and devoted to the authority of the priests and to tradition. The Jansenists are enthusiasts, and zealous promoters of the passionate devotion, and of the inward life, little influenced by authority, and, in a word, but half catholics. The Jesuits are the tyrants of the people, and the slaves of the court, and the Jansenists preserve alive the small sparks of the love of liberty which are to be found in the French nation." This was written by Hume about 1742.

You will now comprehend the manner in which religious disputes gave occasion to a constant series of hostilities between the court and parliaments from the time of Louis XIV. inclusive. The details of this struggle I cannot enter into, but you may read a sufficient account of them in Voltaire and Lacretelle: and you ought to read them; first, because you will thus read the beginning, in some respects, of the late Revolution in France; and, 2dly, because the history of such contentions may teach you forbearance and magnanimity, and a little good sense in your own conduct on all similar occasions; occasions which can never be wanting.

I cannot, I say, enter into the details of this struggle, but I

will now mention to you the steps through which the parties
proceeded in the course of it. You may observe them while I
read them, and draw conclusions, without any comment of mine.

1st. Orders came from the archbishop and the clergy (the
Jesuit side) to refuse the sacraments.

2nd. Censures and prosecutions from the parliament (the
Jansenists' side) against those who obeyed such orders.

3rd. A mandate from the court to stay all such prosecutions
of the parliament.

4th. Remonstrances from the parliament.

5th. The royal commands renewed.

6th. Fresh remonstrances from the parliament.

7th. References from the king to his former commands.

8th. Suspension of all business on the part of the parliaments
(which you will remember were judicial bodies).

9th. Orders from the crown to revoke these resolutions of
suspension.

10th. The parliament attempts to attach the revenue of the
archbishop.

11th. At length lettres de cachet are issued : all the members
of two of the courts of parliament are exiled ; four others are sent
to the state prisons ; letters patent are issued, and an attempt is
made to form new courts of justice instead of the parliaments.

But these letters patent were not valued till they were judi-
cially enregistered. The inferior courts refused therefore to
register them.

The nation was at length inflamed ; the provincial parliaments remonstrated and justified the parliament of Paris ; the
clergy who refused the sacraments were everywhere prosecuted ;
and what then could the court now do ? And what had the
archbishops and the clergy next to advise ? They had evidently
no measure left. Conceive in what a situation this great kingdom was now placed ; on the one hand the legal business of the
country, and on the other the most solemn rites of the religion
of the country, had ceased ; social existence seemed to stop and
be suspended. The parliament was therefore recalled, and the
archbishop exiled. Such is the specimen I have to offer of these
contests.

But how was the breach thus produced between the king and
his parliaments to be ever properly healed ? How was the
folly of the court, and indeed of the clergy, to be ever repaired ?
What folly could be greater than for the court to take a part in
religious disputes like these between the Jesuits and the Janse-

nists? What more unskilful than to give the parliaments an opportunity of resisting the crown in points where men are least of all disposed to be obedient—on subjects of religion; where resistance to authority assumes the highest tone and character that can belong to it; and men seem driven at once to the alternative of choosing whether they shall obey God or man.

The original controversy came at length to be forgotten; the cause of the parliaments was supposed to be the cause of the nation; the secret of the constitution, as must have been known both to the court and to the clergy, lay in the resistance which the parliaments could or could not legally make to the commands of the monarch; and the seeds were thus sown of that revolution which at last broke out to the destruction of the court, the clergy, and all the established orders together.

And now with respect to the financial disputes.

It was in the course of the religious disputes on the subject of Jansenism that appeared the celebrated Provincial Letters of Pascal.

"The comedies of Molière," says Voltaire, "have not more wit than the former part of these letters, nor the writings of Bossuet more sublimity than the latter."

The Jesuits seem never to have recovered from the effects produced by these celebrated compositions.

The intolerant part which the Jesuits took in these political and religious disputes raised them up enemies in the parliament and nation, who were not to be appeased. The whole order was suppressed in the middle of the last century.

You will see very interesting particulars in the relation which Lacretelle gives to explain this very extraordinary event. Various circumstances concurred in producing it; but the accusations of their enemies formed a splendid eulogium on their talents, if not their virtues; and their order must always be mentioned, whenever the history of the human mind is to be given, the nature of its faculties to be illustrated, or the progress of its improvement explained.

So much for the religious contests between the parliaments and the court.

In my next lecture I must proceed to the *financial* disputes between the court and the parliament, and I must advert also to the progress of the new opinions, as concurring with the religious and financial disputes to make the court unpopular, and at length to produce the Revolution.

But before I conclude my present lecture, I must allude to a subject which I have already mentioned to you as belonging to this reign of Louis XV.—the conquest of Corsica; a sort of insulated event, but one which may be reckoned up among the foreign transactions of the kingdom, and which I might have mentioned at the close of them; but as it must have always been introduced as a sort of digression from the main subject, whenever I had noticed it, I thought it less likely to interrupt the train of your thoughts if I presented it to you now, while concluding this present lecture, and before I begin the lecture of to-morrow.

It was under the administration of the Duc de Choiseul, in the year 1768, that this conquest of Corsica was accomplished. The Genoese had long exercised a sort of sovereignty over the island, but were unable properly to secure its obedience. France had been applied to, and at last the Genoese surrendered all their rights to the crown of France, and armies were sent by the Duc de Choiseul no longer to assist the Genoese, but to bring the country under subjection to Louis XV.

Voltaire gives a regular account of the fortunes of this island from the earliest times, and of the whole transaction; but as you can easily turn to his work hereafter, and even now can anticipate what he would say on the subject of the conquest itself, it may be at present more interesting to you to allude to the terms lately made use of by Lacretelle, in giving the history of this conquest.

Lacretelle is an historian, you will remember, writing under the government of Buonaparte; not a word, therefore, of the natural rights of mankind, the laws of nations, or the infamy of this transaction on the part of the French nation.

" A conquest," says Lacretelle, " more important than this of Avignon, and which the Duc de Choiseul had the good fortune to achieve, without disturbing the general peace, attested the dexterity of this minister—the conquest of Corsica. After giving a history of the island, as Voltaire had done, the Duc de Choiseul (says he) received but coldly the Genoese, who came to offer him considerable sums for our soldiers, to be employed in the reduction of Corsica. But he soon after began to offer to the Genoese, in his turn, sums far more considerable, for the cession to France of a possession much too burdensome and uncertain for a republic like theirs; the negotiation was conducted with a secrecy that prevented all jealousy in the English; the king of France announced himself to the Corsicans as a mediator, who was disposed to have their independence acknowledged. Their chief Paoli gave credit to these assurances. In the month of May, 1768, Europe learned with surprise that the Genoese had by treaty ceded Corsica to France; in truth, this cession was not announced as final and irrevocable; the Genoese reserved the right of resuming their sovereignty when they could reimburse the French their expenses. This illusory clause was only intended, says Lacretelle, to soften the resentment of the English; the king of France soon showed the fallacy of the whole, by assuming the title of king of Corsica."

The Corsicans displayed all the indignation of a people abused by vain promises. The English animated their resistance by promises of their own, equally fallacious. Lacretelle then proceeds to state shortly, that the war was for some time, on the part of the French, not successful: that the French general represented the enterprise to be as foolish as it was expensive; that the king hesitated, but that the minister insisted on the importance of the island, &c., and that his decision prevailed.

"No movement," the historian goes on to say, "was observed in the ports of England, and it was impossible not to form a high idea of the talents of a minister who had thus deceived or intimidated a government so jealous and so haughty; a new general was sent; the Corsicans, outraged by the inaction of the English, lost all courage; Paoli, who had made them expect their assistance, partook of the general despair. After being chased from post to post, he was fortunate enough to reach a sea-port and embark for England; Corsica was reduced, and the Duc de Choiseul had the glory of having given a new province to his master, of having made a conquest merely by means of his political address, and of having thrown down the gauntlet to the English, even when intoxicated with all their triumphs, which they did not think proper to take up. "Why," says, Lacretelle, "was England so timid on this occasion? On account of the troubles in her American colonies."

What says our own historian? "The transfer of Corsica to France," says Adolphus, "was an early topic of debate, but produced no interesting remark or useful information; a motion for the correspondence between the British and French ministry, and for instructions and other papers, introduced a discussion on the value of the acquisition. The opposition maintained that every accession of power to France was dangerous to this country; and as great attention had been paid for so many years to. the maintenance of a proper equilibrium among the powers of Europe, the invasion of that island ought to have been considered as a violent breach of treaty, and subversive of that equilibrium. It was replied, that Corsica was a place of no importance, destitute of a good harbour, and an acquisition that would prove rather an evil than a benefit to France; but, at all events, loaded as we already were with debt, folly and madness alone could impel us to engage in a war for so small an object."

To the ministers of England, and apparently to this historian of England, there was nothing then at issue but the mere possession of a barren island in the Mediterranean. Ministers of the same temperament had in their proclamation at the peace forbidden the king's subjects to afford assistance to the Corsicans, and had even presumed to call them rebels. "I expected not this from England," said their gallant chieftain. From England he could not have received such an outrage; the public sentiment was in his favour, and sufficiently clear, and it will be an ill omen for England when on such an occasion it is not so:

> "For he who values Liberty, confines
> His zeal for her predominance within
> No narrow bounds, her cause engages him
> Wherever pleaded—'tis the cause of man."

So was it on this occasion. It was the cause of man, and not of the weeds on the sea shore, or the heath upon the mountains of Corsica, but that of the security of every unoffending community, however small; the security and the shelter that are thrown around every nation by the common pact and guarantee of the republic of nations, while it is content with its own possessions, and neither insults nor invades those of others, and this too in the very view and vicinity of nations more powerful and wealthy, who, like the affluent and the great on the smaller scale of the social and civil connexions of men, are to respect the innocence, and to beat off the spoiler from the cottage of their neighbour, not themselves to become the murderers and the robbers, the Ahabs of sacred writ, who annex to their own wide extent of possessions, and their own assemblage of enjoyments, the humble pittance which the villager has placed upon his board, and the little spot that he has loved, as the inheritance of his fathers.

The author of the Annual Register, who gives a very good account of these transactions, very properly observes, "that it was evident, from the difficulties which the French encountered and the losses they sustained, without any other opposition than the single virtue of the natives, that this attempt might have been easily rendered abortive, and that nothing but the most unaccountable supineness in states, that were not only interested in the preservation of this island, but much more in preventing any new accession of power or dominion to France, could have given it even a probability of success."—Ann. Reg. 1769, p. 46.

The efforts of these heroic islanders to resist the power of France, even as related by Voltaire, were, as you will find, of the most extraordinary nature. The carnage was dreadful.

These are the events in history that it is so painful to observe. The description of the Romans must not be confined to those conquerors of the world; it is but too true of every great people, " Si locuples hostis est, avari, si pauper, ambitiosi sunt." The new world is no sooner discovered, the riches of the west and of the east are no sooner exposed to view, than out rush from every port and haven the iron men of Europe, to rifle and to massacre the unhappy possessors of these fatal treasures. We have the conquest of Mexico and the conquest of Peru, the Dutch East India Company, and the French East India Company, and the honourable Company (honourable, did I say?) of British merchants trading to the East Indies. We have one quarter of the world given away by the Pope, and we have another quarter purchased from the Mogul; and because the Corsicans, it seems, had neither the mines of the west nor the gems and spices of the east, these islanders were to be envied, the first rude gifts that Nature has to bestow, the trees of their mountains, and the sinews of their frames; navies, it seems, might be drawn from their woods, and soldiers from their population; they breathed the free air of their wild country, without asking the leave of France; they loved and hated, and hoped and feared, without orders from Versailles.

How little could the Duc de Choiseul suspect, while he was sending his countrymen, the troops of his king, to perish, battalion after battalion: while he was calling upon the gallant officers of France to perpetrate his foul butcheries of an unoffending people, hemming in the brave with his bayonets, and corrupting the irresolute with his gold; waging a sacrilegious war against human virtue under every form;—how little could this triumphant minister of the court of Louis suspect, that from out of the freemen he was thus bribing, pursuing, and murdering, that from out of those very men who were thus to be converted into subjects of the French monarchy, should arise in the next generation—how little could the Duc de Choiseul suspect it—the man, the very Buonaparte, who was to usurp the throne of his master, and from the very palaces of the Bourbons, where he was himself sitting, issue orders to execute like traitors and outcasts the princes of their race; trample under his feet " the pride, the pomp and the circumstance" not only of that House of Bourbon, but even of that House of Austria, which the Duc de Choiseul had so cherished and united to the throne of France; realize more of empire than the proudest of the Bourbons had ever fancied in their most splendid visions; and ministers like himself, and monarchs like his master, the helpless or unworthy potentates of the continent, " catch in his fury, and make nothing of."

Yet these things have we seen; such is the eventful era in which we live, and such the mysterious dispensations of that Providence, which not unfrequently seems to mock the councils of the worldly wise, and which suffers no course of conduct ultimately to deserve the character of real wisdom or sane ambition, but that conduct on which nations, as well as individuals, had best confide; that conduct which is independent of all changes of events, by being founded on the eternal rules of humanity and justice.

Several years have elapsed since what I have just delivered was first written. During this period what changes have we not seen? Buonaparte was then in the zenith of his power, the lord of the ascendant; but has any thing since happened to invalidate the force of what I then said? Is he to whom I have just alluded an example to the contrary?

I must confess that I do not so interpret the events we have witnessed.

I am conscious, indeed, that I speak of the dispensations of that awful Being, in whose sight a thousand years are but as one day; that this, our sublunary state, is rather a state of probation, than of present reward and punishment; but, when due attention has been paid to these considerations, where, I may still ask, where during this extraordinary era, of five and twenty years, from the breaking out of the French Revolution, where are the instances in the conduct of any of the nations of Europe, or of their rulers; where are the instances of violence, of injustice, of inhumanity, that have ultimately been of benefit to their perpetrators?

Be assured that the magnanimity of uprightness, and all the elevating and all the attractive qualities of the human mind, are the best protection of nations, as well as individuals; that the path of honour is the path of true policy; and that the great Governor of the world, in public, as well as in private life, has indissolubiy connected, even on this side the grave, the happiness of his creatures, with the exercise of their virtues, and the fulfilment of their duties.

LECTURE IV.

LOUIS XV.

My last lecture endeavoured to call your attention to the reign of Louis XV. The task must have been easy, when I had once announced to you that this reign, long as it was, extending through a great part of the last century, was but a prelude to the French Revolution.

I endeavoured to state to you the great points to which you should direct your observation; the wars in which France was engaged, and why they were impolitic (to say nothing of the injustice of them) to a degree of infatuation. Afterwards, I attempted to exhibit to you the reasons why the public mind, while the national debt was thus increasing, advanced fast into a state of alienation from the monarchy and the existing establishments. This alienation took place partly in consequence of the disputes between the parliaments and the court, and partly from the progress of the new opinions. The disputes between the parliaments and the court were of a twofold nature; they were religious and they were financial. In the last lecture we alluded to the religious disputes : to-day we must first allude to those of a financial nature, and at length to the effects produced by the progress of the new opinions.

It will readily be supposed that the opposition of the parliaments to the crown was not confined to religious matters. The finances, it will easily be conceived, were a constant subject of complaint and ill-humour. The secret of the French constitution, as I must often repeat, lay in the power or right which the Parliaments had to deny their sanction to the king's edicts, and therefore to the taxes. The power of thus legalizing the king's taxes would not have been contested with the States General; but the parliament only claimed as the representative of the States General, in the intervals of their sittings; and the right was therefore open to dispute.

Now, whether their claim was, or was not, well founded, still, as the right was a great constitutional question, the obvious policy of the crown was to give the parliament as few opportunities as possible of asserting it.

But this could only be done, as far as taxation was concerned, in three modes:

1st, By keeping the expenses of the crown and court as low as possible.

2dly, By abstaining from foreign wars.

Or, lastly, by persuading or obliging the clergy or nobility to pay their shares of the public burthen.

Now, it was impossible for any ministers of finance to produce any reform in the first two modes of diminishing the public expense; no system of economy, no system of peace, and avoidance of foreign wars, was possible. But neither, on the other hand, was the third mode possible; for neither the nobility nor the clergy had virtue to do what it was both their duty and ultimate interest to do, to pay their shares of the public burthen. The finances, therefore, got at length into irremediable embarrassment. The situation of a minister of finance may be easily conceived, and is not ill-described by Lacretelle. " If one of these unhappy functionaries," says he, " endeavoured to ascertain the real situation of the public revenue, he was disgraced, he was in danger if he talked of any existing evil, and ruined if he proposed any remedy. Did he speak of any reduction in the expenses, the court were furious; of any equalizing of the imposts, the parliaments, the clergy, and the nobility were in an uproar; was he exact and methodical in conducting business, the financiers ridiculed him as a man of little mind and of no genius; did he endeavour in his edicts to disguise and conceal the new impositions which he laid, the economists denounced him not only as guilty of oppression, but of the most egregious folly. To escape from difficulties like these, what resource, but to anticipate, from year to year, the coming revenue; and yet what expedient so ruinous? One really knows not," continues the historian, " what were the views of the different comptrollers-general that succeeded to each other. One talks of the Moris, the Bretagnes, and the Sechelles; and one seems to be speaking but of the same person; so like are they to each other in the expedients to which they resorted and in their compliances, the obscurity of their march, and the rapidity of their fall."

You will observe that the parliaments were, in the mean time, the chief enemies which the court had to fear; they imposed the only restraint that could be imposed on its expenses, whether of domestic profligacy or foreign war; they did so, by the remonstrances and the opposition which they regularly made to the enregistering of the taxes. This opposition had more or less existed for a long period. We have alluded in a former lecture to the subject of the taxes; and the extraordinary measures proposed by the celebrated John Law, and acceded to by the regent. To these measures the parliaments made every resistance in their power, and had at least the comfort of reflecting, amid the general distress, that they had laboured to protect the public from the evils they were suffering; still, they had thus been thrown, which is a circumstance more immediately to our present purpose, into a state of opposition to government.

This opposition was again renewed in the administration of the Duc de Bourbon in 1725, when his ministers of finance had recourse to the only expedient that could meet the profusion of the court; an impost of one-fifth on all the revenues of the kingdom, those of the privileged orders not excepted. Such was the weight of opinion in favour of the authority of the crown at *that time* in France, (though only about seventy years before the trial and execution of the late king,) that even this measure, the measure of an impost of one shilling and five pence on all the revenues of the kingdom, in opposition to the nobles, to the clergy, to the parliaments in Paris, and the provinces, was actually, from the mere authority of the crown, enregistered by the parliament in Paris, and carried; though the impost was such that it was understood that it would bear away not one fifth, but one-fourth of the net revenue of every man of property in the kingdom; and even though the Duke of Bourbon, the minister, was not respected by the public.

The next year, indeed, on the elevation of Fleury, this impost which he had opposed, though perhaps somewhat faintly, was by the cardinal removed.

The receipt had been injured by the opposition that had been made. Under such a feeble government as the duke's, it had not been levied with any strictness. Fleury endeavoured to meet the financial difficulties by economy and financial expedients. He could not, however, escape the remonstrances of the parliament, who predicted loudly a national bankruptcy, and did no service by such language and conduct to the authority of the crown.

On the whole, however, Fleury must be considered as successful in his management of the finances.

But the scene was altered when he was no more; and when the economy, which he had maintained by every expedient in his power, died with him; when the reign of indifferent ministers and expensive mistresses succeeded.

I may not now be able to advert further to the profusion of the court and the history of the taxes. But the same general idea of the subject of the parties concerned, and their modes of behaviour, on all occasions, may perhaps be formed from a slight allusion to an affair which excited considerable interest at the time, and deservedly. Mᵉ. de Pompadour, the mistress of Louis XV., made and unmade the treasurers at her pleasure, and, of course, the treasury lay at her mercy. She at length introduced the practice of drawing bills on the treasury which had no other sanction but the mere signature of the king, no service specified. Of these, as it may be supposed, the more the king signed, the more he had to sign; one compliance leading to another; and it was easier to sign his name than to take the trouble of refusing.

A practice like this, as the historian observes, was enough to bring the best-established monarchy to ruin. The comptrollers-general were in despair.

At length one of these comptrollers-general, Machault, formed a regular design, the only measure left him, to tax, if not the nobility, at least the clergy. He wanted not firmness nor address; and the parliament were less disposed to resist the edicts of the crown, when it was found that they were directed exclusively against the clergy. The clergy, however, warded the blow in the following manner. They had got the court leagued with them in their resistance to the parliament on the subject of Jansenism. This dispute, as I mentioned, at the end of my last lecture, came to a crisis. You may remember that it was found expedient by the court to recall the parliaments from their exile, and to persuade the clergy to waive their intolerant measures, the refusal of the sacraments, the rites of sepulture, &c. &c.

The clergy therefore, on this occasion, made their bargain with the court; and procured, in return for their compliance, with respect to the sacraments, rites of sepulture, &c., the dismissal of Machault, the comptroller-general, who had proposed to tax them.

They left the kingdom, therefore, and the finances to their fate. No doubt they congratulated themselves not a little on thus defeating a scheme which they probably declared in the blindness of their selfishness would have been the ruin of their order and of all religion. And no doubt the same blindness of selfishness would have been visible in the conduct of the nobility if *they* also had been required, as they ought to have been, to pay their contingent to the general burthens. Such a measure they would have declared aloud was a direct attack on the privileges of their order, and tended only to destroy their constitutional importance;

was an attack on the monarchy itself, proceeded only from a secret hostility to all government, &c. &c.

The clergy escaped the tax, the nobility were not even threatened. The finances, therefore, advanced further and further into embarrassment and disgrace. The subsequent events (the Revolution) are but too well known.

Such particulars as these (I can only glance at them) may serve to illustrate the general nature of the subject. The folly and profligacy of Louis and the court: the blindness and disgusting selfishness of the privileged orders; and the difficulties that the ministers of finance were under from the moment they attempted to serve their country; while in the meantime that country was evidently journeying on, in an accelerated progress, to a national bankruptcy.

It is to be observed, too, that France, all this time, took her part in the affairs of Europe, and engaged in foreign wars, as if under no financial difficulties whatever.

The Seven Years' War, in which she engaged, contributed materially to these embarrassments. Neither the death of the queen, nor of Madame de Pompadour, produced any beneficial effect on the mind of the king. His excesses, after the year 1763, were but the more disgraceful; and M^e. Dubarri, a new mistress, succeeded M^e. de Pompadour, with all the faults, and none of the merits of the former.

You will now, I conceive, be able to form a general idea of the opposition that always, more or less, existed between the parliaments and the crown during this long reign of Louis XV. Opposition, partly arising on the subject of religion, partly of finance; and, on the whole, you are to bear away an impression that, all through the reign, publicly and privately, such a series of outrages were offered to public opinion, by unfeeling profusion, by intolerance, by levies of money, and abominable immoralities, as could not but be at least a preparative for the Revolution that followed.

Before, however, I entirely conclude this part of my general subject, the financial disputes, I must at least mention, and direct your attention to the very remarkable affair of the Duc D'Aiguillon. The detail of it is too long for me to do more than mention it. I have not time now to enter into it; but you must remember that it ended in the actual suppression of the parliaments. And you are to consider what must have been at every step, as you read the particulars, the irritation of the public mind, and the national indignation that must have accompanied so violent a measure as the destruction of their parliaments.

This very striking event, however, seems not to have produced such visible effects as might have been expected ; and the real situation of France was not generally apprehended by those who lived at the time, either in or out of the kingdom.

" The noble efforts," says the author of the Annual Register, in 1771, " of that faithful repository of the laws, and remembrancer of the ancient rights of the people, the parliament of Paris, in the cause of liberty and mankind, have fatally terminated in its own final dissolution.

" Its fall was not more glorious from the cause in which it was engaged, than from the circumstances which attended it ; several of the other parliaments having become voluntary sacrifices at its funeral pyre.

" That ancient spirit from which the Franks derive their name, though still gloriously alive in the breasts of a few, no longer exists in the bulk of the people. Long dazzled with the splendour of a magnificent and voluptuous court, with the glare of a vast military power, and with the glory of some great monarchs, they cannot now, in the grave light of the shade, behold things in their natural state ; nor can those who have been long used to submit without inquiry to every act of power, who have been successfully encouraged in dissipation, and been taught to trifle with the most important subjects, suddenly acquire that strength and tenor of mind which is alone capable of forming strong resolutions, and of undertaking arduous and dangerous tasks. Thus has this great revolution in the history and government of France taken place without the smallest commotion, or without the opposition that in other periods would have attended an infraction of the heritable jurisdiction of a petty vassal."

This paragraph was written in the year 1771, by no less a man than Mr. Burke, and is, no doubt, a fair specimen of the opinions which intelligent men formed of the situation of France at the time. In general, therefore, they seem not to have been aware of the changes that were to ensue. Had Burke, however, set himself to reason on the subject with the same philosophic spirit with which we are soon after to see him survey the situation of the North American colonies, no doubt he would have perceived that there were great principles in existence, and even in action in France, which might indeed be counteracted by circumstances, but which certainly were capable at least of producing great alterations, whether favourable or not to the monarchy and to the kingdom. Particular circumstances, the personal character of a monarch or a minister, for instance, may disturb the natural operation of such general principles, suspend them for a time, or even nullify them altogether. The tide, too, of human affairs runs with a very different rapidity at different periods; sometimes seems to pause even for long intervals, and then rushes forward with a force and a swiftness that exceed all possible anticipation. In these cases the state of quiescence has been more imaginary than real. The lesson, however, of the whole is certainly this, that men of education and influence should be very attentive to observe all the general principles that are fitted to act upon a community, and that may be found at any particular time to exist in it, and that the fault of men, especially the rulers of mankind, is that of neglecting these general principles too much. But this fault arises not always from mere want of intelligence, it is often rather from apathy and indolence—no effect without a cause, but no cause without a tendency to produce an effect. Of this men are aware; nor do they suppose that they are to gather grapes from thorns, or figs from thistles. But it is easier to repose upon an existing system and contribute to its dangers, than by virtuous conduct to alter it in time, and prevent the calamities which it is calculated to produce. Louis XV. is himself a specimen of rulers of this ordinary description. He began with personal indolence, which soon ripened into sensuality, its natural consequence; this again into a sort of languid indifference to public affairs, and even to the situation of the monarchy itself. He amused himself with knowing all the little anecdotes and scandal in every court of Europe; but he interested not himself in the literature and philosophy of his own country. He was aware of, and felt a sort of vague disquietude at the extraordinary movement that was going on in the public mind; but he talked only with ill-humour or disdain of the philosophers, the Encyclopedists, and, above all, of Voltaire. "Those people," he would sometimes say, "will destroy the monarchy;" but he seemed to console himself with the thought that after all he was not the monarch that was menaced; and in Louis, on this occasion, in his indolence, apathy, quiescence, and want of active virtue, we may no doubt see the portrait of the greater part of the privileged orders of France almost to the very moment when the States General were assembled at the beginning of the Revolution.

In the Memoirs of Madame de Hausset, lady's-maid to Madame de Pompadour, appears an anonymous letter that was addressed to Louis XV.; and whatever might be the motives of the writer, the picture that he gives the king of the state of his affairs is accurate and striking.

" Your finances," says he, in the course of the letter, " are in the greatest disorder, and the great majority of states have perished through this cause.

" Your ministers are without genius and capacity.

" A seditious flame has sprung up in the very bosom of your parliaments ; you seek to corrupt them, and the remedy is worse than the disease.

" Open war is carried on against religion.

" The Encyclopedists, under pretence of enlightening mankind, are sapping the foundations of religion.

" All the different kinds of liberty are connected ; the philosophers and the Protestants tend towards republicanism as well as the Jansenists ; the philosophers strike at the root, the others lop the branches, and their efforts, without being concerted, will one day lay the tree low.

" Add to these the Economists, whose object is political liberty, as that of others is liberty of worship, and the government may find itself in twenty or thirty years undermined in every direction, and will then fall with a crash.

" Lose no time in restoring order to the state of the finances. Embarrassments necessitate fresh taxes, which grind the people, and induce them towards revolt.

" A time will come, sire, when the people shall be enlightened ; and that time is probably approaching."

This letter, it is said, produced a strong impression on the king, Mᵉ. de Pompadour, and the Duc de Choiseul.

Again—" the regent," said the king, one day (p. 37), " was very wrong in restoring to the parliaments the right of remonstrating. They will end in ruining the state." " Oh, sire," said one of his courtiers, " it is too strong to be shaken by a set of petty justices."

" They are an assembly of republicans," replied the king; " however, here is enough of the subject ; things will last as they are, as long as I shall."

I proceed now to the second point to be considered in the domestic concerns of the reign of Louis XV.—the progress of the new opinions. Not meaning to give any regular history of the French Revolution, still less to enter into the different writings that belong to this part of the general subject, my observations must be very short, and I am happy to have it in my power to refer you to the author I have already mentioned, Lacretelle, to whose authority, on this very delicate subject of the influence of the new opinions, I do not at present see that any objection can

well be made. He has already written a Précis of the French
Revolution, highly and generally esteemed. He is represented
to me as attached in reality to the principles of free government, and yet he writes under the protection of the government
of Buonaparte. It could not have been the wish of that or of
any government that the principles which produced irreligion
and anarchy should be favoured—the doctrines of levellers or republicans—lest they should prove fatal to itself : nor, again, that
the old government should be favoured—its evils, the vices and
the faults of its court and of its nobles—lest the new order of
things which had been established on their overthrow, should
appear less necessary or less desirable. There seems, therefore,
on the whole, from the character and situation of the writer, a
sufficient chance for impartiality. Lacretelle is a man of letters,
and has more opportunities of information, and more incite-
ments to inform himself on these particular points, than those
not resident in France can possibly have ; and it will therefore
be sufficient for me just to mention to you for the present a few
of his opinions, and leave you to consider more regularly what
he has to offer when you come to read his work, and when you
can perhaps compare it with what you may be able to learn from
other sources of inquiry.

He conceives, then, that the writers to whom, among other
causes, the events of the French Revolution are attributed, acted
not in that concert, which has been supposed, either against the
throne or the altar, or at least but for a very short interval ; that
to the year 1748 (the peace of Aix-la-Chapelle) the philosophers,
as they are called, formed no distinct party ; that Voltaire had
but feeble auxiliaries ; that Montesquieu soared too high ; that
changes, however, had taken place in manners, and gave a pre-
sage of similar changes in opinions ; that even in the reign of
Louis XIV. two different succeeding ages of literature may be
observed ; during the best part of his reign, literature, he thinks,
like every thing else, tended only to the support of order and
authority ; that men were libertines rather than unbelievers,
but that to this golden age of Louis XIV. succeeded even in the
same reign a second age, beginning about 1685, marked in the
government of the country by the repeal of the edict of Nantz,
and by intolerance, and in the history of literature distinguished
by the appearance of the Télémaque of Fénélon.

That the French had begun to make remarks upon their government, and that the Télémaque furnished them with their
lessons ; that religion then met its first adversary in Bayle ;

that manners had in the mean time declined, and were not to be favourably influenced by the austerities of Louis XIV.; thus they were, however unfavourably, influenced by the more distinguished writers of the time.

During the regency of the Duke of Orleans, Lacretelle conceives that literature sacrificed less than the arts did, to the corruptions and vices of the day; but he observes, that men of letters then first began to be animated with the ambition of succeeding in society; men of fashion and rank became their friends rather than their patrons; that it was thus by their conversation rather than by their writings, that they were elevated into a sort of invisible legislators; that in this situation of things at length shone forth Voltaire and Montesquieu.

Voltaire must be considered as the great literary character in France during the last century; his Œdipus appeared so early as 1716; he died not till 1778.

As far as relates to our present subject, he must be looked upon as the great adversary not only of the particular Roman Catholic religion of his country, but of Christianity itself under every form and description. Fanaticism was at first, and indeed always, the avowed object of his attack; but as he advanced in years, the destruction of Christianity itself seems to have been the great passion of his life.

Lacretelle, with great propriety, is very particular in his account of Voltaire; his character, the great events of his life, and his writings. To him I must refer you.

Montesquieu must be considered as addressing himself to the statesmen of the world, and as not suffering to expire in France the flame which had first been raised into existence by the Télémaque of Fénélon. He and Voltaire both passed over into England, and the one afterwards exhibited to his countrymen the picture of the philosophy of England, and the other that of the grandeur of the Romans. Montesquieu was long applauded rather than comprehended; but both he and Voltaire were eminently successful, and, on the whole, freedom of thought was thus introduced into France, and soon after exercised in a very great degree.

In this manner we arrive at the close of the administration of Fleury; and Lacretelle observes, that the contest which always exists between the favourers of new opinions and the followers of old, in literature as well as politics, began now to turn in favour of the former, the favourers of new opinions.

As soon as the peace of Aix-la-Chapelle was concluded (in

1748), a great fermentation existed. The monarch was devoted to pleasure, and relaxed the reins of government, and the parliaments and clergy were each candidates for the authority he had thus abandoned.

At this interval appeared the second great work of Montesquieu, L'Esprit des Loix.

Voltaire in the mean time found favour at court; M^e. de Pompadour patronised him, though not so Louis XV., who saw in him, as he thought and declared, a man who would endeavour to hurry along in the current of public opinion even the monarchy itself.

The influence of the work of Montesquieu is evidently considered by Lacretelle as very great. The success was for a long time undecided. But at length, says he, the most frivolous would have thought that they were betraying their incapacity, by only *moderately* admiring his Spirit of Laws. But after Montesquieu, who died in 1755, appeared Buffon, Diderot, D'Alembert, Du Clos, Condillac, Helvetius, and above all, Rousseau. To Rousseau the attention of Lacretelle is more particularly directed; a sort of life is given of him, his writings and their influence carefully noted. I must refer you to his account of Rousseau, as I have already done to his account of Voltaire.

It is with some difficulty that I can restrain myself from endeavouring to turn to your advantage (here and immediately) the description which Lacretelle has given of both these distinguished men, but I am always as careful of your time, particularly while in this place, as I know well how to be, and must depend on your reading for yourselves his narratives and observations.

Soon after the peace of 1748 (about the years 1751 and 1752), Paris became the great resort for men of letters. Diderot is represented as the real centre round which they revolved, and to him is applied by Lacretelle the description of Catiline by Sallust—" Vastus animus immoderata, incredibilia, nimis alta semper cupiebat."

Diderot is considered as being not only, like Voltaire, a furious enemy to Christianity, but as at length becoming an atheist, lest he should be outstripped in the race of incredulousness.

Lastly, he is said to have formed the project of the French Encyclopédie as a means of diffusing what he called light to all Europe, as well as France, and of destroying all ancient prejudices, that is, all modes of belief.

D'Alembert was his associate, the great friend of Voltaire, and apparently the idol of all men of literature and science, not only for the extent and depth of his genius, but his amiable and estimable qualities. Two volumes of the work appeared in 1751.

This date will strike us, on a little reflection, as a very early one—the time of George II., only five years after the crown of this country was fought for in this very island, in the rebellion of 1745.

The clergy, the Jesuits, the government, were at first alarmed. The work early in the next year was suppressed, as contrary to religion and to the state; the principal authors menaced.

But Madame de Pompadour was a lady who on this occasion personated the Goddess of Fortune, and her caprices or her views of her own interest happening to shift about into a contrary direction, the suppression was taken off, and the storm, to which the work had been exposed, passed over.

Voltaire continued his attacks on Christianity under every form, but is considered by Lacretelle as stopping at this point, and as opposing, not favouring, the new opinions on other subjects. He sharply condemned those new opinions which menaced the stability of the state, and very indignantly those which affected the principles of good taste. Voltaire was the philosopher of the court, not of the nation. "Why do you not stop where Voltaire does?" was the language held by the Duc de Choiseul and the people of fashion to the philosophers of the day. "Him we can comprehend; amid all his sallies, *he* respects authority, but *you*—you are mysterious and obscure, and discuss and lay down your doctrines in a pedantic, suspicious, and disagreeable manner. We abandon to you religion and the clergy. Is not this sufficient? many, too, of our prejudices; why cannot you have some regard for those at least that are useful?"

But we must now observe, that we are arrived at a second stage in our present subject—the minds of men of talents in France ten years *after* the publication of the Encyclopédie had begun, it seems, to require a master more powerful than could be found in Voltaire, or any disciple of his school.

The great rival genius of the century had appeared—the eloquent Rousseau; and in the effusions of his ardent and irritated mind, a new world had been displayed, to which the world, then existing, constituted on the ancient system, seemed " weary, stale, flat, and unprofitable."

It was Rousseau, though abominated by Voltaire, and though disliked by the philosophers, who could neither hold him in his transports, nor direct him in his march—it was Rousseau that became the philosopher of the young, the young of both sexes, of that rising generation destined so materially to influence the fortunes of the ancient government of France, and the happiness of mankind.

His prize declamation against the arts and sciences; his discourse on the Inequality of Conditions—(it was Diderot that had whispered to him the nature and the force of his talents)—the new Eloise, the Emile, the Social Contract, the Letters from the Mountains—these were the writings that so awakened the enthusiasm of the readers of France soon after the middle of the last century; these were the writings, that as their influence descended through the different ranks of society, from year to year, bewildered the speculations of the inexperienced, amid the evils inseparable from our condition, and the visions of unattainable perfection.

Such effects it may be thought took place very naturally among the readers of France, during the close of the last century, situated as France then was. But this is not sufficiently to apprehend the powers of Rousseau. Even now, and in England, let every man, let every young man more particularly, be careful how he approaches these productions with too great a confidence in himself, and too regardless of the fate of others. To this hour, even, after all the calamitous events of the French Revolution, at a distance from all contagion then experienced—the contagion of a thousand fermenting minds, importunate hopes and benevolent aspirations—in the absence of every thing that can mislead and inflame, that can call away the understanding from its perceptions of truth, or the sentiments from their impressions of duty—in the very calm and solitude of domestic happiness or political tranquillity, even *thus* happily situated, let no man presume to suppose himself safe, when exposed to the eloquence of Rousseau, safe when placed within the circle of that mighty magician. His is the spell that can teach the heart to wander till it knows not, and cares not, whither it is going, or how fatally it is lost; his is the wand under whose influence, as it waves around, crimes the deepest change their colour, absurdities the most lowly elevate their aspect and their form; suicide, seduction, the equality of civilized man, the happiness of savage existence.—Extraordinary being! Intelligence and insanity mingling their streams into one wild current of strange and uncertain brightness! The moralist and the logician; the estimator of man and of society through every stage of their existence; the believing sceptic; the, master of the heart; the agitator of the understanding; attracting, and yet repelling; fascinating, and yet wearying our attention; disgustful, yet of a sensibility too tender and unhappy not to be pitied and almost beloved; ridiculous, yet of a genius and a wisdom too sublime not to be respected, and almost revered!

There are other writers besides those already mentioned that are enumerated by Lacretelle—Helvetius, for instance, and the materialists. Helvetius and his school must also be considered as principal figures in the general picture which we are now sketching. From the year 1758 to 1770, Lacretelle observes, that the French literature was disgraced by a great number of publications, where atheism was openly professed; the authors seem to have been anonymous. The true philosophers, Turgot, Malesherbes, and their associates, lamented over these perversions of the human intellect; and Voltaire protested against the principles of many of those who ranged themselves under his standard. Marmontel, La Harpe, and other men of letters did the same. The works against Revelation, continues Lacretelle, were still more numerous: some with all the grossness, he says, which generally marks them; others recommended by graces of style, like those of Voltaire; others, again, by logical subtleties, like those of Rousseau.

The stage was, it seems, not overlooked, as affording an opportunity to wage war against opinions that were old. Lastly, men of talents made it a practice to entertain society by their sallies against the doctrine of religion, till, at length, the conversation which at the beginning of the century disgraced the private parties of the regent, descended, as the century advanced, through the intermediate ranks, down even to the night cellars of the metropolis.

Such are the remarks I have to offer respecting the new opinions of France, borrowing my facts from Lacretelle. And in this manner we are conducted to the end of the reign of Louis XV. But I have selected these facts, as those more immediately important, from a large mass stated by Lacretelle, in about three hundred pages of his work, in his ninth and twelfth books. In reading these books, I would recommend it to the reader to do what Lacretelle has not done: set apart as much as possible those writings which may be supposed to have affected the opinions of the public on the subjects of *morality, religion,* and *government,* and distinguish them carefully from those that belong to *general literature only,* or even to *science.* It is the former that are evidently *alone* deserving your attention, while you are en-

deavouring to form a philosophic estimate of the rise of the
French Revolution; and the mind is drawn aside from its
object, when others are mentioned; any others but those which
affected morality, religion, and government. I have found some
difficulty in making the selection and separation which I am
proposing to your imitation, and I may not have entirely succeeded. I conceive, however, that the important features are
those I have enumerated: Voltaire, Montesquieu, L'Encyclopédie, Rousseau, Helvetius, and the materialists; finally, the
low publications of the atheistical school: these are the *authors*
and the *writings*.

The *circumstances* more particularly are, the introduction of
allusions and invectives against old opinions and prejudices on
the stage; the circulation of remarks and witticisms of an irreligious nature in the conversation of society; and, finally, the
alteration that gradually took place in the manners and views
both of society and men of letters themselves, in consequence of
which the authors of books were no longer solitary students, insulated and unseen, but men of the world, ambitious to shine in
society; forming its taste, influencing its opinions, and producing, by visible and rapid agency, that alteration in the views,
sentiments, and habits of the community, which had always
before appeared the slow and silent effect of time alone.

It may be added, that the natural progress of the prosperity
of France, in despite of its wars, must have extended very widely
the circle of men of intelligence and independence; that circle
which comprehends within it what in every country may be
called (as far as politics are concerned) the effective public.

Now, reflect for a moment, on the few particulars that have
been mentioned.

The writings of Voltaire—how were these to be resisted by
the doctrines and practices of the Roman Catholic communion?
What materials were not in his works supplied for the ridicule
of what was thought to be Christianity, in a nation of which
gaiety has been always the passion, and thoughtlessness the
reproach?

Who can refute, as it has been well said, a sneer or a witticism? But what Frenchman, it may be added, would have ever
tried?

Again, the writings of Montesquieu—how were the great views
of this estimator of ages and nations, how were they to be shut
out from the minds of men of intelligence in France?—By the
transactions of their own times, and the scenes of their own

history?—the wars and mistresses of their monarchs?—the lettres de cachet of their ministers?—their exiled and ruined parliaments?—their shades and spectres of their constitution and government?

But again, how was the public (the effective public in the sense just explained) to be indifferent to the pages of Rousseau? the piercing invectives, the soothing sophistries, the warm and splendid visions of this most eloquent of men; the deceiver of the imagination of others, the victim of his own—how were these to be rendered harmless and of no avail?—By the extremes of wretchedness exhibited in the metropolis of France?—the painted emptiness of its vanities, in the absence of the domestic virtues?—the ignorance and profligacy of its populace, set off by the dissolute effrontery of its court and nobles?

But, lastly, amid this general debasement of maxims and of manners, was it for the low schools, the materialists, the atheists, and the obscene writers, to blush and to stand silent and appalled?

I must leave this subject to your own reflections. Assuredly the reign of Louis XV. will afford you ample materials. In what a rapid manner have we passed along the surface of them, yet how many and how weighty have been the topics to which your curiosity has been directed!

Through nearly the whole of the last century, the great kingdom of France has been seen under the direction of cabinets that continued to indulge themselves in every enterprise of ambition and injustice.

Beginning with a debt to which her revenue was unequal, and persevering still further to accumulate a weight so dangerous to her monarchy; determined always to take the same part in the politics of Europe, and incur the same expenses as if she had been possessed of funds adequate to discharge the interest of her old debts, and even to meet the interest of new ones. Unhappy country, destroying and destroyed! disturbing every potentate and neighbour, and ruled in the meantime by debauched kings, with their impudent mistresses and daring ministers, who could waste not only in wars, but in excesses of every kind of ostentation or of profligacy, the earnings that could be wrung from the hands of peasants, and from the incomes of the laborious and virtuous classes of the community. Continue the picture: the clergy and the nobility, you will remember, are in the meantime seen to refuse their contingents to the general expense; and the hereditary maxim of the privileged orders is to be this—" that they, forsooth, are not to be taxed." Every outrage is in the meantime to be offered to public opinion. The parliaments, the only images of the nation, then constitutionally existing, are to be kept by the court in a continual warfare, sometimes of a religious, sometimes of a financial nature.

At length a bold and bad man, the Duc d'Aiguillon, because he is a peer of the realm and a favourite, is to be protected in the mal-administration of one of the provinces; every contempt of national justice is to be shown, and at last the very parliaments themselves are by violence to be extinguished and put down, as if no law and no will were to be left in the land but that of the king and his mistresses, or some base parasite like the chancellor Maupeou, who could prefer the smiles and honours of beings like Louis XV. and la Comtesse Dubarri to the consciousness of rectitude, and the approbation of the wise and good.

But while the dreadful harvest of all these offences is ripening, present at this moment to your imagination men like Voltaire, Montesquieu, Rousseau, and Diderot. The doctrines and corruptions, for instance, of an ecclesiastical establishment, where ceremony was to supply the place of piety, and a wretch like Du Bois could be made a dignitary, were ridiculed and exposed by one writer; just views of policy and government were exhibited in the meantime by another; lastly, the enthusiasm that sighs for unattainable perfection was excited by a third; the abused and the oppressed were told their wrongs, but the giddy and the ignorant were called upon to redress them. Government, it appeared, was to exercise authority without any assistance from the natural associations of the human mind. The members of society were to go through the duties of common life without the virtue of self-denial; at length, even the wise man (such are sometimes the awful follies of the wise)—even the wise man was to say in his heart, " There is no God."

These are the materials for your reflection as you close the history of Louis XV. Fewer and less than these they cannot possibly be. Where are you to find lessons if not here?

The rulers of mankind—the gentry, the nobility, the clergy, the magistrates of a country, its princes and its monarchs, by no means excluding its still more powerful monarchs, the men of genius—all these seem but too often to suppose that the general laws of the moral world are to be suspended or new-modelled for their particular convenience, enjoyments, or repose.

They gratify their passions, whether of literary vanity, political ambition, or personal sensuality; they exercise no self government, and show no public spirit; they are base and selfish or they are daring and dissolute, or they are profane and irreligious; they disregard the ordinances of their country, corrupt its manners, or destroy its opinions, each according to his own particular temperament or temptation; and then they know not, it seems, how it happens that the public opinion becomes unfavourable to the establishments of the state; that the lower orders are wretched and immoral; that whenever an occasion offers, they are even mutinous and savage.

These things are, however, but too intelligible.

But even more may ensue, and calamities still more dreadful —a revolution may ensue—a community declines, the storm gathers, the scene sinks deeper and deeper into shade, the darkness at length comes, and the tempest. But who shall abide their coming? The cry is then heard, and the lamentation; there is at length silence, for the judgment is accomplished.

The historian shudders as he draws aside the rent and bloody veil, and the philosopher sees traced in the footsteps of the Destroying Angel the dreadful lesson that he has so often explained in vain.

LECTURE V.

LOUIS XVI.—TURGOT.—NECKER, &c.

The first Course of these Lectures on the French Revolution, down to the close of the Constituent Assembly, was delivered in 1826; the subsequent Course in 1827.

THE four lectures that you have last heard were originally intended to be the conclusion of my labours, and at the same time to prepare my hearers for the future study of the French Revolution. The Revolution itself I always thought too vast a subject for me to attempt, and that it must be left to my successors; but I became at last uneasy, on observing the hourly importance of every thing connected with this great event. It was but too plain that the youth of this place should not be suffered by me to go into the world without having had their attention directed in some general manner, however imperfect, to those opinions and events which would affect the interests and politics of it, not only while they were allowed to exist in it, but long after they were passed away and were no more. Sentiments like these were only impressed more deeply upon my mind by further reflection, and I therefore now proceed to offer you what I have written, only under what appeared to me the necessity of the case, and the duty of making every effort in my power, and not from the slightest expectation that I could deliver lectures on the French Revolution, which I could for a moment consider as worthy of a theme so extensive and so important.

In the lectures that I delivered on the reign of Louis XIV., I endeavoured to give some general notion of the monarchy which he may be said to have created ; of the splendid edifice which the Revolution levelled with the dust. Unless you know what it was, you cannot understand what the patriots and agitators of that period either attempted or effected. Voltaire's Age of Louis XIV. will afford you the best account of it, and in the shortest time.

In the lectures that followed in the long reign of Louis XV., I endeavoured to explain how the minds of the French people became alienated from their government. I alluded to the financial disputes and the religious disputes between the court and parliaments ; the manner in which these parliaments (judicial bodies) were exiled and recalled, broken up, and at last destroyed ; how the public feelings, political, moral, and religious, were in every way outraged and defied ; how an opening was thus made for any new opinions that could be proposed.

I then endeavoured to give you some notion of the new opinions that in fact were proposed ; their various nature, philosophic, visionary, anarchical, sceptical, and atheistical, immoral and licentious, obscene and disgusting ; and again, of the various descriptions of men, and of the very extraordinary men, by whom they were exhibited to the country ; and you will now, I hope, be prepared to receive the description I am about to give of the late French Revolution ; to give in a very few words. It was the conflict of the new opinions with the old ; apparently it was only the fall of a government under the weight of its financial engagements. But there was no reason why Louis might not have called the States General or any public 'assemblies together, to provide for the contingencies of the state, without being precipitated from his throne, unless the times had been of a very peculiar nature. They certainly were so, and I have endeavoured to describe how they became so ; the conduct of the rulers, and the privileged orders, and the conduct and writings of the men of genius of every description so acted and re-acted upon each other, and upon the community, that the Revolution we have seen—the conflict of the new opinions and the old—was the result.

I must now, and in the succeeding lectures, enter a little into the detail, and you must observe the statements and opinions I make, and remember them while you read the history for yourselves. Public lectures are always but a preparation for subsequent study. It is not easy to form reasonable views, and you must be therefore patient while you find me hereafter endeavouring to estimate the motives and conduct of every person and party that appears, in a manner that may seem to you somewhat minute and tedious.

But it is from such descriptions that instruction is to be gathered; it is during the first opening scenes, and during the approach of revolutions, that lessons are to be found; the wisdom or folly of the parties is then of the greatest consequence. The point is always how revolutions are to be avoided while reforms are accomplished; and during the present lectures, the patience of my hearers must be often exercised, while I endeavour to exhibit what were the mistakes and faults that were committed by all parties in their turn.

I have been assured that no fair relative justice has been done to those who took a part in these memorable transactions; the French historians of the Revolution, Mignet, Thiers, and others, are totally intolerable; introducing into the subject the doctrine of necessity, and resolving everything into a sort of concatenated series of events, of which no further account need be given, but that they could not have happened otherwise. The province of a reflecting historian, on a supposition of this kind, is at an end.

I shall advert to this point hereafter; it is sufficient for the present to enter a protest against all such views of history or its concerns.

I enter upon my subject with views far different, hoping to exhibit to you the relative merits and demerits of all concerned for the purposes of your instruction; and this may not be so easy a task, as has been theirs, who have neither praise nor censure which they can morally bestow; but it is a task which must be performed, or at least attempted; and aware of its difficulty, I have not presumed to present myself here, and read to you what has not been considered by others as well as myself. I have requested and received the assistance of one whom I think eminently fitted to render me this kind and necessary office; a very judicious and intelligent man on all occasions, and one well conversant with the occurrences and actors in these memorable scenes—Mr. Mallet. In consequence of his suggestions, I have made additions to the lectures, as they originally stood; in consequence of his objections, I have made modifications of what I had written, that are material, and when our sentiments differed (they sometimes did so, though rather in degree than in kind), and when I could not sincerely give up my opinion, I have incorporated his remarks into my lectures, and they will appear in conjunction with my own, in such a manner that you will, without observing it, in fact, be left to judge between us; nor do I think that the distrust of my own judgment, which I have thus described to you, should be forgotten by any of you on any public occasion; such are the imperfections of the mind, and such its occasional eclipses.

To proceed, then, to the consideration of the great subject before us.

My first observation is a startling one. The French Revolution must be considered as having failed: in every immediate and proper sense of the word, it failed.

No beautiful system of civil and religious liberty was seen to arise in France, and they, who wished well to the happiness of mankind, and who had looked forward to the progressive improvement of the human species, saw swept from their view all the splendid visions on which they had so fondly gazed. What cause for so cruel a disappointment to the expectations of the wise and good? There had been long a conflict between the old opinions and the new; the government was lost in public estimation; the king was without energy, ill fitted for his situation; the privileged orders were too selfish; the patriots too violent; the great military powers of Europe interfered.

Such is a short explanation of this deplorable event—the failure of this great experiment.

It is a great calamity to mankind when the patriots of a country fail; they are the salt of the earth. We are placed by our Almighty Master in a world where nothing can be obtained without enterprise and effort; but the conclusion from the failure of such men is, that enterprise and effort are in vain.

It may be, however, useful to allude in such passing manner as the nature of these lectures will admit, to the great scenes of this interesting history, to see what instruction can be reaped from it, and what estimate can be formed of it, asking ourselves what we could have done, what attempted in each different situation, each crisis that will be presented to us. It is easy to blame; of two different courses that might have been pursued, it is easy to see, when one has failed, that the other should have been preferred; but what we are to do is this: we are to try to place ourselves in the situation of those who had alternatives, before them, and were obliged to act; we must, above all, try not to judge from the event. Mistakes were no doubt committed, but the great lesson of the whole is the wisdom, the duty in all political affairs, of moderation; a lesson that will be thought by some too trite to be worth the drawing, and by others too tame and uninteresting to be likely to be observed by such absurd and furious beings as mankind are composed of; yet it is the great lesson of the whole, and it is the lesson that by me, at least, must for ever be inculcated.

The first book I would have you turn to is Lacretelle's History of the Eighteenth Century—not his Précis of the Revolution, but his History of the Eighteenth Century.

We have already passed through the reign of Louis XV. We can now go on with the fourteenth book, the Accession of Louis XVI. to the throne. You will find the situation of things to be something of the following nature. The young king was grave, decorous, sensible, modest, pious, virtuous, and deeply interested in the happiness of his people—such was the young king. Louis, just twenty, was happy to call to his assistance the experience of the Count de Maurepas, a statesman that was old enough to have been a counsellor to Louis XIV. The ministers of Louis XV., you will see, were dismissed; among them the chancellor Maupeou, who had contrived the destruction of the parliaments. The celebrated Turgot was called into office.

A new system was therefore evidently adopted. Turgot was the favourite of the philosophers, and he was soon removed from the marine, where the old minister had originally thought proper to place him, to the situation of comptroller-general of the finances. You will now remember what I have said of the new opinions. It was in the finances that Turgot was expected to introduce the most important reforms, those to be followed by reforms in the laws, and these again, by reforms in the manners of the country and all the ancient institutions of the monarchy.

Now that such hopes should be entertained not only by men of intelligence, but by the young monarch himself, was highly natural. Benevolence was the ruling passion of his nature; this may assuredly be asserted, and must never through the whole of this history be forgotten; but he was born a king, no doubt, and had his appropriate difficulties and temptations : hitherto we see no mistake. You will find in the notes of Lacretelle an affecting letter from Turgot, addressed to the young king.

" We will have no bankruptcies," said the philosophic min-

ister, " no augmentation of the imposts, no loans. I shall have
to combat abuses of every kind ; to combat those who are benefited by them, and even the kindness, sire, of your own nature.
I shall be feared, hated, and calumniated ; but the affecting goodness with which you pressed my hands in yours, to witness your
acceptance of my devotion to your service, is never to be obliterated from my recollection, and must support me under every
trial."

This letter is surely very creditable to both parties. The minister had said, you will observe, " we will have no bankruptcies ;" and I will now stop for a moment to mention, that there
is in the community a great looseness of thought upon this subject of a national bankruptcy. You hear people speaking " of a
national sponge," of " sweeping away the stocks at once," as if
the whole was a castle in the air, which might be made to disappear, and no one be affected.

It is a pity that such light reasoners do not ask themselves
what must be the consequence if those who now receive their
dividends were to receive them no longer ? This is a very short
and intelligible question. Do they not know, does not every
one know, that they who receive dividends are not so much a
few rich capitalists as widows and orphans—the helpless and
the unprotected, particularly the female part of the community :
the old and the infirm ; public institutions of every description ;
hospitals, places of education ; suppose all these without their
usual means of support ? a partial earthquake or a deluge would
in comparison be a trifling calamity.

But to return. The finances were the great point to be considered ; the minister had no doubt directed his view to the real
difficulty. The revenue, through a long succession of years, had
continually fallen short of the expenditure. There could be no
repose for the monarch, no real security for his crown, unless
some happy alteration could be effected in the management of
the finances. You have already, in considering the reign of
Louis XV., seen sufficiently the importance of this part of the subject; but the question was, what could be attempted, supposing,
as was the case, that the minister was enlightened, and the monarch benevolent. Great improvements in the system of taxation ; in the nature of the taxes, in the collection of them, in the
expenditure of them ; again, great reforms in the expenditure of
the court; an active and skilful resistance, a sort of war to be
waged against abuses of every kind, against profligacy and folly,
wherever they might appear ; these improvements were possible.

But when all this was done, all this it was evident would be insufficient unless something more could be accomplished.

The fact was, that the privileged orders were exempted to a certain degree from the taxes to which the rest of the country was exposed. Now, unless they could be brought to bear their part, no real relief could be afforded to the monarchy. The accumulated deficit, the annual deficit, were each too great.

To accomplish so desirable an end was the great object, was the great hinge on which turned the happiness of the community, the authority of the monarch, the safety of the privileged orders themselves; and unless these orders could be brought to rise superior to their own views of self-interest, and the prejudices of their birth, and even their views of the constitution of their country, there could, in truth, be no chance for the improvement or even the welfare of France, in the state of things which had arisen from the expenses of government on one side, and the prevalence of the new opinions on the other.

Of all this Turgot seems to have been well aware. He had announced himself as decidedly of opinion that an impost must be fairly and equally levied upon proprietors of every description; and certainly this was a doctrine perfectly right and just. What meanness in the privileged orders to resist it! what selfishness, what guilt! but what folly, particularly when the country had evidently begun to inquire and to think! What truth so obvious as this, that nothing can be secure that is not agreeable to the moral feelings of mankind? Still the minister and the monarch were to take into their account the inherent baseness and stupidity of mankind on all such occasions; and the student should himself now consider how, in the situation of the monarch and the minister, he would have endeavoured to procure from the privileged orders so reasonable and so necessary a sacrifice.

It will not be easy for him to determine upon his measure, but certainly he will not, I think, propose the measure that really was adopted—the recall of the parliaments.

If he turns to the reign of Louis XV., he will see in what manner these bodies were superseded and destroyed. But why renew their existence? They were connected with the privileged orders rather than with the king or the people.

Their doctrine had been, that a tax could not be legally levied, unless first enregistered by them. What chance for any great scheme of improvement in the finances, such as the minister contemplated, if their consent was first to be made necessary? Their proper office was the administration of justice; other courts had been, on their suppression, erected: what need of their revival?

What but opposition could be expected from them to such measures as intelligent men would have proposed, such as the minister himself no doubt meditated, and as he had probably, already, in the whole or in part, introduced to the consideration of the young monarch. The free commerce of grain, for instance; the suppression of oppressive duties—that on salt, the gabelle; the abolition of the corvées, or the repairing of the roads by the peasantry; the abolition of tyrannical feudal usages; the imposition of a land-tax, from which the nobles and clergy should not be exempt; a more merciful criminal code; a civil code, improved, and throughout the whole of France consistent and every where the same. What hope for projects like these, particularly the last, if they were to pass through the ordeals of the parliaments?

Turgot was well aware how unfavourable to his plans would be the restoration of the parliaments, and he opposed it, as did the minister of war; but the old courtier, the Count de Maurepas, prevailed, and the parliaments were in an evil hour recalled. It is not easy to say what could be the motive with Maurepas, unless jealousy of Turgot; but with the king, at least, it was surely a mistake. The measure was indeed popular—no reason this for its adoption, but rather the contrary. The king was on this account only the more likely to create a power which he could not control; Malesherbes was added to the ministry, a valuable auxiliary to Turgot; but in the event, what was the fate of this minister of reform, of Turgot? Maurepas was not faithful to him; the privileged orders were soon united against him and the parliaments and the clergy forgot their differences, the better to oppose him. The queen committed the mistake of uniting with the old minister and the noblesse against the reformers, as they were called; and when Turgot at length produced his six edicts, a clamour arose, that seemed to indicate that all the very elements of the public safety had been endangered. The five last of these edicts had reference only to the proper management of the interior traffic and business of the metropolis, more particularly the commerce of grain, but the first was the suppression of the abominable corvées; and the roads were, by the new edict, to be repaired, and the expense defrayed by a contribution, from which the privileged orders were *not* to be exempt; hinc illæ lacrymæ—the nobles and the prelates, it seems, considered themselves degraded if they were to contribute to the repair of roads; and they would no doubt have declared that their dignity and their existence, the very rights of property itself, were endangered, if they were now for the first time, they would have said, in the history of the monarchy, to be subjected to the visits of the tax-gatherer. It is in the sentiments and the conduct of these privileged orders, on this and on all similar occasions, former or subsequent, that you are to find *one* of the greatest lessons to be derived from this French Revolution. Nothing, as I must for ever repeat, that is not agreeable to the fair, obvious conclusions of the moral feelings of mankind, can be in politics secure. These moral feelings may slumber for years, for ages, but if by any chance they are awakened, the wise and the good will conform to them in time, will conform to them with all possible expedition, will make what sacrifices are necessary, and the truth is, that if sacrifices are made early, such sacrifices may be found light and be little felt; not so if delayed; no wisdom, no moral sensibility of this kind, was on *this* occasion shown by the parliaments and the privileged orders, and it never was on any subsequent occasion shown, till too late. They saw not exactly their situation, probably no one in France at the time did; but were they not calling for reforms and sacrifices from the king, from every one but themselves? Was not this at least plain? And was it not plain, also, that the peasants and the public were alone contributing to an expense which they themselves were bound in common justice to share? ¬Were they not taking the business of reform from the king and his ministers, where alone it could be safely lodged, to be undertaken by themselves? And with whose assistance, it may be asked, if they moved not in concert with the king and his masters—with whose assistance, but as in the former times of the parliaments, the assistance of the people—the assistance of the people! And this, then, was the expedient of the parliaments and the privileged orders, for the accomplishment of their own, and the happiness and prosperity of the community. In the event, you will see, that the minister Turgot was dismissed, that the excellent Malesherbes retired, and that the nobles, the parliaments, and the clergy were triumphant. But triumphant over whom? Over a benevolent monarch, and a patriotic minister. Turgot soon after died, early in 1781; his epitaph might have been the couplet of the poet:

> " Truths would you teach, or save a sinking land,
> All fear, none aid you, and few understand."

No doubt the possibility of a revolution little occurred to the privileged orders, yet there is a remarkable passage in a letter of our own Lord Chesterfield, so early as the year 1753, twenty-three years *before* these proceedings of the parliaments, and before the times of Turgot, which shows plainly that this possibility was clearly seen by him. "Wherever you are," says he, writing to his son, "inform yourself minutely of, and attend particularly to the affairs of France; they grow serious, and in my opinion will grow more and more so every day; . . . . . . the people are poor, consequently discontented: those who have religion are divided in their notions of it, which is saying, that they hate one another; the clergy will not forgive the parliament, nor the parliament forgive them: the army must, without doubt, take (in their own minds at least) different parts in all these disputes, which upon occasion would break out; armies, though always the supporters and tools of absolute power for the time being, are always the destroyers of it too, by frequently changing the hands in which they think proper to lodge it . . . . The French nation reasons freely, which they never did before, upon matters of religion and government, and begin to be spregiudicati, to have got rid of their prejudices; the officers do so too; in short, all the symptoms which I have ever met with in history, previous to great changes and revolutions in government, now exist, and daily increase in France."

This was written in the year 1753. His lordship seems to have fixed his eye more particularly on the religious dissensions between the court and the parliaments, the Jesuits and the Jansenists, but he had observed also the freedom of discussion that was making its appearance. A civil war seems to have been his expectation, and the privileged orders, therefore, twenty-three years afterwards, should have shown a little more discernment than they did. His concluding remark was not exactly verified by the event. "I am glad of it," says he; "the rest of Europe will be the quieter, and have time to recover." He had been evidently in the habit of considering France as the great disturber of the peace of mankind.

Expectations of changes and revolutions, views of this kind, are no doubt often entertained lightly, taken up hastily, and produced at random. But this is not a passage of any such nature; and it comes from a man of the world and a statesman.

Of what value would such a man as Lord Chesterfield have been to his order in France on the occasions which followed, and how reasonable and prophetic would have been the advice he would have given! I shall have quite failed in what I have already delivered in this lecture, if I have not excited your curiosity with regard to the origin and first opening of this

French Revolution. It is in these opening scenes that the great lessons of instruction are to be always found. No philosopher, no statesman can render his country or mankind so great a service as to advance their civil or religious liberties, and yet secure them from these dreadful revolutions; to reform, to improve, but without violence and bloodshed: and to attain a wisdom of this exalted cast, no means so natural as the long and careful meditation of the rise and first progress of great changes, like these we are now surveying.

I have already given you a faint, general sketch of this part of the subject; but I will dwell upon it a little longer.

The situation of the king is the great point of curiosity; he is benevolent, and wishes the happiness of his people; he is calm and sensible, and therefore summons to his assistance an ancient counsellor, M. de Maurepas, and at the same time a man then celebrated for his intelligence, and for those more enlarged views which the gradual progress of civilization and knowledge had introduced to the notice of the French nation—M. Turgot. All this Louis does; but Louis was born a king, and had the feelings natural to his birth and situation; he could not mean so to alter the institutions of his country that he should appear to himself to be king no longer; and any philosopher and any patriot that required this of him was unfeeling and unjust. He was surrounded, too, by a court (the queen at his head) who could not be expected to see any merit in any minister or any system that at all disturbed their usual routine of opinions and enjoyments; beside him stood a noblesse and a clergy, among whom many men of intelligence and patriotism might be found; of more, indeed, than could be expected to belong to those bodies in their collective capacity; but the question was, whether those bodies could be persuaded to act with any feeling for the lower orders, with any due sense of the sacrifices that were now required of them; for on this depended the safety of their monarchy, the repose of their king, the real security of themselves. Their organ at this time seemed to be the parliaments, particularly the parliaments of Paris, the members of which had long been engaged in struggles with the crown, appeared to be animated with a wish to save the country from oppression, more particularly from taxation, but seemed ready to unite with the privileged orders in resistance to every measure that the king could propose, if any taxation was thus to reach the privileged orders themselves, as well as the rest of the community.

Now, I ask what more unhappy state of things can be conceived for the monarch ? What is he to do, and where is his power ? He is quite young; the patriotic minister Turgot would go far greater lengths than could be intelligible to him, than could be agreeable to his other minister, to an old courtier, the experienced friend on whom the king naturally depended, than could be endured by the privileged orders, or thought of with any patience by the court.

What now could the king do ? What but endeavour to turn to the best advantage he could the intelligence and sentiments of all concerned, and make such attempts for the welfare of the community as might appear likely to succeed. He therefore proposes the six edicts of Turgot, which I have mentioned, to the parliaments. The privileged orders are in these edicts only required to contribute like the rest of the community to the repair of the roads, nothing more; but no, the edicts are resisted by the parliaments (the privileged orders had taken the alarm). The king then insists upon their being enregistered, and calls a bed of justice.

But the result of the whole is, that the patriotic minister is dismissed, and the edicts gradually forgotten. This no doubt the king should not have submitted to; though young, he should have seen that nothing unreasonable had been proposed, and that his patriotic minister must be supported while he was only proposing what was reasonable, and while it was clear that, sooner or later, and in some way or other, sacrifices of their personal interests must be procured from the privileged orders, or the finances fall into the most irremediable confusion, his own happiness be at an end, and possibly even his crown endangered.

The student should, I think, fix his attention very earnestly on this particular part of the history.

It is probable that a monarch not only of benevolence but of decision of character, who would have insisted upon these edicts, and carried his minister through all his difficulties, might thus have prevented the Revolution; if the king could but have seen his danger at so early a period as this, all might have been well; but he did not, nor indeed did any one at the time. He was young and inexperienced, and even if he had speculated more deeply and successfully on his situation, he was not of a temperament to confront and overpower resistance.

All through the history of the Revolution, and from the very first appearance of it, this want of character in the king must be considered as the great misfortune of all; as contributing to its progress and failure, as fatal to his people, and still more fatal to himself.

On this occasion it operated most unhappily, and whatever we may say of the king in his existing situation of youthfulness and ignorance, his counsellors at least are not to be forgiven; nor is he himself, if Turgot, as probably he did, made proper representations to him, and presented to his consideration views that were reasonable, and such as were fitted somewhat to alarm him, anxious and uneasy as he already was. The case before them all, the king included, was simple, the steps few : the finances, for instance, were to be repaired ; the immunities, therefore, or the privileged orders were to be disturbed, modified, more or less conceded : this could not be done without a struggle; but it was evident if the king gave up his minister, and retired from this struggle, that the struggle might then come to be, not between the privileged orders and the king, but between them and the community; the king withdrawn from the field, to be rendered insignificant, and perhaps put aside or trampled down amid the chances of the combat.

These are reflections, it may be said, only obvious from the event; the danger, it may, however, be replied, the danger might not be obvious, but the faults that the king was committing, these really were obvious; and he is not to be pardoned for the commission of them. He should have prevented Turgot from producing these edicts, or supported him in them ; he did worst of all, he suffered them to be proposed; he made the parliaments, as I have already mentioned, enregister them by a bed of justice, that is, by force; and he then gradually and silently abandoned the minister and the edicts together. But the defects of the character of Louis—for defects he had—were but too important ; a want of rational confidence in himself, an unwillingness to rule any one, while born the ruler of millions, born and not created by his own choice, and this is his excuse, and must always be remembered ; and positive vices and outrageous faults would have been less fatal to himself and to his country than was this unhappy failing (this want of character) at this singular crisis.

What was to be his situation when both the edicts and the minister were gone ? Probity and wisdom, if attempting any opposition to the privileged orders, had evidently no chance at court, even when honoured by his protection. But what hope was there then for the finances, that is, for his own repose, perhaps security ? You will easily conceive the situation of the court, and what must necessarily have been the character of any *new* comptroller of the finances. How little agreeable were the sounds of economy, of reform, the total want of all real ability, that must have belonged to any minister that could now undertake, on any opposite system, the post from which Turgot had been driven.

One remark is indeed to be made; the king, amidst all the frivolity and folly, whether grave or gay, that surrounded him, had still his anxieties directed to the right point. He was never at ease about the finances; his attention was still fixed upon them—this is merit and sense. And at last, in a very singular manner, which you will see explained in the histories, a Swiss banker, M. Necker, was called to the administration of them; the old minister, Maurepas, still remaining the minister, and at the head of affairs. The maxim of Turgot was "no new loans and no new impositions." This was tolerably hardy, when the annual deficit was twenty-five millions of livres; but Necker's was even more so, "new loans, and yet no new taxes."

This system might indeed save him and the king from contests with the parliaments, the nobility, and the clergy, but how was the interest of these loans to be paid? By the suppression of offices, Necker would have replied, reforms in the expenditure of the court, in the collection of the taxes, and by all the savings of a very vigilant economy; but economy was apparently a very inadequate resource for a minister of finance, of French finance, to depend upon. The loans, however, succeeded; they were made, and they were registered by the parliaments, though not without difficulty.

But, in the midst of these transactions came on the perilous question of war with England. The North American colonies had declared themselves independent. An opportunity was offered to France of humbling her ancient rival; how was it to be resisted? how, by a French cabinet? by the French people? It is understood that the king, when he signed the treaty with the revolted colonies, could not help saying to the minister, Vergennes, "You will remember, sir, that this is contrary to my opinion." The king was surely right; it was no time for France to engage herself in a war when the finances were already in a state of confusion. She had received no offence from England; had no grounds of interference between her and her colonies; the war was unjust on the part of France, as well as impolitic; either reason should have been sufficient. No doubt it would have been difficult to have preserved a neutrality, and the king would have thus rendered himself unpopular; but his want of firmness on this second great occasion, and the want of honour and good faith to England in the ministers of France, must be considered as having mutually contributed, and most materially, to the Revolution that followed. Dodsley's Annual Register for 1789, opens with a statement of the effects produced upon the affairs of France by her interference in the American contest; the influence attributed to it is very great, and I do not conceive exaggerated. I refer you to the work itself. Those of the young French officers who distinguished themselves in America (Fayette and others), became afterwards the patriots and heroes of the French Revolution. The appearance of Franklin at Paris was quite an event.

While the war with England continues, the history of this French Revolution seems suspended. Necker is the minister of finance, and is employed in making provision for the expenses of the war by all the possible expedients of economy. This would have surely been but a strange system of finance—loans, and the interest to be paid by particular measures of economy— even if there had been no war, and even if the court had been virtuous and patriotic; but the court was not so; it was giddy, frivolous, and expensive. The king was too easily satisfied with his own privations and sacrifices, and thought that doing this, he had done every thing; and he was too indulgent to the queen and the light troop of pleasure by which she was surrounded. The situation of Necker was indeed deplorable; the apathy of Maurepas, the facility of the king, the caprices and folly of the court. "Never shall I forget," he says in a work he published in 1791, "the long dark staircase of M. de Maurepas, the terror and the melancholy with which I used to ascend it, uncertain of the success of some idea that had occurred to me, likely, if carried into effect, to produce an increase of the revenue; but likely, at the same time, to fall severely, though justly, on some one or other; the address, the expedients, I had to make use of to succeed; the sort of hesitation and diffidence with which I ventured to intermingle in my representations any of those great fundamental truths, those maxims of justice and of right, with which my own heart was animated. I was really like the ancient Sully when he stood surrounded by the young and tittering courtiers of Louis XIII." Victories, it seems, were the hopes of Necker in this unseasonable war; and then an honourable peace, he thought, would open all the world to the French commerce, and the influx from the customs would render other taxes unnecessary.

Necker was popular with the monied men, and carried his loans and his annuities very successfully. They were enregistered, but with some difficulty, by the parliament of Paris. He met there, however, an acute and violent opponent in D'Esprémesnil, who inspired his colleagues, young and old, with an ardour and a boldness like his own; turned the grave legal court of the parliament of Paris into a political assembly, like the House of Commons in England, and at last talked of an appeal to the States General. The words fell with little effect upon the ear of the public at this moment; but twelve years after, they were the signal of the Revolution.

Opposition of this kind from the parliaments, and many secret misgivings, must no doubt have not a little disquieted the mind of Necker. He meant well to the country, but was in the first place faithful to the king he served. He saw the wonders produced by credit in England. He had been in that country, and a free government must have appeared to him the secret of the whole.

Publicity of accounts, and representation of the people, these must have occurred to him as the real remedies for all the miseries of the great empire of France; for the disorders of the finances; the oppressions of the people; the vices of the nobility and of the privileged orders; the anxieties and insecurity of the monarch.

But how were such objects to be accomplished or to be approached? The kingdom of France, as you are already aware, was originally composed of a number of small and separate kingdoms, which had gradually been forced or persuaded to accumulate round one great central province. The great merit of Henry IV. was, that he kept them together; and, during the time of Richelieu and Louis XIV. the whole kingdom got consolidated, and became at last one and indivisible; but each province had its laws and its customs; many of them (the Pays d'Etat, as they were called*) had made distinct bargains with

---

* The great vassals of France had always endeavoured to have seignorial possessions in France; it had been the object of every succeeding monarch to reunite the great fiefs to the crown.

They accomplished their object so far, that at the accession of Louis XIII. the seventy-two great fiefs of France were united to the crown, and all the feudal lords attended at the States General in 1614. (Louis XIII.) In Butler you will see a table of the re-union of the fiefs to the crown, and an enumeration of the additions that were thus made by each monarch, from Hugh Capet to Louis XV.

With respect to law, each seignory had its particular usages, scarcely two

the crown, which were still in full effect; and any rational system of commercial intercourse, certainly any system of uniform jurisprudence, seemed impossible. (You will easily understand this part of the subject from Mr. C. Butler's publications, his Horæ Juridicæ, and his work on the Revolutions of the German Empire.) How could a minister like Necker, a Protestant from Geneva, reduce to order such a chaos of feudal usages and opinions? What, again, could he effect on the subject of the representation of the people? The States General, the original representation of the country, had been long disused, and it was evidently a most perilous experiment to revive them. The parliament was sufficiently factious and troublesome; and these difficulties, that must have presented themselves to the meditations of this philosophic minister, would only have appeared more alarming and insuperable if he had endeavoured to discuss them with his youthful sovereign; who, benevolent as he was, was neither enterprising nor resolute, was still a pupil to his ancient counsellor Maurepas, and devoted to the queen; who, like the court around her, could have little taste for reforms and improvements, and the timely counsels of prospective wisdom.

But one of the measures which Necker now adopted was of a very important nature, and in itself not a little objectionable. He published his Compte Rendû; that is, the Report he had furnished to the king, of the finances; in other words, he gave publicity to the national accounts. He unveiled every mystery that they contained; that is, he threw himself, for the support of his financial schemes, on the candour and intelligence of the community.

No doubt, what he meant by this measure was to persuade or morally oblige the privileged orders to contribute to the public burden. It was but too evident to him, as it must have always been to every thinking man, as it had been to Turgot, as it must have been to the king himself, that this contribution of the privileged orders was the great remedy, was at least the first more immediate and practical remedy for the evils that embarrassed the government.

But surely this publication of the Compte Rendû was, on the

alike. Charles VII., in 1453, endeavoured to ascertain them. Forty-two years elapsed before the customs of any one place were verified. The measure lingered, and was resumed in the reign of Louis XII., and about the year 1619 (time of Louis XIII.) was completed. The customs of each place, formed into one collection, was called the Grand Coutumier de France. The best edition of it is in four volumes folio.

whole, a measure, the expediency of which may be very reasonably doubted, if not entirely denied. What good could have been expected to result from it, by any very sensible and sagacious man? The new opinions did not then want fresh fuel, or any new and authentic means of attack. Necker knew enough of the privileged orders to doubt the influence of reasonable motives on their minds. The great accusation against this minister has been always that of personal vanity, a love, a passion for public applause.

Materials for such an accusation may perhaps be here found. It is not very agreeable to see defects of this kind in the character of a benevolent, virtuous, and enlightened man; but if they appear, they must be noted.

But the next great measure of Necker, was to improve, if possible, the constitution of the country; to introduce some representation of the community into the system of the government; to create some bodies that should be the organs of the respectable and intelligent part of the people. In this manner he might have hoped gradually and silently to extinguish the political importance of the parliament of Paris, and eventually to control the selfish passions of the privileged orders. He seems to have done what alone could be done; to have availed himself of existing institutions, and to have endeavoured to modify and wield them to his purposes. Good was chiefly to be expected, he must have thought, from gradual amelioration, and training the people to better habits, and modes of political thought and government. He was, perhaps, too late: but this was his misfortune, not his fault. He revived the idea of Turgot, and formed a project of provincial administrations. According to Necker's management, these bodies would have become a sort of States General, not collected at Paris, but established in every province, consisting of nobility, clergy, and (equal in number to the other two) of Tiers Etat.

The provinces of the Pays d'Etat, Languedoc, Burgundy, &c. had assemblies already of this description. Many advantages would have been thus obtained; the vexations arising from the immediate agency of the officers of the crown, the taxgatherers, the intendants of the provinces, would have been thus avoided; the dangers to be feared from the parliament of Paris weakened; the dangers to be feared from Paris itself escaped; and a step made, an important one no doubt, yet on the whole a cautious one, towards the accomplishment of those objects which the patriotic minister and benevolent monarch had equally at heart. You will see some account of this part of our subject in the work

of M^e. de Staël; it has not, I conceive, been considered with
sufficient attention by the writers on the French Revolution, not
even by M^e. de Staël herself.   Yet what she says is valuable and
curious. To me it appears among the first measures that the king
should have attempted to carry, and he should have attached himself firmly to Necker, as the only minister fitted to serve him.
The experiment is considered by M^e. de Staël as having been successful in the two provinces where it was tried ; but a work upon
the subject, addressed to the king by Necker himself, in which
his ultimate views were displayed, having come to the knowledge of the parliament, so much opposition was excited, that the
minister was overpowered.   The minister, it seems, had no object but economy and the welfare of the state ; and no powerful
friend in the court but the monarch himself, who, in a crisis like
this, was unhappily from his nature unfitted for the office.
    The parliament saw from Necker's own work, that their own
influence, that their own existence, as a political body, if his provincial assemblies succeeded, would gradually cease ; and the
privileged orders saw, that new powers and authorities were,
according to Necker's plan, to arise in the state, which could be
of no advantage to them ; but, on the contrary, must eventually,
more or less, deprive them of their immunities, and withdraw
from them their prerogatives.   The old minister therefore combined with every one around him, in and about the court and
his more immediate sphere, and Necker was disposed of as a
common grievance, and dismissed from the ministry.
    You will, I hope, not be unwilling to know a little more of
this measure of provincial assemblies proposed by Necker, so
early as 1780 and 1781.
    1st. There is a Memoir of Turgot relative to the subject ; and
2dly, a Memoir of Necker.   Both ministers had seen that it was
desirable to emancipate the crown from the interference of the
parliaments, that it was necessary to make the privileged orders
contribute ; and that these points could not be accomplished without borrowing for the sovereign some authority from the community.
    Turgot seems to have referred himself entirely to the Tiers Etat,
and to have made use of no other order in his organization of these
provincial assemblies ; but Necker avoided this error, and composed his assemblies of all the orders in the state, in the way,
you will see hereafter, that the States General were composed,
one-fourth clergy, one-fourth nobility, one-half Tiers Etat.
    The views of Turgot, you will also see, were more popular,

were probably too popular.   Necker's were much less so.   These
provincial assemblies, consisting of all the three orders, nobility,
clergy, and Tiers Etat, seem to have been M. Necker's measure,
in truth, his expedient, to make as near an approach as consist-
ently with his duty to his master he thought he could, to the
system of representation established in England.   The privileged orders, though it must be allowed that, in one way or other,
they paid much more than is supposed, still were more exempted
from the taxes that were paid by the country, than, on the one
hand, he thought just or agreeable to the interest of the monarchy;
yet still, on the other, by force to compel them to pay their quota,
and with or without their acquiescence to abolish their privileges,
was not what Necker at all considered as practicable, or even as
very reasonable ; and, on the whole, therefore, he rather hoped
insensibly and in due time to accomplish these great objects, by
mixing the privileged orders in this manner with the Tiers Etat,
and introducing them gradually to the benefits and practices of
the representative system.   M. Necker, in this first administration, was certainly ready to compound, to balance, and capitulate
with evils ; and no idle taste for innovation and experiment
seems to have formed any part of his character.

You will find the difficulties of Necker's situation and the
difficulties of the state well described by Mᵉ. de Staël.   You will
see the evils he hoped to remedy, the advantages he hoped to
procure, by the establishment of the provincial administrations ;
even from what I have already said you will have a general notion of them.   You will sufficiently comprehend them from her
work, and only from her work.

You will then turn to the detail of the history, and you will understand that the old minister, Maurepas, became jealous of Necker,
whose merits and virtues, and whose importance at that time to
the state he did not properly comprehend ; you will find that
the king gave way ; and you will see, I think, some reason to
suspect that Necker was at the time more interested in his own
personal consequence than was exactly necessary ; was, in short,
too vain.   I consider this part of the work of Mᵉ. de Staël as
valuable and curious, and I conceive it will be sufficient for me
to direct your attention very particularly to it.

It is quite impossible to offer any abridgment or representation of the pages of such a writer.   She herself gives only a rapid
sketch, all beaming with light and beauty ; and it is in vain to
provide for the case of those who would not meditate with delight and interest, everything that can be said by such a writer
on such a subject as the French Revolution.

If Necker had succeeded, as he ought to have done, in this, his first administration, the Revolution might have been adjourned, and possibly even prevented. If he had continued to succeed, as he went on, and if the king's mind had gradually opened to the crisis in which he and his kingdom were in truth placed, and to the necessity he lay under of being steady and decisive, there can be little doubt that the government would thus have been regularly ameliorated, and the country at length advanced to a new and more becoming situation of general intelligence and happiness. No such good fortune awaited France or Europe ; and with Necker, in 1781, as it appears to me, departed all real hope for any peaceful alterations in the objectional institutions, in convenient usages, and unfortunate opinions of the inhabitants of this great country.

One word on the subject of the parliaments, and I conclude.

It was the parliaments that were the great obstacles in the way of Necker. It was these bodies that most effectually resisted the plans of Necker for the safety of the monarchy. They were acting perhaps according to the natural prejudices of their situation ; but they have been praised by respectable writers, and thought patriotic at this period of their history and at periods immediately succeeding it. I do not, I confess, see any great reason for such approbation of their conduct. What did they mean, what was the end and intention of their eternal complaints and opposition ? Did they wish to impede the benevolent efforts of the king, and to depress the lower orders, more than they were already depressed ? No. Their language was that of a general zeal for the public good. Did they mean to render the privileges of the higher orders less injurious to the interests of the community ? No. For they resisted Turgot, and more especially Necker, while endeavouring to effect these ends, at every moment and at every turn. Would they do good themselves ? No. Would they suffer others to attempt it ? No. What other description than this can be given of men who are factious or wrong-headed ?

Their great leader, M. D'Esprémesnil, saw his mistake too late. He united himself afterwards to the king, and perished, like him, a victim to the Revolution.

There is a passage in the Memoirs of Baron de Grimm, on the subject of these parliaments, which you should by all means peruse attentively. He was led to the consideration of them in April, 1789, by the situation of France and the approaching meeting of the States General. He had been long in the country, was by profession an observer, and on every subject was one, very acute and intelligent. You will find his description of these important bodies very unfavourable; and I have myself just expressed sentiments unfavourable also. No doubt I must not forget, nor must the student, that these bodies were the only representatives òf the civil and religious liberties of the country, that ever appeared or could well be found. The merit of such resistance, under any arbitrary government, must not be lightly estimated; and the temptations of their situation, and the treatment they had often and even lately received, must not be overlooked. But the question is not that of their prior merits and their general merits, which were very great; but what was the nature of their opposition during the periods we are now more immediately considering—whether that opposition had not all the marks of a factious and seditious opposition. Was it not vague and inextinguishable; not to be either satisfied or pacified; without precise object expressed, or intelligible system proposed; and therefore factious and seditious? Surely it was most injurious to the public weal at this particular juncture, while Turgot, Necker, Calonne, and others, were endeavouring to assist the king in settling the disordered affairs of this great kingdom.

LECTURE VI.

CALONNE.

My last lecture was employed in endeavouring to describe to you the manner in which the opportunity of probably preventing the Revolution was lost during the earlier part of the king's reign; lost by the want of character in the king, and by the selfishness and blindness of the privileged orders.

My chief topics were the efforts of Turgot to introduce a tax on the nobility and clergy, and the fault the king committed in suffering him to be overpowered by the court and privileged orders, and driven into retirement.

Again, the fault that was next committed by his ministers rather than himself, when they engaged in a manner so impolitic and unjust in our American war, and thus gave such circulation and energy to the new opinions.

I next alluded to the efforts that were made by Necker for the improvement of the finances, and more particularly the amelioration of the constitution of France by his measure of the provincial administrations, and the fault that was again committed by the king in suffering this minister, like his predecessor Turgot, to be overpowered by the court and privileged orders, and driven, in like manner, into retirement.

I concluded with giving a very unfavourable opinion of the parliaments. Whatever might be their former merits, I represented them as having acted at this period in a manner very unreasonable, perverse, and factious, highly unfavourable to the interests of their country.

I now proceed. When Necker was dismissed, the king took his two next financial ministers from the parliament, to lessen, perhaps, their opposition ; but these ministers seem to have been wholly inefficient, though the return of peace gave them opportunities more favourable than any which Necker had enjoyed. Regular magistrates, like these new ministers, and privileged bodies, like the parliaments they came from, have naturally, as Madame de Staël observes, a dread of innovations, and yet some change was surely to be attempted, when things, if left to themselves, were evidently journeying on to disorder and ruin.

This was probably in some way or other understood or felt by the court, for M. de Calonne was called to the administration of the finances, a man of brilliant talents, and probably in every respect the contrast of the worthy magistrates who had thus preceded him. You will see a great deal deserving of your attention on the subject of M. de Calonne, in the books I have referred you to.

You will find no difficulty, in the mean time, to conceive the situation of the king, the minister, and the kingdom.

The writings of the philosophers, the success of the American cause, and the disorder of the finances, the publications of Necker, the distresses of the state, every thing conspired to agitate the public mind; to lead men to find a pleasure in political speculations ; to induce them to form extravagant expectations of the reforms that were to be introduced into France; of the wonders that were to be achieved by men of intelligence and patriotism ; before the century yet closed, it seems to have been agreed that the last half of the eighteenth was to do more for mankind than all the ages that had preceded it.

It was certainly most unfortunate that a sentiment, a sort of enthusiasm like this, should have got possession of a nation like the French, capable, as a nation, of every thing and of any thing but calmness and sobriety of thinking ; a virtue, this last, that is the safeguard of all the rest.

The manners and the talents of Calonne you will see, as I have already mentioned, fully described in the works and histories I have referred to. Always agreeable and accommodating, he seemed to find no difficulties, and to make none. Did a courtier want a post? It was ready. Did the queen wish for a little place or pension for a favourite? It was ready also. The money was ready in like manner, if a prince of the blood had a debt to discharge, contracted, perhaps, at a gaming-house; the minister was always cheerful and at leisure, and perfectly happy to listen to the wishes of every one.

But in the midst of this new era of felicity, this golden age, as it must have appeared to the courtiers and the court, the minister became sensible that the expenses of the state far exceeded the revenues, and the king found himself brought to the same point as before, that there could be for him and his kingdom no comfort and no security, unless the privileged orders could be induced to take their share of the general burden, and unless some provision that might really be effective could in this manner be made for the restoration of the finances.

Nothing can be more painful than to consider, in however brief and passing a manner, the situation of this unfortunate monarch, and this great kingdom, at this particular period. It was now the year 1785, two years after the peace. The parliament had registered the last loan not till after three remonstrances, after a formal protest, after being summoned to Versailles. The king very properly concluded, that when he was obliged to have recourse to force, he was losing the character of the father of his people. He was disquieted and unhappy; but if the parliaments were refractory, and if the privileged orders could not be managed, and if the middle classes of the community were becoming more intelligent, and if there was nothing around the monarch but dissatisfaction and restlessness, and vague aspirations after some settlement and improvement, which he knew not how to procure, nor exactly to comprehend, what expedient was there left him, and what measure was he to adopt? He was too benevolent to join the courtiers, and by force and fury, banishing the parliaments, and trampling on all privileges of every kind, collect the revenue he wanted by the undisguised exertions of absolute power; nor was he of an understanding sufficiently decisive, enterprising, and elevated, to strike into some path of wisdom for himself, and, like a man of genius, control men, circumstances, and every thing around him, and convert them to his purposes. Unfortunately for himself, and indeed for his country, he had no pretensions of the kind. But we must return to the history.

His minister, M. de Calonne, had; and he therefore proposed what he considered as a grand measure, and what he represented to the king as an infallible method of saving him from all new loans, all new imposts, and above all, from all further opposition from the parliaments.

The monarch could perceive that these were the great problems to be solved; and how was this to be effected? The answer was, by new management of the imposts, and by an abolition of those privileges which the timidity of the government (the minister observed) had allowed not only to the Pays d'Etat, but to the two orders, the most powerful of the kingdom—the nobility and the clergy. No doubt the king might have thought these two orders should on no account be exempted.

But what, then, was M. de Calonne's measure? He referred very properly to the history of the ancient practices and institutions of the country, the right point to turn to for any reformer; and he proposed to call together the assembly that had appeared in 1627—the assembly of the Notables; in other words, an assembly of the chief people of France; and for what purpose? To consider the whole of the case, and to give their advice; and what advice was expected? The only advice that was reasonable would have answered M. de Calonne, that all orders in the state should make common cause, and the privileged orders contribute; and then with the sanction of such advice, the king, it was intended, should afterwards proceed to carry the measure into execution, and make himself and his people happy. Such were the views of Calonne.

And were, then, the privileged orders themselves, who constituted the main body of this assembly, expected to *give* this advice, this disinterested patriotic advice; to forego their own privileges, and submit themselves to the taxgatherers? Now, if there was any one measure more to be avoided than another, it was a measure like this.

M. de Calonne had seen what had been the result of reviving the parliaments. What assistance had these bodies rendered to the king or his ministers, or M. de Calonne himself, in the settlement of the finances? And what material difference could be shown between the parliaments and the Notables? What folly greater than to call bodies of men together, to discuss things in general; men collected from all quarters on a sudden (and, as it were, for the first time), to talk over the affairs of the nation;

an ingenious expedient this for settling the disordered concerns of a great country! "But no," would have said the minister, "I had propositions to make, evils to state, remedies to propose." —But to whom? and when did a body of men act otherwise than with the spirit and prejudices of that body? Individuals may be disinterested, may be virtuous, may be wise, may rise superior to their temptations, but bodies of men never, if collected and addressed as a body; and no dream could be more shadowy than a delusion like this; more unworthy of the talents and situation of the minister, or even of the natural good sense of the king himself.

It is very true that Calonne could demonstrate the utility and reasonableness of his plans, to those who would listen to him; and on this he depended—a vain dependence, if the only dependence, as every one will find, who has to deal with bodies of men, or even individuals, and has points to obtain, and measures to carry.

> "On life's vast ocean diversely we sail,
> Reason the card, but passion is the gale."

Calonne has published a work on the French Revolution— "De l'Etat de France présent et à venir." At the end of it he gives an outline of his plan; nothing can be more reasonable, and it remains an eternal indictment on the people of consequence then in France, more particularly on that part of them that composed the assembly of the Notables.

"What difficulties," he says in the close, "can be placed in the balance against such advantages; what pretext can there be for any disquietudes on the subject?"

"More will be paid," he continues, "no doubt; but paid by whom? By those who now do not pay enough. They will hereafter pay every one in due proportion, and no one will be aggrieved.

"'But privileges will be sacrificed.'—Why, yes," he replies, "but then justice ordains and necessity requires it. Would it be better to overcharge those who are not privileged—the people? 'But there will be a great outcry raised.' This must be expected. Can one ever effect any general good without running counter to particular interests? Can any one introduce reforms, and no complaint be heard?"

"The voice of patriotism," he goes on to say, "that attachment due to a sovereign, who concerts with his subjects the means of assuring the public tranquillity, the very sentiment of honour, a sentiment so powerful in the breast of Frenchmen, can one doubt a moment that considerations of this kind will not triumph over every other?"

In this manner did the minister express himself in March, 1787. But, alas! in his postscript in 1790—" Such," he says, " is the address that was considered as an incendiary production ; not that the truth of its statements has been ever contradicted ; it was discovered (it seems) that I had not spoken in terms sufficiently measured of the privileged orders, and to appease them I have been sacrificed." These are, as it were, the last words of Calonne.

Lacretelle, at the close of his seventeenth chapter, gives the reasonings that may probably have passed through the mind of the minister, and made a part of his conversation with his friends at the time. At the end of the chapter there is a list of the Notables, their divisions into seven chambers, and the names are given ; princes of the blood, archbishops and bishops, marshals, counsellors of state and presidents of parliaments, prévôts and mayors ; a selection from all the rank, official dignity, and talents of the kingdom.

Unfortunately for Calonne, the minister Vergennes died about a week before the opening of the assembly.

Opposition had been for some time preparing against him. Nothing could be more ingenious than his management of the assembly, as far as mechanical divisions went, for while it was only a minority of the whole body that favoured his projects, by breaking up the assembly into different chambers, and parcelling out his minority with skill, he had a majority of the chambers ; but all was vain : the parliaments, the intriguing Bishop of Toulouse, the clergy, the people of consequence, even the queen, were against him.

At last he seemed to have no friend, and he was actually obliged to fly. The same aristocracy and clergy that thus beat him off and banished him as a public enemy, and a sort of swindler, he lived to see flying, in like manner, for their lives, from the senseless and unprincipled demagogues, the rulers that but too soon succeeded him, the popular, furious tyrants from whom the plans of Calonne gave the privileged orders their only chance of a timely escape.

" It is to Calonne," says Me. de Stael, " that the Revolution is to be imputed, if such an event can be attributed to any single individual." No doubt the minister was too sanguine, was too presumptuous ; attended too little to the obvious principles of human nature ; but to whom is the fault, is the guilt of this calamity to be attributed ? To the minister who has depended too confidently on the disinterestedness, the sense of justice, the reasonableness of the privileged orders, or to those privileged orders themselves, who, in a great crisis of public affairs, have been wanting to their country in such necessary qualities?

You will see in the books I have referred to, Lacretelle, the Annual Register, &c., a very sufficient account of the proceedings that took place, the speeches of the king and the minister, and the views and movements of his opponents in and out of the assembly. Some circumstances were unfavourable to him; but I consider the whole as a memorable example to prove what I have announced to you—first, that no minister is to collect bodies of men together with no other dependence than the reasonableness of his own views, opposed to their natural prejudices and selfish interests; and secondly, that the adherence which bodies of men (I do not say individuals) show to their prejudices and selfish interests is always most infatuated and most blind, and in situations of a critical nature may be, and generally is, fatal to themselves and to their country.

But these observations, I must remind you, might be urged with much more reason in every period *preceding* the ministry of Calonne. Turgot and Necker were patriotic ministers, of virtuous and respectable character, the representatives of the king and the people. Calonne was of a different description, of licentious character, and the minister of the queen and the court. What might be properly conceded by the privileged orders to the former, might not be equally so to the latter; the privileged orders were to give up their exemptions from taxation, that is, to give up part of their property; but property is never given up, whatever may be the arguments of the reasoner in the closet, without some very serious compensation, or the application of something like necessity and force.

Great want of magnanimity, of patriotism, of knowledge of human nature, was shown by the different parties on this occasien. The king and court, particularly the king, should have offered distinct and important ameliorations in the government, in lieu of the privileges to be conceded; and on the part of the privileged orders, if the concession of privileges was to be by them denied, it should have been denied, not, as it was, without any reason given, but because patriotic concessions on the part of the court and monarch were not at the same time proposed.

Still, and finally, after all the weight that may be allowed to observations of this kind, the conduct of the privileged orders on this occasion must for ever be held up to mankind as an example of the selfish blindness of which all such orders are capable; they would not concede in time. Animated by no one generous or patriotic feeling that can be mentioned, they would not concede; and they, and every thing that they loved and honoured, were consequently buried in one common destruction. But they saw not their danger—let others, then, take warning.

The usual routine of the administration of public affairs in France had now been violated in vain; an assembly of Notables had appeared, and yet no great salutary effect had been produced.

This ought of itself to have been considered as a very serious calamity by the monarch, and all those who wished well to his authority.

The assembly and he parted in apparent good humour; every thing had seemed to go on smoothly when the minister was given up; they appear even to have assented· to many of his proposals, and these proposals devolved as a sort of legacy upon his successor (his real, not his more immediate successor), the Bishop of Toulouse.

They were many of them of an important nature; the second of the six articles was the establishment of provincial assemblies for the equal collection of the imposts. To read the summary of the labours of the assembly, with which the keeper of the seals, Lamoignon, put an end to their sittings, one should suppose that a new era was now to commence, that the most important improvements were to be realized, and every thing from this moment to be regularity, peace, and mutual satisfaction on the part of the king and his people; but by some strange fatality, some miserable want of capacity in the new ministry, some melancholy want of character, it must be confessed, in the king, no such happy alteration of circumstances in the affairs of this great country is seen to take place; and one more precious year, the most precious, perhaps, and critical of all, is wretchedly thrown away and lost. The edicts to which the Notables had agreed are neither immediately brought to the parliament of Paris, nor acted upon without its authority, as having received the sanction of the Notables. Time is given to the parliament to recover, to their members to confer with each other, to speculate upon the interests of the kingdom, and in one way and another, even to unite the people against the crown, while they are thus maintaining the rights and interests not in truth of the people, but of the privileged orders. You will see in the Annual Register, far better than in Lacretelle, a detail of the contest that ensued between the parliament and the crown.

It is important; for it was during these twelve months (parts of the years 1786 and 1787), that reasonable efforts should have been made for the restoration of the finances and the happiness of the French people; but the parliaments did nothing; they entered into a contest with the crown, instead of making the best of what had been done and been proposed by the Notables. Observe what had been done, and recommended, and approved by that assembly, and you will then judge of the conduct of the parliament; for instance, many of the important proposals of Calonne had been sanctioned by this assembly of the Notables; they were the wish and desire of the king: the abolition of the corvée, the removal of the barriers between the different provinces, the abolition of internal taxes, duties, and restrictions upon the transit of commodities from one to another, a decree for laying open and rendering free the commerce of grain throughout the kingdom, a decree for the relief of protestants, the abolition of the gabelle; all this was intended, and the king had pledged himself to the last measure of the gabelle. The king's wish to promote the ease, content, and happiness of his people, was not a passion or secret disposition indulged only in speculation—it was embodied and brought fully into action, it was universally acknowledged.

Extraordinary adulations, continues the Annual Register, marked the speeches in the assembly of the Notables on the day of their rising. The mayor of Paris declared, that Louis XVI. would have been the exemplar and model on which Henry the Great would have formed himself, if the partial destiny of the present generation of Frenchmen had not reserved him to complete their happiness.

The Notables had indeed deserted Calonne and the king in the grand measure of all, the territorial revenue or land tax, which would have fallen upon the nobility and clergy, and thereby removed, so far as it went, those exemptions which had been so long considered as an intolerable grievance; here the patriotism of the assembly failed them, or they were awed by the potent bodies, the parliaments and privileged orders, whose interests, as well as their own, were concerned; still it is here to be observed, that the Notables were not totally wanting to their country—the people, according to the views and notions of the Notables, were evidently to be relieved from a number of the most crying grievances. The people had every rational ground to expect, that what was already done by the Notables was only introductory to a progressive course of measures for the melioration of the constitution and the improvement of all the departments of government, and nothing more was wanting, but an accommodating and conciliatory disposition in the parliament of Paris, by filling up the sketch traced out by the Notables, to have established eventually the prosperity of their country and even the permanent improvement of its constitution, or rather of its arbitrary monarchy.

For what was wanting to the community? Some power of criticism and control on the public expenditure; some public bodies of a representative nature. A power like this might have been generated by means of the provincial assemblies. These assemblies were themselves of a representative nature; they were the measures of Turgot and Necker, popular and acknowledged patriots; they would have been a sacrifice on the part of the crown; it was fit that this sacrifice should have been answered by a corresponding one on the part of the privileged orders—an admission of the land tax.

What then could possibly be the meaning of the parliament and the privileged orders in thwarting every measure that the king could propose, in doing every thing to offend him, every thing to force him to a measure so unexampled and so perilous, as the call of the States General? You will see the detail of these strange transactions, these revived contests between the king and parliament of Paris, in Lacretelle and in the Annual Register. The Duke of Orleans, whose very name is infamy, is one of the heroes of these scenes, and D'Esprémesnil and others are united with him, whose names, on the contrary, are never mentioned but with honour.

At last you will see the parliament is animated with a spirit of opposition, so determined, with an enthusiasm so patriotic, that they even declare their own incompetency to legalize the imposts of the crown. The words "States General" are pronounced, and no other authority is proclaimed to be sufficient. And what then will become of us, (the parliament,) it was observed to D'Esprémesnil, when the States General appear? "The States General will be grateful to us," he replied, "for our magnanimity; and in the interval of their sittings they will continue to delegate to us their power." "Heaven will punish thee," replied one of his colleagues, "by listening to thy vows." This prediction was but too speedily and too fatally accomplished.

As I have already said, you may easily see, in the Annual Register, the remonstrances of the parliament and the answers of the king. The language and the sentiments are sometimes of a querulous and wearisome, sometimes of an elevated and patriotic cast, and fitted to remind you of similar state papers that occur in the history of your own country during the contest between Charles and his parliaments; but there is one important difference which you should never lose sight of; Charles was a prince who had ruled illegally, and even tyrannically, who had for eleven years endeavoured to carry on his government without the representative assemblies of the country; assemblies long established, and that were a regular part of the constitution of the government.   In Louis, the parliaments and parliament of Paris and its patriots had to do with a benevolent monarch, who had no object so dear as the happiness of his people; to whose nature tyranny of every sort was abhorrent; who had the prejudices, no doubt, of his birth and situation, but who was only asking for measures that would have been of permanent improvement to the country; who would even have admitted changes that would have made the constitution of the country more free; who was indeed surrounded by a court and courtiers, that thought only of themselves, their privileges, and enjoyments, but who was himself of all men the most removed, both as a king and as a man, from every thing that was selfish, unreasonable, or harsh.

The parliaments, instead of lecturing the king in the tedious, not to say disrespectful manner in which they did, on the virtue and necessity of economy, and on the faults of his ministers, that is, his own, would have done better to have schooled themselves and their privileged orders, on the duty of equal justice to the community—to have reduced the difficulties of the case to some few and intelligible issues.   On the part of the community they must have been aware that what was wanting, was, some constitutional power of criticising and controlling the expenses of the government, and on the part of the crown, some mode of providing for the disorders in the finances; that this was the whole that was to be accomplished,· at least first and mainly to be accomplished; that the first might be accomplished eventually, and to all practical purposes, by a proper attention to the expedients proposed by Turgot and Necker, by a proper modification of the provincial assemblies; and the latter, by a proper management of the privileges of the nobility and clergy; that these were the lines of direction which their patriotism and wisdom should have taken, and that by patience and proper management they had every thing to expect from the real interest which it was evident the king took in the happiness of his people; that the minds of men were obviously in a state of great ferment and agitation, and continually more and more turned to the discussion of political subjects; that the crown had hitherto failed in every attempt to restore the finances, had even failed in the extraordinary measure of the assembly of the Notables, and that it was high time for the privileged orders and the monarch to proceed on a system of accommodation and peace, and of mutual sacrifice and attention to the interests and welfare at least, if not to the rights, of the whole community.

But all this, it would have been said by the leading men of the parliament, all this is what will be best effected, and can alone be effected, by the measure we have proposed, the only measure that can furnish a legal provision for the difficulties of the state, a call of the States General—a call of the States General! And what good has been produced, in fact, by a call of the Notables? What good to be produced by summoning large bodies of men, inexperienced in business, and unused to the possession of power, to discuss public grievances? Would it not be wiser to let the States General hereafter arise out of the provincial assemblies, when the minds of men have been thus familiarized to the images of representative power, when men of intelligence and consequence in their different provinces Rave been accustomed to the duties and the temptations of an authority so important? But with how little effect would reasonings of this humble and moderate nature have been addressed to D'Esprémesnil, or l'Abbé Sabathier, or to Fretau, or Duport, or other active members of the parliament: or again, to the young, lively, ingenious, sanguine, theatric men of talents in the capital of Paris, or the great cities of the provinces. It was unhappily more agreeable to the feelings of such men, and even of the parliament, and they considered it as far better wisdom, to say to their monarch in July, 1787, " that they wished to see the whole nation assembled before they registered any new impost; that the nation alone thus assembled and instructed in the true state of the finances might extirpate the great abuses that are existing at present, and offer great resources to obviate them in future; that the monarch of France could never be so great as when surrounded by his happy subjects; that he had really nothing to fear but the excess of their attachment; that he had no other precaution to take but to be upon his guard against issuing orders that may be beyond their power to accomplish."

Such was the conduct and such was the parting language of the parliament in July, 1787; and these are among the lessons of this great event, this Revolution in France. Men are not to see, indifferent and unmoved, their country miserable; the people depressed; the privileged orders unjust · and profligate and unfeeling; but they are not to let loose the community upon the existing rulers of it: they are to proceed step by step; they are not to depend upon vague, general, sanguine estimates, like those I have just quoted, but to be precise, cautious, and practical; above all, to fly from every thing that tends to revolution, because revolutions are not favourable to civil freedom. It is quite a mistake to suppose, as many noble-minded and virtuous men do, and always have done, that revolutions are the proper remedies of national grievances: that they naturally lead to the establishment of the rights of mankind; nothing can be further from the fact: they break up society, and then the violent alone bear sway. If the country has before been free, all this may end ultimately in the revival and in some improvement of the former state of freedom, as was the case (but most fortunately the case) in our own country.

But it is only in cases of this kind that such salutary changes can be at all expected from revolutions. Even in such cases, civil freedom will best be gained or rather generated by the long-continued exertions of wise and good men, by the dexterous management of times and circumstances; by doing anything rather than run into the extremes of violence and bloodshed. But will governors and governments, it will be replied, ever make any concessions, ever part with any power for the benefit of the people, unless they are terrified, unless they are compelled to do so? There is too much truth, I must allow, and it is mournful to me to acknowledge it, there is too much truth in this observation; and when it is added to the observations I have already made, the whole difficulty of the subject is then seen:—the merit of those patriots who are not only generous and gallant and noble-minded, but wise, that is, patient; the merit of those rulers who respect public opinion, and respect it in time.

In the instance before us, the instance of France, I must contend that the patriotic leaders in the parliaments had always before them the spectacle of a most benevolent monarch, who, though affected by the prejudices of his birth, never ceased to mean well. I must indeed admit, that they had to do with a thoughtless, expensive court, with courtiers of very arbitrary principles, and with privileged orders (they themselves most of them belonged to these privileged orders,) that were unjust and unfeeling; but at the head of them, I must again repeat, was a monarch unhappily not fitted to rule them, but a sensible, virtuous, religious man, from whom anything and everything might be expected, that his country could require, if but managed with proper forbearance and skill; if due advantage was made of his good qualities, and care taken not to give too much opportunity for the unhappy influence of his defects and failings.

But the words " States General" had been pronounced—pronounced by the parliament itself. In France—in Paris—the mode is everything. The idea of the States General became popular, became fashionable; every wise man and every foolish man had now got a resting place for his thoughts, and one at which his speculations could arrive with confidence, and in a moment; every one could see that something ought to be done, for neither people, king, court, nor privileged orders were at ease; and it was now evident, forsooth, to every the meanest capacity, that it was only necessary to assemble all the wisdom and consequence of the country together, to unite them to the benevolent wishes of the good king; and that *then*, to suppose any further doubt, or difficulty, or impediment remaining to the happiness of the country, to what was called " the regeneration of France," was perfectly ridiculous.

You will see in Lacretelle, and more particularly in the Annual Register, that a spirited and even able effort (though ill managed) was made by the king and Lamoignon to transact the business of the kingdom without the parliament of Paris, and probably to preclude the necessity of calling the States General. This was the institution of what was called the " Cour Plénière ;" but the people of rank and consequence, both of the nobility and clergy, deserted their monarch (such is the term used by the writer in the Annual Register) on this critical occasion. The Dukes of Rochefoucault, De Noailles, Luxembourg, and several others, rejected the king's nomination, and refused to sit in the Cour Plénière, this new assembly that was to supersede the parliament. The king was condemned, it is said by the same writer, to submit to this public insult, and to retract all he had done. Thus was the court sunk to the lowest ebb of degradation, while the parliaments were raised to the pinnacle of triumph and power.

I have in these few words given you the representation rather of the respectable writer in the Annual Register, Dr. Lawrence, than my own; for I must observe that it was a serious thing, and so it must have been thought by the Dukes of Rochefoucault and Luxembourg, to sweep away the parliaments, and substi-

tute in their room merely a Cour Plénière, whilst the nobles were
so attached or even dependent on the court, and while the people
were nothing, and certainly could find in this court no proper
representative; finally, that the same Cour Plénière that might
be valuable to the community under Louis XVI. might be only
an instrument of tyranny under his successors.   I do not, therefore, know how to blame these men of rank on this occasion;
but what are we to say of the king and his advisers, who were
to commit themselves on a measure like this, without having
first felt their way, or ascertained the opinions and intentions of
such distinguished men as have just been mentioned?

   This measure, however, having failed, the king had no resource, for he was neither fierce nor arbitrary, and he therefore
dismissed his minister, the Cardinal de Brienne, from a post to
which he ought never to have suffered him to be promoted. He
recalled Necker, and the States General were promised for the
May of the ensuing year.

   I will now proceed to give you, before I conclude my lecture,
some general notion of what was thought of the situation of France
by different observers at this particular period.   I do not necessarily adopt or require you to subscribe to any sentiment that I
shall thus exhibit before you; my meaning is, to put you in possession, as well as I can, of the whole of the case, to give you
an interest in the scene, by enabling you the better to understand
its bearings and its circumstances, its unhappy difficulties and
various perils.   I will first refer you to the representations of the
Baron de Grimm, an eye-witness at the time. He is writing at
the very period now before us.

   " Never was there a minister," says he, " who showed such
talents for throwing everything into confusion, as M. de Brienne
(the cardinal).   He has shaken to pieces the whole political
machine in the space of a few months; thanks to the happy ascendant of his genius, one may truly say, that there is not a
single public body in France that remains in its place, or retains
its natural movements.   The parliament has on a sudden adopted
a system the most directly opposed to its own interests, one that
it has anathematized a hundred and a hundred times; the nobility, the existence of which seems the most intimately connected
with the rights of the throne, has an air of being disposed to
separate itself.   Even the military spirit seems overpowered by
some spirit, I know not what, of patriotism, laudable in itself
perhaps, but rather difficult to reconcile with that character of
subordination, without which there can be neither discipline nor
army; the clergy no longer preach obedience, the soldiers seem

no longer disposed to maintain it. What is still more remarkable is, that this universal discontent has been preceded by declarations from the king the most favourable to public liberty. He has just been making more sacrifices of his authority than any of his predecessors have ever ventured to do. The parliaments have called aloud for the assistance of that which of all other things they had most to fear, a meeting of the States General, carried away by a man totally without consideration among them, an Abbé de Sabathier; all, as if actuated by some supernatural influence, have demanded the convocation of the States General; making as it were in this manner the amende honourable to the nation for having so long usurped the most capital of its rights."

" It was under these desperate circumstances," says the Baron de Grimm, " that Necker was recalled."

Such was the general notion formed at the time of the situation of France by the Baron de Grimm, an agent of an arbitrary court (of Prussia), but a man of a very experienced, improved, and penetrating mind.

I will next refer you to the views that were formed at the time by men of the old régime in France itself. I will allude to the Memoirs of the Marquise de Bouillé. He was the very humane and respectable man who commanded the French forces in the West Indies during the great American War, and so conducted himself, that on his visiting England a public dinner was given to him by the planters and the West Indian merchants, and he was everywhere received, at court and by the public, in the most flattering manner. The opinions and feelings of a man like this (you must, as you read the history, always refer to this memoir) are on every occasion entitled to our consideration.

After some observations, he goes on to say—" The French nation, in the corrupt state to which it had arrived, could no longer be governed but by a firm and severe government, by a sceptre like that of Louis XIV.; and this was too weighty for the hands of Louis XVI. His aged counsellor recommended mildness instead of severity, and the king was easily made to believe that the love of his people ought to be preferred to their fear." Here you see the soldier, the veteran general, the man accustomed to the exercise of regular authority, and who depends upon authority alone. He afterwards admits, that the most numerous and most useful class of the king's subjects, the labouring poor, were at that time harassed and rendered unhappy by the avarice and rapacity, not only of the courtiers, but of an immense crowd, some of whom by intrigue, others sheltering themselves beneath the privileges of their order or situation, threw the whole weight of the public burden upon the inferior ranks of society. He continues thus:—" His Majesty suffered himself to be persuaded, and his ministers persuaded themselves, that the enlightened (he must now mean to speak of the patrons of the new opinions,) but at the same time restless, jealous, insatiable, and corrupt description of men, who inhabited the court, the capital, and the great cities, composed the mass of the people. These, however, in reality, formed a very small part of the nation, and that, the most depraved in its morals and the most dangerous from the turbulent spirit with which it was agitated. Thenceforth the opinion of this part of the public became the uncertain guide of government." The marquis (I say) must here refer to those who had become imbued with the new opinions ; he probably quite under-estimated their number and importance, and even their respectability. He goes on to refer every measure of the king, ministers, and court, to their wish to propitiate this public opinion ; the recall of the parliaments, the exhausting of the treasury, the dismissal of the officers and attendants of the monarch, the assistance given to America; " in fine," says he, " so totally was every principle of policy and of morality disregarded, that the public mind was already democratical, while the monarchy still existed ; the Notables could do no service, nor could the States General ; the magistracy was ambitious, the clergy jealous of their privileges, a spirit of innovation prevailed among the nobility, whilst there was a total want of subordination in the army, particularly among the chiefs; licentiousness and insolence pervaded the middle ranks of society, whilst the lower class experienced the extreme of misery, and the rich indulged themselves in the most unbounded luxury."

This is a fearful picture, and the marquis does not attempt to offer any remedy for these calamities of the state. An assertion, however, of the rights of the old monarchy, of the old régime, authority, force, a trial of the bayonet, would have been probably his advice, his only resource; no composition, no conciliation, no terms to be kept with the new opinions, no escape from them, resistance to the utmost, war; at least such would have been his counsels certainly at any time after the formation of the constituent assembly, and probably at the period we are now alluding to, the year 1788. Such are the men and such the opinions that must be considered as existing at the time, and as forming, I must repeat, a part of the case.

For another specimen of this kind we may turn to the annals of Bertrand de Moleville, another respectable supporter of the old régime. I will allude to them for a moment, and conclude. Speaking of this period, he says—" With these important sacrifices made by the princes of the blood and the nobility, the Tiers Etat ought to have been satisfied, and grateful for them; but they were sometimes represented as acts of hypocrisy, which ought not to be relied on; sometimes as indications of fear, which should encourage that order to rise in their demands. By such perfidious insinuations the factious kept alive the distrust and agitation of the people, and disposed them to revolt. The most inflammatory pamphlets against the clergy and the nobility were circulated through the whole kingdom without the least opposition; the most shameful caricatures, exposed to view in the squares, on the quays, and at the print shops in Paris, excited the crowds they collected to insult not only the ecclesiastics, but every well-dressed man who happened to be passing.

" The letters for convoking the States General," he goes on to say, " were issued at this crisis. The affectionate and truly paternal sentiments expressed in them by the king ought to have allayed all discontent and dissipated all uneasiness; and no doubt they did produce that effect among the reasonable, honest, and well-affected persons of the three orders; but the turbulent and ambitious, the intriguing and the revolutionary fanatics, did not relax the least on that account in the project for overturning everything, but continued preparing the means for carrying it into execution."

Such were the views of Bertrand de Moleville, of the Marquis de Bouillé, and the Baron de Grimm: represent now to your minds, as well as you can, the fermentation that had long existed in the minds of the people of France, and particularly of Paris; consider what the court and government had been, and what the new opinions were; the opportunity that now appeared to offer itself for what was called the regeneration of France; and combining thus the effect of the old and new opinions, together with the particular circumstances of the monarchy, you will be able to form some general notion, such at least as can now be formed, at this happy distance of time and place, of the state of this distracted kingdom, when Necker was recalled to undertake once more the office from which he had been a few years before most unfortunately and improperly dismissed.

LECTURE VII.

NECKER.

In my last lecture I adverted to the administration of M. de Calonne.

I described his efforts to restore the finances by a call of the Notables. This was his expedient for procuring assistance from the privileged orders. He had hoped that these privileged orders might be induced, by the advice and authority of the Notables, to pay their share of the public burdens; but this advice the Notables would not give. They attended to his recommendations, but with this most important exception.

He had been too sanguine, was disappointed, and obliged to fly the country.

Even the measures which the Notables did approve and recommended were not carried into execution, though they would have been highly beneficial to France, and might have somewhat allayed the storm.

I then alluded to the conduct of the parliament, who crowned what has always appeared to me their prior very unreasonable conduct, by calling for the States General.

I quoted a paragraph from the Baron de Grimm, giving his opinion of the situation of the kingdom, and of the injudicious administration of the Cardinal de Brienne.

I gave two quotations, one from M. de Bouillé, and one from M. de Moleville, to exhibit to you what were the sentiments of the patrons of the old régime, and then, reminding you of what were in the mean time the disorder and confusion of opinions and interests every where prevailing, I concluded by stating that the meeting of the States General had been promised by the king, and that in this crisis of the state Necker was recalled.

My present lecture must be devoted to his administration; but I must first say a word of the Cardinal de Brienne. This predecessor of Necker, the Archbishop of Sens, was a man of family, fortune, and influence, with all the penetration of an experienced courtier, and great talents for intrigue. Owing to these circumstances, and his having taken a lead in the opposition to Calonne, he acquired the great object of his ambition, the post of prime minister; but it was a post of which he was not at any period worthy, and one for which he was peculiarly unfit at the particular period before us. His administration, as you have already been given to understand by the Baron de Grimm, was full of mistakes and inconsistencies; at a time, too, when they could not but be fatal to the king he served. The last fault that it was in his power to commit, he seems to have taken care to commit as he was going out of office: the States General were promised, and he actually invited all the writers and philosophers in France, in the king's name, to give their opinions on the proper mode of assembling them!

It must be confessed, therefore, that Necker returned to power, in August, 1788, under very unfavourable circumstances; the critical year and a half of the archbishop's administration was for ever lost; and the time that might have been employed by a popular minister in saving the monarchy from a revolution, had been only used in making a revolution inevitable.

The loss of these fifteen months was deeply lamented by M. Necker, and he considers himself as having been called for too late. This lamentation of M. Necker is ridiculed by M. de Bailleul, a democratic writer, the declared opponent of the work of Me. de Stael, over the pages of which he hopes to pass, like a pestilential blast over a fair country, withering its fruits and flowers as he goes along. He is a very odious, though an able writer; and thus to ridicule the natural sentiment of M. Necker, is to suppose that things are to be left to take their course, that evils cannot be prevented, and that it is of no consequence to a country, in very critical times, whether its counsels are guided by men of conciliatory dispositions and intelligent minds, or the contrary; and it is in this strain that M. de Bailleul proceeds all through his work, as do indeed the French historians Mignet and Thiers.

When, however, M. Necker came into administration, he appears to have himself committed all the faults that now remained possible; to have been quite overpowered by the force of public opinion; to have had no object but to ascertain it, and then no plan but to submit to it. Woe to the country where ministers do not respect public opinion; but woe equally to the land, to the monarchy at least, whether absolute or mixed, where the minister has no other master! As if to rival the incapable measure of his predecessor, M. Necker, in the first place, thought proper to summon the Notables once more together, to deliberate, forsooth, as the States General were now to be called,— 1st, how they were to be composed; 2dly, the form of convocation; 3dly, the order of the elections; 4thly, the manner in which were to be held the different assemblies, which were to give instructions to their deputies to the states. As if the royal authority had not been already sufficiently degraded and damaged by the irrational conduct of his predecessor, he must now proceed to abandon in this manner to the result of a public discussion, to surrender up to others, formally, voluntarily, and without the slightest apparent utility, the regulation of all those important points, which it was the natural office of the king to adjust and decide himself. M. Necker may speak, as he pleases, of the force of public opinion, as may his daughter, Mᵉ. de Stael; but the minister was unfit for his situation, at this extraordinary juncture, who saw not that every thing had turned against the crown; who saw not, that what authority was still left it, must be turned to every purpose of its protection and illustration of its dignity, and must, as much as possible, be produced and exercised, that it might not expire and appear voted out of the world by common consent. What I now say of this measure of calling the Notables together, for the purpose of consulting them, is still more to be applied to the measures which he subsequently adopted. The Notables, on this second occasion, seem to have been somewhat more aware of their danger, than they were when called together by Calonne. They were composed, as before, chiefly of the privileged orders; and with the exception of one bureau, where, singularly enough, his present majesty of France, Louis XVIII., then the king's brother, presided, the six were chiefly of opinion that the number of the Tiers Etat in the ensuing assembly should *not* equal the joint numbers of the two other orders, the clergy and the nobility. This was evidently the great question of all. On one side, that is, against it, were this decided majority of the Notables, a great part of the clergy and nobility, the noblesse of Britany, and the magistrates. This opinion (against the double representation) was likewise fortified by the inference to be drawn from the example of the states of Britany, Burgundy, and Artois, and by the support of most of the princes of the blood.

On the other side were ranged (that is, in favour of the double representation) this small minority of the Notables, the three orders of Dauphiny, the bureaux of the provincial assemblies, supported by the inference to be drawn from the ancient constitution of the states of Languedoc, and the formation of the recent estates of Provence and Hainault, the opinion of the publicists, of the parliament of Paris, of the towns and commons of the realm, and public opinion in general. Such was the state of things in December 1788, and at the end of the month the ordinance or declaration of the king appeared, determining that the number of the deputies should be one thousand, be formed on a basis of population and taxation, and that the number of the Tiers Etat should equal that of the other two orders united.

This was in December 1788. A month after, in January, 1789, the Marquis de Bouillé mentions that he had a conversation with Necker. " I represented to him with force and with truth the danger of assembling the States General in the manner he intended. I told him that he was arming the people against the first orders of the state, and that when thus delivered up unarmed, they would soon feel the effect of their vengeance, urged on by the two most active passions of the human heart, interest and self-love. I entered into particulars, but he coldly answered me, raising his eyes to heaven, that it was necessary to rely on the moral virtues of mankind. I replied that this was a fine romance, but he would see a horrible and bloody tragedy, of which I advised him to avoid the catastrophe. At this he smiled, and M. Necker told me that my apprehensions were extravagant."

I must enter a little more into the particulars of the conduct of the minister at this critical period of the Revolution.

It would have been very difficult for M. Necker to have recovered the false step he had made in consulting the Notables, in calling upon them to decide questions which the king should have himself decided in virtue of his own prerogative and as a matter of course.

The mind of the public had been thrown into a high state of fermentation before the close of the year 1788, when this second assembly of the Notables broke up. The current had begun to set strongly in favour of new opinions ; still it is understood that the monarch was respected, his authority, as such, had never been called in question, and they who speculate upon this great subject of the French Revolution, who can extend their sympathy to every class and description of men in society, to the high as well as the low, and who shrink with a just terror from any counsels or opinions that are likely to lead to scenes of confusion and bloodshed, all such humane and reasonable philosophers have never ceased to accuse Necker of a great want of political courage on this most momentous occasion. They consider him as waiting to be directed by the public opinion, instead of taking his ground early, and directing it where to flow, and within what bounds to confine itself. Every credit is given him for his intentions and his integrity, that he meant to give security to the crown, yet civil liberty to the country ; properly to limit the powers of the monarch, but of the people also; that he had no selfish views, and sought neither rank nor riches, nor any reward but that of honest fame and the consciousness of doing good to others; still they consider him as accommodating himself to the new opinions, at this particular crisis, in a manner that proved in the event quite calamitous to the country, and fatal to every object that could have animated his benevolence or rewarded his ambition.

The two great points which should have been settled as of course by Necker, and should have appeared in the king's declaration, were, 1st, whether the number of the Tiers Etat should equal the numbers of the two other orders conjointly; 2ndly, whether these orders were to vote in different houses or in one, to be three assemblies or one, to vote by orders or by head.

You will easily see the importance of these points and the direction which the new and old opinions naturally took. What chance for the Tiers Etat, if each of the other two privileged orders was to have a negative on their measures? What chance on the other side for the king or for those very orders, if all were to be assembled together, and everything to be decided by a majority of the whole? More particularly if the numbers of the Tiers Etat were to be equal to the numbers of the other two conjointly.

When points of this nature were thrown upon the public for discussion in the improvident manner they were, by the prior minister, the Archbishop of Sens, and even afterwards by Necker himself, the fermentation that would be occasioned in such a place as Paris, in such a country as France, at such a period as the close of the year 1788, cannot possibly be conceived.

Me. de Stael is obliged to allow her father's mistake in calling this second assembly of the Notables: she is willing to defend him in every subsequent measure: But he has defended himself very ably, very anxiously, and at considerable length. I have already referred you to his book on the French Revolution, and I have also mentioned to you his work on his own administration, printed in 1791, which is very interesting. The subject matter, with which we are now concerned, was then fresh in his memory. He was a philosopher, a patriot, and an actor in the scene. He has on every account a perfect right to be heard.

I must remind you, as I have never ceased to remind you, that it is when you are employed in considering points of this nature, that you are best employed. It is here that you are to meet your lessons of instruction, that you are to learn how you are to manage the affairs of mankind. You are to find the greatest interest in those points where a common reader finds the least. The questions before you are of the following nature : Could Necker have prevented the Revolution and yet have allowed France to have attained a rational system of liberty ? or rather, perhaps, an intermediate situation that would necessarily have led to one ? Did he make mistakes ? Were they important ? Such are the questions you are to consider. I mean in the remainder of this lecture to occupy you with the conduct of M. Necker. I shall do little more than make quotations from his later work on the Revolution, and this may not be very interesting to you, unless you consider attentively the nature of the subject before you.

You who have not exactly lived during the times of the French Revolution, cannot at all imagine how long and how deeply it affected the thoughts, the feelings, and the interests of every human being, without any exception, that then existed in the civilized world; the lives, the properties, the affections, the daily anxieties of millions—but you must endeavour to conceive it ; and I cannot but believe, that with a little reflection, you will be able to do so to a considerable degree ; to a degree sufficient, at least, to enable you to listen to the detail of what passed in the mind of one of the most important actors in the scene, M. Necker, at a moment when the business of the scene was of the most critical nature.

Recollect what has been already intimated to you ; the manner in which the affairs of the kingdom have been now for some time journeying on to a state of the greatest difficulty and danger: figure to yourselves the court and the patrons of the old régime on the one side, the patriots and the patrons of the new opinions on the other ; the king and his minister, Necker, between the two ; the convocation of an assembly promised that was to be the image of the whole nation, the assembly consisting of three orders ; of two that would be naturally leagued with the old opinions ; of one that would be as naturally animated with all the ardour and enthusiasm of the new ; and the questions to be determined then are, whether the popular part was to equal in number the other two, and whether the three orders were to meet in three houses or in one ; that is, as you will easily see, whether the new opinions were entirely to bear sway or not. This consequence, at least, was pretty evident even then ; but to us who live after the events, it is difficult to say, what consequences, and what calamitous consequences, may not be traced up to the manner in which, on whatever account, these great questions were now determined; and as this determination seems to be the hinge on which the Revolution may be said to have turned, you can surely think no time lost that is employed in considering what were the views of M. Necker, by what circumstances he was surrounded, if misled and mistaken, how and why; and whether any instruction can be derived for ourselves from the conduct of all parties on this occasion, the minister and those whom he undoubtedly wished to serve. You will observe then, with respect to Necker and his book, that nothing can be more reasonable or manly, than all his preliminary observations and admissions. He seeks not to withdraw himself from responsibility in any part of the discussion. Add to this, he affirms, and no doubt with perfect truth, that he never ceased to speak to the king of the wants and unhappy situation of his people; nor to the people of the virtues and benevolent intentions of the king; that it was the object of all his efforts to defend the monarchy without concealing from the monarch how useful it was, to have the constitution of a government properly balanced; and at every turn and on every occasion through the whole of his adminstration, he insists, to use his own words, that so far from accelerating, as has been supposed by his accusers, the descent of a car that was already running down with such velocity, he did everything he could to stop the wheels of it, and never ceased, while by the side of it, to call aloud for help.

In the first place, he says that the States General were promised before he returned to power. He shows very satisfactorily that it was then totally impossible to prevent their assembling; that this fault, at least, he did not commit. " I must declare, too," he says, " to the honour of the prince, that he never for a moment made it a question, whether he was to keep an engagement so distinctly entered into."

" Great changes are always so hazardous," he says, " that had not the States been promised, I should have made every possible effort to *serve* France by means of the provincial assemblies, and yet *save* her from disturbance and convulsion; and why should I disguise the truth? Like the nation, I was full of hope—hope that I then could not suppose vain—Alas! how can one now think, without tears, on the hopes and expectations then every where felt by all good Frenchmen, by every friend of humanity?" He then goes on to describe how the new opinions were brought to bear, in the most unfortunate manner, on every existing principle, and institution, and usage in the state;

on the confused and contradictory nature of the different powers existing in the constitution; how easy were the improvements, it was thought, that must result from the assembling of the representatives of the nation; how beneficial and how certain, as it was supposed, the regeneration of the whole system : and he thus arrives at the consideration of his own particular case.

The States General, he says, were promised, no doubt; nothing more; but the same public opinion, he observes, that had extorted from the king this meeting of the States General, was sure to have its influence on their formation. M. De Brienne, his predecessor, he says, requested opinions on the subject from the municipalities, the provincial administrations, and even the academies and the men of letters; and the nation, even if before not disposed to rest much on the authority of its own opinion, was thus taught to refer to it from the very doubts and apparent uncertainty of government itself.

He perceived, he says, that the nation looked forward to the States General not as a mere ceremony and spectacle. He then shows that the forms and proceedings in the year 1614, to which the parliaments had referred, could have afforded no proper precedent for the assembly that was to be summoned in 1789; and that it was so necessary that the States should not only be called, but called· in some form and manner, that would be agreeable to the ideas of the public, that, he says, his proposition of consulting the Notables was considered as a fortunate expedient, as a sort of lucky thought to have occurred to him. The labours of the Notables he holds to have been eminently useful, and he considers them as settling many things of an uncertain, yet important nature, that could not have been well settled by the king's council on their own authority.

This is a striking difference from the opinion of Necker's critics, who conceive that the king in council should have settled every thing, and even from Mᵉ. de Stael, who does not defend this consulting of the Notables.

These Notables were divided into six bureaux, of twenty-four each, princes of the blood, archbishops, &c. One of the most important questions of the whole subject, the number of the deputies to the States General, they did not touch upon; and on the still more important question, the relative numbers of the orders, the bureau in which Monsieur presided, determined that the number of the Tiers Etat should be double that of either of the other two orders; but not so the other five bureaux. Necker ultimately decided for the double representation. How came then Necker, after calling the Notables and asking their advice, not to take it, when it now appears it was most important to have followed it ?

You will see his reasons—that is, his defence against the serious accusations that were brought against him. On the whole, they seem to resolve themselves into the following propositions :—

That if the ancient formulary of the convocation of the States had been adhered to, such a liberty would have been allowed, that the number of deputies returned by the Tiers Etat under the existing circumstances of political fermentation and enthusiasm, would have turned out to be far more than double that of the other two ; that the writs that must have been made use of by the crown would have admitted an almost indefinite latitude of election : this may be, and is a sufficient answer to those who would have had the election form of 1614 adhered to. But again—that if the king and council were obliged to take upon themselves to fix the relative numbers of the orders, they were in truth obliged also to conform themselves to the public wishes. They were under a strict moral necessity to do so ; they could not venture to do otherwise. And their only part to take was to be content with the double representation, and to proclaim this as their measure as soon as possible, that the king might have the credit of a popular measure, and the state escape the confusion that would have resulted, if the council had left the point undetermined by repeating the ancient forms of convocation.

But this is for Necker to say, in other words, that he durst not oppose the public opinion.

Reasoners on the case now will think, on the contrary, that he ought, and that he might and ought, in the king's declaration to have settled this point, and the second point also, of their mode of voting, which we have mentioned, in favour of the crown ; but he settled neither the one nor the other. He announced in the king's declaration that the number of the Tiers Etat should be double. He said nothing of the manner in which they were to vote—in three houses or one ; and this point was to be determined by the States when they met ; and, as the number given to the Tiers Etat was double, it could not but be determined like the other, sooner or later, against the crown. We must, however, again hear his defence. When I refer to it, I must observe that it is quite impossible for me, on this occasion, to impress upon your minds the full weight of his arguments. He is a very good writer, and gives his reasonings, which are always respectable, every advantage of style and manner. You must read this part of his work very attentively; you will then see that I could not possibly be so unjust as to leave his case entirely to depend upon any imperfect description or unworthy abridgment of his book, which I could myself make, and that I have necessarily referred you to the work itself. It is, moreover, a very critical part of the whole subject; and one which I conceive you cannot be better occupied than by studying thoroughly. To make a revolution may be easy; to prevent one, and yet not be wanting to the great cause of liberty, is indeed a labour worthy the ambition of the highest faculties, and necessarily implying the exercise of the greatest virtues; and this is the subject before you.

Some general notion of M. Necker's views I can give you, but some general notion only; but before I give them, you will observe that I consider them as reasons not sufficient to justify him in the conduct he pursued, but rather as fitted to show that he should have done what he did not do; what we have already mentioned that he should have done; that is, decided every thing in the king's declaration, on the king's own authority. In his work on the French Revolution, to which I am all along referring, you will see him exhibit the difficulties of the case. They were very great. You will then see, that in the event, and after the States had met, he was at last obliged to propose a system of conciliation and accommodation to all the parties, as a remedy for all these difficulties. Now, it would have been better, or rather, perhaps, it would have been the only chance to have made this system, which he had afterwards to *propose*, his measure from the first, and to have announced it as the king's will in the declaration, in the instrument, by which the king did the public the favour of calling the States together at all. M. Necker's representations are of the following nature: —A long interval, he observes, had elapsed since the last assembly of the States; and, from being veiled in a distant obscurity, they were embellished by all the colours of the imagination. Almost all the former assemblies had been convoked for the mere will and purposes of the crown; an ephemeral senate, which the sovereign could dissolve at pleasure. Subsidies were demanded, and grievances brought forward, which might or might not be afterwards attended to.

But times of this nature were passed, says M. Necker. Louis XVI. had scarcely ten millions of feudal revenue, and it was for the entire sum of the public expenses, of the whole interest to be provided for an immense debt, that he found himself under the necessity of having recourse to the States; a necessity imposed upon him, not only by a resolution of the sovereign courts, but even by the parliament of Paris, which declared itself incompetent legally to register either impost or loan any longer.

What power, what authority would not naturally be obtained, says M. Necker, by the deputies of the Tiers Etat, the representatives of those who had chiefly to contribute, while they were called to deliberate upon all the conditions and all the reasons for which they were to make an annual sacrifice of five hundred millions.

The clergy of France, he says, were at one time so situated, that superstition combined with religion to elevate and sustain their supremacy. The nobility were *once* aided by all the consideration with which the feudal system had environed them. But these two orders, even in all the splendour of their former greatness, if they had been called to deliberate with the Tiers Etat on the form and mode of collecting an immense contribution of this kind, would have found it quite impossible to maintain their ascendant; but what hope for them, when the relative importance of the two orders, and of the third, had actually changed situations, and been transferred from the one to the other. But here, it may be replied to M. Necker, if this was the case, as it certainly was, ought not M. Necker to have foreseen what must be the event, if the question of voting or any other material question was left to be decided by the States, when met together? Was he not to have tried to anticipate their decision by one from the king? Commerce alone, he continues, among other things, had entirely changed the solid importance of the Tiers Etat in the social system. It was to their talents and industry that the existence of national wealth was owing; that is, the existence, as every day more and more proclaimed, of national power. Education, admission to offices in the provincial assemblies, a thousand causes had placed their intelligence and their knowledge in a rapid state of progress and improvement. There was little resemblance between the Tiers Etat of 1789 and those of former periods. Once more, too, with regard to the other orders, M. Necker goes on to say, the prelates and clergy naturally owed their influence in the first place to the general respect that prevailed for religion itself: but this had unhappily been weakened. Other causes had conspired to diminish their authority.

Every thing contributed to engage them to support the royal authority, but it was no longer in their power to afford it any material assistance by their influence over the Tiers Etat and the nation.

And with regard to the nobility, Necker observes, that many circumstances (which he mentions) had contributed to rob them of all their constitutional dignity and lustre, in the eyes of the nation. There were those among them, no doubt, of historic name; but the greater part consisted of those who had been ennobled only in more modern times by the crown. The whole composition of the body was altered, the most ancient and most honourable of distinctions had been made a subject of traffic; each sort of nobility had equally a right to vote; at least one-half the order consisted of families ennobled within the last two centuries. This disposition of things might do very well for Louis XIV.; he had various court contrivances of ceremony, indulgence, and decoration, by which he kept the two sorts of nobility distinguished from each other: so had Louis XV.: but all this was in vain when the whole body was to rally round the throne, and effect, by its political consideration, the Tiers Etat and the nation.

"What a subject here for reflection," says Necker, "this relative importance of the Tiers Etat and the other two orders, to suppose that it could be balanced by any contrivance of the respective numbers of the two orders!" But to this it may be surely answered, that to suppose that there was no contrivance by which it could be balanced, and no preparatory measures to be adopted, is to surrender at discretion; to give up the cause of the crown (that is, the cause of peaceful or temperate improvement) at once. It is in vain to dissemble, he continues, that the power of the crown had attained its height in the best days of Louis XIV., and had from that period declined. Louis XV. himself, perhaps, had indulged but too imprudently in a taste for popularity, Louis XVI. and the queen, their love of the ease and the comforts of a private station. The personal dignity of a crowned head can never equal the conventional grandeur of a monarch.

These are not trifling considerations, he says: the conduct of the court was affected by the examples of the king and queen, and the manners were changing. Great effects are produced by the union of an infinity of small causes.

A strange situation of things, says Necker: it might well be doubted, whether even the re-establishment of the States themselves could sufficiently provide for it. He then mentions a notion entertained by himself and others at the time, that all would have been well if something like the constitution of England could have been proposed and accepted. Was it unnatural for a statesman, he says, to cast his eyes on the constitution of England? The order of nobility in France, mixed as it was, could no longer discharge its office in the political system; but a House of Peers like the English might.

There were difficulties, he continues, as France then stood, with regard to the contributions of the Tiers Etat; but there was an end of them, by supposing the people of property (the Peers excepted) represented in a House of Commons, as in England. It was necessary that something should be done for France immediately; but what could be expected from the discordant views and mutual disgusts of a legislature divided into three orders? Not so, if divided only into two, as in England. "And why again should I dissemble," says Necker, "that both my first and my last thoughts have leaned in favour of a system of government like that of England, with which neither states in three orders, nor any form of monarchy, can be put in comparison?

"The king, unfortunately for any views I might have entertained of this kind, had a prejudice against whatever might resemble the usages and institutions of England. His opinion afterwards altered, but it was then too late."

At the time that the Cour Plénière was attempted by the Archbishop of Sens, a Chamber of Peers and a House of Representatives would have been received from the king with acclamations; but it is in vain to regret, says Necker, thoughts of foresight, of prevention—the generality of people have nothing to say to them; the tocsin of events must sound before they can be awakened or instructed.

There was nothing for it then, concludes Necker, but to embark upon this sea of troubles; to take the chances of these States, thus called, and their three orders: a scene of rivalry that the dispositions of men had made so dangerous. An exact line of conduct it was not possible to trace; it was evident, however, that the two orders could not sufficiently support the crown; that the crown must get assistance from public opinion; that great address would be necessary to manage the general movement in the public mind; that the love of the people was to be sought to regain for the king what royalty had on various accounts lost.

These are the representations of Necker, written in 1795, and after the events.

Now, surely, under the circumstances thus described, it was not the best chance, (and that is the turn of the whole question,) it was not the *best* chance, as he seems to take for granted, to let things take their course; to let the different orders meet, and abide by the result. This was not the best chance. This result could not possibly, even under his own view of the case, be favourable to the crown. Surely any other chance would have been more promising. Such, however, was the part taken; the consequence was, what appears to us now, a consequence, from the first, inevitable. A dispute immediately arose. The Tiers Etat insisted that the whole should form *one* assembly; that the different orders should deliberate and vote in common; while the nobility and clergy insisted that the orders should all vote separately, and in their own houses. The public of course took the part of the Tiers Etat. Some of the members of the two privileged orders wavered and went over, and the monarch was at last obliged to interpose his authority, and invite the whole into one great assembly, for the sake of the general tranquillity, and for the sake of retaining for himself some share of the public affection and respect.

The public, says M. Necker, took part with the Tiers Etat. The whole meeting of the States, it was conceived by them, would have become a mere pageant, unless the orders were united and voted in common. It was thus that the deputies, it was everywhere observed, did business together in the provincial assemblies with perfect harmony and success. Why not in the States General? The deputies from Dauphiny appeared in the assembly so united, as of course, and the place resounded with applauses.

The nation had expected, says Necker, every thing from their deputies; they had ordered them to settle the constitution before they granted the supplies. The most difficult of enterprises was thus to be attempted before the most urgent of necessities was to be provided for. In the mean time government itself could not be at ease if nothing was done. The exigencies of its situation were most pressing.

Some have held, continues Necker, that the king should have opposed, before the meeting, any deliberation in common, and should have decided for the nobility and clergy at once. Some, on the contrary, that he should have ordered the union of the orders—certainly they have supposed the first, and with great

reason.   All, alas! he says, was impossible.   Supposing the
nobility and clergy disposed to unite with the Tiers Etat, the
king had no right to prevent them, nor was it in his power.
He might indeed have ordered them to *unite*, for *there* the public
would have been with him; but why was he to take away that
merit from the two orders?

Surely this is but loose reasoning in M. Necker.   It is to
suppose that the minister and the king had only to consider
what would be the wish of the popular party.

On the whole, then, we hold, that M. Necker made a mistake
in not having taken the best chance which the case afforded, that
of settling these disputable points in favour of the crown, by the
king's own authority, in the king's declaration.

But one word more from M. Necker.   He conceives that the
two privileged orders were in fault on the first meeting of the
States.   These two orders, continues Necker, I must for ever
reproach, bitterly reproach, for not having seen the course which
reason, policy, and, above all, perhaps, a just estimation of the necessity of their situation, prescribed to them.   Necker seems to
have wished that the two orders should immediately, and without making any further difficulties, have *united* with the Tiers
Etat.   Had they but taken, he continues, the direction which
government recommended to them, all would have been well;
the minds of men would have been settled, and we should not
have seen what we have seen.   The two superior orders could
perceive, observes Necker, as clearly as I could, the changes of
times and circumstances, they could see the power of public
opinion, the great effects it had produced, the necessity of making
an alliance with it; that it had concentrated its force to procure
the meeting of the States; that its hopes were entirely fixed on
the assembly, and that these hopes were not to perish blighted
and destroyed by the enemies of the public welfare; that the
nation would receive with gratitude any sacrifices that were
made to it; and it was for the privileged orders to have contended with the Tiers Etat for the good opinion of the public,
for their affection and their support, not leaving that popularity,
as they did, to fall entirely (by a succession of improvident
measures) into the possession of the Tiers Etat.   They ought
themselves to have been the first to propose to unite themselves
to the Tiers Etat, and to deliberate in common for the public
good; on the same account, to have surrendered their pecuniary
privileges.   They might have made proper reservations with
regard to their particular prerogatives and rights.

It is not to be told, concludes Necker, what would have been the sensation thus produced, the authority they would have thus acquired, and the opportunity that would thus have been afforded to so many of the Tiers Etat, to have rallied round them in support of the general weal, to be accomplished by every rational and peaceable method; and, after all, they would but thus have anticipated the necessity they were afterwards obliged to submit to; it was evident these privileges would have to be sacrificed, and that the national concerns could not at that particular period be treated of by three separate assemblies. But circumstances, says Necker, often are such, that the part of wisdom is not to wrestle with them, but to leave them behind, and seize in advance some good position. A wisdom indeed this, he says, of all the most rare. The common course is to suppose one makes a sacrifice, when one only submits to necessity; and one loses one's opportunity to negotiate, as it were, on free terms, while one is yet free and competent to do so.

Such are the representations of Necker, and may be admitted. All this may be very true, but forms no proper defence for M. Necker for his *prior* mistakes. He may indeed show the subsequent want of policy or temper in the privileged orders; but this is a great question, and one that we arrive at after we have determined the question of the prior and preparatory conduct of M. Necker, and *not before*.

There was no reconciling the respective pretensions, continues M. Necker, of the three orders; the king became quite uneasy; he required them to send commissioners to discuss them before him in council; they did so: it was in vain; long debates ensued.

I endeavoured to accommodate all difficulties, says Necker. I submitted propositions to the commissioners for that purpose; there seemed to be no objection to them. The nobility, however, made reserves and distinctions which were equivalent to a refusal, and as such were seized upon by the Tiers Etat, who then declared themselves the National Assembly. The nobility afterwards wished to have recovered the false step they had made, but it was too late.

No doubt the Tiers Etat, in voting themselves the National Assembly, in affecting thus to supersede the necessity of the concurrence of the other two orders, says M. Necker, were guilty of every fault that can belong to an usurping power; but the two orders, at this period, particularly the nobility, committed every error that could result from a want of policy, circumspection, and foresight.

Such are the general representations of Necker; and the two orders may have conducted themselves with the want of prudence, the Tiers Etat with the spirit of encroachment he describes; but the question is, whether any of the parties acted differently from what might have been expected; and whether their subsequent ill-conduct forms any justification of his prior imprudence? M. Necker made a distinct and a reasonable effort afterwards to conciliate all parties. Now, the question is, whether all the efforts he afterwards made might not have found their place in the king's declaration *originally*? Might he not have anticipated and provided some measure to prevent the difficulties which he might have foreseen would otherwise arise? And is not M. Necker to be asked whether the king, by first, and originally, pronouncing and determining what Necker afterwards proposed, would not have taken his best course? Whether this would not have been the best chance of preventing the collision, the exasperation, that afterwards ensued, and that could not but ensue; the best chance of preventing the mistakes of the privileged orders, the usurpations of the Tiers Etat, the unhappy diminution of that royal authority which it was so much the wish of Necker, and of all wise and good Frenchmen at the time, to defend from disrespect and violence?

No doubt, it is easy for us, or for any one, to be wise after the event; but Necker, from the first, saw and felt the force of public opinion; no one more so; indeed too much so: it was his business, therefore, as soon as possible, to take some position, such that he might either secure the best chance of avoiding a contest with public opinion altogether, or, that he might contend with the best advantage.

Circumstances are not easily appreciated at a distance of time or place; the precise influence and effect that each or any of them ought to have upon a reasonable mind, called to decide at the moment; but Necker seems to have been of a temperament too sanguine. He had expected more wisdom, more disinterestedness, from the parties than was reasonable; more than they afterwards showed. As a man of sense and humanity, he was desirous that something should be done for France; he must have supposed, that nothing would, if the double representation was not conceded to the popular party. He therefore granted it. He had expected, no doubt, to influence afterwards all parties, by showing them, from time to time, what it was just, and right, and wise to do; but he should have prescribed what was just, and right, and wise, by the royal authority in the first declaration, and he should have left nothing that he could possibly avoid to be settled by the result of the general fermentation and the conflict of the three orders.

I do not see that these general conclusions will be disturbed by turning to the pages of Mᵉ. de Stael. She mentions the sufferings of Necker during the seven years that intervened between his first dismissal and first recall, between 1781 and 1788; with what anxiety, with what melancholy, he saw the precious years elapse, within which he thought a system of political happiness might have been created for France; observing every project of his own neglected or overthrown. She shows that the times, views, and opinions of the three orders and of society, when the States of 1614 assembled, to which the aristocratic accusers of her father continually appealed, were in every respect different from any that could be supposed to exist in 1789; that, on the whole, neither the assembling of the States themselves, nor the doubling of the Tiers Etat, could have been avoided by Necker. This last position she labours at great length to establish.

"But," says Mᵉ. de Stael, "the natural consequence of the doubling of the Tiers Etat was, according to the notions of Necker's accusers, the voting by head, not by order."

"No," she replies, "it was rather the voting in two chambers, and to this there could be no objection, but the contrary. Why, then," she continues, "why, then, according to the same accusers, did not M. Necker make the king pronounce upon this point, when he granted the doubling of the Tiers?"

"He did not do this," she replies, "for he thought an alteration like this ought to be concerted with the representatives of the nation." Here I apprehend lay the whole mistake of M. Necker; and it is in vain that Mᵉ. de Stael immediately subjoins, "Two houses were recommended by M. Necker afterwards, when the representatives had been assembled, as above, but in vain;" and France was thus destroyed, she thinks.

France may thus, as she supposes, have been destroyed, with its aristocracy and monarch; but it is not by such reasonings and statements that M. Necker can be extricated from the censures of his critics; and if France was ruined by any one mistake more than another, it was apparently by this mistake of M. Necker.

I do not say that the king should have resolved to establish two chambers, and have altered the whole constitution of France in this manner by his own authority, but that some measure should have been well weighed beforehand, and then converted into a part of the original declaration—the measure, for instance, not of two houses, but those that Necker, on the part of the king, afterwards proposed; at all events, some measure by which he and the royal authority were to stand or fall. Fall they could not but do ultimately, if, without ordaining from the first some measure of their own they were to abide by the result of a conflict between the Tiers Etat and the two orders, in the existing state of Paris and the kingdom. On the whole, and as a sort of explanation, it must be remembered, that in the interval of his first and second administration, Necker carried on a controversy with Calonne, in which he was assisted and supported by his philosophical friends and the adherents of the new opinions. This controversy had no very good consequences, nor could have. It exposed the evils of the existing system (not very necessary this, at the time,) and exposed all the indecisions and weakness of the court. Those who were then of the court, and were Necker's friends, must notwithstanding have thought well of the measures of Calonne, and have become at length indisposed to Necker. Necker was thus placed in a sort of opposition to the court, got entangled in the new opinions, and could not disengage himself from the influence of his Paris coterie in the consideration of the questions which arose on the assembling of the States. This was probably the real fact. Influence arising from circumstances like these might affect his mind without his being well aware of it. He had also, as he himself confesses, his own too sanguine hopes and aspirations, and he shared them with the generality of wise and benevolent men at the time. It might not be that he wanted decision, that he wanted foresight: *these* might not be the *only* solutions of his conduct, when he left the questions open which we contend he should have anticipated and decided. It might be that his wishes and his opinions were, that they should be decided on popular grounds, and the wishes and opinions of the court being the contrary, a sort of tacit compromise took place in his mind, and he, on the whole, thought it best that nothing should be settled, and therefore nothing was settled.

Turning, however, from Necker, and casting, as I conclude, one glance on the court during this period of French history, surely the want of statesman-like talents in the king and his ministers, and ignorance of every thing that it imported them to know, were never so apparent. What are we to say to this court and ministers, who could, but the year before, mix themselves with the politics of Holland, and even engage on the popular side; taking no warning from what they had experienced from a similar conduct in the case of America—and again

engage on the popular side, when from their own embarrassments, and the state of public affairs at home, they could not
possibly engage with effect; fanning the flame of liberty, which
at the very time they thought was ready to consume themselves;
and as if their opponents around them were not already sufficiently animated and enterprizing, make them still more contemptuous, powerful, and determined, by yielding the palm to
England and tarnishing the national glory in the face of Europe,
and this, too, fo the illustration of their hated rival?   All this
time there were Sieyes, and Target, and a hundred other writers,
leading up the public to the overthrow of the monarchy.   But
the truth must be confessed: governments who thus deport
themselves in the midst of their difficulties and dangers, appear
rather to earn their destruction than to meet it.

LECTURE VIII.

TIERS ETAT.

I HAVE described in the last lecture the views of Necker and his
situation, referring myself in the main to his own works and to
his own statement of the case, as he drew it up at a subsequent
period, deliberately considering it in the calmness of his retirement.   It is difficult to judge of the conduct of statesmen, no
doubt; for, in politics, existing circumstances are every thing.
On the present occasion, however, we judge not a little from the
materials which he himself submits to our consideration; and
though no mistake was of more importance to the world than
his, if it was one, we may determine, as I conceive, on the
nature of it in this instance, with rather more confidence than
in most others.

In politics, I have just said, existing circumstances are every
thing.   Not that the general rules of justice and right are to be
made light of or forgotten, but that wise and good men must in
politics look earnestly to discover the expediency of the case, and
that this can only be judged of by the circumstances.   Very
painful struggles are sometimes occasioned by the doubts that
arise, which of two general rules of obligation it is best, that is,
it is ultimately most expedient to prefer; including in the word
expedient, as must never be forgotten, the importance and
sanctity of all moral obligations.   But a statesman, above every
other moralist, (he is only a moralist on a larger scale,) is bound

to mark well the nature of every thing around him at the moment, and to adapt well his means to his end. With him, above all others, success is included in the idea of his merit : not only must his objects be noble, but the expedients he uses to accomplish them must be adequate to their purpose. He must not injure his fellow-creatures, however good his intentions ; it is wisely ordained, as has been well shown by Adam Smith, in his "Moral Sentiments," a work which I must earnestly recommend to you, that intentions are not sufficient, lest men should rest satisfied with their good intentions. And if a minister, an actor in the scene, is to be so affected by the circumstances under which he is to act, so must you be, when you are to judge of his conduct. The period now before us in the history of the Revolution, is, of all others, the most critical. After the preparatory lectures I have given, I might now proceed at once to the opening of the States General, in May 1789 ; but the circumstances, as I have said, are in politics every thing, and I must still endeavour to give you some further specimens of those that were connected with this memorable scene, that the scene itself may be better understood. You must meditate these things hereafter in the detail of the history, but in the mean time I must provide you with any general notions of it I can, by any slight sketch that it is in my power to make.

Before, therefore, I advert to the opening of the States General, which I shall do before I finish this lecture, I shall endeavour to afford you, in the first place, some view of the situations and opinions of the different parties concerned, by some quotations from the speeches or writings of those who may be considered as the representatives of those leading divisions of sentiment that then agitated this great kingdom. After this is done, which may or may not be a little tedious, I will proceed to the opening of the States. The three great classes, as you will easily comprehend, were first, the moderate men ; secondly, the supporters of the old régime ; and thirdly, the followers of the new opinions.

To allude, therefore, to each :—Of the moderate men, the best example that I can produce is Mounier. He was one of the most enlightened and virtuous members of the Constituent Assembly ; he has left some works behind him, and it is in these that you must look for such opinions and feelings as may be said in general to have belonged to wise and good men at the time. Referring, then, to such matters as we have been discussing, he seems clearly of opinion, that the king had a right according to ancient usage, and might certainly, according to every principle of political expediency, have prevented all the discussions and disputes that afterwards took place, by settling himself the forms and constitution of the States General.

Great mistakes he conceives to have been committed; he is far from blaming the intentions of the king's advisers, but their mistakes, he thinks, were clear and very important. He had been a considerable man in the states of Dauphiny; and there, and afterwards in the Constituent Assembly, his object had always been a limited monarchy; where the power of the crown and the rights of the people should mutually support and guarantee the existence of each other.

M. Necker must have depended on the number and weight of the moderate men that were to be found in the States General and in the nation.

Such men (there were many of them in the Constituent Assembly) sympathized with the new opinions, but were not out of reach of the old; they were willing to improve the situation of France by an admixture of both; to advance her political situation, to secure her civil and religious liberties, but not by violence, not by means of a revolution.

So much for the moderate men, of whom Mounier is the best specimen; Necker is another; and you will see what were their views by referring to their works.

I will now allude to those who sympathized with the old opinions *only*, and afterwards to those who were the supporters of the new.

About the time that Necker prevailed on the king and council to adopt the double representation (in December, 1788), five princes of the blood addressed a memorial to the king, which showed the views and feelings of that high aristocratic party, which then, and ever after, existed in France; those who were destined to support, under all circumstances, and at all hazards, the ancient forms and modes of proceeding, and the ancient spirit, principles, and ranks of the monarchy.

" Sire," they say to the king, " the state is in danger—(this is in December, 1788, the States meet in the following May of 1789)—the virtues of the monarch ensure him the homage of the nation; but, Sire, a revolution is taking place in the principles of the government, brought on by a ferment in the minds of the people; institutions held sacred, and by which this monarchy has prospered for so many ages, are made subjects of debate, and even decried as replete with injustice. The writings which have appeared since the assembly of the Notables has been sitting, and the memorials which have been delivered to the undersigned princes, the petitions drawn up by several provincial towns or societies, the object and style of these petitions and memorials, all proclaim and prove a digested system of disorder and contempt for the laws of the state. Every author sets himself up for a legislator. Eloquence and the art of writing, even though destitute of study, knowledge, or experience, seem to bestow a sufficient title to regulate the constitutions of empires. Whoever advances a bold proposition, whoever proposes a change of the laws, is sure to find readers and partisans. Such is the unhappy progress of this effervescence," continues this petition or remonstrance, " that opinions which some time ago would have appeared entirely reprehensible, are now thought just and reasonable ; and what good men are now hurt at, will, in a short time, perhaps, pass as regular and legal. Who can say where this rashness of opinion will stop ?"

They then advert to the subjects more particularly before them, the double representation, &c., and at last observe :—

" Let the Tiers Etat then cease from attacking the rights of the other two orders ; rights, which being as old as the monarchy, ought to be as unalterable as the constitution of it ; and let them confine themselves to soliciting a decrease of the taxes with which they may be surcharged ; then might the two higher orders, finding in the third countrymen who are dear to them, generally renounce pecuniary privileges, and consent to support the public burdens with the most perfect equality."

Here, indeed, we have language from these princes of the blood, which, if but addressed to the sovereign *a few years before*, might have saved them and the sovereign from destruction.

" Then might the two orders," they say, " finding in the third countrymen who are dear to them, generally renounce pecuniary privileges."

And why could they not, *before*, find in the third estate countrymen who were dear to them ? Why could they not before do upon the general principles of humanity and benevolence, not to say of justice, what they were now, it seems, ready to do, but only when they had just before pronounced the words " Sire ! the state is in danger."

But the trial of the two privileged orders, their temptations to abuse their power, was now past. They had failed ; that of the Tiers Etat was now to begin, and they were destined to fail also. It is but too often thus. " Let the Tiers Etat," (these princes of the blood observe, these princes who had now become moni-

tors to others), "let the Tiers Etat reflect what in the end might
be the consequence of invading the rights of the clergy and nobility, and the result of the confusion of the orders. The French
monarchy must degenerate into despotism or become a democracy; two different kinds of revolution, but both deplorable."
This was but too true, but what had been done by themselves to
prevent it? The peers of the realm, about the same time with
these five princes of the blood, addressed a letter to his majesty,
in which they supplicate him to receive their solemn wishes to
bear a just proportion of the taxes and public burdens according
to their fortunes, without any pecuniary privilege whatever; and
they had no doubt, they said, that the same sentiments would
be unanimously expressed by the gentlemen (that is the smaller
nobility) of the kingdom, if assembled. And so the event proved;
the same wishes being expressed in the instructions of the nobility of almost all the bailiwicks of the kingdom, when they sent
deputies to the States General. All this wisdom was, alas! too
late. Of this tardy wisdom I will just give another specimen,
that of the parliament, and then proceed further to the views
and opinions of other patrons of the old régime.

The parliament during the general fermentation, at the close
of the year 1788, had ceased to occupy public attention; but
when the Notables broke up, on the 7th of December, 1788, its
members made an effort to regain their popularity, in a decree,
which seems to include their general notions on the principal
points of French liberty. They contend for the periodical return of the States General; no subsidy to be allowed that was
not granted by the States; the responsibility of ministers; the
protection of personal liberty; the lawful freedom of the press;
the suppression of all those taxes which marked a distinction between the orders, and that they should be replaced by common
subsidies equally imposed on all.

Here again in this last article we see the same tardy wisdom
in the parliament that has been witnessed in the two privileged
orders; an equal taxation in vain proposed at the close of 1788,
which, if conceded to the sovereign at the time he required it, a
few years before, might have prevented the Revolution.

This Revolution was now approaching fast, and this celebrated parliament of Paris, that had for the sake of the public,
resisted so often, (and in prior reigns more particularly, though
not in the reign of Louis XVI.) resisted so virtuously the monarch and his ministers, and suffered so often exile and imprisonment, was cast aside by the public (after their manner) as an

assembly now without use or meaning, and was never thought of more. But to return to the patrons of the old régime.

In January, 1789, the Marquis de Bouillé saw a terrible storm, as he tells us, ready to burst upon the kingdom, and dreaded the consequences; troubles appeared to him inevitable; he was apprehensive of a civil war. Speaking of the States General, he considers Necker as having made no proper exertion for its composition.

He mentions facts that are important. "The ecclesiastical members," he says, "were principally chosen from among the inferior clergy, without livings or property; among the representatives of the nobility were many subtle, daring, and intriguing men, who meant but to corrupt and divide the order; and the third estate," he says, "was laid open to a description of men, numerous and dangerous in France, those who lived by their talents, their literary abilities, and their industry; lawyers, principally of the lowest class; physicians, artists, writers of little or no eminence, and men without either rank or property. Of three hundred members who represented the clergy, two hundred and eight were possessed of no ecclesiastical dignity. Of six hundred who represented the Tiers Etat, three hundred and seventy-four were professors of the law. These were important facts no doubt, and of awful augury. Indeed, it appears," he says, "that however the clergy and nobility had been summoned, much of their relative importance had been lost since the former periods of their sittings.

"In the order of the clergy, the dignities of the profession had not been, as formerly, the reward of virtue, piety, and an active discharge of duty; the higher clergy were composed of the young nobility of the court and provinces. The order, therefore, had lost much of its consideration, especially as the respect for religion itself had been gradually weakened."

His representations go on in the following manner:—The nobility had lost much of its ancient splendour. There were in France nearly thirty thousand noble families. Four thousand civil offices either gave or transmitted nobility. The king granted patents of noblesse. There were about one thousand families whose origin was lost in the remote periods of the French monarchy: of these, scarcely two or three hundred had escaped indigence and misfortune. There were two hundred families whose names existed in history. If honorary titles were borne by some old and illustrious families, they were likewise shared by a multitude of new nobles, who by their riches had acquired the right of assuming them. The nobility had nothing to distinguish them but the favours of the court and exemption from taxes. Much of what the nobility and clergy had lost of their riches, power, and importance, had been gained, according to the marquis, "by the third estate." Commerce had enriched the third order, not the nobility, who would not engage in trade. Many of this part of society had become superior to the nobility in wealth, and talents, and personal merit, yet they were excluded from rank in the army, from high ecclesiastical preferments in the church, and even from the higher class of the magistracy; the major part of the sovereign courts admitting only the nobility into their bodies. The States General of 1789 were thus, says the marquis, "opened under very unfavourable circumstances. The people had become inclined to intrigue and licentiousness; in all their ranks was remarked an aversion to the established authorities, and a contempt for the persons of those who exercised them;" and finally and on the whole, the marquis conceives, "that it would have required the greatest energy and address, not merely to guide their labours to useful objects, but even to prevent them from overturning everything from the foundation."

The same general conclusions that are thus presented to you by the Marquise de Bouillé, you will see also in the Memoirs and Annals of Bertrand de Moleville. All these works are extremely interesting and valuable. They exhibit to you the notions of the court and the privileged orders; and at the same time show the unhappy case, that, by the folly of their prejudices and the injustice of an ill-digested system of government, had at length arisen.

But while, in the manner you have seen, the princes of the blood and the privileged orders were now desirous only to support the ancient system of the monarchy, very different were the notions that had circulated through society, and got possession of the minds of the most intelligent part of the country, had from them descended to the multitude, and become the conversation of statesmen of every description; the young and the old, the low and the high, the ignorant and the well-informed. I will, therefore, now introduce you to the advocates of the new opinions.

I have mentioned two works, the History of the Revolution, par Deux Amis de la Liberté, and the Précis, by Rabaud de St. Etienne. You will be able, by turning to their pages, to form some idea, though probably a most faint one, of the general fermentation that then existed. As a specimen, I will allude to

the work of Rabaud de St. Etienne.   He writes in 1791, immediately after the close of the Constituent Assembly, and produces
the sentiments and opinions which he must have entertained
from the first, or rather such as he still entertained, notwithstanding all the intermediate events, since May 1789.   Observe
the general tone of what I quote.

" The French nation," says he, " has for ages been submitted
to arbitrary laws.   The people, that is every thing in free countries, and nothing in those that are despotic, with us, have been
subjected to a number of tyrannies, so great, that the best part
of its substance has been dissipated in imposts levied by force or
fraud, by superstition, or under the pretence of privilege.

" The sovereign has raised more than most of the great princes
of Europe together.   The clergy has drawn one-fifth of the net
produce of the territorial revenues of the kingdom ; the nobles,
by their feudal rights, have in reality levied taxes, yet have nothing paid themselves.   A crowd, in like manner, of those that
have been privileged, and those that have been ennobled, have
acquired by purchase a right of exemption from the public expenses.

" Wars, which kings," continues St. Etienne, " seem never to
have been able to do without, have furnished a pretext for levying soldiers, and then soldiers have in their turn been the pretext
and means of new wars.   See a regular army, and you may say,
There goes a tyrant, or one who will soon become so.   In a
vast extended monarchy like ours, kings could only see by their
ministers ; and this has ended in the ministers being the government, with all their apparatus of *lettres de cachet*, sinecure offices
for the support of their creatures, &c. &c.

" Never has nation been depressed in so insulting a manner as
ours from the time of Richelieu to the States General of 1789."

He then gives the history, passing through the times of Louis
XIV. and XV.   " And thus," says he, " journeyed on to its
total decline and fall, one of the greatest kingdoms of Europe.
The national character has been effaced ; and it is to write the
history of the Revolution to trace the steps by which the public
mind had advanced at last to complete annihilation."   He then
describes the labours and the merits of those who had broken
the fetters of tyranny—Voltaire, the philosophers of England,
the Encyclopédie, Montesquieu, Rousseau, and Raynal.   Every
tribute is then paid to the good intentions of the king, and he
describes his successive ministers ; " but reform," he says, " was
impossible.   It was above the powers of Necker, or any single

man. It was for the nation alone to attempt it; and one has seen, in attempting it, to what perils have been exposed the Constituent Assembly and the public welfare." Rabaud was a member, and wrote in 1791. " What an immense coalition," he says, " had indeed a minister, or even the king himself, to assist him, when he was contending with others—sixty thousand men, nobles or ennobled, them and their dependants; the military men, noble or pretending to be so; one hundred thousand privileged persons, who are not to pay taxes, it seems; two hundred thousand priests, sixty thousand religious; the farmers general, and all the agents of the revenue, with their army, fifty thousand strong, and the multitude of those who had offices, extended even into the smallest towns; finally, the men of the robe, the parliaments, the superior courts, the inferior, and all the people of business, who in one way or another thus lived upon the nation, and became an impost which it would be terrifying to the imagination to calculate. Such was the formidable mass of people that had got possession of France, that held it down by a thousand chains, and that formed the nation, while the rest were supposed to be mere people. This was that mass," says St. Etienne, " that one has seen afterwards unite its voice and its clamours against the National Assembly, because with a spirit and a courage unexampled the Assembly suppressed all the abuses on which *it* depended for its existence.

" From the moment," he afterwards observes, " that the word 'the States General' was once pronounced, that they were demanded by the parliament, and promised by the king, events rushed on, one after another, so as scarcely to be distinguishable. While the nation was only occupied with the delightful thought of some approaching regeneration, that should for ever remove it out of the reach of tyranny, those who then held the mastery of the nation were only occupied with the means of retaining their empire. But the imposing colossus of the majesty of the people found, every hour, its growth advancing, and trampled under its feet successfully every fantastic authority by which it had been so long subjugated.

" The provinces in the meantime abandoned themselves to all that excitation of mind that naturally arose from a sense of all the evils to which France was exposed, all the indignities and the outrages which it had suffered, and the hope of a better order of things. Dauphiny led the way. Innumerable writers," he says, " recalled the Tiers Etat to a sense of their rights. Some mounted up to the origin of the monarchy, and traced in characters of fire, the progress of despotism, the absolute power of twenty tyrants, and the consequent degradation of the nation. Others found, in the history of the States General, the proofs of the national authority, and that it was the nation that was the sovereign. Others mounted still higher to the original and imprescriptible rights of every people.

" Paris became the very concentration of intelligence and light. Societies, correspondencies, were formed. The press was in fact free. Publications were every where dispersed adapted to the comprehension of the lowest orders.

" The government was without resource, and could only leave every thing to be said or written without further stay or molestation."

These passages, written by an active, able, and respected member of the Constituent Assembly, even so late as about the time of its termination, will give you some slight notion of the situation of Paris and of France in the months that more immediately preceded and that followed the meeting of the States General in 1789 ; some notion also of the general views whch had been formed by the more ardent and leading members of the Constituent Assembly.

When these general views of Rabaud de St. Etienne had been but too successful, he retired, and was soon dragged from his retreat to perish under the guillotine.

In the history of the Two Friends of Liberty, the sentiments and opinions are of a nature so similar, that I do not occupy your time with producing them ; it is one of the histories which you should read.

But the extracts I have given from Rabaud de St. Etienne, and even the perusal of both these histories, will give you but a very inadequate notion, I am satisfied, of the spirit in which the new opinions were conceived, and the ardour and sweeping fury with which they were at this period every where in France circulated and maintained.

It was under these ominous circumstances that the meeting of the States General took place in May 1789. To this memorable meeting we will now advert. And to give you a sort of general picture of the first and ceremonial part of it, I will quote a few paragraphs from a writer, the most beautiful of all, M^e. de Stael ; one who, from the liveliness of her imagination, and the quickness of her feelings, could sympathise with whatever was reasonable or affecting in the opinions or situation of every party, and therefore appears to belong to every party in its turn ; but who was in truth most deeply and most honourably attached to the principles of civil and religious liberty and to their cause in France, but could not do otherwise than be disappointed and grieve over the failure of her father, and mourn over the calamities of her country.

" I shall never forget the moment," says Me. de Stael, " when I saw the one thousand two hundred deputies of France, moving on in procession to hear mass, the evening *before* the opening of the States General. A striking spectacle for the French, and one unexampled.

" All the inhabitants of Versailles and people of curiosity from Paris assembled to see it. A new sort of authority thus arisen in the state, of which one knew not either the nature or the force, quite amazed the generality of those who had not reflected on the rights of nations.

" The high clergy had lost something of their consideration, for many of the prelates had not been sufficiently regular in their conduct.

" A long peace had left the nobles little or no opportunity, however desirous they might have been, to recall the memory of their ancestors. Those of the second order (of the nobles) had been equally without opportunities of distinguishing themselves, for no career was open to them but that of arms. Those who were ennobled, and who were seen marching in great number in the ranks of the nobility, seemed to carry with but little grace their plume of feathers and their sword; and one asked oneself why they were to be thus placed in the first order of the state, merely because they had *bought* the right of not contributing their part to the public imposts.

" But whatever was lost to the nobility and the clergy was added to the importance of the Tiers Etat. Their habits and black cloaks, their fixed looks, and their imposing number, drew every eye upon them.

" Men of letters, merchants, and a great number of lawyers, composed this third order. Some nobles had got made deputies, and among these was above all to be remarked the Count de Mirabeau. The opinion that one entertained of his powers of mind was singularly increased by the terror inspired by his licentiousness; yet was it that very licentiousness that diminished the influence which his astonishing faculties were fitted to procure him. It was difficult to take one's eyes away, when one had once seen him. His immense head of hair distinguished him; one should have supposed that, like Samson, his strength depended on it. The countenance of the man borrowed expression from its very ugliness, and the whole appearance of him gave me an idea of some great irregular force and power, in short, such as one should expect to find in a tribune of the people.

" I was in a window," she continues, " by the side of Mᵉ. de Montmorin, wife of the minister of foreign affairs, and I abandoned myself, I confess, to the most lively hope and exultation at seeing, for the first time in France, the representatives of the nation. Mᵉ. de Montmorin, in whose mind and talents there was nothing at all remarkable, observed to me in a decided tone, which afterwards impressed me much, ' You are quite wrong to be in such spirits on this occasion; great calamities will be the result of all this to France and to us.'

" This unhappy lady," continues Mᵉ. de Stael, " perished on a scaffold with one of her sons, another drowned himself, her husband was massacred on the 2d September, her eldest daughter perished in the hospital of one of the prisons, her youngest before thirty, borne down with her afflictions. The family of Niobe herself suffered not more. She must have had a presentiment, one would have said."

Mᵉ. de Montmorin was probably a woman of ordinary good sense, whose judgment was not disturbed by any irregular impressions of the feelings or wanderings of the imagination, like that of Mᵉ. de Stael; and such women, by a sort of general tact, which operates like instinct, the result of mere commerce with the world, and the common feelings and vulgar interests which form the history of it, are generally able to form a far more accurate opinion on any practical case before them, than women of genius like Mᵉ. de Stael; and the same observation may be extended to the men of talents at this period, not only in France, but all over Europe. In proportion to the intelligence and the powers of each individual mind, with one illustrious exception (Mr. Burke), was the enthusiasm, the hope, and the expectation, entertained of the future liberties of France, and the cause of liberty there and throughout the world.

The States General assembled, therefore, as you see on the whole, under favourable circumstances—the king indecisive, the minister too sanguine, the court bigoted to the old opinions, the Tiers Etat unreasonably inflamed with the new, the populace tumultuous and ferocious.

A riot had just occurred; the house of an innocent and respectable man had been, in consequence of some idle report, attacked and pillaged, and as the first party of soldiers was too weak, it had been found necessary to order out a large party of the French and Swiss guards, with two pieces of artillery, to quell the insurgents. Above one hundred had been killed, some also of the military; a considerable number wounded. This specimen of the populace had just been witnessed. Again, the evening before the opening of the Assembly, the bishop of Nancy, in his sermon, had alluded in some strange manner to the salt tax, and applauses resounded from every part of the church, as if it had been a theatre. The sensibility of the public to the political grievances was, therefore, clearly shown to be of the most intemperate nature.

Nothing, however, could be more august than the opening of the Assembly. You will see, in such books as I have mentioned, a description of the scene. All, however, was false and hollow. The Tiers Etat were determined that the public business should be conducted on one system, the court and the privileged orders on another; and on the first possible opportunity this original cause of dissension was sure to appear, and the most alarming consequences ensue.

In the mean time you will observe the speech of the amiable and unfortunate king, the expressions he uses in his address to the collected wisdom of his people.

" The convocation of this Assembly has fallen into disuse, but I have not hesitated to re-establish a custom from which the kingdom may derive new force, and which may open to the nation a new source of happiness.

" I have already ordered considerable retrenchments in the expenditure. I shall direct the exact state of the finances to be laid before you.

" The public mind is agitated, but an assembly of the representatives of the nation will without doubt only listen to the counsels of wisdom and prudence. You must yourselves have felt that these counsels have been swerved from on many recent occasions; but the reigning spirit of your deliberations will correspond with the true sentiments of a generous nation, whose love for its king has ever been its most distinguishing characteristic. I discard every other recollection. All that can be expected from the tenderest interest in the public welfare, all that can be asked of a sovereign, the firm friend of his people, you may and ought to hope for from me. That a happy harmony may reign in this Assembly, and that this epoch may become ever memorable for the happiness and prosperity of the kingdom, is the wish of my heart, the most ardent of my vows; it is, in short, the prize that I expect from the rectitude of my own intentions and my love for my people."

Such was the general tenor of the king's address; a very favourable impression, it seems, was made upon the audience; the simple dignity of the king, the air, the tone, the cordial expression with which he delivered his speech, were not without their effect on a people ever quick to feel, could they but be steady enough to retain, the sentiments that do them honour; but nothing was pronounced by the king on the real subject of difficulty, the mode of voting.

The keeper of the seals followed, but with a feeble voice, ill-heard, and what reference he *did* make to the great point at issue might have been better spared, " that the king left it to the States to consider of the best manner of collecting the votes, though the vote by head appeared, by giving one general result, to evidence better the general wish."

Necker followed, but seems to have disappointed every one. His discourse was considered as tedious, declamatory, and academical; above all, as contributing nothing to the instruction of the Assembly on political subjects; as deciding nothing with regard to the real difficulty, the mode of voting. This point, the mode of voting, whether by order or by head, it might still appear to have been (legally at least) within the competence of the king to have determined; the different orders of the Assembly had not yet verified their powers; they had as yet obtained no legal existence; the king was as yet the only constituted authority in the state; but the state was now distempered in the extreme; the opportunity, if it ever existed, was lost by Necker, lost, most unhappily, and for ever.

The democratic leaders of the Tiers Etat made haste to strike the first blow; they sent a civil message to the two orders, inviting them, as if it had been a matter of course, to unite with them in order to verify in common their writs of return.

Nothing could be more assuming and improper; such I confess it appears to me, but it may not to others. The natural course was, for the members of each order to lay their writs of return on their own table, and for commissioners of their own to report upon their validity to their own separate house. Why were the other two bodies to exhibit themselves before the Tiers Etat? It was not the Tiers Etat that had called the Assembly together; who had made the Tiers Etat a ruler and a judge? Indeed, strictly speaking, the verification should have taken place before the king in council, since none of the deputies was competent, before the verification of his own powers, to verify those of others: and if this mode was objectionable, as giving opportunity to the king and court dishonestly to reject particular deputies, the only alternative seemed to be the mode we have mentioned; indeed, had the king even on the day of opening observed in his speech, that the verification of the powers was a necessary preliminary to all deliberation in the States General, and had he directed that the deputies should declare their titles to the keeper of the seals, in order to be verified by committees of the council, it is possible that no one would have questioned the regularity of such an order, and it might have been executed, perhaps, as of course and without opposition—all this is, however, doubtful. The public had been long in a high state of fermentation, were evidently animated in the extreme with the expectations that had been held out to them by popular writers; and the nature of the new opinions was now to be exhibited. The democratic leaders were determined that nothing in the shape of public business should begin to exist, but upon the system which they thought conducive to the public welfare, the system of voting by head; they concluded, that if each assembly once assumed a legal and separate existence, the three could never afterwards be made to vote in common; they conceived that nothing would be done for the public if the deliberation was to be carried on by orders. The public were with them; so was upon the whole the minister Necker. The nobles were not unanimous, still less the clergy; and not only the rash and enterprising patriots, but even the men of sense and good intentions among the Tiers Etat, appear all to have concurred in these violent proceedings, in the measures of unjustifiable pretension and usurpation that now took place.

The nobility saw the crisis in which they were placed, and made every effort to preserve their consequence; but with the community they were in no favour; the king and his ministers had imposed upon them a contest from which they ought to have saved them, and which they should have undertaken themselves; and of the order of the clergy, a large part consisted of those of an inferior rank, the curés, little inclined to be favourable to the interests or even the particular rights of their superiors. This distracted state of things existed for some weeks, and this suspense, by giving opportunity to the public mind to get inflamed, was of the most fatal consequence; and, at last, the ministers seem to have been alarmed. M. Necker, on June the 4th, came forward with a conciliatory plan, the sum and substance of which was—

That the three orders should trust each other with regard to the verification of those writs on which no difficulties had arisen, and that if any should arise, they should be carried before a commission chosen out of all the orders, and finally, if necessary, the dispute should be referred to the king.

This scheme, which would have satisfied all parties if the dispute had been sincere, entirely failed; and the Tiers Etat at last proceeded to declare, that the names of the clergy and nobility should be called over as well as their own, that they would then constitute themselves an active assembly, and proceed to public business with or without them.

It would not have been now easy to have contrived a safe measure for the court, or a prudent one for the nobility and clergy.

In the event, when the Tiers Etat called over the members, as they had announced their intention of doing, three curates appeared; they were, of course, received with the loudest acclamations, embraced and hailed as the saviours of France.

The Tiers Etat were sure that the example of these three curés would be soon followed, and that ultimately, both the clergy and the nobles would be left, those that resisted, in an insignificant minority, and obliged to submit to whatever terms might be imposed on them.

Five weeks had now elapsed, no public business done, no effort made for the happiness of France; it was the obstinacy of the nobles that was supposed in fault by an impatient public; little attention was paid to the unjustifiable nature of the pretensions of the commons, who now not only required the nobles to submit the verification of their powers to them, but that they should sit (the real point to be attained) in the same house with them. More of the clergy now joined the Tiers Etat, and the Tiers Etat at last proceeded to drop entirely the notion, that they were only *one* part of the great assembly of the States General, and they actually assumed to themselves the character of the whole concentrated wisdom and representative consequence of the kingdom; they resolved to call themselves at once "the National Assembly;" the vote, their own vote, was carried by a large majority, and the air resounded with the cry of "Long live the king! long live the National Assembly!"

One thing more remained, not only to assume, but to exercise the power of sovereignty; the power of sovereignty, or what was in effect, under the circumstances of the case, a very near approach to it; and to this they proceeded.

They issued what they called a decree to the following effect: "that inasmuch as the contributions now levied in the kingdom, not having been consented to by the nation, were all illegal, and consequently null; the National Assembly declared that they consented provisorily for the nation, that the taxes and contributions, though illegally established and levied, should continue to be levied till the day of the separation of the Assembly, after which they were to cease if not regranted by the Assembly."

By these acts of supremacy, made without the concurrence of the other two orders, and without waiting for the approbation of the king, they not only decided the two former questions about the mode of voting, but they acted as a sort of legislature, as a complete assembly authorized of themselves and alone to reform the old government, in fact to form a new government—certainly to present themselves as such—the government of the National Assembly.

Now, certainly to me, I confess, who turn to look on this scene as a matter of history, nothing can appear more unjustifiable than the whole of a conduct like this; but it may not to others; what had the king done, or even the court, to make it necessary? Why was the king to be made so soon to repent of his calling the states together for his own and the public advantage? What indifference had he shown to the public welfare? What measure had he rejected? What effect could usurpation on their part produce, but irritation and hostility on his, and rage and violence on the part of the court? What benefit could hence accrue to the community? Was peace no object? Was not order and regularity, and a system of conciliation and mutual sacrifices, the best, and indeed the only, chance for the permanent improvement of the constitution? It seems indeed to have been taken for granted, that unless the states were to vote by poll, no benefit could result from their meeting; but this was an assumption, and in truth a very violent assumption. The Tiers Etat seem quite to have overlooked the most important circumstances of the case: the progress of the new opinions; the ferment of the public mind; the influence of public opinion; the intensity of the expectation of the community; the difficulties that the king and court would be under if they ventured often or very materially to disappoint that expectation. It might have been asked them, what measure of clear importance and benefit to the state, if pressed for by the Tiers Etat, could long have been withheld by the king and the other two orders. Suppose the privileged orders had been made to contribute equally to the public taxes, and suppose provision had been made for the future meeting of the States General, would not even this have been sufficient to secure eventually, in the existing state of the world, a complete though gradual amelioration of the whole system of the government? Why was the Assembly to rush forward in this manner, and assume to themselves the office of what they called the regeneration of France; to set aside all the existing authorities, the king included, or only to consider them as subservient to themselves, as only useful or estimable as they would contribute to forward their own particular views of political expediency; as they would or would not assist them in new organizing society, or in giving, as they termed it, a new constitution to France?

There is no doubt that the majority of the Tiers Etat meant well, there is no doubt that very wise and very good men concurred in these proceedings, there is no doubt that the greatest blessing that can be procured for a nation is civil liberty, that just allowance must be made for men who step forward in a cause so noble and so animating; but it is on these very accounts the more necessary for history to criticise such men; because the mistakes of bad men and arbitrary rulers do not necessarily lead to liberty, while those of good men and virtuous patriots inevitably do to the loss of it.

These are, I confess, the opinions that I have found myself obliged, with whatever hesitation, and indeed with some surprise, at last to form; but I am well aware, that other views may be taken of these proceedings by the friends of liberty, and I shall endeavour to put you in possession of the whole of the case by adverting to them in my lecture of to-morrow.

LECTURE IX.

TWENTY-THIRD OF JUNE.

At the close of my lecture of yesterday, I referred to the first proceedings of the Constituent Assembly, and I submitted to your consideration the reasons why I thought them so objectionable; they were objectionable, in a word, because they were more or less violent and assuming at a time when everything depended upon the moderation of the parties; and as the Assembly were on this occasion the first to quit the path of peace, it is they who are to be most visited with censure, because in all disputes they who are first wrong, are most wrong. But to such observations as I have made in my last lecture, it will be replied by those who, though friends to liberty, are as deeply impressed with the necessity of peace and order as I can be, or as any one can be, that the nature and situation of the French people, of the king and court, of the patriots themselves, the time, the occasion, the circumstances, and all the exigencies of the case must be considered; and that then, such animadversions as I have made on the conduct of the Assembly, must be materially modified, if not entirely abandoned.

It will contribute, I think, to the clear understanding of this, by far the most difficult discussion and the most important that the history of this Revolution affords, if the different measures which I have presumed to blame are separated from each other and surveyed apart, and if we proceed step by step:

The first and great point was, in truth, the mode of voting, whether by orders or by head, whether in one Assembly or in three Chambers.

This was the first and great point; the dangers and difficulties on each side of the question were always sufficiently apparent, and they have been already exhibited to you. But in defence of the strong measures just adopted by the Assembly, it will be observed, that the States General had now met; the Tiers Etat been assembled; the members of it now brought into contact with each other mutually to explain their grievances and expectations; that the prior and existing fermentation of the public was very great; and that in this situation of things, the doubling of the Tiers Etat in the original formation of the Assembly was considered a virtual concession of the right of voting by head; that Necker and his friends so understood it; that they considered it as a popular concession, and meant the crown to have the credit of it; but why popular, if it had no popular object, and no distinct object? The Tiers Etat followed up this virtual concession by assuming at once that the three estates should act together; and how are they to be blamed? What other chance in the known temper of the court for any reform in the administration of the government? What other chance for tranquillity amid the general hopes and fears and impatience of the public? A majority in any one house obtained against them, what probability of any reform?

In return rather than in answer to this reasoning, it must be first remarked, that it is here we find the accusation of Necker, it is here that his fault appears. If Necker left these points open, it was but too probable that the leaders of the Tiers Etat would reason thus; it was impossible that the public should not sympathize with them; it was impossible that a ferment should not

arise, which the king and the court were little fitted, either by
gentle means or by force, to encounter and subdue.

But when all this has been allowed, may not then the observations I have made be suffered to find their place? Are the patriots of a country, are the more wise and enlightened leaders of
the public emotion, to rise superior to the temptations of their
situation, or not? They are to be praised, highly praised, if
they do; but are they not to be blamed, if they do not? What
is ever human virtue but some elevation of the character more or
less of this description? What chance for the public weal but
in the prudence of the court on the one side, and the moderation
of the Tiers Etat on the other? But what moderation did the
Tiers Etat exhibit in thus requiring the king and the two privileged orders to abandon all their inherited notions and feelings?
What moderation in requiring them to take the chance of one
great assembly in which all ranks and orders were to be confounded; an assembly where everything was to abide the decision
of a majority; an assembly where the Tiers Etat already constituted one half? Why was the first step of the Tiers Etat to be
that of relatively annihilating the personal consideration, the
legal and long established dignity of every individual in the country but themselves? Why were they to suppose that no one
had any interest in the public good but themselves? What measure, calculated to promote the public good, had been as yet rejected by the king? What opposition as yet made to the reasonable wishes of the public? Why was it to be taken for
granted by the Tiers Etat that all wisdom and benevolence were
monopolized by themselves? What was hereafter to be expected
from them if this was to be the first specimen of their views
and character? What respect for the nobility and clergy of the
land? What safety for the monarch? What peace for the people? What was meant, or what could be meant, by all this
ferment in the public mind, this cry for the regeneration of
France? Was it or was it not meant, that nothing at the time
established should eventually exist; and was it then the scheme
of the Tiers Etat to merge all the dignity and authority of the
country in one Assembly, and that their own? And was this
the first measure for the purpose or not? Would language of
this kind then, let it be asked on the whole of the case, would
language of this kind have been unnatural or even exaggerated,
or materially unjust, if held by any of the members of the two
higher orders at the time? And if so, is not the charge of violence, of want of reasonableness, of want of moderation in the

Tiers Etat made out : and if this charge be made out, has not blame been incurred ?

The subject must be here left, I conceive, to the decision of every man for himself.   There seems to have been little doubt among the members of the Tiers Etat upon these questions at the time, but the lesson of instruction for after-ages, I must still think, is what I have presumed to draw, and only the more necessary to be drawn on that very account; the next question is, what was to be done by the court and the privileged orders ?   That is, supposing that the Tiers Etat were unreasonable in their expectations, and insisted on the voting by head, what was then the best policy, the proper conduct of the privileged orders ?

Necker bitterly complains that these points were not given up, and the union which the Tiers Etat required made with a good grace and at once.

It is possible, it may, I think, on the whole be allowed, that in the situation in which Necker had placed them, or suffered them to be placed, the best measure with a view to the public good and their own safety, was the union which he wished.   It was a most fearful measure to be obliged to take, but on the whole it was the least objectionable.   In the state of general irritation that prevailed, the public expectation was to be gratified within any tolerable bounds, as quickly as possible.   If the Tiers Etat were to be resisted, some better point was to be taken than one, which would appear to the public only a point of form ; whether it involved an important principle or not (it certanly did one most important), still it would not be so considered by the public, and would be thought by them to have no effect or meaning but that of paralysing all public business ; of indicating, perhaps, the resolution of the king and court to escape from all measures of reform whatever.   The Tiers Etat were not likely to give up the point without a protracted struggle ; and in civil contentions delay is sure to be fatal to the party which is the *least* popular : it was therefore clear, that the point must be conceded eventually, and therefore the sooner the better.

The chance of resistance to the Tiers Etat was to be taken on some other occasion, when the strong passions, that were evidently ready to burst their holds, had been first soothed, and a large portion of the Tiers Etat and of the moderate men in the two orders had been conciliated by such prompt measures for the removal of public grievances and the amelioration of the constitution, as would have shown a real sympathy with the public wishes and opinions ; and, in short, whatever was the chance of the three orders meeting in one Assembly, whether unpromising or not (it was most unpromising), there was now no other, unless an open rupture; a dissolution of the States and a civil war was on the whole preferred.

But they who at all admit the remarks I have made on the first point, the voting by head or by order, in one house or three, will readily concur with the same train of reasoning, when applied to the succeeding point, the vote by which the Tiers Etat constituted themselves the National Assembly: this vote was carried by a majority of four hundred and eighty to eighty-nine, or something more than five to one; an immense majority this, on a question that was to set every thing aside in the state but themselves, to propose to the public no other object on which they were to look with respect or expectation.   The vote for independence in America was not carried till a war with Great Britain had been for some time raging; in the instance before us, on the contrary, a vote is carried in the popular assembly of France for an independence of all the other established authorities of the state, after a contest only of a month, not of violence and arms and bloodshed, but of pamphlets and disputation; not a single act of harsh authority yet exercised, not a reasonable cause of offence yet given.   Indecision and perplexity and disunion are indeed very sufficiently evidenced in the conduct of their political opponents; folly, if you please, nothing more; a vain and helpless unwillingness to relinquish in time the constitutional privileges, of their birth, and supposed rights of their condition in society; but were these sufficient reasons for a vote, like this, from the Assembly; for standing on no terms with them any longer?   Was the sympathy of the public, which they found continually increasing, and rendering them every hour more and more powerful, to be turned to no better purpose than that of rendering the sincere co-operation of the king and court in their designs for the public good, from that moment impossible?   Wise and good men concurred in this vote at the time; this must be admitted: but whatever explanation I may see of it, I confess I see no proper defence.

This lecture was written many years ago, but in the work lately published, the posthumous work of M. Dumont, it appears that Mirabeau said to him, when dying, " Oh, my friend, how right we were when we endeavoured at the first to prevent the commons from declaring themselves the National Assembly! It is this that has been the source of all our evils.   From the moment they carried that victory, they have never ceased to show themselves unworthy of it."

The next point is their decree relative to the levying of taxes; they evidently voted that they were illegal, without consent of the National Assembly.

No one will deny that this was a very strong measure, scarcely justifiable, as appearing too like an assumption of the legislative functions, by one only of the three estates. Still it will be contended, that it is going too far to consider it as an act of sovereignty. The states, it will be observed, were met, among other objects, for the purpose of consenting to taxes. They assumed, that whenever former States General had met, they had consented to taxes and given subsidies; and, although the crown had exercised this power for centuries without control, the States might with propriety contend that the right had now been recognised anew. The king had himself lately declined any further attempts to raise new taxes on his own authority; the decree therefore only went to declare, as a constitutional principle, what had already been virtually acknowledged. Such will be the view that will be taken of this subject by many of the friends of freedom. It will be asked, at the same time, who could tell whether the king might not, any day, change his ministry and dissolve the States? What greater calamity for France; what calamity which it more imported the patriots to provide against? How could they better provide, than by making it difficult for the king to raise money without their consent?

It is probable that reasonings of this kind were very current with the most distinguished members of the Assembly at the time; but if so, they afford a memorable instance of the unhappy nature of civil contentions, how readily men of the first intelligence become inflamed amid a general ferment, and how easily they overlook the most obvious distinctions of propriety and right. Taxes and subsidies, as every one knew, were voted by the *States General*, not by the *Tiers État*—by all the *three* orders, not by *one* of them, acting for and assuming the authority of the whole. But the Tiers Etat had not yet been joined by the nobility and clergy. The more the origin and nature of these general assemblies were inquired into, when the times of Tacitus and the Germans were once left behind, the less important would appear the Tiers Etat, that now called themselves, single as they stood, the National Assembly, and arrogated the office and functions of the whole legislature of the state. The king might decline the exercise of the powers which his ancestors had so long usurped, but surely never meant to devolve it on the Tiers Etat. The king might any day change his minister, and dissolve the States, but the proper defence against such a contingency, when any defence really became necessary, was a resolution, not a decree—a resolution by the Tiers Etat declaratory of the nature of this constitutional power, explaining, asserting, and recording it, where it lay, and by whom it could be exercised; not a decree, assuming to themselves all the legislative authority that belonged, in fact, to the States General. A disrelish of the new opinions, an indisposition to any new order of things, might be suspected by the patriots in the court and the privileged orders; a change of counsels in the king, and some arbitrary measure to dissolve them, might be thought possible by the Tiers Etat; but were they, therefore, thus to provoke it and to justify it? Were they, therefore, to be the *first* to set an example of violence and usurpation? Were they to keep no terms with the sovereign, and to leave him no sentiment but that of regret and that of terror at having summoned them to his assistance at all? Certainly the very eminent men who were now leaders in this Assembly must have totally distrusted the court and the privileged orders, must have strangely overestimated the power of their opponents, must have thought it their duty, not only to make a revolution, but their policy to take the whole management of it instantly into their own hands, lest nothing should be done for the country—to avail themselves of their popularity as soon as possible, and at once; to keep alive their popularity, and to paralyze all opposition by the energy or rather violence of their proceedings. And the welfare of their country, the noble objects which they meant to accomplish, must have justified in their own minds the irregular means they were using.

Such must be the explanation of their conduct, but, as I have already ventured to say, it is not, I think, their defence.

To return to the history.

The Tiers Etat having now, so early as the 17th of June, voted themselves the National Assembly, and assumed, or so nearly assumed, the sovereign power of the state, it was high time for some measure on the part of the king. Even Necker himself must have been ill at ease. It never could have been his intention or his wish (whatever might be his popular feelings) that the monarchy should be endangered, or all the power of the state be merged into that of the Tiers Etat. It was therefore resolved that the king should hold a sitting on the 23rd.

This sitting of the 23rd is the next great step in the Revolution. You must observe it well. You are in this sitting to see the terms offered by the king and the court to the popular party. But some unhappy fatality seems to have overruled the destinies of this great kingdom; not only to have made her patriots intemperate, but her ministers or the court thoughtless and imprudent to a degree exceeding all belief; and many circumstances left no fair chance for this reasonable measure, this royal sitting of the 23rd.   The hall in which the Commons assembled was the place, on account of its size, where the king had met and harangued the States.   Workmen were therefore sent in to erect a throne; a party of guards took possession of the place for the king; the royal sitting was formally proclaimed, (through the streets of Versailles, indeed,) by the heralds, but unfortunately no proper notice had been given, no formal communication made, to the Assembly or the president, of what was intended; and M. Bailly, the president, with other members of the Commons, when they repaired, as of course, to hold their sitting in their own hall, were repulsed without ceremony from their own door.

The Commons very naturally conceived, not that terms were to be offered to them, but that an immediate dissolution was in fact intended: they must have been conscious that their own proceedings had been irregular and violent, and they must reasonably have expected some violent measure in return from the king and the court; they therefore hurried away, through a severe storm of rain, to a tennis-court, where, with proper spirit and firmness, though in something of a theatric manner, they bound themselves with a solemn oath never to part until the constitution was completed; even on this occasion, it must be confessed by the nature of their oath, plainly showing the unlimited extent of their views.   They seemed to proclaim that France had no constitution, and that they were determined to create one, and to proceed to lengths which had certainly not been in the contemplation of the king when he called them together, nor of those whom they represented.   Still, as they were now at issue with the court (whether by their own fault or not, it was in vain to inquire), and all seemed lost if they ceased to exist, no other expedient was left them but some resolution of this kind: some vote or decree that should intimate that they were superior to fear, and would not desert what had become the cause of their country.   M. Mounier, one of the most virtuous men in the Assembly, was the proposer and framer of the oath; but it was his measure to prevent an adjournment to Paris and more violent proceedings.   All these were circumstances that very much indisposed them to listen to the king with any proper temper or moderation when he addressed them, a few days after, at the royal sitting, and brought forward his intended measure.

The next day, immediately after this day of the tennis-court, was signalized by a most important event, the union of a body of the clergy with the Tiers Etat. The nobility had not yet given way. It does not appear very intelligible why the clergy should have fixed upon this particular moment for their junction, when the king was evidently at issue with the Tiers Etat, and when the royal sitting was expected in two days. It was probably from the feeling excited by the scene in the tennis-court and a measure of sympathy. They were received with fraternal embraces, and loaded with praises as a band of patriots who had come in a moment of imminent danger to save their country.

How far the Assembly afterwards remembered, with proper gratitude, the service that was now rendered them by the clergy, you will have occasion in due time to observe.

This union of the clergy naturally made the Tiers Etat more confident that they should, ere long, be joined by the nobility; and this persuasion could not but tend to make them less ready to receive the offers of the king, though it should have made them more so. Again, besides the shutting up of their hall, to which we have alluded, other marks of neglect were shown to the Tiers Etat; and on the day of the Royal sitting, they were kept waiting till the other two orders had arranged themselves in their proper places—waiting in the rain with little shelter, while they not only saw the ostentatious procession of the court, the embroidered heralds, and an unusual display of the pompous carriages and gaudy livery of the noblesse, but military detachments patrolling the streets of Versailles, and even posted around the very hall of the Assembly, where they were at last admitted, apparently to receive their orders.

All these unhappy circumstances are for ever to be deplored, and those by whom they might or ought to have been prevented (the king could have nothing to say to them), are never to be forgiven. For this measure of the sitting of the 23rd you will see fail, and, as I conceive, most fatally for France. Men will be men. Allowance must be made for the irritations to which the members of the Tiers Etat were thus exposed.

In the course of this lecture, my humble censure, such as it is, must fall on the members of the Constituent Assembly; but the student must never suppose me insensible to the merit of all expressions of patriotism, if they be but sincere—of all generous exertions in the cause of civil liberty, if they be but well-meant —of all resistance to unworthy indignities and to oppression, if but honest. It is my province, however, to draw lessons from history—to make patriotism prudent, a love of civil liberty wise, and a resistance to authority, of whatever kind, careful, circumspect, and fitted for the nature of man and of society.

The royal sitting was held on the 23rd. The king ascended the throne, and produced the plan of a new constitution or system of government; it was read to the assembled orders, and was a piece of considerable length. You must consider it with great attention, for it is a most important document in the history of the Revolution.

It was, on the whole, a great outline of a system of government; it was, in short, an offer from the king and court to the patriots—the extent of the concessions that could be admitted by the retainers of the old opinions to the patrons of the new.

The question, therefore, is, what should the patriots have done? To me it appears that this was an offer with which the patriots should have instantly closed.

Whatever objections, deficiencies, or imperfections were to be found in the system proposed, there were none that might not hereafter have been provided for. The main points were secured, and the dictatorial style which was too often assumed by the king might have been overlooked, as the ancient form of expression, and pardoned, from a spirit of forbearance and conciliation, for the sake of the peace of the community, and the great advantages that were evidently on the point of being for ever established.

It was observed, however, that M. Necker was not in his place. The fact was, that the plan had been originally drawn up by that minister, but having been altered, and materially altered, and made, in his judgment, less fitted for its purpose, he had thought it improper to sanction it by his presence. This was the most unfortunate circumstance of all. He was very popular at the time, and no plan was likely to succeed with the Assembly, or rather with the public, which he did not countenance; and it was a grievous mistake on the part of the court not to have taken his advice in the perilous situation in which they stood,—at least not to have come to some understanding on the conduct which he meant to pursue. Better to have given up their measure, than left him to remain in visible opposition to them.

It is probable that no system of government founded essentially on old opinions would have satisfied the majority of the Assembly, who were heated with the new opinions, and who longed for some great experiment for what they believed the happiness of France and of mankind. Still it must be remembered that Mirabeau was in the Assembly. He never seems to have meant to destroy the monarchy; a limited monarchy and a representative Assembly seems to have been his notion of civil liberty.

It is possible that great assistance might have been derived from him, if Necker's original plan had been produced, and if Mirabeau had been in time consulted and propitiated, as he might have been. All the wise and moderate patriots of the Revolution, Mounier and others, were then in the Assembly, and still in possession of the public favour, and might have been consulted and conciliated also; but there was no prudence in the court, nor attention to their situation, and everything turned out unfortunately, as has always been the case when the civil liberties of this great country were at issue. In England it has often been the reverse. Setting out from nearly the same beginnings, I have repeatedly had to observe to you how different were the points at which the constitutions of the two kingdoms from time to time arrived.

I consider this royal sitting of the 23rd of June as so important an event in the history of the French Revolution, that I particularly wish to direct your attention to it, and must exhibit it to you a little more distinctly.

M. Necker has dedicated his fourth section of his first volume of the French Revolution to the consideration of it. He explains the notions which he himself had formed of the situation of the monarchy and the kingdom, and nothing can appear more reasonable.

His object was to assert and support, as much as possible, the rights and consequence of the monarch, which he saw were visibly and really sinking fast; he therefore drew up a declaration for the king to produce at the royal sitting, and with the ministers that acted in concert with him and the king in council, his success had been complete; in fact, the council was just on the point of breaking up, every thing settled and agreed to, when an officer came to the king, and having whispered him, the king immediately got up, and desiring the ministers to await his return, left them sitting, and went out.

" This can only be a message from the queen," said M. de

Montmorin to Necker; " the princes of the blood have got her to interfere, and persuade the king to adjourn his decision."

So it turned out. The king, after being absent half an hour, returned, and, in spite of every consideration that could be suggested to him, adjourned the debate to the next council. It was not held till two days after, and two princes of the blood and four magistrates were added, new to the subject, which had now to be discussed entirely afresh.

It was soon evident to Necker that his original measure was not to be carried. He was desired to confer confidentially with some of the new counsellors. He made what concessions he could, as he thought, with effect; but no : the whole plan was in the event, as he thought, so materially changed, as to be no longer one which he could intimate his approval of by personally appearing at the sitting. He resisted to the utmost, protested against the whole measure, and announced his intention of resigning. His brother ministers, even M. de Montmorin, seem to have agreed with him.

He does not give the original declaration as he had intended it to stand; the MS. was burnt during the subsequent terrors of the Revolution; and though he points out some of the alterations that were made by the court, he might, on this part of the subject, have entered more into detail, with some advantage to his reader and to his own character, as he was accused by the court of unreasonable pertinacity, of perversely, of factiously absenting himself from the sitting, and as it was his object to show that all such accusations were unfeeling and unjust. But, fortunately, in the appendix to Bertrand de Moleville's Memoir, the declaration and the articles are given.

B. de Moleville is very loud and decided in his censures of the conduct of Necker, and you will find no difficulty in judging of the plan as Necker originally proposed it, and as it was subsequently altered and read by the king. I must repeat to you, that this is quite a crisis in the history of the Revolution.

You will see, I think, that it was a plan to which, even as it was at last left to stand, the Tiers Etat should have acceded ; but that it was altered so essentially that Necker had a right to say it was no longer his measure, and that he would not be responsible for it as minister of the king. Still, you will see, I think, that it was a plan to which the patriots should have acceded. It was essentially altered, for the very first article in the declaration, as really delivered by the king, annulled the decree of the Tiers Etat by which they voted themselves the National

Assembly, with all the resolutions that followed, as illegal and unconstitutional. Necker had thought it best (as it certainly was) to be silent, and to declare nothing of the kind ; and it was but too evident (to all but the court) that the king had no longer the power to control the Assembly in any manner like this.

Necker observes that the king in his own proposed declaration, had *enjoined* the *three* orders to unite in common when deliberating on affairs of a common interest ; that in the *altered* declaration, the first *two* orders only were addressed, and only *exhorted*, not enjoined. And again, that at the end of the declaration, the three orders very unwisely, and, as it turned out, very fatally, were ordered to separate, and to repair to their own halls to renew their sittings the next day.

Necker, in his plan, had made the king reserve to himself the power of *sanctioning* any future scheme of the States General with respect to their future constitution, declaring, however, that the Assembly must be composed of at least two chambers ; but in the altered plan, the king was made to reserve to himself the adjustment of the future form that was to be given to the States General.

The alterations were evidently all on the side of the crown, all tending to make the whole measure less likely to succeed with the Tiers Etat. And as Necker contends, and very justly, that he had ventured upon certain articles in favour of the crown (he mentions those which were sufficiently important and unpopular), the alterations must be considered as on the whole very injudicious, and such as Necker could not possibly admit.

Now all these are points which deserve the attention of the student. Whatever shows the wisdom of Necker shows the folly of the court, and becoming one of the reasons why the Revolution did *not* succeed, becomes in fact one of the lessons of history.

For the student must not forget, that it was a great calamity to mankind that the Revolution did not succeed—that the cause of liberty, the noblest of all causes, was thus on the whole lost.

But it was lost, I conceive, because the Tiers Etat did not on this occasion consent to close with the king, and proceed on the terms and in the spirit of the declaration, to the settlement of the kingdom.

The points of the subject are, then, first, that the court most improperly and unpardonably altered the declaration, and made it more irritating to the Tiers Etat than M. Necker had thought wise ; more than this, that they had made it of such a nature that he thought it could not succeed with them, and that he, therefore, declined appearing as the author of it on the day of the royal sitting.

2ndly. That though this might be the case, still there were left in the measure such common grounds for the king and the Assembly to have stood upon, that the leaders of the popular party should have received the measure in a spirit of kindness and conciliation, and proceeded upon it immediately, to the establishment of proper provisions for the present and future happiness of their country, the danger to the state being so very great on every other supposition.

This they did not. The most dreadful consequences ensued, and were sure to ensue, fatal to the monarch, to France, to the great experiment in the cause of liberty which they were themselves attempting to make, and therefore very injurious to the best interests of Europe and of mankind, perhaps for ages.

This last point as well as the first you will consider. Whatever caused or contributed to the event, is a lesson of history.

Observe what were some of the articles of the king's declaration, as they were finally suffered to stand by the queen and her advisers. I mention them as reasons which should have induced the patriots to have acceded to the declaration. No new tax was to be levied, no old one prolonged beyond the time fixed by the laws, without the consent of the representatives of the nation. Such as existed were only to remain in force till the next meeting of the States. Consider how much was contained in these concessions. When the right of the purse was thus yielded up and a new meeting of the States was thus secured, what further concession was necessary? Every further improvement and security would gradually have been obtained, as in England, by this power of the purse.

No new loans were to be made without the consent of the States General, with a particular exception, reasonable in itself, which was mentioned.

The public finances, the revenues, the expenses were all to be submitted to the examination of the States. Every concession in matters of this nature was offered.

The clergy and the nobility were to be sanctioned by the king in that renunciation of their pecuniary privileges which they had already promised. The taille was to be abolished.

Every thing that could be said, according to the existing notions of France and the real difficulty of the case, really *was* said, on the subject of *lettres de cachet.*

A very reasonable declaration was made on the delicate subject of the liberty of the press.

Provincial assemblies were promised—assemblies that, apparently, would have created a respectable magistracy throughout the kingdom.

Upon a variety of other articles, some of great importance,—the king's demesnes, for instance, the internal custom-houses, the tax on salt, &c. &c.—nothing could be more reasonable and benevolent than the articles of the declaration.

The corvées, the capitinaries, were to be abolished.

The value of these articles of the declaration will be seen by the student, if he will look into one of the chapters in Young's Tour in France; a work, several parts of which will be found entertaining, instructive, and very much to our purpose, the concluding chapters more especially.

The declaration, no doubt, laid down the sacred nature of all property, tithes and feudal rents included.

The king also willed that the ancient distinction of the three orders should be preserved entire, as essentially connected with the constitution, and declared null the deliberations taken by the Deputies of the Third Estate on the 17th of the month, as well as all others that might have followed it, as illegal and unconstitutional.

This was, you are aware, the decree of the Tiers Etat voting themselves the National Assembly, assuming the right of taxation, and in fact the sovereign power. Upon these acts of usurpation Necker had thought it best to say nothing. He seems rather to have hoped hereafter, by a proper adjustment of the powers of the crown and the Assembly, to render them null and void in effect, avoiding, in the meantime, a subject of certain controversy and irritation; but this was a wisdom which the court could not reach.

The fifteenth article was unhappily but of too much importance. " A proper regard to good order," says the article, " to decency, to the very freedom of the Assembly, all require that his majesty should prohibit, as he expressly does, that any persons, except the members of the three orders composing the States General, should be present at their deliberations, whether held in common or in their separate houses."

The student will have abundant occasion hereafter to remark the influence of the galleries on the events of the Revolution. It had been already shown but too strongly when this article appeared.

The galleries, however, were the means which the Tiers Etat made use of to awe and control the court, and most unfortunately the popular leaders could neither do with them nor without them.

This was certainly, during these more early periods of the Revolution, the great difficulty. The difficulty was not properly disposed of by this article of the declaration, but it was clear that the *interference* of the galleries was, at all events, to be prevented, if not their presence.

The concluding article was, that having called together the States to effect, in concert with him, the great objects of public utility, he was obliged to say expressly that he reserved to himself the army, the police, the military power, such as it had always been exercised and enjoyed by the monarchs of France.

He had before, in the first part of the declaration, observed, that he wished to lay before the states the different benefits "that he intended to concede to his people; that he wished not to circumscribe their zeal within any limits which he might trace out; that he should adopt with pleasure any views of the public advantage which should be pointed out to him by the States; that he might say, he thought, without flattering himself, that never had monarch done more for any nation, but that no nation had ever better deserved it from a monarch, than the French nation; that he had no fear of saying this, but that they who, by exaggerated pretensions, by unseasonable difficulties, still retarded the effect of his benevolent intentions, were no longer worthy the name of Frenchmen."

These were his expressions in the opening of his declaration, and he ended the whole by saying—

" You now see the result of my wishes and my views; they are agreeable to the lively anxiety I feel to effect the public good; and if, by a fatality, which is the furthest from my expectations, you abandon me in so noble an enterprise, I will myself accomplish the welfare of my people—I will consider myself as their true representative; and, knowing as I do the instructions you have received, and the conformity that exists between the wishes of the nation and my own intentions, I shall derive every confidence that is the necessary result of such a harmony between us, and I shall proceed forward to effect an end so desirable with all the courage and firmness by which I ought to be inspired.

" You will consider that none of your projects or dispositions can have the force of law without my special approbation. It is thus that I am the natural guarantee of your respective rights.

" All orders of the state may repose upon my equitable impartiality; any distrust on your part would be to me the highest injustice. It is I who have hitherto been doing everything for the welfare of my people, and it is very rare that the only ambition of a sovereign has been, to obtain from his subjects a disposition in them to receive his benefits."

It was in this sort of dignified, and on the whole not unbecoming, though somewhat impolitic manner, all circumstances considered, that the monarch of the French people concluded the declaration of his sentiments, views, and intentions, on this great occasion.   It would have been happy for themselves, and for the world, if the National Assembly had been in a temper sufficiently composed, and of a wisdom sufficiently prospective and steady, to have borne this representation of the hitherto acknowledged rights and natural expectations of their monarch; if they had made due allowance for what they might have supposed the prejudices of his education and the temptations of his situation; and if at all events they had taken care to provide for the public peace, by proceeding on a system of conciliation, without which conciliation they with their galleries, and the court with its army, were not likely to do much for the cause of liberty, in any rational sense of the word, then or eventually.

But all such modest expectations, such moderate views, that may even now, to many friends of the liberties of mankind, appear ill suited to the occasion, were considered, by the leaders of the popular party at the time, as totally unworthy, or rather were never considered at all.

Some years after I had written what you have now heard, I had the satisfaction of finding that the same view of the case was taken, even at the time, by Mr. Jefferson, who was then the American ambassador, and who says in his Memoirs, that he remonstrated with the French patriots, and advised them by all means to close with the proposals of the court.

The measure of the royal sitting totally failed; the king's address was received with a cold and ominous silence; the concessions not duly estimated; the situation of the king not considered; the acknowledged rights of the sovereign overlooked; and the usual tone and language of all addresses from the throne totally forgotten.   Very different, indeed, are the feelings and opinions with which we now read this part of the history, from the feelings and opinions which then animated the great patriotic leaders, and indeed the more intelligent men, not only of France but of Europe.   On this last point you may refer to the violent notice taken of this royal sitting in the Vindiciæ Gallicæ; the author, the late Sir James Mackintosh, who then meant to be, what he has ever since been, an enlightened upholder of the rights and happiness of his fellow creatures.

To us who live at the present period, however sincerely we may feel the love of civil liberty, the difficulty of procuring it by violence and revolution is sufficiently apparent; the sort of hope and confidence with which we speak on such subjects is very different from what it was, on the breaking out of the French Revolution. The value of all concessions from power, of all steps to improvement, of all progressive advances to amelioration, are by this time duly estimated (I speak of men of sense and experience). We no longer talk of organizing a community afresh, of regenerating a kingdom, of giving a constitution to a great people, with all the ease and dispatch which at the breaking out of the French Revolution was thought possible. The wisest men and the best, at that period were, no doubt, dazzled and made confident by the delusive and irrelevant example of America; and nothing was thought of but the original rights of the people, the imperfections of society as it then existed, and the dignity and the happines to which a people might be exalted; exalted by no more difficult process, it was understood, than their own wishes. It was a favourite maxim, that a people had only to will to be free and to be so. Doctrines like these may be so modified and veiled as to be reducible to salutary practice; they may be, in secret, the principle of vitality to the free constitution of a great people; but it was a little too much to expect that they should be the maxims which should prompt the feelings and colour the language of a monarch of France, when now only for the *first time* addressing the States General of his kingdom.

This is the unreasonableness, this is the intolerance for all old opinions, that distinguished, at that time, the holders of the new. Bristling with their logic, and confident in the superiority of their reason, everything, they thought (for they were generally young men), might be safely intrusted to the prevalence of reason among mankind; and as this will ever be the case on all such occasions, and with all such men who are also on such occasions the most effective part of the community, this becomes one of the lessons of history.

Again, and on the contrary side of the question, little less intolerance of the *new* opinions, it must be observed, was felt by the court and the holders of the old opinions; either now or at any subsequent period; "all or nothing" was always their maxim, and this is *also* the lesson of this history. But on the present occasion, on the occasion of this royal sitting, it should be considered, that concessions many and important had been

made; they afforded a sufficient ground on which to have proceeded to the settlement of the kingdom, and the main blame
must rest with the Tiers Etat, after deducting the blame that
rests with the court—for great blame certainly does rest with
the court; and out of common justice to the leaders of the Constituent Assembly it must be remembered: on occasions of this
kind, imprudence is fault.

You must observe then, that the concessions made by the
king, considered with reference to the state of the government
de facto for some centuries past, were, no doubt, very great, and
as such, should have been felt and acknowledged, and acted
upon; but whether they were so, with reference to the state of
opinion and the public expectations *at the time,* is more doubtful.
The royal prerogative was now so injured in general estimation,
and the many experiments made with a view of avoiding the
present necessity had been so unsuccessful, and had so damaged
the government, that it was hardly considered to be in a situation to propose terms, still less to determine the extent of the
concessions to be made.   There was no longer a disposition to
accept a constitution as a boon.   The popular writers all agree
in representing this measure as one of the most doubtful expediency; and the circumstances by which it was attended, as
well as the declaration of the king respecting the voting of the
orders separately, and the rights of the privileged orders, completed its unpopularity.   Until this sitting of the 23rd of June,
Mirabeau seems to have hesitated, and to have kept his eye
upon the court.   He had been against the measure of the Tiers
Etat constituting itself a National Assembly, but from the
moment of the sitting of the 23rd, from the moment that he
saw the folly of the court, he seems to have thought there was
no chance for them, and threw himself headlong into popular
measures.   I apprehend that Mounier and other moderate men
felt their influence decline from this period, and that a most unfortunate weight was thus thrown into the scale of the violent
party, headed by Sieyes, Chapelier, Target, and others.   Unless
Necker could have obtained the concurrence of the moderate men,
the measure of a royal sitting should never have been resorted to.
And again, who could conceive it possible, that the king should
have been advised by any one, or should have himself consented
to come down to an Assembly, already exasperated and strong
in popular opinion, with a scheme that had not been discussed
with some of the principal leaders among them?   Who could
dream at that time of keeping the three orders separate, merely

by a royal direction; the clergy, in fact, gone over, and the noblesse divided? What can we say of a king who could turn away from Necker, the only person near him capable of forming an estimate of all the circumstances by which he was surrounded, and who could even suffer the violent people of his court so to alter the minister's measure, that the minister could not even appear in his place lest he should seem to approve it? Surely it must be allowed, that a king and a government so unmindful of the temper and circumstances of the time, and of all the plain dictates of the most obvious common sense that belonged to the case, could not possibly avoid their ruin, and by many will be thought even to have deserved it. But it is ever thus: a court and its more immediate supporters can never see either wisdom or virtue in the feelings and opinions of moderate men, and a king but too naturally listens to those who echo his own sentiments. Such conduct, however, is not the lesson of this Revolution.

I turn with pain to mention to you in a few words the scene that immediately followed the delivery of the king's declaration. The preparatory circumstances of this royal sitting had been such, that the popular leaders and the public had been induced to think that a dissolution of the National Assembly by force was intended by the court. The king had himself intimated in his speech, that if they would not concur with him in his wishes and intentions, he would himself attempt to effect the happiness of France alone.

This seemed, no doubt, a threat of dissolution; and troops and artillery had been coming up in a very unusual and therefore alarming manner; four thousand guards were under arms all the day of the session, and seven or eight regiments were assembled in the neighbourhood of Versailles.

The speech of the king had been heard with gloomy silence, and it ended, most unfortunately, with ordering the three orders to separate, and to repair to their appropriate chambers; there, the next day, to resume their sittings. But this was apparently to carry into practice that part (the most offensive) of the declaration of the king, by which he had just annulled the decree of the Tiers Etat, constituting themselves the National Assembly.

It was a very unskilful conclusion of the speech, unless the strongest measures were, if necessary, resolved upon.

The king left the hall; almost all the bishops, some priests, and the greater part of the nobility, retired in obedience to his commands.

The rest of the deputies remained in their places, apparently at a loss what part to take. According to Bertrand de Moleville, all might have been well, though this is totally improbable, and the means of conciliation announced by his majesty accepted, when Mirabeau arose and in an instant changed the disposition of the Assembly by a speech to which I will just allude for a moment, where the new opinions, as usual, appear, and more particularly the leading notion which so inflamed all France and Europe at the time, "that the States were to make immediately a new constitution for France." "I confess," said Mirabeau, "that what you have just heard might be for the welfare of the country, if the gifts of despotism were not always dangerous. Why this dictatorial language, this train of arms, this violation of the National Temple, to command you to be happy? Who gives you the command? Your vicegerent. Who makes imperious laws for you? Your vicegerent! Your vicegerent! he who should receive them from you; from us, gentlemen, who are invested with a political and inviolable supremacy; from us, to whom alone twenty-five millions of men are looking for certain happiness, as it must be granted, given and received by all. But the freedom of your debates is fettered; a military force encircles the States. Where are the enemies of the nation? Is Catiline at our gates? I insist that, arming yourselves with your dignity and legislative authority, you recollect the religious force of your oath, an oath that does not suffer you to separate until you have established the constitution."

This harangue is represented by Bertrand de Moleville as having had great effect on the deputies; they were warmed and irritated as if the king had really dissolved the Assembly. He certainly had endeavoured to reduce the National Assembly to its former situation and office, as a part only of a whole, as the Tiers Etat only, of the States General, but not more. The Assembly, however, did not retire; the master of the ceremonies, therefore, advanced into the middle of the hall, and observed to them, "that they had heard the king's intentions."

"Yes, sir," said Mirabeau, "we have heard the intentions of the king; and you who cannot be his agent at the States General, you who have here neither seat, nor voice, nor a right to speak, are not the person to remind us of his speech. Go tell your master that we are here by the power of the people, and that nothing but the power of the bayonet shall expel us."

"Yes, yes," said a great number of the deputies, "nothing but force can drive us hence; the Assembly are determined."

The Marquis de Brezé appeared to refer to the president, who told him that " the Assembly resolved yesterday that they would continue to sit after the royal session, and that he could make no change in that resolution—that it must be discussed by the Assembly."

" Am I to carry that answer to the king ?" said the marquis. " Yes, sir," replied the president.   The marquis departed.

The Assembly, therefore, and the king, were now in a state of direct opposition.

The king had proposed a limited and modified monarchy built upon the ancient system.

The Assembly had turned away from his declaration and resisted his commands ; they had renewed their name of National Assembly, and they had clearly shown that they meant to persist in the exercise of the sovereignty they had assumed; their support, too, it was clear, they meant to be the public ; under this term by no means excluding the populace, to whom their galleries were now thrown open.

LECTURE X.

FOURTEENTH OF JULY.   THE BASTILE.

It was now but too clearly shown, that no composition could be made between the old opinions and the new.

The Tiers Etat had not even entertained the question ; they had not even received or noticed the proposals of the king : no doubt he had resisted their assumption of power, and in a manner most unskilful ; but they had made no representation ; they had offered no address nor remonstrance complaining of any measure or any conduct of his to which they objected ; they had shown no disposition to come to any terms.   The country, it seems, was to be regenerated ; the views *he* had taken were inconsistent with *theirs* ; *his* ideas of the prosperity of France not the same ; nor his notions of the claims of the monarch or the duties of the subject.

The king and the court, more especially the king, were now, therefore, thrown into a most perplexing situation ; to do nothing, was to surrender themselves to the Assembly ; and yet to take any effective measure that led not to violence and bloodshed, was, to all appearance, impossible.   The humanity of the king shrunk from every expedient that was to be supported by military execution; while to the favourers of the old opinions, no option but the dissolution of the Assembly appeared to remain.

This seems to have been thought by Bertrand de Moleville the only measure left. He declares it to be so in his Annals, and describes the manner in which he would have had it carried into effect.

Properly softened down, and more accommodated to the difficult circumstances of the case than Moleville thought necessary, it was, perhaps, one of the expedients, however doubtful, which the king might now have adopted.

For instance, he might have dissolved the existing States General, calling, at the same time, another meeting of them; remarking upon the assumption of the sovereign power by the present Assembly, and publishing the declarations he had made, and the scheme of government he had proposed on the sitting of the 23rd; promising to adhere to it, and to listen to any further proposals for the benefit of the community.

After some manner of this kind he might have justified his measure, and called upon all good Frenchmen to come forward in his support.

No doubt the difficulty was, the opposition that would have been made by the more violent leaders of the Assembly and their partisans out of doors; and the consideration, that new Assemblies, returned on occasions like this, are in general even more refractory than those dissolved.

Still it seems to have been one of the measures left. The provinces were not as yet raised to that state of irritation and enthusiasm, in which were, at this period, Versailles and the metropolis. The clergy and the nobility had not as yet stood in any direct opposition to the crown, and they, and all men capable of sober thinking, at the time, *might* have seen, I am far from saying that they really *did* see, but they might have seen, on comparing the decrees of the Tiers Etat with the declarations of the king, that the monarchy was in the greatest danger, and that the peace of the kingdom was not likely to be long maintained, unless the parties at issue were brought to some immediate agreement; and, on the whole, unless the crown was supported.

Thus far, at least, the conclusions of every thinking man might have been expected, might have been fairly hoped by the king and his advisers, to have gone along with the court; and the experiment properly introduced, explained, and limited, would, on the whole, have been a reasonable one, at least, a possible one.

What was attempted by the king, however, though in a spirit

of conciliation, was an experiment of a directly opposite nature ;
the only other alternative.   For instance, a large body of the
clergy, one hundred and forty-nine (making up now a majority
of the whole), and two or three of the nobility, had joined the
Tiers Etat in the church of St. Louis, even before the sitting of
the 23rd.

But the remaining body of the clergy were pretty equally
divided, though on the 24th, half even of the remainder joined
the Assembly ; the nobility were more firm and attached to what
they thought the interests of their order and the safety of the
monarchy ; forty-four members, indeed, out of three hundred,
the Duke of Orleans at their head (but some of them men of the
first estimation for talents and virtue), joined on the 25th, but
the main body of the nobility appeared inflexible.

What, however, they did, was to wait upon the king, and
after expressing themselves in the most dutiful manner to him
in every respect, particularly with regard to his late declaration
on the 23rd, to pray him to convene the nobility of the bailiwicks, that they might receive fresh instructions from their
constituents.

The king, therefore, now interfered for the sake of the peace
of the community.   He desired the Duke of Luxembourg to tell
the nobility, that he entreated them to join the other two orders ;
if that was not enough, that he commanded them to do it, as
their king ; that it was his will.

Afterwards he wrote letters to his " loyal nobility," and to
"his faithful clergy," urging them to join the other orders without delay, to accelerate the accomplishment of his paternal intentions, making their compliance a sort of personal favour.

But still the order of the nobility was divided ; more than
eighty of them thought the union of the three orders would be
fatal to the king and to the state, and they seem only at last to
have acquiesced from an apprehension that the life of the king
might be endangered by their longer resistance.

Thus was, at length, effected the complete triumph of the
patriotic leaders.

The nobility and clergy were all merged in the Tiers Etat ;
the title of National Assembly, the assumption of sovereign power
had been resisted by the king and the privileged orders in vain ;
and if, indeed, it was necessary for the future prosperity and
the civil and religious liberties of France, that the new opinions should entirely prevail, and some great experiment be made
to exemplify and establish them, then must the more distin-

guished members of the Tiers Etat be considered as having deserved well of their country, and of mankind, by the boldness,
the perseverance, and the fortitude with which they had obtained their victory. But it is *only*, I conceive, on this supposition, and whether this supposition ought or ought not to be
admitted, *this necessity of the entire establishment of the new opinions to the exclusion of the old*, seems to be one of the leading
questions on which the student will be called to exercise his
judgment, and to give or withhold his praise accordingly. My
own opinion, such as it is, that no such necessity existed, you
have already received.

But, with whatever hesitation the student may or may not
form his own, he can surely have no difficulty in determining,
with regard to another point, that the conduct of the court during
all this period was most unskilful, and entirely to be lamented.

In times of difficulty, the governing powers are always, as on
this occasion, too late with their concessions.

The wishes and intentions of the king in favour of the people,
as seen in the declaration of the 23rd of June, should have been
produced long before; before the Tiers Etat had committed
themselves, before they had voted themselves the National Assembly, taken the oath in the Tennis Court, and even before they
had raised the question of voting by orders or by head.

Neither the king nor his secret advisers can be excused for
not showing that timely wisdom, or at least that reasonable decision, which provides for events, and which may, therefore, be
said, to a certain degree, to control them; above all, which
makes concessions at the proper moment, when they can be
offered with dignity and received with gratitude.

We may now, I think, consider ourselves as having arrived at
a very particular epoch in the history of this Revolution. We
may now, I think, pause, and retrace, in some general manner,
the scenes through which we have passed. Such occasional re-
views, I conceive, to be useful; and a work occurs to me, which
will enable us to do this, and even more; it is the Journal of
Arthur Young. He travelled over France as a speculative farmer,
in the important years of 1787 and 1789; but being very active
and intelligent, he could not fail to be struck with the political
situation of this great kingdom.

The great instruction of history, as I have often observed to
you, lies in the comparison of existing notions with subsequent
events; this instruction we may here derive, while, at the same

time, we may revive the memory of the leading facts of the history, and the conclusions to which they gave rise.

I shall produce for you then some extracts from this book, and you may compare what occurred to him at the moment, with the events that afterwards took place; and this is to be your instruction.

Some years afterwards, Arthur Young became what was termed a great alarmist; he did not succeed in his farming, was not affluent, and was at last considered as no very great friend to liberty.

I know not with what reason: it is sufficient for me to say, that he certainly was, when he wrote the work to which I shall now refer. Indeed, there is one of his notes, which shows him to have been very violent and revolutionary in the views which he sometimes took, at least at this period, on political subjects. He was, indeed, a critic, and a sort of discerner of mistakes and faults by profession. The note I allude to would not be unfitted for one of our demagogues, addressing from a stage the populace of one of our manufacturing towns in some unhappy season of their distress; it is in p. 556 of his first quarto volume of his Tour to France. He is insisting, that experiment is as necessary a means of knowledge in relation to government, as in agriculture or in any other branch of natural philosophy; and he concludes thus :—" The British government has been experimented, with what result? Let a debt of two hundred and forty millions, let severe wars, let Bengal and Gibraltar, let thirty millions sterling of national burdens, taxes, rates, tithes, and monopolies, let these answer."

To refer, therefore, to his work, as coming from one sufficiently inclined to popular feelings at the time he wrote, in the year 1787, two years before the Revolution. He speaks thus :——

" One opinion pervaded the whole company, that they are on the eve of some great revolution in the government; that every thing points to it : the confusion in the finances great; with a *deficit* impossible to provide for without the States General of the kingdom, yet no ideas formed of what would be the consequence of their meeting : no minister existing, or to be looked to, in or out of power, with such decisive talents as to promise any other remedy, than palliative ones : a prince on the throne, with excellent dispositions, but without the resources of a mind that could govern in such a moment; without ministers; a court buried in pleasure and dissipation, and adding to the distress, instead of endeavouring to be placed in a more independent situation : a great ferment amongst all ranks of men, who are eager for some change, without knowing what to look to, or to hope for : and a strong leaven of liberty, increasing every hour since the American Revolution ; these, altogether, form a combination of circumstances, that promise, ere long, to ferment into motion, if some master-hand, of very superior talents, and inflexible courage, is not found at the helm to guide events, instead of being driven by them. It is very remarkable, that such conversation never occurs, but a bankruptcy is a topic : the curious question on which is, *would a bankruptcy occasion a civil war, and a total overthrow of the government ?* The answers that I have received to this question, appear to be just : such a measure, conducted by a man of abilities, vigour, and firmness, would certainly not occasion either one or the other. But the same measure, attempted by a man of a different character, might possibly do both. All agree, that the States of the kingdom cannot assemble without more liberty being the consequence ; but I meet with so few men that have any just ideas of freedom, that I question much the species of this new liberty that is to arise. They know not how to value the privileges of the people ; as to the nobility and the clergy, if a revolution added any thing to their scale, I think it would do more mischief than good."

This was in 1787. You will now observe in what manner Arthur Young writes from Paris, on June 9th, 1789 ; a most critical month : the royal sitting, you may remember, was on the 23rd.

" The business going forward at present in the pamphlet shops of Paris is incredible. I went to the Palais Royal to see what new things were published, and to procure a catalogue of all. Every hour produces something new. Thirteen came out to-day, sixteen yesterday, and ninety-two last week. We think sometimes that Debrett's or Stockdale's shops in London are crowded, but they are mere deserts compared to Desein's, and some others here, in which one can scarcely squeeze from the door to the counter. The price of printing two years ago was from 27 liv. to 30 liv. per sheet, but now it is from 60 liv. to 80 liv. This spirit of reading political tracts, they say, spreads into the provinces, so that all the presses of France are equally employed. Nineteen-twentieths of these productions are in favour of liberty, and commonly violent against the clergy and nobility ; I have to-day bespoken many of this description, that have reputation ; but inquiring for such as had appeared on the other side of the question, to my astonishment I find there are but two or three that have merit enough to be known. Is it not wonderful, that while the press teems with the most levelling and even seditious principles, that if put into execution would overturn the monarchy, nothing in reply appears, not the least step is taken by the court to restrain this extreme licentiousness of publication? It is easy to conceive the spirit that must thus be raised among the people. But the coffee-houses in the Palais Royal present yet more singular and astonishing spectacles; they are not only crowded within, but other expectant crowds are at the doors and windows, listening *à gorge déployée* to certain orators, who from chairs or tables harangue each his little audience : the eagerness with which they are heard, and the thunder of applause they receive for every sentiment of more than common hardiness or violence against the present government, cannot easily be imagined. I am all amazement at the ministry permitting such nests and hotbeds of sedition and revolt, which disseminate amongst the people, every hour, principles that by and by must be opposed with vigour, and therefore it seems little short of madness to allow the propagation at present."

This is but a description, as you will see, drawn from the life, of what is meant by the progress of new opinions ; of the public opinion having taken a turn against the government of the country; of the current setting strong and furiously : a very fit subject of consternation in any unhappy country to all who mean well.

Again, on June the 11th, he writes thus :—" In these most interesting discussions, I find a general ignorance of the principles of government; a strange and unaccountable appeal, on one side, to ideal and visionary rights of nature ; and on the other, no settled plan that shall give security to the people for being in future in a much better situation than hitherto ; a security absolutely necessary. But the nobility, with the principles of great lords, that I converse with, are most disgustingly tenacious of all old rights, however hard they may bear on the people ; they will not hear of giving way in the least to the spirit of liberty, beyond the point of paying equal land taxes ; which they hold to be all that can with reason be demanded. The popular party, on the other hand, seem to consider all liberty as depending on the privileged classes being lost and outvoted in the order of the commons, at least for making the new constitution ; and when I urge the great probability, that should they once unite, there will remain no power of ever separating them ; and that in such case, they will have a very questionable constitution, perhaps a very bad one ; I am always told, that the first object must be for the people to get the power of doing good;

and that it is no argument against such a conduct to urge that an ill use may be made of it. But among such men, the common idea is, that any thing tending towards a separate order, like our house of lords, is absolutely inconsistent with liberty; all which seems perfectly wild and unfounded.

Here we have the picture so constantly presented to us.

" On one side," he says, " a strange and unaccountable appeal to ideas and visionary rights of nature."

But this will ever be the case in disorderly times, but more particularly when on the other side, as he says, " the privileged orders are most disgustingly tenacious of all old rights, however hard they may bear on the people."

" They will not hear," he says, " of giving way to the spirit of liberty, beyond the point of paying equal land-taxes."

It was only very late, and when too late, that they reached even this point; and they who have power never are in time with their concessions.

A few days after, on the 13th of June, it seems to have been discovered by the public, that all was not harmony in the cabinet. Young writes thus:—

" All this day I hear nothing but anxiety of expectation for what the crisis in the States will produce. The embarrassment of the moment is extreme. Every one agrees that there is no ministry; the queen is closely connecting herself with the party of the princes, with the Count d'Artois at their head; who are all so adverse to M. Necker, that every thing is in confusion: but the king, who is personally the honestest man in the world, has but one wish, which is to do right; yet, being without those decisive parts that enable a man to foresee difficulties and to avoid them, finds himself in a moment of such extreme perplexity, that he knows not what council to take refuge in."

This was on June 13th; ten days after, on the 23rd, the king came forward with his *séance royale;* with his views of the state of the country, and the proper remedies of it; or rather with Necker's, but so unfortunately modified, that, as you may remember, Necker would not sanction them by his appearance. Before, however, this meeting of the 23rd, Arthur Young makes a few observations on the hall of the Assembly, the manner of debating, &c.; important points.

" We went immediately," he says, " to the hall of the States to secure good seats in the gallery; we found some deputies already there, and a pretty numerous audience collected. The room is too large, none but Stentorian lungs, or the finest, clearest voices can be heard (and Young might have added, none but violent men). However, the very size of the apartment, which admits two thousand people, gave a dignity to the scene. It was indeed an interesting one. The spectacle of the representatives of twenty-five millions of people, just merging from the evils of two hundred years of arbitrary power, and rising to the blessings of a freer constitution, assembled with open doors under the eye of the public, was framed to call into animated feelings every latent spark, every emotion of a liberal bosom. To banish whatever ideas might intrude of their being a people too often hostile to my own country, and to dwell with pleasure on the glorious idea of happiness to a great nation—of felicity to millions yet unborn."

Again, on June 15th:—" In regard to their general method of proceeding, there are two circumstances in which they are very deficient: the spectators in the galleries are allowed to interfere in the debates by clapping their hands, and other noisy expressions of approbation: this is grossly indecent; it is also dangerous; for, if they are permitted to express approbation, they are, by parity of reason, allowed expressions of dissent; and they may hiss as well as clap; which, it is said, they have sometimes done: this would be, to overrule the debate, and influence the deliberations. Another circumstance is, the want of order among themselves; more than once to-day there were a hundred members on their legs at a time, and M. Bailly absolutely without power to keep order."

The importance of these remarks was in the event but too unhappily shown.

At last he alludes to the sitting of the 23rd of June, which I have just represented to you as one of the important turns of the whole history; nor do I see that his opinion, when on the spot and at the time, is different from my own, writing thirty years afterwards, with all the intervening instruction of events.

He says, " The important day is over: in the morning Versailles seemed filled with troops: the streets, about ten o'clock, were lined with the French guards, and some Swiss regiments, &c.: the hall of the States was surrounded, and sentinels fixed in all the passages, and at the doors; and none but deputies admitted. This military preparation was ill judged, for it seemed admitting the impropriety and unpopularity of the intended measure, and the expectation, perhaps fear, of popular commotions. They pronounced, before the king left the chateau, that his plan was adverse to the people, from the military parade with which it was ushered in. The contrary, however, proved to be the fact; the propositions are known to all the world : the plan was a good one; much was granted to the people in great and essential points; and as it was granted before they had provided for those public necessities of finance, which occasioned the States being called together, and consequently left them at full power, in future, to procure for the people all that opportunity might present, they apparently ought to accept them, provided some security is given for the future meetings of the States, without which all the rest would be insecure ; but as a little negotiation may easily secure this, I apprehend the deputies will accept them conditionally : the use of soldiers, and some imprudencies in the manner of forcing the king's system, relative to the interior constitution, and assembling of the deputies, as well as the ill blood which had time to brood for three days past in their minds, prevented the commons from receiving the king with any expressions of applause ; the clergy, and some of the nobility, cried *Vive le Roi !* but treble the number of mouths being silent, took off all effect."

"The plan, you see," Arthur Young says, "was a good one; much was granted to the people in great and essential points."

"I apprehend," he says, "the deputies will accept them conditionally."

Arthur Young seems here to have expected too much from the reasonableness of the Assembly. I venture to say reasonableness, for I have always considered the conduct of the great leaders of the Assembly, on that occasion, for they certainly meant well, as exhibiting the most fatal mistake which they committed.

The next day, the 24th, he writes thus :—" The ferment at Paris is beyond conception ; ten thousand people have been all this day in the Palais Royal ; a full detail of yesterday's proceedings was brought this morning, and read by many apparent readers of little parties, with comments, to the people. To my surprise, the king's propositions are received with universal disgust. He said nothing explicit on the periodical meeting of the States ; he declared all the old feudal rights to be retained as property. These, and the change in the balance of representation in the Provincial Assemblies, are the articles that give the greatest offence. But, instead of looking to, or hoping for further concessions on these points, in order to make them more consonant to the general wishes, the people seem, with a sort of frenzy, to reject all idea of compromise, and to insist on the necessity of the orders uniting, that full power may consequently reside in the commons, to effect what they call the regeneration of the kingdom; a favourite term, to which they affix no precise idea, but add the indefinite explanation of the general reform of all abuses. They are also full of suspicions at M. Necker's offering to resign, to which circumstance they seem to look more than to much more essential points. It is plain to me, from many conversations and harangues I have been witness to, that the constant meetings at the Palais Royal, which are carried to a degree of licentiousness and fury of liberty that is scarcely credible, united with the innumerable inflammatory publications that have been hourly appearing since the assembly of the States, have so heated the people's expectations, and given them the idea of such total changes, that nothing the king or court could do, would now satisfy them."

Again, 24th June :—" If, on the side of the people it is urged, that the vices of the old government make a new system necessary, and that it can only be by the firmest measures that the people can be put in possession of the blessings of a free government; it is to be replied, on the other hand, that the personal character of the king is a just foundation for relying, that no measures of actual violence can be seriously feared : that the state of the finances, under any possible regimen, whether of faith or bankruptcy, must secure their existence, at least for time sufficient to secure by negotiation, what may be hazarded by violence : that by driving things to extremities, they (the patriots) risk an union between all the other orders of the state, with the parliaments, army, and a great body even of the people, who must disapprove of all extremities; and when to this is added the possibility of involving the kingdom in a civil war, now so familiarly talked of, that it is upon the lips of all the world, we must confess, that the commons, if they steadily refuse what is now held out to them, put immense and certain benefits to the chance of fortune, to that hazard which may make posterity curse instead of bless their memories as real patriots, who had nothing in view but the happiness of their country."   This appears to me a remarkable paragraph.

Two days after, on the 26th, he writes thus :—" Every hour that passes seems to give the people fresh spirit : the meetings at the Palais Royal are more numerous, more violent, and more assured; and in the Assembly of Electors, chosen for the purpose of sending a deputation to the National Assembly, the language that was talked, by all ranks of people, was nothing less than a revolution in the government, and the establishment of a free constitution: what they mean by a free constitution is easily understood—*a republic;* for the doctrine of the times runs every day more and more to that point; yet they profess that the kingdom ought to be a monarchy too, or, at least, that there ought to be a king. In the streets one is stunned by the hawkers of seditious pamphlets, and descriptions of pretended events, that all tend to keep the people equally ignorant and alarmed. The supineness, and even stupidity of the court, is without example: the moment demands the greatest decision; and yesterday, while it was actually a question whether he should be a doge of Venice or a king of France, the king went a-hunting!"

Such were the views and observations that occurred to Arthur Young, while only a visitor in the country, and before the unfortunate events that subsequently occurred. They appear to me very creditable to his sagacity and good sense, and very creditable to the country he had left, and the constitution of England under which he had lived—a constitution that had evidently taught him the value of civil liberty, but taught him also the dangers to which it is exposed, and the mistakes that may be committed by its friends and assertors.

We will now return to the history. The royal sitting of the 23rd has been held; it has failed: the Assembly and the court are entirely at issue; and the king, turning away apparently from all counsels of violence, adopts other resolutions, and personally interferes in procuring the immediate union of the two privileged orders with the Tiers Etat in one great Assembly.

The student might expect, therefore, that nothing would *now* remain for him to witness, but the labours of this National Assembly for the regeneration of France; that no further interruption would be given by the king and court to their wishes or their plans; that a civil war had been happily avoided by the concessions of the king; and that some experiment of the new opinions, some union and mixture of the claims of the monarch with those of the people, would now be accomplished.

"How honourable," said Mirabeau, "will it be for France, that this great Revolution has cost humanity neither offences nor crimes." After referring to England and America, their struggles and their sufferings,—"*We*, on the contrary, have the happiness," he said, "to see a revolution of the same nature brought about by the mere union of enlightened minds with patriotic intentions; our battles are mere discussions; our enemies are only prejudices, that may, indeed, be pardoned; our victories, our triumphs, so far from being cruel, will be blessed by the very conquered themselves.

" History, too, often records actions which are worthy only of the most ferocious animals ; among whom, at long intervals, we can sometimes distinguish heroes : there is now reason to hope that we have begun the history of man, the history of brothers, who, born for mutual happiness, agree when they vary, since their objects are the same, and their means only are different."

Such were the observations of Mirabeau, such his views, and such might be also the views of the reader of the history, if he could be ignorant of what followed.

But on a sudden a new scene opens, and one that cannot be explained except in a very general manner, no particular account having as yet reached the public ; it is no other than this : troops are brought up and made to approach nearer and nearer Paris and Versailles, Marshal Broglio is appointed to the command of them, and there is every appearance that violence is intended, that the Assembly at Versailles is to be dissolved by force, and that in some way or other, and to some extent or other, the military are to be called in, and the cause of the monarchy of France and of the old opinions to be by their means asserted.

Nothing short of all this can well be supposed from all the circumstances that now took place. There is, however, another solution of all these phenomena, to which I shall hereafter allude ; it is this : that the court meant only to maintain the peace of the metropolis and the community ; but in the mean time observe the facts, and consent to proceed with me, for the present, on a different, and, as I conceive, more reasonable supposition.

Necker, who, after the 23d, had become the great idol of the public, intended to have resigned, and was indeed to have been dismissed, but he was so beset and affected by the entreaties of the people, that he complied with their wishes, and those of the king, and remained in his situation of minister. While this was the case, the public considered themselves in a state of security. Necker himself seems not at all to have participated in this new and extraordinary change in the counsels of the king. He declares positively that he knew nothing of these military movements till it was impossible that they could be concealed from any one. " The war minister," he says, " talked of necessary precaution, in consequence of the late seditious appearance at Paris and Versailles, and the explication was natural enough ; but could no longer be admitted when Marshal

Broglio was called to court. I could never ascertain," he adds, " to what lengths their projects really went. There were secrets upon secrets; and I believe that even the king himself was far from being acquainted with all of them. What was intended was probably to draw the monarch on, as circumstances admitted, to measures, of which they durst not at first have spoken to him. Time," he continues, " can alone unveil the mystery; with me, above all others, a reserve was maintained, and reasonably, for my indisposition to everything of the kind was decided."

Such is Necker's account. The mystery seems to have been, that the court could not bear the assumption of authority which the National Assembly had displayed, and that when they saw that the two orders had united themselves to the Tiers Etat, they conceived that an assembly like this would trample down the monarch and all the privileged orders without hesitation or delay, and that, therefore, in self-defence, they must try to dissolve the Assembly by military force.

But neither can the court be excused in making this experiment, nor the king in suffering it to be made. The opportunity of trying force had been lost. After the king had desired and commanded the nobility and clergy to join the Tiers Etat, the National Assembly had a right to suppose that their legal existence was acknowledged, and the measures they had adopted forgiven, at least admitted; that it was only by their subsequent conduct they could forfeit the good will of the king; that, in short, all was now to be a system of harmony and peace. Nothing could appear more treacherous, nothing more unjust, than for the king, in this situation of things, to bring up troops from all quarters, as if he had before meant only to lull them into security, the more easily to dissolve the Assembly, and, perhaps, seize, banish, confine, or even execute for treason, some of their most obnoxious leaders.

It is difficult to understand how the king, a man of integrity and virtue, could be so blind to the very objectionable nature of the course of measures which he saw himself gradually adopting. He must have really supposed, as the court pretended, that they were necessary to secure the tranquillity of Paris, and the peace and order of the community. What, however, was the reasoning of the court? How could they possibly suppose that the king would not fail them when the moment of trial came? They knew that it was his great maxim that the blood of Frenchmen was not to be shed in what he called his quarrel; how could they expect such a prince to run the chance of a civil war? But what more cruel injury could they do to the monarch and the privileged orders, than, under such circumstances, to try, or rather to *appear* to try, the experiment of military force?

Another consideration still remained behind: were they sure of the soldiery? Unhappy is the government, and at its last gasp, when the military are to be set apart from the community, and the rulers are to depend on the one to subdue the other. There was nothing, on this occasion, to encourage the court to suppose that they could with safety venture upon this fearful appeal. The public had been long in the highest state of inflammation; nothing was expected from the old opinions, everything from the new; the monarchy had become nothing, the National Assembly everything; it was from them, and from them only, no longer from the king or the privileged orders, that laws, liberty, prosperity, national grandeur, were expected; the three orders had now united; the Assembly seemed just, as it were, on the point of beginning their great work of the regeneration, as they called it, of France; all eyes were turned upon them, all hearts participated in their feelings of every kind: and this was the moment which the court fixed upon to call out the soldiery to disperse and put them down by force, and all the time to expect that such a metropolis as Paris, in its existing state of excitement, was to look quietly on and submit in silence, while they saw their representatives dismissed, the image of their national greatness dishonoured, and all their cherished dreams of happiness and glory dissipated, at once and for ever, by the rude assault, for such it would have appeared to them, of mere brutal and unenlightened power.

Certainly never was a time so ill chosen for an experiment like this, a prince so ill fitted, a soldiery so unpromising; and, as in judging of all political measures, the probability of success must be carefully and fully taken into account (whatever may be the right), nothing can appear more unpardonable than the conduct of the court on this most critical occasion.

These general reflections will be entirely confirmed by an appeal to the history, into the detail of which I cannot enter. You will see an account given in all the writers to which I have directed your attention. The most full is given in the modern publication of Dulaure.

It will be found that the most common provisions of prudence were neglected; the soldiery suffered to approach Paris, to mingle with the inhabitants; no decision, no alertness of movement; nothing secured from the populace—the Bastile, the depôts of arms; nothing arranged or managed as if any measures of hostility or force were to be adopted.

Yet was sufficient warning given to the court, that neither were the Assembly asleep, nor its partisans in the metropolis, nor the daring and bad men that are always afloat and prepared for mischief in every great metropolis.

In the first place, the soldiery, by mixing with the populace of Paris, had become so disorderly, that it had been necessary to confine them in their barracks; at last eleven of them were picked out and sent to the prison of the Abbaye, till they could be tried by a court-martial. But you will see in the history that the gates were broken open by the populace, and these victims of their patriotism, so they voted themselves, were rescued. In their return from the prison the mob was met by a troop of dragoons and another of hussars, who, in short, at last joined the crowd in their cry of *Vive la nation!*

It was then determined to send a deputation to the National Assembly in favour of the prisoners.

This was done; an address was presented to the king; and the soldiers, having been first returned to the prison as a necessary formality, were by his order set at liberty.

This was but an ominous specimen of the soldiery and of the populace, to those who were intending to overpower the one by means of the other.

Other particulars of this kind you will see in the history.

With respect to the Assembly, on the 8th of July (this affair of the eleven soldiers had taken place about the 1st) they were addressed by Mirabeau in one of his most celebrated speeches, and this speech was followed by a sort of remonstrance addressed to the king on the subject of the troops that had been brought around them; and both of these documents you will read with great attention, not only as specimens of the powers of this extraordinary man, on a very difficult and important occasion, but as forming a sort of epoch in the history of this great event.

"Nevertheless," said Mirabeau, in the course of his speech, "what hath been the issue of those declarations and of our respectful behaviour? Already are we surrounded by a multitude of soldiers; more are arrived, are arriving every day; they are hastening hither from all quarters; thirty-five thousand men are already cantoned in Paris and Versailles, twenty thousand more are expected; they are followed by trains of artillery; spots are marked out for batteries; every communication is secured, every pass is blocked up; our streets, our bridges, our public walks are converted into military stations; events of public notoriety, concealed facts, secret orders, precipitate counter-orders—in a word, preparations for war strike every eye, and fill every heart with indignation."

The speech grows more and more violent as it proceeds, and was followed by the celebrated address to the king for the removal of the troops, which you will of course read with attention. A few sentences from it may serve to give you, for the present, a slight idea of it, sufficient for my purpose.

"In the emotions of your own heart, sire, we look for the true safety of the French. When troops advance from every quarter, when camps are forming around us, when the capital is besieged, we ask one another with astonishment, Hath the king distrusted the fidelity of his people? What mean these menacing preparations? Where are the enemies of the state and of the king that are to be subdued? ... The sway of Louis IX., of Louis XII., of Henry IV., is the only sway worthy of you.

"We should deceive you, sire, if, forced as we are by circumstances, we neglected to add, that such a sway is the only one which at the present day it is possible to exercise in France. ... Where then, our enemies will affect to say, is the danger to be apprehended from the soldiery?

"The danger, sire, is urgent, is universal, is beyond all the calculations of human prudence.

"The danger is for the provinces. Should they once be alarmed for our liberty, we should no longer have it in our power to restrain their impetuosity," &c. &c.

"The danger is for the capital. With what sensations will the people, in their state of indigence, and tortured with the keenest anguish, see the relics of its subsistence disputed for by a throng of threatening soldiers," &c. &c.

"The danger is for the troops. They may forget that the ceremony of enlisting made them soldiers, and recollect that nature made them men.

"The danger, sire, menaces those labours which are our primary duty, and which will only obtain their full success and a real permanency as long as the people considers the Assembly as altogether free.

"The danger, sire, is yet more terrible; and judge of its extent by the alarms which bring us before you. Mighty revolutions have arisen from causes far less striking. . . . . .

"Sire, we conjure you in the name of our country, in the

name of your own happiness and your own glory, to send back your soldiers to the posts from which your counsellors have drawn them—send back that artillery," &c. &c.

These few extracts may be sufficient to afford you, for the present, some general notion of what you will hereafter read ; as may the following extracts of the answer of the king :—

" No person is ignorant," replied the king, " of the disorders and the scandalous scenes which have been acted and repeated at Paris and Versailles, before my eyes and before the eyes of the States General ; it is necessary that I should make use of the means which are in my power to restore and maintain order in the capital and the environs ; it is one of my principal duties to watch over the public safety : these were the motives which determined me to assemble the troops round Paris," &c. &c.

" If, however, the needful presence of the troops in the neighbourhood of Paris still gives umbrage, I am ready, at the desire of the Assembly, to transfer the States General to Noyon or to Soissons, and shall then repair to Compiegne, in order to maintain the communication which ought to subsist between the Assembly and myself."

This answer met with some applause, but not with the applause of Mirabeau.

" The king's answer," he said, " is a downright refusal."

" We have requested the dismissal of the troops ; we have not asked leave to run away from the troops, but merely desired that the troops should be at a distance from the capital," &c. &c.

The king's answer was given on the 11th ; on that day M. Necker was dismissed. On the 12th the new ministers, Breteuil, Broglio, &c. took their seats in the council ; but on the 13th the Assembly decreed that Necker and the dismissed ministers were regretted by the Assembly ; that the advisers of his majesty, of what rank and station soever, were personally responsible for the troubles then existing, and for all those which might ensue.

On the 14th the Bastile was taken, and on the 15th the Assembly at Versailles, which had been sitting night and day since the morning of the 13th, and had already sent two deputations to the king, on the subject of the troops, in vain, were prevented from sending a third by the appearance of the king *himself*, to announce to them that he had just ordered the troops to remove from Paris and Versailles, and that all was to be now a system of confidence and peace.

So rapid was the course of these most memorable events.

I must allude to them a little longer, that you may bear away from the lecture a distinct impression of them.

The dismissal of Nécker happened on the 11th, and this was followed by the immediate appointment of a new administration, at the head of which were M. de Breteuil and Marshal Broglio.   This was the first event.

It was impossible that this should not cause the greatest alarm and indignation.

Paris was filled with consternation.   The busts of Necker and the Duke of Orleans were paraded through the city, covered with crape.   A party of dragoons was ordered to attack the multitude.   The Prince de Lambesc was at the head of a body of foreign cavalry; stones were thrown, a charge made, people wounded, the populace cried "To arms!" the alarm-bells were sounded, the armourers' shops broken open; but, above all, many of the French guards left their barracks to join the people, and the foreign cavalry were obliged to give way; and, on the whole, it appeared, judging from this first experiment, that the Parisian populace were not likely to be much restrained or kept down by the military force of the crown.

This was the second event; but it gave occasion in conjunction with the increasing terrors and expectation of an attack from Broglio, for a third, and the most important event of all; which was no other than the sudden rise and appearance of forty-eight thousand men in arms, the citizens of Paris, followed immediately afterwards in the provinces by similar bodies of volunteers, so that on a sudden all the regular forces of the crown seemed surrounded, kept in check, and in fact taken prisoners, by the whole effective population of this great kingdom; and all the real power of the monarch, the power, at least, by which he was to defend the prerogatives of his crown and the claims of the privileged orders, in opposition to the will of the National Assembly, at once annihilated.

This was the great result.   You will see the particulars in the histories.

The insurrectionary movements of the populace in Paris, the forcing of the Hospital of Invalids, where thirty thousand muskets were found; the assault and even destruction of the fortress of the Bastile; the disgusting outrages, the bloody exhibitions that ensued: all this happened at Paris on the 14th; while, on the morning of the 15th, the Assembly at Versailles were still drawing up representations to the king, who seems, from some lamentable want of character, or from the effect of that system of deception and flattery which is so practised in the courts and chambers of princes, never actually to have known the

o 2

dangerous situation in which his crown and dignity were placed, and the astonishing scenes of popular violence, still more the decisive exertions of public spirit, which his capital had exhibited.

One honourable man, one faithful friend to the monarchy and to the liberties of the country, was at last found, the Duc de Liancourt. In the middle of the night of the 14th he made his way into the king's chamber, and disclosed at once all the melancholy truths which had come to his own knowledge, and in a total ignorance of which the king slumbered on, as if he was unconscious that he was never to know repose again.

" It is a revolt," said the king. " It is a revolution, sire !" said the duke.

It was indeed a revolution, to which now no further opposition could be made ; and the measure adopted by the king was the only one that could be now advised.

He repaired in the morning to the Assembly, which, as I have mentioned, had been sitting two days and two nights ; repaired to them without pomp, almost without attendants, and in the plainest dress : standing, and uncovered, he addressed them in the most conciliatory terms ; professed his sorrow for the disorders at Paris, his regard for the Assembly, and ended by declaring that he had ordered the troops to remove from the neighbourhood of the capital.

It must be mentioned to the honour of the Assembly, that this effort of the king to regain the affection of his people was not made in vain. This Assembly was, after all, an Assembly, where men of character, and rank, and education, and feeling were to be found,—far removed above the level of those Assemblies that succeeded.

The hall resounded with shouts of applause. As he withdrew, they surrounded him in a respectful manner, attended him to his palace, and a deputation of eighty-four of the most distinguished of them was sent to Paris to conciliate the minds of the citizens, to place the conduct of the king in the least unfavourable point of view, and to assure them of his wishes for the happiness of the people. From the Hotel de Ville the deputies were conducted to the church of Notre Dame, and Te Deum was performed for the happy agreement between the king and the national representatives, and for the public prosperity which was expected to be the consequence.

More still remained. You will see, in the history, that the offensive ministry is dismissed, Necker recalled, and contrary to the wish, and to the great terror of the queen and court, the king actually repairs to the town house of Paris, and appears with the national cockade in his hat, to render his reconciliation with its inhabitants and his acceptance of the Revolution more public and more complete.

Such was the end of the great monarchy of France, and such is, I conceive, in a few words, a fair general account of this astonishing Revolution, this appalling spectacle of the instability of every thing human.

But it is necessary, before I conclude, that I should remind you of what I have already mentioned, that there are two different accounts or explanations given of these memorable events, and that you are not to accede to the representation I have just given without due examination of one of a totally opposite nature.

Some assert, not what I have stated, that an unseasonable, ill-conducted, and on the whole unjust attempt, was made by the court to put down the National Assembly, to control the new opinions by military force, and to destroy ultimately the liberties of France; but, on the contrary, that the court intended nothing of the kind, that the court only wished to assert the proper authority of the king as guardian of the public peace, to repress the licentiousness of Paris, to counteract the factious or even republican designs of furious and bad men, and to save the National Assembly itself from being overawed by the populace; that this populace, amid the real miseries of a scarcity, were exposed without bread to all the inflammatory representations of the orators of the Palais Royal—orators that were never for a moment quiet, imputing all the evils that were suffered to the fault of the government, to the court, to foreigners, to foreign troops, and to those they called by the general name of traitors in and out of the walls of Paris.

This is the great question before the student, at this most important part of the history of the Revolution. My own view of it is what I have given, fortified by the direct evidence of Necker, and supported, as I conceive, by all the probabilities of the case in its different stages.

But you must judge for yourselves; and, in my next lecture, I will endeavour to exhibit to you what may be considered as the case of the court.

LECTURE XI.

FOURTEENTH OF JULY.

In the course of my last lecture I alluded to the great crisis in the history of this Revolution, the production of military force by the court—the production rather than the employment of it; the astonishing effects by which this menace was almost instantly followed, the sudden rise of a citizen army in Paris, the taking of the Bastile on the 14th, the visit of the king to the National Assembly, afterwards to Paris, and his public and avowed adoption of the Revolution in the presence of his people.

I then mentioned the different explanations that have been given of this sort of appeal on the part of the king and court to military force: the two explanations are quite at variance with each other; and having adopted one of them myself, and proposed it to your consideration, I told you at the close of my lecture, that it was fitting I should exhibit to you the other, and that this I would do to-day, by laying before you various passages from different authors, those who think well of the intentions of the court.

I will just mention, before I refer to these books (as the extracts are desultory, and not always sufficiently distinct), that the court party contend, in opposition to such views of the case as I have hitherto described to you, that it was necessary to produce the troops to awe and to restrain the disorderly and mutinous populace of Paris, and that no counter-revolution was intended.

You will observe, however, that in Paris the interpretation of this approach of the troops was, that the city was to be besieged and starved into submission, and even, if necessary, given up to military execution; and that it was under the terror of such calamities that the demagogues raised an insurrection of the populace and stormed the Bastile; and that the more regular inhabitants formed themselves into a company of volunteers, forty thousand strong, to defend themselves and the capital from Marshal Broglio and his troops.

These are the terrors and alarms on each side, and these the transactions that occasioned all the confusion and uncertainty of mind and purpose in the parties, which you will see alluded to in the extracts which I shall bring forward from different writers; the National Assembly, who were sitting at Versailles, never knowing what was passing at Paris, nor they at Paris what was doing in the Assembly and the palace.

But to proceed. The first author I shall allude to is Marmontel. Marmontel was a man of letters, who resided at Paris at this period; a successful writer, and of an amiable and elegant mind. His Memoirs have been published: they were much read and admired when they first came out, and in the latter part of them you will find an account of the whole Revolution, rapid and concise, but perfectly entitled to your consideration.

He was for some time an eyewitness, and even took a part in it. He was at length happy to retire and to die in silence and obscurity. Having, in the course of his Memoirs, proceeded through the earlier stages of the Revolution, he at last arrives at the scenes that took place in Paris, such as I have slightly described, immediately after the royal sitting of the 23rd.

And then more immediately, in allusion to our present subject, he says, p. 158 (I quote from the English translation):—
"The adventure of the two soldiers of the guards, the spirit of insubordination with which the people inspired them, the audacity of this people, the tone it had assumed, &c., &c., had been forcibly seized upon in the council, as means to persuade the king, that the greatest of evils, both for the state and for himself, would be, to suffer the authority which he held in his hands to be despised, and that it would infallibly be despised, if it were seen disarmed. It was represented to the king, according to Marmontel—and this is very probable—that the multitude must tremble, or it would make all tremble; that it would have been desirable, without doubt, that the sessions of the States should have passed in complete security, without having around them any display of military force; but that so long as the people came to mix insult and menace with the deliberations of the States General, public force had a right to arm itself in order to repress them."

"There are those," it was observed to the king, "who think they can appease the populace as easily as they irritate it. After they have made it serve their purpose of subverting the whole kingdom, they will want to bring the tiger back to his cage, but it will be too late; the ferocious beast will have felt his own force and the weakness of his chains: above all, what will he be if he has tasted blood? Teach this people then, that in your hands it has still justice to dread.

"If the members of the National Association had all your loyalty, sire, they would all unite to demand, around the sanctuary of legislation, some impenetrable barrier, inaccessible to the troops on one side and to the people on the other, and then all would be equal. But no; it is in order to leave to this populace full license and complete impunity, that they wish the troops to be withdrawn. . . . .

"It is by the people that they seek to reign: the name of

liberty, which for the populace means only license, has resounded like a general signal of insurrection and anarchy.

"Independence, and contempt for every species of authority, this is what the face of the kingdom presents; and it is on the ruins of the monarchy, and with its wrecks, that the revolutionary faction boasts of creating a democratic empire. It is a vile mass of vagabonds, without morals, without employment, without home, that is called the sovereign people. . . . .

"No, sire, it is no longer in the name of the clergy or of the nobility, it is in the name of a good people, of which you are the father, that we conjure you not to abandon it to the most cruel of tyrannies—to that of the populace and of its perfidious leaders."

"It is thus," says Marmontel, "that the king was persuaded, that in displaying to the people a military power, he should only repress force by force, and should leave public liberty protected and uninjured."

And here we may observe, that it is very probable, that it is very certain, that the king was addressed in the manner Marmontel describes. Many questions, however, and difficulties remain, both of prudence and honour, such as I have endeavoured to submit to your consideration, with respect to the advice itself and the acceptance of it; the time, the occasion, the circumstances, under which the king was placed, the quantity of the force produced, the style and manner of it, the natural interpretation of it in the community.

Marmontel opens the next book with a statement of the incapacity of the ministers. "The king then," he says, "ordered some troops to advance; but in forming a vigorous resolution, the ministers should have foreseen its consequences, the difficulties, the dangers.

"But they calculated nothing, they provided for nothing, they did not even think of securing the troops from the corruption of the populace of Paris. . . . And in the Fauxbourgs of Paris, the only imposing post, the Bastile, was neither furnished with a sufficient garrison, nor with provisions to support the few soldiers who were there. . . . .

"To this species of stupor into which the court and council had fallen, the adverse party opposed," he continues, "a measured, progressive, and constant march, proceeding from post to post towards dominion, without ever losing a moment or retrograding a step. Resolved to suffer no collection of troops, either around Paris or Versailles, this party determined on an address to the king," &c., &c.

He then goes on to describe Mirabeau's address to the king, Mirabeau himself, the king's answer, the necessity of a new system, and the consequent necessity of the dismissal of Necker, and the scenes that followed—the scenes that I have already described to you.

" Thus Paris," he at last observes, " without courts of justice, without police, without a guard, at the mercy of one hundred thousand men, who were wandering wildly in the middle of the night, and for the most part wanting bread, believing itself on the point of being besieged from without and pillaged from within ; believed that twenty-five thousand soldiers were posted around to blockade it and cut off all supplies of provisions, and that it would be a prey to a starving populace."

Such was the terrible picture which, in the night between the 12th and 13th of July, was present to every fancy.

Marmontel then goes on to describe the events that followed in a manner very animated and striking.   " If the National Assembly," he at last observes, " could have had any presentiment of the evils with which the kingdom was threatened by this dreadful anarchy ; if it had foreseen how impotent its own efforts would be, to force back into the bounds of legitimate authority this ferocious beast which it was eager to unchain ; if those who flattered it had thought that they themselves might perhaps one day be its prey, they would have shuddered with a salutary fear. But to procure for themselves a reigning authority, they only thought of disarming that which alone could have saved all."

Again,—" A blockade," he says, " a siege, a famine, a massacre, were the black phantoms which had been employed to frighten the Parisians ; and in seeing the troops retire, that were supposed to be charged with the commission of these crimes, Paris thought it had nothing more to fear.   It was under the eyes of six Swiss battalions and of eight hundred horse, all motionless in their camp, that the Hotel des Invalides was opened to the people—a very positive proof, as Bezenval, who was in command at the moment, has since affirmed it to be, that the troops were forbidden to fire on the citizens ; and *there*," says Marmontel, " was the great advantage of the people ; they knew that the king would only suffer them to be curbed, without ever consenting that they should either be treated as enemies or rebels."

" It is true," says Marmontel, " that if the governor of the Bastile had made use of his artillery, he would have struck Paris with awe."   He recollected, without doubt, that he served a good king, and among the people every man knew it as well as

he. All Paris had hastened towards the Bastile. Sexes and
ages, all were confounded around those ramparts that were
loaded with cannon; what is it, then, that heartened them?
"The king consents that his people should be threatened, but
not that his people should be crushed."

These sentences, and sometimes half sentences, which I have
extracted from Marmontel, will give you some general notion of
the view he took of these extraordinary scenes. He was, as I
have already mentioned, a distinguished man of letters, lived at
the time, and you will of course read what he has written, with
curiosity, as I hope, and with care.

His Memoirs, he says, are not a history of the Revolution;
they are addressed to his children, and they are rather meant to
give a history of himself; but as he concludes, he observes,
"The events which I have just recalled to my memory have so
occupied my fancy, that amid so many public calamities I have
almost forgotten myself; the impression which this mass of
misery made on me was, indeed, so lively and so deep, that it
was very natural, that what only concerned myself should have
been very often forgotten."

"If the life of man," he says, "be a journey, can I recount
mine, without telling through what events and by what torrents,
what abysses, what wilds, peopled by tigers and by serpents, it
has passed? It is thus that I retrace to myself our ten years of
misfortunes, almost doubting whether it be not a violent and
fatal dream." He died on the 31st of December, 1799.

It is probable, that in these Memoirs of Marmontel may be
seen such sentiments and opinions as would have passed through
the student's own mind, if of gentle nature, and if intelligent,
and an eye-witness at the time; and this must constitute the interest and value of the perusal of them. I will now refer to the
memoirs of Bertrand de Moleville; they must be attentively
perused by the student, who cannot be better employed, than in
comparing the opposite representations of men of different characters and views, and in endeavouring to form a right judgment
on the whole. Such opposite accounts become, after the events,
a sort of representation of what was the real scene actually in
existence, amidst the contending passions and opinions of which
the student would have had to decide, if he had been a statesman or a man of influence himself at the time. And similar col-
lisions he will always have to witness, when large masses of
mankind are put into a state of agitation; and it is in the midst
of the embarrassments of such perplexing and contradictory cir-

cumstances and representations, that men of education are to learn to judge of any scene that may hereafter be placed before them in real life, and may thus be enabled, by the remembrance of what history has shown them, and by the exercise of their good feelings, and good sense, and superior information, to influence the conduct of those around them at the hour of need, and do good to their fellow-creatures on occasions the most difficult and important.

The view that Bertrand de Moleville takes of the transactions we have been adverting to is much the same; that the metropolis had become disorderly and seditious, and that it was necessary to march up troops from all quarters to preserve the peace of the community. That the attempt was not on the part of the court to destroy the Assembly, but on the part of the democratic leaders in and out of the Assembly, by means of the populace, to overthrow all the legitimate authority of the king, at the same time with an intention to make the Duke of Orleans lieutenant-governor of the kingdom.

I must observe to you, before I proceed further to allude to the opinions of Bertrand de Moleville, either now or at any other time, that I give them to you as opinions that were held by the patrons of the old régime, not as necessarily true. Bertrand writes in 1799, from his lodgings in London, and describes what he had himself seen and known, and what he had understood from those on whom he was confident he could depend. He was a man of character and veracity, and a man of ability: his facts, however, are one thing, and his opinions another; the former may be (insensibly to the writer himself) affected by the other; still more so, whenever they are given, not on his own authority, but on the authority of others. He was called to the ministry, not because he was a friend to moderate opinions, and a friend to a mixed and constitutional government, but because he was a man of daring character, and of considerable resource in all those minor expedients, by which the court were at the time endeavouring to tide the torrent. His counter police, of which you will see an account in his Memoirs, cost very large sums, and answered, probably, little or no purpose. He was a man that would have brought back the old régime without the slightest compunction; nor would he have hesitated, if necessary, to adopt measures of the most arbitrary character. No one cared less for constitutional principles. Still, as a man of character and ability, and of eminence at the time, his sentiments and opinions must be considered. He is one of a class;

they form part of the general case; a part that at every period must be duly estimated.

I will now allude to his view of the scenes, and the crisis before us.

After a variety of details and observations, which you will attentively read, he reaches the subject of the dismissal of Necker. This is, evidently, a very curious part of it; and, as I conceive, in itself and alone, decisive of the whole question of the intentions of the court.

With regard, then, to Necker, he observes: " It is certain, that all the parties labouring to subvert the monarchy, or at least to change the nature of it, depended upon the support or on the indulgence of that minister, and that the staunch royalists had no reliance upon him. These motives at length determined the king to remove him."

This is his explanation, short and clear, but surely not satisfactory. He then gives a description of the effect produced in Paris by this certainly very alarming measure. His picture of the state of that capital on the 12th of July is most appalling: it was on that day that M. Necker's departure was known. He describes the manner in which Camille Desmoulins, one of the demagogues, mounting upon a table in the Palais Royal, cried out, " Citizens, there is not a moment to be lost; M. Necker is dismissed; this dismission is the alarm bell for another St. Bartholomew of patriots. To-night all the Swiss and German battalions will come from the Champ de Mars and cut our throats," &c. &c.

The parading of the busts of the Duke of Orleans and M. Necker is then described by Moleville; the affair of the Prince de Lambesc. "It would be difficult," he goes on to say, " to paint the disorder, fermentation, and alarm, that prevailed in the capital during this dreadful day : a city taken by storm and delivered up to the soldiers' fury, could not present a more dreadful picture. Imagine detachments of cavalry and dragoons making their way through different parts of the town at full gallop to the posts assigned them ; trains of artillery rolling over the pavement with a monstrous noise; bands of ill-armed ruffians and women, drunk with brandy, running through the streets like furies, breaking the shops open, and spreading terror every where by their howlings, mingled with frequent reports from guns or pistols fired in the air; all the barriers on fire; thousands of smugglers taking advantage of the tumult to hurry in their goods ; the alarm bell ringing in almost all the churches;

a great part of the citizens shutting themselves up at home, loading their guns, and burying their money, papers, and valuable effects in cellars and gardens; and, during the night, the town paraded by numerous patrols of citizens of every class, and even of both sexes; for many women were seen with muskets or pikes upon their shoulders."

" Such," he says, " is the exact picture of the state of Paris on the 12th of July."

" At Versailles," he says, " the new ministry were busily debating sometimes in the council, sometimes in committees, without knowing what resolution to take; the general officers were constantly going for orders, were made to wait long, and received none at last," &c.

" The king," he observes, " could not have dismissed M. Necker at a more critical juncture, than that in which the people, alarmed with famine, fixed all their hopes on the attentions of that minister, and on the credit and resources they attributed to him."

" The Revolution," he says, " though in its cradle at the time, assumed one of its distinguishing characters; the Parisians in arming the populace and ruffians, in order to oppose them to the troops of the line, were anxious to anticipate a danger with which they were *not* threatened, and thought nothing of that, arising from putting the public force into the hands of those who, on the contrary, should always be awed by it. The consequence was, that the next day, July 13th, at three in the morning, an immense crowd, armed with clubs, bludgeons, and pikes, under pretence of the dearth of provisions, attacked the convent of St. Lazarus, crying out, ' Bread! bread!' They then demanded arms," &c.

He afterwards describes the manner in which the populace forced the doors of the *garde meuble*, carrying off all the rich and curious arms there deposited; then the forcing of the prisons of La Force, and the inaction of the minister, M. de Bezenval, who had troops at his disposal without once employing them while all these enormities were committing; and then at last the manner in which a Parisian bourgeois militia was formed, provisionally settled at forty-eight thousand men.

" The promptness," he observes, " with which the Parisians organized at once this provisional magistracy, the bourgeois militia, and the sixty district assemblies, has been made too much a wonder. To M. Necker's imprudence belongs the honour of this melancholy miracle, without which the city of Paris would have been under the necessity of submitting to the king's authority, and of imploring his protection against the plunderers. It was the innovating genius of that minister which engendered that electoral assembly, and that division of the capital into sixty districts or rounds for the appointment of their respective electors; without reflecting, that in so immense a city as Paris, where the populace is too numerous not to be turbulent, it is always very dangerous to establish or point out to the people a settled place of assembling in each quarter; it is removing the greatest obstacle to a general insurrection. It was thus that this modern patchwork of an electoral assembly, and assemblies of districts, devised for the appointment of deputies to the States General, became the corner-stone of the Revolution."

Bertrand goes on to describe the exertions made by the populace to provide themselves with arms; the attack on the Bastile, of which he gives a more intelligible detail than will be easily found elsewhere. He enumerates the terrible atrocities that followed, nor can on this subject his natural indignation be too great.

He next turns to the king and the National Assembly. "It was late at night, on the 14th of July, before the Assembly were informed of a part of the outrages committed at Paris . . . . . The king was not better informed." . . . . He then describes the deputations of the Assembly, and the answers of the king on the subject of the troops.

"Can it be conceived," he at last observes, "that during an insurrection, in which the people, armed and constantly committing acts of violence, were everywhere but feebly resisted by the troops, the removal of these could have been considered and solicited by the Assembly, as the only means of suppressing the insurrection and preventing new ones?

"But it was too clear," says he, "that they neither wished to suppress the insurrection nor prevent new ones, but to ensure the triumph of the rebels."

"The night of the 14th of July," he says, "was another night of anxiety and horror for the Parisians. Terrified at the enormity of their crimes, and particularly dreading the exemplary punishment they deserved, they firmly believed all the projects of vengeance with which the king was charged, and were in constant expectation of the bombardment of the capital, or the arrival of squadrons upon squadrons of hussars," &c.

"When it was known that nothing had passed at Versailles, and that the Assembly continued to hold their sittings unmolested, it was rumoured that the project of the ministers had failed, because the cannoniers, commanded by M. Broglio, had refused to obey him. The fact was, that M. Broglio had proposed to escort the king and royal family safely to Metz with the army, and that his majesty, instead of adopting this measure, which might have saved everything, had determined, from the representations and entreaties of the Duke of Liancourt, to throw himself confidently upon the Assembly, and to consent to all they asked."

He then describes what passed between the Assembly and the king, and concludes this part of his subject in the following manner :—

" Thus terminated that memorable sitting, in which Louis XVI., ever impelled by his fatal reliance on the love and allegiance of the French, voluntarily stripped himself of all the means of supporting his authority, at a moment when the most powerful would scarcely have been sufficient to preserve it. He chose rather to leave his throne, without support, to the mercy of all the factious who wished to overthrow it ; and his own person, without defence, to the discretion of a people, armed and delirious, than to shed the blood of any one of his subjects."

Such are the representations of Bertrand de Moleville, at every point different from what I conceive to be reasonable and fair, except his account of the feelings of the king.

The want of character in the king was, no doubt, in itself fatal to all the views of the followers of the old régime ; but this want of character was known, and should have been taken into their calculation, and materially influenced their measures.

That their measures would have been a trial of force and a dissolution of the Assembly, seems sufficiently clear, even from the general tone of these passages, taken from Bertrand de Moleville ; but from what is now known of Paris, and the prevalence of the new opinions, the result must have been a civil war ; nor do I deny, but rather I contend, that these sentiments in the court and its adherents, and the probable chance of a civil war, were the natural consequences of the first strong measures of the patriotic party on the opening of the States. They certainly were ; and they constitute, what I conceive, and what I have represented to be, the very objectionable nature of their proceedings.

But to return to the subject before us.

You see what were the representations of Bertrand de Moleville.

I will now allude to what were the sentiments at the time of Mirabeau. In this, as in the former case, the sentiments given are not necessarily just. Mirabeau is an orator, a rhetorician, not a philosopher or an historian; but he, too, is a sort of representative of a class. His address of the 16th of July, to which I shall now allude, was applauded by the National Assembly, and was to have been presented to the king. It is quite clear what were the real opinions of the more eminent and efficient leaders of the Constituent Assembly at the time, and their opinions must be considered as of great weight at such a moment—eye-witnesses and actors in the scene. "It is a matter of certainty," says the address, "that only for those perfidious counsels, the troops, which your majesty has condescended to dismiss, would never have been summoned hither.

"Sire! whither did they pretend to lead you? What was the object of that fatal plan which they had the audacity to meditate? There is not one of us who can doubt that they proposed to disperse the National Assembly, and even lay their sacrilegious hands on the representatives of the nation," &c. &c.

After many strong observations, he concluded—"We pretend not to dictate to you the choice of your ministers: they ought to be such as please you; but, sire, when you come to consider the fatal course into which your advisers would have seduced you; when you reflect on the discontent of the capital, which they besieged, and would have starved—on the blood with which they drenched it—on the horrors, which can be imputed to themselves alone—all Europe will think you clement if you deign to pardon them."

Such are passages in the address. Mirabeau afterwards, in one of his letters to his constituents (the 19th), speaking of the scenes to which we have alluded, thus expresses himself:—

"So many extraordinary changes," he says—" the capital passing from despotism to liberty; from the most extreme terror to a state of the most perfect tranquillity; a militia of citizens established; the Bastile taken by assault; a conspiracy averted; perverse counsellors dissipated and dispersed; a powerful faction obliged to fly; ministers that were clandestinely exiled, recalled in triumph; their successors preventing their ignominy by a sudden retirement; the king, whom they had deceived, restoring to us his confidence, and demanding a return of ours; coming to show himself to his people, to collect the public interests, and to assure us that he is entirely ours;—all these events, astonishing in themselves, and, from their rapidity, almost incredible, will never remain barren, or without producing effects, and those effects not to be calculated."

In an earlier part of the same letter, alluding to the excesses of the populace, " How many," says he, " were the causes that prepared the materials of this explosion ! Ministers, that were dear to the people, exiled; those that were marked by the public scorn, brought forward to replace them ; the sanctuary of the laws profaned; the National Assembly menaced; foreign troops; artillery; the capital besieged or invaded ; the preparations of a civil war—what did I say ?—of a horrible butchery, where all the friends of the people, known or supposed, were to fall, surprised and without arms, under the swords of the soldiery ; and two centuries, in short, of oppression, public and private, political and fiscal, feudal and judicial, were to be crowned by the most horrible conspiracy which the annals of the world have ever displayed. Such are the provocations of the people. Terrible indeed is the rage of the people ; but the cold-bloodedness of despotism is atrocious, and its systematic cruelties make more men miserable in a single day, than are destroyed by the vengeance of popular insurrections in years."

Such were the different views that were taken of these memorable scenes at the time by those who were eye-witnesses and actors in them.

I will now allude to a publication that appeared about this time, under the name of Groenvelt.

I was struck with the good sense of the author. He writes as an eye-witness. I always suspected that he was some Englishman then at Paris, and from information I have subsequently received, I believe that he was one, afterwards much distinguished and admired among our public men.*

After alluding to the affair of the imprisoned soldiers, &c. &c., he proceeds thus, writing on the 7th of July :—" This town of Versailles wears in every part a military appearance, and one cannot stir a step without being struck with the idea how ill these preparations of war can be reconciled with free debate ; but what alarms men still more, is the nomination of Marshal Broglio," &c. &c.

But Groenvelt then adds—" It is impossible for any one in his senses to believe, that the slight tumults at Paris and Versailles

---

* Not so : Sir S. Romilly was only the translator of the work ; the author was Dumont.

are the real cause, though they may be the pretext, for drawing together so great an army; those insurrections were completely quelled before these preparations were made," &c. &c.

"Indeed I cannot but suspect that some great event is at hand, and that the king will not abandon the declarations which he made at the royal session (of the 23rd) without some attempt to enforce them.

"The disposition of the army, however, appears every day more favourable to the people," &c. &c.

This he writes on the 7th of July, a week before the Revolution of the 14th.

On the Saturday afterwards, on the 11th of July, "I went," he says, "to Paris, where I found, to my astonishment, that though the troops were collecting on every side, the king's answer had produced such a degree of security in people's minds, as had at least banished all idea of any immediate danger; every body looked up to the National Assembly; and if no danger was apprehended *there*, none, it was supposed, *ought* to be apprehended.

"The next day news arrived at the Palais Royal, that Necker was out of office. . . . . The people were extremely agitated; at length grief and indignation became universal. . . . . All the theatres were immediately shut. . . . . The bust of Necker was carried about the streets, covered with a crape.

"The Prince de Lambesc, at the head of a troop of foreign soldiers, galloped amidst a multitude in the garden of the Tuileries." . . . . "A general alarm was given, the bells rung. The inhabitants, who had been, as usual on a Sunday, amusing themselves in the environs of the city, hurried home; others armed themselves, crying out that the city was to be sacked with fire and sword that very night. The night (the night of the 12th) was terrible," &c. &c.

"On the Monday (the 13th) the appearance of the capital seemed perfectly miraculous. In a single day a municipal commonwealth was established, and an army set on foot. One would have thought that the six hundred thousand inhabitants of Paris had been all animated with one soul. All passions were absorbed in one, the love of liberty; all objects were neglected but the public safety." . . . . "In a single day more than forty thousand men had enlisted themselves," &c. &c.

These extracts will enable you to judge of the general manner of Groenvelt.

"Not foreseeing," he says, "all that was to happen at Paris, I hastened back to Versailles on the evening of Monday, that I

might observe the unequal contest that was to take place between
the dark and insidious policy of a court faction, and the frank
and ingenuous courage of a popular assembly."

He then goes on to describe the addresses and replies that
passed between the king and the Assembly on the subject of the
troops ; the ignorance in which the king was kept of the real
state of Paris ; his imperious and inauspicious answer (such it
appeared to Groenvelt) ; and the consequent resolutions voted by
the Assembly, " that Necker was regretted, the present ministers
responsible," &c. &c.

" In this alarming situation," he proceeds to say, " the Assembly resolved not to adjourn during the night. They dreaded
every moment receiving the news that an attack was made on
Paris by the army, and they were apprehensive that some of their
own members might be carried away clandestinely. A report
was circulated to that effect ; the Abbé Sieyes, Mirabeau, &c.,
were named. No business was proceeded on during the night,
but the Assembly sat, prepared for whatever might be the event.

" The next day, the 14th of July (a day ever memorable), the
Assembly resumed its proceedings, but in a state of the most
perplexing anxiety. The more imminent the danger which
threatened the intended constitution, the more important did it
seem to proceed to its establishment." . . . . They appointed a
committee to draw up and report to them without delay the plan
of a constitution.

" But it was in the evening that the spectacle exhibited by
the Assembly was truly sublime. I shall not attempt to describe to you," he continues, " the various emotions of joy, grief,
and terror, which at different moments agitated those who were
merely spectators and strangers in the Assembly. But the expression is improper : we were none of us strangers. For myself,
I felt as a Frenchman, because I felt as a man ; I waited for the
catastrophe in the same state of mind as I should wait for a sentence on which my own life depended. Nothing could be more
distracting than our uncertainty concerning the state of Paris,
from whence no person was suffered to stir. The Viscount de
Noailles, after repeated interruptions, had contrived at last to get
away ; but the intelligence which he brought served only to
quicken our impatience and increase our alarms. He knew that
a multitude of people in search of arms had forced their way
into the Hospital for Military Invalids ; that the Bastile was besieged ; that there had been already much bloodshed ; that the
troops encamped in the Champ de Mars were expected every mo-

ment to march to the relief of that fortress, which could not be effected without deluging all Paris in blood. At this dreadful news the Assembly was penetrated with horror. A number of the members started from their seats by a kind of involuntary impulse, as if determined to hasten to the defence of their fellow-citizens; others were for bursting immediately into the king's presence, to remonstrate with him on what had happened—to tell him, 'Behold the fruits of your counsels! hear the cries of your victims! see the destruction which is about to overwhelm your capital! saȳ, are you the king or the murderer of your people?' But these tumultuous emotions gave place to the more temperate measure of sending a numerous deputation to the king, to represent to him the calamities that threatened Paris, and again to conjure him to remove the army.

"A long time elapsed," says Groenvelt, "and the deputation did not return; no one could account for the delay. In the meantime there came a message, that two deputies from the body of electors at Paris desired admittance. They were instantly ordered in; not a breath was heard; every ear was attentive, every eye was strained, every mind was upon the rack. From some unaccountable mistake, it was a long time before the deputies entered. Never was impatience wrought up to a higher pitch; the interval was dreadful: at last the deputies appeared at the bar. 'Having been deputed,' they said, 'by the body of electors of Paris, to the Bastile, they had been fired on, and had seen several of their fellow-citizens murdered by their side, while a flag of truce was displayed, and they were negotiating with the governor.' . . . . The whole assembly was filled with indignation. A confused cry was heard: 'Revenge!' 'No, justice!' 'Justice on the guilty!' resounded in different parts of the hall. . . : . The king's answer arrived: it was less imperious, but less clear than the former. . . . .

"A third deputation was immediately sent. . . . . This new solicitation was as ineffectual as the former," &c. &c.

"This inconceivable perseverance," says Groenvelt, "in so fatal a resolution, convinced many men, that no means of resistance to the faction of the court remained but force, and several deputies, whom I talked with during the night, considered a civil war as inevitable."

Groenvelt then proceeds to describe, which he does in a very animated manner, the scenes that followed: the deputation to the king that was once more proposed, the speech of Mirabeau—and at last the turn of the whole—the appearance of the king in the assembly, &c. &c., the speech, the applauses, &c. &c.

" I have heard it observed," he afterwards says, " that the king deserved all this enthusiastic popularity at a moment when he came to save the nation.   He did save it, it is true, but from whom ?   Who had brought it into danger ?   Who was the enemy that threatened it ?   Was it not in the king's own council, or perhaps in his own heart, that the plot was formed ?   Who but his own favourites. his own ministers, and his own family, were the conspirators ?   And was he not, till the very moment when he found his own person in danger, inexorable to the prayers and entreaties of the nation ?"

This is very unjust to the king; but allowance must be made for the excited feelings of a spectator of the scene.

" I regret very much," he says, " that I was prevented going to Paris on the 15th, when the eighty delegates from the National Assembly arrived there.   I should have been very glad to have been present at their reception, to have followed them to the Town House, to the Bastile, and the Cathedral; to have enjoyed the lively emotions of the people, to have sympathized in their happiness, to have caught their enthusiasm, and to have adored the first rays of their rising liberty.   I think I should not have had to reproach myself with being a cold or indifferent spectator, or with hearing unmoved, amidst the conquerors of the Bastile, and under their torn banners, that sublime Te Deum which drew tears from the eyes of the whole congregation.   A more glorious spectacle, surely cannot be conceived, than that of a nation, which had just thrown off its bondage, beginning a new existence, and becoming an example to all the enslaved nations of the earth. It would seem, indeed, that it is at this period that the history of mankind is to commence."

I have produced these passages from Groenvelt for your consideration.   The feelings and opinions of an eye-witness (probably some Englishman) are here before you, and I leave you to convert them, by reflecting upon them, to your own instruction. My own opinions I consider of no importance, and I rather wish to furnish you with the means of forming opinions for yourselves.

" I was impatient," says the same writer, " to see the Bastile, to walk over it, and to enjoy my liberty in its cells and in its dungeons. . . . . When we arrived there, we found a great crowd of spectators before it, gazing at the towers, examining the batteries, contemplating the depth of the ditches, and inquiring about the circumstances of the siege. . . . .

" I could not help shuddering, as I passed over the drawbridges which used to be let down to receive the prisoners, and drawn up the moment they had passed.   We proceeded into the inte-

rior court, which is so narrow, and surrounded by such high
walls, that I doubt whether the rays of the sun ever entered it.
The whole prison, its dark staircases, its mysterious passages,
its triple doors plated with iron and fastened by enormous bolts,
its cells, which resembled graves, prepared for the reception of
living bodies; its dungeons, gloomy, damp, and unwholesome,
with walls eight feet in thickness; the great stone in the midst
of each, which served the double purpose of a bed and a chair;
the chain in the middle of the stone, which from its thickness
seemed intended to bind a wild beast, and not a man; in short,
every object that met our eyes inspired us with sentiments of
dread and horror. We saw many instruments of torture, the
names and the uses of which were entirely unknown to us. Among
others, we observed an iron suit of armour, made to press upon
all the joints, and to seize, as it were, with one gripe, the knees,
the hips, the stomach, the arms, and the neck, of the wretch on
whom it was fixed. It may be considered as a precious relic of
tyranny. I know that it is a long time since these abominable
engines have been used, but they were once used; and it is not
uninstructive to remember what torments have been invented by
slaves to revenge themselves on those who refused to share their
slavery, and disdained to partake of the infamy of their honours."

Such is the description, and such the sentiments of Groenvelt.

I produce them, not to excite in you any crude, irrational, and
vague hostility against authority, but because it is not uninstructive to see, how cruel man has been and may be; to note the
progress of society; to consider what in free countries he now
is; to reflect on what are the sources of this improvement; the
virtue of those who, though in possession of power, do not abuse
it; the merit of those who resist oppression, and who make
sacrifices, of what ever kind, for the happiness and advancement
of their fellow-creatures.

The conquest of this fortress was not, it seems, the result of
any preconcerted design, but was achieved by enthusiastic ardour,
favoured by accidental good fortune. Some account of this conquest is given by Groenvelt, and some of those particulars mentioned, which may be expected to occur, when the varying passions of the populace are so tremendously excited. A capitulation had been proposed and agreed to, but it was impossible, from
the confusion, to make the capitulation publicly known; at least,
it was impossible to stop the multitude, who rushed forward
thirsting for victims, whose blood might atone for what had
been already shed. The leaders did all they could to disarm the
fury of the people, but in vain.

De Launay, the governor, was immediately murdered, and not far from him the major of the Bastile, De Losme Solbay, a man who was worthy of a better fate, for he had proved himself a friend to the unfortunate, while himself in a situation (an officer in the Bastile) not favourable to the milder virtues of the human character. A young man was seen exerting himself in defence of this unfortunate officer, with a degree of strength and courage which seemed perfectly miraculous—miraculous to those who know not the strength and courage that are inspired by the consciousness of a generous cause: though repeatedly struck to the ground, he rose again with redoubled vigour, and rushed upon the assassins—but in vain.

This youthful hero, this hero of gratitude and humanity, was the Marquise de Pelleport, who, during an imprisonment of five years, had experienced the kindness of Solbay, and had come to the attack of the Bastile for the purpose, if possible, of protecting the life of his benefactor.

Other victims were sacrificed: the barbarous cry was " No forgiveness for traitors !"

Flesselles, the first municipal magistrate in Paris, was shot by a pistol, and his bleeding body torn into pieces by a mob who appeared no longer to possess the common attributes of our nature. The soldiers of the Bastile were with difficulty saved by the French guards, and the bleeding heads of those who had suffered were placed by their murderers on poles. And this was, alas ! the triumph that was now to proceed along the streets of the most splendid city of the most civilized portion of the globe.

Some incidents occurred that afford the mind a passing relief amid such scenes of horror.

A young man, by his courage and contrivances, saved the life of his father, then an invalid, and one of those who defended the fortress.

Again,—in the midst of the assault, a young girl was observed in one of the courts. The assailants, who mistook her for the daughter of the governor, were brutal enough to call aloud that they would murder her if the governor did not surrender. Her real father was a witness from the ramparts of this abominable scene, saw that it was his daughter, heard the words of her executioners, and was rushing forward to speak to them and to save her, when he was killed by a musket ball. At this moment, for the honour of human nature, thus debased and fallen, one of the citizens pressed forward, beat down the wretches who had seized on the girl, bore her away in his arms amid the shouts and applauses of many of the spectators, conveyed her to a place of safety, and then returned to the charge.

During all these days of tumult and disorder, none of the people appear to have been actuated by the desire of plunder. Those few who did so appear, were instantly tried, convicted, and hanged by their companions. Money, plate, and jewels, were brought to the Town House by men covered with rags, and the same men seemed at successive moments, now to be debased by the most savage, and now to be elevated by the most disinterested passions of our nature.

Groenvelt afterwards describes the visit of the king to Paris; the waving forest of pikes and bayonets, stretching out for the space of four or five miles, through which he had to pass; the order which every where prevailed; the regular army that, from amidst the citizens of Paris, had started up, as it were, in a single day; the grave and solemn manner in which he was received; the free and spirited harangues at the Town House; the national cockade; the people, to all appearance, unanimously demanding new laws and a new constitution.

"Thus every thing," he at last concludes, "is awed, submissive, and humbled before the nation. The whole difficulty," he says, "which the Assembly can now experience, is in stopping the ravages which may be caused by the overflowing of popular power. That species of difficulty, however," he says, "is neither so great nor so dangerous as those which must have arisen in a perpetual struggle with the faction of the court, in the compromises that must have been made with the existing powers, and in the necessity of only correcting what ought to be totally abolished, and of merely reforming, where every thing was to be created anew.

This opinion pronounced by Groenvelt, was shared at the time by all the friends of freedom; but it is the great question of the whole subject, and this decision must now, I conceive, be considered as wrong. To stop the overflowings of popular power, when the power is really popular, and once triumphant, must now be thought the most invincible of all difficulties. Timely compromises with existing powers, to correct, not totally abolish, to reform, not create anew, must now be deemed the only practical wisdom.

From the day of the royal session (June 23), it is the opinion of Groenvelt, that the court was only bent on maintaining the system which it had there avowed. Necker was to be dismissed, and a new ministry named entirely devoted to the court. Breteuil was consulted, it is said; and it was supposed that, with an army of fifty thousand men, it would be an easy thing to over-awe Paris, and to govern or dissolve the National Assembly.

"As to the intended siege of Paris, the devoting the city to plunder and conflagration, and a proscription of the members of the Assembly, I consider them," he says, "merely as the dreams of fear; but at the same time it must be confessed, that the most violent measures, though they had not been coolly preme-ditated, were not absolutely rejected from the plan which the court adopted; they were thought worth risking in the dreadful hazard that was to be encountered. Such indeed is the common course of human affairs. Nothing more than an extraordinary exertion of authority is at first intended, but the maintenance of that authority, and the necessity of advancing in order not to recede, leads insensibly to the most bloody proscriptions.

"All the measures of the court," he then affirms, "have been false, ill-concerted, ill-executed, and marked in every instance with weakness, levity, and infatuation.

"Breteuil and Broglio," he says, "found the king too virtuous, or too feeble, for the execution of their bold designs. If they could have ventured openly to advise him to quit Versailles, to retire to Metz, there to put himself at the head of his army, to have called to his aid religion, the nobility and the parliament, and to have convoked another assembly according to the ancient form, a civil war would have ensued.

"But what," he continues, "would have been the event of it? From the temper of Paris we may judge of the rest of France. The whole nation would have united under the auspices of the Assembly in the common cause of liberty, which would certainly in the end have proved victorious, but not perhaps until after such a series of calamities, as might make it doubtful whether even liberty be worth so great a price."

Such are the opinions and representations of Groenvelt of all he saw or heard, and you have now had those of other writers and eye-witnesses laid before you, in that sort of brief and gene-ral manner which I can alone attempt in lectures like these: and when you come to consider these materials for your reflec-tion more attentively, you must judge for yourselves.

You will in the mean time observe, that the National As-sembly were quite clear and decided in their sentiments on this occasion, and they certainly considered the court as bringing up the troops, not to maintain the tranquillity of Paris and the cause of good government, but to dissolve them by force, and to put an end to the Revolution by violence.

On the whole, it appears to me, that there can be no doubt that a great design had been formed by the court for the dissolution of the National Assembly, and the assertion of the power of the crown. That military force was to have been produced, and according to the measure of its success would in all probability have been the depression of the spirit of liberty, even of rational liberty, then existing in France.

Less than this cannot well be supposed; much more may be believed.

And such was the notion every where entertained of the arbitrary nature of the old government of France; such were the expectations formed of the National Assembly; such was the fermentation produced in the minds of benevolent and intelligent men, by the example of America and the captivating nature of the new opinions, that such sentiments as I have quoted, even from Mirabeau, were those that prevailed over Europe: and in this country at least, and in all free countries, the fall of the Bastile, and the arming of the French people, with the disappearance of the regular soldiery, were every where celebrated by poets and orators, and considered by all those who loved liberty, and knew its value, as the astonishing but virtuous insurrection of a great people, in assertion of every thing that could do honour to human nature, or give a promise of happiness to succeeding generations.

LECTURE XII.

BAILLY.

You have been now conducted to a striking point in this great subject of the French Revolution. You have passed through a series of events, that at last transferred the old monarchy of France into the hands of the National Assembly; the old monarchy of France, and even the fate of the monarch himself. Many reasonings and opinions have been proposed to your consideration while you were journeying on to a result like this. I have already mentioned to you several books and memoirs to which you may apply for information.

There are other writers besides those I have referred to, that deserve your attention; writers that give their opinions on many of the subjects which have now passed in review before you. On these subjects you cannot be too well informed; it is the first stages of this great Revolution that are more particularly instructive. Men are not to be indifferent to one of the noblest of all causes, the cause of liberty ; but they are to be very careful how they proceed in the assertion of it. Those who naturally take a part are the young, the high-spirited, the fearless, and the presumptuous. I add the presumptuous, for those who deserve this last epithet will assuredly be mixed, at least, with those of generous and patriotic feelings ; nay, more, be likely, sooner or later, to take a lead among them ; and it is therefore the duty of a lecturer on history to exhibit, if possible, the first reasonings and views of those who interfered in the earlier scenes of a Revolution like this, that every chance may be taken of giving instruction to all who mean well; whether those of the privileged orders, who are to give way for the sake of the common good, or those who are, as patriots, to bring forward their schemes of improvement.

I shall, therefore, still further direct your attention to the testimonies of those who were actors in the scene; and, at the hazard of appearing tedious to you, I shall proceed to the memoirs of two more, who were members of the Constituent Assembly; they sat on opposite sides, M. Bailly and the Marquis de Ferrieres, and they are on that account of more value to us. I must suppose you now sufficiently familiar with the leading topics, and I shall allude to such passages in their works as I think most worthy of observation.

M. Bailly was one of the most celebrated men of his time. He was a philosopher well known for his writings all over Europe ; a person of unblemished character, and of the best intentions; and he saw his country, after he had taken a leading part in her concerns, brought to a state of anarchy and confusion, while he was himself led out to perish on a scaffold. There can be no want of interest in the opinions and views of a man like this. He had been member of the Academy of Sciences, of the Academy of Belles Lettres, of the French Academy; he was member and president of the first National Assembly, and twice mayor of Paris, he was at the time, in the full maturity and vigour of his intellectual powers ; he was put to death at the end of the year 1793, and was then at the age of fifty-seven.

His Memoirs were written in 1792, and he intended to have given the whole of his political life, a period of thirty-one months; but his account terminates in October, 1789, and comprises, therefore, only an interval of about five months and a half; but it is a most memorable interval. He was too good a man to have been admitted to all the secrets of the Revolution, but his book will on that account be only more instructive to all good men like himself. He intends but a journal, and his reader, he says, shall see his heart, and the thoughts of it (such as they were), exhibited before him in all their naked simplicity and truth.

It was on the 29th of December, 1786, when he was dining with the Maréchal de Beauvan, that he first heard the news of the calling together of the Notables. He was struck with it, he says; he thought it a great event; that it would lead to changes, and changes even in the form of government; but certainly he foresaw no Revolution such as afterwards took place, nor does he conceive (and he is very right) that any one at that time did (December, 1786); but the deplorable state of the finances sufficiently, he thought, justified him in such conjectures as those he made. He then gives a short general view of what passed before the winter of 1788, and he observes :—" It was thus, and with arms like these, that men prepared themselves for the States General, and for the recovery of the rights of the nation, and of the Tiers Etat. But if these rights," he adds, " have been recovered, we must not forget, that it is to Necker and to the king that this is owing—to the minister who proposed, and to the king who consented : both the one and the other have given the means of the regeneration of the empire, a point this that has been sometimes too much forgotten. Despotism is what never entered into the character of the king; he never had any wish but the happiness of his people, and this was the only consideration that could be ever employed as a means of influencing him; and if any acts of authority were to be resorted to, he was never to be persuaded, but by showing him that some good was to be thus attained, or some evil to be avoided; some relief for the nation was to be held out in prospect before him, or the prosperity of the empire, and the happiness of all. I am convinced," continues M. Bailly, " that his authority was never considered by him, nor did he wish to maintain it, but as the best means of supporting and securing the tranquillity and peace of the community. As we are now speaking of the causes," says he, " that produced this regeneration of the country, let us state the first to be the character of Louis XVI.; a king less of a good man, and ministers more adroit, and we should have had no Revolution."

This is a very full, strong, and (coming from M. Bailly) unobjectionable testimony to the merits of the king; to his patriotism, at least, and good intentions; to his moral if not political merits.

At the first sittings of the Assembly of the Electors of Paris, M. Bailly was made, very unexpectedly to himself, deputy to the States General. He was not fit for it, he says: without facility in speaking, and timid to an excess.

"The men of letters," he observes, "did not act a prominent part, but the advocates did; the men connected with the law; distinguished everywhere by their numbers and their opinions, in the capital, in the bailliages, in the Electoral Assemblies, in the legislative body and the constituent: it is to them that the success of the Revolution is to be attributed." By the success I fear M. Bailly must mean the progress.

You may remember that the lawyers took the same distinguished part in the revolution in America; this, on many accounts, was to be expected.

"The men of letters," says Bailly, "were far from being popular in the National Assembly. I may say so, for I speak with the exception of myself; and yet men of letters are of all the most enlightened, if not on particular subjects, on subjects in general; they have more exercised their faculties, and know best how to apply them; but they were not numerous enough to make their part good; the trading interest and the advocates were the prevailing descriptions in the Assembly. But there had always been a rivalry between the men of letters and the advocates, though they of all others should have been most united. Power had never been able to shut the mouth of a courageous advocate, and power had always stood in awe of the enlightened minds, and free and fierce language, of distinguished men of letters. Exile and *iettres de cachet* had often been their reward; how was it then that so few of the men of letters took the lead in the Revolution? I must not dissemble, that many of them mixed a little worldly prudence in their politics, and chose to see the side that was likely to prevail. These were, indeed, but the poor creatures of this particular class, but in others of the class the same hesitation may be traced to causes of a more dignified nature. For instance, the philosopher loves liberty, he knows the dignity of man, but he first, and above all, asks for peace. Let the light, he says, expand around him; let humanity recover its rights; but by degrees and without effort. He is in terror of concussions and violent revolutions. The reason is simple: he compares the purchase with the price to be paid. Efforts can only accelerate things; when they are ripened and come to maturity, their very necessity inevitably produces them. If a great people once thinks of liberty, at liberty they must arrive. The time when, the natural epoch, the philosopher thinks, and wisely thinks, must not be precipitated; his calculations turn only on the more and the less. He would have less rather than more, if that more is to be purchased by public calamities and the shedding of blood. However the men of loftier minds, who vote themselves the only children of liberty, may look down upon, as spurious, those who condescend to consider and calculate, they cannot but allow that such calculations are not altogether unreasonable; and I have always thought, and I think still, that a little more of this sort of philosophic reasoning would have done us no harm in the Constituent Assembly."

Now I must recommend this paragraph that I have quoted to your recollection. You will see, hereafter, that M. Bailly was an assertor of the new opinions, voted and acted with La Fayette and his friends, yet he seems here to have been aware, perhaps too late, that the march of reformers should be slow. Those who love liberty, and who have ardour and talents enough to obtain an audience in their country, should be warned by passages like these, coming from a man like this, of the most undeniable benevolence, and of intelligence the most acknowledged. Principles like those which M. Bailly has here laid down, might have saved the National Assembly and the state. But Bailly immediately subjoins:—" Such were my principles; my conduct, indeed, has been that of my duties; my first law was the national will; when the nation was once assembled, I had no other law but that sovereign will."

Principles like these last, on the contrary, which M. Bailly has thus expressed, ruined all. To vote that no question was to be asked beyond the sovereign will of the people, was to leave everything to the disposal, first, of sanguine, intemperate, and therefore dangerous men, and ultimately of bad, designing men, and of furious and ferocious men. Nothing can be so base in itself, and so fatal to the state, as to act in subserviency to the popular will, when it is felt to be wrong.

The great points of interest when the States met, were such as I have already proposed to your consideration, the verification of the powers, the early votes of the Assembly, the struggle, and the result, as far as we have yet proceeded in the history. It will be curious to observe, what such a man as Bailly has to say on such important subjects. I will, immediately, endeavour to give you some notion of what seems to have occurred to him, but I will first allude to a few particulars which I think are of a preliminary nature. For instance, Bailly lays down the propriety and necessity of a particular dress for people in public situations. He laments that the costume appropriated to each order in the National Assembly was at last abandoned. One of the notions (a very convenient one at the time) to which the French Revolution gave currency, was, that every thing ought to be rested entirely on its own merit; that a magistrate or a king was but a man, and was, therefore, only to appear as such. This is very much the tone and language of all republics; directly opposed to that of monarchies and courts: each carries its notions to an extreme. But Bailly's testimony is clearly against the republican extreme, and is somewhat remarkable, considering the times in which he lived, and that he was by profession himself a philosopher. He had every temptation to be wrong; but being president of the National Assembly, he probably discovered, that there were other things which affected large masses of mankind besides merit, and that the natural associations of the mind and feelings of the heart should be made available to the great cause of peace and order and law.

Again,—One of the main causes of the failure of the Revolution was, the liberty which the people in the tribunes assumed of expressing their applause or censure of what was going on in the Assembly. It is curious, therefore, to observe the first approaches of a power so fatal, and the reasonings which led to its introduction.

The line taken by our own House of Commons seems the right one; that strangers, as they are called, should be admitted (for advantages quite inestimable result from the publicity of their debates), but that any member should have a power of ordering them instantly to withdraw, which secures, and can alone secure, their non-interference: a point that is on one side quite as indispensable, as is the publicity of the debates on the other, and even more so.

"Just as we were going to deliberate," says Bailly, "a deputy demanded that the strangers should withdraw; the proposition was rejected. It was settled, that there could be no discussion that ought not to have the greatest publicity, for there could be none that had not for its object the interest of every citizen. The strangers were, therefore, only given to understand, that they were not to seat themselves among the members, and carefully to abstain from all expressions of censure or approbation;"—"an engagement," says Bailly, "made with the public, which the public has not always observed." They were sure not to observe it, it may be replied ; and the deputy's motion should have been carried, and the rule made what it is with us. There was, no doubt, a difficulty in the case of the National Assembly, who thought themselves in need of the constant sympathy and support of the public ; but it was not so necessary as they supposed, and they bought it too dearly. In a subsequent part of his Memoirs, you will find many curious particulars on this very important subject ; Bailly was always aware of the fatal, at least very dangerous, consequences of the interference of the galleries.

You will find, too, observations on the first rise of the clubs, and of their objectionable nature ; the Assembly seem not at first to have admired them.

I will now proceed to the main subjects on which the notions of Bailly should be observed.

You must remark, as I read, the tone and manner of his reasonings : they must have been those of wise and good patriots, like himself, at the time ; they are specimens of the effect of the new opinions. I produce them as a sort of picture of the Revolution ; and you must not be repelled by the dry and tedious nature of exhibitions like these, now or at any other time, for I conceive them to offer the best chance of your instruction.

The National Assembly had been sitting some time before Bailly and the deputies for Paris had joined them.

The great question of the verification of the powers was now in full agitation. Bailly discusses and gives the history of it, but seems not to have seen the dangers that were to be apprehended from the vote by head, instead of by order, which was the question really at issue ; and an issue which was to determine another point of still more importance, whether the Revolution was to go on step by step, and with due moderation and delay, or to proceed with a rapidity that even Bailly might have seen at the time would be very dangerous. On the contrary, his apprehensions seem to have taken no other but an opposite direction ; and this, I conceive to be one of the lessons of his work. " To divide and rule," says he (80), " has been always the maxim of governments, (he alludes to the wish of the court for the vote by orders,) and the application of it seems to be thought useful, even in such new circumstances as ours ; and at the moment, when it has become prejudicial to the public weal, and dangerous to those who so make use of it. It is on the contrary," says he, " quite necessary that every power should be united to make the constitution ; and above all things, that the constitution, as it proceeds, should trample down all difficulties and resistance." This is not very agreeable to Bailly's earlier and more sound mode of reasoning, such as I have quoted at the opening of the lecture.

But to proceed. You will see still further in the passages I shall now quote, how distinctly the new opinions appear in the views and reasonings of this eminent philosopher; a philosopher of some standing, but a somewhat-newly made statesman.

" The nobles," he says, " decreed, that the deliberation by order, and the power of each order to put a veto on the proceedings of the other two, were part of the very constitution of the monarchy, and that they must maintain them as the defenders of the throne and of freedom.

" What a strange decree !" says Bailly ; " the representatives of about two hundred thousand individuals or more, who are noble, take upon themselves to decide, and in their own favour, a question that concerns twenty-five millions of men. They assume for themselves the right of the veto; they declare the powers and the principles of the constitution ; and who are they, more than others, who thus declare ?" M. Bailly, a calm and most intelligent philosopher, appears thus, at this particular period— such was the effect of the new opinions—to have seen nothing in an order of nobility but a collection of so many individuals ; a most vulgar and miserable misconception. But Bailly was not merely a man of science; he had even lived in Paris, and was at the time enjoying a pension from the crown as a man of letters : so strong had set the current of public opinion against privileged orders, even so early in the Revolution as May, 1789. He seems never for a moment to have seen or to have regarded the importance of their body, as a body ; the weight of their argument, even with reference to the safety of the monarchy.

Again, on the fifth of June, probably for the first time, the language of democracy was sounded in the palace of Versailles. A deputation of the Tiers Etat was to wait upon the king. Bailly was the president; he had to adjust the ceremonies with the keeper of the seals. " It is not," said the keeper of the seals, " that one would insist upon any ancient custom (the going down upon the knee), any that would hurt the Tiers Etat, or that the king has any intention of exacting any observance of this kind ; yet still, as this custom has existed from time immemorial, and if the king should will it—" " But if twenty-five millions of men should *not* will it," interrupted Bailly, " where would be the means of forcing them ?" This, to be sure, was a question not hitherto asked at Versailles, in the palace of Louis

XIV., and shows in Bailly's mind the inroad of the new opinions.
—With respect to the struggle that ensued between the Tiers
Etat and the privileged orders, M. Bailly describes it much in the
way you will see it given by others.

At last the Tiers Etat, it seems, having first dropped that
name, and called themselves " the Commons," voted themselves
" the National Assembly."

" There was some little awkwardness," says Bailly,—(undoubtedly there was,)—" in thus declaring ourselves to be the
nation. In the first place, it was not exactly true," says he,
" while there was assembled at the time a Chamber of the Clergy,
and a Chamber also of the Noblesse, with a right to be so assembled ; and yet it was certain that the French in mass (the clergy
and nobility excluded) were such a majority, that they might be
considered as the whole nation. Usage was on one side," says
he, " reason on the other : usage, which divided the nation into
three portions, one immense, and two very diminutive ; reason,
that wished to unite them all, or that thought the one larger
should absorb the two small ones." Now here I must observe, on
this passage of M. Bailly, that this is revolutionary language ;
that it is by reasonings of this kind that men on all these occasions colour their usurpations, deceive others and themselves.
Men are to be numbered by the head ; things are to be reduced
to their first elements ; what is called reason is to be brought
forward to put aside all usage and custom ; that is, to put aside
all existing feelings and associations ; and the nation is to take
the chance of a new set, better or worse (as it may happen), to
be formed with difficulty, and, after a collision, a conflict with
the old, ending probably in a civil war.

Acts of usurpation should be also, on another account, most
carefully avoided, not only from the justice of the case, from the
possible inexpediency of the proceeding, but from the impossibility of receding, when a public body has once committed itself.
An accidental circumstance is here to be remarked. It was one
misfortune among others, that the Tiers Etat had got into the
great hall, where the States General would naturally assemble :
there they were ; and it appeared more in course for the other
orders to be found there too, that is, to come to them, than the
contrary ; that is, the Tiers Etat were themselves profiting by the
very associations which they were calling on reason to destroy.

But this act of usurpation was, in fact, not proposed in the
assembly of the Tiers Etat without exciting the greatest sensation ; not without tumult and noise the most frightful and over-

powering; and this is a very curious circumstance. M. Bailly
evidently gives himself the greatest credit for the calmness and
the sort of *vis inertiæ* that he displayed. He was president.
Three or four hundred members among them, " the brave Bre-
tons," as he calls them, stood bawling for the question before
him; behind him, about one hundred endeavouring to cause an
adjournment, by making, if possible, a still greater uproar, that
all business might be impracticable; the great table that stretched
along the hall and divided the parties, alone prevented them
from coming to blows : a scene this, which might have taught
M. Bailly and the patriots how much more easy it was for men
to feel than to think, and that the reason to which he and they
were referring every thing was only one element among others
in the composition of human nature.

I cannot but think this portion of M. Bailly's account somewhat edifying. It is my office to denounce to you all acts of
usurpation whenever they appear, whether committed by the
friends of liberty or its enemies. Acts of usurpation are violence; violence must be followed by violence, by hatred, dissension, bloodshed, by individual and national calamity. It is
natural for me to turn my own eyes, and to wish to direct yours,
to the beginning of these things : when the flood-gate is once
opened, it is in vain to lament the rushing out of the torrent.

But to proceed. After a more orderly sitting the next day,
the following resolutions were decreed, and were the first constitutional acts of the Assembly, by a majority of four hundred
and ninety-one to ninety; something more than five to one.
Observe now the nature of the resolutions of the Assembly, and
of Bailly's reasons while considering these resolutions. The
point to be effected was, to show how and why the Assembly
were to be every thing, and every other authority in the state
nothing. Observe, then, I repeat, the revolutionary, special
pleading of the Assembly in the first instance, and of their
commentator, the philosopher, in the second.

" The Assembly," says the first paragraph of these resolutions, " the Assembly, deliberating after the verification of its
powers, perceives that it is already composed of representatives
sent directly by ninety-six hundredths, at least, of the whole
nation." Very well : " Nothing," says Bailly, " can be more
exact than this assertion."

Again : " Such a mass of deputation," continues the resolution of this Assembly, " cannot remain inactive on account of
the absence of the deputies of some particular bailliages, or of

some classes of citizens; for the absent, who have been summoned, cannot prevent those who are present from the full exercise of their rights, particularly when the exercise of those
rights is a duty imperious and pressing."

"Nothing," says Bailly, "can be more regular than this;
there the principle, here the consequence: quite unanswerable.
The four-hundredths that are absent, but duly summoned, cannot impede the ninety-six-hundredths that are present. Certainly not. To show the contrary, one has only indeed," says
Bailly, "to cite usage, custom; but reason," he replies, "that
has now awaked, stifles all murmurs of this kind about usage
and custom;" and reason having thus done its office, M. Bailly
can proceed, as can the resolution of the Assembly, to the desired
point, and that, after the following manner :—

"Moreover, as it belongs to those representatives only, who
are verified, to concur with the national will, and as all the representatives verified must be in this Assembly, it follows in-
dispensably that it belongs to this Assembly, and to this Assembly only, to interpret and to produce the general will of the
nation." All right again, it seems, according to Bailly: "The
principle," says he, "that all the representations should be verified, is incontestable; that the representatives ought all to find
themselves in the Assembly, incontestable also (it can be contested only by the two orders). And this last principle admitted, the assertion that it belongs to the Assembly, and to the
Assembly only, to declare the will of the nation, has in it nothing
rash, and nothing that is not perfectly well founded;" that is,
in other words, according to M. Bailly, for the king's will, which
was formerly the term, the national will was to be substituted;
and by the national will was meant the will of the Assembly;
and so it comes out (according to *this* reasoning at least) that the
States General had been called together by the king, that a part
of them, the Tiers Etat, might be made king instead of him.
Certainly usage and custom were against all this, but reason was
then adequate, according to M. Bailly, to settle every thing.

Particularly it seems, as the Assembly went on to decree, that
"there could exist between the throne and the Assembly no veto,
no negative power;" and as the Assembly declared further,
"that the common work of the national restoration could and
ought to begin without further delay by the deputies present,
and that they ought to pursue it, as without interruption, so also
without obstacle." Further, "That the name of National Assembly is the only one that befits the Assembly in the present
state of things; as well because the members who compose it

are the only representatives lawfully and publicly known and
verified, as because also they are sent by almost the whole of
the nation; and because, finally, the representation being one
and indivisible, no one of the deputies (for whatever order or
class they may be chosen) can have the right of exercising their
functions separately from this Assembly.

"Here," says Bailly (still proud of the reasoning and wisdom
of the Assembly), "here, then, we finish by a principle which
confirms and legitimatizes all the rest, the unity of the national
representation. What sort of a state," says he, "is that, where
the nation has three voices? and what then is to be the result
of these three voices? Is it the majority of the three that is to
decide? Would it not then be of course, that the nobles and
the clergy, four in the hundred, would in the event be the majority over the remaining ninety-six? But who then will at
last have to decide between the two orders and the Tiers Etat?
The king. But then the nation has no longer a will. Be the
following truths, then, agreed to:—No more orders in the representation of the nation; deliberation in common; unity in
the representation. Let me admire," says he, "the wise and
firm march of the Assembly;" and the movements of this march
are then by him again recapitulated.

Something, however, of civility, of haughty civility, that
must have been more offensive than the usurpation itself, was
to bring up the rear of this column of reasoning.

"The Assembly," said the last clause of the whole resolution,
"will never lose the hope of uniting in its bosom all the deputies that are now absent: will never cease to call upon them to
fulfil the obligation that has been imposed upon them of concurring with the sitting of the States General. At whatever
moment the absent deputies may present themselves in the
session about to open, the Assembly declares beforehand that it
will hasten to receive them, to share with them, after the verification of their powers, the continuance of the great labours
which cannot but procure the regeneration of France."

After these resolutions, it seems the Assembly voted what they
and M. Bailly considered a respectful address to the king, to apprize him what the resolutions were; that is, to apprize him
that he was to descend from his throne and to seat himself by
the president: this, or something very like it; and then the hall
resounded with reiterated shouts of *Vive le Roi!*

Such is the account given by M. Bailly of the revolutionary
logic that was used, and of the proceedings that followed. I

know not how to give you a better idea of the situation of France
at the time, than that such logic should be tolerated and such
proceedings ensue.   M. Bailly was, as I must again and again
repeat, an amiable and sensible man, a calm and distinguished
philosopher, a disinterested patriot; yet could M. Bailly not perceive, that while the Assembly were thus usurping, in fact, the
whole power of the state, the king in the meantime had done
nothing to justify them in thus setting him aside, and all the
rules, and maxims, and orders of the ancient monarchy aside
also ; that they were standing away full sail from the shore, and
embarking on an untried ocean, with no star to guide them but
their reason, as they termed it; or rather, perhaps, with no
other light but the flashes that might issue from the thunder-
storms of the multitude.   The injustice, the rashness, the folly
of all this, seems never for a moment to have reached the apprehension of this most respectable member of the Assembly.
The regeneration of his country was his object; the sovereign
will of the people his means.

Such was M. Bailly ; such were thousands of intelligent men
around him.   What could be expected, what could be hoped,
from the majority of a nation, when such were the most distinguished of the wise?   But those who consider themselves as the
wise also, either now or hereafter, may here find their instruction.

The next act of the Assembly was in course.   M. Bailly, and
no doubt the members themselves, were conscious that the act
by which they had thus constituted the Tiers Etat the National
Assembly, comprehended in its meaning and operation the destruction of the two privileged orders.   " In establishing," says
he, " that we could do without them, we showed their inability
and their abuse. Government," he says, " could not but see that
this act seized upon that authority which had, till that time,
been exclusively royal, to throw it into the hands of the nation
and its legitimate representatives."   And now, you will observe,
as one usurpation was to be followed up by another (and this is
always one of the great objections to anything that bears the very
appearance of usurpation), it became necessary to the Assembly,
as acquiescence in their proceedings could not possibly be expected from the court, to provide for the permanence of their
sitting, lest their dissolution should be attempted, and their leading members seized and imprisoned; and they, therefore, proceeded next to vote, that the existing taxes, not having been
consented to by the nation, were illegal; but that they consented to them provisorily, and legalized them, till the day of

their dissolution, after which none were to be legal which they had not expressly made so.

Now here it may surely be asked, was this the manner in which the king was to be treated, or even the two privileged orders? These two privileged orders had formally (however late) given up their immunity from taxation. Is there not always in the affairs of mankind, as in the action of bodies, a reaction to be expected? Is it to be wondered at that the court should urge the king to bring up the army to dissolve the Assembly?—that the king should consent to it? It is very true, that if things had b en left to take their natural course, the Tiers Etat might have und great opposition from the other two bodies, voting by or r, not by head; their Revolution would not have proceede at the rate they wished: but was this a reason for their putti everything to issue; for their making their terms so hard the king and the patrons of the old régime; for their runn the chance of a civil war?

B uch, it will be said, was the nature of the times. Then such reply, is the lesson of the times, and as such I propose it, a with the antecedent selfishness and folly of the privilege ders, to your most careful consideration. There is selfishness the one side, rashness on the other.

B have gone more into this subject before, and explained mys ore calmly. It is difficult to be calm when the very reas gs that have led to fatal consequences are, as in the memoi Bailly, exhibited to our more immediate view: when thei gerous pretensions, their shuffling sophistry, their triumphal justice, can be seen through.

S fter, you will remark new circumstances appearing: the vote re printed and published; the members of the Assembly, the y particularly, were, therefore, hooted or applauded by the lace. M. Bailly, it is true, makes here the proper observ s; but it should have taught him, and have taught oth take care that such statesmen as these, the populace of did not interfere in the debates of the Assembly. M. Bai tes this as the commencement of that war that was afte ls waged by the Sansculottes and hired armies of Paris; tha was the commencement of the destruction of the cause of r and of M. Bailly and his fellow-patriots.

w you will observe that the lesson is to *alter*, and you are called upon to remark an extraordinary want of skill an nspection in the conduct of the king and the court.

pposition was of course to be made to these proceedings of embly, and, as you may remember, a royal sitting was determined upon (the sitting of the 23rd of June); that is, the king was to occupy the hall of the Assembly, while he summoned to his presence and addressed there the three orders of the States General.

Instead, therefore, of notifying his intention in an official manner, as he would have done to the parliaments, M. Bailly, the president, received no proper official notice, and he and the members of the Assembly had to say to themselves and to each other, " Is it decent that the members of the National Assembly, or even the deputies of the Commons, as you may still please to consider them, is it decent that they should thus be apprized of the intentions of the king, of the suspension of their own sittings, and of the shutting up of their hall, only by public criers, and by notices posted on the wall, as the inhabitants of a town would be made acquainted with the shutting up of a theatre?"

These are the words of M. Bailly, and are but too reasonable; and the conclusions that were drawn by him and others were but too natural—that what the court intended was to prevent the Assembly from sitting at all; to prevent any more resolutions like those we have just alluded to, of the 17th, till some great blow should be struck (probably at the sitting of the 23rd); to prevent the union of the clergy at all events; and to allow no time to the Assembly to take measures in opposition to the royal sitting. These seem to have been the notions of M. Bailly, and no doubt of the rest of the Assembly; and it must be confessed that they were very fair conclusions for them to draw, and that they afterwards under these impressions defended themselves from the court, and supported their late usurpation of the powers of the state, with great firmness and spirit.

The facts as related by Bailly himself, one of the principal persons concerned, are the same that have been given you by other writers, and you are already acquainted with them. The deputies of the Tiers Etat were shut out from their hall, when they came to renew their sitting agreeably to their adjournment; they therefore assembled in a tennis court, and the opportunity was taken to declare, and indeed, under the circumstance of the case, it was necessary to declare, that wherever its members could meet, there was the National Assembly, and to enter into a solemn engagement never to separate; an oath with uplifted hands was the form adopted, after the theatric manner of the nation; it was pronounced aloud by the president, heard outside the doors, re-echoed in all the streets, and all around accompanied and followed up (one cannot immediately see why) by universal shouts of. *Vive le Roi!*

The revolutionary language, however, in which the decree sets out is remarkable. "The National Assembly" (the words are) "considering, that called upon to fix the constitution of the kingdom, and to effect 'the regeneration of public order," it is then added indeed, "and to maintain the true principles of the monarchy, resolves," &c. On these last words, M. Bailly seems to rest his thoughts with some complacency. "The Assembly," says he, "took proper precautions against the ministry, and armed itself against its despotism, but was heart and soul with the king, and had no intention to do any thing in opposition to his lawful authority; and it was against despotism, not against the monarchy, that its proceedings were directed."

No doubt these were the views of Bailly and the majority of the Tiers Etat; but their new opinions, their contempt for precedent, for experience, and the established forms and notions of the monarchy, assisted by the original perverseness, the blindness, the stupidity I had almost called it, of the court, and the lamentable want of character in the king, soon rendered their good intentions vain, soon threw everything into a state of difficulty, from which no wisdom of theirs could ever afterwards extricate the unhappy country they had wished to serve; but had endeavoured to serve by such rash and dangerous proceedings.

"What has inevitably brought on and hastened the Revolution," says M. Bailly, "is, that the ministers would never see that the state of things was everywhere changed.

"Time was, when one led the people with ease; for cabinets were then so superior in intelligence; but this superiority has been lost, and has at last even changed places, and a new manner of governing must now be adopted; a truth which ministers have not yet felt the force of."

On the whole, therefore, it turned out that the expected royal sitting was considered as a bed of justice. Troops, too, were perceived to be approaching; the sitting was put off from the 22nd to the 23rd. In the middle of the night Bailly was called up, and privately informed that Necker disapproved of the measures adopted, that he would not attend the sitting, and would probably be dismissed. It had been settled between Bailly and the Assembly that no reply should be made to the king, whatever he might say to them; it was afterwards intimated to Bailly by the king that he wished no reply to be made; and under these most unfortunate circumstances the royal sitting opened on the morning of the 23rd.

I have already mentioned to you that I consider this sitting of the 23rd as one of the most important turns in the history of the Revolution. The patriots, I conceive, should have been content with the king's proposals then delivered, but they seem to have had no notion of the kind; and it becomes a point of curiosity to see what occurred to a man like Bailly at the time.

The detail which he gives is what is given by others, and what you know. The most deplorable want of contrivance was shown by the ministers even in so insignificant a matter as the admission of the Tiers Etat into the hall : they were kept waiting, as you are aware, and in the rain, till the other two orders were seated ; apparently lest they should mix themselves along with them. The majority of the clergy had joined them the day before.

" One was astonished," says Bailly, " to observe that the king had been made to use the old phrases, ' the king wills,' ' the king understands,' &c. ; that he had been made to nullify the resolutions of the Assembly, when as the chief head, the hereditary representative of the nation, he could only have a veto. Many deputies observed upon such expressions as ' the benefits which the king has granted to his people,' &c. &c. The king sole master, indeed, and sole legislator in the *absence* of the nation, can he thus speak to the nation assembled in the form of its States General !" Here we see new opinions. " The Commons," he continues, " during the reading of the king's declarations, remained in a silence the most profound. Not so the majority of the noblesse and the majority of the clergy, who accompanied and followed these two declarations with the most frequent bursts of applause. Well they might, indeed, for they were partly their work."

" Unhappy prince," says Bailly, commenting on the conclusion of the king's speech (the spirited part of it), " unhappy prince ! to what have they pledged you, and how have they deceived you ?"

He then gives the minute particulars of what passed, all of which, on such an occasion, are important. He told the master of the ceremonies, he says, that the Assembly, having adjourned till after the royal sitting, could not separate without first deliberating, and that it was not (as had been reported) to the master of the ceremonies, M. de Brizé, but to those around him, that he added, " I conceive that the nation assembled can receive no orders."

" I respected," says Bailly, " the king too much, and knew

too well what was due to the Assembly, to send any such message without their direction.

"It was, in truth," he continues, "it was Mirabeau that took upon himself to be angry with M. de Brizé, and he said pretty nearly what has been reported:—' Go tell those who sent you, that the force of bayonets is of no avail against the will of the nation.'

"This has been praised," says Bailly, "as an answer; but it is no answer, it is a sort of apostrophe, which he was under no necessity of making; which he had no right to make, for it was the president alone who was called upon to speak. No one had said a word to us of bayonets; no force had been announced to us; no menace had issued from the mouth of M. de Brizé: nothing of the kind. He had reminded us, as it was his duty, of the order of the king; had the king a right to give that order? The Assembly, by continuing its sitting, had decreed—no; and I," says Bailly, "in declaring that the Assembly could not be separated till it had deliberated on the point, had maintained its rights and its dignity, and had kept within that sort of limit and restraint which an assembly and its president should never fail to observe." These are the words of Bailly.

I had long, I confess, before I read these remarks of Bailly, considered the address of Mirabeau (as reported) to the master of the ceremonies as entirely uncalled for, and as a very ostentatious flourish, which the Assembly should not have appeared to adopt; and it is agreeable to perceive that a reasonable man like Bailly, however patriotic, however a disciple of the new opinions and an actor in the scene (though the actor interfered with), so considered it. Violent sallies, such as catch the applause of public assemblies at the time, are always very suspicious in point of wisdom, sometimes in point of principle, and are upon the whole to be avoided, and neither to be produced nor applauded by those who mean well.

There was then a pitiful attempt made by the court to disturb the Assembly by workmen, and make them quit the hall. The result of the whole was, that the Assembly unanimously declared, that it persisted in its former resolutions; and as those had been in the royal sitting formerly annulled by the king, the royal authority and that of the Assembly were thus placed entirely at issue; and Bailly observes, that the Assembly was never so great as at that moment; rendered so, by a declaration so simple, so precise, and, all circumstances considered, so firm. What the ministers gained, says he, by this strange sitting, so

he terms it, was only to make the nation exhibit a new act of
sovereignty, and by a solemn act to decide, and in favour of the
nation, the conflict that then existed between the powers of the
nation and the king. The Assembly concluded by declaring their
persons inviolable.

Four pages now follow in M. Bailly, which will show the
student very distinctly the views that were taken of this singular crisis, probably by the most intelligent and patriotic men
of France, at this particular period.

I have already announced to you that the Assembly should, I
conceive, have closed with the proposals of the king, and saved
their country from the storm that evidently was impending;
but this is the great question, and you must well observe what
are the sentiments and expressions of such a man as Bailly at
the time.

In the first place, he begins with representing the conduct
of the Assembly, as ' above all Grecian and all Roman fame.'
" Nothing in antiquity," says he, " can be opposed to these resolutions in point of wisdom, and nothing to the firmness of those
by whom they were adopted." But at the close of this discussion,
while endeavouring to show the injudicious conduct of the ministers, " where," says he, " was their force to carry their measures?
were they sure of the soldiers? The event proved not. Could
they believe in their numbers, &c.; this was the cause of the
people, but the soldiers are people; what then could they have attempted? Imprisonment—but imprisonments are to have some
term or other; they durst not have done it. But besides, however they might have deceived the king with regard to measures,
of which he saw not the probable result, measures of rigour
were foreign to his heart, and such, I am sure, he would have
revolted from." But here it may be observed, in answer to M.
Bailly, where was then this Roman firmness in the Assembly
if they had no enemy to fear? and with respect to their wisdom,
if such was the king, it might have surely been asked M.
Bailly, why was the Assembly thus to erect their power upon
the ruins of his? Why were they to force on this tremendous
issue of a distinct struggle between their king and the Assembly?
They saw the ministers and the military force ranged around
the king: behind themselves were placed the people of Versailles
and Paris, who were to be taught, at all hazards, the doctrines
of insurrection. These were the parties, this their situation, this
the field of battle—and what an issue! Suppose the soldiers

were to stand by the monarch while he maintained his late declarations, what was to become of the Assembly and eventually of the cause of Freedom? Suppose, on the contrary, the soldiers were to side with the Assembly and the people, what was then to become of the royal authority? What various chances here of confusion and bloodshed! and on what account? Because France, upon a system of moderation and conciliation with the king and court, was then not to be regenerated, as it was called; because all that had been expected by the followers of the new opinions was then not to be realized; because the whole was then to proceed on a system of mutual tolerance, mutual concessions, checks, and balances; and because the old opinions were then not to be entirely scoffed and hooted out of the world by the new. Such were the calamities to ensue. Now was this wisdom in the Assembly? Was this the conduct of statesmen? Our own ancestors had a very different case before them, while acting in the Long Parliament. Charles I. had shown that his principles and feelings were perfectly arbitrary: far from calling together the free assemblies of the country, he had endeavoured for eleven years together to rule without them. Louis XVI., on the contrary, was a prince acknowledged, by the most furious of the assertors of these new opinions, to be peaceful, benevolent, patriotic—to be anything but a tyrant. I am not now arguing the question with revolutionary, daring men, who enjoy disorder, and whose dreadful talents and propensities are called into full triumph and display, on such occasions, to the gratification of their personal pride or selfishness; but I speak to those who mean well, who deserve the venerable name of patriot, but who get enamoured of their own notions of political right; who are strong, as they suppose, in their powers of reason; who become, by sympathy, warm and heated; and who, by turning away from counsels of expediency, and of moderation, by not being reasonable in time, by not striking balances, by not being content with what is practicable, without further experiment or hazard; in short, by despising everything of this sane and necessary kind, become, in truth, political enthusiasts, and mere enthusiasts, dangerous to themselves, and enemies to the best interests of their country.

Now I apprehend this to be one, at least, of the great lessons of the French Revolution.

The first lesson, no doubt, is the restiveness of the privileged orders, who will never give way at all, and never, even if they do, concede in time. But the next is the possibility and danger of political enthusiasm, enthusiasm in support of a theory, in support of some supposed intuitions of the understanding, rights of human nature, dictates of common sense ; and these two opposite lessons I have taken, and shall continue to take every opportunity of holding up to your observation, (and this even at the chance of wearying you,) on account of what I conceive to be their supereminent importance.

Observe the confession of M. Bailly himself. "In the second declaration of the 23rd," he says, "where the intentions of the king are manifested, it must be admitted, many things are settled by the king in a manner perfectly paternal ; many which must have come within the view of the States General. There was to be no impost, for instance, without the consent of the representatives of the nation, none was to last beyond a session," says he. "All this was very good ; but was this to be the form, when the nation, when the enlightened nation was present ? 'Why are you not satisfied ?'" he continues, "said one of his ministers to me : 'had the king made a declaration like this ten years ago, would it not have been received with enthusiasm ?' 'Oh, yes,' I replied, 'no doubt, ten years ago.' 'Why, what then does the Assembly want or wish to do ?' 'Every thing itself,' I replied ; 'not for you to do it.'"

Now this conduct in M. Bailly and in the Assembly, I consider first, as following but too surely in the natural progress of political collision at all times; but secondly, as the folly, the enthusiasm of new opinions, and such folly as new opinions will, on every occasion, display.

Matters now began to look very ominous. You remember the affair of the eleven soldiers. Bailly consulted Necker what was to be done, for in this case they had but one wish and sentiment.

Necker recommended the course that was afterwards adopted, but advised a city guard, as M. Bonneville had done, at an assembly of the electors a few days before ; a scheme that was afterwards executed in an instant, and carried to an extent that overthrew all the existing executive authority in the kingdom, in the extraordinary manner you have seen, during the crisis of the 14th of July ; but it is curious to observe, the first hints and origin of great events like these.

We have next appearances still more gloomy ; the troops, the artillery every where drawing round Versailles, and Mirabeau's spirited speeches and addresses to the king. Bailly seems to have talked with some of the ministers, and remonstrated with them. They told him that the troops were only meant to maintain peace and order in Paris. The philosopher, however, set himself to work, and from the visible appearances and known facts, seems to have reasoned out (what I conceive to have been) the real state of the case, and the views of the court, with sufficient success.

He seems afterwards to have been very much captivated with Mirabeau's celebrated address to the king for the removal of the troops. He refers particularly to that part of it where it is said, "We should but deceive you, Sire, if we were not to add, under the impulse of our present circumstances, that this empire of peace and order is the only one which it is now possible to exercise in France."

"It is not to be dissembled," says Bailly, "that Mirabeau was in the Assembly, its principle of force. Nothing could be more grand, more firm, more worthy of the occasion than this address to the king; with every proper form of respect, it is agreeable to the resolution of the 23rd, where the Assembly declares that it will persist; here, then, it tells the king himself the same. The great quality of Mirabeau was boldness; it was this that fortified his talents, directed him in the management of them, and developed their force. Whatever might be his moral character, when he was once elevated by circumstances, he assumed a grandeur and a purity, and was exalted by his genius to the full height of courage and of virtue."

The remainder of the first volume of Bailly is chiefly occupied with the crisis of affairs that immediately took place, and which was terminated by the taking of the Bastile, the sudden appearance of an armed national force, or rather of an armed nation resisting the court and adopting the measures of the Assembly, and taking the chance of what was called the regeneration of France. M. Bailly seems not to have been in the secret of affairs, but he describes, much in the way you have already seen, the anxiety of the National Assembly, and at the same time his own—the anxiety and terror of a good man, during a crisis so tremendous.

Nothing was wanting but the visible acquiescence of the king, which was given, and given with every appearance of sincerity and good will. The particulars are described by Bailly in the beginning of his second volume.

The king seems, according to Bailly's representation, never to have had any pleasure greater than that of being considered the father and benefactor of his people. He orders the troops to withdraw; gives up all idea of force, and without ceremony, and accompanied only by his brothers, repairs to the Assembly to make his peace with them. Expressions in his speech so move the Assembly, that they surround and attend him in his return to his palace. Nothing is heard but the sounds of "Vive le Roi!" The trees, the gates, the walls, the statues, are all covered with spectators; the air is fine, the day brilliant; the people tell the king that he has need of no other guards. M. Villeroi answers, that he may resign his office, as the nation has taken his duty upon itself. "The walk is fatiguing to your majesty," said an attendant to him. "Not at all, not at all fatiguing," replied the king, pointing to the delighted crowd that escorted him. "These acclamations render homage to your character, Sire," said another. "How could they ever have misconceived me?" answered the king. The music sounded as they approached the palace. The air was that of the song, "How can you be so well as in the midst of your children?" The queen was seen waiting in the balcony with the dauphin in her arms to be presented to the spectators; and the king, the court, the Assembly, and the people, dissolve in an universal sentiment of peace, and tenderness, and joy. And thus far, at least, historians seem agreed.

Alas! the contrast between scenes like these and those that were so soon to succeed them; between these amiable effusions of a generous, loyal, I had almost said forgiving people, and the dark suspicions, the unreasonable clamours, the tumultuous inroad of a ferocious and bloody populace; the queen flying through her palace from assassins, and the king conducted captive to the metropolis!

LECTURE XIII.

FERRIERES.

In my last lecture I endeavoured to introduce to your observation the views and reasonings of the philosophic Bailly in the earlier stages of the Revolution. I must continue a little longer this species of lecture: the leading and more critical points will thus be revived in your memories; the instruction belonging to them; different portraits of the Revolution will be offered you in their own fresh and natural colours; you will not have to receive my representations; you will see the materials upon which my own judgment, such as it is, has been formed.

To-day I shall therefore produce specimens of the views and

reasonings of the Marquis de Ferrieres, a deputy of the Nobility, a patron of the old opinions, and who, an eye-witness of the scene, and apparently one of the most respectable of men, has every right to be heard.

The Marquis de Ferrieres was born at Poictiers in 1741, was a member of the Constituent Assembly, and was at the time about the age of fifty, and in the full vigour of his faculties.

He relates, he says, the facts that he witnessed, or that were reported to him by those on whom he could depend, and he neglected no written accounts that seemed likely to afford him information; he hopes to furnish materials for future historians.

He had early retired to the country, where he lived occupied with his duties and his studies. Of a religious turn of mind, he had written in defence of the best interests of mankind against the philosophers who had improved, as they supposed, on the doctrines of Montesquieu, Voltaire, and Rousseau; and when sent, therefore, by the universal respect of the nobility of his bailliage, as their deputy to the States General, his birth, his education, his religious habits of thought, all concurred to render him the defender of the old opinions, and to seat him on the opposition side of the Assembly, where he always voted, with the majority of the nobility, against the union of the orders, in concurrence with them on all the principal questions, and finally, against the great work of the Assembly, the Constitution of 1791.

He was not a speaker, but he was occasionally a writer, and, fortunately for us, he wrote on the subject of the French Revolution, or rather of the Constituent Assembly, and he seems to exhibit to us very faithfully the different impressions he received from what he saw and heard.

It is agreeable to find, that a respectable and good man like this was allowed to return to his tranquil pleasures and duties, and to die in peace, a few years afterwards, in 1804.

He opens his narrative by observing, that he was chosen deputy very unexpectedly to himself, but "I could soon discover," says he, "all the selfish interests that were actuating all the great bodies of the kingdom: the parliaments hoped to receive all that the States General could take away from the king; the high nobility to shake off the ministerial yoke, which had been imposed upon them by Cardinal Richelieu; the capitalists and the renters to pledge the state for the debt due by the king; and the Commons affected only to wish for a reform of abuses, while the double representation, which would have been null if the orders were to vote separately, showed plainly, that they meant to vote by head, and to make themselves masters of the deliberations that were to follow.

"The nobles in the provinces would have nothing to say to the great lords; their interests, they thought, would be sacrificed. My situation, which rendered me indifferent to all views of ambition, fixed their choice, and still more my principles, which were well known, but very far removed from any tendency to despotism; in me they believed they had found the mean, between abandoning everything and conceding nothing: as I was not one that was bound to the court, what I was likely to retrench from the monarch would be all gain to the nation. Such is the history of my elevation; or it may be, that the Almighty, to punish my foolish pride, chose to show me, that all my supposed virtues, all my vain science, upon which I so plumed myself, that all were of no avail in the great affairs of the world; that out of the confined circle in which his fatherly goodness had traced out for me, they could be of no use either to myself or my country, and that I might thus be taught to bless that compassionate wisdom which I had so often but little understood; for often has it happened to me, in thoughtless moments, to murmur in secret at being limited to the exercise of the mere good qualities of a private individual, and removed from those employments which would have furnished me with an opportunity of exhibiting the talents and the virtues of a public man.

"I confess, that having participated in no intrigue to procure my deputation, it was with much secret congratulation that I saw myself now about to produce the fruits of twenty years of thought and study, and that I was now to be useful to my country. I was soon cruelly undeceived.

"But if I have not laboured for my cotemporaries, I have for posterity at least. I now place before their eyes a faithful picture of the Constituent Assembly. It may be, that the experience of those who go before will not always be useless to those who follow.

"I write," says he, "not the history of the French Revolution, but of the Constituent Assembly. I mean to exhibit the speakers and actors just as they spoke and acted, and at the moment, and on the spot. It is of no consequence what they would say or do *now*; let them only ask themselves, did they or did they not so speak and act at *the time?*

"No sooner," says he, "had the deputies arrived at Paris, than they all seemed to give vent at once to their particular feelings; a general restlessness seemed to have got possession of all their understandings, a vague desire of change. The French, confined till that moment by a vigilant and severe police, which watched and controlled their every movement, their every thought, were totally unacquainted with all notions of the social compact, the rights of the nation, the rights of the monarch, those of individuals, those of different classes of citizens; and they hurried everything into a state of exaggeration, everything—even truth itself, to which they would have preferred error, as far more imposing and grand; they abandoned themselves to the utmost intemperance of sentiments and language, as if, issuing from some long enchantment, they had now recovered the faculty of speaking and thinking. It was in the coffee-houses of the Palais Royal that was shown in its true colours this new development of the national character; everything was to be understood, everything was to be known, everything was to be communicated, and therefore every day was there assembled a crowd of people. Here came one with a draught of a constitution in his hand, which he assured every one, in the most confident manner, must necessarily occupy the labours of the States General; then came another with a composition, which he read aloud with all his might, drawn up to suit the circumstances of the particular case of the nation; a third thundered away against the ministers, the nobles, the priests, thus clearing away the stage for what *he* also had to propose; while a fourth had climbed upon a table, and was discussing the great question of voting by head, or proposing chimerical plans of government of his own; each had its auditory, more or less numerous, that listened to him, and approved or censured." Such is the lively and, I have no doubt, very faithful picture given by the marquis.

Ferrieres takes the earliest opportunity of speaking of the Duke of Orleans (Bailly, you may observe, says little of him); but Ferrieres represents him as becoming, from a chain of circumstances, the idol of the people, and the chief of a party composed of nobles discontented with the court; philosophers greedy of honours and the good things of this world; men mortified at being nothing, when this was not the case with others; adventurers and bankrupts, who immediately after the meeting of the States General, and the rapid march of public opinion, indulged themselves in all possible hopes and expectations. " The duke," says he, " was himself without talents, and debased by a life of drunkenness; greedy of money to a degree that would have been perfectly reprehensible in a private man, but which was disgraceful and degrading in a prince; he had every vice which can

R 2

make crime odious, and none of the brilliant qualities by which it can be in some degree illustrated in the eyes of posterity. The dead feelings of the duke," he says, "it was necessary to animate, in some way or other, that he might appear to have a wish for something, and so they held out to him the supreme power, under the title of lieutenant-general of the kingdom; all the public money at his disposal, and, in the events which it was for him to hasten, the crown for his children, and himself thus made the commencement of a new dynasty."

This is the account of Ferrieres; and something of this kind must be supposed, the concurrence of opinion, reaching to similar conclusions, is so very great. There is a passage even in Bailly which seems to look the same way; but this part of the secret history of the Revolution has never yet been brought to light, and there is some difference of opinion on the subject. Mirabeau, you may remember, has been always suspected of having for some time connected himself with this desperate faction.

Ferrieres seems to have thought very unjustly of Necker on every occasion, his talents, his intentions; this you will see at the commencement of his work; he even supposes him to have been connected with the Duke of Orleans. With more reason, he represents the philosophers, the authors, the journalists, as turning against the parliament when the States General, a body more adapted to their purposes, had once been called for and granted by the king.

The meeting of the States General seems extremely to have affected the Marquis de Ferrieres, as indeed it did others. He saw the procession and the ceremonies of this great event, with all the pious emotions of a religious man, and all the hopes and fears of a patriot : his description of what he saw and what he felt is striking; and you have placed before you in this part of his work, the man whose opinions and observations you are going to read.

He makes such observations on what passed at the opening of the States, and afterwards on the Tiers Etat, as you might expect, but seems to think that great want of skill and capacity was shown by those who had the management, particularly Necker.

The description that he gives of the different people and parties that appeared around him is not very favourable; and a well-meaning man, he at length observes, like himself, insulated and left alone in the midst of such a multitude as this, knew not where to repose his confidence. One trait of the general picture,

not being as much insisted upon by others as it deserves, I will
give you; more concisely, but as much as possible in his own
words. All through this lecture, you will observe, I make a
sort of running translation of his work.

He is speaking of the part taken by the women in the Revolution, particularly those about court, of whom he is no great admirer. " A great wish," says he, " to be of consequence, to be
busy; little jealousies and animosities, and attachments still more
trifling; spleen, weariness, &c.; hearts emptied of all the natural affections; all these things concurred to throw most of the
women about court into the popular party. With that eternal
frivolity which marked their character, a revolution, which was
to decide the fate of France, was treated by them as would have
been an intrigue that was to displace a minister, or advance a lover.
Seated at their toilettes, or lost in all the soft luxuriance of their
boudoirs, ' What a charming thing,' they cried, ' is a revolution !'
—Gallantry is the great means on which the sex have to depend;
this was always so, and it was thus that they were enabled to
play a distinguished part in the wars of the League and of the
Fronde. This means of influence was not neglected now; their
lovers were members of the minority of the noblesse, and that
was already much in their favour. But the harsh, yet firm and
vigorous rudeness of the deputies of the Commons frightened
them not; a new sort of language and of people had at least the
merit of exciting curiosity. But what a triumph to decide a
vote by their influence in one of the houses; to animate by a gesture, by a look, a patriot while pouring out from the tribune the
flaming language of liberty ! and again, how delightful to be
eternally in motion, coming here and going there, to have mysterious conferences at one's house, to have the great interests of
twenty-four millions of people discussed there; a people, too,
that were regenerating themselves; to have cards at Paris, to
harangue about constitutions, and to assure every one that one
hated despotism and all its agents !

" Madame de Stael, the daughter of Necker, became one of
the most zealous propagators of democracy. Born with great
powers of mind, very active faculties, a lively imagination, and a
passion for celebrity, secret interviews, morning billets, evening
meetings, parties of pleasure, intrigues, she was equal to everything; at one and the same time, was she to be found at Paris,
at Versailles, in the saloon, in the boudoir, always at work,
and perfectly indefatigable. Me. de Luines, d'Aiguillon, de Cas-
telane, de Tessé, de Coigni, each had their post, gave dinners,

assisted regularly at the sittings of the Assembly, cajoled the
patriot deputies, got them to write pamphlets, animated the
weary, and supported the failing : politics took the place of
topics of gallantry, and anecdotes of scandal ; liberty was in
every mouth, a love of rule in every heart ; society became an
arena that exhibited an universal combat, a combat marked, indeed, with rudeness and impropriety ; difference of opinion furnished those who hated each other in secret, a pretext to hate
each other openly,—all their affectations of sensibility, virtue,
benevolence, and religion disappeared; down went the masks,
and in some of these women all their moral deformity was shown
in open day, and they seemed perfect monsters.''

There is some spleen and ill-humour probably in this description, but no doubt a great deal of truth, and of important truth.
The marquis, a grave, studious man from one of the provinces,
was not likely to be a very favourable critic of these ladies, or to
be very favourably criticised in return.

Necker himself does not fare better with the marquis than his
daughter. " This man," says he, " citizen of a small republic,
ignorant of our manners, of our history, or having read it very
superficially, having no clear idea of what is called a monarchy,
had persuaded himself that the word king brought along with it
the exercise of a power unlimited, and that all the opposition he
had to fear to his ministerial speculations was to arise from the
nobility and the clergy. At the house of Necker every thing
was considered and decided ; this minister-banker had conceived,
it was said, vast projects ; and what were they ? Three successive loans of twenty-four millions, an augmentation of the leases
of the farms, an extension of the imposts, a consolidation of the
public debt, that new loans might be effected ; and these were
the objects called by his hirelings the restoration, the regeneration of the state ; and it was for these objects (he sought no
more) that he contributed, without knowing it, without suspect-
ing it, to the overthrow of the laws and of the ancient constitution.''

But the marquis proceeds further than this. " The minority
of the noblesse," he continues, " entered into the views of Necker;
they met every day at his house : but Necker and the greatest
part of these members of the minority were but mere instruments
in the hands of others, men with designs far more extensive and
profound. There existed a secret committee, where all the
leading chiefs of the Revolution united ; deputies of the three
orders were there indifferently received, there was no difficulty

made in the selection. This committee exercised a great influence over the deliberations of the three chambers; there were events prepared, there were concerted the manœuvres that were to be employed in the provinces to inflame the minds of the people, and to produce insurrections : every where it was in the meantime circulated in Paris, that there could be no States General but by an union of the three orders, that a bankruptcy was the necessary consequence of their separation. A crowd of Parisians came to the Assemblies of the third estate ; there they heard pronounced with emphasis, I should rather say hurled out with fury, the vague terms of liberty, patriotism, and sovereignty of the people. From the Assembly they issued quite intoxicated with what they had heard, and breathing nothing but hatred and vengeance against the noblesse ; a profusion of incendiary libels, hawked about in Paris, and transmitted to the provinces, diffused every where sentiments of the same kind, and the language was, and it was even heard aloud, that the horrors of St. Bartholomew were to be renewed, that the very race of aristocrats and tyrants were to be swept away from the earth."

The secret committee, that the marquis here talks of, if it existed at all, must have consisted of those who espoused the new opinions ; but the marquis is very indistinct on such subjects, and this is the greatest fault that can be objected to him. He confounds together all those who espoused the new opinions in a very improper and perplexing manner. But in other respects, I do not conceive that the account of the marquis is at all exaggerated, and I do not believe that any adequate idea can now be formed, even from his work or from any work, of the fermentation that existed in every class of society, in Paris and Versailles, soon after the meeting of the States General.

I do not see any thing very particular in the account which the marquis gives of the transactions that took place during the struggle between the orders, except, indeed, the most unfair and unfavourable turn given to every motive and measure of the minister Necker. The most important point to be observed in the account of the marquis is, that he does not at all conceal the intentions of the court, as other writers with his opinions have done, and I shall, therefore, quote largely from him, translating, as I go along, in the sort of general running manner that I have announced to you : and you must listen patiently ; for it is often difficult to judge, amidst the different representations that are given by different writers ; and here we have a man of character, rank, and intelligence, himself an actor in the scene, and describing what passed and the views and conduct of all concerned, apparently, in the most impartial and fearless manner.

" The court," says he, " unable any longer to hide from themselves the real truth, that all their petty expedients to separate the orders served only to bring on their union, resolved to dissolve the States General. It was necessary to remove the king from Versailles; to get Necker and the ministers attached to him out of the way; a journey to Marli was arranged; the pretext was the death of the dauphin. The mind of the king was successfully worked upon; he was told it was high time to stop the unheard-of enterprises of the third estate; that he would soon have only the name of king. The Cardinal Rochefoucault and the Archbishop of Paris threw themselves at the feet of the king, and supplicated him to save the clergy and protect religion. The parliament sent a secret deputation, proposing a scheme for getting rid of the States General. The keeper of the seals, the Comte d'Artois, the queen, all united. They persuaded the king that to satisfy the people was easy; and all that was wanted was a declaration accommodated to the wishes of the cahiers, that the noblesse and high clergy would accept it with gratitude. All was therefore settled; and an order from the king announced a royal sitting, and suspended the States under a pretence of making arrangements in the hall."

Now deliberations of this kind may, as the marquis describes them, have taken place; they were very natural, when the Assembly had ventured upon such acts of encroachment and usurpation as they very early did; and it is indeed clear that they took place from that interference of the court, which Necker afterwards experienced: but the measure of the *séance royale* was the minister's own; and if the proposals, which the king was to have made to the National Assembly, had been left what he made them, the measure might have saved France, or at least the popular party would have been then placed in the wrong.

But nothing could be more unskilful than appeared even to the Marquis de Ferrieres, the manner and every circumstance that was suffered to accompany this last critical effort of the king, and court, this *séance royale*. "It had the semblance," says the marquis, " of a bed of justice. The hall was surrounded by soldiers and by guards; every thing about the throne was silent and melancholy; the declaration itself satisfied no one; and the king spoke rather like a despot who commanded, than a monarch who discussed with the representatives of his people the interests of a great nation."

This testimony is very strong, coming from the marquis; and what followed is related by him as you have received it from others.

Every where you must observe, however, that the marquis expresses the most unfavourable opinion of Necker during all these transactions, while, it is quite certain, that mixed with a little personal vanity, the most sincere wish for the happiness of France and the happiness of mankind was the ruling motive with Necker. He is, however, considered by the marquis as thinking only of his place, in the most vulgar and wretched manner; in short, I consider the marquis as singularly unjust to Necker. But his great fault is always not to make sufficient distinction between one man and another.

We will now advert to what he says of his own order. You may remember that it was very late, and only by the interference of the king, that they could be persuaded to join the Tiers Etat. What passed was, according to the marquis, as follows: " In the chamber of the nobles, in the mean time, the most violent dissensions prevailed. ' Let us join the Tiers Etat,' said Lally Tollendal, ' as the king has recommended us to do; there is a force of circumstances which is above every consideration of place and power, a great Revolution has begun, nothing can prevent it, it only remains for the nobility to concur with it, and to assign for themselves an honourable place.' ' You understand then at last,' said D'Espremenil, (the D'Espremenil you have heard before of), ' you understand then that a great Revolution is begun; and it is even in this chamber of the nobility that there are found those who can dare to pronounce such a sound, that we are to be invited even to join it? No, gentlemen, no; our duty is to preserve the monarchy; the monarchy which the factious are going to destroy.'"

Every thing was agitation through the whole of this assembly of the nobles. Hostile passions, hostile interests appeared in the words, the gestures, the animated expressions of every one. (Ferrieres, who gives this account, was himself a member.)

It was now a grievous mortification and affliction to the nobility to join the third estate. The Vicomte de Noailles assured the nobles, that the union would be but temporary; that the troops were coming up, and that in fifteen days every thing would be changed. The king sent a second letter, assuring the nobles that the safety of the state and his own personal security depended upon the union. ' Let us hasten to the palace,' said the Marquis de St. Simon, ' and make a rampart of our bodies round him.' It was with the greatest earnestness that the Duc de Luxembourg had to oppose himself to the general enthusiasm, to represent the embarrassing situation into which the king would thus be thrown. 'We can no longer deliberate,' said the duke, 'we must save the king, we must save the country ; the person of the king is in danger. Who can hesitate? who can venture to hesitate for a moment?' The assembly rose in a tumultuous manner, they were joined by the minority of the clergy, and entered," says the marquis, "in silence the hall of the Tiers Etat."

This step had no sooner been taken, in compliance with the wishes of the court, than the court repented of it ; and the description which the marquis now gives of the state of affairs is very candid, and entitled to the perfect confidence of the reader. Observe the freedom with which he speaks of all parties and persons. I shall use his words for some time. "The court, recovered from its terror," says he, "repented of it ; they saw the intentions of the Commons ; what they had already done sufficiently announced it. The new constitution, supported by general opinion, by the unanimous wish of the public, was now acquiring," says he, "a force which was likely to sweep away every abuse : the court knew that the nobility and high clergy would seize with eagerness any opportunity of dissolving these States General that intended their ruin. But a military force was necessary to keep down Paris, to break up the Assembly, and to enforce the acceptance of the declaration of the 23rd of June. Many of the nobles would have quitted the Assembly, but a partial secession would have done nothing : they were assured that the troops were coming up ; were praised for their honourable feelings, for the resistance they had already made : that they must dissemble a little longer. And indeed," says the marquis, "thirty regiments were now marching upon Paris. The pretext was the public tranquillity ; the real object, the dissolution of the Assembly. Difficulties without end kept retarding their march ; provisions were not furnished them, money very sparingly. The Marshal de Broglio took the command, established himself at the palace of Versailles, surrounded by a brilliant staff ; every thing was at his disposal. In the mean time, a part of the majority of the nobility continued to assemble at the Duke of Luxembourg's ; protests were there entered into against the union with the Tiers ; their mandates from their constituents were appealed to ; the decrees of the National Assembly were declared to be null and void. Pretexts were discovered for its approaching dissolution; and their manœuvres, which were soon every where divulged, every where united all other descriptions of men to the National Assembly. The hall of the Assembly became, to all Frenchmen, their common country (I am all along giving the important representations of the marquis, and shall continue to translate his paragraphs). The Assembly was made acquainted with every movement and every thought; and the absolute monarchy of France, betrayed by the very persons who drew from it all their consequence and all their support, remained alone and unassisted, though placed in the middle of its own people and agents. The queen, the Comte d'Artois, the princes, the courtiers, the ministers, the bishops, the nobles, were all surrounded by spies, by treacherous domestics, pursued by them into the most intimate recesses of their retirement, the very repose of the night: and they expressed not a sentiment, made not a gesture, that was not reported; and thus was generated that violent antipathy that took place against the nobles and the clergy. The Commons perceived, that these two bodies attached to despotism, as the true aliment on which they lived, would reject liberty, and would insist upon having in preference a brilliant servitude; and they therefore said to themselves, ' It is for us then, for us alone to make the Revolution.' And as they resolved that nothing should resist them, the destruction of the nobility was resolved.

"The Assembly, in the mean time, while these intrigues were going on at court, represented in reality the sovereignty of the people. It took its own measures, formed thirty committees for the dispatch of business, and France saw with joy that it was at last going to set about that regeneration of the state that had been so long desired and so long expected.

"The National Assembly," says the marquis, "sought in the people a support against the court; secret embassies, spread over every quarter of Paris, denounced the projects of the ministry. 'France,' they said, 'is going to become the prey of courtiers, nobles, and priests. This yoke, now imposed again upon us by force, will be more intolerable than ever. The monarch, disengaged from his promises, and entering again, by the dissolution of the Assembly, upon the full plenitude of his power, will know no other limit to his will but such as the most unlimited whims and fantasies may prescribe.'

"The capitalists," he continues, "the rent-holders, terrified at the prospect of a general bankruptcy, united themselves to the Assembly as to a common and only hope; they employed

in the support of it the powerful means that were afforded them
by money, by credit, by very extended connexions. Paris,
agitated by every possible passion, by every possible interest,
peopled by men who had every thing to hope and nothing to
fear from a Revolution, was the central point from which every
movement issued. The court, accustomed to see Paris kept in
awe by a lieutenant of police and a guard of eight hundred horse,
little thought of any resistance, foresaw nothing, calculated nothing ; did not even take care to assure itself of the very soldiers
that were to be the instruments of its designs. The French
guards were lost by giving the command to M. de Chalelet.
The Assembly, in the mean time, neglected not the provinces ;
their correspondencies were multiplied, their agents every where
inflaming the minds of the people, concerting insurrections,
painting the projects of the court in the blackest colours, representing the nobility and the clergy as resisting the reform of
those abuses by which they themselves so profited, as refusing
to take their share in the public burdens, refusing to abandon
their odious and unjust privileges, as secretly plotting the dissolution of the States General. Innumerable addresses and assurances of attachment were the consequence ; and this unanimous concert and co-operation of every part of the kingdom,
elevated the courage of the Commons, gave them an energy like
that of the senate of Rome in the trying moments of the republic ; and France, animated by a similar spirit, seemed a sort of
immense forum, where the great questions of government were
discussed in the presence of twenty-five millions of citizens.

" In this state of things," continues the marquis, " the Comte
de Mirabeau made his celebrated address in the Assembly (the
address for the removal of the troops)." And you will observe,
that the marquis having admitted all the circumstances of the
case that I have now laid before you, while I have thus been
translating from his pages, admits finally the insincerity of the
court in the king's answer, for, says he, " The Assembly easily
saw through the snare that was spread for them ; they would
have lost all their hold if they had once removed themselves
from the security which the vicinity of Paris afforded. Enclosed
between the two camps, they would have found themselves at
the mercy of the court."

These are the words of the marquis. I have called them his
admissions, but it is an improper word. He seems to me a fair
historian, giving his account fully and honestly (as far as public
matters are concerned, though he is unfair to individuals), with-

out favour, or affection, or any wish of his own to gratify, but the honourable love of truth.

In addition to what I have already quoted, the marquis seems clearly to suppose, that what is called the Orleans Faction existed in Paris, filling the minds of the populace with the most dreadful apprehensions; that the citizens were to be massacred, the Palais Royal abandoned to the pillage of the army, chiefly composed, it was observed, of foreign regiments; that a bankruptcy was then to be declared: and the marquis proceeds to suppose, that Mirabeau was in reality at the head of this faction, and meant to have transferred the royal authority to the Duke of Orleans. All this has been both confidently asserted and much questioned. But the great misfortune was, that during all this period a scarcity existed in Paris, and under such circumstances there was no event, however outrageous, that might not possibly happen. Bailly mentions in his Memoirs, that while mayor, he was repeatedly uncertain one day whether Paris would have a sufficient supply of bread the next. And there was something singularly defective (and unintelligibly so) in the management of this article of prime necessity.

The Memoirs of the marquis now become particularly interesting, not only because he was a member of the Constituent Assembly at the time, but because he was a partisan of the old opinions and a lover of the monarchy; and yet the account he gives is not materially different from what has been delivered by men of opposite principles: and this is the great point which I must urge upon your attention. Nothing can be more interesting than the situation of Paris, of Versailles, and of France, of the popular party, of the Assembly, of the court, of the king, and finally of the army, during those three or four days and nights that preceded and followed the memorable 14th of July. In the first place it was clear, to the popular party, that the army was to be brought to act, and the Assembly to be put down. The approach of the troops and the appearance of Marshal Broglio left no doubt remaining on that head. The Marquis de Ferrieres first describes the manner in which an insurrection of the populace was begun by Camille Desmoulins, in the Palais Royal. "He mounted upon a table," says the marquis; "'Citizens!' he cried, 'I am just come from Versailles; there is not a moment to be lost: M. Necker is dismissed, his dismissal is the tocsin that sounds a St. Bartholomew to all patriots. This very evening the Swiss and German battalions are to come from the Champ de Mars to butcher us. To arms! to arms! We have no other resource.'"

What followed you will easily conceive, and conceive it as Ferrieres describes it to have taken place. The orator, with a pistol in each hand, rushes out into the streets, followed by his audience; they pass through the most populous streets; the crowd gathers; the barriers of the city are set on fire; the public spectacles closed; and all is alarm, confusion, and uproar. The insurrection is made more and more furious, and rendered triumphant, by the rencontre with the Prince of Lambesc, at the head of a detachment of his German troops. The night comes on; the tocsins keep sounding; armed men with lighted torches, continually passing, give the city the appearance of a place sacked by an enemy; and everything is thus prepared for the alarmists to organize their insurrection by means of a regular committee communicating with the rest of the citizens.

In the meantime, nothing, according to the same account of Ferrieres, nothing could exceed the disquietude of the Assembly at Versailles. Many of the members met in the hall on Sunday, the 12th, but having been adjourned to the 13th, it was early on that day, the 13th, that a regular meeting took place. The members seemed differently affected. The revolutionists, in groups and in different parts of the hall, seemed considering what was to be done, terrifying each other or inflaming each other against the ministers. "The better part of the Assembly," he says, "strangers to all the intrigues that might be going forward, was filled with alarm at the sad reports that were circulating, and terrified at the designs of the court, which they were assured went to the seizing of Paris, the dissolution of the Assembly, and the massacre of the citizens. These members preserved a mournful and thoughtful silence, while the greatest part of the Assembly were evidently in the greatest agitation; on their countenances were painted anxiety, fierceness, fury, notwithstanding all their efforts to disguise their emotions. In the meantime the partisans of the court concealed their joy under an appearance of indifference. They came to the sitting to see what turn the deliberations would take, to enjoy their triumph and the humiliation of the Assembly. The Assembly they looked upon as annihilated; they had no doubt that it would have to accept the declaration of the 23rd of June, the States be separated, and things then be left to take their ancient course.

"Such," says the marquis, "was the blind folly and infatuation of these people."

He then goes on to describe the debate that followed: the speech of Mounier, recommending an address to the king in sup-

port of Necker and the disgraced ministers, followed by a beautiful defence of him by his friend Lally Tollendal, and the whole
closed by a spirited harangue from the Comte de Virien; who
described, in the most glowing colours, what had probably been
passing during the night at Paris, and the necessity there was
for all the members of the Assembly to pledge themselves to the
country and to each other to stand by the noble resolutions they
had already voted, and never to separate till they had discharged
the great duties imposed upon them.   An oath was immediately
taken to this effect by all the members present; and an address
and a deputation sent to the king.

"The court had hitherto," says the marquis, "remained tranquil spectators of the movements in Paris.   The troops posted
at the Champ de Mars, at St. Denis, at Sèvres, at St. Cloud, remained in a state of inaction.   One would have said that the
new ministers, assured of success, left the insurrection to go on,
and authorize at last those measures of rigour which they were
resolved to employ; that they looked upon the situation of Paris
as merely arising from a sort of passing insurrection; that they
had no doubt that at the approach of the troops the people would
disperse, and their terrified leaders come to solicit the clemency
of the king.

"In the meantime, however, the tocsins kept everywhere
sounding; the shops," he says, "were shut up; the streets
crowded with armed men, some running from house to house,
talking of murder, and fire, and pillage; others marching with
tambours and trumpets, with the soldiers of the regiment of
French guards at their head; others forcing open the prisons
of La Force and Du Chatelet, and announcing their intention
of pillaging the great hotels, and the houses of all the people of
affluence."

This led, as you have already understood, to the seizing of
the great depôt at the Hotel des Invalides.   The National Assembly, in the mean time, supported by what they could hear
of the spirit of resistance that had now broken out in the metropolis, continued to debate and to address the king, who kept
returning them civil and respectful, but by no means satisfactory
answers; nothing that indicated that the troops would not be
employed, the real point at issue.   An account of what had
passed at Paris, of the rise and progress of the insurrection, had
reached the Assembly; had been highly grateful to some, and
had elevated the courage of the most timid.   "Every floating
opinion," says the marquis, "was at last united, and the famous

resolution was unanimously carried, ' That the exiled ministers had the confidence of the nation, that the Assembly would not cease to insist on the removal of the troops, and that it persisted in its former resolutions;' a resolution this," he continues, " which under existing circumstances, was, in fact, a declaration of war. These vigorous resolutions," says he, " astonished the court, but did not induce them to abandon their plan : it was only put off to the next day ; but there was no longer now a time," he continues ; " the fate of France was from this moment irrevocably united to the fate of the Assembly ; and no choice was left to the people but that of liberty or the most overwhelming despotism."

This is a very striking account, and these are very striking expressions from such a man as the Marquis de Ferrieres. " The greater part of the deputies," he goes on to say, " passed the night in the hall of the Assembly, less with the view of deliberating there or continuing the sitting, than with the hope of putting themselves into a state of security from the enterprises of the court. Many had received secret intimation that they were to be arrested. They thought with reason that the sanctuary of the national representation would be to ·them an asylum, and that the court would not dare so openly to violate the majesty and the liberty of the French people."

Through all this part of his Memoirs, the marquis, a deputy from the noblesse, and on every account removed from all popular prejudices, leads his reader to suppose, that the Assembly, and the popular leaders, and the city of Paris, were entirely on the defensive. I shall continue to give you his representation of these momentous transactions.

" The insurrection," he says, " was at last regularly organized by means of the committee of the districts into which Paris had been divided ; every preparation was made to resist the expected attack of the Marshal de Broglio ; and at last, as the Bastile might have been made use of against the city by the marshal, it was voted, that this fortress should be taken possession of, at least surrendered into the hands of the magistrates of the city of Paris."

The tumultuous siege, and the sudden and most unexpected capture of it was the consequence, and such atrocities as you have already been made acquainted with.

" After these atrocities all Paris," says the marquis, " men, women, children, priests, and those connected with religious houses, all united to put the city into a state of defence : ditches were dug, the pavement taken up, pikes fabricated, and a deputation sent to the National Assembly."

The paragraph that now follows, coming from the marquis, is very remarkable. " The court," he says, " were resolved to act that very night ; the foreign regiments were ordered to be under arms, the hussars were stationed at the palace, the guards in the courts, and in the midst of these menacing preparations, the court had an air of festivity that added insult to cruelty. The Comte d'Artois, the Polignacs, and M^e. d'Artois appeared on the terrace of the orangerie ; the music of the two regiments was made to play ; the soldiers, on whom wine had not been spared, formed dances ; a sort of insolent and brutal joy resounded on every side, and applauses from all the abandoned women and men that surveyed so strange a spectacle with delight. Such was the frivolity, or rather the wickedness of those beings, that assured, as they supposed, of success, already indulged themselves in the most insulting triumph. Very different was, in the mean time, the aspect of the Assembly : a majestic calmness, a firm countenance, a wise but quiet activity, all announced the great interests with which they were occupied, and the dangerous situation of public affairs. There was no ignorance of the designs of the court : the Assembly knew very well, that at the moment of the attack of Paris, the foreign regiments were to surround their hall, carry off their most distinguished members, and, in case of resistance, employ force ; they knew very well, that the king was on the morrow to come and make them accept the declaration of the 23rd, and dissolve the Assembly ; that already more than forty thousand copies had been sent to the intendants and their inferior officers, to be published and posted up in every place and corner of the kingdom. The Assembly, however, was resolved to brave every outrage rather than consent to any illegal proceeding like this, or betray the confidence of the people in sacrificing its rights to their own personal security. Nor were the Assembly," says the marquis, " without resources ; the slightest attack upon them would have been the signal of a massacre, which would have involved in it the king himself, and all the royal family : a numerous populace, in a sort of dark and fierce silence, and a suppressed feeling, that could in an instant have been converted into fury, surrounded the hall of the States, uneasy at the movements that it saw everywhere around, and waiting but a word to be transported into all the violences and extremities of despair.

" We had a confused notion," says he, " of what was going

on in Paris. The posts were guarded, and the communication stopped; but every now and then a courier reached us, satisfying first the impatient curiosity of the multitude, and then reporting to us in our hall. We sent deputations to the king: the composed and severe air of the deputies showed the imperturbable courage of the Assembly. The people made way for them in the most respectful manner. On their return their looks and sorrowful air showed the people that their mission had been fruitless.

" To the first deputation the answer of the king had been, though not harsh and determined, evasive ; to the second, in his agitation, he had replied, ' You tear me to pieces by the recital you give me, of what has passed in Paris ; it is not possible that the orders I have given can be the cause.' Proper answers were now sent to Paris by the Assembly, and Clermont Tonnerre prevailed upon the Assembly to pause, and not send a third deputation to the king till the next day.

" At eight the next morning, on the 15th, the day after the taking of the Bastile, various addresses were proposed in the Assembly, till the reading of them was on a sudden interrupted by Mirabeau, who, unable to contain himself any longer, burst forth into a furious invective against the court, and what he said he insisted should be made into a message to the king : and the deputation was moving away for the purpose, when the Duc de Liancourt appeared, and announced to the Assembly that the king was on his way to them.

" The fact was," says the marquis, " that the night had passed at the palace in the utmost agitation and indecision ; council after council was held ; the ministers insisted that the troops should act ; but, besides the unhappy consequences that it was possible might ensue from so violent a measure, of which the success was very uncertain, Louis XVI. had an invincible repugnance to every measure that could give occasion to the shedding of the blood of Frenchmen.

" The Duc de Liancourt had availed himself of his opportunities to address the king in the sincerity of his heart; and the king, moved by his arguments, by the concurring opinion of Monsieur, his brother, and the tenderness of his own nature, had given way, and consented to repair to the Assembly.

" The arrival of the king," says the marquis, " produced different effects on the different parties ; the first impression was a general one of surprise, then sentiments followed that were more the result of a little reflection. Well-meaning men, re-

lieved from their terrors, abandoned themselves to their emotions
of love and gratitude to the king.

" The Orleanists, mute and motionless, seemed struck with
stupid astonishment; the Duke, Sieyes, Latouche, retired into
a corner of the hall, and seemed to reproach each other for not
having foreseen all this, and prevented it by some decisive measure of their own; every look, gesture, and movement appeared
to paint their vexation and their uncertainty what to do. The
members of the old régime revolted from a condescension of the
king, which they thought weakness, and considered themselves
as deserted. Many members of the commons, whose pride and
jealousy were not yet satisfied, notwithstanding this brilliant
triumph, appeared quite out of humour, that they could not
push still further the humiliation of the throne."

Of the remainder of the scene, what passed in the Assembly,
and on the return of the king to the palace, the Marquis de
Ferrieres afterwards gives the same account that you have seen
given by Bailly and others. But he does not give the same account that Bailly does of the subsequent visit to Paris. This
visit he considers as brought about by the partisans of the Revolution; that Louis might thus authorize, in a public manner, all
that had been done, and in fact the new form of government that
had just been given to the capital, the organization of the national force, an organization that was to be extended to every
part of the kingdom. Louis was told that this step alone could
quiet Paris, and give confidence in the sincerity of his intentions.

" A thousand fears, in the meantime," says he, " distracted
the palace; the Parisians might seize and detain the king;
some hired wretch might assassinate him; but Louis was resolved. Accepting the offer of a numerous deputation to accompany him from the Assembly, he set off, surrounded by the new
militia of Versailles, that armed in haste, with any weapon that occurred, and clothed in rags, seemed rather a troop of vagabonds, collected together for the purposes of pillage, than an escort for the
king of a great nation. The avenue of Paris was filled with a crowd
of spectators: all in thoughtful silence, but with very different
feelings, gazed upon Louis XVI. as he passed by. Yet this procession of the greatest monarch of Europe," continues the marquis, " could not but inspire the most melancholy reflections on
the instability of all human grandeur. In the carriage with the
king, were the Dukes of Villeroi and de Villequiers; the marks
of anxiety and chagrin were visibly painted on his countenance,
a little dissipated for the moment by some appearances of interest
shown him by the deputies and inhabitants of Versailles.

" His body-guards were at the barrier of Passy, and intended
to have formed his cortège ; but they were left at the gates of
the city, and four only allowed to enter.

" Bailly, at the head of the municipal corps, presented the
keys of the city to the king, with this singular expression :—
' These are the keys which were presented to Henry IV. He
made a conquest of his people ; to-day it is the people that make
conquest of their king.'

" In truth, every thing announced a victory. One hundred
and fifty thousand men armed with scythes, pick-axes, pikes,
muskets, offered a spectacle majestic at the same time, and terrible : cannons on the bridges, and at the entrance of the streets,
through which Louis had to pass, seemed to say but too clearly,
It is a great captive, and not a king, that is now coming into
his capital, into the midst of his subjects.

" An immense mass of people, like a great and troubled ocean,
smoothness, indeed, on its surface, but hollow murmuring in its
depths, gave a mournful air to this vast and imposing spectacle.
Every countenance seemed sombre, every look seemed cold, and
every heart seemed closed against all the sentiments that once
used to animate the hearts of Frenchmen for their king. The
carriage moved on, surrounded by a numerous troop of people
on horseback and on foot; the French guards with their artillery at the head of the column ; a confused sound of musketry.
The cries were a thousand times repeated of ' Vive la nation !'
Not a word of the king ; the most offensive silence ; every where
the humiliating haughtiness that proclaimed a triumph."

The marquis then makes the terms of his narrative concise.
" Louis," he says, " got out at the Hotel de Ville ; walked under
the arms and pikes that were crossed over his head. He was
placed on a throne that was prepared for him in the great hall.
Some natural tears, it seems, he dropped : he attempted to speak ;
a sudden oppression seized him ; he could only say, ' My people
may always depend upon my affection.'

" Bailly presented to Louis XVI. the national cockade ; and
the national cockade was taken by Louis XVI. and placed in his
hat : he appeared in it at the window; and this act of condescension excited numerous applauses.

" Louis XVI. confirmed the nomination of Bailly, of La Fayette,
and retired. The Paris militia no longer maintaining its menacing appearance, reversed its arms in token of peace. The same
cortège reconducted Louis XVI. to the barrier of Passy, where
he found his body-guards, who brought him back to Versailles."

This is the sort of melancholy account given by the marquis of the visit to the capital ; a visit which it must be allowed by every one, showed but too plainly that the old régime and the ancient monarchy of France had passed away, and that the authority of the state was transferred from the monarch at Versailles to the National Assembly and the commune of Paris. This inference was instantly drawn by those more immediately about the court. The Comte d'Artois, the ministers, Marshal Broglio, disappeared ; and the king must be now considered as left alone in his magnificent palace, that told of the grandeur of his ancestors, no longer of his own, terrified by the past, and uncertain of the future ; without confidence in himself, with little hope from the counsels of others, and with no consolation or support but the affection of his family, and that last appeal which is not denied even in this world to those who, however unfortunate, have meant well.

LECTURE XIV.

NECESSITY OF EXECUTIVE POWER.

I HAVE already observed to you how desirable it is that you should attend well to the opening scenes of this great Revolution. It is here that your instruction will best be found. I have also remarked to you, that it is not always easy to form just opinons on these momentous transactions, and that you may not as yet be exactly aware of the value of such just opinions when they can be attained. I can have no wish that you should adopt what are delivered by me, any further than they are reasonable ; and I am naturally anxious to fortify them by any testimonies that are within my reach.

I must therefore now mention to you a particular circumstance.

You will have remarked, that though I represent myself as deeply interested in the great cause of the liberties of mankind, still that I have distinctly protested against the conduct of the patriots of France during these earlier sittings of the Assembly, of the Tiers Etat ; and above all, I have rested much on a particular crisis—on the declaration of the king on the 23rd of June. All through these lectures I have taken upon me to assert, that it behoved the patriots to have closed with the king and the court on this occasion, and however altered and impaired the original measure of M. Necker might be, still to have accepted what was offered, and on such ground as was thus made solid under them, to have stood firm, and to have been satisfied with their success.

In these views, assertions and final decision on the whole of the case, I have always considered myself as adopting an opinion at the hazard, or rather the certainty, of censure from those who think otherwise; and it was therefore with considerable satisfaction, that long after my lectures were written, I met with a passage in the Memoirs of Jefferson, from which it appears that he actually came to the same decision on this important crisis of the 23rd of June that I myself had done, when himself in Paris at the time, in the situation of ambassador from America.

Mr. Jefferson, as it is well known, was a person of very warm, not to say violent temperament, and of opinions entirely democratic.

After describing events much in the way you have understood them from me, he proceeds thus :—" M. Necker's draught of a declaration was entirely broken up, and that of the Comte d'Artois inserted into it. Himself and Montmorin offered their resignation, which was refused, the Comte d'Artois saying to M. Necker, ' No, sir, you must be kept as the hostage; we hold you responsible for all the ill which shall happen.' This change of plan was immediately whispered without doors. The noblesse were in triumph, the people in consternation. I was quite alarmed at this state of things. The soldiery had not yet indicated which side they should take; and that which they should support would be sure to prevail. I considered a successful reformation in France as ensuring a general reformation through Europe, and the resurrection to a new life, of their people, now ground to dust by the abuses of the governing powers. I was much acquainted with the leading patriots of the Assembly. Being from a country which had successfully passed through a similar reformation, they were disposed to my acquaintance, and had some confidence in me. I urged most strenuously an immediate compromise, to secure what the government was now ready to yield, and trust to future occasions for what might still be wanting. It was well understood that the king would grant at this time,—first, freedom of the person by Habeas Corpus; secondly, freedom of conscience; thirdly, freedom of the press; fourthly, trial by jury; fifthly, a representative legislature; sixthly, annual meetings; seventhly, the origination of laws; eighthly, the exclusive right of taxation and appropriation; and, ninthly, the responsibility of ministers; and, with the exercise of these powers they could obtain in future whatever might be further necessary to improve and preserve their constitution. They thought otherwise, however, and events have proved their lamentable error ; for, after thirty years of war, foreign and domestic, the loss of millions of lives, the prostration of private happiness, and the foreign subjugation of their own country for a time, they have obtained no more, nor even that securely."

I must mention, too, that long after these lectures were written, I have found such objections as are made in them to the proceedings of the National Assembly abundantly confirmed by the publication of M. Dumont, the friend and assistant of Mirabeau, a very able and enlightened man, at the time deeply interested in the liberties of France, and the fortunes of mankind.

But to proceed to my lecture.

The first events that occurred after the king had adopted the Revolution promised ill ; Foulon and Berthier were massacred in the streets of Paris by the multitude ; and every where through the interior of the kingdom the people of condition saw their country-seats burnt and pillaged, and themselves and their families exposed to the most dreadful outrages. Popular victories in the Assembly seem never to have had any effect on the ferocious passions of the people. It is no light matter to withdraw a community from the influence of established authority ; it is never easy, it may not be possible, to substitute for some time any new system of control. In the interval the lower orders are ready for any enormity that their own passions or the passions of designing or bad men may propose to them. It is very true that patriots must expose the faults of their rulers and the vices of their government, or they can hope for no reform in either ; but every distinction should be always made, that can possibly be made, between governors and government itself ; the selfish, unfeeling, odious vices of the rulers are to be resisted, but care must be taken not to pander to the base and brutal passions of the multitude. To do this, however, it will be replied, is pretty nearly to effect impossibilities. It may be so ; yet such is the task to be held up to the virtuous ambition of brave and good men ; and such men, the patriots of a country, must endeavour to accomplish it according to the varying opportunities of the case, and the qualities of mind and body with which they have been intrusted. Much of this task was accomplished by the patriots of America in the great revolution that separated them from this country ; a favourable one, totally unlike that of France or of any European country; cases with which it is so often confounded : and you may remember, even in this case of America, the confusion, the shame, the anguish with which the mind of Washington was but too often overwhelmed by the indisposition of his countrymen to the necessary restraint of regular authority, and the proper machinery of executive government.

The difficulty, you will remember, is, and it is most intelligible, how to restrain the selfish passions of mankind, how to procure any attention to the common obligations of law and justice, when the former ministers of law and justice have been displaced and lost their authority.

To return to the instance of America. One of my lectures on the American Revolution was chiefly intended to show you, how much Washington suffered, how much the best interests, present and future, of the great continent of America were endangered from that absence of executive power, which necessarily took place, when the contest with Great Britain was terminated. The difficulty will always occur. In the case before us, the patriots of the French Revolution had talked of the sovereign will of the people, and had made such large references to their wisdom and their power, that the multitude seem to have taken them at their word, and to have concluded that every thing that was agreeable to them, must necessarily be right. All government is instituted for the happiness of the people; this is the first step, and one of which there can be no doubt; but the second is, that of this happiness they can be themselves the only and the best judges ; a position totally different, and which requires many limitations, distinctions, and explanations, and which, when thrown out to the multitude, as it continually was, by the patriotic leaders in the most unqualified manner, could lead only to those unhappy excesses, which it is the grief of every friend to the liberties of mankind to read and hear of, and which constitute so much of the history of the French Revolution.

I have now made three distinct accusations. I have accused the people of Paris (the multitude at least) of taking the law into their own hands, and in defiance of what authority yet remained, of massacreing those who had offended them in the public streets. I have accused the common people all over France, when the authority of the old government was removed, of committing the most disgraceful and cruel outrages on the property and persons of the aristocracy of the country. I have

accused the leaders of the Revolution of addressing such language
to the people (that of their sovereignty and their sovereign will)
as could only be fatal to the people and to themselves; such as
was unworthy of them as statesmen; such as could never have
been necessary, if they had acted during the first weeks of the
Revolution in a spirit of temper and moderation, and made the
best of their case with the king, who was, according to the limits
of his views and feelings, as patriotic as themselves.

Now these are accusations which you must consider in the
detail of the history, as you read it for yourselves. Of the two
first there can be no doubt; of the last there may, and it will
require your best attention. But even of this last position, that
the leaders used fatal language to the people, the truth is sufficiently apparent; and after the first lessons that are given to
rulers, the next are, those that are afforded to all who love freedom, and more particularly those who are ready to resist, or
even overturn, a government for the sake of bettering the condition of their country. Patriots have their temptations and
their mistakes, as well as those who govern; and you must
keep your attention directed to the faults that were committed
(and by them committed) on the subject of executive power.
The great cause of the French Revolution failed for want of
executive power. This is indeed a difficult subject, and one
which I ought not thus to decide and anticipate—this conduct,
I mean, of the Assembly with respect to the executive power;
but this at least I may say, that the first and most important
point of all others to be accomplished when the king had resigned himself to the Revolution, in the Hotel de Ville, was the
immediate establishment (more particularly in Paris) of something like an effective power. The next point was, when the
constitution came afterwards to be regularly settled, to make
the executive power sufficiently strong. Now, the Constituent
Assembly did neither. These are, I think, the two great lessons of
instruction for you during all the earlier parts of the French
Revolution, during the sitting of the Constituent Assembly;
their failures on the subject of executive power.

You will see a very good description of the situation of Paris,
immediately after the king's visit, in Groenvelt. You must
read this part of the history also in Bailly's Memoirs, and in the
Memoirs of the Marquis de Ferrieres. There is a good account
in Dodsley's Annual Register. And now you will observe, that
there seems to have been in Paris, all through the Revolution, a
set of wretches among the multitude always ready to undertake

any projects of insurrection and bloodshed : these were always
considered as the followers and hired ruffians of the Duke of
Orleans, though I know not with what sufficient reason : money
may have been given, and a certain effect in consequence produced, but no such effect, I conceive, as was unhappily witnessed : and it is quite out of the question to suppose that such
a spirit and such excesses, as were witnessed, could have been
produced by money; far different, and far more awful, was the
origin of such frightful phenomena in the history of our species.
There was in the houses of legislature also, at all times and from
the first, a party that were always urging every thing to extremes, and seemed to have no relish for any counsels but those
of fury and violence.   Now men of both these descriptions,
whether men of bad designs and desperate characters, or men
inflamed to a sort of madness by the intoxicating nature of
new opinions, men both like the one and like the other, must
always be expected to appear, must always be taken into account in all revolutions.   They are naturally the favourites
of the multitude, and it is very difficult, it is almost impossible, to save a community from their destructive influence.
You will see them in action all through the Revolution; the
low party of the Constituent, the republicans of the Legislative Assembly, the mountain of the Convention, the leaders
of the Jacobin club, the demagogues of the Palais Royal.   Observe their speeches, the decrees they propose, their conduct ;
these (after the first lessons have been given) are the next lessons of the Revolution.   Such men will arise, will necessarily
be found in public mobs, in public assemblies; but these are
the men against whom real patriots, the real friends of liberty,
are to be more particularly on their guard.   I must now make a
painful reference, in some slight and passing manner, to subjects
of this nature.

M. Bailly gives a regular account of the massacre of M. de
Berthier.   He presided that day at the town hall.   All the way
to Paris, it was but too clear, as M. de Berthier was brought
along, under the conduct of the civil power, that no civil power
would be sufficient for his protection.   The savages that had
just murdered his father-in-law, Foulon, brought the head upon
a pike, close to the carriage where he was sitting ; M de la
Riviere, his conductor, exerted himself very humanely, made
him turn aside his eyes, and told him it was the head of M. de
Quesnay ; but the sufferings of the unhappy man were extreme,
and M. de la Riviere was unable to lodge him, according to his
orders, in the prison of the Abbaye, and he could only bring him

to the town hall.   M. Bailly had procured a strong guard from La Fayette; it was their object to remove Berthier to prison, if possible, preparatory to his trial; but even while they were interrogating the prisoner, the blood-thirsty impatience of the crowd had become uncontrollable, and he no sooner appeared on the steps, than he was torn away from the guard, and massacred on the spot.   A dragoon brought his heart to the council; he was repulsed with horror.   The multitude next attempted to bring his head on a pike, and were already on the staircase; the helpless committee were obliged to send word, that no admission could be allowed, as they were, at the moment, sitting and engaged in business.   "In these terrible moments," says M. Bailly, "pretexts were to be made use of to escape from these atrocities; there was a real danger," he continues, "to those (it was useless to brave it) who attempted to speak the language of justice and humanity; the people could hear nothing; whoever thought not with them was supposed a traitor."

This is an awful specimen of the rude passions of mankind. The dragoon, however, it is said, was pursued to death by his indignant comrades, and was killed in the first duel with one of them.   The honour of the military character was justly felt; and these, the very murderers of Foulon and Berthier, brought their money and trinkets to the Assembly.   These incidents speak something in favour of human nature.   But in the notes to Bailly's Memoirs, you will see a sort of pamphlet, or hand-bill, that appeared at the time, written by some bad man, but one evidently of intelligence and of literary talents.   What are we to say, what are we to think of the frail nature of the peace of society, and of the danger of loosening its bands, when even such a man could deliver to his fellow-creatures a detail of the abominations of these massacres, decorated by the refined expressions of pleasantry and good writing?   "But to lose no more time," says this hand-bill, "we strangled him; and then, as he was an ex-administrator, we took off his head, in a manner the most respectful; we took from him his heart and his entrails; the head walked off on the one side, and the body on the other, —the first time that these two intimate connections had found themselves separated from each other."   Other passages, and more disgusting, occur; the whole is properly given by the present editor of Bailly, to show to what an extent the human mind may be hardened by political fury.

After all, it is very strange that no resistance could be made to such atrocious proceedings, and it seems difficult to suppose, that the mere mob were alone concerned ; not that, if they were, this would be any justification of the Assembly. Where was all the force of the capital ? Why did not the Assembly call aloud, in the cause of everything that should have been dear to them? When the citizens of Paris, a few days before, expected their town to be attacked by Broglio and the army, the body of electors had assembled, had created a regular force, La Fayette was at the head of it; afterwards, when the king repaired to the capital, wherever he looked, he had seen the population under arms ; where were they all ? They must have constituted much of the respectable part of the population of Paris. Efforts were made by La Fayette and by Bailly, by the military and civil powers, all in vain. What the editors of Bailly have to say is only this, that at the time of these massacres the armed force was not properly organized ; that the officers scarcely knew each other, and that their persons were scarcely known to those who were to obey them ; that it was an irregular mass, divided in sentiment, over which no general influence could be exercised. Divided in sentiment, but how ? on an occasion like this ? To be able to say no more than this for the people of Paris is to say but little. La Fayette, it is added, had saved from popular fury, at different times, seventeen persons just before : a melancholy addition this to the crimes of the populace, and a new cause of reproach to the Assembly and the respectable part of the community.

La Fayette on every occasion, it will be found, all circumstances considered, did everything that could possibly be done by a brave and good man, often at great personal risk, often with very eminent success. In this instance, La Fayette was not wanting to his own character, or to his country ; the cause of civil order and of the law was evidently at issue. He must have been deeply mortified at this early specimen of the Revolution. He wrote to Bailly, and to the districts, to throw up his command, and he was able to write to them a calm and reasonable letter. Every effort was made to appease his just indignation, and he at last resumed the command, as he had always secretly intended, on a promise of proper obedience to him, given by the electors and deputies of the districts in the name of the citizens of Paris ; " that his zeal," they said, " seconded by their common efforts, might conduct to perfection the great work of the public liberty."

How ill this promise was observed, is but too well known ; these massacres produced some sensation in the districts of Paris, and occasioned a seasonable proclamation, but they should have far more powerfully affected the National Assembly. It was evident how dreadful was the monster that they had unchained, while endeavouring to free their country from a system of bad government and the oppressions of a court ; but no proper sentiment seems to have been awakened in the democratic party. The virtuous M. de Lally Tollendal exerted himself with no adequate success.   This distinguished patriot had taken a reasonable view of the situation of France, even before these dreadful events.   "From the point where we then were," he says, "immediately after the king's visit to the town hall, it was evident that nothing more was to be feared for liberty, but the projects of faction, and the dangers of anarchy ; the National Assembly had only to put itself on its guard against the excess of its power.   There was not a moment to lose to re-establish public order ; news had been already received that the commotions, which had shaken the capital, had been felt not only in the neighbouring cities, but in the distant provinces."

With his hands full of letters, that attested the excesses everywhere committed with impunity, Tollendal repaired to the National Assembly, and proposed his proclamation on the 20th. On the first and on the second reading his project was received with acclamation, but to his astonishment he saw a party rise to oppose it.   " According to one," says he, " my sensibility had seduced my reason ; these fires, these imprisonments, these assassinations, were crosses that we should learn to support, because we ought to have expected them :—according to another, my imagination had created dangers which did not exist : there was no danger but in my motion ; danger for liberty, because it would take from the people a salutary fear and alarm for their freedom, which should rather be encouraged than suppressed; danger for the Assembly, that would see Paris declare against it.

" The next day," continues Lally Tollendal (the 21st of July), " I was awaked by the cries of grief.   I saw enter my chamber a young man, pale, disfigured, who hastened eagerly to throw his arms around me, and who said to me, as he sobbed aloud, ' Sir, you have passed fifteen years of your life in defending the memory of your own father ; save the life of mine, let him be heard by his judges.'   It was the son of the unfortunate Berthier.   I conducted him instantly to the president of the Assembly.   As ill fortune would have it, there was no sitting in the morning ; in the evening it was too late.   The father-in-law and the son-in-law had been, in the mean time, in the course of the day, torn in pieces." Such is the account of Tollendal. Such are the scenes of a Revolution.

" You may imagine," continues Tollendal, " that at the very first sitting I hastened to fix the general attention on this hor- rible event. I spoke in the name of a son whose father had been just massacred ; and Barnave, a son who was in mourning for his own father at the time, dared to reproach me with feel- ing, when I should only reason. He added, ' Was then the blood, which has been shed, so very precious ?' And every time he raised his arms in the midst of his sanguinary declamations, he showed to every eye the mournful marks of his own recent afflictions, the weepers (for his own father) that made a part of his dress, the incontestable witnesses of his barbarous insensi- bility." You will see hereafter in the history, that Lally Tol- lendal at last rushed forth from the Constituent Assembly, unable to bear the presence and the language of the democratic party any longer.

The conduct of Barnave on this question, shows the repub- lican character in that odious point of view in which it is but too ready to present itself. You remember the incidents of the Roman story. These often mislead ; and cool cruelty is some- times supposed to be virtue, and humanity to be weakness. But it is agreeable to remember, that Barnave lived to melt over the misfortunes of the king and queen, and to show the more amiable feelings of our common nature. But no such amiable, such in- dispensable feelings were witnessed in an important portion of the National Assembly. Lally Tollendal was expostulated with, checked, and opposed. " I discharge my conscience," he cried aloud, " of the evils that will result from your refusals of what I propose. I wash my hands of the blood which will flow." Cries of fury resounded on every side, and Mirabeau observed, with a ferocious look, " Nations must have their victims ; to the calamities of individuals one must be hardened ; it is only at this price that one can become a citizen." Mirabeau afterwards addressed a letter on the general subject to his constituents ; and he called forth all the powers of his eloquence to palliate the excesses of the people, and rather to throw the blame on their former rulers. Admitting that there was too much of truth in some of his remarks on their former rulers, this was surely not a time to have produced them.

" Observe now," said he, " how many have been the causes that concurred to produce this explosion, these massacres (he enumerated many of these causes), in short," said he, " two centuries of oppression, public and private, political and fiscal, feudal and judicial, crowned by that most horrible conspiracy (Broglio and the court) which the annals of the world will for ever transmit to memory ; these are what have so provoked the people; the people have punished a few of those whom the public voice has declared the authors of these evils. Let those who have so managed as to fear no other tribunal, fear this of the public.

" It would make a volume to show by examples that in these seasons of severity exercised upon government, governments but reap the harvest of their own iniquities. The people are despised, and are then expected to be always gentle and passive; but no, it is instruction which must be drawn from these events, the injustice of the other classes to the people makes them find justice in barbarity itself."

Such were some of the passages in the letter of Mirabeau. The oppressions of the old government are here seen, no doubt, but extremely exaggerated and very unseasonably produced, even admitting that there is but too much truth in the moral which he draws. What could be the interpretation or effect of such observations at that particular juncture ? He who justifies a crime is little to be distinguished from the criminal ; and this is a fault of constant occurrence among men, especially when parties run high. The proclamation that was issued by the Assembly, turned out to be spiritless and inefficient. The Assembly, in this proclamation, after stating (reasonably enough) its own merits with the public, those of the king, and the consequences of such proceedings, informed the public that a tribunal would be immediately created for the regular trial of cases of treason ; and they were then invited to peace (*invited to peace*), to the maintenance of order and the public tranquillity, to the confidence which they owed their king and their representatives, and that respect for the laws, without which (it was observed) there can be no liberty. " These were the sentiments and principles," says M. Bailly, " of the National Assembly ;" and he seems to think them so adequate to the occasion, as to be quite pleased with his fellow legislators. He pronounces them excellent.

The proclamation issued was the one that had been proposed by Lally, even before the murders of Foulon and Berthier had taken place, but the most important paragraph, even as it first stood, was left out; the paragraph was this :—" That punishment the most just, pronounced on crimes the most clear, became itself an injustice and a crime, unless ordered by the law, and the judge, the proper organ of the law."

Once more, and to close for a time the subject.

The scenes I have alluded to are highly disgraceful to the Assembly, and all the constituted authorities of Paris. They show, no doubt, the necessity of some executive power. This is the first lesson; but more is to be considered. The two unhappy men who were massacred were literally torn in pieces by the multitude. Their heads were carried on pikes, and led in a sort of triumphal procession through the streets. A fiend in the shape of a man, as I have already mentioned, actually thrust his hand into the entrails of one of these unfortunate victims, tore out the heart, and brought it to the council table, where the committee was sitting in the town hall. These are the great facts to be remembered.

Now horrors of this kind, and they are innumerable through the French Revolution, show, as I have mentioned, in the first place, the necessity of some executive government; but in the second place, they have been always considered as the most decisive proofs that can possibly be produced to show the necessity, after all, of the Revolution itself, and the badness of the old French government. What must have been the rulers, or at least the system of government, when such were the people? What further justification can be required?—Now whether this rapid mode of reasoning be or be not entirely conclusive, one thing must, I think, be admitted; that the moral situation of the lower orders in France at the time of the Revolution, forms an eternal answer to those who would give the people no instruction and no freedom. How is the brute to be taken out of the human animal but by the influence of that moral and religious knowledge, which alone distinguish him from other animals in the desert? But give him instruction, it will be answered, and he will then be a more intelligent and discerning critic on the vices and follies of his superiors. No doubt they must behave better; and why not? Is not this in other words to say, that the community will in every class and in every direction be advanced and improved.

But the community will never be safe, it will be again answered, if every man is thus to be converted into a judge of his betters and erected into a statesman. This is a gross exaggeration: the generality of mankind must be occupied in making provision for themselves and their families; the knowledge they

can acquire must be very limited, little more than what may
save them from the brutal vices; the political power which will
sufficiently gratify them and make them respectable in their own
eyes and those of their superiors is in truth, generally speaking,
and in any ordinary state of the world, very little; and at all
events the community can never for a moment be safe, when
the multitude are degraded and despised.   They will, on some
opportunity or other, rise, as they did in France, first in the Jac-
querie, next at the Revolution; on both occasions, but too much
after the manner of slaves in a West India island.   And even
in regular and good governments, like our own, in times of any
difficulty or danger, the visitation of a scarcity, a fall in the
price of labour, a stoppage of the manufactures, to whom has a
factious demagogue the best chance of successfully addressing
himself—to an ignorant creature that can understand no voice
but the clamour of his wants and passions, or to one that has
been accustomed to consider occasionally the nature of his duties,
moral and religious, occasionally to exercise his thoughts, occasionally, in the language of the poet, " to look before and
after?"   Again, to which of the two can a wise and good man
address himself in these seasons of public calamity with the best
chance of success ?   Which is most likely to understand what
even a wise and good man can then only say—the wisdom of
patience; the necessity of suffering; that governments cannot
perform impossibilities; that the best will be abused; the wisest
make mistakes; that perfection, that happiness, in our sublunary
state, are not to be expected;—of such things, which of the two
is likely to be the best auditor, the ignorant man or the more
improved ?

But to return to our subject of the want of executive power.
The Revolution failed not a little on account of the tumultuary
mobs of Paris.   The student's attention should always be directed
to this point; why and how it came about that there was no proper executive power in the metropolis and in the country; why
the Constituent Assembly never seemed sufficiently aware of the
necessity of one; why democratic principles of the most unqualified nature so uniformly prevailed.

This subject of executive power is at all times so important,
and is so intimately connected with every part of the French
Revolution, that I will endeavour, in the remainder of the lecture, to furnish you with such particulars of a general nature, as
may give you some notion of what it was, during the period we
are now considering, and long after.

A sort of slight history of it seems the following.

This first executive power that existed in France prior to the Revolution, was of course the ancient power, prerogative, and authority of the crown.   The king was, under the old régime, the great executive, and indeed legislative power.

But this executive power grew weaker as the Revolution proceeded, and might be said to be suspended, when the king was thought to have brought up Marshal Broglio and his troops to put down the Revolution and to subdue Paris.   His authority, on the failure of this measure, was virtually at an end, and a new sort of executive power was created.

Recourse was had to the body of Parisian electors, about three hundred in number, those who originally chose the deputies that were sent to the States General, and they became the first magistracy, or executive and civil power ; and, in the revolutionary state of things then existing, were highly fitted to be so.   They arranged and formed the military force, that appeared as by enchantment, and probably saved Paris, not only from Marshal Broglio, but from internal pillage and destruction at that terrible crisis.

But it was afterwards found that they and the military force, with all the assistance of La Fayette and Bailly, were insufficient to secure the peace and order of the community ; they had not been able, or they had not sufficiently exerted themselves, to prevent the massacres we have lately alluded to ; and the real executive power became little to be distinguished from the mere will of the multitude, the will of the sovereign people.   This was in truth the law ; there was no other, and none could be worse.   The electors were not at ease or pleased with their situation ; they seemed to have understood the nature of their fellow-citizens, the Parisians, perfectly well ; they were not very desirous to retain their authority ; and they therefore persuaded the sixty districts of the capital to elect each two deputies, who should constitute a temporary administration, make proper provision for a future municipal government, and being the acknowledged representatives of the community, could assume the appearance of regular legitimate authority, according to the new opinions.

These one hundred and twenty deputies then constituted the second municipal authority or acting executive power of the capital ; and these might have succeeded eventually in maintaining some appearance of order in the community, but for one unfortunate circumstance : it was this ; they were the immediate representatives each of their own districts ; and these districts had each of them, most unhappily, General Assemblies.   In these Assemblies every inhabitant was permitted to speak (each inhabitant, a Frenchman), permitted, I say, to speak and vote. These Assemblies, in this manner, framed resolutions, which were laws in their own districts, issued proclamations, and granted passports. They became themselves, rather than the deputies, the effective executive power; and the result of this was, that the great city of Paris became at once tormented with sixty republics, each with a General Assembly, where all the citizens, meeting, speaking, voting at the same time, each Assembly became a cave of Æolus, but with no master-spirit to control its inmates. This, then, was a dreadful species of executive power or municipal authority. Such Assemblies, with such representatives, the Assemblies constantly sitting, the representatives the mere organs of their will—this was a miserable specimen of the sovereignty of the people, a melancholy caricature of the doctrines of freedom.

Groenvelt, an enthusiastic friend of liberty, who was on the spot at the time, thus expresses himself:—" The noise which prevails in these Assemblies is enough to distract any one who is not accustomed to it. Every speech is followed or interrupted by the loudest and most clamorous applause, or the most tumultuous signs of disapprobation. The president of one of these Assemblies, finding it impossible to command silence by any other means, has stationed a drummer behind him; and when all is noise, tumult, and confusion, he gives the signal to beat the drum till tranquillity is restored." Groenvelt, however, finishes the paragraph by a consolatory reference to the usual subject of vituperation, the old government. " If a man will have his house repaired," says he, " he must not complain that he is *incommoded* during the operation by dust and noise." " Incommoded " seems a very faint term to be used by one who had been present at these Assemblies.

When such was the great source of executive power, that is, of the authority of the community, the next step in the progress of destruction, as the student will easily conceive, would be, that these Assemblies would fall under the management of wrongheaded, furious demagogues; that sensible people in disgust would withdraw (a constant but most lamentable consequence at all times of a disorderly public assembly); that these demagogues, in each district, would communicate and correspond with each other, and at last would fall into a great united club (as they did, the Jacobin club); be there joined by the more violent members of the National Assembly; and by forming a similar organization in the great towns and all over the kingdom, influence these Assemblies, organize these districts, and in fact constitute the real effective government of the empire, and give the law to the National Assembly itself, under whatever form or name it appeared. All this took place.

Now a more tremendous executive (or rather legislative and executive power) than this, to exist in any country, no imagination can conceive. It was highly fitted, it must be allowed, to beat off an invading enemy; to raise armies, that might be let loose upon the rest of Europe : but it was the least fitted in the world to build up the regular constitution, and lay the foundations of the future peace and prosperity of a great empire. You will often hear of the municipality of Paris, as you read the history ; that is, of the body composed of the representatives of the sixty districts, each district having its own Assembly. You will often hear of the Jacobin club : bear in mind this slight sketch of these dreadful ministers of authority that I have given you ; the nature of the power, its organization, and extent ; and all the enormities that disgraced the Revolution, and destroyed all the efforts of good men, will not surprise you.

But other circumstances must be mentioned that concurred to the same end ; concurred to the debasement and destruction of all regular executive power, of all the proper authority of the community.

"There is a very numerous class of men," says Groenvelt, "in this metropolis, who, though they do not frequent the Assemblies of the districts, are by no means indifferent about politics, but hold Assemblies of their own in public places, in the Palais Royal, in the streets, wherever they happen accidentally to collect together. They are, in general, men of distressed circumstances, with little or no employment; some supporting a precarious existence by alms, condemned to a life of misery, and consequently restless, dissatisfied, greedy after news, or rather impatient for change. Nearly one hundred thousand individuals (of the upper ranks) are supposed to have emigrated. Judge from this circumstance what an army of servants out of place, labourers out of work, men wholly dependent on the luxuries of the great, and now stripped of all resources, must have been turned loose upon the public. Again : the levity and inconstancy of the Parisians had been always proverbial; so had their gross ignorance ; so had their blind credulity : and yet they were suspicious in the extreme ; they imagined treachery or villany in the most indifferent, innocent, or praiseworthy

actions ; so that no men could preserve their favour or conduct
their business.

"Falsehood," says Groenvelt, "is the constant and the favourite
resource of the cabals which prevail here.   You cannot form an
idea of the impudence with which the most palpable lies are
published and propagated among the people.   The most positive
assertions, the most minute detail of facts, the strongest appearance of probability, are made to accompany the grossest falsehoods.   Foulon and Bezenval were the victims of pretended letters, of which one thousand copies, but no original, was ever
seen.   The convent of Montmartre has been twice beset by
twenty or thirty thousand men, who threatened it with destruction for having engrossed the provender of Paris ; it was searched,
and there was scarcely found provision enough to supply the
house.   At one moment it is affirmed that the aristocratical conspirators have thrown a great quantity of bread into the Seine ;
at another, that they mowed the green corn.   The public is
overwhelmed with lies and calumnies."

Nor was this credulity and this unhappy suspiciousness of
temper confined to Paris.   These prevailed all over the kingdom, and instances the most ludicrous might be produced.

Now I must turn for an instant to observe, that the picture of
general ignorance in the people of France, as you see, is very
complete ; and yet, as you also see, the old government was not
in this way made secure, as it should have been, according to
those who contend against the instruction of the lower orders :
quite the contrary ; there was no chance left for it.   But in this
general state of public ignorance the political press seems
to have been active and unprincipled to the most extraordinary
degree.   In Paris, thirteen or even sixteen pamphlets a day
were no matter of surprise.   These innumerable productions
were spread from the capital through every part of the kingdom
with the greatest dispatch ; it is said they were given away : a
circumstance which, like many others, leads to the belief of an
Orleans faction existing to a certain extent at least, and exercising all their abominable machinations for the propagation
of disorder.   Lastly, as a supereminent difficulty for good patriots to struggle with, a scarcity, a famine, was sorely felt in
Paris, and more or less in other parts of France, during these
earlier parts of the Revolution.   Demagogues, and revolutionists,
and all the artificers of confusion, can have no instrument in
their hands like this—the rich man eating bread while the poor
man is famished.   How vain to talk to the latter of order and

law! how easy, of the necessity of insurrection and a better government! Bailly mentions, that he was often uncertain at
midnight of the proper supply for the city the next day. To all
these causes of disorder and calamity must, I conceive, after all,
be added the immense fortune of the Duke of Orleans, and the
manner in which he suffered it to be employed. And lastly,
and above all, the nature of the new opinions, intoxicating alike
to the speaker and the hearer, to the writer and the reader, to
the thousands of demagogues and literary men who supposed
they were already wiser than all who had gone before them, and
to the crowds and multitudes, more particularly those, rising
into life, who thought they were now to become so. The very
nature of these opinions was to suppose that there was a new
era to commence in the religion, morals, and governments of
mankind; and when, in this state of things, even the wise and
the people of property seemed no longer to respect any established
system of conduct or opinion, and openly to avow it, what was
to become of the mass of the community?

You will now, I hope, be able to form some general notion of
the state of Paris and of France when the king adopted the Revolution, and for some time after; a notion sufficiently clear to
enable you to understand what I am delivering on the subject of
executive power in this lecture; and the question now is, What
was done by the Constituent Assembly from the moment that
all the regular and legitimate power was transferred from the
king to them? what was done for the preservation of their own
consequence; for the security of the public; for the very success
of any measures they could possibly prepare; for the improvement of the constitution of their country? Are they, or are
they not, to be blamed for their want of sense and spirit? And
if Lally Tollendal and others were helpless, and unable to carry
proper measures with the Assembly, are the friends of freedom
to be warned or not by the example of the Assembly? What
has been the event is now known, and what the event *could not
but be* might have been foreseen (so it must now be thought) by
all intelligent men at the time. I do not deny their difficulties,
but they were intoxicated with the new opinions, as men will
always be; and they made no efforts, or thought none necessary,
to form a proper executive power for their own defence, the
protection of the community, in fact, the protection of their own
Revolution.

You will of course consider the subject more thoroughly hereafter. It was on the whole a most perilous and unhappy situa-

tion of affairs, though it appeared not so at the time to the friends of liberty in this country, in America, and in Europe. The question in reality was, whether the National Assembly (for this was the only hope), consisting of so many enlightened and respectable men, could restrain the general ardour, and could by their own virtues, wisdom, and moderation, compensate for all the tendencies to evil which we have thus briefly and very imperfectly described.

As I leave this subject, and before I conclude my lecture, I must announce to you the subject of the lecture of to-morrow—one, indeed, connected with the subject of this lecture, the want of executive power.

The truth was, that the most dreadful outrages had followed all through France the first success of what must be considered as the first insurrection of the people, on the 14th of July.

A report was made to the Assembly on the 3rd of August; the committee stated, to use their own words, that "letters and memorials received from all the provinces had proved, that property of every kind was everywhere the prey of the most atrocious plunderers; that throughout the country the houses were burned, the convents destroyed, and farms given up to pillage; imposts, seignorial services, all, every thing is annihilated; the laws are without force, the magistrates without authority, and justice is no longer more than a phantom, which it is vain to seek in the courts."

Such was the language of the report made to the Assembly on the 3rd.

Dreadful accounts had also reached many individual members of the Assembly on the morning of the 4th.

The question then was, what was the course to be pursued? The result was the proceedings of the night of the 4th of August: among the most memorable in the course of the Revolution. They must be well considered by you in every part, and I must call your attention to them in my lecture of to-morrow. They must be well observed, because they are connected with the nature of the rights and privileges of property, particularly ecclesiastical property. They show how these subjects are naturally affected by revolutions. These proceedings of the night of the 4th of August put an end, in a word, to all feudal rights and privileges, and led at last to the destruction of the property of the clergy in France and of her ecclesiastical orders; and, as a specimen of revolutions, and the reasonings and consequences by which they are accompanied, are for ever memorable in the history of mankind.

LECTURE XV.

FOURTH OF AUGUST. DESTRUCTION OF FEUDAL RIGHTS AND CHURCH ESTABLISHMENT.

THE governments of Europe were all founded on feudal principles; but customs continue long after the original reasons of them have ceased, and nothing could be less agreeable to the views and reasonings of a philosopher than the rights and observances, which had been thus transmitted from one generation to another, and, however modified and disguised, had thus descended down to us, even so late as the close of the eighteenth century.

With these feudal notions, it was impossible that the new opinions should not be in a state of hostility from the first. The distinctions of society itself were scarcely tolerated by Rousseau. There was then little chance for the oppressions of the feudal system, when men began to speculate upon the nature of society and the happiness of their fellow-creatures; and with all our reverence for antiquity, and whatever be the difficulties and dangers which are connected with the breaking up of the habits and customs of a community, still we must allow that the feudal system, as it then existed in France, was a burden from which it was very naturally the wish of the patriots of France to deliver their country. The new philosophy was more especially anxious (and very properly so) to elevate the condition of the lower orders; and, as applied to this part of society, the feudal system assumed no appearances but those of oppression and injustice. Reference must be had to some sufferings of this kind in the people, or we shall be unable to explain some of the outrages that took place, and not indeed in Paris and the great towns, but through the interior of France, in the earlier periods of the Revolution. These sufferings of the peasantry have, I apprehend, been overstated by very respectable writers; among the rest, our own Arthur Young.

It may be observed, for instance, that the chateaux and the title-deeds might be burned, because the cultivators of the soil, the métayers, were always in debt to the proprietors. Still, sufferings and oppressions to a certain extent must be supposed. The most dreadful disorders took place.

Accounts to this effect had reached the members of the Constituent Assembly, as I have already mentioned, from all parts of France; and it now became an object of serious anxiety to all those who had privileges or possessions, to determine immediately what could best be done, as well for themselves as for others.   Many letters had been received on the 4th of August; and when the Assembly met in the evening, strong symptoms of vexation, anxiety, and terror, were visible in the countenances of the members, particularly those belonging to the two first orders.

But you will see, on the slightest reflection, the difficulty that belongs to the subject.

Privileges, however fantastic and unjust, if long enjoyed, become a species of right and property; and they are retained as such; they are often more dear to their possessors than more substantial goods; to be required to give them up is thought very unreasonable; to have them taken away by force, very unjust.   A dispute much of this kind led to our own civil war between Charles I. and his parliaments. One of the greatest merits of the Long Parliament was the clearing away from landed property some of the inconvenient and oppressive usages of the feudal system; a merit which the parliament of Charles II., without acknowledgment, immediately assumed, as its own, on the Restoration.

People may no doubt surrender, if they please, their privileges and enjoyments, but they are not very likely to do so; and, therefore, the first operation of revolutions is in general to exercise compulsion upon them, and thus to fill the houses and families of many distinguished individuals, sometimes of whole classes of the community, with misery, indignation, and complaints.

When the Assembly met on the evening of the 4th of August, some proposed resolutions were read by Target; the general import of which was, that the ancient laws, imposts, &c. &c., were to remain, till new modified by the Assembly; but the Viscount de Noailles seemed aware that no such temporizing conduct in the Assembly would now be sufficient, and he instantly arose to propose measures, which alone could produce, he said, the public tranquillity, and which went immediately to ordain that all public charges should be equally supported by the whole community; all taxes levied in proportion to income; above all, that all feudal claims should be redeemable at a fair valuation, and that corvées and all rights of the lords to the services of the peasantry, with other grievances of the kind, should be abolished.

You will see his reasonable speech in the notes to the Memoirs of Bailly. He was immediately seconded by the Duc d'Aguillon, whose speech created even more surprise, on account of his very ample estate and extensive royalties. This speech appears to me so humane and yet so considerate, and to touch with so much propriety on all the leading points of the subject, that I will offer to your remembrance some of its leading passages.

"Gentlemen," said the Duke, "there is no one who must not groan over the scenes of horror which are now exhibited in France: it is not only that brigands, with arms in their hands, are enriching themselves at the expense of the public calamity; in many provinces, the whole population forms a species of league to destroy the chateaux, to ravage the lands, and, above all, to possess itself of the places where the titles to feudal properties are deposited. Men are everywhere eager to throw off a yoke that has for so many ages pressed upon them so heavily; and it must be confessed, gentlemen, that this insurrection, though in itself to be blamed, as all violent aggression must be, may still find its excuse in those vexations of which the people are the victims. The proprietors of the fiefs and seignories are themselves, indeed, but seldom to be blamed for the excesses of which their vassals complain, but their agents are often without pity; and the unhappy cultivator groans under the barbarous remains of those feudal laws which still subsist in France. These rights, it cannot be concealed, are a property, and all property is sacred; but then they are burdensome to the people, and all the world agree, how heavy is this oppression.

"In this enlightened age, when a sound philosophy has resumed its empire; at this fortunate epoch, when united for the good of the public, and disengaged from every personal interest, we labour together for the regeneration of the state, it appears to me, that it is for us, before we establish the constitution expected from us by the nation, it is for us, I say, to prove to all our fellow-citizens, that our intention and our wish is, to anticipate their desires, and to establish, as soon as we can, that equality of rights, which ought to exist amongst all men, and which can alone assure to them their freedom. I doubt not that these proprietors of fiefs, these lords of the seignories, far from their refusing their assent to this great truth, will of themselves be disposed to make every sacrifice of their rights that justice can require: they have already renounced their privileges and pecuniary exemptions. One cannot, at this moment, demand from them the pure and simple renunciation of their feudal rights: these rights are their property, of many individuals their only possession; and justice requires from us, not to exact the delivering up of any property from those, to whom we have not first granted a just indemnity ; and I therefore propose, for the sake of rendering them duly sensible that we are not inattentive to their interests, that we should offer them a compensation for the sacrifice of their own convenience to the public good." He then went on to propose resolutions agreeably to those of the Duke de Noailles ; the import of which was, that the National Assembly, considering, moreover, that the feudal and seignorial rights are an oppressive tribute, which injures agriculture and desolates the country, but unable to conceal from itself that all rights are in reality a property, and that all property is inviolable, resolves, &c. &c., " that these rights were to be redeemable after a fixed standard, accommodated by the Assembly to the nature of the case," &c. &c. &c.

Expressions of joy and exclamation followed (and very reasonably) these very generous proposals on the part of the viscount and the duke.

A deputy then arose, Leguen de Kerengal, clad in the habit of a peasant, and gave the Assembly a very full and eloquent description of the feudal abuses.

" You would have prevented," said he, " these burnings of the chateaux, if you had been more early in declaring, that the terrible instruments of oppression, which they contain, were now to exist no more. Let us be just, and let us bring here and annihilate for ever these feudal rights and titles, that outrage all modesty and humanity ; that degrade the human species ; that tie men to a car or a plough, and make them draw it, as if they were beasts : that make men pass whole nights in beating the ponds, lest the frogs, by their noise, should disturb the slumbers of the voluptuous lord. Who is there in an enlightened age like this, that would not make an expiatory bonfire of these infamous parchments ? who that would not seize a torch and offer them up as a sacrifice on the altar of the public good ? There is no peace for France till there is an end of these things : tell the people that you acknowledge the injustice of these rights, acquired in times of ignorance and darkness. You have not a moment to lose.

" The fall of empires has often been announced by less noise than you now hear : do you mean to give laws to France only when in a state of devastation ?"

From these few passages, you will, for the present, sufficiently conceive the nature of a speech, that was followed by redoubled applauses, and by acclamations too loud, to leave any chance of a hearing to those among the nobles who in vain protested, and probably with very great reason, against the truth of the orator's assertions.

This orator was soon after followed by another, Laponte, who completed the picture of feudal tyranny, by the description, probably a most unfair and exaggerated description, of abominations still more disgusting, and even talked of a right which the lords in certain districts were possessed of, actually to warm their feet in the entrails of their vassals when returning cold from the chase. The nobles here, as may well be supposed, could contain themselves no longer; and amid their natural cries of remonstrance, and the equally loud cries of horror and indignation of the Assembly, the uproar was so great, that the orator sat down. Each deputy, as you will now easily imagine, rushed forward to make sacrifices of his particular rights and privileges, many more sacrifices than could be enumerated by any writer or observer of these transactions, and many more than could by us be understood.

The night was, no doubt, a night of tumult and disorder, and the Assembly had little the appearance of the Assembly of a great nation, a meeting of legislators, who were, by their deliberate wisdom, to regenerate an empire. All this is true; and this, and much more than this, you will read in the histories and memoirs that I have offered to your attention. It has been called the night of dupes, and I cannot but allow, that rights and institutions, of whatever kind, if found existing in a community, should be treated with a little more ceremony than was now paid; and every accommodation should be given, and every respect shown, to the convenience and feelings of all concerned. Considerations of this kind you will see strongly urged in the Annual Register, and some of the French works; but it would have been well for France and for mankind, if the Assembly had committed no greater faults than those of this memorable night, and if their enthusiasm, their folly, if you please, had been always not only so noble and so generous in itself, but directed to purposes equally just and intelligent.

Whoever considers subjects of the kind now before us, will find, that they at last resolve themselves into questions of feeling. Why am I to give up my right? says a possessor of an ancient privilege. You should feel for the public good, it is replied; what other answer can be made him? If he *does* feel, he is a man of virtue, and to be had in honour; and so are these patriots of the Constituent Assembly. Men act from mixed motives: it is impossible to enter into all that may have affected the conduct of the different nobles and privileged persons who distinguished themselves on this occasion; it is never very useful to occupy ourselves with disquisitions of this nature. The main feelings and principles concerned, were generosity, humanity, disinterestedness, a sense of justice, a sympathy with others, an interest in the public good, a hope for the improvement and regeneration of France; patriotism, in every sense of the word that can belong to it. The natural impetuosity of the French character was, no doubt, shown; perhaps, that unhappy taste for scenic effect, by which it is so degraded; but, on the whole, humanity has here much to be proud of, and an effort was now made for the happiness of the people of France, the benefit of which France now feels, and will never cease to feel, while the very distinctions of society subsist, while the land is cultivated and property enjoyed, whatever be the fortunes of her government.

The Viscount de Montmorency at last proposed, that the various motions that had been made should be converted into a decree, and the president Chapelier was proceeding accordingly, when he suddenly made a pause—" However," said he, " none of the clergy have yet had an opportunity of being heard; I should reproach myself if I closed this interesting discussion before those of the clergy, who are disposed to speak, have made their sentiments known."

We have now arrived, you will immediately see, at a part of the general subject more particularly interesting—the nature of the sacrifices made by the clergy, and the treatment they received.

It was impossible for the clergy not to come forward, whatever might, or might not, have been their original intentions, when thus called upon by the president; they seem to have managed ill, not to have settled beforehand the part they were to take. The crisis was probably too sudden and unexpected, but they do not appear to have wanted a proper interest in the welfare of the state when they *did* speak, or in the sufferings of others.

Lafare, the bishop of Nancy, in the name of his brethren, expressed his approbation of the abolition of feudal rights, &c. &c.; and proposed that the ransom of ecclesiastical feudalities should not go to the profit of the actual incumbent, but to the assistance of the poorer benefices, for the better relief of the indigent.

Luberac, the bishop of Chartres, expressed his regret at not having sooner seen that the time for political sacrifices was at last arrived. He proposed the suppression of the game laws, and the rights of the chase, describing them as they deserved.

These two speeches excited the greatest enthusiasm and applause in the Assembly, the sitting seemed suspended by them; the nobility were excited more than ever to a renewal and redoubling of their generous efforts for the happiness of the community; more of the nobles came forward with their sacrifices, and more of the clergy; then came the deputies of the different provinces, with the renunciation of their privileges, charters, franchises, and capitulations (you remember how the great monarchy of France was formed, by the continued accretion, piece by piece, if I may so speak, of one part after another, till it became what you see it); a crowd of other renunciations followed, and the Assembly was, at last, in such a situation of tumultuous excitement, that the Bishop of Paris must be considered as having laid the Assembly under the greatest obligation by hitting off a finale, that might with proper grace and effect terminate so extraordinary a scene. He proposed a Te Deum, which was received with the loudest acclamations.

The Duke de Liancourt next proposed a medal, and Lally Tollendal succeeded in reminding the Assembly of the poor king, and in proposing that he should be proclaimed the restorer of French liberty.

Thus ended the celebrated sitting of the 4th of August: but not thus did it end to the clergy, who were affected by consequences a little more important to them than the procession to Notre Dame, a medal, and a new title given to the king.

A committee was appointed to reduce all these rival emotions of magnanimity and patriotism (for such they were) into a law, and the decree that followed, in the shape of nineteen articles, you will find in the notes of Bailly: the fifth is the important one to the clergy. The committee in this fifth article abolished tithes of every species, and they were only to be paid till the Assembly had made proper provision, and their present possessors had entered into the enjoyment of what the Assembly called the "replacement" that was intended for them. And on the 13th of August the Assembly decreed, that by this word they did not mean (as it might naturally have been supposed) that they would furnish them with an equivalent, but with what should be a suitable and honourable support.

A sad difference of opinion seems immediately to have appeared. The committee considered tithes as a feudal vassalage or tax levied on the lands, and as such, with other feudal vassalages or taxes to be abolished; the clergy themselves considered ecclesiastical tithes as a rent-charge for the maintenance of the church, and they could not see how the legislature could transfer this rent-charge from the church, whose property it was, to the landlords, who had no claim to it whatever. Several warm debates followed. Some idea may be formed of them from the Mercure* of the month of August, 1789. From the nature of this journal these debates are given in a broken, inconvenient, and imperfect manner, yet are they still sufficient, as they appear in different months, to enable you to mark the progress of revolutionary violence and injustice.

The great defender of the rights of the church was the great supporter of the Revolution itself, the Abbé Sieyes; like other celebrated statesmen that might be mentioned of our own, and of every other country, powerful when concurring with the public sentiment, weak when opposing it; proudly eminent when hallooing on the passions of the public, hooted down and disregarded when breathing the sounds of justice and of peace.

The arrêt containing the nineteen articles that I have just alluded to, was the result of the 4th, 6th, 7th, 8th, and 11th, of August. As the debate went on, the original rights of the clergy were treated with less and less ceremony; but while the argument was placed only on the issue which I have just mentioned, that the tithe was a rent-charge, the argument at least was entirely in their favour.

You will see at the close of the Mercure of August, an extract from the abbé's speech, which will perfectly enable you to judge of his reasonings. They seem to be entirely just, but the latter part as here given, should come first. At the close of the extract, " the National Assembly," says he, " on the 4th of August decreed that the tithes were redeemable, and you now propose," says he, " that the tithe should not be redeemable ; and this is only a difference in the statement you say ; pleasant enough this. If the ecclesiastical tithe is to be suppressed without any indemnity, will it not rest in the hands of those who owe it, instead of going to those to whom it is due? Is there an estate that has not been bought and sold since the establishment of

---

* The Mercure was a periodical work, the literary part by La Harpe and others, the political part by Mallet du Pan, published before and during the earlier parts of the French Revolution. Having made much use of it, and finding that it was now scarce, I have suggested to M. Mallet and his family, on account of what I esteemed its importance, my wish that it should be presented to the public library of the University of Cambridge ; and, in compliance with my representations, this has been done.

tithes? Was purchase ever made without the charges being taken into calculation?"

You will easily see that while the abbé was proceeding in this strain, his reasonings were totally unanswerable; but he had before, as you will observe in the opening of this extract, taken a much more general view of the subject. He said not a word of the divine origin of tithes. This seems to have been a doctrine which he either did not hold, or did not think it prudent to produce; and the most philosophic layman, while the word philosophic is pronounced in its proper and natural sense, as a title of respect, will not, I conceive, find it necessary to proceed further than the abbé, who states as the sum and substance of what he meant to say,—" first, that the tithe ought not to be compared to any impost or tax laid upon the land, but considered as a real rent-charge, left upon different estates by those who once possessed them; secondly, that the tithe ought not to be suppressed, for the sake of the actual proprietors of the land, who know very well that at all events it does not belong to them; nevertheless, thirdly, that the tithe has been with reason classed with that species of property which, however lawful (perfectly so in itself), is still answerable to the public good, and is liable to be extinguished, as all property of this kind is, after an indemnity offered to the present holders; fourthly, that the redemption ought to be settled by agreement freely between the parties concerned, or according to a fair estimate proposed by the Assembly: fifthly and lastly, that by due management, the sums so arising from the redemption might be so disposed of as properly to answer all the original purposes of the tithe, and yet furnish to the revenue of the state a resource infinitely precious to it in its present circumstances." These were the abbé's general statements and conclusions. I must again observe, that they were such as the most philosophic laymen could not object to, and could not in common reason and justice go beyond. His reasonings and remonstrances with those the more violent of his opponents, do him in every point of view great honour; and he cried out at last, and his words have been ever since very properly remembered, " You wish to be free, and you know not how to be just." He appears to have published his speech on the 12th of August, and to have made it on the 10th.

There seems to have been a violent debate on the 10th, in the morning sitting, and in the evening.

You will see a sketch given in the Mercure. Mirabeau took a part. You may look at the second volume of his speeches. I will make a reference to it, that after seeing what in the main was said by the Abbé Sieyes on the one side, and by Mirabeau on the other (men so distinguished), you may judge of the general views that were entertained on this subject by the different reasoners in the Assembly and in France at the time. " No, gentlemen," said Mirabeau, " tithe is not a property; property is that which a man can dispose of: this the clergy never could do; they never had more than a life interest in their tithes. Tithes are a sort of tenure, a sort of enjoyment from year to year; they are merely possessions revocable at the will of the sovereign power: nay, more, the tithe is not even a possession, as it has been supposed to be; it is a mere contribution, devoted to that part of the public service which concerns the ministers of the altar; it is the subsidy with which the nation provides for the salary of those who are to take care of their morals and instruction. At the word salary, which I have used, a great murmur has, I perceive, arisen; there are those, then, who are now saying that I wound the dignity of the priesthood. Gentlemen, it is high time that in a revolution which has brought to light sentiments, and those so many just and generous, it is high time that we should abjure these prejudices of haughty ignorance which would disdain these words of salaries and salaried. For my part, I know of but three ways of living in society—to beg, to rob, or to be salaried." These were words which Mirabeau thundered out into the Assembly with all the energy of his voice and manner. " What is the proprietor of land himself," he continued, " more than the first of these salaried persons? What is vulgarly called his property? Is it anything more than the price which society pays him for the distribution which he makes to others, in the shape of his consumption and his expenses?

" No doubt they who are charged with the morals and instruction of society must hold a distinguished place in its hierarchy. Consideration must be paid them, that they may show themselves worthy of it. It is just and proper that they should be accommodated and endowed in a manner agreeable to the dignity of their ministry and the importance of their functions: but it cannot be necessary that they should insist upon a particular mode of contribution from society, as if it was their property, when it is not agreeable to the interests of the public. I know not why it is disputed that the tithe is a national ordinance; it is so in point of fact, and it is on this very account that the nation has a right to revoke it, and substitute another. If it were not, that one is at length arrived at a period when one may disdain the frivolous authority of these mere men of learning, in matters of natural and public right, I would defy the best of them to find in all their capitularies of Charlemagne, where tithes are mentioned, the word ' solverint;' the word is always ' dederint,' not pay, but give : but of what consequence is all this ? The nation abolishes ecclesiastical tithes because they are a mode of paying that part of the public service, to which they are destined, and because it is easy to replace them in a manner less expensive and more equal."

Such was the general view of the subject taken by Mirabeau. I have already described to you the reasonings of the Abbé Sieyes. It may be instructive to you to see the notions of such distinguished men on so interesting a subject.

The notions of Mirabeau, vague as they may be, still remain ; though trust property is a very common species of property, and obviously the nature of church property. But observe the light manner in which the same Mirabeau speaks of such an element in the constitution of all civil society, as property ; think of such a man as Mirabeau, under the existing circumstances of an actual revolution, while the populace were lawless, and all ancient authority at an end, talking of property " as the price which society pays a man for the distribution which he makes to others, in the shape of his consumption and expenses."

Observe, too, as you read the debates, for I have not time to comment upon them, the careless and unphilosophic terms in which the members of the Constituent Assembly, too many of them, spoke on this vital subject of property, property of whatever sort, at all times. It was this total disregard of what men hold most sacred in civilized society, which led to the extreme and pertinacious resistance of the privileged orders, the horrors of the Revolution, and the determined and ultimately successful resistance of all Europe to the new principles upon which the Revolution was founded.

The debate was in the same evening renewed. " I demand," said the Bishop of Rhodes, " as indispensable, the preservation of the ecclesiastical benefices, and the conversion of the tithes into pecuniary payments. Your present resolution attacks, and would go to destroy religion itself. The tithe is destined to the support of the pastor; it has subsisted from the earliest ages of Christianity ; it has been confirmed both by Pepin and Charlemagne. There must be divine worship; there must be priests ; there must be funds for their support, when abstracted from the world, and for their comfort. Without this, parishes would soon be without pastors, confessionals without confessors, the sick without assistance, the poor without relief, the afflicted without consolation."

"An enumeration of the payments and expenses of the clergy would show the extent of the charge to which the state will have hereafter to be exposed, if ecclesiastical property is to be destroyed." The bishop went on, but though, as you see, very reasonably, he could no longer obtain an audience.

No better fortune attended the Abbé Sieyes, who followed; the same clamours, the same interruptions. "What, then," said the abbé, "no truths are here to be spoken but those that are agreeable." In spite of all opposition, however, he delivered the speech to which I have just alluded, and which he published. He was followed by other speakers on each side the question; but the tribune became at last inaccessible, surrounded on all sides by candidates and clamours. Various efforts were made, and schemes proposed, to come at the sense of the Assembly; all in vain: the disorder, the tumult, the interruptions, increased; the members left their seats, and got all mixed and confused together in the middle of the hall; at last the Assembly dispersed.

These are the scenes over which the friends of liberty must droop and hang their heads in mortification and grief, for they show the disgraceful violence of which men are capable, when they have been once excited in her cause, and collected into any popular assembly. They show likewise the inexpediency of leaving questions of state to be determined by one House of Assembly, exposed to such excitements; and the necessity of constituting a second, a subsequent one, by which a pause may be introduced, and reason, and justice, and humanity have some chance of protection.

The next morning (the 11th), when the subject was renewed, one of the secretaries but too naturally complained of the tumultuous sitting of the preceding evening. One of the members of the Commons made a furious attack on the clergy; the deputy from Toulon followed with an attack less violent, but more elaborate, concluding with an éloge on those of the clergy, who had already sacrificed their tithes, and a distinct enumeration of their names. This produced on a French assembly the effect intended, the curates rushing forward, as on the 4th, to give in their renunciation at the bureau. The Abbé de Plaquet resigned a priory: "and yet," said he, "notwithstanding the enumerating eloquence of M. de Mirabeau, I am, first, too old to get a salary; secondly, too honest to rob; thirdly, my past services have been such that I cannot think I ought to be left to beg." Applauses always ready, as ready as the hootings and clamours, resounded from all sides; and the Archbishop of Paris could not for some time obtain a hearing to deliver, as at the last he was allowed to do, his own and the general sentiment of the clergy.

"Our colleagues," he said, "have only anticipated the sacrifices which we have now universally to offer to our country. We return into the hands of the nation the ecclesiastical tithes, and we must trust ourselves entirely to its wisdom. Let the gospel be preached, let Divine worship lose nothing of its decency, let the poor be still relieved and comforted; such are the objects of our wishes, the end and meaning of our ministry: from your enlightened wisdom we hope to find every necessary support and security for objects so important."

The fifth article then passed, as you see it, after some reasonable distinctions and objections had been offered, but which were not attended to, though they deserved attention, and with the dissent, firmly urged, of the Abbé Sieyes and one of the nobles.

It cannot be supposed that a concession like this from the bishops, so unlimited and so unconditional, was freely and voluntarily made by the clergy; the revolutionary tide had begun to run violently against them, and it was for them to endeavour, if possible, to evade it, and not to render it more rapid and furious, by attempting openly to resist it.

In all times of disorder the officers of the law, and more particularly the clergy, are the first objects of popular hatred and persecution: it has been the necessary business of these two descriptions of men to restrain the passions of mankind; and mankind, in these unhappy seasons, do not choose to be restrained any longer; they therefore first dislike and soon detest those whose very presence admonishes them of the folly, the injustice, the guilt, of the course they are pursuing.

Such is a general account of the fall of the French church establishment; but I will now enter a little more into the detail.

It must have already occurred to you that the property of the clergy offered an easy means of repairing the finances of the nation, and very early in the sittings of the National Assembly it must have presented itself on this point of view to those of its members who were the most violent and the most unprincipled. Even admitting the truth of some of the observations of Mirabeau, with regard to the possessions of the clergy, it is one thing to negotiate with a particular description of men, to enter into adjustments, and even obtain concessions from the necessity of the case, and it is quite another to use no right but that of the strongest, to violate their principles and feelings, disappoint their reasonable expectations, take away their property (what they had been allowed to consider as such), and draw out one set of men from the midst of society, like sheep, to be sacrificed and butchered for the support of the remainder.

We will try to allude to the progress of the fortunes of the clergy from the first. Observe while we do so, how far these harsh words, which I have just used, are or are not applicable to the proceedings of the National Assembly, or rather the violent members of it; for it is to this point to which I must for ever remind you that my humble efforts all through these lectures are directed, not for a moment against the moderate and reasonable friends of liberty, but against the cruel, unjust, and fatal conduct of violent men; those whom the Marquis de Ferrieres calls the revolutionists; those who were in truth not the friends, but the enemies of Liberty; those who have brought her great cause into suspicion and disgust, even with the virtuous and good.

But to return to the fortunes of the clergy, and to gather up some particulars of the history, as yet not mentioned. Soon after the 4th of August, the Marquis la Coste, when Necker had called the attention of the Assembly to the subject of the finances, had insisted upon it, that the people could not furnish the succour that was wanted, but that there was *one* resource still remaining. "Declare," said he, "that the ecclesiastical possessions belong to the nation:" this was the first distinct and open assault. Alexander Lameth laboured to show, that to seize the possessions of the clergy was not to attack property in general. These attacks on the property of the clergy excited some murmurs. No measure at the time followed; "but this notion thus thrown out," says De Ferrieres, "thus cast into the nation, germinated everywhere; it was adopted with enthusiasm by the monied men; and the people thought, that by thus extinguishing the public debt, they should get rid of the taxes."

The next attack on the possessions of the clergy consisted of the debates, subsequent to the 4th of August, the debates on the 5th article respecting tithes; to these I have already alluded.

But on the 30th of October the motion of the Marquis de la Coste was revived by the Bishop of Autun, the celebrated Talleyrand. You will see his elaborate speech in the Mercure. This was a very serious attack indeed, coming from an ecclesi-

astic, high in rank, and of distinguished ability. His measure
went to the destruction of the church property ; but necessary
provision, he said, must be made for the support of the altars
and the ministers of religion. No minister of a parish was to
have less than twelve hundred livres annually, house and glebe
not included, &c. &c.

Loud applauses followed from the revolutionists and capitalists.
The Abbés de Rastignac and d'Aymar, however, combated the
project of the Bishop of Autun, and showed how unjust it was
and how dangerous to religion to leave its ministers at the mercy
of the caprice of a nation, already little attached to its worship,
and a government necessarily expensive and prodigal ; no funds
assigned, nothing upon which any dependence could be placed.

" You will plunge them into a state of indigence, two hundred thousand of your fellow-citizens," said the Abbé Maury ;
" you talk of a *general* interest, and in the meantime, we are to
see one part seizing the property of another part." Observations
of this kind were of no effect. The business was indeed adjourned, till the Assembly could be removed from Versailles to
Paris, " but in the meantime," says De Ferrieres, " every effort
was made to render the priesthood odious and contemptible.
Men were hired," he says, " to represent to crowds in the streets,
that the riches of the clergy must be seized, or a national bankruptcy ensue. The pride and hauteur of the bishops was not
forgotten ; the incontinence and drunkenness of the monks ; the
soft, voluptuous lives of the abbés. Pamphlets on pamphlets
succeeded to each other ; some affected to be profound, and demonstrate the right of the nation to the possessions of the clergy.

" At the theatre was acted the tragedy of Charles IX., who
reigned, you may remember, during the massacre of St. Bartholomew ; acted with the most unhappy effect, from the nature of
its misrepresentations, on the minds of the audience."

Such are the very credible accounts of De Ferrieres.

The project of the Bishop of Autun was, after these preparations, revived by Thouret ; now attached to the revolutionists.
" No public body," he said, " the nation excepted, can have in
itself either property or existence, for it owes both to the nation,
who protects it and allows it to have either ; the nation may
therefore resume its grant." Applauses followed a long and able
and laboured speech, which he regularly delivered. Opinions,
however, were still somewhat undecided, and Mirabeau, who
knew the importance of phrases, " say rather," he cried, " in
your decree, not that the possessions of the clergy belong to the
state, but that they are ' at the disposal of the state.' "

An ordinary mind, in its simple honesty, will see here, perhaps, no very material distinction, but the amendment was applauded, as if of importance, and was violently resisted by the nobles and the clergy; and a base and shuffling crowd of the members affected not to see the consequences of the principle they thus established, and uniting themselves to the revolutionists, the decree thus worded passed on the 2nd of November, 1789, by a large majority. For some time, however, it was only a decree, not acted upon; the first attempt to make a practical use of it was a succeeding decree, which ordered the sale of four hundred millions of the property to the different municipalities. The clergy hoped, however, that the remnant would be left them undisturbed; they offered to raise by a loan, and present to the state, the four hundred millions wanted.

But all their hopes were dispelled by a motion made on the 3rd of April, 1790, by Chapel, who, on that day, proposed that the possessions of the clergy should, in each district, be transferred to the administration of the department, and proper provision being made for the clergy and the public worship, the whole be then disengaged and made available to the exigencies of the state. The Bishop of Nancy, the Archbishop of Aix, in vain protested against the motion, complained of the perfidious manner in which the clergy had been treated, and renewed the offer of four hundred millions to be freely given to the service of the state. The Abbé de Montesquieu, so endeared by his amiable qualities, both to one party and the other, found that it was in vain he endeavoured to engage the Assembly in favour of the clergy.

At last he said, "When I mounted this tribune, I was addressed on all sides; 'What are you doing?' they cried; 'the business is already settled; the committees have already decided.' It is too true: I have only then to descend from this tribune; I have only to implore the God of our fathers that he will preserve to you the religion of St. Louis; that he will still grant you his protection: the truly unhappy, those most to be pitied, are not they who suffer injustice, but they who commit it." This brought up a member of the monastic order, who said, it was easy for the Assembly to put an end to calumnies vented against them on the subject of religion, by declaring, as he now proposed that they should do, that the religion Catholic, Apostolic, and Roman, was, and was for ever, to remain the religion of the state, and its worship the only one to be authorized.

You will easily see how inconvenient and unexpected a mo-

tion like this must necessarily have been to the Assembly at this
particular moment: the advantage which the one party would
endeavour to make of it, the embarrassment and distress of the
other   Having mentioned it, I need do no more : your curiosity
will be sufficiently excited.

You will see a good account of the scene that took place;
among other writers, more particularly by the Marquis de Ferrieres.

The motion, as you may suppose, was got rid of as irrelevant
and unnecessary ; but the fate of the clergy and their possessions was soon after, in subsequent sittings, decided.

The number of bishops and archbishops was reduced to one
for each department ; their stipends, in future, to twenty-five,
fifteen, or ten thousand livres, that is, from about one thousand
to four hundred pounds per annum, or under, according to the
population ; the stipends of parish priests, to about one hundred
pounds per annum ; and of curates, to about forty pounds each,
with a parsonage in addition.

This was but indifferent provision for the future clergy ; but
the present bishops were to have the whole of what they received,
if not exceeding five or six hundred pounds per annum ; one
half of what it did exceed, if the *whole* did not exceed about
fifteen hundred pounds per annum : they had before five, ten,
fifteen, and in some cases as much as thirty or forty thousand
pounds per annum.

The abbés, priors, dignitaries, &c. &c., and other beneficed
clergymen, if their ecclesiastical revenue did not exceed fifty
pounds, had the whole ; if it did, half the excess, as before ; but
the whole revenue was never to exceed about three hundred
pounds.

The incomes, therefore, of the existing priests and dignitaries,
were miserably curtailed.   The triumph of the Jansenists and
revolutionary reasoners was very evident : these two were descriptions of men, who, in their notion of the priestly character,
its offices, and its proper rewards, not a little agreed.

In a word, the total expense of divine worship, including the
stipends of its ministers, to the number of forty-eight thousand,
the provisions of the friars and nuns, the necessary succours for
the hospitals, colleges, &c. &c., and the expenses of erecting and
repairing buildings, was fixed at about seven millions.

The plan of the ecclesiastical committee was to add the raising
of this sum to the general mass of taxes and contributions to be
raised from the nation ; suppressing tithes, and placing the whole
amount of ecclesiastical property in the hands of the nation.
This was in April, 1790.

At a prior meeting of the Assembly, in February, 1790, the monastic establishments had been suppressed for ever, and their lands confiscated. The existing friars and nuns were, however, allowed to continue in the observance of their monastic vows; moderate stipends were granted for their maintenance; and the nuns were not to be removed from the convents in which they then resided without their own consent.

It should seem, in this last instance, as if the ancient gallantry of the French nation had still survived to produce something like a parting emotion of humanity and politeness, when the fate of these inoffensive females was ultimately to be decided.

But, on the whole, these proceedings must be considered as marked with the most unequivocal tyranny and injustice, though little or nothing of this kind is said by the popular French writers, who are often to be censured, not only as too indifferent to the humanity of the case, but as inattentive to the great leading principles on which constitutional governments are founded, and from which they derive so inestimable a value. The clergy were told, indeed, that they were to be paid in money; but no real property was left as a security for their stipends, the whole was swept away: assignats were to be issued; the church property was to be pledged or sold for the regular payment of these assignats. If a system of paper money was to be resorted to, as a measure of the state, there was little chance that the state would pay the clergy in money. The paper money of America had been just before a subject of historic experience; depreciated, so as at last not to be worth the counting. On the whole, the indignant exclamation of one of the curés, in some of the earlier stages of these ecclesiastical discussions, is recalled to our remembrance. "Was it for this, then," said the unhappy man, when he saw, as he thought, how the proceedings of the Assembly were likely to terminate, "was it for this that you invited us to join you in the name of the God of peace?"

But the last and finishing acts of tyranny and injustice yet remained: this was the interference of the National Assembly, not only in the temporal but in the spiritual concerns of the church. Various decrees were proposed for what was called the organization of the church; every benefice, for instance, from a curacy to a bishopric, was to be rendered elective; people of all religions were to vote; the long-established limits and extent of dioceses were to be altered. The discussions to which a scheme of church government like this gave occasion, occupy a certain portion of the histories which you will have to read. You will

easily, in the meantime, comprehend, that this new civil constitution of the church was totally inconsistent with all the notions
and feelings, whether right or wrong, which had been so long
transmitted from age to age, and considered as sacred by the
members of the Roman Catholic church, a church that refers
every thing in their spiritual economy to the first Apostles and
to the Saviour himself. It was in vain that they expostulated,
argued, and remonstrated; that they proposed the calling of a
National Council to consider what concessions could be made.
No such measure as a general council was likely to be very agreeable to the Assembly; and they, on the contrary, imposed an
oath of submission and acceptance of the new civil constitution,
as already decreed, to be taken by the clergy, under the penalty
of expulsion from their benefices in cases of non-compliance.

This is surely a sad specimen of revolutions; this is surely to
legislate and to act with the rude and savage spirit of those who,
in the carelessness of power, exercise only the right of the
strongest; this is surely to disregard and outrage the most sacred
feelings of the human heart, and the most ennobling principles
of human conduct.

There is, indeed, no limit to be put to our indignation on the
present occasion.

The French clergy had, at the moment of the Revolution, essentially contributed to the success even of the popular party;
their reunion with the Tiers Etat was to be written, according
to Bailly the president, in letters of gold. They had shown no
want of interest in the public welfare at any period of the Revolution; could then no better terms than these be made with them,
no better means than these be found for reconciling them to the
new order of things? Suppose them enemies to it, and fallen
and helpless, could no better mercy be shown them, than first
stripping them of their property, and then violating their consciences?

All these proceedings were then defended in the Assembly,
and since in the patriotic histories, as measures of self-preserva-
tion, as necessary to the cause of liberty, as arising from the re-
fractoriness of the clergy, from their efforts to put down the Revolution, particularly in the interior; but this is to confound
dates and misrepresent the history. I do not deny that there
was, originally, great difficulty in the case. The clergy could
not be expected to be very favourable to the Revolution originally; but how could they be favourable to the progress of the
Revolution afterwards, if it was to sweep away, in its torrent,

their property and their establishments ; and where was the necessity that this should be the case : where was the necessity, after they had joined the Tiers Etat, that their possessions should be menaced, their rights disputed and denied ;· that when they argued and remonstrated, no concessions should be admitted ; that the Revolution should be made fatal, to them at least ; and because they were then no longer any friends to it, that their destruction should be resolved upon ?

It could not have been the wise and the good men of the National Assembly (the earlier majorities were not great, about twelve to seven), it must have been the furious, violent revolutionists, whom I can never sufficiently denounce to you, who originated, conducted (the moderate men committed their usual fault of being too torpid), and at length step by step succeeded in their scheme of carrying into execution these arbitrary, and unjust, and cruel measures ; impolitic too as they were cruel : and the only consolation that can now be derived from the subject is, that the clergy of France, though ruined, were not disgraced ; that they refused to take the oath required from them, and were not wanting, either to themselves or to mankind, on this trying occasion.   Certainly they were acting on the theatre of the world, and in the presence of all posterity, and still more in the presence of their Almighty Master ; and they showed, as men of real piety always will show, a sense of duty, and the faith that was within them.   They were to be cast, indeed, like the traveller in holy writ, to the compassion of the Samaritan, (and for much the same reason, for they had fallen among robbers); they were thus to be thrown into the highway, in any stage, whatever it might be, of age and infirmity, but they were still to show, and they did show to the bad men of a world of violence, the plunderers that had encompassed them, that powerful as they might think themselves, still there were those, the innocent and the helpless, who would resist them—resist them, and in all the power of unoffending piety, resist them to the death ; that there were those whom they might despoil of their possessions, but who had that within which their decrees could not reach ; who, wretched as they might be thought, and who, outcasts as they might be, seen flying from their country, or lingering in its hiding places, without a benefice and without an altar, had still a character to enjoy and a God to serve.

What then are the facts ?   You must observe them.   You will see them all from the first, very fully in the Marquis de Ferrieres, and very easily in Bertrand de Moleville.   In the sitting of the 2nd of January, 1791, the Bishop of Clermont proposed an oath which he would have taken, and which it was the height of the most intolerable injustice in the Assembly to refuse.

"He would be true," he said, "to the nation, to the law, and to the king, and would maintain with all his power, in all that related to political order, the constitution decreed by the National Assembly, and accepted by the king, with the express exception of those matters which depend particularly upon the authority of the church." "This oath I can take," he said; "the oath you propose I do not think I conscientiously can take."

But this sort of declaration would not satisfy the Assembly.

Barnave moved, that the time for taking the oath should expire at one o'clock the next day. The Abbé Grégoire attempted explanations of the oath, but the Assembly refused to avow them formally, by any decree, and the president at last informed the ecclesiastical members that they must answer to the call of names which was going to be made, and take the oath or refuse it. A dead silence followed, interrupted by the howlings of the mob who surrounded the hall; by the cries of "To the Lanterne! Away with the nonjurors to the Lanterne!"

The Bishop of Agen was named the first; and he desired to speak. "No speaking," cried out several members of the coté gouche; "will you take the oath or not?"

The bishop at length obtained a hearing; he had never spoken before in the Assembly. "I feel no regret," said he, "for the loss of my preferment" (the courteous, the polite humility of the Christian character did not desert him), "I feel no regret for my fortune, but I shall regret the loss of your esteem, which I am determined to deserve at least; believe me then, that I feel great pain at not being able to take the oath you require."

M. Fournés was next called.

"I glory," said he, "in following my bishop, as St. Lawrence did his pastor."

M. Le Clerc was the third called upon: he had scarcely pronounced the words "I am a member of the Apostolical Catholic Church," when he was interrupted by the most violent murmurs. "Take the oath," said Roederer, "or refuse to take it."

"This," said M. de Feriault, "is tyranny indeed; the very emperors suffered the martyrs to pronounce the name of God, to utter the testimonies of their fidelity to religion."

At last the president persisted no longer in the call of names, but required the public ecclesiastical functionaries collectively to ascend the tribune. A motion had been made to that effect, and carried. The good part of the Assembly had feared that those who refused the oath would be marked out and massacred; and the bad had perceived that the triumph of religious principle was becoming too distinct and solemn.

A curate of the name of Landrin was the only one who took the oath. Two offered to take it with the restrictions proposed by the Bishop of Clermont, but were refused. No concession could afterwards be obtained from the Assembly; they would not say distinctly, by a decree, that they meant not the control of spiritual affairs. "To the order of the day" was the only answer.

The Bishop of Poitiers ascended the tribune. "I am seventy years old," said he; "I have passed thirty-five in the episcopacy; I have done my best to discharge my duty; I will not dishonour my old age; I cannot take an oath against my conscience." "Say yes or no." "I prefer then living in poverty, and will take my fate in the spirit of penitence."

After some more vain efforts by the clergy to obtain concessions and explanations from the Assembly, the president for the last time called upon the public ecclesiastical functionaries to take the oath conformably to the decree.

The Assembly waited in vain: no one presented himself; no bishop, no priest spoke; and all heard in silence, serene and unmoved, the decree that pronounced their deprivation. Such was the conduct of the French clergy: such the cruel and unjust proceedings of the National Assembly. But these proceedings were impolitic as well as cruel and unjust, for they inevitably threw the clergy into the most decided opposition to the Revolution, and all whom they could influence.

I will cast a parting glance on this part of the subject, and conclude.

"I do not think," said afterwards M. de Montlosier, "that the bishops *can be forced* to quit their sees. Driven from their episcopal palaces, they will retire to the huts of the cottagers who have fed upon their bounty; take from them their golden crosses, they will find those of wood. The cross was of wood—the cross that saved the world."

M. de Cazales insisted on the necessity of suspending the execution of the decree. "A schism," said he, "is preparing, the whole body of the bishops of France and the great majority of the inferior clergy believe that the principles of religion forbid them to obey your decrees; their principles are of a nature superior to your laws. Expelling bishops from their sees, and priests from their parishes, in order to overcome this resistance, is not the way to overcome it. You will be but at the commencement of the course of persecution that opens before you. The victims of the Revolution will be multiplied, and the kingdom be divided." Nor was M. de Cazales materially mistaken in his prediction.

In the metropolis, no doubt, the populace took little interest in the fate of the church, but all the unhappy effects of religious schism were everywhere else but too visible, as M. de Cazales had predicted. The bishops refused to give up their sees; protested against the spiritual authority of those who were to replace them; forbade all good Catholics from communicating with them in any of the sacred offices of the church; declared the marriages illegal, &c.

The effect was very unfavourable to the National Assembly all over France, though not exactly in Paris; for the revolutionists, in the mean time, filled the streets and shops of Paris with indecent caricatures and dramatic exhibitions, ridiculing and reflecting on the clergy. In a contest like this it was very clear who were likely to bear away the triumph in the midst of the Revolution and in the streets of Paris; and while the thoughtful and the grave, the few that there were, turned away with pain or disgust from prints and spectacles of the nature we have described, the rest of the population, laughing and amused, were content to be entertained at any expense, and the interests of religion were no longer regarded, if found not to harmonize with the interests, such as they were supposed, of the Revolution.

The violent party in the Assembly had always depended on the inferior clergy, who were to be tempted with the benefices and sees of their superiors, and were from the first less attached to the ancient system. And it is very true, that though a great majority was firm, a sufficient minority, on one account or another, took the oath; so that there was no danger of the entire cessation of public worship.

The rites of religion necessary to society could still be performed. And the people everywhere, in the great towns more particularly, supposed, that the only chance which France had of escaping from tithes, and even feudal oppressions, as well as from taxes and public burdens, was the spoliation of the clergy, and the submission of the clergy to the new constitution proposed to them.

Still all the interior of France was long harassed by civil and religious dissensions, and by local wars; always very disgraceful to the country, often very bloody, and sometimes not a little dangerous to the success even of the more violent and popular party. These, and above all, the dreadful war of La Vendée, sufficiently proved the original impolicy as well as injustice of the National Assembly, and the wisdom of the very humane observations I have just quoted from M. de Cazales and M. de Montlosier; and all that the former predicted in the remainder of his speech to a similar effect would have been fully verified, if the subsequent fury and violence of the Revolution had not swept away from the minds of the people of France all the ordinary feelings and associations of their nature. Such is the general sketch that I have to offer to your consideration of this very remarkable portion of the French Revolution: the destruction of the feudal system and church establishment of France.

You will easily conceive that the different writers of histories and memoirs will see these transactions from very different points of view.

I can have afforded you, in a short lecture like this, but a very imperfect notion of their reasonings, and of the subject itself, but you will read for yourselves, and you will see a very able and spirited *précis* of the whole subject in M^e. de Stael.

You will find a general account of it in both of our Annual Registers; a general though more detailed account in Lacretelle; one also from which I have quoted, in Bertrand de Moleville. The most full and complete account is in the Memoirs of the Marquis de Ferrieres, which you may compare with the very full account on the other side, furnished by the history of the Two Friends of Liberty. In this last work you will meet with everything that can be urged on the revolutionary side of the question, all the philosophy that can be produced, and all the ecclesiastical learning; the same philosophy you will also find, united to all the eloquence of which that side of the question was susceptible, in the different speeches of Mirabeau (there are several of them), appearing in the different volumes of the octavo collection of them. And if you look through the different volumes of the Mercure, you will acquire a very adequate idea of the debates that took place, and the different speeches and various reasonings by which the interests of the clergy were assailed and defended. And, indeed, everything relative to the subject in the course of these volumes is more or less found, particularly the unanswerable pleadings of the Abbé Sieyes. Lastly, in our own writers, you will see all the powers of Burke engaged on the one side, and the rising eloquence of Mackintosh on the other. These are very splendid portions of their great performances. You will find in the public library a short treatise by Sarpi, his " Treatise on Beneficiary Matters," and you will very easily refer to a learned and very able history and defence of church property in the Quarterly Review for July, 1823, and again the subject continued in the number for January, 1830.

A few words more, for the sake of making a few necessary distinctions on the general subject of the destruction of the church establishment of France, and I conclude my lecture.

Society cannot exist (any state, at least, that deserves the name of society) without the institution of property, but it may without the institution of church property. The foundation, therefore, of the two is not the same—this must be admitted; the property of the individual is necessary to the very constitution of society—not so, the property of the clergyman.

It may be very possible, that an establishment may be the best method of providing society with the consolations of religion, the best method of explaining its doctrines and exhibiting its evidences, of securing mankind from degrading or dangerous fanaticism on the one side, or even on the other, from licentious indifference: it is very possible, that the best method of securing these most important ends, may be the establishment of an ecclesiastical body, and the furnishing of that body with a permanent, independent, visible, real support, like that of land or its produce. All this may be very true; and as this possession is from age to age continued, it may not, in the common estimation of mankind, or in a court of law, be distinguished from any other possession or property; and an estate of land or tithes may thus be enjoyed by an ecclesiastical body, or by a minister of religion, as an estate is by any other individual: still it must be allowed, that the original nature of the possession is different; that society cannot exist without the one sort of property, but may without the other; that the one is a case of necessity, the other of legislative wisdom.

But when this sort of reasoning has been admitted, with Mirabeau, still it must be laid down, with the Abbé de Sieyes, that men must be just; and when a state has long proceeded, from age to age, on a certain system; has long suffered men to educate themselves for a specific purpose; has at all times, and in all places, dedicated, or allowed individuals to dedicate, which is the same thing, real possessions to that specific purpose, and suffered their possessions to assume the office and character of property; it surely can have no right to turn round on a sudden, to tell such a body of men, that it has altered its system, that they are no longer wanted, and that they were mistaken in supposing their land or their tithes property; that the original elementary difference of property was now to be acted upon; that they must give up the whole, or any part of it, which the legislature now found it convenient to resume, or to annul the right of. Language of this kind, the language of the revolutionists, is surely not, for a moment, to be considered as consistent with humanity or justice. A wide distinction even exists between what a state may do as regards the future, and as regards the present; a future hierarchy it may treat according to its new system and views, or it may in future dispense with an hierarchy altogether; this may be a matter of legislative wisdom, and no more; but it is not to proceed in this speculative manner with those in whom it has already raised rational expectations, and whose thoughts, opinions, feelings, and habits, whose ideas of comfort, respectability, and happiness, it has suffered to grow up and be fashioned to a particular model of its own approving or proposing. Indemnity, compensation, voluntary adjustment, these are the only sounds that can now be heard.

In these observations I have not insisted on the nature of *trust* property, that it is inviolable if the duty be performed; I have consented to take the ground which the enemies of church property propose. They may, however, be reminded, that what is now church property was never in possession of the state; that it was originally given by those who possessed it to ecclesiastical bodies and functionaries, who were thus to be supported while they dispensed the offices of religion; and that while therefore they do faithfully dispense the offices of religion, their part of the obligation is performed, and the property must remain with them according to the intention of the original possessor and giver of it; the property is trust property.

There never was, as is supposed, any gift of property made by the state; the state is only indirectly the giver, as allowing such gifts to be legal. As far as the state has interfered, it has not been to give property, but rather to prevent the gift of it, that is, to prevent persons of religious feelings, by statutes of mortmain and other legal expedients, from giving away their property to pious uses, in a manner that became at last injurious to the community.

But, as I have already intimated, France, it will be said, and it has been said by two most distinguished writers, France had to perfect its Revolution, and the existence of the great Roman Catholic hierarchy of France was inconsistent with its hopes of freedom; the whole body was therefore to be dissolved.

I do not think it necessary now, at the termination of my lecture, and after all that I have already said, to enter into this sort of reasoning. I hope that I love liberty, and that I teach the love of it to others, and that it will be sufficient for me to answer, that liberty itself, even if it could, must not be thus procured.

LECTURE XVI.

MOUNIER. LA FAYETTE. NO PROPER EXECUTIVE POWER.

The fall of the church establishment in France was not the result of a single sitting of the Assembly, as in the case of the feudal privileges of the aristocracy and the nobility; the transactions, to which we have just alluded, were, one after another, the consequences, and the subject-matter of many debates and discussions, from the middle of the year 1789 to the 12th of June, 1790. It took a year to overthrow the hierarchy of this great kingdom, but this was an interval fearfully short for such an event; and the destruction of a body of men so numerous, so connected, so elevated by their education, in their office so sacred, even so useful, to say the least of them, in their occupation, as the civilizers of the main portions of mankind, a body of men for ages had in honour, and considered as an indispensable element in society,—the destruction of their privileges, their property, and their influence, so soon to be accomplished and so completely, —was, indeed, a most striking specimen of the hardness of the nature of the members of the Constituent Assembly, and well fitted to show how reckless men may be made by the sympathy and fury of new opinions, and how unpitying, indeed, is the nature of enthusiasm, on whatever occasion, and of whatever kind.

A milder fate might have awaited the clergy, but the current of these new opinions had begun to run more and more strongly in favour of innovation and democracy from the moment that the Assembly and the people had triumphed, and the court had tried their experiment of menaces and force in vain. It would often be happy for mankind, if the victorious party could abstain from abusing their victory; but this is not to be expected from human nature, and governments must not proceed upon any supposition of this kind: they must abide their mistakes, and the consequences of their faults, which will certainly be followed by faults in their opponents.

Melancholy were the events that intervened during the struggles of the clergy with the National Assembly, all most unfavourable to the clergy; for then there was no hope, nor ever had been, but in the due maintenance of the respectability and efficiency of the royal power.

But this respectability and efficiency had constantly declined from the month of July, 1789; it had been deeply injured by the sweeping and totally unqualified sacrifices of the night of the 4th of August; every movement and every event continued to operate to its prejudice; that is, as it may now be perceived, when it is too late, continued to operate to the failure of the experiment of this French Revolution. These movements and events should be carefully marked by the student, for they are now the lessons of history.

To us, who live at some distance of time and place, it is somewhat surprising to observe, that the very enlightened, and most of them virtuous men, who composed the patriotic part of the National Assembly, for some time after the month of July, were not more aware than they seem to have been, how completely the executive power was now destroyed. It is scarcely too much to say, that the king was, indeed, seated on the throne, but that a baby sceptre was in his hand, and that he was a phantom only, and a name.

The troops of the line, all the former supports of his power, had acceded to the new order of things, and the nation itself had suddenly taken up arms; and the regular soldiers of France, if favourable to the king, were surrounded, and had, in truth, become mere prisoners of war. What single wish of the king could now be accomplished, if leave were not first asked of the National Assembly? In theory, indeed, and as a component part of a good constitution, and of any that could be well intended for France, these patriotic leaders saw the necessity of a king, and of executive power; but they seem by no means to have been sufficiently aware, that they had now nothing to fear, whatever they might once have had to fear, but from the violence of democratic principles. No doubt they would have had great difficulties to contend with, in the midst of a people so giddy, licentious, and ignorant, however just had been their estimate of their situation; but they had formed no such estimate, and they seem by no means to have taken sufficiently into their ac-

count the extraordinary advantages which they possessed, not
only in the complete triumph of the Assembly, but in the known
disposition of the monarch, so marked by gentleness and amiable
qualities.

Whatever might be their difficulties, arising whether from the
people or the court, the monarch, at least, as they knew very
well, had no wish but the happiness of his people; no terror
but that of shedding their blood; no fear but that of a civil war.
This they knew, and they knew that his mind was open to
schemes of improvement, to any change and experiment, not obviously inconsistent with his long-established opinions and the
proper dignity of his crown.

This was their great advantage. In the patriotic feelings of
the court and the princes, they could look for no assistance;
every thing the reverse: but they *could* in those of the king;
and it was their business to make their terms as mild and
equitable to him as possible; to furnish him with as good a
case as they could against those who surrounded him, while he
was endeavouring to be patriotic, while he was listening to the
suggestions of Necker, or other friendly counsellors, or acceding
to the measures of the Assembly. Here lies, I conceive, their
great accusation. The mildness of his disposition, his real benevolence, his genuine patriotism, had no proper effect upon them;
it did not, for a moment, check their usurpations on the royal
power; it did not, for a moment, dispose them to the wisdom
of offering honourable terms to a fallen foe, if a foe he was to
be esteemed; it did not animate them, as it ought to have
done, to encircle him with their protection, and shield him from
the violent and disorderly spirits which they saw in the Palais
Royal, and in their own Assembly; there was no generous sympathy with gentleness and goodness (I speak not of Mounier
and his friends, Lally Tollendal and others, I speak of the main
body of the patriots). These French patriots were not situated
as were our English patriots in the time of what is denominated
the great rebellion. Louis XVI. was not Charles I. Our patriots had, indeed, difficulties; for there was in their king no
proper mildness, no general benevolence, no sympathy with
civil liberty on which they could depend. It was otherwise
with the French monarch; and not only this, but the violent
counsellors of his more immediate court had tried their experiment, and had been defeated and overpowered. They were, no
doubt, to be watched and distrusted, but they were no longer to
be feared. The king had shown that he could be no instrument

in their hands; that there were certain limits, distinct measures of tyranny, a civil war, bloodshed, beyond which they could not hurry him; that wanting character as he did, still, as far as benevolence to his people was concerned, he did not want character; and that if they did not give the court an opportunity of saying, that as a king of France he was insulted and extinguished, all might yet be well. The main body of the men of talents and patriotism in the National Assembly, the main body of the assertors of the new opinions are not to be forgiven for their want of forbearance, caution, and conciliatory wisdom. I must appeal to the great leading facts.

You will observe, then, that from the period of their victory in July, every measure and every change was continually more and more unfavourable to the royal power.

In the first place, the proceedings of the night of the 4th of August could not have been altogether relished by the king, for whatever might be, in general, their beneficial and reasonable import, they were in a style of revolutionary rapidity and violence, that could not but be alarming to any one like himself, a regular and constituted authority of the state.

He made, therefore, very natural observations when these proceedings were reported to him, and, while he approved their general spirit and meaning, talked of modifications and indemnities, and, with the love he bore his people, spoke of the protection he owed also to the principles of justice. On the general subject, however, as he said, there could be no difference between him and the Assembly; their wishes being the same.

The Assembly were not pleased with his measured acquiescence, with his reasonable criticisms, important remarks, nor did many of the members at all conceal their displeasure.

But now, in the second place, it must be observed, that the great subject of the future constitution of France was also brought forward, and that every change and every measure was continually unfavourable to the royal power, visibly, offensively so, in the eyes of himself, his friends, and all Europe. Was it thus that he was to be reconciled to the Revolution?

This part of our general subject is so important, that I must present it to you under every possible point of view that I can contrive. My mode of doing this will be by exhibiting to you the different notices that were taken of these transactions by intelligent writers and reasoners at the time. I wish you to proceed as little as possible upon any authority of mine; and do not be offended by my tediousness of detail or dulness of quotation, or repetitions of the same facts or reasonings.

This cause of the French Revolution was one of the greatest that has existed in the annals of mankind since the times of the Reformation. It failed—in every proper sense of the word, it failed; and the point of the subject now more immediately before us is, how far the friends of freedom themselves were in fault; how far they, too, did or did not take their turn, and commit their particular faults; faults to be marked and condemned, after those that had been committed by the court and privileged orders have been first stated and duly reprobated. I certainly conceive that this was the case. How far these faults and mistakes were or were not but too natural, is not the point; if they really were committed, they must be produced, and made to serve as a warning to wise and virtuous men hereafter.

With respect, then, to the great subject of the formation of the constitution, you will observe that among the patriotic members of the Assembly, there was one particular band, headed by Mounier, consisting of Lally Tollendal, Clermont, Tonnerre, and others, who were men (as I conceive) of real wisdom, as well as of patriotic feeling, to whom the business of the constitution was first referred, and who were the committee of five, and who really *did* make on the whole a very reasonable report to the Assembly, who did not press too hard on the royal executive power in the existing state of things, and who in fact proposed a scheme of a constitution somewhat after the model of that of England. This is the first point.

But that this scheme was overruled by the Assembly, and one of a much more democratic nature, after much discussion, ultimately adopted: this was, I apprehend, fatal to the Revolution. This is the second point.

This second scheme of a constitution was made much more democratic. For, in the formation of any constitution that could be proposed for France at this particular period, the great questions at issue were—

1st. The veto of the king on the proceedings of the Assembly.

2ndly. Whether the Assembly should consist of two houses or one.

3rdly. Whether be dissolved at the pleasure of the king.

All these three questions were determined in *favour* of the crown by Mounier and his friends in their first scheme of government; and determined reasonably, as I conceive: but other patriotic members of the Assembly thought differently, as did the majority of the Assembly; and in their scheme of government these points were determined *against* the crown; and

in this manner the cause of the Revolution was, I also conceive,
lost—lost in the interval that passed between the middle of July
and the beginning of October.

And now I have two observations to make. Those patriotic
members, La Fayette and others, who thus made another constitution, more democratic in its nature; a constitution in which
these questions were determined against the crown, were not a
little led away by the example of America, as well as by the
intoxicating nature of the new opinions. This is my first observation.

Lastly, by a reference to the debates that took place, you will
see that these patriots and the people of France had sufficient
warning, from the reasonings and speeches of intelligent men, of
the mistakes they were committing. This is my second observation.

Such is my general statement, which I must request you to
remember while I journey on through the varying opinions and
statements of different actors in the scene, and while I go a little
more into the detail than I have yet done, on account of what I
suppose to be the importance of this part of the general subject.

One of the most distinguished men among the leaders of the
popular party at this particular epoch was the celebrated La
Fayette. He had been the hero of the American Revolution;
and however then favourable (as indeed in practice at least, he
always remained) to the monarchy of France, it was still impossible that he should not bear away from that Revolution a strong
impression of those great democratic principles of liberty, which
he had seen in America successfully established, and to whose
triumph he had so materially, in the face of the world and of
posterity, contributed.

His fellow patriots must have been caught by the same flame,
and influenced by the same example. Even Mounier, Lally
Tollendal, and the most virtuous and the wisest members of the
Assembly, could not have been otherwise than affected by the
influence of this memorable assertion of what they considered as
the great, the original rights of mankind; and, therefore, even
in moments of depression, and while they thought the court and
the royal authority were likely to overwhelm them, and before
the Bastile was destroyed, they had busied themselves in preparing a declaration of their rights, to leave, if it were necessary,
as a legacy to their countrymen.

It happened that the issue of the struggle, as you have seen,
turned out entirely in their favour; and, therefore, they now

renéwed their intention of exhibiting these great principles of
civil liberty, as had been done in America, and of laying the
foundations of the future constitution of France so deeply, as
they conceived, that the edifice could never hereafter be shaken
by any efforts of tyranny or usurpation.   It is at this moment
that begin our first thoughts of doubt, and even of censure, in
this business of the formation of the constitution; for this their
resolution, though wise and magnanimous in the first instance,
and before the 14th of July, might not be exactly expedient
afterwards.   The conduct to be pursued in a situation of danger
or defeat was one thing, and in a situation of victory and triumph
might be quite another.

Considerations, however, of this kind, seem never to have occurred to La Fayette or his friends, and the consequences were
very lamentable.

We will refer a little to the great example that on this occasion betrayed them—to America.

In America, not long after the declaration of independence by
the Congress, the different provinces of that great continent
began to form constitutions for themselves, and these were generally prefaced or accompanied by assertions of the original rights
of mankind and the popular origin of all free government.

" All men are born free and equal," says the first article of
the declaration of Massachusetts, " and have certain natural,
essential, and unalienable rights;" and it proceeds to enumerate them.

Again, in the constitution of Pennsylvania :—" All men are
born equally free and independent, and have certain inherent
and indefeasible rights." " All power is inherent in the people;
all free governments are founded on their authority," says the
ninth article.   " All government of right originates from the
people," says the first article of the declaration of the state of
Delaware.   So the declarations of Maryland, and of North Carolina; so the ninth article in that of South Carolina; and so the
rest.   " All men are born equally free and independent, and
have certain natural, inherent, and unalienable rights," says the
declaration of the inhabitants of Vermont.   " We hold these
truths to be self-evident," said the Declaration of Independence
issued by Congress in 1776, " that all men are created equal;
that they are endowed by their Creator with certain unalienable
rights; that among these are life, liberty, and the pursuit of
happiness; that to secure these rights governments are instituted among them, deriving their just powers from the consent

of the governed." "That whenever any form of government becomes destructive of these ends, it is the right of the people to alter or abolish it." "That governments long established should not be changed for light and transient causes; but when a long train of abuses and usurpations evinces a design to reduce men under absolute despotism, it is their right, it is their duty, to throw off such government, and to provide new guards for their future security."

Here we see the school in which the French patriots had studied. La Fayette talked afterwards, you may remember (but in cases of necessity arising from oppression), "of the sacred duty of insurrection;" nor can it be denied that these manly principles are founded in nature and in truth, that they are deeply engraven on the hearts of all men, and that they form the proper protection of the social order among men. These are the theories upon which legislators and governors are to proceed while they are endeavouring to administer to the happiness of their fellow-creatures; and these are, no doubt, the great principles and sentiments of human nature to which an appeal must ultimately be made by the people and their patriots, when governments abuse and persevere in abusing their trust.

The only question is the manner in which these principles and sentiments are to be applied to the concerns of mankind; the time, the occasion, the form, under which they are to be exhibited to the consideration of the people. The limitation made even by the American Congress, while throwing off the yoke, as they thought it, of Great Britain, is very remarkable. "Prudence will dictate," they say, "that governments long established should not be changed for light and transient causes;" and they reduce the case to a design of absolute despotism—to a case "of a long train of abuses and usurpations," such are their words, and "that evince a design to reduce men under absolute despotism."

It therefore well became the wise and virtuous men of the National Assembly of France to consider carefully what were the doctrines they were scattering broad-cast upon the land, and upon what soil they were to fall. Without disputing their abstract truth, we may protest against the propriety of their being proclaimed, as they were, at the moment when the king and the court had ceased to contend, and when the Assembly, or rather perhaps the people themselves, were now supreme. The true wisdom would have been to have left these abstract rights, where they were found, in the intuitions of the understanding and in the first and inevitable feelings of the heart ; to have left them there, acknowledged and undisturbed, and then to have proceeded immediately, as it were, to business ; and as the night of the 4th of August had cleared away the stage, first to have secured the proper existence of the king and the executive power, and then to have made such reforms in the laws and the system of taxation as would have reconciled all Frenchmen, who meant well, to the Revolution and the new order of things ; proclaiming aloud, not the doctrines that might flatter the people into madness and folly, but those that showed them the danger of their situation ; the necessity, to them, of peace and order ; the benevolent nature of their king ; how fruitless must be the effort that could now be made by the court to resist the labours of the Assembly ; and how evident it was that the community could have now no enemy but its own irritability and rashness.

I do not deny, I am happy to acknowledge, that great wisdom and caution were shown by Mounier and his friends ; that it will be an eternal honour to their memory that they made great provisions for the stability of the royal power. You must never forget, what I have already announced to you, that they (the first committee of five) determined the three great questions, on which the future existence of the royal power depended, quite right and in favour of it. This was great merit in them, considering the times and circumstances in which they were placed ; and had they been properly countenanced and assisted by others, all might have been well. Very different were, however, the views and feelings of but too many of the most enlightened and powerful men of the Assembly at the time. These men (and the Assembly unfortunately followed them) went far greater lengths than Mounier and the admirers of the English constitution ; and the first thing they had to do, as they supposed, was, after the example of America, to teach the people their rights, and to exhibit the principles upon which the existing government was to be swept away, and a new one substituted in its room. Mounier's scheme was therefore rejected, and a new declaration of the rights of man and of the citizens (followed by most important alterations in the intended constitution) was drawn up and presented to the king. In this declaration, by the first article it was laid down that all men were born and remained free and equal, and that social distinctions could only be founded on common utility. The natural rights of man were declared by the second to be liberty, property, security, and resistance against oppression; and by the third, that the principle of sovereignty resided essentially in the nation, and that no body of men and no individual could exercise an authority that did not emanate expressly from that source.

In the preface to the Declaration, it was said, that these natural, unalienable, and sacred rights of man were thus exhibited, in order that being ever present to all the members of the social body, they might be incessantly reminded of their rights and their duties, and that the acts of the legislative power and those of the executive power being every moment compared with the end of all political institutions, both might require the more respect. Finally, that the remonstrances of the citizens, being thus founded henceforward on simple and incontestable principles, might ever tend to maintain the constitution and to promote the general good.

Now what we contend for is, that, independent of the democratic provisions of the constitution, by which they were followed, doctrines and prefaces like these, however fitted for America in June 1776, at the beginning of a doubtful and even unpromising contest with the king of Great Britain and a parliament that would not listen to petitions, were far from being fitted to the situation of France, and more particularly of Paris, in August 1789—to the case of a benevolent monarch with a people in a state of triumphant insurrection, headed by an assembly, a single Assembly, that were the representatives of the whole community, and that were exercising all the powers of it. Our argument would not be affected by supposing the court and the royal party more powerful than they are here conceived to be. If they were, it then became still more a matter of prudence to offer them better terms, and to keep out of their sight such principles as must necessarily be offensive to them. But the National Assembly must at all events be considered, in this stage of the Revolution, as the triumphant party; and it is impossible for us, at this distance of time, not to contrast, as Mr. Burke did at an earlier period, the moderation and the good sense of the Whigs in 1688, with the rashness and enthusiasm of the leaders of the Constituent Assembly a century afterwards, in August 1789; for so far these two very dissimilar cases may be compared.

These principles of the rights of man, you will see very fully and earnestly discussed in the works you will have to read, more especially in Burke and Mackintosh. They were afterwards produced by Paine, in his celebrated pamphlet "Rights of Man," and applied to our own constitution. The propagation of these doctrines gave the greatest alarm to the generality of the people of property of this country, and you will therefore consider the first appearance of these principles in France with a more than usual interest ; and you may now do it with impartiality and calmness, unaffected by the passions which were most tremendously excited by the situation of France, and indeed of Europe, at this particular period.

In the meantime, there is one observation which may be very obviously made, and which I must even now present to your consideration; and it is this : that these rights of man, under whatever form presented, are in fact abstract political maxims; are to be received, if received at all, as the intuitions of the understanding, when applying itself to the subject of politics; as the metaphysical or moral axioms of the science.

Now what may or may not be justly so esteemed, under what limitations and what exceptions must be ever a matter of discussion ; and as it is the business of statesmen and reformers, as much as possible, to avoid subjects of debate and collision, all such men, if they are wise, will keep at the greatest possible distance from all elementary rights and principles. They will in reality proceed upon them, and take such of them for granted as are clearly connected with the public happiness; but they will say little or nothing about them, and certainly not preface their measures or open their discussions with abstract positions and metaphysical generalities of this kind, but hasten on to practice and to the real wants and wishes of their fellow-citizens, as they see them plainly existing before them, not expecting too much from themselves or others, and above all things losing no time.

I have already intimated to you, that when Mounier's scheme had been rejected, a new one was at last formed.   This new Declaration of Rights (of the 17th of August) consisted of seventeen articles, and this was immediately followed by nineteen supplementary articles of the constitution, October 1st, 1789 ; and of these last articles, it must be remarked, that, by the fifth, the legislature was to consist only of one house; by the eleventh, the king was only to have a suspensive veto; and by the fourth, the Assembly was to be permanent: that is, the king was not to have the power of dissolving the Assembly, and he was to have no army; so that the democratic principles announced in the Declaration were very decidedly carried into full effect in these proceedings of the Assembly; and it was very clear, that while the government was declared to be monarchical, the authority of the monarchy was to be most materially changed, was indeed to be virtually destroyed.

For ourselves, we conceive that it was the business of the friends of freedom at this period to have taken security, as much as possible, against the exasperated popular feelings, against demagogues and mobs for the present, and against democracy for the future. But, on the contrary, the friends of freedom, most of them, seem to have been anxious chiefly and in the first place to provide against the court and the nobility and clergy for the present; and, secondly, against the renewal of the royal power, with its ancient tyrannies and abuses, for the future; and to have thought of little else.

To recapitulate, therefore, the subject as far as we have hitherto alluded to it.

You will now, I hope, have a general notion, first, of the reasonable attempt that was made by Mounier and his friends to raise up a constitution somewhat after the English model.

Next, of the manner in which the minds of many patriotic members of the Assembly became inflamed by the new opinions, and particularly by the example of America.

Next, that in consequence, they formed a scheme of government of a much more democratic nature than Mounier's, consisting of seventeen articles, and nineteen supplementary articles.

And lastly, you will have, I hope, a general notion of these articles, and of the nature of the elements on which they were founded, the rights of man; on the whole, that the royal power was unreasonably and fatally weakened.

But I have also said, that the patriots and people of France had sufficient warning, in the different reasonings and speeches of intelligent men, of the mistakes they were committing.

Much light is thrown on points of this nature by the weekly journal the Mercure. Slight sketches of the debates are occasionally given, and a general notion may hence be formed of the violence of parties, the endless variety of human opinion, and the difficulties which the counsels of wise and good men have inevitably to encounter when they are to address themselves to the passions and abide the decisions of any large and popular assembly. I will endeavour to give you some notion of the debates furnished by this journal; but you will not find your time thrown away (very much otherwise) if you refer to the journal yourselves.

Turning, then, to this journal, and as a specimen of the manner in which the majority of the Assembly neglected the reason-

able observations that were made to them, I shall first allude
to the report that was delivered to them by the committee of
five (Mounier and his friends) on the very important point,
whether there should be two houses or one. I shall then give a
specimen of the debates on the subject of the declaration of the
Rights of Man.

"Some persons," says the report, "are attached to the system
of one chamber; they appeal to the happy effects produced in
the instance of the National Assembly already; they argue, that
it is the common will that should make the law; and that it is
best seen in a single chamber; that every division of the legislative body, by destroying its unity, often renders impossible the
most desirable institutions and the most salutary reforms; that
such a division would introduce a constant struggle and combat
into the very heart of the nation, the result of which must be
either a political torpor and inertness, or the most unhappy dissensions; that by the two chambers we should be also exposed
to the dangers of a new aristocracy, which it is equally the wish
and the interest of the nation to avoid."

The report has here fairly stated the arguments in favour of
one chamber, but observe how just are the arguments urged in
reply.

"Others," says the report, "on the contrary, contend that
this division of the legislative body into two chambers is entirely
necessary; that though one chamber might be more desirable
in the moment of regeneration, when every obstacle was to be
resisted, two chambers are still the proper measure, and are indispensable for the preservation and stability of the constitution
afterwards, and when it shall once have been determined upon;
that two chambers are necessary to prevent all surprise and all
precipitation, and to secure mature deliberation; that the intervention of the king in the legislation will be vain, illusory, and
without effect, if it is to be opposed to the irresistible mass of
the national will, brought forward and exhibited in one single
assembly; that meaning first, and above all things, to make a
constitution durable and solid, the National Assembly should
take care to avoid every system which, throwing all the real
power into the hands of the legislative body, could only render
the monarch anxious to seize any opportunity to modify and
change it, and expose the empire to new convulsions; that by
giving the legislative body a great facility of movement, which
is done by leaving it to act in one body, you expose it very idly
to resolutions that are too sudden—resolutions inspired perhaps

by some eloquent speech, some hasty enthusiasm, some intrigue in favour of ministers or against them, and that such precipitate resolutions must lead to despotism or to anarchy; finally, that the examples of England and America show the utility of two chambers, and are a sufficient answer to those who insist upon their inconvenience."

Such were the reasonings which this report of the five (of Mounier, Lally Tollendal, and others) exhibited on the great question of the two chambers; and the fate of the reasonings in favour of the two chambers, their real wisdom and total *failure* with the Assembly, is surely now, after all that we have seen, very remarkable.

And next, with respect to the second point, the Declaration of the Rights of Man.

I have already announced to you that very reasonable speeches were occasionally made in the Assembly; and the Assembly and the people of France were not in the end wrong without having been first distinctly warned of the mistakes they might commit.

Observe some of the speeches that were made on this subject, that so agitated mankind at this period and long after, the rights of man.

M. de Riauzat protested against these printed formularies of declarations of rights. Liberty, according to him, was to emanate from the constitution and the decrees of the Assembly. Man could only be considered in a state of society : to take him in a state of nature, is to found political institutions upon bases merely chimerical.

M. Malonet could not see how a declaration of this kind was at all necessary to the destruction of tyranny; the constitution itself would be sufficient for this purpose. "Metaphysical maxims," he said, "are always little intelligible to the generality of mankind. It is dangerous to present the people with a system of rights of which their understandings can neither seize the proper character nor the limits. America was in a different situation. The rights proposed should be quite simplified and joined to the constitution itself."

A speech of greater length, by M. de Landine, is then given, who seems, in this speech at least, to have been one of the few men of letters disposed rather to practice than to theory.

"Far," said he, "from mounting up to the first origin of the social order, let us improve that in which we are placed; let us turn from the man in a natural state, let us consider him in a civilized. Without inquiring what we have been, or even what we are, let us fix our eyes on what we ought to be. Locke, Cumberland, Smith, Hume, Rousseau, and many others, have developed the great principles of laws; but we want now the practice, not the theory. We are not likely to lose sight of those principles, but it is the immediate application of them that is the business before us. The law itself will be better than a thousand prefaces to it. Our wisdom is to gain time, now that we have lost so much of it, and have no more to lose; and on no account to open wide to the public mind a vast field for disputes, and commentaries, and opinions. When points are made the subjects of long discussion, even among ourselves can we suppose that the imaginations of others will not take fire? and the divisions, the controversial writings, and the debates that will ensue, will they not necessarily weaken the profound respect with which every thing that comes from the Assembly of the representatives of the nation should be received?"

This slight notice of what passed in the Assembly on the 3rd of August will give you a general notion of the style and import of the observations that were occasionally made there. There was no want of discussion, however stormy, or of intelligence, however unavailing.

I will now briefly allude to the events that took place, and to the constitution that really was formed.

And to give you, in the shortest manner I can, some general notion of the spirit in which the framers of it proceeded, I will also quote to you some of the sentiments that were expressed on the subject of the constitution of England. I will then conclude.

In the first place, then, on the 17th of August, when Mirabeau presented his report from Mounier's committee of five (he was one of the five), he accompanied it with a modest and sensible speech, stating the difficulties with which they had to struggle; and he renewed observations of this kind on the 18th. You will see his remarks in the Mercure, and still more at length in the printed account of his speeches. Great diversity of opinion prevailed. But this report as drawn up by the committee, though in itself so reasonable, though presented by Mirabeau, and though coming from Mounier and other men of such high authority, did not at all succeed; and this (you will remember) I consider as one of the fatal events of the Revolution.

A new effort to make a constitution was almost unanimously required; other schemes of government were afterwards considered, and the votes of the Assembly were taken. Forty appeared in favour of one by La Fayette; two hundred and forty for one by the Abbé de Sieyes; six hundred and forty for one attributed to the Bishop of Nancy.

On the 20th this last more favoured scheme was discussed. Great difference of opinion still prevailed on the whole and every part of it.

The great points of debate were, as I have already intimated, those more immediately connected with the prerogative of the king.

In the opening week of September, questions such as I have mentioned, had already agitated the Assembly.

An appeal was of course made to the example of England.

It had chanced that Rousseau, who was then the highest authority, had observed in his Letters from the Mountains, that the veto of the king of England was, after all, so checked, and tempered, and controlled, as not to be formidable to liberty, and he counselled the representatives of Geneva not to deny their magistrates a similar power, if they wished for it : but now in France the orators and writers of the day still insisted that to give the veto was to establish despotism ; that the English had given their kings the veto in feudal times of barbarism, and that they now repented.

It was in vain to reply that the English did not repent, and that they certainly flattered themselves that they were free. The same Rousseau was now again produced to prove that they were otherwise.

" The people of England," so went the quotation, " suppose themselves free, but they are quite mistaken ; they are only so during the election of the members of parliament; when these are once elected, the people are then slaves ; they are a mere nothing : this modern idea of representation is quite absurd, the offspring of the feudal governments," &c. &c.

When such sentiments as these could be quoted from Rousseau, and when Rousseau was to be considered not only as a moral sage, but as a political writer and a legislator, in what a bewildered state must have been the understandings of too many of the Assembly and of the community !

In the Mercure will be found a very full debate that took place on the 2nd of September. M. de Landnies seems to have spoken at great length.

" At every moment," said he, " the government of England is referred to. No doubt, considering the age in which it was formed, the government of England is a noble monument erected to the liberty of man ; it is an enlightened system for that period, no doubt; but let us lay aside all prejudice. Does any one suppose that there is nothing there defective, that the English statesmen and reasoners see nothing there to correct? Are we to suppose that if England was now labouring, as we are labouring, to make a constitution, that she would establish it on the same bases which she has done; that she would retain even the House of Peers, very often indeed useful to the king, but always perfectly useless to the people?

"Never believe it, gentlemen, that England has done everything for the happiness of mankind, and that we have nothing left but to copy her. Let us dare to do something better; let us have the elevated boldness to place the statue of Liberty on a base, that it will be still more impossible to overturn."

This paragraph will give you a notion of the sentiments of a large description of those who were unfortunately considered among the wisest at this particular period. "Talk not to me," said the celebrated Barnave in the same debate, "of the British constitution, formed not by the liberal use of reason, but the result of time and custom, and in the midst of wars and political events. It would be against all natural reason that the people should make their king into their legislator; it would be unjust to submit a whole nation to the caprices of a single man."

These were the notions that unhappily had taken possession of the patrons of the new opinions, and it was in vain that Mounier, as virtuous and intrepid as he was wise, defended, apparently at the risk of his life, the views of the committee of the constitution, the plurality of chambers, the senate for life, and the absolute veto.

The debates through the whole month of September, 1789, continued to turn on the great points connected with the future constitution, but were still marked by violence and disorder. Nothing could exceed the commotion when M. de Virieux observed with a good sense, that was but too prophetic, "It is my duty strongly to warn you of the dangers that result from the unity of the Assembly; all numerous assemblies, if singly left to act, are hurried away by demagogues and popular fury, and they have always been the destruction of free states, after first tearing them to pieces by their factions."

Lally Tollendal afterwards appeared at the tribune; and such was the treatment he received, that the president, the Bishop of Langres, was at last so offended, that he threw up his post, and put an end to the sitting.

The question, upon which the fortunes of the Revolution

might be almost said to turn, was the next day decided (the 10th of September), and most unfortunately decided; eight hundred and forty-nine were for the single chamber, only eighty-nine for the double, and one hundred and twenty-two did not vote at all.

The next sitting was not less confused and stormy, so numerous were the different propositions made by different members—made, accepted, rejected, again and again.

It was at last voted that the royal consent was necessary to the constitution; seven hundred and thirty to one hundred and forty-three, one hundred and twenty-two not voting, and in favour of the absolute veto were three hundred and twenty-five; six hundred and seventy-three in favour of the suspension, eleven not voting. M. de St. Farzeau and Robespierre, afterwards so well known, were for an annual election of the Assembly; the Abbé de Maury was for a duration of four years; M. de Virieux, for three; M. Demeunier, for two: there seemed no probable end to the debates.

Mounier, Lally Tollendal, Borgasse, and Clermont Tonnerre almost immediately gave in their resignations as members of the committee of constitution, the committee of five. These were the men that after the sitting of the 23rd of June, would have given the Revolution its second best chance of success. They failed; they were outvoted by La Fayette and his friends, by a large majority of the Constituent Assembly, who are therefore answerable for the event.

That these latter patriots, like the former, meant well, there can be no doubt. Their mistake (such I esteem it) I have endeavoured to explain; but of this mistake (they suffered for it severely) I shall often have to remind you, if I should hereafter come to consider the proceedings of the second or Legislative Assembly.

The lecture you have just heard was written some years ago, but I have just met a passage in Jefferson's Memoirs that illustrates many of the statements and opinions it contains. Jefferson, you may remember, was the American minister, resident at Paris at the time. He is speaking of the popular leaders. "When they proceeded to subordinate developments, many and various shades of opinion came into conflict; and schism, strongly marked, broke the patriots into fragments of very discordant principles. The first question, whether there should be a king, met with no open opposition; and it was readily agreed that the government of France should be mo-

narchical and hereditary. Shall the king have a negative
on the laws? Shall that negative be absolute or suspensive
only? Shall there be two chambers of legislation? Or one
only? If two, shall one of them be hereditary? Or for life?
Or for a fixed term? And named by the king? Or elected
by the people? These questions found strong differences of
opinion, and produced repulsive combinations among the patriots.
The aristocracy was cemented by a common principle, of preserving the ancient régime, or whatever should be nearest to it.
Making this their polar star, they moved in phalanx, gave preponderance on every question to the minorities of the patriots,
and always to those who advocated the least change. The features of the new constitution were thus assuming a fearful aspect, and great alarm was produced among the honest patriots
by these dissensions in their ranks. In this uneasy state of
things, I received one day a note from the Marquis de La Fayette,
informing me that he should bring a party of six or eight friends
to ask a dinner of me the next day. I assured him of their welcome. When they arrived they were, La Fayette himself, Duport, Barnave, Alexander Lameth, Blacon, Mounier, Maubourg,
and Dagout. These were leading patriots of honest but differing
opinions, sensible of the necessity of effecting a coalition by mutual sacrifices, knowing each other, and not afraid, therefore, to
unbosom themselves mutually. This last was a material principle in the selection. With this view the Marquis had invited the conference, and had fixed the time and place inadvert-
ently, as to the embarrassment under which it might place me.
The cloth being removed, and wine set on the table after the
American manner, the Marquis introduced the objects of the
conference, by summarily reminding them of the state of things
in the Assembly, the course which the principles of the constitution were taking, and the inevitable result, unless checked by
more concord among the patriots themselves. He observed, that
although he also had his opinion, he was ready to sacrifice it to
that of his brethren of the same cause; but a common opinion
must now be formed, or the aristocracy would carry everything,
and that, whatever they should now agree on, he, at the head of
the national force, would maintain. The discussions began at
the hour of four, and were continued till ten o'clock in the
evening; during which time I was a silent witness to a coolness
and candour of argument, unusual in the conflicts of political
opinion; to a logical reasoning, and chaste eloquence, disfigured
by no gaudy tinsel of rhetoric or declamation, and truly worthy

of being placed in parallel with the finest dialogues of antiquity, as handed to us by Xenophon, by Plato, and Cicero. The result was, that the king should have a suspensive veto on the laws, that the legislature should be composed of a single body only, and that to be chosen by the people. This concordat decided the fate of the constitution. The patriots all rallied to the principles thus settled, carried every question agreeably to them, and reduced the aristocracy to insignificance and impotence."

Such is the account of Jefferson. Such, you see, were then the patriots of France; the logic and the eloquence of Xenophon, Plato, and Cicero; and with the best intentions. But all in vain amidst the enthusiasm of the new opinions—an enthusiasm which I must for ever represent to you as one of the great lessons of the French Revolution.

LECTURE XVII.

VIEWS OF DIFFERENT WRITERS.

I will now proceed to refer to some of the histories and commentaries on the French Revolution, drawn up by actors in the scene, or those who lived at the time. These accounts will present you with the same transactions and topics again and again repeated; but this, as I have mentioned to you, will only impress the leading points of this great subject more and more on your memories. To men of intelligence, to those who mean well, to all who are really interested in the liberties of mankind, and in the best happiness of their country, I consider this portion of the Revolutionary story to be most particularly important: such men were at this period, as I conceive, wanting in caution, in respect for those who had gone before them; were too sanguine, too enthusiastic in their good feelings, too confident in the people. And if these things be so, they ought to operate as an example to others hereafter; to other wise and good men; to other patriots, who must be taught, that it is not sufficient to have good intentions or great talents; that they must have prudence, circumspection, and many other virtues, which those who engage in revolutions are too apt to despise. Look, therefore, at the portraits of this singular period, which I am holding up to your view; for this is what I am now doing, while I am quoting from the writings or speeches of those who lived at the time. It might be more easy, and more regular, and less tedious, to offer you my own estimates of these things; but I choose rather, while I am exhibiting to you my own opinions, to lay before you, as well as I can, the materials on which those opinions have been formed, and you can then judge of both the one and the other, in a general and rough manner, if I may so speak, now, while you hear me, and more regularly hereafter, when you come to meditate these subjects and read for yourselves. The interval that elapsed between the 14th of July and the 5th and 6th of October was the precious season when the Constituent Assembly were in power, and when it might have been possible for them to have carried their new opinions into effect, and have laid the foundations of the happiness of France; and you cannot, therefore, examine too patiently the opinions and views of all concerned.

It is on this account that I am now endeavouring to call them up to appear before you, speak in their own language, tell their own story, give their own evidence, and leave you sitting in quality of jurors to bring in your verdict on the case.

I will add one consideration more, and then proceed.

One of the most celebrated productions in our language is the work of Mr. Burke, his Reflections on the French Revolution. This is a work that can never die; not only on account of its own merits and its reference to the great principles of human nature, but because it must be always connected with an event that can never be blotted from the history of Europe.

I have already declared to you, that I should hold it no mean praise, but esteem it an important reward, for the labour of these lectures, if I could at all contribute to your accurately appreciating the proper value of this great performance: if I could enable you the better to distinguish its spirit and its fire from its enthusiasm, its profound philosophy from its declamation; in a word, if I could enable you to discern, while you are reading with delight, when it is that your understanding, and when it is that your imagination only is affected. But this can best be done by entering into such particulars and submitting to such details as I am now exhibiting to your observation. Mr. Burke's work is a critique on the conduct of the Constituent Assembly, and of that conduct a most important portion is that now before us. But to proceed. I have already mentioned to you Rabaud de St. Etienne, a lawyer, a man of letters, a minister of the reformed religion, and a distinguished member of the Constituent Assembly. He is a specimen of a numerous description of men

of the time; a friend to freedom and a virtuous man, but a convert to the new opinions, and an enthusiast in their favour.
His story is shortly told : he supported these new opinions, but
he supported order also, on every occasion ; he voted against
the death of the king ; and for these crimes, or rather virtues,
he was in the course of the year (1793) denounced, and at the
end of it perished under the guillotine.

I shall now make some references to the accounts he gives.
In the fourth book of his Précis of the Revolution, he observes,
that at the period we are at present alluding to, " France was
like an immense chaos, in which all the elements of order subsisted, and waited but the hand of the Creator ; every thing,"
says he, " seemed to indicate that the kingdom would be a prey
to anarchy ;" and this was the great fear of the good, and the
hope of all bad citizens, who thus looked for the renewal of the
ancient despotism.

" But the men of property," he continues, " got armed, and
this was the safety of France. France was covered with three
millions of men clothed in the national uniform. It was the
nation that protected the nation, and force was wisdom.

" The Assembly thus placed in security (this you see he
admits), proceeded to the Declaration of Rights, and to lay down
the principles of the monarchy, which they did, as they had been
required to do by the people.

" When they came, however, to discuss the share which the
king was to have in the legislation, then arose the great
struggle in the bosom of the Assembly. There were those on
the one side whom long-established associations had prepared
for a blind tenderness for the name and person of the king—the
king, who, or whatever he was ; who were for things as they
found them ; who thought the only legislator was the king ;
and, in short, who hoped to regain by the king what they had
lost by the people.

" On the other side there were those who were terrified, who
were rendered wild, at the very shadow and appearance of despotism, and who could conceive no safety for liberty but in the
permanence of the legislative body—a body first making the
laws and then presenting them to the sanction of the monarch.
These two parties the president saw ranged on his right hand
and on his left, and the same was the division through the whole
of the kingdom."

Rabaud de St. Etienne then proceeds to the discussions that
took place on the subject of the veto. These will be edifying

to you, but still more so, those which related to the National Assembly itself.

You are never to suppose in political questions that much is not to be said on each side; it is for good sense to compare and decide.

" While the minds of men," says Rabaud, " without doors got influenced on this subject of the veto, the Assembly proceeded to decide upon the permanence of its body, and the famous question of the two chambers. Before the meeting of the States General, the numerous partisans of the English constitution had declared their opinion. To this opinion great weight was given by the authority of Montesquieu, and the recent publication of De Lolme. But the advocates for the one chamber considered this equilibrium in the English constitution, but as a treaty of peace between three powers then existing; and however adapted to England this system of adjustment might be, France, they contended, was in no similar situation. Personal interests, however, mixed themselves in the discussion.

The high clergy were for the two chambers in the hope of obtaining a place in the upper; so was a great part of the nobility : but a division ensued : the noblesse of the provinces were for a representation of the whole order, the noblesse of the court wished to have the rights of the peerage conferred on them alone, and many of the nobility feared, that in some way or other, it would be contrived by the National Assembly, that the high chamber should be composed only of the forty-seven that had first gone over to the Tiers Etat.

The curés, those that were not devoted to their bishops, were for the unity of the Assembly. The majority of the deputies saw in the upper house but a constitutional refuge for aristocracy, and a preservative of the feudal system. Their distrust of it was but strengthened by the continuance, as they thought, of that triple league which existed between the two privileged orders and the court, and was again confirmed by the intrigues that were practised to prevent the king from giving his sanction to the decrees of the 4th of August. The result of all this was a sort of uncertainty and obscurity thrown over the measure of an upper house, and this diminished the number, at least the warmth of its partisans. No one could exactly see what the Assembly was to be, or what share he was to have in it; and in affairs of this kind, and in all politics, personal interests will necessarily find their way into the minds of men.

Nothing better, as it seemed, could be made of a senate for life, composed of citizens of all descriptions, for this might easily be corrupted by the court; nor of a senate taken from the whole of the Assembly for the time, and of which it would only be a fraction; and with respect to those who objected that no restraint could be imposed upon a single assembly, and no counterpoise contrived for it, it was answered, says Rabaud de St. Etienne (you will observe the answer), "that means enough could be found in the Assembly itself to stop its course by introducing delays into its proceedings; that a counterpoise would naturally be found in the veto of the king, which veto might be considered as representing the negative will of the nation, as the Assembly did the affirmative: that if they abused their power by making decrees contrary to the interests of the community, the king would find his merit with the community in saving them from the tyranny of the Assembly; that these two counter powers of the king and the Assembly were far better for the people than three, of which two would be naturally united against them. And so the Assembly," continues the historian, " decreed by a majority of nine hundred and eleven to eighty-nine voices, that there should be only one chamber;" and again, " that the Assembly should be created afresh, by new elections every two years; and this term of two years be called a legislature."

You see here the nature of the plausible but superficial and unfortunate reasonings of the more warm partisans of liberty at this time. Even so early as August 1789, the king was expected, without an army, without a power of dissolving the Assembly, and without a second house of any kind whatever, to oppose his veto to the representatives of the people, not indeed whenever, in his own judgment, their measures were wrong, the natural meaning of a veto, but when it was also clear that the people would be with him. And this was to be the situation of the executive power; and this was to be the king's chance for the necessary prerogatives of his station; and these his means of supporting his crown and dignity; and this the treatment of one of the great authorities in the state, already constituted, acknowledged, and existing, and hitherto considered as supreme.

Now I do not see a single remark of this kind in the historian, though he was writing, as he says in the preface, not in 1789, but some time after, when the constitution was made, and when the mistakes of it were already, one might have thought, sufficiently displayed.

We will now refer to the other history which I mentioned, the history of the Two Friends of Liberty : the state of the Assembly and of Paris, and the warning it holds out to all who love freedom, is still more distinctly seen in this history of the " Two Friends of Liberty." The whole subject of the constitution, as it appears from this work, was thoroughly discussed both within the Assembly and without ; the nature of the rights of man, the veto, and the two chambers, all were made matter of the most lively contest and debate.

Of the rights of man three different systems were, it seems, offered to the Assembly ; one by La Fayette, one by the Abbé de Sièyes, and one by Mounier. Each had, it was supposed, its merits and defects, of course. The Assembly referred them to a committee, who were to report and produce a new one: this was done, but in vain. In politics, the incurable nature of human dissent should be taken always into the calculation by those who are criticising old systems, or are ready to propose new ones. Mirabeau, it appears, interfered with all his commanding powers, very reasonably proposing that the prefatory rights and the constitution, the theory and the application, the tree and the fruits of it, should be all seen hereafter, and all at one and the same time—in vain.

The more warm partisans of liberty insisted on the danger of any delay ; talked of pretexts, subterfuges, and chicanery ; expressed their suspicions of Mirabeau himself and of the steadiness of his principles.

These are, I think, among the lessons of the Revolution, and are admitted by those historians who lived and wrote at the time. Men must love liberty, but, if possible, even in perilous times, should be conciliatory and ready to come to adjustments, and deeply aware of the controversial nature of independent minds.

The declaration was at last agreed upon, such as you see it. I must now digress for a moment, to make an observation on the general subject of these declarations, or rather to contrast the conduct of the statesmen of America with those of France on this occasion. I have already pointed your thoughts in this direction ; I must do it once more.

It is remarkable, then, even in the case of America, when in 1776 the people of the continent were to be worked up into resistance to Great Britain by Congress, and soon after by the state legislatures, that though the rights of man were *then* brought forward and drawn up in battle-array, and very naturally ; yet when a general constitution was to be formed by the convention in 1787, eleven years after, some lessons had been received in the mean time by Washington and the best patriots of America, and, therefore, their preface is then simple and calm, and there is nothing said about rights of man and elementary principles. " We, the people," they say, " of the United States, in order to form a more perfect union, establish justice, ensure domestic tranquillity, provide for the common defence, promote the general welfare, and secure the blessings of liberty to ourselves and our posterity, do ordain and establish this constitution for the United States of America." This is their language ; and then (to use a common phrase) they immediately proceed to business. " All legislative power herein granted," they declare, " shall be vested in a Congress," &c. &c. ; and the sensible men engaged in this work concluded it with saying, " the ratification of nine estates shall be sufficient for the establishment of this constitution between the states so ratifying the same." The form of government which they chose was that of a republic, agreeably to the inherited and existing notions and manners of those for whom they were acting ; but there was nothing of arrogance or rashness in their proceedings, and no longer any metaphysics.

But to return to France. France, at the period we are now considering, chose a monarchy ; but a monarch could not be set up, like a tall column on the surface of a plain, single and unsupported, and then expected to stand. Yet was this pretty nearly what the patriots of the National Assembly attempted. One of them talked of a " royal democracy." The question of the veto was, as you will see in the history of "The Two Friends," very fully discussed. I cannot, in a lecture like this, exhibit to you all these reasonings, which you ought to read fully stated in this history. In my last lecture, indeed, I referred to them, and gave you a specimen of them.

Mounier, Lally Tollendal, and others, above all Mirabeau, were for giving the monarch a veto absolutely and entirely, on all laws presented to him ; Garat the younger, and other distinguished members, were quite of an opposite opinion ; and both perfectly united in rejecting all compromise, all idea of a suspensive veto. Here, therefore, the three parties might have remained ; but it was impossible that the sages of the Palais Royal and the statesmen of the streets of Paris should rest undisturbed spectators of these discussions, and the part they were likely to take may be easily imagined. You will have some proper notion of it from the " History of the Two Friends."

The prospect of falling again under the yoke of the nobles and the priests filled every mind, it seems, according to these historians, with indignation. No one could conceive, they said, how the representatives of the nation could dare to propose in the National Assembly to arm the royal authority with such a power as that of the veto absolute. It was in vain that wiser men endeavoured to restore a calm; nothing but perfidies and treasons were talked of; and in short it was resolved at the Café de Foy that a deputation should be sent to Versailles, to declare to the Assembly, " that the secret practices of the aristocracy to procure the veto were well known, as were all the accomplices in this odious plot : that if they did not instantly renounce this their criminal league, that five thousand men were ready to march ; that the nation would be desired to recall such faithless representatives, and replace them with good citizens; and that the king and his son would be requested to repair to the Louvre, there to live secure in the midst of his faithful Parisians."

With great difficulty, by the exertions of the constituted authorities, of La Fayette, and some of the more reasonable of the popular orators, the storm was at last appeased. Some of the deputies from the Palais Royal, however, reached Versailles and the house of Lally Tollendal ; they came to inform him, they said, " that Paris was not for the veto : that it regarded as traitors, those that were ; and that it punished traitors ;" and many of the members were named and already menaced with proscription.

Lally Tollendal replied with spirit and propriety, and went with them to the Assembly. Similar communications, it was there found, had been made to others ; anonymous letters to the president and secretaries, filled with the most furious menaces. Two hundred torches were ready to set fire to the chateaux of certain of the members, as an intimation, in the first place, of what they were afterwards to expect. The Assembly was universally indignant. Clermont de Tonnerre and Mounier spoke with their usual force and eloquence.

Such, according to these historians, were the beginnings of troubles, and as such I mention them to you. They ought to have warned the more warm partisans of liberty how perilous was the situation in which the Revolution was already placed.

The next great question was the permanency of the Assembly and its organization, whether two houses or one. The reasonings were all founded on a terror of the executive power. It was evident, they said, that a permanent body, for instance, would more easily restrain the executive power within its proper

limits.   The moral force of the Assembly, if consisting of only
one house, and the consequent spirit of its deliberations, would
form a much better counterpoise than could be found if the Assembly were to be divided into two, and by its very composition
be thrown into a state of equilibrium.   On the first supposition
the veto of the king would have its meaning and necessity,
but in the second it was but a wheel useless, and therefore dangerous, to the machinery.   In this manner proceeded the reasoning, according to the historians ; and in short the conclusion was,
that there was a necessity that the constitution should be settled and strengthened ; that incessant efforts were required from
the constantly recurring exigencies of the community ; that details of every kind made it expedient that the whole system
should be regenerated ; and that all these concurred in powerfully demanding from the community an universal vote for the
presence, the activity, and decidedly the permanence, or rather
the constant existence, every year renewed, of the National Assembly.

Such were the general notions of the public, according to these
historians, at this critical period.   Calling to mind all that we
have seen, it is very grievous to observe the mistaken apprehensions that were entertained, the total blindness that prevailed,
with regard to the real seat of the danger.   No doubt it is a
testimony to prove how wretched and how oppressive had been
the ancient government, with its own abuses, and the abuses of
its aristocracy, when men seemed to have no terror but of its return.   But the whole may still be held up as a warning to all
future patriots, of whatever country, never to withdraw a society
entirely from its accustomed restraints ; to alter, to modify them,
to substitute others more convenient, but never to clear away
the ground in the first place, and remove the old building, as the
necessary preparation for the erection of a new one.   We have
not to deal with the insensate materials of stone and mortar, but
human beings incapable of rest, or even suspense, if roused ; exposed to misapprehension, highly selfish, and always the mere
slaves of the present uneasiness.

The conduct of the friends of freedom at this particular epoch
of the Revolution is the more inexcusable, because the great
leader, Mirabeau, spoke the words, and in his own forcible manner, both of wisdom and even prophecy.

" For myself," said he from the tribune, " I consider the
veto of the king as so necessary, that I would rather live in Constantinople than in France, if it be not granted.   Yes, I do

declare it, I know of nothing so terrible as a sovereign aristocracy, of six hundred persons, who, making themselves permanent to-morrow, will make themselves hereditary the next day,
and finish, as the aristocrats of every country on the face of the
globe have always done, by leaving no power in existence that
they did not invade and absorb."

It is but justice, too, to Lally Tollendal, Mounier, and other
wise and good men, that they proposed to their countrymen, as
I have already mentioned to you, a system of government, which,
if it could but have met the opinions and expectations of the Assembly and the public, all might have been well. The friends
of freedom would have had a good case, its enemies none; the
king would have been satisfied, and the nation happy; and Europe
saved from a series of the most tremendous crimes and miseries
that ever afflicted and terrified the civilized world since the
irruptions of the northern nations.

You will observe, or rather remember, what I intimated yesterday, that in the name of the committee of the constitution
(the committee of five), M. de Lally Tollendal had made the following report:—

"1st. The legislative body shall be composed of three parts,
the king, a senate, and the representatives of the nation." Two
houses, you observe, as in England, and the king.

"2ndly. It is the right and duty of the king to convoke the
legislative body at epochs fixed by the constitution. He may
prorogue and even dissolve it, if at the same time he call a new
one." The power of dissolution, you see, given, without which
anything else that might be given was totally vain.

"3rdly. The taxes are in every respect to come from the representative body on the requisition of the king, and the senate
are on this occasion merely to consent or reject simply, and no
more.

"4thly. The senate is to be the tribunal in all state delin-
quencies.

"5thly. Each house is to judge of what concerns its own
police and particular rights."

By the 7th article, the royal sanction is necessary to every law.

"8thly. The initiative of every law and the mode of enactment belongs to the two houses; the sanction, to the king."

"10thly. The two houses are to have the negatives each upon
the other; the king upon them both. The senate to be elected
for life."

Even here there was nothing said of the army and the neces-

sary patronage of the crown; but the whole was evidently in the
right tone and spirit.   The example of England was taken advantage of; experience was made a guide.   Proper prerogatives
might have been introduced into the system for the support of
the executive power; the whole might have been rendered such,
that the king might have acceded to it without degradation, and
therefore with sincerity.   And now there is seen the accusation
of the more warm and enthusiastic supporters of the new opinions in the National Assembly.   No system of this kind was
thought possible for France.—

A scheme of organization like this, say the historians, the Two
Friends of Liberty, was universally disrelished.   The basis of
it was, as every one saw, the famous balance of the three powers,
and the example of the constitution of England.   But neither
the authority of Montesquieu, they observe, nor the logical reasoning of Mounier, nor the eloquence of Lally, could reconcile it
to the friends of freedom.   They could see in it but an asylum
for the ancient aristocracy, the cradle of a new one, still more
dangerous, as it planted corruption in the very bosom of the Assembly; an allurement to the ambitious, and a nourishment for
all those unhappy prejudices of distinction and pre-eminence, so
contrary to the spirit of the new constitution.

The Assembly, indeed, ordered it to be printed out of respect
to its own committee; but submitted it not to discussion, article
by article, out of respect to the judgment of the public, already
most clearly expressed.

It was, however, examined, continues the historian, and refuted in all its points (refuted, you will observe), during the
discussion of the three great questions at issue, the veto, the permanence, and the organization of the Assembly.   Due homage
was paid to the wisdom of the English constitution, but examples, it was said, are in politics apt to deceive.   The constitution of a people ought to be accommodated to its character, opinions, and manners: often modified by local circumstances; so
that an institution that will prosper in one country will cause
the ruin of another.   Such were the reasonings of too many of
the assertors of liberty at this period.

And in this manner, and from considerations of this kind, was
the example of England, its long and eventful history, and its
successful Revolution, to be set aside, through the case of a
monarchy; and the constitution of America to be preferred as a
model, and even that model not properly followed (for in that
constitution there are two Houses of Assembly, not one); though

this was a case of thirteen confederated republics, resisting the harsh government of the mother country; and though, at the same time, the people were republicans from their first origin: a case in no respect similar to that of France.

No scheme of government, no measure in politics, can ever be without its appropriate recommendations; no men, who take a side, can be without their arguments; but every thing in this world is a choice of difficulties or a comparison of advantages; and, as I have already observed, and as you must remember, it is for those who mean well to do more than mean well, and, after due reflection, to labour, if possible, to judge well.

Rabaud de St. Etienne, and no doubt many others, depended on such arguments as the following, which I quote from him, and which were urged with all the triumph of the most irresistible logic.

"The very nature of things," says he, "resists this division of the legislative authority. The nation is one; so should then be the body that represents it.

"The National Assembly is to collect and proclaim the general will; that will is one and indivisible; it is illogical, therefore, to divide the Assembly into two, that there may issue from it a will that is one.

"If the two chambers have not a veto upon each other, their division is without meaning; if they have this veto, they are then so formed as to do nothing.

"If the senators are for life, they will think no more of the nation, and be corrupted by the crown; if for a time, they will never acquire a consistency, or a character, on an individual interest, sufficient to fit them to be a weight in any political scale."

And so the result of all this exquisite logic, the very quintessence of smartness and infallibility, was, that the country and the monarch were to be left to the mercy of one great Assembly, that was sure, as Mirabeau predicted, to render Constantinople itself a more eligible residence.

"The Two Friends of Freedom" bring their historical observations on this critical period to a sort of conclusion by saying, "The National Assembly advanced rapidly in their career. In less than eight days they had proclaimed as many truths and political axioms as the teachers of superstition and the ministers of tyranny had proscribed or obscured during the course of ten centuries. They had restored to the laws their supremacy, which despotism had usurped (this was no doubt true); they had ennobled the sceptre itself by submitting it to their empire; and they had consecrated the royal authority by deducing it from the first great original source of all authority.   They had defined the nature and fixed the boundaries of the different powers of the state; acknowledged the inviolability of the person of the king; restored to the nation the legislative power, to be exercised by its representatives; assured to the subject personal liberty; and conferred on the monarch the supreme executive power."

Such is the panegyric of these historians, and it is in some of its particulars a panegyric perfectly just.   Many things had certainly been done by the Assembly; their difficulties and their exertions are not to be forgotten; and if the last thing mentioned by the historians had been done also, if the supreme executive power had been conferred on the king, fairly, fully, and justly conferred, their labours might have been crowned with success, and the Assembly might have received and deserved the title which they had bestowed on their unfortunate monarch, that of " Restorer of French liberty."

These remarks, and notices, and quotations, will give you some general idea of the views taken by the popular historians and by the popular reasoners of the time.   You see how the minds of men were influenced by the thought of their escape from the old government of France, by their ardour to make a new one; one that should secure them from the return of the oppressions which they had experienced.   Mounier and his friends, you see, were not listened to.   What Necker, a man of intelligence, thought at the time is sufficiently known, not only from his measure of the suspensive veto, the best terms he could make with the Assembly, but from all that he has published in remarks on their conduct, and in his work on executive power.   To these I may hereafter allude.

His daughter, M⁵. de Stael, to whom I shall now, in the last place, refer, takes the same ground with her father, having been, like him, an eye-witness of the scene, though still more animated with the generous enthusiasm of liberty.   She sees very clearly the crisis of this particular period, and thinks that the example of the English constitution should have prevailed.

" On the right hand of the president," she says, " was ranged the aristocratic party, composed chiefly of nobles, members of the parliament, and prelates.   There were on this side scarcely thirty of the Tiers Etat.   This aristocratic party had constantly protested against every resolution that had been taken by the

Assembly, whose insolent movements they found it difficult to treat with seriousness; and the discovery of the eighteenth century, that there was such a thing as a nation, they considered as somewhat ridiculous, accustomed as they had themselves been, to see and hear of nothing but nobles, priests, and people. To the popular party they addressed only reproaches and abuse; and then, with a total contempt of the circumstances in which they were placed, their receipt for doing good, was to make what they thought bad, worse; regardless of what was to become of themselves, if they could but have the satisfaction of having been prophets."

This is a picture of human nature, and of the privileged orders, and of any fallen party, but too faithful, and yet very melancholy.

" The more violent of the two parties," she says, " were on the more elevated benches on the opposite sides. As the eye moved down the right, it reached the plain, where sat the moderate men, for the most part the defenders of the constitution of England.

" The principal people here were, Malouet, Lally, Mounier. Men more conscientious (says Mᵉ. de Stael) in the Assembly were not to be found; but though the eloquence of Lally was quite superb, though Mounier was a publicist of the most elevated wisdom, and Malouet an administrator of the first efficiency, though from without they were supported by the ministers, with Necker at their head, and though often in the Assembly, men of the greatest merit rallied round their opinions, still did the more violent of the two parties never fail to overpower them in every thing they proposed or said; courageous though they were, and pure, and of all in the Assembly the more so; they never ceased, indeed, to cry aloud in this wilderness of disorder : but the high aristocrats could not bear men like these, whose object it was to establish a constitution wise and free, and therefore durable; and one often saw them, rather than assist such real patriots, giving their hand to unprincipled demagogues, whose follies menaced France, as well as themselves, with the most frightful anarchy." This you see is a repetition of the most serious accusation possible that can be urged against the privileged orders at this period; their desperate perverseness and impolitic blindness.

" Proceeding now from the moderate and the impartial to the popular party," she says, " however united on more important questions, they had fallen into different divisions. There were those attached to La Fayette; Mirabeau, though without what could exactly be called a party, had a great ascendant over the whole by the admirable powers of his mind.   There was Barnave, of all the most fitted by the nature of his talents to be an orator after the English manner; there was the Abbé Sièyes, who enveloped himself in a sort of mysterious wisdom; he was supposed to be possessed of secrets on the subjects of government from which the most extraordinary effects were expected when he should think proper to disclose them; and there were the Mountaineers, as they were called; they sat the highest on the right; Robespierre was already seen there, and Jacobinism was preparing in the clubs.

The chiefs of the majority of the popular party rather amused themselves with the exaggerations and violence of the Jacobins, and were pleased with the air of wisdom which they thought they might assume, when they *complacently* compared themselves with these factious conspirators.   These pretended modérés, one might have said, followed after, and attended these violent democrats, as a huntsman does his pack, priding himself that he can stop them at a call.

" It has been asked," continues M^e. de Stael, " who were those in the Assembly that could be called the Orleans party ?

" Perhaps no one, for no one would have acknowledged the duke for a chief, nor did he wish for it.   Mirabeau had sounded all the depths of his character, and thought no enterprise could be rested upon it.

" But he gave money to the populace, it is said.   Whether he did or no, it is little to understand the Revolution, to suppose that this could have the slightest influence.   It is not by such means that a whole people can be put in motion; this has always been the mistake of the people connected with the court. In some facts of mere detail they seek for the cause of sentiments expressed by the whole nation.

" The leaders of the popular party," says M^e. de Stael (and what she says contains, I think, the lesson which from the love I bear to civil liberty I ought to enforce, no matter at what risk of tediousness and repetition), " the leaders," says she, " on the left side (on the popular side), might have made the project of the English constitution succeed, if they had but united in this object with M. de Necker among the ministers, and with his friends in the Assembly; but then they would have been but secondary agents in the march of events, and they wished to take the lead; they chose, therefore, to draw their support from without, from the collections of men who were preparing commotions; they gained an ascendant in the Assembly by mocking at the moderate men, as if moderation were weakness, and they themselves alone possessed of any character of strength. One saw them in the hall, and on the seats of it, turning into ridicule any member who ventured to observe, that really men had existed in society before, that they themselves had so existed, and certainly that there were writers who had supposed that England was in possession of some little liberty; one would have thought it was the tales of the nursery that one was thus telling them; with such impatience did they listen, with such disdain did they pronounce their particular phrases and positions, highly exaggerated and peremptory, 'that it was quite impossible to admit an hereditary senate,' ' or a senate even for life,' ' or the absolute veto,' ' or any condition of property,' ' or, in short, any thing that, as they said, trenched upon the sovereignty of the people.' These leaders of the popular party were of more elegant manners and wished to be in the ministry; and would have conducted affairs, if they could, to the very point, when it would have been necessary to have called for their interference; but in a rapid descent like that of a revolution, the car could not have been stopped, because they were a relay to be harnessed to it; they were not indeed conspirators and traitors, but they trusted too much to their powers over the Assembly, and they flattered themselves that they could again raise up the throne after they had brought it within their disposal. But it turned out that when really, and in good truth and faith, they wished to repair the ill they had done, it was impossible: It is not easy to say how many misfortunes might not have been spared to France if this part of the younger members had but united with the moderate men. Before the events of the 6th of October," she continues, " when the king had not yet been brought away from Versailles, and the French army, scattered over the provinces, still retained some respect for the throne, circumstances were such that a reasonable monarchy might have been established in France. Vulgar philosophy, indeed, is pleased to believe that all that has happened could not but have happened." (This you will find hereafter is the philosophy of her opponent Bailleul; often of still more weighty and respectable writers, Mignet and Thiers); "but to what purpose, then, the reason and liberty of mankind, if the same will that evidently *accomplished* things could not also have *prevented* them?"

Such are the views and sentiments of M⁰. de Stael; and I know not how better to impress you with what seem to me reasonable opinions on this portion of the French Revolution, than by continuing to borrow passages from some of the chapters of her first volume.

"All the power of the government," she says, "had fallen into the hands of the Assembly after the 14th of July, which yet had only functions that were legislative; their distrust, however, of the intentions of the king, or rather of the court, prevented them from confiding to him the necessary powers for the re-establishment of order.   M. Necker was the intermediate person between the royal authority and the Assembly.

"But those deputies who were attached to him, notwithstanding his moderate politics, thought that the aristocrats were deceiving him; that he was their dupe.   This was not so, but Necker knew that the privileged persons, under the former régime, would reconcile themselves to any party rather than the *first* friends of liberty: but he did his duty in endeavouring to restore force to the government; for a free constitution can never be the result of a general relaxation of its restraints, but rather a despotism.

"The Constituent Assembly could not depose a sovereign, virtuous as Louis XVI., though England had deposed James II., and yet it wished to have a constitution that was free; the consequence was, that it came to consider the executive power as an enemy to liberty, instead of making it one of its safeguards; it combined the constitution, as it would the plan of an attack; everything followed from this mistake.   Whether the king was or was not reconciled in his heart to the limits which the national interest required, this was not the point; it was not for the Assembly to examine his secret thoughts, but to found the royal authority, independently of what one might exactly hope or fear from the monarch.   Institutions are at length more easily conformed to than broken through; and to retain a king, and yet strip him of his necessary prerogatives, was, of all parts that could be acted, the most absurd and reprehensible; a constitution which comprehended within its elements the humiliation either of the sovereign or the people, could not but be necessarily overthrown by one or the other."

These observations of M⁰. de Stael are surely very reasonable.

With respect to the second House of Assembly.   "M. de Lally," she says, "wished for a House of Peers.   It could not even be proposed, and M. de Lally therefore wished to supply its place by at least a senate for life.

" But the popular party had got irritated against the privileged persons, who had always separated themselves from the nation, and they therefore rejected a durable institution of this kind, from the prejudices of the moment: A very great fault this," she says, " not only because a high chamber was necessary as an intermediate body between the sovereign and the deputies of the nation, but because there was no other method to make fall into oblivion that noblesse of the second order so numerous in France; a noblesse not known to history, not recommended by many considerations of public utility, and continually displaying, even more than did the first rank, a contempt for the Tiers Etat, lest it should not be sufficiently distinguished by them.

" The right side of the Assembly," she goes on to say, " that is, the aristocrats, might have carried this measure of a senate for life, by uniting themselves to Lally and my father; but they voted for one chamber rather than two, that they might make things hereafter better, as they thought, by making them first as bad as possible—a detestable and unprincipled speculation, that seduced the mind, by appearing to be so profound.

" The next subject," she continues, " was the veto. Was it to be absolute or suspensive ?

" The word 'absolute' sounded to the ears of the vulgar like despotism, and one saw now begin the unhappy influence of the cries of the people against men the most enlightened.   It is scarcely possible for any mind to place within its view all the questions that may be connected with a political institution; what, then, more calamitous than to leave such questions to the reasonings, and often to the pleasantries of the multitude ?   In the streets of Paris they spoke of the veto as of some monster that was to devour all the children."

She then goes on to describe the views taken by the opposite parties, and the reasonings of her father, and at last observes, that under the existing circumstances, it was impossible to think of irritating the public by the word " veto absolute," when, in fact, the royal veto in every country always gives way more or less to the national wish.   " The high-sounding nature of the word," she says, " one may, indeed, regret; at the same time one must not overlook the danger of placing the king alone in the presence of one great assembly, no gradations of rank near him, and left singly, as it were, to confront his people, and to oppose in the balance the insulated will of himself against that of twenty-four millions.

" M. Necker, however, protested, so to speak, against this means of conciliation, this suspensive veto, even while he proposed it; for at the moment that he was showing that it was the necessary result of the single chamber, he continually insisted that a single chamber was wholly inconsistent with anything that could be durable or good.

" This institution of a single chamber, and many other decrees relative to the constitution, which so entirely departed from the political system of England, occasioned Necker," says his daughter, " the greatest possible concern, for in this democracy royal, as they called it, he saw (as he thought) every danger both for the throne and liberty. The spirit of party has always only one fear, wisdom has always two. One sees in his writings the respect he always bore to the constitution of England, and the arguments on which he depended, while wishing to adapt the great bases of it to France.

" But on this occasion it was amongst the popular deputies, then all powerful, that he encountered obstacles as great as those he had hitherto met with in the council of the king. As minister and as writer his language has been always the same.

" The Chamber of Peers," continues Mᵉ. de Stael, " was a project that displeased both parties; the one as reducing the whole noblesse to one hundred or one hundred and fifty families of names known in history, the other as renewing those hereditary distinctions to which so many were entirely hostile; for the whole nation had been deeply wounded by the privileges and pretensions of the nobility.

" M. Necker reasoned in vain with the one and with the other; simple and sincere, he could little prevail over the passions of which selfishness and vanity are the leading springs; and the factious, perceiving that the king, guided by his ministers, was gaining popularity, resolved to deprive him even of his moral influence, after having deprived him of every other.

" All hope of a constitutional monarchy was thus once more lost for France at a time when the nation, as yet unsullied by any very serious crimes, retained its own proper self-esteem, and the esteem of the rest of Europe."

These views of Mᵉ. de Stael I conceive to be very just, and I therefore now leave them to your meditation.

To-morrow I will offer you the general impressions of particular men on this most critical period—men who were actors in the scene; impressions such as arose in their minds at the moment, and therefore highly worthy of your consideration. On such impressions, on their minds and the minds of those around them, in the Assembly and out, hung the fate and fortunes, the joys and sorrows of millions of human beings; for all Europe, and all the world, and ages present and to come, were to be affected by the course that the Revolution was now to take.

LECTURE XVIII.

QUESTION OF MONARCHICAL POWER, AND CONDUCT OF PARTIES.

I must continue, for one lecture more, to exhibit to you the sentiments and opinions of those who took a part in the memorable scene before us. I have already explained to you, why I dwell so long on this particular period, and why I treat it in this particular manner. Before the 14th of July, the Assembly were engaged in a struggle with the crown; after the 5th and 6th of October, they were removed from Versailles to Paris, and were brought too much under the influence of the violent party; but in the interval which we are now considering, between these two periods, if the patriots had but seen the path of wisdom, and the court had acquiesced, or even if the patriots alone had been moderate and firm, France might yet have been saved, and Europe might have been saved, from what they were both to suffer; and the noblest of all causes, the cause of liberty, not been marked by those outrages and crimes, which can never cease to be lamented by all, who wish well to the best interests of mankind.

Among those who were distinguished at this particular era, it is impossible to overlook Bailly, the philosophic mayor of Paris. The observations of such a man, on this occasion, are particularly deserving of regard. He was, as I have already described to you, a man of intelligence, of patriotism, and virtue; and yet, though he seems to have been aware of the nature of the people, he never carried his reasonable apprehensions into practice, nor ever laboured for a proper establishment of executive power. Such being the patriot and the man, I consider his example as one among many others, that are highly edifying.

" This memorable day," says Bailly, " of the 14th of July, was scarcely over, when other memorable days succeeded. The Assembly, however, in the midst of its anxieties, returned to its labours. The great point was the constitution, but how to begin or proceed, if every one was to be heard? The diversity of objects, the confusion of different opinions, how were such wishes and opinions to be reconciled, in any moderate portion of time, on questions so profound, and amid interests so weighty? Pétion proposed a committee of eight, who were to trace out a plan of a constitution, and then submit it to the Assembly: this was agreed to. It was a question, whether a declaration should be inserted in the scheme of the constitution, or placed before it. It was insisted, that the laws to which liberty must be subjected, should be laid down before liberty was produced and established in its mere principles; that men must be taught how to enjoy liberty in a social state: liberty may otherwise be the destruction of men, and destroy itself. It were to be wished," says Bailly, writing in February, 1792, nearly two years after, " that the Assembly had been controlled by considerations of this kind, and that it had perceived, that provisions must be made to supply the place of the barriers that it was going to remove.

" The meaning of the Assembly, at least so I believed at the time," says Bailly, " was to withdraw the existing constitution from its foundations, and to place it on those that were more solid and lasting. If the scheme of Barrere de Vieusac had been followed, and the principal articles only decreed *provisionally,* the Revolution would have been less complete, but we should have been saved from the anarchy which threatens the constitution, and has so long threatened it." These are admissions that are now remarkable. " But one must admire," says he, " the Assembly, deliberating in the midst of such scenes of horror (the July of 1789), discussing with calmness and consideration, and then pronouncing the oracles of wisdom.

" Among the eight members," says he, " of the committee, the chief were Talleyrand, Lally Tollendal, Clermont de Tonnerre, Mounier, and the Abbé Sieyes.

" These were to be supplied by eight others, among whom were La Fayette, Mirabeau, Bailly, Rabaud de St. Etienne, and Pétion.

" It was in the midst of the anxiety and terror of the celebrated 14th of July, that, with much of a Roman firmness, the Assembly were occupied on the subject of their rights as men and as citizens, and that La Fayette first proposed his declaration of them: this was the groundwork of all that followed. The subject was considered on the 1st of August and the 4th, and the declaration, that is now a preface to the constitution of

1791, was selected from many others, particularly from those presented by La Fayette, Sieyes, and Mounier: it was adopted on the 27th.

"In this Assembly, Mounier," he says, "read a project from the committee of the constitution." He now alludes to the committee of five. "He expressed," says he, "those manifest truths, that are a lesson to the Assembly, and to the king: 'That when the government does not clearly emanate from the will of the people, there is no constitution.' We have in France, therefore," says Bailly, "no constitution, but we have some fundamental laws, monarchy, the hereditary nature of the crown, &c. &c. We must have a constitution, that determines precisely the rights of the nation, and of the king; this constitution cannot be found in a despotism royal, nor in a feudal aristocracy, nor in a liberty without restraint; which last would place an arbitrary power in the multitude, which would but lead to anarchy, and that to despotism, which always follows in its train, to reunite and devour whatever has been thus torn in pieces."

You will now note attentively what Bailly observes upon this Declaration of the Rights of Man.

"M. Mounier," says Bailly, "prefaced his scheme of a constitution by a declaration of rights, but thought as I did, that they should go together. Abstract and philosophic ideas, if not accompanied by a statement of the consequences intended, allow people to suppose other consequences than those which are afterwards to be admitted by the Assembly. Such," he continues, "was the event. This precipitate publication of rights gave occasion to an infinity of misapplications and usurpations, and when these were to be stopped, when the violators of order were to be stripped of their imagined rights, the multitude resisted. We had to meet force opposed to us, and a sort of right acquired in opposition to the law. The law itself was perceived to be without support; order could not be re-established but by means difficult in themselves, uncertain in their success, and that cost us much. This anarchy, defended by the multitude, who rejoiced in it, has had consequences of which one cannot yet see the duration or the result; one must hope, that it will not be despotism."

This remarkable sentence was probably written in 1792, when it was now too late. Bailly, like his friends, was no doubt too sanguine originally, and yet he seems often to have acted contrary to his better judgment, and to have had a great notion of the authority due to public opinion. He afterwards notices the difference that existed between his own sentiments and those of Lally Tollendal.

"Lally Tollendal," he says, "had with him the example of England, where the royal prerogative, and the rights of the barons, were made sacred, along with those of the people." With Bailly and his friends there were no rights sacred but those of the people: observe then his statement. "Myself," he says, " and the rest of us, *we* were more for the assertion of the great principles of society. If we succeed, reason is with us, and we shall have done better ; but if we fail, we shall have lost an opportunity that can never be recovered, and we shall have lost the happiness of France."

These are remarkable words to be used by so celebrated an actor in the scene : for the question now is, whether the happiness of France was not lost, and lost, as Bailly here himself declares, that it was *possible* it might be lost. What need of so perilous an experiment ? it may now be asked; but how feeble at the time, in August 1798, would have been an expostulation like this !

From Bailly we will now turn to the Marquis de Ferrieres, one of the most respectable of the high party, as Bailly is of the low. In his second book, he gives an account of the communication made by Mounier to the Assembly, from the committee of the constitution, in the sitting of the 9th of July. He mentions what were the very reasonable wishes of Mounier, that the deliberations of the Assembly on such a subject as the constitution, affecting the happiness of twenty-five millions of men, should not be precipitated, but should be continued from week to week, three general sittings in each, but he objects to Mounier, the rashness and expediency of his notions, in their origin and from the first, on this great subject of a constitution. The Marquis de Ferrieres, though a sensible, virtuous man, was, you will recollect, of the order of the nobility, and never makes sufficient distinction between men, who though of popular opinions, were of very different popular opinions : a most common species of mistake or injustice this. He is quite unfair, for instance, to Mounier. What I am going to read to you, he addresses to that excellent man ; I would rather address it to the more ardent friends of liberty who thwarted Mounier.

"It is impossible," says the Marquis, "not to reproach Mounier for not having sufficiently reflected on the danger of placing a great people, arrived at a state of civilization, which has advanced their intelligence, developed their passions, and affected every man with the vice of selfishness, a people so corrupted, a people among whom the inequality of fortune and condition had left many without any interest in the community, or chance of procuring any—it is impossible, I say, not to reproach him for placing a great people like this out of the reach of all laws of restraint. What are we to say to Mounier for reporting it to be in a state of nature; for considering it as if now in the infancy of society, and that for the sake of giving it a constitution, and one different to that under which it has lived for fourteen hundred years: without examining whether a people like this is fit for such a constitution; without examining whether it has not now sunk into such a state of degeneracy, that it can only be suited by a government which, though just and moderate, shall be firm and active; and competent to repress this ignorant fermentation, a fermentation which can only lead to the dissolution of society itself; without examining whether this new constitution is accommodated to the manners, to the political situation of a people surrounded by nations civilized and corrupted like itself? It is impossible," says the Marquis de Ferrieres, "not to reproach Mounier with not having sufficiently reflected on what must be the consequence of thus fatally destroying all ancient principles, habits, and prejudices, and of abandoning to the influence of an order of things, whose laws no longer exist, a multitude of men that have hitherto lived but in their intrigues and their vices, totally removed from all the purity and virtue of the primitive man, such as he is supposed to be in a state of nature; men, on the contrary, hitherto kept in order, and with difficulty, only by a vigilant police.

"Mounier ought to have known," he continues, "that the interval that must elapse before laws could be re-established, however short it might be, would open a wide field for the ambitious, for the speculations of the wild, and the machinations of the bad. The whole of the constitution, therefore, should have been presented gradually, and each part in succession, so that the people should have seen in these alterations only reforms, however they might, in fact, have been receiving a real constitution; that in obeying the new laws they should have believed themselves ruled by the old; for as to laws, it is quite necessary that the people should have been long in the habit of respecting them; their origin, like that of illustrious families, should be lost in the obscurity of ages. True, there was no need of announcing a new constitution, it was only necessary to re-establish that which had existed in France for fourteen hundred years; to disengage it from the abuses with which it was encumbered; to reform it in those points where the difference of times and circumstances made a change expedient; to pursue the track which had been pointed out to us by our mandates; they were, in truth, the expression of the general will. In this way, and after this manner, might the constitution have been established, and upon the basis which the committee proposed; no obstacle would have been encountered, and everything would have remained in a state of peace and order: but the philosophers, the intriguers, the men of ambition, were determined on a Revolution; they were determined to realize,—some their senseless systems, others the unbounded hopes which they had conceived."

These views and reasonings of the Marquis de Ferrieres must appear to men of reflection at the present moment, in the abstract at least, sufficiently just and wise. I must repeat, however, that he does not sufficiently distinguish Mounier and his friends from the other patriots; his observations should have been rather addressed to the latter; and he takes no notice of any difficulties in the case before him. Mounier was obliged to make sacrifices to the opinions of others; and so far were the generality of the friends of liberty at the time from relishing such notions as these expressed by the marquis, that to them appeared more reasonable the elevated sentiments of La Fayette, " that for a people to love liberty, it was only necessary that they should know it; and to be free, that they should will to be so."

Ferrieres afterwards alludes, at some length, to the discussions that took place on the great subjects of the veto and the two chambers.

" The popular party," he says, " were afraid that the king would exercise his veto, if given to him, on the decrees of the night of the 4th of August, and the same popular party were unwilling to be checked in their schemes of a total renovation of the government, and they thought they might be so checked by the existence of a second house of legislature. This was a fault in those among them who meant well," says the marquis: " the second house might have been composed, and would have been most evidently and naturally composed, of the two orders, formed in the case of the National Assembly, and then thrown into one house; or a senate might have been contrived according to the plan of Mounier and Lally; but their exertions, and they made every possible exertion, were in vain. The more violent of the popular party made it their business to deride the senate and the senators; and those of the nobility, who considered the minority of their order, who had joined the Tiers Etat, as having betrayed them, unhappily indulged their sentiments of hatred and vengeance on this occasion, and joined in rejecting the projects of the two chambers. It was in vain that Lally mounted the tribune, and that Mounier (this is a very curious fact) went from rank to rank, assuring the deputies of the commons, that the nobles and the aristocrats, who resisted the measure, did so only that the Revolution might fail. Every effort within doors and without was vain, and the decision was at last made, eight hundred and forty-nine to eighty-nine, almost ten to one."

After Bailly and Ferrieres, I will now turn to this most respectable patriot, who has just been mentioned, to Mounier.

The sentiments of Mounier, who was, as you may have perceived for some time, one of the most distinguished leaders of the Revolution, are such as, from what you have heard of his character, and of his projects of a constitution, might be expected. I will give you a short quotation from his book; observe it well. He means, no doubt, to describe the causes of the *failure* of the Revolution, and he is great authority. He had originally materially contributed to the formation of the National Assembly.

" I am far," says he, afterwards, in his work printed in 1792, at Geneva, p. 233, " I am far from priding myself on the efforts I then made. Like so many others, the friends of humanity, I was guilty of the fault of having hopes too sanguine; but what had passed in my own province had contributed to delude and betray me, when I reflected on all that we had obtained in Dauphiny by the mere force of justice and reason ; I now see, how I was led on to believe that the French, in like manner, might deserve to be free. The lower classes of the people in my own province awaited calmly the result of our labours ; never had the multitude any influence on our assemblies, the spectators restrained themselves always within the bounds of decency ; our votes were perfectly free ; the clergy and the nobility showed themselves generous, the commons moderate; many of those who now distinguish themselves in Dauphiny by their zeal for new institutions, were not then, as now, the vile agents of despotism ; there was nothing then to indicate that they would one day seduce and deceive the multitude, so as even to make the people suppose that they were attached to

liberty. Some, indeed, of the members of our states had endeavoured to gain celebrity by ranking themselves as enemies of
the throne, but in general their opinions were my own : they
published in favour of the two houses ; they tempered the effervescence of hot-headed men ; and they told the people, that
there was no arriving at liberty, unless they knew how to limit
their desires, and not make the advantages they obtained pretexts for requiring more."

Mounier, as I have just intimated to you, is here, no doubt,
describing the great causes which he thought, whatever might
be their origin, contributed to the failure of the Revolution.

"Many persons," he afterwards observes in a note, " have
blamed me for the Declaration of Rights. I did every thing I
could to resist this project ; I presented one to the committee,
in which I took care to insert no article that I thought dangerous. I had done better, no doubt, to have maintained, as
did some of the deputies, that *all* abstract ideas on the rights of
man admitted into legislation might be exposed to misinterpre-
tation, and produce the most unhappy consequences."

Afterwards in his work he argues with great earnestness
against any suspensive veto in the king, and contends for the
power absolute and unlimited.

"The States General," says he, (note, p. 8) " owed their
very existence to an act of the king : their deliberations could
have no force without his free consent, and every friend to
royalty should have acknowledged, without any reservation
whatever, the necessity of the free consent of the king, even to
the very decrees that related to the constitution.

" How rapid," says he, " has been the progress of the degradation of the royal power since the establishment of this suspensive veto : before, the representatives of the people, even in
their acts of menace, had been humbled in their supplications,
and called themselves the subjects of the king ; but from the
moment that they had reserved to themselves the legislative
power, the monarch was to be designated under the title of ' the
executive power,' a title which could only indicate a subordinate
magistracy, of which the legislative body could modify the rights
or even pronounce the extinction, as of any other subaltern employment. .From this moment, in every publict act the king
was not named till after the Assembly, and the ministers themselves submitted to adopt a language like this, so injurious to
the crown.

" The suspensive veto prepared the minds of men to see the

decisions of the king, and the orders which he gave the administrative bodies, submitted to the examination of the Assembly, which could annul them in consequence of their supreme power; it prepared the minds of men to see him excluded from all participation in the laws relative to the imposts, and in all changes in them relative to the constitution; it has demolished the throne, and substituted for the throne nothing but a mere simple seat by the side of the president, who is to treat the king as his equal on public occasions of ceremony, and as his inferior on every other.

"The absolute veto left the king in possession of a great part of his sovereignty; the suspensive made him at once a subject.

"It is no matter of wonder," he goes on to say, "that the majority of the committee of the constitution attached such great importance to the absolute veto; and if the royalists who were there (he is speaking of himself and his friends) gave in their resignation, when they found that the legislative body was to consist of one chamber only, that the Assembly was to be permanent, and the veto of the king suspensive, it was only because, after such a triumph of the democratic party, there was no alternative left, but to contribute to the destruction of the throne, or discontinue their labours."

Such were the sentiments of this reasonable and virtuous patriot, when he contemplated, in his retirement, a short time afterwards, the scenes in which he had been engaged.

I will now turn to the works of the more violent men on each side, to Bertrand de Moleville, of the court party, and M. de Bailleul, of the democratic party.

Bertrand de Moleville takes notice of the transactions of the period we are now considering, much in the way you would expect.

"Jacobinism," says he, "has formed the sovereignty of the people into a principle, in order to make it the rallying cry of rebellion, and the essential dogma of revolution."

And again. "The factious, whose intention it was to annihilate the monarchy, took great care not to let it be known that their object was to seize the supreme power themselves. It is to you, say they to the multitude, it is to you that the sovereignty belongs, from you it has been usurped; there was people before there were kings; kings were made by the people, therefore it is you who are the sovereign, and all we want is to restore you to your rights.

"Those," he continues, "who combated these sophisms were by far too metaphysical in their reasonings. The principle of sovereignty, they said, is in the people, but the exercise of the sovereignty must be always separated from the principle. The people are to discover it only in a visible and commanding representation, which impresses them with obedience." Bertrand may object to this reasoning, but I know of no other possible.

Bertrand de Moleville then produces his own theory and reasonings, which are also both long and metaphysical, and would probably not have been more easily understood by the populace than those he rejected. In defiance of them, this populace would have gone on to reason, as he says, they did reason ; the nation is the sovereign, the sovereign is king; we are the nation, and therefore we are king ; and the cry of *Vive le Roi* became *Vive la Nation*.

Certainly this doctrine of the sovereignty of the people, though in itself perfectly just and true, when it means, as in practice it can only mean, that in all government the great justification of rule, restraint, authority, the great end to be accomplished, the great and the only end, is the happiness of the community ; certainly this doctrine was a dangerous doctrine, (and thus much we may concede to Bertrand de Moleville,) to be produced and thrown broad-cast among the people, in the way it was proclaimed by the great leaders of the French Revolution ; and we must allow that from the first it was sure to be interpreted in the manner Bertrand de Moleville describes, and though fatal to the court originally (this it might be), was sure to be afterwards fatal to the patriots themselves. It is, on the whole, a doctrine that might be inscribed with good effect on the chairs of a cabinet council, but not, therefore, on the tribunes of a popular assembly.

Our author goes on to describe the efforts of the Palais Royal to reign over the assembly at the crisis we are now considering, and much in the way we have seen them described in the Memoirs we have just alluded to. I will, however, give you a specimen. "The anonymous letter," says he, "which the president received was couched in these words : ' The Patriotic Assembly of the Palais Royal have the honour to make it known to you, that if the aristocratic faction formed by some of the nobility, clergy, and one hundred and twenty ignorant and corrupt members, continue to disturb the general harmony, and still insist upon the absolute assent, fifteen thousand men are ready to enlighten their country seats and houses, and particularly your own.'

"The heads of the motion," he says, "delivered to M. Lally were, ' We are arrived at the critical moment of French liberty (this was but too true), we think it time to recall several of our deputies: they may be impeached after their recall; the veto does not belong to one man, but to twenty-five millions. It has been unanimously resolved to go immediately to Versailles, as well to put a stop to the aristocratic effervescence there, as to protect the lives of the worthy deputies, which are in danger.' Such was the sort of manifesto presented to M. Lally." These were pretty strong symptoms, no doubt; of the movements that were afterwards to be expected, and that actually took place; and though these letters might be dismissed with contempt, as they were by a majority of the Assembly, they should have been the signal to all, who meant well, to rally round the king and the executive power immediately, and with all their strength. To Bertrand it appeared, and I think with reason, that the king should have accepted no veto unless the power of dissolving the Assembly was granted him.

And indeed this power, as it existed at the time in the example of the English constitution, should have been the point contended for, if necessary, by the king, or rather should have been from the first proposed by the patriots. To have the veto without the power of dissolving the Assembly, was only to be exposed to a combat without the means of defence. Bertrand de Moleville is a writer that you must read attentively, and I need not further allude to him. If you do not read him, you will never know the case of the court.

I will now refer to M. de Bailleul, who drew up his work expressly to confute what he considered the errors of M^e. de Stael. He is a very good representative of the most violent patriots of these times; decisive, able, authoritative; very ready with sweeping statements, little affected by difficulties, contemptuous of the privileged orders, and considerably unfeeling. In his pages you will always find the democratic view of the question when you wish to know it; as in Bertrand you see that of the court. He forms, as you may suppose, a very different estimate of such questions as we have been considering, and of the situation of France during these important months, in the middle of the year 1789. "The short explanation of the events of the Revolution," says he (vol. i. p. 244), is this: "a nation chooses to have laws and liberty; its government refuses; but the supreme power placed, as it happened to be, under the influence of a well-meaning minister, like M. Necker, shows symptoms that are favourable and encouraging. Hopes are therefore entertained by the nation: the one has, however, promised more

than it exactly meant to give, and the other has pushed its pretensions further ; calling for its rights and for justice ; a struggle
ensues ; force is produced : it is impossible to retreat without
being in a worse situation than ever, at least such is the apprehension ; and so the nation rushes onward into a profound
abyss, which, indeed, could not have been avoided even if the
nation had foreseen it." Such is the account of Bailleul. But
this is rather a description of the facts than an estimate of what
might and ought to have been the conduct of the parties.
" How," he continues, " does M^e. de Stael torment herself, to
show in what a thousand different ways M. de Necker would
have directed, retarded, or modified the Revolution ; as if to scat-
ter a few handfuls of dust were sufficient to disperse two armies
already in presence of each other, and who have begun to engage."

This, we contend, in opposition to reasoners like M. de Bailleul, is not a proper statement of the case. The question rather
is, first, whether the parties cannot be prevented from assuming
the form and character of armies disposed to engage ; and secondly, what is the one army, what is the popular party to do,
when the other, the king and the court, has declined or given
up the combat, has been unable or unwilling to contend. Wisdom
too, and the counsels of peace and kindness, may not at the time
have been heard, though breathed by M. Necker and other good
men, by the Lallys and the Mouniers of the period ; but it
does not thence follow that they ought not to have been, or as
M. de Bailleul supposes, that they might not have been ; and it
is the business of those who speculate on the events of history,
to mark these wild and senseless movements of the passions of
mankind, and to hold them up as a warning to those who are to
come after ; not to vote them inevitable and irresistible. All
reason and reasoning are at an end, as M^e. de Stael has observed,
if everything that leads to violence and revolution is, after the
manner of democratic thinkers, to be thus voted inevitable.
" The moment," says M. de Bailleul (247), " that the monarch
took refuge in the ranks of the privileged orders, and that an
army was in march to dissolve the National Assembly, as Necker
was informed, and as M^e. de Stael agrees, nothing but extremities were to be expected."

The king, however, it must be observed, never did, even on
the 14th of July, properly speaking, take refuge in the ranks of
the privileged orders. And again,—the National Assembly,
long before, were the first to encroach upon his authority, and
if nothing but extremes were to be expected in the case of the

14th of July, as thus described, this was owing originally to the mistake or the fault of the patriots, not to any meritorious conduct that can be ascribed to them, in this instance at least.

"The 14th of July did not," he afterwards observes (249), "overthrow the monarchy, as M*e*. de Stael supposes; it only purified it, and prepared it for a new existence?" How is this? it will be said. "Because," says M. de Bailleul, "the court, instructed by this terrible experience, had only to adopt, with sincerity, the principles which afterwards could alone bear sway in France."

Now the question is, whether the patriots made their terms such, that it was possible they could be received by either the court or the king, with the sincerity here required.

"Every one," continues M. de Bailleul, "should, according to M*e*. de Stael, be in full possession of his rights, or what chance for his sincerity?" It is curious to observe what will here be the answer of M. de Bailleul; it is this:

"But was the king then," he says, "in the possession of his rights, when in the midst of the people of a court, rebels both to the real interests of his throne and to the wishes of the nation? Was he then in possession of them; or was he not rather in possession of them when in the midst of his people (the good people of Paris, you will observe), who only required him to acknowledge those rights (that is his own rights) and to maintain them?"

This is the sort of unfeeling declamation which everywhere pervades the work of M. de Bailleul, as it must have done the conversation and writings of all violent men at the time. But again,—no doubt M. de Bailleul is at issue with us on the great fact of the whole case, whether the court and the old régime were still the main object to be dreaded. "Three descriptions of opinion," says he (299), "existed, according to M*e* de Stael, in the bosom of the Assembly: the partisans of the ancient régime, the partisans of the royal prerogative, and the demagogues. Now these last," says he, "were always from the first the majority. It was amongst these that in fact were found the men of talents and enlightened minds. Indeed? The second were but a handful (he must here allude to Mounier and his friend), their intentions were good, their objects laudable, but they deluded themselves about the facts. It was not true that the Revolution had disarmed the partisans of the old régime; these men still deliberated in the councils of the king; they still had all the employments and disposed of the public force

(M. de Bailleul seems here to forget the 14th of July and the
events of it).   The patriots could not possibly withdraw themselves from the consideration of circumstances so real as these ;
they therefore rejected all propositions that were too favourable
to the royal authority, not that they meant to overthrow the
royal authority, but that while that authority was placed under
aristocratic influence, they trembled to give it an independence
of the Assembly, which it appeared likely to use, even at the
very moment against liberty."

This, in opposition to M. de Bailleul, we must contend, was
a mistake.   No doubt the king, though benevolent and patriotic,
wanted character ; no doubt his advisers (the court and its followers) were unfavourable to the Revolution ; but this is no
sufficient reason why the Assembly should have rejected all
propositions, not only those too favourable, but those that were
at all favourable to the royal authority ; that they should act, at
least, whatever they might intend, as if they really did mean to
overthrow it ; that they should not only tremble to give it an
independence of the Assembly, but that they should leave it no
power that was not at the mercy of the Assembly ; that they
should make no terms, and should enter into no composition
with the old opinions ; that they should not see that in August,
September, and October, 1789 (I am speaking of the period
before me, not of any period prior), the court and the old
régime were not so much the proper objects of terror as the
popular party and the new opinions, whose victory on the 14th
of July was complete.   But you must read Bailleul all through
the History of the Revolution, when you wish to know the
democratic view and representation of the case.

A word now in reference to Mirabeau.   It is but justice to
Mirabeau to say, that he seems at this particular period to have
seen the difficulties of the situation of the patriots.   He insisted
upon a veto for the king, but his own personal ambition was
unhappily in the way of the project of the two houses, perhaps
too an inordinate fear of the returning power of the crown.   In
his Courier de Provence, he observes, " Truth would command
me to say every thing, wisdom to temporize.   On the one side,
for the sake of justice, we are to burst through and disregard
the timid expostulations of prudence ; but on the other, the fear
of exciting a fermentation that may be dangerous, will reasonably alarm those who do not choose to buy the welfare of posterity at the price of calamity for the existing generation.   With
the philosopher who labours for the future as for the present,

with him, indeed, circumspection may be weakness, and the
tolerance of abuses prevarication; but it is not so with the
statesman, who, in the first place, must act for the present; he
will not give arms to the people till he has taught them how
they are to be used, lest in their first paroxysms, the people
should be only agitated with fury, turn them against each other,
and abandon them with remorse and terror.

" It is necessary, therefore," continues Mirabeau, " that a
declaration of rights should be promulgated only in conjunction
with the constitution, of which it is to be the foundation; that
the principles of liberty should be accompanied by the laws
which are to direct its exercise. Upon the people, one should
act in every way at once: upon their minds, to enlighten them;
their passions, to restrain them; their sentiments and feelings,
to temper their bitterness, and to inspire them with a hope of
better things." These, the views of Mirabeau, are the views of
a man of sense and reflection; and in his speech to the Assembly, when he had to speak as a member of the committee of
constitution, there was nothing of confidence or presumption.
He seemed quite aware of the incurable nature of human dissent, of the difficulty of coming to right decisions, of the danger
of coming to none, when so many had to propose their opinions.

I will digress for a moment. There is a remarkable paragraph, and one somewhat amusing on the subject of committees,
which any one who has attended them will know how to appreciate. " One man," says he, " offers to a committee the result
of his reflections, another proposes retrenchments of the plan, a
third additions, and so on, till there is no longer any plan or
coherence left. And yet one must submit, for the very first
duty of a committee is to produce a report, in which all are
agreed. In all human circumstances and affairs," says he, " I
know but of one in which despotism is not only good but necessary—it is so in a committee; to make it digest and do something."

Mirabeau was never without his sense of the necessity of
order, or even his attachment to the royal power; but on some
account or other, the want of skill in the court, his dread of their
returning power, his want of timely prudence, the rashness of
his ambition, on some or on all of these accounts he put not forth
his strength at the proper time in favour of the executive power,
and never properly united with the first more wise and sound
patriots of the Assembly, when it was possible, that with his
assistance, they might have prevailed.

His great mistake seems to have been that he supposed a king might be left alone with his people to settle every thing to their mutual advantage, and that there was no necessity for the intervention of any aristocracy; no necessity to surround a monarch with natural defenders, and furnish the people with safe leaders.

An annual assembly, an annual army, annual taxes, responsibility of ministers, and an absolute veto in the crown, which might be absolute in theory, as he said, but could never be so in practice; these were his views: two chambers of legislation, if they were but two sections of one and the same chamber, for the purposes of more complete deliberation; but only one, rather than have two and leave each to exercise a veto on the other, which would end, he thought, either in collision or inaction:— views these of too democratic a nature at any time, but entirely out of the question on the supposition, then accepted and reasoned upon, that France was to remain a monarchy.

These general references and quotations will serve, I hope, sufficiently to give you some notion of the sentiments and opinions of, the different descriptions of men and of patriots that existed in France during these very critical weeks that intervened between the middle of July 1789, and the beginning of October.

And now, while I am concluding my lecture, I must again remind you, that the period that elapsed between the middle of July and middle of October 1789, was the interval during which all reasonable hope of the peaceful success of the Revolution was lost. It is, therefore, that interval which should, I think, be most particularly studied; studied by those who are friends to liberty, and who will always find it so difficult to restrain their ardour and limit their expectations, when engaged in their animating cause. I dwell, therefore, on this part of the subject, and repeat the same lessons again and again; and I exhibit the faults to which patriotic men and patriotic assemblies are exposed, not for the purpose of reconciling you to despotism, but from the hope of teaching you how best to escape from it. I must again and again remind you, that the mistakes of arbitrary rulers, the greater or less quantity of oppression or harsh government which they exercise are, within certain bounds, of little comparative import to the general stability of their own cause: advantage cannot be taken of their errors and faults by the friends of freedom so readily and with such effect. But it is not so with those who are endeavouring to establish the rights of mankind and the civil happiness of the community : their golden opportunities are like angel visits, short and far between ; and if they seize them not and improve them not to the utmost, if they do not even exercise virtues of a most high and some-times almost of an inconsistent and contradictory nature, caution in the midst of enthusiasm, and forbearance and conciliation in the midst of a high sense of indignation and wrong, all is lost.

The purport then of this part of my present course of lectures is to warn you of the possible mistakes of men of elevated and generous natures, of men of ardent and sanguine minds, of men, of young men more particularly (they were almost all young men that took a lead in this Revolution), of men of presumptu-ous and conceited understandings, such is naturally the character (I mean not to offend), but such is naturally the character of men at an early period of life, especially when they are men of talents ; such men, as in the instance of France before us, and in any other instance that can be expected to arise, will always start up from society, the supporters of new opinions, the scoffers of prejudices and antiquated notions, the patrons of sweeping measures and daring experiments ; and they will undertake to manage mankind as they would the pieces on their chess-boards ; and suppose that what is clear to their own particular understandings, must necessarily be so to that of the com-munity ; and conceive that when a reasonable doctrine or system, or what appears such to themselves, has once been held up to the acceptance of men, no further difficulty remains.

The fact is always otherwise ; and, if the system which the patriots adopt has not been from the first one of compromise and conciliation, opposition, determined opposition, is engendered ; the multitude are then to be called in, the violent prevail ; and for the early patriots, and for the friends of peace and order, there is no longer any hope ; they find that they become un-popular, they lose their power.

> ———" Carceribus sese effudêre quadrigæ,
> Addunt se in spatia : et frustra retinacula tendens
> Fertur equis auriga, neque audit currus habenas."

I must now conclude ; but I must make one parting observa-tion on the noblesse of France at this period, which will enable me to do equal justice to all parties, and exercise my censure (such as it is) on both the descriptions of offenders that appeared in these memorable scenes.

It is melancholy then to reflect upon the conduct of the no-

bility, during these discussions on the constitution ; what chance
for them, what chance for the king, what chance for their country, even according to their own particular notions, but in the
formation of two houses ?   Yet mark now their miserable
jealousies and small views.   From the superabundant noblesse of
France, only a small portion could be chosen to form an upper
chamber ; those, who saw no chance of their being themselves
elected, were against the measure of two houses.   Some imagined
that the forty-seven who had first joined the Tiers Etat would
be first promoted to the upper house, and this again was intolerable ; and of the rest too many of the higher orders, who
were enemies to the Revolution in any form, thought that such
a regulation would give stability to it, and prevent that discord,
precipitancy, and anarchy, of which they already saw the seeds
and the beginnings in the present Assembly, and from which
they augured its overthrow and the restoration of the old régime.

The question was, therefore, lost by an immense majority :
the higher orders and the royalists voted *against* the two chambers, uniting with their enemies ; and this conduct of the noblesse, which was the destruction of France, is but too much the
conduct of privileged orders at all times and in all countries :
they can never rise superior to the temptations of their situation,
whether in religion or politics ; and the well-wisher to the civil
and religious liberties of mankind, the historian or the philosopher, who comes afterwards to weigh them in his balance, loses all
his proper calmness and consideration, and in the impatience of
his indignation, when public disorder and ruin have been the
consequence, pronounces them to be as selfish, contracted, and
improvident in their notions, as the lowliest of the rabble which
surround their carriages in the streets.

The mistake of the noblesse, to which I have just alluded,
was not only one very obvious and very unpardonable, but it
was a late one.   They and the court had already made their
mistakes before, and they now repeated them ; but the people
also and the popular leaders had now to make their mistakes,
and I think, as we have just seen, they did make them.   I
speak not of bad and wicked men, such as will always be found,
such as must always be taken into all calculations in political
affairs : I speak of men of enlightened minds and patriotic feelings, such as I have no right to suppose meant ill to their country.   To these men, the patriotic leaders of 1789, and to the
privileged orders who preceded them in their mistakes, to both
descriptions of men the words of Mr. Burke, in one of his cele-

brated passages, are strictly applicable, and were not only a lesson to them which they ought to have observed, but they are also a memorable lesson to those who are to come after them; for a sort of conflict between old and new opinions in the history of this world of ours will never cease.

"Early reformations," says Burke, in a well-known paragraph in his well-known speech on economical reform, "are amicable arrangements with a friend in power; late reformations are terms imposed upon a conquered enemy. Early reformations are made in cold blood; late reformations are made under a state of inflammation. In that state of things the people behold in government nothing that is respectable; they see the abuse, and they will see nothing else."

Weighty words these, and universally applicable; uttered many years before, and prophetic, if applied to France; for the privileged orders never could see the wisdom of early reformations, and the patriotic leaders (too many of them) could afterwards behold in government nothing that was respectable. They saw the abuse, as Mr. Burke says, and would see nothing else. "They fell into the temper," as he continues, "of a furious populace, provoked at the disorder of a house of ill fame: they never attempted to correct or regulate; they went to work by the shortest way: they abated the nuisance, they pulled down the house."

LECTURE XIX.

FIFTH AND SIXTH OF OCTOBER.

In the three last lectures, I have endeavoured to draw your attention to the period that intervened between the 14th of July and the beginning of October 1789. I have endeavoured to place it before you in every point of view: the different questions that were then discussed, the different opinions that were then expressed; and I have done this at great length (reckless of any charge of tediousness and repetition), on account of what I believe to be the importance of the lessons that this period offers to all who are disposed to engage in public concerns, more especially to the friends of freedom. During this period, had Mounier and his friends been properly supported, the Revolution might have been adjusted upon a system of mutual sacrifices, conciliation, and peace; but the opportunity was lost. No proper terms were kept with the king and with the court. The friends of freedom, some of them, still entertained their terror of the return of arbitrary power, while others of them were animated with hopes of a new order of things, more favourable, as they thought, to liberty, but evidently of a nature far too vague and unqualified, far too democratic to be admitted into a system like that of the French monarchy, without much positive injustice, great violence, the certainty of much commotion, and the hazard of a civil war.

Now these I conceive to have been serious mistakes made by the friends of freedom on this occasion in the one way and in the other; and I am now, you will observe, speaking only of those men who are entitled to our respect, those who meant well, who supposed that they were friends to their country and mankind. I speak not of daring, selfish, unprincipled men, such as always come forward on occasions of public agitation : I speak not of those; of such men it is in vain to speak; I am directing my observations to those who were too full of their own opinions to respect those of others; who expected too much from the influence of truth and reason; who considered not the perilous and uncertain nature of all political dissensions; who were too sanguine to be wise. Men like these will, as I conceive, always exist : nay, more; unless men of generous minds and ardent temperaments are continually found in society, freedom cannot be maintained in it. No point, therefore, can be a point of greater anxiety than to teach men like these, the temptations of their situation; to warn them, by the example of a period like this in the French Revolution, that they are to keep a guard upon their very virtues and upon some of the most indispensable and highest qualities of their nature. In revolutions, the history is always much the same. There are those of warm passions, of ready eloquence, of fearless minds : these are the men who put a revolution into motion; dangerous from the very elevation of their characters, from the very purity of their enthusiasm; young men, for the most part, caught by novelty, disposed to experiment, offensive by their presumption, and who turn away with contempt from what are proposed to them as the lessons of experience. These are found on the *one* side ; and on the *other* are ranged those more advanced in age, more especially those of the privileged orders, accustomed to a certain routine of duties and opinions, and too much disposed to consider, as still in existence, those sentiments and prejudices, good and bad, which, amid the changes of the world, *may* have passed away.

Now, between these descriptions of men stand the men of intelligence and reflection, too young for the one, too old for the
other; who are by nature, as by wisdom, placed between the
two, and whose wish and whose labour it will be to conciliate
and to harmonize, to estimate and to provide at once for the
past, the present, and the future. But what will naturally be the
fate of such men? Belonging not to the violent on either side,
they will persuade neither, they will displease both; they will
fail, they will be disappointed; they will be found in the company of the first that come forward while the revolution is
ripening, but they will be also among the first who will have to
retire or perish, if the revolution proceeds.

Such may be in general the melancholy history of revolutions;
but the question is, ought these things to be so? This may be
indeed the history, but *ought* this to be the history?

Democratic writers continually speak as if there was a progress in these affairs totally inevitable. Such, since I have drawn
up these lectures, I have found to be the language even of the
late able writers, Mignet and Thiers, in their Histories of the
French Revolution. That it is in vain for the men of wisdom
and counsel to raise their voice when revolutions are begun;
that the wind bloweth as it listeth; that the wind becomes a
storm, and the storm a hurricane, raging till the air be purified:
this is their excuse for the measures of violence and guilt that
too often occur. But reverse the picture, and the same is the
reasoning of writers whose principles are those of an opposite
and arbitrary cast; and it is *their* excuse, on the contrary, for
listening to *no* projects of reform, and for ruling men from the
first by mere force and authority; not perceiving, that it is for
them at all times to consider whether what is proposed be
just and reasonable or not; to concede nothing indeed to fear,
but every thing to reason.

It is for those who read history, above all, for those who comment upon history, to resist these sweeping conclusions on the
one side and on the other, these doctrines of despair, these views
of human nature, that can lead to nothing but slavery on the one
side, or bloodshed and anarchy on the other. Men must be
called upon to observe the mistakes and the crimes of those who
went before them; and they must be required to avoid and fly
them, as they are rational creatures, as they are beings " that
look before and after." In like manner, in domestic and social
life, men will be selfish, hard-hearted, licentious, wicked. It
must needs be that offences will come; but it does not follow

that our sages and our divines are not still to labour on, in the
duties of their callings, are not still to cry aloud and spare not.
The cause of human nature must never be abandoned; nor need
it, it may be added, for it can never be sufficiently known or estimated what may have been even the *success* of those, who toil
for the benefit of mankind; because the evils they have prevented
do not appear, and cannot be brought to the credit of their account; while those they have in vain resisted, are seen but too
plainly, and operate against them.

In the history of our own country, in the times of the great
rebellion, Charles I. was so arbitrary and obstinate, and the religious principle got so interwoven into the disputes between the
monarch and his parliaments, that the moderate men, the men of
wisdom and counsel (who had been always, however, far too
torpid), were at last obliged to give way, and a civil war ensued;
but it was not so at the period of the Revolution of 1688; in
this instance they prevailed, and this is the eternal glory of the
Whigs of that era.   What was then done, however, may again
be done; and this splendid instance in the annals of mankind
must ever be of avail to encourage the friends of freedom in their
virtuous struggles, must ever be sufficient to show them that
efforts for the welfare of the community do not necessarily fail;
that resistance to oppression is not necessarily followed by anarchy and civil war; that the friends of their country and of mankind *may* succeed, if they can but to their high virtues add other
virtues that are equally indispensable, though they may at
first sight appear scarcely necessary, and, indeed, to bold and
generous men may always appear virtues of a very lowly and
ordinary nature.   Patience, moderation, modesty of temperament, candour, attention to the feelings of others, to the arguments of their opponents; a disposition to make the ground
solid under them as they go along; a deep sense of the infirmi-
ties of their own nature, and of the irritable nature of the passions of mankind; these are the virtues not less necessary than
those of a more popular nature, to the proper completion of their
character as patriots and reformers.   The union of these qualities is difficult, but a fair object of virtuous ambition; it is
within the reach of human nature, and it may and ought to be
produced.   On the whole, then, of the case, opposite lessons
must be directed to the different portions of the community.
Those in the political system, who in the first place want instruction, are, on the one side, the grave and the old, and the
privileged orders, who will suffer no alteration, and make no

provision for the new circumstances that may have occurred, the changes that time may have operated upon their own community and the world : and, in the second place, are those on the other side, who will make no allowance for what they may esteem the prejudices of others, and who forget that, at all events, reformers must proceed upon a system of conciliation and peace, for if a temperament of this sort once cease, the violent will alone succeed, and they themselves be no longer listened to ; lastly, and above all, that if, when they have the power, they make their terms too hard, their opponents cannot be expected (I speak not of the point of duty, but they cannot in *practice* be expected) to keep good faith with them, and nothing durable or solid will have in reality been accomplished. So was it in France on this present occasion : the friends of freedom did not sufficiently assist Mounier, and the men of moderation and wisdom ; they would not accommodate themselves to what they esteemed the prejudices of their opponents ; they proceeded not sufficiently on a system of peace and conciliation ; they had more splendid views, we will suppose, of the happiness of France and of mankind, and, in a word, they made their terms with the king and court too hard, and their Revolution failed : it could not but fail : and it failed, though the king was not of a temperament to resist them ; was too gentle, and too benevolent : had he been of an ordinary complexion, a civil war would have ensued ; and this also I should call the failure of a revolution, as I do the subsequent disorder and anarchy.

I do not, as I must again repeat, now speak of the licentious, daring, bad men, in the Assembly and out of it, the higher rabble or the lower, which unhappily then existed in Paris. I speak of the first more sanguine and ardent leaders of the Revolution, of those whom I conceive to have meant well, and who cannot be supposed to have meant otherwise, and with whom so many in their own country, and in this country also, at the time entirely sympathized.

But the daring, licentious, and bad men of every description, such as were to be found in Paris at the time, and such as must be always taken into the calculation, when wise and good men speculate upon the affairs of their country—such men found assistants to their wickedness in these first sanguine and unreasonable leaders of the Revolution ; a system of peace and adjustment would have put an end at once to *their* consequence and their hopes ; wicked and bad men would have had no opportunity of appearing ; but the want of character in the king, the want of prudence in the court, and the want of caution and moderation, not to say of moral feeling, and a sense of justice in the more young and able leaders of the Constituent Assembly, gave full play, circumstanced as France was at the opening of the States, and for some time after, to these daring and unprincipled men, and they had full opportunity to display their courage, their ambition, their unfeeling insolence, their lawless fury, their atrocious cruelty.

Paris and France, Paris more particularly, were extremely agitated during all the discussions to which we have alluded during the months of July, August, and September.   Such questions as these " of the two houses," " the permanency of the Assembly," and " the veto of the king," were dreadful questions to be debated in such a place as Paris, when the royal power had just been put down by the people, and their sovereignty proclaimed.

We have already alluded to the manner in which, immediately after the 14th of July, the metropolis became a scene of different assemblies and constituted authorities, all debating at the same time ; each of sixty districts, assuming to itself legislative power, and conferring executive power on its committees ; the manner in which soldiers, tradesmen, artisans, and domestic servants, all in their separate classes and places of rendezvous, were haranguing and disputing (and more particularly at the Palais Royal), discussing and settling the same questions, which occupied the National Assembly ; and to all this unhappy fermentation was to be added a real scarcity, sufficient of itself to have collected the people together in troops and mobs in the streets, ripe for disorder from their sufferings, and ready, however unreasonably, to attribute to the mere fault of the government their want of bread, and the privations and wretchedness to which themselves and their children were exposed.

To talk to a metropolis, in a situation like this, of limits to be assigned to different powers in the state, more especially to their own power, and of the veto of the king, was to speak a language that only irritated them to fury.   They had some confidence in the Assembly, and therefore the Assembly was to do every thing ; in the king they had none, and therefore the king was to do nothing : to give any power to the king and the court was only to restore, as they supposed, the old régime, and to bring on a counter revolution.   A public sentiment in Paris soon vents itself in songs and pasquinades, and the king and queen were sung about the streets as Monsieur and Madame Veto : and this was to be the manner in which the great question of the executive power of the country was to be decided; and menacing letters, as we have already mentioned, were issued from the Palais Royal, to virtuous patriots like Mounier and Lally Tollendal, to tell them that they were to be cashiered, and that the legislators of Paris were about to march against Versailles, and clear away the faithless legislators of the Constituent Assembly. Such is the sad description I have to give of what may be called the more violent party, and of the lower orders of Paris at this particular juncture.

We must now reverse the picture, and turn to the king and the court. On all occasions violence in one direction produces it in another. When the decision of every question in the National Assembly went unfavourably to the executive power, what were to be the feelings of those who were attached to the royal authority? When the Assembly, who were summoned by the king to assist him in reforming the state, assumed all power to themselves, and evidently set the king entirely aside, referred every thing to the sovereignty of the people, and considered themselves as its only legitimate representative;—when to those who spoke of the ancient institutions and established principles of the French monarchy, it was only replied that France was to be now regenerated, that a new constitution was to be given, and that the king was not even to concur in its formation, was not to sanction, but was only to accept it;—when these were to be the results of the experiment, which the king had made in calling the States General, partly, no doubt, from the necessities of the state, but surely from motives of benevolence and patriotism also;—when these were to be the results of his efforts for the general happiness, with what sentiments was the king to be affected, with what sentiments but those of indignation and anger? And what were to be the feelings of his courtiers, and the court, and the privileged orders, who had neither his benevolence nor his patriotism; what but the feelings of horror at the populace, and of hatred of their leaders, rage at the patriots in the Assembly, an abjuration of all measures of change and reform, and thoughts only of an appeal to arms, the succour of foreign powers, and a civil war? How impossible was it that effects of this kind should not be produced in the one party by the hard terms that had been imposed, by the unlimited pretensions that had been advanced by the other! But what was to be done? The royal authority had been produced on the 23rd of June, and the king's system of a constitution offered, in vain.

The soldiery had been drawn out, and force had been all but employed on and before the 14th of July—in vain also. What measure was left? To the court there could appear none but flight and a civil war; this therefore was supposed by the Assembly and the patriots to be the intention of the king; it was concluded that he would retire to Metz, to the Marquis de Bouillé and his army, that he would there summon the nobility and aristocracy of France to his assistance, and what troops yet remained faithful to him; denounce the National Assembly; and if he could not restore the ancient régime, at least establish the system that he had himself proposed in his declaration of the 23rd of June.

And all this reasoning would have not only proceeded very smoothly, but been probably just, both with respect to the court and the king, if the king had been a man of energy and decision; but this was not the case, and it was known not to be the case; and therefore the leaders in the Constituent Assembly could not reasonably believe it to be the case, as far at least as the king was concerned, and were guilty of a great fault, while they acted as if they supposed it to be the case; and the violent and the bad men in and out of the Assembly, with or without believing it, very readily persuaded themselves that for them there was no measure but that of transferring the king and the Assembly to Paris, where both the one and the other might be placed, in fact, under their superintendence and control.

Such is but too often the unhappy progress of civil dissensions—no magnanimity, no moderation, no kindness, no peace, no opportunity for the wise and good; violence, fury alone, bearing sway; and the happiness of a community, if accomplished at all, the result rather of its good fortune than its merit. Melancholy reflections of this kind will obtrude themselves; but we must not speak thus, though not to feel thus is sometimes impossible. The lesson is everywhere and always the same; moderation — timely moderation — the despised, unpalatable lesson of moderation, disdained by the high-minded, ridiculed by the thoughtless, forgotten by all, and most so when most needed.

But we must not, I say, speak thus, but continue to note, as well as we can, the mistakes and faults of every party in its turn; the whole of our lesson being still comprised, as I have just intimated, in the single word, moderation. And now, then, what were the events that took place? what was the more immediate history? The two great parties in the state were in the situation we have described. The history was sure to become important : the adherents of the old opinions could not possibly acquiesce, with any sincerity, in the terms which the assertors of the new opinions had imposed upon them. There were very violent, unreasonable men among the former, the adherents of the old opinions; they might and did wish only for a counter revolution ; but again, there were very violent and unreasonable men among the latter, the assertors of the new opinions ; and to these latter also were united many daring and bad men—the lower orders of the lower fauxbourgs of Paris, and the mobs and orators of the Palais Royal—and these were determined to secure themselves and their Revolution, as they supposed, and to bring the king to Paris. A collision could not well be escaped, the moderate men in the National Assembly having failed—and a collision *did* take place, a dreadful one—the crisis, so well known in history under the general name of the events of the 5th and 6th of October, and I must consider it at some length.

The immediate causes were soon found ; these were, 1st, a scarcity in Paris ; and 2ndly, some imprudence on the part of the court at Versailles. Nothing is so easy as to rouse the people to acts of violence when they want bread : and in this situation they will believe any thing of their rulers or their government that is told them. What was told them, too, in this instance, of the intentions of the court to retire and prepare a civil war, was not in itself improbable.

When a train of this kind was laid, the slightest spark from the imprudence of the court was sure to produce an explosion. But this slight spark was produced by the imprudence of the court, and in the following manner.

The critical state of affairs in Paris seems to have been apprehended at Versailles, and among others by the Count D'Estaing, who wrote a letter to the queen, on the 14th of September, detailing to her the conversation he had lately heard in the metropolis, to the effect we have just described, the rumours and suspicions that prevailed, and requesting an audience. This was granted. What passed is not known, but the result probably was, that the queen satisfied the count that the machinations he talked of meant only the safety of the king and the royal family. This is, indeed, sufficiently clear from what followed. The old French guards, who had joined the popular cause, and were at Paris, talked of returning to Versailles to re-assume their post of duty around the king ; La Fayette wrote to St.

Priest, who was in the confidence of the court, on the 17th of September, not to be alarmed, for he was sure he had influence enough with the troops to prevent this measure of their return. But this assurance from La Fayette could not satisfy the court; there was no force to be opposed to them; four hundred body guards and one hundred chasseurs were all; the town militia of Versailles could not be depended upon; and by a decree of the National Assembly, no troops of the line could be brought up without a requisition from the municipality.   Now this requisition the Count D'Estaing made it his business to procure from the municipality of Versailles, by representing to them that La Fayette was favourable to the measure; that the king was alarmed; that the royal family, that the very National Assembly would be endangered by the presence of two thousand of the French guards, who were coming to resume their post, as they called it, round the king, and that a regiment of the line must be brought up immediately.   The regiment of Flanders was fixed upon; the court thought they could best depend upon them, for they had refused the civic oath; and, on the contrary, their colonel was a member of the Assembly, and attached to the popular cause; this consideration, therefore, it was thought would tend to quiet the fears of the Assembly.   The Assembly seem not to have behaved improperly on this occasion, though the measure had, on the whole, (however prudent and necessary in itself,) somewhat of the appearance of an intrigue.

You will immediately see how fast were now collecting together the materials of future commotion.   The municipal force, or national guards, of Versailles were to be made to coalesce as much as possible with the regiment of Flanders; they had not yet been organized; the queen was to give them their colours; there was to be a day appointed for the benediction, a sort of joint review of them and the body guards to take place.   This was all very well, and would have been so at any common juncture, but on the present occasion all this was interpreted by the people of Paris as the beginning and the preparations of a counter revolution; which was therefore to be prevented by sending to Versailles the old French guards disguised, and women of the town, to detach the soldiers from their allegiance.   These old French guards, as I have mentioned, were not satisfied that, because they had become patriots, they were no longer to occupy their posts of honour about the palace of the king; who, on his part, could not be well disposed to those who seemed now rather to belong to the city of Paris than to

him; and the Assembly itself had already proposed its decrees
and votes on the future constitution of France, of a nature far
too democratic to be sincerely admitted by the king, or to be at
all relished by those who wished well to his authority. Lastly,
and above all, it must have been well known to the court, that
the popular party meant, if possible, to accomplish the removal
of the king and the Assembly to Paris; and the queen and the
court could not but have surveyed any project of this kind with
sentiments of perfect horror.

This was a most calamitous state of things, and the slightest
untoward accident, or unfortunate mistake, or offensive imprudence, might evidently lead to consequences the most important.
Such an accident, or mistake, or offensive imprudence, did immediately occur. What it was is well known; it was after the
following manner. The gardes du corps (the king's body guards
at Versailles) gave an entertainment to the officers of the regiment of Flanders, to which they invited several officers of the
national guard, of the rangers, and other military corps; the
king, at their request, lent them the theatre of the palace for
the purpose; the dinner was served to near three hundred
guests; the lights of the house, the crowd of spectators who
filled the boxes, the music of the different regimental bands,
gave to the repast the brilliancy and gaiety of a festival. During
the first course all was decency and order; in the second, the
company drank, very naturally, to the health of the king, the
queen, the dauphin, and the royal family, and the cries of " Vive
le Roi!" " Vive la Reine!" " Vive la Famille Royale!" of
course resounded from every quarter. All this was innocent
enough, but the health of the nation was feebly proposed by
some one of the company, more patriotic than wise, for the present was not the precise moment for a toast like this, and the
toast (though not exactly rejected) after all was not drunk.
" Vive la Nation" had not as yet become a national cry. But
this was the first offence committed, and it was an offence, and
was afterwards not a little dwelt upon. It was but a matter of
course, that some of the ladies of the palace should run to the
queen, to tell her how prosperously went on the banquet, and to
beg her to send the dauphin. The queen was in no spirits; she
was requested to come herself; the spectacle might amuse her;
she hesitated, and some mysterious, inexplicable presentiment
seemed to say, that sad might be the consequences of what in
itself appeared so innocent and unimportant. The king returned from hunting—would he accompany her? The king

complied, and with the dauphin, the royal visitors placed themselves in one of the latticed boxes; but they were soon discovered, and a thousand cries of "Vive le Roi!" "Vive la Reine!" "Vive M. le Dauphin!" resounded from all parts of the theatre. The poor king was unable to resist these testimonies of affection, they had become to him of late more than ever precious; he descended from his box, and the queen, with the dauphin in her arms, made the tour of the table amid the most loud and reiterated acclamations and applauses.

This was a sight not likely to be unaffecting to such a company, and on such an occasion. The graces and elegance of the queen's deportment had been long the subject of general admiration in a court, and amid a nation, where graces were virtues, and elegance was the ambition of all; the dauphin, too, always made the idol of the nation, was seen reposing on the bosom of his mother in all the affecting innocence and simplicity of childhood; and both were now more than ever recommended, as well as the father near them, to the courage and the loyalty of every true Frenchman—to their courage and loyalty; for the necessity of such virtues must have been deeply felt at the moment, amid a thousand apprehensions of unknown and mysterious danger, that seemed to be gathering around them, menacing with insult their dignity and honour, and threatening even the security of their throne, and the very tenure of their existence.

The swords were drawn and flourished in the air; the healths were again repeated; the acclamations again and again resounded, and the queen seemed to renew the image of her august mother, Maria Theresa, addressing herself to her Hungarian subjects, with the young emperor in her arms, and like her, appealing for compassion, and requesting their protection against the daring and unfeeling men who were going to drive her from her throne, and plunder her possessions.

At this moment, as the royal family was retiring, the bands struck up the air of Gretry, in his musical romance of Richard Cœur de Lion, the well-known air, "O Richard, O mon Roi, l'univers t'abandonne." Never were sounds that so completely convey the sentiment that is to be expressed. They are put into the mouth of the queen, addressing her song, disguised as a minstrel, to the captive king—"O Richard, O my love, by the tyrant world forgot," as the original words were translated for the English stage. It is many years since I heard them delivered at one of our own theatres, no doubt by the sweetest voice that theatre ever listened to; and to this hour I can recollect the melting of the heart, and the indignation that was excited against the oppressor and an unfeeling world, that thus abandoned the royal captive to his brutal tyrant; all this I well recollect, (allow me to speak of myself,) and if at the distance of so many ages from the real event, sitting only for my amusement at a public spectacle, I could thus be affected, as I remember myself to have been, by the mere delusion of the scene, what, (I can readily conceive), what must have been the effect produced by the same music upon the hearts of Frenchmen, of young officers, men of honour and of arms, fearless of the future and prodigal of life, each animated by the banquet and the sympathy of surrounding minds, while they saw palpably standing before them, with his queen and dauphin, their own unhappy Richard, whom surely the world seemed to abandon; for where was he to look for aid, and how had he offended?

What followed at this unfortunate entertainment may be without difficulty imagined. Imprudences without number: "Down with the tricoloured cockade!" "Long live the white!" "The white for ever!" these were the cries that were heard. The boxes were scaled; the guests were intoxicated; uproar and noisy merriment everywhere prevailed; white cockades were noticed in the king's anti-chamber; in the evening, ladies of the court, it is said, took the white ribbons of their head-dresses, and put them into the hats of officers of the national guard, who had asked for them.

" But what," as the Marquis de Ferrieres very naturally asks, " what have follies and extravagances of this kind to do with the plan of a civil war and a counter revolution? What is there in all this but the natural effects of the French character; of a people full of enthusiasm, never reflecting, ever in extremes, accustomed for ages to see the nation and the state only in the person of its king? Again, the conduct of the queen, what is it? what is there," says the marquis, " in the expression she made use of to those who came to thank her the next day for their regimental colours, ' that she was delighted with yesterday?' what wonder that, amid the cruel griefs and mortifications that she must of late have suffered, she should be alive to the marks of attachment that were offered her, or that, deserted by the ungrateful beings whom she had loaded with her favours, without succour, and made the object, by designing men, of the hatred of the people, what wonder that she should rest herself upon the first prop and stay that was presented to her? Certainly I can believe," continues the marquis, "that the ladies of the court, that enthusiasts, that courtiers without forethought, might have imagined they saw an infallible means of a counter revolution in the momentary exultation produced by wine on four or five thousand people; that they might abandon themselves to the most indiscreet projects; that they might cry, ' Long live the white cockade, it is alone the true one;' all this I can believe," says he, " but that the court and the ministers, with so little force, should now think of doing what they could not dare to attempt on the 14th of July, with forty thousand troops of the line, one hundred pieces of cannon, and a general, this, indeed, is what I certainly do not believe, nor will any man believe, of any sense."

Such were the observations of the Marquis de Ferrieres; but very different were the conclusions drawn at Paris, and no doubt the imprudences of the court had been very great; any thing and every thing was believed, and these transactions produced the most lively indignation. Other imprudences (they were now, alas! becoming follies and faults) in the meantime took place at Versailles: the banquet was repeated the next day, the 2nd of October, and the company indulged in even greater excesses of revelry; the ladies were more bold and active with their cockades, and black cockades appeared even in Paris. The people were irritated; and with perfect reason; for these were the beginnings of a civil war, after a national cockade, the tricoloured, had been once established, and the king had himself once adopted it.

Follies and faults, or experiments (as they were thought) of this kind called into full activity the revolutionists in Paris; they could now perceive, that every thing was prepared for the execution of their own projects, in front of which was placed the removal of the king to Paris. Symptoms of a counter revolution at Versailles, and a populace in want of bread in the metropolis, these were sufficient hinges on which to move the metropolis and the kingdom.

You will see in the histories the gradual progress of the insurrection which was at last brought to the point desired, and "Bread!" "Bread!" "To Versailles!" "To Versailles!" became in Paris the universal cry. The town house was on the point of being burnt; the constituted authorities exerted themselves in vain; La Fayette harangued, exhorted, and conjured them, equally in vain; his life was in danger; and the Assembly of the Commune at last sent him word, that he must go with the people, as they desired, to Versailles, since there was no alternative.

As La Fayette was one of the first movers of the Revolution, no proper justice is ever done to his character by those who were unfriendly to the Revolution; it must, therefore, be mentioned that it is quite clear, from the concurring accounts of all writers, that he made every possible exertion to prevent this fatal measure, this march to Versailles, and that, with an afflicted and foreboding heart, he accompanied the populace and the soldiers, to take the chance of moderating and directing, as well as he could, a dreadful mass of men, whom he could no longer control or bring to reason.

In the meantime, the agitation was at Versailles only less than at Paris: from the first opening of the sitting, this agitation appeared not only in the Assembly but in the tribunes, and in the looks and gestures of the multitudes that surrounded the hall.

You will see a short and good account of what passed in Ferrieres. It happened that, at the time, very unfortunately, the president had to report the answer of the king to the Constitutional Decrees and the Declaration of Rights. This answer was not sufficiently favourable and agreeable to the more ardent part of the Assembly; violent language ensued; strong allusions were made to the unfortunate fêtes that we have just described; to orgies, as they were called; to menaces uttered; to counter revolutions intended; to the national cockade trampled under foot. "It is not the cries of 'Vive le Roi,' or 'Vive la Reine,'" said Pétion, "that we complain of, they are ever welcome to our hearts; but in these military orgies, have not imprecations been vented against the National Assembly, and against liberty? Have the body-guards taken the oath? What means this black cockade?" One of the members of the nobility, shocked at these misrepresentations, moved that Pétion's denunciation should be signed by him, and laid upon the table. Pétion was embarrassed; but Mirabeau, formed for such conjunctures, instantly started up, and cried out, that he would himself denounce and sign, if the Assembly would first declare, that all but the king were within the reach of the law. "I will then," said he, audibly enough to be heard by those around him, "denounce the queen and the Duke de Guiche."

This unexpected proposition soon made it necessary for the president, who luckily happened to be Mounier, to call for the order of the day, and get rid of such a perilous discussion. The result was, that the president, at the head of a deputation, was ordered to wait upon the king, to beseech him to give his assent, pure and unconditional, to the articles of the constitution, and the Declaration of Rights, that had been just presented to him. But in the midst of this debate, four hours before the brigands arrived, Mirabeau had gone behind the president's chair, and apprized him that there were forty thousand men marching upon them from Paris—" You had better break up the sitting."

Mirabeau, it is thought, wanted a clear stage, the better to ensure the success of his operations; and this notion is somewhat strengthened by the cold and pointed reply of the president, " So much the better, they have but to kill us all—all—and the affairs of the republic (a sarcastic word) will go on better." " That's prettily said," replied Mirabeau, and retired.

It is possible, however, that Mirabeau only wished, as a well-meaning man naturally might, on the first impulse, at least, to get the Assembly out of the way, when such a storm was approaching. Bertrand de Moleville blames La Fayette for not sending off intelligence of the formidable body of men that was coming. Only women and brigands were expected; it was thought enough to shut the iron gates of the palace, and to draw out on the Place d'Armes the regiment of Flanders, the rangers, the gardes du corps, and some other military force; the national guards of Versailles were in their neighbouring barracks. About three o'clock the phalanx of the women arrived, Maillard at their head, the man who had played the chief part in the attack of the Bastile.

A disgusting scene soon ensued; Maillard presented himself at the bar of the Assembly with his retinue, and set forth, that for three days past there had absolutely been no bread in Paris; that they were come to Versailles to ask for it, and, at the same time, to have the gardes du corps punished for having insulted the national cockade; that the aristocrats wanted to starve them. The Assembly were able to pacify tolerably well this first orator and his deputation; but other women soon forced their way into the Hall of Assembly, mounted upon the benches, crying for bread (all at once), the dismission of the regiment of Flanders, the punishment of the gardes du corps, and uttering, at the same time, the most horrid imprecations against the queen; some insulted the deputies, particularly those of the clergy. " Speak, you deputy there," they said to one; " Silence, you deputy there," to another; and, in short, the scene soon became so scandalous, that the Assembly had no measure left but to charge the president to go immediately to the palace, at the head of a deputation, and represent the calamitous situation of

Paris to the king. This was done, some of the women accompanied, and the king received and was able to soothe and tranquillize them.

These were, indeed, the occasions on which the unfortunate monarch appeared to such an advantage : his genuine benevolence, his ready sensibility, his calm patience, his dignified fearlessness, his anxiety to do every thing that was or could be required of him, his gentleness, his politeness, his humanity, lawless as these women were, women they still were, and such qualities it was impossible should not have some effect upon them. One of them, a girl of seventeen, fainted, and they all retired, crying in the court, " Vive le Roi !" "God bless the king and his family !" " We shall have bread to-morrow !"

But the situation of the king and the palace was, in truth, most unprotected and most deplorable. The regiment of Flanders seems to have been ordered away from the palace ; it had been corrupted by the municipal force of Versailles. Most of the body guards, too, were sent to Rambouillet by the king from motives of humanity, lest they should be massacred ; they were gentlemen all, from the nature of the institution. The king then sent for the National Assembly, meaning to place himself under their protection ; but such part of the National Assembly as still remained in their hall, was mixed up, and reduced almost to a level, with the poissardes and first banditti that had arrived from the metropolis, and no use could be made of them. And afterwards, while Mounier, the president, was endeavouring, by beat of drum, to collect a proper representation of the nation, with which to surround the king, La Fayette arrived, and their protection was thought, after an interview with him, no longer necessary.

But the disgraceful scenes to which we have just alluded in the Assembly, were but the beginnings of troubles. It is impossible to give here the slightest idea of what passed for many hours afterwards in and about the palace. Bertrand de Moleville was on the spot, and gives a very detailed account, and you must refer to it. You will easily see what were the great component parts of this dreadful whole : the royal family who were to be protected ; the body guards, who were now left few in number, and who were alone faithful, and who wanted protection also ; the old French guards who had come to resume their posts about the king ; the national guards of Versailles, whose fidelity to the king and whose attachment were of a very wavering nature, or rather were extinct and void ; and lastly, the military bodies that were coming up with La Fayette, the national guards or militia of Paris; these were not favourable to the king, and not favourable to the old body guards : and again, mixed up with the whole, and first making their appearance with the women, and afterwards in fresh crowds with La Fayette's army, were to be enumerated, as actors in the scene, a description of people called by the general name of brigands, the most ferocious and brutal men and women that could issue from the most desperate part of the population of Paris; supposed by most writers to have been hired for purposes of mischief, and even for the destruction of the queen, by the Duke of Orleans and his party; but at all events engaged and brought up by the revolutionists to accomplish their one great end, that of forcing the king and royal family to Paris, that they and the Assembly might be under their control, and not only all chance of a counter revolution, or the king's flight, be prevented, but the Revolution itself made to proceed according to their pleasure.

Mirabeau and the Duke of Orleans were so accused of being the prime movers of the dreadful occurrences which now took place in and about the palace, that a judicial inquiry was afterwards instituted, which ended, as such inquiries generally do, in an exhibition of evidence, which it is impossible to weigh, and fatiguing to read, and in the acquittal of the accused. Even Bertrand's account, though comprised within a couple of chapters, it is in vain to attempt minutely to understand.

But the general history of what now took place, in a word, is this : the body guards are insulted and assaulted; La Fayette appears, answers for his troops, pacifies the court, quiets the National Assembly, and tranquillizes the king and royal family; the old French guards, who had lately gone over to the nation, resume their old posts about the king, which was their particular object and wish, as guards of the palace. Every thing is at last quiet, and at a late hour, the general, overcome with the fatigues and anxieties of such a day and such a night, sinks for a short interval to rest. The brigands, the horrible wretches that we have mentioned, early in the morning get into the palace; they make for the queen's apartment; she has just time to fly for her life to the king; her guard at the door is left for dead; many of the gentlemen of the palace and distinguished officers of the different corps are murdered, or left mangled and expiring; La Fayette is roused from his unfortunate repose; by his personal courage and activity, and the exertions and steadiness of

the king, the body guards (the gentlemen about the king) were
saved from massacre, and at length something of the appearance
of peace and good will and order are procured, but at a most
fatal price; the removal of the king to Paris, which is the cry
at last heard, and to which no refusal, it seems, could then
be given.

This is, in a few words, I can offer no more, the general description, of which you will see all the interesting particulars in
the historians and memoir writers. You will have to mark, as
happens on these occasions, at one moment, perfect prodigies of
human virtue, and at the next, the most repulsive acts of cruelty and abomination. I know not what is to be concluded
from instances like these, but that every exertion is to be made
by every means, of moral and religious instruction, to civilize
and to purify the human animal, since he is thus at once capable
of the highest elevation, and yet also capable of a degradation,
the most afflicting, ferocious, and appalling.

I will dwell a little longer, before I conclude my lecture, on
these scenes of the 5th and 6th of October. You must remember how distinguished a figure they make in the eloquent
reflections of Mr. Burke. The most complete account of these
unfortunate transactions is to be found in the history by the
Two Friends of Liberty. These writers are, no doubt, not of
the school of Mounier, or the first moderate leaders of the Revolution, but they are friends to order, and, as far as they have understood them, to the best interests of mankind. The reader
will find no difficulty in perceiving where he is to receive with
hesitation, and where he is not to receive at all the representations that are offered to him; and the detail, extended through
six chapters, will put him in full possession of the facts, which
appear to me, on a comparison with the account of Bertrand de
Moleville and Ferrieres, to be exhibited with sufficient fairness
and impartiality. I must just allude to the account they give,
and afterwards to the account given by Weber; that is, to some
particulars furnished by each writer.

It appears that a communication from La Fayette *did* arrive
at nine o'clock in the evening, sufficient to throw the whole
palace into confusion and alarm. The departure of the king instantly from the palace was certainly a measure much agitated.
The two historians mention various particulars, and then observe, " It will be difficult not to suppose, that it was amongst
the projects of the league at Versailles to avail themselves of
these events to alarm the king, determine him to fly, and thus

hurry him into a civil war, so desired by the bloodsuckers of
the court, as their last chance for despotism and aristocracy.
But Louis XVI. was immoveable, and amid the fluctuations of
the council he adhered constantly to this principle, ' that it was
very doubtful whether his withdrawing from Versailles would
place him in safety, but that it was very certain that it would
be the signal of a war, that would shed torrents of blood.   I
would rather perish for my people than have thousands of them
perish in my quarrel; happen what will, I will not move.' "
This is the account given by the two historians, the Two Friends
of Liberty, themselves, and the account that is to be received.
It is affecting to see this unfortunate monarch devoting himself
in this manner.   This was his language at all times : " It was
his quarrel," he said; " no blood shall be shed." But his people
were unworthy of him; they saw not what was due to his
gentle nature ; they dragged to a prison the helpless being who
had no wish but their happiness, and at last they executed on a
scaffold the king that could not bear, lest he should shed their
blood, even to defend himself.   But the king who thus devoted
himself, as these two historians acknowledge, so generously for
the nation, was, however, still a husband and a father, and he
trembled, when he heard from his apartment the ferocious cries,
the horrid imprecations of the multitude, who mixed the name
of the queen with that of the gardes du corps, and clamoured
aloud for their blood.   Every instant augmented the irresolution
of the council on the measures to be taken for the preservation
of the royal family, and every effort was made to persuade the
queen to retire.   But when it was at last clear that the king
was determined to stay, and that the rage of the Parisians
threatened her alone, she declared, that she would perish at
the king's feet, but would never leave him.   And in the midst
of the general consternation, say the same historians (the Two
Friends of Liberty), the queen alone displayed a countenance
calm and serene, supported and animated those who were sinking
with terror on her account, and made even those admire her
courage who condemned her principles, and whom the remembrance, still present, of her faults inspired with every prejudice
to her disadvantage.

Abundant testimony is paid by these historians to La Fayette,
and it appears that he did not retire to rest till five o'clock in
the morning, and till every thing seemed calm and composed.
It is clear, too, that he afterwards made every effort for the
safety and for the honour of the king and the royal family, and

finally, that he saved the gardes du corps from being massacred. "Gentlemen," he cried to his soldiers, " I have pledged my word to the king, that nothing which belongs to him shall come to harm; if you murder his guards I shall be dishonoured, and can be no more your general."

Two of the body-guards had just before been cut down by the mob, and their heads were on pikes for the gratification of such spectators at the very time. " The king," says Weber (he was foster-brother of the queen), " threw open the window, and from the balcony implored the people to spare the lives of these his unfortunate servants. Those of them who had taken refuge near the person of the king, threw their bandoleers to the people, and cried, ' Vive la nation !' 'Vive le roi !' was immediately echoed from all quarters; and the body-guards saw themselves on a sudden embraced and caressed by the very tigers who had been disputing in what manner they were to be murdered. La Fayette was able to rouse some proper feelings in the old French guards, but was obliged to depend on them, and more particularly on his own officers. The common soldiers of the national guards, the militia of Paris, would not fire on their fellow citizens, as they called them, and these fellow citizens happened now to be the dreadful fiends, who were ready to pillage and murder." Weber, who gives a very interesting account of these transactions (he was at Versailles at the time), cannot forgive La Fayette for his mistaken confidence, at least for going to rest any where but in the antechamber of the king; others excuse him. La Fayette and his officers, and the grenadiers of the old guards, having now allayed the murderous fury of the multitude, and saved the body-guards, the king was obliged to intimate his willingness to go to Paris, and he came at last to the balcony to reiterate his assurances to this effect. The joy of the populace knew no bounds, but " the queen !" " the queen !" became every where the cry; and she was given to understand that it was necessary for her to come forward: she advanced into the balcony immediately, leading the dauphin in one hand, and the young princess in the other. " No children !" was then the cry; " no children !" An ominous sound, as if she alone was to be made the victim. The queen, with a movement of her hand, returned them both back to the inside of the apartment, and with a calm countenance of repose and dignity, her hands folded upon her bosom, stood alone—unprotected indeed, and alone; like one, that thought death might at the moment await her, and that did not mean to brave it; but still like one that was a queen, and the daughter of Maria Theresa, and did not fear it. The multitude gazed for a moment, and the elevated grandeur of a mind, that corresponded with its high station of dignity and rule, awed their rude passions into obedience, and prevailed. The admiration was universal, and the clapping of hands and the shouts of " Vive la reine ! " made the courts of the palace re-echo to her applause; an applause, which, having been won by her magnanimity, she had a right to enjoy, and which it is to be hoped, for one short passing moment, she did enjoy—the short and passing moment of conscious exultation and triumph, to be set in contrast with all the agonies she had lately endured, and was yet to suffer.

Her great danger and her very imminent danger (as from previous circumstances that had occurred she well knew) was the possibility that she might be fired at by some of the many assassins that were mixed with the mob below ; her being ordered to put away the children seemed to intimate something of this kind. Pieces were levelled at her. Weber says, he saw one, and that the man who was next the ruffian struck the barrel down, and almost massacred him on the spot: others say that many were levelled. " Finding," says Weber, " that all resistance was thought vain, and that the royal family must at all events go to Paris, my anxiety," says he, " became extreme. I equipped myself in the uniform of a staff-officer, got a horse from the royal stables, and placed myself as near as possible to the carriage of the king.

" First went the main body of the Parisians," he continues, " each soldier with a loaf on his bayonet; then came the poissardes, drunk with fury, exultation, and wine, astride on the cannons, mounted on the horses of the body-guard, surrounded by the brigands and workmen that had come from Paris ; waggons of flour and grain formed a convoy, followed by the grenadiers, who still kept under their protection the body-guards, whose lives had been purchased by the king; these captives were led, one by one, disarmed, bare-headed, and on foot, some of them with the grenadier caps instead of their hats; the dragoons, the soldiers of the regiment of Flanders, and the hundred Swiss guards then surrounded and followed the carriage of the king, where were seated his majesty, the royal family, and the governess. It would be difficult to describe," says Weber, " the confusion and tediousness of a procession like this, which lasted six hours : it began with a general discharge of musketry at Versailles ; halts were made from time to time to give opportunity for new salutes: the poissardes on these occasions descended from the cannons and the horses, to dance around the carriage of the king, and to sing their songs. But the horror," says he, " of this dreadful day, cold and rainy as it was; this infamous soldiery, wading in the mud; these harpies, these monsters in human form; and in the middle of his captive guards a monarch dragged along thus ignominiously with his family, all together, formed a spectacle so terrible, a mixture of every possible affliction and shame so piteous, that my imagination cannot to this hour recall the remembrance without an almost instant oversetting and annihilation of my faculties. No idea can be formed," he continues, " of all that was said and uttered by the populace as we went along. For three parts of the whole time I kept myself at the right door of the carriage; at any discharge of the musketry, at any explosion of the cries and vociferations of the populace, I cast a look into the carriage, and their majesties had the goodness to express to me, by their gestures, and their eyes cast up to heaven, their perfect astonishment at the state at which it had been possible to make the people at last arrive."

The remainder of the history is well known. The king and the royal family came to Paris; they were received by the mayor, by Bailly, the man of science, who called the day of their arrival a beautiful day, a strange and most unfortunate expression, which Bailly was not a man to have used in its more obvious and offensive sense. It was an expression that never was or could be forgotten, apparently so completely at variance with every sentiment and reflection that could at the time, and on the spot, be entertained by any wise and good man like M. Bailly, who might wish, indeed, for freedom and the fall of tyranny, but who surely could not see a tyrant in Louis, or freedom in excesses like these.

The king was then transferred to the Tuilleries, and the palace of his ancestors became his prison.

LECTURE XX.

LALLY TOLLENDAL—MOUNIER—BURKE—FOX—DARWIN—COWPER—MRS. BARBAULD—SIR JAMES MACKINTOSH.

THE violent party must now be considered as having entirely succeeded. They had got possession of the king and the royal family, and they had lodged them in the Tuilleries.

The National Assembly was next transferred to Paris, and all the real power was thus placed within the inspection and control of the tumultuous inhabitants of the metropolis.

The Assembly, it might have been at first sight hoped, would still have been able to maintain its consequence, and protect the king, by the assistance of La Fayette and the national guards, and by the influence of its own weight and character.

But all constituted authority had just been found inadequate to the preservation of order. Nothing but the most lawless fury had of late prevailed, and no friend of the Revolution or of mankind, who had actually witnessed these scenes, could have been otherwise than deeply afflicted at the past, and surely, as it might have been expected, somewhat appalled at the prospect of the future.

Yet these do not appear to have been exactly the sentiments generally felt in and out of Paris (such was the enthusiasm of the season), felt, I mean, among the more ardent friends of liberty.

Excesses and enormities, it was thought, could not but be expected from a populace just broke loose from oppression; they were of a temporary nature, it was held, and such excesses and enormities now, and at every period of the Revolution, were always considered as in themselves a proof how bad had been the system of government under which the people of this great country had formerly lived; a reflection that afforded a general answer, of a most convenient nature, to every complaint that could be uttered, or accusation that could be made.

But very different was the impression which these and other events had made on the more reasonable friends of liberty; on the more moderate part of the Assembly itself; on Mounier and his associates; on those who wished for a limited monarchy and a free constitution; free, at least, after the measure and the manner of the constitution established in England.

Very different were the feelings of such men; and Mounier and his friends, immediately after these outrages at Versailles on the 5th and 6th of October, and before the Assembly had left the place, held a meeting, and considered the situation of their country and their own.

Nothing could have been more deplorable than must have appeared to patriots like these, the circumstances of both; themselves defeated and disappointed in their dearest hopes, without the chance of being further useful; their country abandoned to the caprices of a giddy and bloody populace; and their king, whom they had not meant *thus* to assist and honour, left to

await his fate, in the midst of his helpless family, and to stand
the result of a revolution which they had themselves so contributed to set first in motion, and which it was now no longer in
their power to direct or to control.

The consciousness of virtuous intention must support men in
situations like these : their reflections, however they may fail,
can never be like those of men who are disappointed in enterprises of guilt; for they have at least meant well, and the
Almighty Master has not left afflicted virtue without its appropriate support—but still what is suffered is severe.   There is
nothing of joy or triumph, there is little of cheerfulness in what
passes in the virtuous mind on these occasions; and we are thus
taught the duty of being prudent, if possible, as well as benevolent ; that laudable intentions are not of themselves sufficient;
that we are not to rest satisfied with them ; that good must not
only be attempted, but accomplished.

The mortification, the indignant feelings, the agonies of men
of high sensibility in great conjunctures of affairs like these, are
best described by what was written by Lally Tollendal himself—
(the measure, you will observe, that these first patriots of the
Revolution resolved upon was a secession from the Assembly
altogether).

"The part I have taken," says he, alluding to this secession,
in a letter to his friend, " is well justified in my own eyes;
and neither has this guilty city, nor its still more guilty Assembly, any claim upon me to justify myself further ; but I have it
at heart, no doubt, that you, and people like you, should not
condemn me.   My health, I solemnly assure you, would render
the discharge of my functions impossible, but setting this aside,
it is quite beyond any power of mine to bear any longer the
horror that I feel at all this blood; these heads carried on
pikes ; this queen all but assassinated ; this king dragged along
as a captive, entering Paris in the midst of his assassins, and
preceded by the heads of his unfortunate body guards ; these
perfidious janizaries (the old French guards he means), these
assassins, these female cannibals ; this cry of ' All the Bishops
to the Lanterne,' at the very moment when the king was entering his capital with the two bishops of his council in his carriage ; the report of a musket which I saw fired into one of the
carriages of the queen; M. Bailly calling this a beautiful day ;
the Assembly declaring coldly, on the morning of this day, that
it did not consist with its dignity to go in a body and environ
the king; M. Mirabeau saying (and with impunity), in that

Assembly, that the vessel of the state, far from being stayed in
its course, would only launch itself forward with greater rapidity
than ever towards regeneration; M. Barnave smiling, as well
as he, when torrents of blood were flowing around us; the virtuous Mounier escaping by a sort of miracle from twenty assassins, that wished to make of his head one trophy more.

"Such are the horrors that make me swear never to set foot
again in that den of cannibals, where I have no longer the
strength to raise my voice at all, where now for six weeks I
have raised it in vain : for myself, Mounier, and every honourable man, the last effort that we could make for the common
good was to fly from this Assembly. Any idea of personal
danger never approached me. I should blush to have to defend
myself from any charge of the kind. I have still received on
my journey, from this people (less guilty are they than those
who have made them drunk with fury), I have received acclamations and applauses, with which others might have been flattered, but which have made me only shudder. It is to the indignation, to the horror, to the physical convulsions which are
excited in me by the very sight of blood, that I have yielded.
Death one can brave; one can brave it when any good is to be
done, again and again ; but no power under heaven, no opinion
public or private, has a right to condemn me to suffer a thousand punishments every minute, and for no possible use, and
condemn me to die of despair and rage, in the midst of triumphs
and of guilt, which I can neither prevent nor stay. They will
proscribe me ; they will confiscate my property : I will dig the
earth ; I shall, at least, see them no longer.

"Such is my justification."

Mounier, in like manner, explained the motives of his secession, and at some length. He thought it would be an useless
sacrifice of himself, he said, to speak the truth either at Versailles or Paris, and yet that to be silent was to be criminal; he
therefore declared openly, that he would neither commit guilt
himself, nor be an accomplice in the guilt of others. He then
describes the circumstances that made it impossible for him to
remain in the Assembly any longer ; the duty, on the contrary,
that was imposed upon him to return to his constituents, and
lay the truth before them. He considers the proceedings of the
5th and 6th of October, as an insurrection against the king. He
considers him as in a state of durance, and the Assembly itself
as no longer free. Even at Versailles, he says, that the galleries expressed their opinions, and that he often saw the effects

produced by proscriptions and menaces. If firmness and good intentions could be of use, he concludes, " I might hope to be useful ; but I cannot show indifference to crimes."

The whole memoir, and the part extracted from Lally Tollendal, are both in the notes to the third volume of Bailly's Memoirs.

These extracts will sufficiently show you what was thought of these transactions, and of the Assembly itself, by those few of the more early movers of the Revolution, at this particular period of its progress, those who first seceded. Whether they were, after all, right in seceding, is indeed another and a very difficult question ; an allusion to which has given occasion to one of the many striking and affecting passages in the writings of Mr. Burke.

" I cannot bring myself," says Mr. Burke, addressing himself to one of the patriots, who had *not* seceded, and alluding to those who *had,* " severely to condemn persons who are wholly unable to bear so much as the sight of those men in the throne of legislation, who are only fit to be the objects of criminal justice. If fatigue, if disgust, if unsurmountable nausea, drive them away from such spectacles, ' ubi miseriarum pars non minima erat, videre et aspici,' I cannot blame them."

" Again ; last and worst," says Mr. Burke, " who could endure to hear .this unnatural, insolent, and savage despotism called liberty ? If at this distance, sitting quietly by my fire, I cannot read their decrees and speeches without indignation, shall I condemn those who had fled from the actual sight and hearing of those horrors ? No, no ; mankind has no title to demand that we should be slaves to their guilt and insolence, or that we should serve them in spite of themselves. Minds, sore with the poignant grief of insulted virtue, filled with high disdain against the pride of triumphant baseness, often have it not in their choice to stand their ground. Their complexion (which might defy the rack) cannot go through such a trial ; something very high must fortify men to that proof ; but when I am driven to comparison, surely I cannot hesitate for a moment to prefer, to such men as are common, those heroes who, in the midst of despair, perform all the tasks of hope ; who subdue their feelings to their duties ; who in the cause of humanity, liberty, and honour, abandon all the satisfactions of life, and every day incur a fresh risk of life itself. Do me the justice to believe that I never can prefer any fastidious virtue (virtue still) to the unconquered perseverance, to the affectionate patience of those who watch night and day by the bedside of their delirious country; who, for their love to that dear and venerable name, bear all the disgusts and the buffets they receive from their frantic mother. Sir, I do look upon you as true martyrs; I regard you as soldiers who act far more in the spirit of our Commander-in-Chief and the Captain of our salvation, than those who have left you; though I must first bolt myself very thoroughly, and know that I could do better, before I can censure them. I assure you, sir, that when I consider your unconquerable fidelity to your sovereign and your country, the courage, fortitude, and magnanimity, and long suffering of yourself and the Abbé Maury and M. Cazales, and of many worthy persons of all orders in your Assembly, I forget, in the lustre of these great qualities, that on your side has been displayed an eloquence so rational, manly, and convincing, that no time or country perhaps has ever excelled. But your talents disappear in my admiration of your virtues. As to M. Mounier and M. Lally, I have always wished to do justice to their parts and their eloquence, and the general purity of their motives. Indeed I saw very well from the beginning the mischiefs which, with all their talents and good intentions, they would do their country, through their confidence in systems.

" But their distemper was an epidemic malady. They were young and inexperienced, and when will young and inexperienced men learn caution and distrust of themselves? and when will men, young and old, if suddenly raised to far higher power than that which absolute kings and emperors commonly enjoy, learn any thing like moderation? These gentlemen conceived that they were chosen to new model the state, and even the whole order of civil society itself. The fault of M. Mounier and M. Lally was great, but it was very general. If those gentlemen stopped when they came to the brink of the gulf of guilt and public misery, that yawned before them, in the abyss of these dark and bottomless speculations, I forgive their first error; in that they were involved with many. Their repentance was their own."

Such were the sentiments of Mr. Burke, and I will dwell a little longer upon this particular part of the history of the Revolution, this secession of the first patriots from the Assembly, both because the propriety of such secessions is a curious and not uncommon question in political science, and because the consideration of it will make you reconsider the past, and will again bring before your view many striking particulars and characters, and an important crisis in the history of the Revolution itself.

I will mention to you the facts of the case as I understand them. You have heard the eloquence of the case; observe now the facts. I will report them to you from Bertrand de Moleville, the minister.

" When the king had left Versailles," says the writer, " the discussions of the Assembly were frequently interrupted by complaints of insults and menaces directed against a great number of the deputies. Many of them, little encouraged by the decree which had declared their persons inviolable, withdrew themselves; and, in the space of two days, the president had been obliged to give passports to about three hundred of his colleagues, among whom were the Bishop of Langres, M. Lally, and M. Mounier.

" It would be a great mistake," says the same author, " to suppose that all the deputies who retired were induced by motives of fear. Those whom I have named cannot certainly be accounted in this class; but they were all as disgusted, as discouraged, at seeing the factious so completely triumph, and compel the king, not only to sanction the new constitutional principles, but to fix his residence at Paris. They could no longer hope to persuade the Assembly to return to their system of two houses; they foresaw the fatal consequences of the outrages of the 5th and 6th of October, and, convinced that they should labour in vain to prevent them, they chose to resign their places, and withdraw from the state of inability and inactivity to which they found themselves reduced. The retreat of nearly half of the bishops ought much less to be attributed to fear than indignation; to the conviction that all was lost, and the embarrassment that would naturally be produced by such criminal violence among men, whose situation and whose habits of tranquil life rendered them strangers to civil commotions.

" I am very far," he continues, " from blaming the motives of the deputies who withdrew themselves at this period; without doubt they were very pure and very laudable; yet it is but too true that the consequences of their withdrawing were disastrous. How many unjust and atrocious decrees might we not cite which passed by a very small majority, and which their votes would have prevented.

" If the nobility and clergy had retired altogether in a body, their retreat might have been of the most important service; but a partial desertion of worthy men from all the orders could but ensure a majority to the factious and triumph to villains. He who deserts his post renders himself answerable, not only

for the loss of all the good he could have done in it, but for all
the evil he might have prevented."

Such is the account given and the opinions offered by Bertrand de Moleville, an account confirmed by all the other historians.   Malouet, Clermont de Tonnerre, and others remained ;
the Abbé de Maury and Cazales continued their gallant warfare
to the last.

And here it may be remembered, in the history of our own
country, that the more moderate party seceded in like manner
from the Long Parliament, and retired to Oxford (Hyde, afterwards Lord Clarendon, among them), and with the same deplorable consequences.   Measures of this kind are always to be
avoided.   In the instance of France before us, the very situation
of the king himself should have decided the question.   Why
was he to be left to suffer, the general victim, the unhappy
being on whom alone the storm was to beat ?   " If the king
goes to Paris," said nobly the Archbishop of Aix to some of his
brother prelates, " *I* go; if he remains, *I* remain.   Wherever
he is, *we* ought to be.   We have no force to defend him, but we
do our duty."

Having thus briefly exhibited the affecting eloquence of Lally
Tollendal, the powerful observations of Burke, and the facts of
the case from Bertrand de Moleville, with his very reasonable
opinions, I will now proceed.

From the moment of the secession of so many distinguished
men, and the transfer of the Assembly itself to the city of Paris,
the cause of the old opinions was on the whole at an end ; the
triumph of the new opinions was complete.   Any system, like
that of the English constitution, of checks and balances, and of
a monarchy supported by posts and places, and defended by
aristocratic orders of clergy and nobility, was now impossible,
and was thought unfavourable to the interests of society and the
general rights of mankind.   Other notions and other views of
the public happiness had become popular ; the new opinions
were more and more entertained ; and the Revolution, as it was
called, was to go on, in defiance of its enemies and in disregard
of its calumniators, till the welfare of France was accomplished,
and a new era had commenced, to be marked by the renovation
and improvement of Europe and the world.

And this is now, as it has been from the first, to become a source
of your instruction.   You are to observe still further these new
opinions; you have already been called to do so, particularly
from the 14th of July : you are now to proceed, and watch the

measures they led to in the Assembly, and the consequences by which they were followed, from the 5th and 6th of October to the close of the Constituent Assembly.

I will first offer you a very general and brief account of those measures; and next an account, first, of the effect produced on the king and higher orders in France, and, again, on the minds of different writers and reasoners, more particularly in our own country.

I conceive this to be a part of the general subject highly fitted to afford you instruction, if you can but meditate it with due calmness, impartiality, and patience.

Of these new opinions, then, the great and visible result produced in the course of about two years, was the Constitution of 1791, the work of the first or Constituent Assembly. This Assembly laboured on, through evil and good report, for these two years, from this last crisis which we have spoken of, that of the 5th and 6th of October, 1789; and then, at the end of September 1791, terminated their sittings, delivering to their fellow-citizens at the same time this the last product of their united exertions for the renovation and happiness of their country, this Constitution of 1791. This was their work, this was the first practical result of the new opinions. It was soon overthrown, and melancholy events followed; but of these we must speak hereafter. We must first attend to the leading decrees in the Assembly, which showed the nature and the progress of the new opinions. We must acquire some general notion, sufficient for the present, of the Constitution of 1791.

These decrees were in brief the following.

The kingdom was, in the first place, immediately divided into eighty-three new departments, and all the former system of different provinces, with their different usages and laws, was swept away. The parliaments followed. The great establishment of the Gallican church was dissolved, as I have already endeavoured to describe to you in a former lecture. All titles of nobility were formally extinguished; that is, there was an end, real and apparent, of the two ancient orders of the clergy and the nobility. The ministers of the crown were not to be members of the Assembly. These great measures marked the progress of the new opinions after the 5th and 6th of October, in addition to those that had marked their progress before, which had also been most important: the rejection, for instance, of the two houses; of the king's absolute veto; and the new and civic organization of the national military force: that is, the army, the clergy, the nobility, were taken away from the crown, and the whole kingdom and its legislation and official business were organized and adjusted on a new and different system.

The Constitution of 1791 therefore turned out at last to be, a sort of experiment to try, with how little patronage, respect, and executive power, a king could maintain and carry on a limited monarchy.

The event was, that such a monarchy did not stand, and was never likely to stand.

We will now proceed to the second part of my subject. What in the meantime, what were the effects produced by their leading decrees on the king and higher orders in France? And secondly, what was the effect produced on our own writers and statesmen? These shall be the subjects of the remainder of my lecture, that you may the better comprehend the nature of this particular period of history, one most memorable and extraordinary.

These proceedings could not be approved by the king, and those who were more or less attached to the old opinions. The king indeed was a prisoner, and he at last, as you will soon see, endeavoured to escape, but he failed; and the progress of the new opinions became then more violent than ever. The court, and all of the old school, resisted the Constituent Assembly in every way they could, and continually turned their eyes to foreign powers for assistance. These foreign powers were more and more disposed to interfere by force in assertion of the old opinions, from what became to them more and more the offensive nature of the new; and while La Fayette and his friends—the last friends that the king and the monarchy had—succeeded to the task of Mounier and his friends (the task of mitigating the new opinions by some adherence to the old), their efforts were continually attended with more and more difficulty, from the continually growing hatred felt by the court on the one side, and continually increasing distrust felt by the patriots on the other.

Such was the effect (and a most unhappy effect) of these great leading decrees of the National Assembly on the king and higher orders of France.

We will now turn to the writers and statesmen out of France, more particularly those of our own country; and we will advert to the sentiments with which these memorable scenes were surveyed by men of intelligence and reflection, not resident in the kingdom, at this singular crisis of the world.

The government of France had long been considered by such

men, as on the whole, in church, a sort of splendid superstition, a most unworthy representation of Christianity; and as in state, a sort of qualified despotism.

The Constituent Assembly was supposed to have freed the country from temporal and spiritual thraldom. This was, in brief, the general view of the subject taken by benevolent and intelligent men; and the means that had been resorted to, and the immediate consequences were not very scrupulously inquired into, the result being apparently so magnificent. The attention too was easily caught by particular objects that had been accomplished, objects in themselves most striking and important. The government had been rested upon free principles; the Bastile had been destroyed; *lettres de cachet* abolished; feudal impediments and oppressions of every kind removed; religious liberty established; the system of law made uniform; the criminal jurisprudence reformed; monasteries abolished; and, by making the military force consist of the citizens of the country, freedom, and all these new and weighty advantages, seemed to be for ever secured from the machinations of arbitrary power.

Such an event, as the appearance of liberty in such a kingdom as France, was naturally hailed by the generality of liberal and good men, of whatever country, as one of the greatest that could have happened. The poets everywhere took fire; they saw

> " O'er the vine-covered hills and gay regions of France,
> The day-star of liberty rise."

The poet of Caledonia, who, like the lark that hovered over his plough, " warbled his native wood-notes wild," the ardent and impetuous Burns, saw a vision of Liberty, that stood " tiptoe on his misty mountain's top."

Another poet, in like manner, Dr. Darwin, a great, though now neglected poet, who was the first that could persuade the Muses to enter the factories of the artisan and the laboratories of the philosopher, expressed himself with all the enthusiasm and the hope that then so generally animated the minds of distinguished men on the subject of the French Revolution. He is speaking of Liberty.

> " Long had the giant form on Gallia's plains
> Inglorious slept, unconscious of his chains:
> Round his large limbs were wound a thousand strings,
> By the weak hands of confessors and kings;
> O'er his closed eyes a triple veil was bound,
> And steely rivets locked him to the ground;

> While stern Bastile with iron cage inthrals
> His folded limbs, and hems in marble walls.
> Touched by the patriot flame, he rent amazed
> The flimsy bonds, and round and round him gazed;
> Starts up from earth, above the admiring throng
> Lifts his colossal form, and towers along;
> High o'er his foes his hundred arms he rears,
> Ploughshares his swords, and pruning-hooks his spears;
> Calls to the good and brave, with voice that rolls
> Like heaven's own thunder round the echoing poles;
> Gives to the winds his banner broad unfurled,
> And gathers in the shade the living world."

A very different, and a still greater poet, that had arisen a few years before, the unhappy Cowper, in the musings of his imagination, had glanced on the Bastile of France, and had anticipated the feelings that were afterwards to animate the bosoms of his countrymen, for assuredly such feelings did animate their bosoms in the month of July 1789.

> " Ye horrid towers, the abode of broken hearts,
> Ye dungeons, and ye cages of despair,
> That monarchs have supplied, from age to age,
> With music, such as suits their sovereign ears,
> The sighs and groans of miserable men!
> There's not an English heart that would not leap
> To hear that ye were fallen at last; to know
> That even our enemies, so oft employed
> In forging chains for us, themselves were free;
> For he who values Liberty, confines
> His zeal for her predominance within
> No narrow bounds; her cause engages him
> Wherever pleaded; 'tis the cause of man."

You can little conceive the feelings of mankind at that extraordinary period of the world, still less what they afterwards became as the revolution advanced; certainly you can little conceive them.

On the contrary, however, the great philosophic statesman of our own country, Mr. Burke, seems on the subject of France to have been very cautious from the first. He seems to have been able, even though living at the time, to have surveyed these events as calmly as we can now.

So early as the 9th of August, 1789, according to the account given by Mr. Prior in his Life of him, he made the following observations in a letter to his friend, Lord Charlemont; and this letter, I find from an application to the present Lord Charlemont, is genuine.

" The thing, indeed (says he), though I thought I saw something like it in progress for several years, has still somewhat in it paradoxical and mysterious.   The spirit it is impossible not to admire : but the old Parisian ferocity has broken out in a shocking manner.   It is true, that this may not be more than a sudden explosion : if so, no indication can be taken from it; but if it should be *character*, rather than *accident*, then that people are not fit for liberty, and must have a strong hand, like that of their former masters, to coerce them.

" Men must have a certain fund of natural moderation to qualify them for freedom, else it becomes noxious to themselves, and a perfect nuisance to everybody else.   What will be the event, it is hard, I think, still to say.   To form a solid constitution requires wisdom as well as spirit; and whether the French have wise heads among them, or if they possess such, whether they have authority equal to their wisdom, is yet to be seen.   In the meantime, the progress of the whole affair is one of the most curious matters of speculation that ever was exhibited."—p. 346.

This was written so early as the 9th of August, 1789, when, on account of the fall of the Bastile, every other friend of liberty was probably, in this country at least, animated with no feelings but those of hope and triumph.

The night of the 4th of August, the destruction of the feudal rights and privileges, or rather of the feudal tyrannies, as they might lawfully be exercised by the great land proprietors, had just before occurred; and early in the month of October, Mr. Burke appears to have written to M. de Menonville, a member of the National Assembly, who requested his opinions.   The letter appears in Prior (p. 348), and has every mark of being authentic.

But in this letter also there is nothing of exultation; all is hesitation, distrust, and doubt.

" The freedom that I love," says he, " is social freedom.   It is that state of things in which the liberty of no man, and of no body of men, is in a condition to trespass on the liberty of any person, or any description of persons, in society.

" I have nothing to check my wishes towards the establishment of a solid and rational scheme of liberty in France.

" When, therefore, I shall learn, that in France the citizen (by whatever description he is qualified) is in a perfect state of legal security with regard to his life, to his property, to the uncontrolled disposal of his person, to the free use of his industry and his faculties; when I hear that he is protected in the bene-

ficial employment of the estates to which, by the favour of settled law, he was born, or is provided with a fair compensation
for them ; when I know all this of France, I shall be as well
pleased as any one must be," &c. &c.

These expressions show plainly enough the state of the mind
of Mr. Burke at the time.

In a second letter, which must have been written *after* the 5th
and 6th of October, he speaks in a manner far more distinct and
determined.

(Page 352.) " If any of those horrid deeds, which surely
have not been misinterpreted to us, were the acts of the rulers,
what are we to think of an armed people under such rulers ?
Or if (which possibly may be the case) there is in reality and
substance no ruler ; and that the chiefs are driven before the people, rather than lead them ; and if the armed corps are composed
of men who have no fixed principle of obedience, and are embodied only by the prevalence of some general inclination ; who
can repute himself safe among a people so furious and so senseless ?

" In all appearance, the new system is a most bungling and
unworkmanlike performance. I confess I see no principle of
coherence, co-operation, or just subordination of parts in this
whole project ; nor any the least aptitude to the conditions and
wants of the state to which it is applied ; nor anything well imagined for the formation, provision, or direction of a common
force. The direct contrary appears to me. I cannot think with
you, that the Assembly have done much. They have, indeed,
*un*done a great deal, and so completely broken up their country
as a state, that, I assure you, there are few here such Antigalli-
cans as not to feel some pity on the deplorable view of the wreck
of France. I confess to you, that till I saw it I could not conceive that any men in public could have shown so little mercy
to their country."

This was very strong language, and must have been the
result of the outrages that he had observed committed by the
populace of Paris, and the sweeping measures that had been
adopted by the National Assembly. The current of the new
opinions had run very high from the fall of the Bastile on the
14th of July ; the night of the 4th of August, the 5th and 6th of
October, had occurred ; and during all the remainder of the year,
the proceedings in France had been carefully watched by Mr.
Burke, and, therefore, soon after the meeting of our own parliament in January 1790, so early as the 9th of February, 1790,
not a year after the first meeting of the States General in May

1789, he took his part in the English House of Commons, directly in opposition to the whole system of the French patriots and rulers, and protested, in the most decided terms, against the principles, proceedings, and tendencies of the French Revolution.

The other great distinguished statesman and friend to liberty, Mr. Fox, on the other hand, had in conversation, and in the house expressed his sympathy with the French people in their struggle for liberty, and his exultation in their success, for success it appeared to him to be ; and the difference of opinion between these illustrious men was so vital, that a rupture was evidently possible, and even to be expected.

A meeting of the Whig party (Mr. Burke included), it is understood, was held at Burlington House immediately after. It lasted from ten at night to three in the morning, but it ended in the breaking up of the assembly amid irreconcilable differences of opinion. Great talents, it is said, were displayed, but no mutual compromise, or general adjustment, could unhappily be effected.

Mr. Burke after this meeting turned his thoughts to the press ; and so early as May 25 of the same year, 1790, he told Lord Charlemont that he was much occupied and much agitated with his employment, and his task was carried on during the summer with his accustomed ardour.

The result was memorable. In the beginning of the following November, 1790, was published his celebrated work, his " Reflections." Its appearance was a sort of event in the history of the revolution. Thirty thousand copies were sold in an instant in London. No previous production ever excited so much attention.

The work must be considered on the whole as a defence of the old, and as a most indignant protest, and most eloquent indictment, preferred against the new opinions ; illustrated by such events and proceedings as had already taken place in the history of the Revolution.

The sovereigns of the continent transmitted to Mr. Burke their approbation.

The University of Dublin and distinguished members of Oxford offered him their tribute of admiration.

The Archbishop of Aix, and others of the dignified clergy of France, very naturally wrote letters of acknowledgment.

In our own country, the most decided effect was produced on the great body, not only of our clergy, but of our nobility, our statesmen, our men of letters, and our people of property. The tide of public opinion was entirely rolled back, as far as these were concerned; but on the other hand, the book was considered by many as assailing the very foundations of liberty. Mr. Fox thought so, and was not a man to conceal his sentiments upon a great subject like this. He had never done so from the first; he had early made allusions to the French Revolution (and even in the House of Commons), in a very different tone and temper from those of Mr. Burke; and he had afterwards, both in public and private, avowed opinions totally in opposition to those of Mr. Burke's book, when it came out.

The subject of the Quebec Bill, therefore, in the ensuing spring of 1791, produced at length an altercation between these two distinguished men, in the presence of the House of Commons of England: and all political friendship between them was from this moment at an end, and for ever.

They had fought together in many a long debate in the cause of freedom, and the mild government of mankind, during the American contest. They had struggled together in what they conceived a generous cause, resistance to the oppressions of the East; they had united against what they considered to be the excessive and undue influence of the crown, in the constitution of their own country; they had been bound together by the most ennobling of all ties, the mutual admiration of the great talents and elevated qualities of each other; even a sort of tender sympathy existed between them. Fox declared that Burke had been his master, and that he had learned everything from him that he could suppose he knew. And at a subsequent period, Mr. Burke, when his end was now fast approaching, declared in like manner, that Mr. Fox " was born to be loved."

He had indeed shown himself born to be loved in this very altercation with Mr. Burke in the House of Commons; but all these mutual merits, these ties of generous sympathy and kindred genius, all at this unhappy moment were overpowered and found to be vain; and this memorable conflict in the history of mankind between the new and the old opinions, which had already produced such extraordinary events in France, and was to be followed by such convulsions in that country and in Europe, was first to be marked by a conflict and a convulsion of two of the greatest minds that had yet been given to our parliaments by the free constitution of England.

There may be those to whom a subject of this kind may be of no material interest. You are not, I trust, of a temperament so unworthy.

He is without genius himself, who can be indifferent to whatever has concerned illustrious men like these; beings of a higher order, who are destined to be ranked with those who have been the glory of our country; the *Dii Majores* of the Pantheon of England, whose memory can never die, while her story is yet to be told.

I must confess indeed, unwillingly confess, that you will have to note, and you may turn it to your instruction, the irritabilities that appear so often, in our common nature, even when that nature is exhibited, as on the present occasion, in its noblest specimens. These irritabilities were fatal, more especially while one of these great defenders of the rights of humanity was contending, as he conceived, for the freedom of mankind, and the other, as he believed, for the peace and good government of the world.

These general views that I have now offered you on this particular period of the Revolution, and the influence that it had on this country, may be further illustrated by one or two more quotations, which I will proceed to give you. When Mr. Burke first spoke in the spring of 1790, so decidedly and at some length in the House of Commons, producing, in fact, the principles and views that he *afterwards* in November so eloquently and so fully exhibited in his book, Mr. Sheridan immediately rose, and among other observations, and after paying some warm compliments to Mr. Burke's general principles, said, that " he could not conceive how it was possible for a man possessing such principles, or for any man who valued our own constitution, or revered the Revolution, that obtained it for us, to unite with such feelings an indignant, unqualified abhorrence of all the proceedings of the patriotic party in France. He conceived theirs to be as just a Revolution as ours, proceeding upon as sound a principle, and a greater provocation. He vehemently defended the general views and conduct of the National Assembly; he could not even understand what was meant by the charge against them, of having overturned the laws, the justice, and the revenues of their country. What were their laws? The arbitrary mandates of capricious despotism. What their justice? The partial adjudications of venal magistrates. What their revenues? National bankruptcy. This he thought the fundamental error of his right honourable friend's argument, that he accused the National Assembly of creating that, which they had found existing in full deformity, at the first hour of their meeting. The public creditor had been defrauded; the manufacturer was without employ; trade was languishing; famine clung upon the poor, despair on all. In this situation the wisdom and feelings of the nation were appealed to by the government; and was it to be wondered at by Englishmen, that a people so circumstanced should search for the cause and source of all their calamities, or that they should find them in the arbitrary constitution of their government, or in the prodigal and corrupt administration of their revenues? For such an evil, when proved, what remedy could be resorted to but a radical amendment of the frame and fabric of the constitution itself? This change was not the object of the National Assembly only; it was the claim and cry of all France united as one man, for one purpose. He joined with Mr. Burke in abhorring the cruelties that had been committed; but what was the striking lesson, the awful moral that was to be gathered from the outrages of the populace? What but a superior abhorrence of that accursed system of despotic government, that set at nought the property, the liberty, and the lives of the subject; a government that dealt in extortion, dungeons and tortures; that set an example of depravity to the slaves it ruled over: and if a day of power came to the wretched populace, it was not to be wondered at, however it was to be regretted, that they acted without those feelings of justice and humanity which the principles and practice of their governors had stripped them of."

This was early in the spring of 1790, and this is the animated speech, as he calls it, of Mr. Sheridan, to which Mr. Burke alludes, when he gives in his works an epitome of his own.

But again, soon after this, it happened that the Dissenters applied for a repeal of the Corporation and Test Acts. This repeal was refused.

Mrs. Barbauld, one of their brightest ornaments at the time, immediately wrote an eloquent and indignant address to the opponents of the measure: a sort of digression to the subject of France, in the course of her remonstrance, will give you some idea of the general feelings of the friends of liberty at this time in Great Britain, and in truth, of the new opinions, wherever they were entertained. In March, 1790, "Can ye not," she says, " discern the signs of the times? The minds of men are in movement, from the Borysthenes to the Atlantic. Agitated with new and strong emotions, they swell and heave beneath oppression, as the seas beneath the polar circle, when at the approach of spring, they grow impatient to burst their icy chains; when what but an instant before seemed so firm, spread for many a dreary league like a flood of solid marble, at once with a tremendous noise gives way, long fissures spread in every direction, and the air resounds with the clash of floating fragments, which every hour are broken from the mass. The Genius of Philosophy is walking abroad, and with the touch of Ithuriel's spear is trying the establishments of the earth. The various forms of prejudice, superstition, and servility, start up in their true shapes, which had long imposed upon the world under the revered semblances of honour, faith, and loyalty. Whatever is loose must be shaken off, whatever is corrupted must be lopped away, whatever is not built on the broad basis of public utility must be thrown to the ground. Obscure murmurs gather, and swell into a tempest; the spirit of inquiry, like a severe and searching wind, penetrates every part of the great body politic; and whatever is unsound, whatever is infirm, shrinks at the visitation. Liberty *here*, with the lifted crozier in her hand, and the crucifix conspicuous on her breast; *there*, led by philosophy, and crowned with the civic wreath, animates men to assert their long-forgotten rights : with a policy far more liberal and comprehensive than the boasted establishments of Greece and Rome, she diffuses her blessings to every class of men, and even extends a smile of hope and promise to the poor African, the victim of hard, impenetrable avarice. Man, as man, becomes an object of respect; tenets are transferred from theory to practice. The glowing sentiment and the lofty speculation no longer serve but to adorn the pages of a book; they are brought home to men's business and bosoms; and what some centuries ago it was daring but to think and dangerous to express, is now realized and carried into effect. Systems are analyzed into their first principles, and principles are fairly pursued to their legitimate consequences. The enemies of reformation, who palliate what they cannot defend, and defer what they dare not refuse, who, with Felix, put off to a more convenient season what, only because it is the present season, is inconvenient, stand aghast! and find they have no power to put back the important hour when Nature is labouring with the birth of great events. Can ye not discern?—but you do discern these signs; you discern them well, and your alarm is apparent.

" You see a mighty empire breaking from bondage, and exerting the energies of recovered freedom; and England, which was used to glory in being the assertor of liberty and refuge of the oppressed; England, who with generous and respectful sympathy, in times not far remote from our own memory, afforded an asylum to so many subjects of that empire, when crushed beneath the iron rod of persecution, and by so doing, circulated a livelier abhorrence of tyranny within her own veins; England, who has long reproached her with being a slave, now censures her for daring to be free; England, who has held the torch to her, is mortified to see it blaze brighter in her hands; England, for whom, and for whose manners and habits of thinking, that empire has, for some time past, felt even an enthusiastic predilection, and to whom, as a model of laws and government, she looks up with affectionate reverence; England, nursed at the breast of liberty, and breathing the finest spirit of enlightened philosophy, views a sister nation with affected scorn and real jealousy, and presumes to ask whether she yet exists? Yes, all of her exists that is worthy to do so. Her dungeons, indeed, exist no longer; the iron doors are forced; the massy walls are thrown down; and the liberated spectres, trembling between joy and horror, may now blazon the infernal secrets of their prison-house. The cloistered monks no longer exist, nor does the soft heart of sensibility beat behind the grate of a convent; but the best affections of the human mind, permitted to flow in their natural channel, diffuse their friendly influence over the brightening prospect of domestic happiness. Nobles, the creatures of kings, exist no longer; but man, the creature of God, exists there, who only now truly begins to exist, and to hail, with shouts of grateful acclamation, the better birthday of his country. Go on, generous nation, set the world an example of virtues, as you have of talents! Be our model as we have been yours! May the spirit of wisdom, the spirit of moderation, the spirit of firmness, guide and bless your counsels!"

This fine effusion of a comprehensive benevolence, and an ardent imagination, was written in March, 1790, when the new opinions had been now strongly asserted in France, and when Mr. Burke (to whom several passages allude) had taken his part in the House of Commons. In the November following his book appeared, and Sir James Mackintosh, then just entering upon the public exercise of his great powers, soon after published his reply. He presumes not, after the meditation of the work of Burke, to give the reins to his sensibility and generous expectations, as does Mrs. Barbauld; still, in the more measured tone and manner of a philosophic reasoner, he ventures to declare "that the discussion of great truths has prepared a body of laws for the National Assembly; the diffusion of political knowledge has almost prepared a people to receive them; and good men are at length permitted to indulge the hope, that the miseries of the human race are about to be alleviated. That hope may be illusion, for the grounds of its enemies are strong,—the folly and villany of men. Yet they who entertain it will feel no shame in defeat, and no envy of the triumphant predictions of their adversaries.

'Mehercule malim cum Platone errare.'

Whatever be the ultimate fate of the French Revolutionists, the friends of freedom must ever consider them as the authors of the greatest attempt that has hitherto been made in the cause of man. They never can cease to rejoice, that in the long catalogue of calamities and crimes which blacken human annals, the year 1789 presents one spot on which the eye of humanity may with complacence dwell.''

In another page, after a sort of summary and general estimate, he observes (p. 202, Vin. Gal.): '' Thus various are the aspects which the French Revolution, not only in its influence on literature, but in its general tenor and spirit, presents to minds occupied by various opinions. To the eye of Mr. Burke,'' he says, '' it exhibits nothing but a scene of horror; in his mind it inspires no emotion but abhorrence of its leaders, commiseration of their victims, and alarms at the influence of an event which menaces the subversion of the policy, the arts, and the manners of the civilized world. Minds who view it through another medium are filled by it with every sentiment of admiration and triumph, inspired by widening prospects of happiness.''

Such are the expressions in the Vindiciæ Gallicæ; and among these minds must therefore be numbered the mind of the author.

I have now, in a general way, exhibited the different views and opinions of the great writers and reasoners of our own country on this interesting occasion, on this memorable crisis of human affairs; it is surely not without a sentiment of melancholy that we can now read these splendid effusions of the wisest and brightest of mankind. We think of what has passed in France, and however variously we may distribute our censure, we have no admiration to bestow, we have no triumph to enjoy; we have only a painful task to endure. We have to meditate, we have to inquire again and again how it could possibly happen, that such natural hopes, such generous feelings, were all disappointed and in vain; how the cause of liberty was lost; and that, following the course of this Revolution, there is little for the eye

to rest upon but violence, and fury, and bloodshed, and guilt—
little but what is fitted to appal the imagination and mortify the
heart of every man who can sympathize with the happiness of
his fellow-creatures, or feel for the dignity of our common nature.

LECTURE XXI.

FROM THE FIFTH AND SIXTH OF OCTOBER TO THE FLIGHT TO VARENNES.

To us, who live at a distance of time and place from the opening of the French Revolution, and who, above all, have the advantage of judging after the event, it appears not a little surprising, that such a crisis in the affairs of that kingdom as this,
should have been hailed with such brilliant anticipations of the
result.   It is even yet more surprising, that the most favourable
expectations should have been retained and persevered in, not
only through the early months of 1789, but through the years of
1790 and 1791 ; by some even beyond the dreadful massacres of
September 1792.   What was the real truth of the case ? From
the first there was every possibility that great changes might
ensue, so lost had been the government in public opinion ; so active and powerful had been the writers who had been agitating
the minds of men on every subject of morality, politics, and religion.   And what could these changes be ; must they not be
perilous in the extreme ?   Immediately after the meeting of the
States, the popular party appeared to have no modesty of expectation, the court party no prudence of management ; and if then
abuses were to be rooted out, and the State to be regenerated, as
it was called, what could be expected ; what, but that the most
violent concussions would take place ? The people were not
used to freedom ; they had no maxims, principles, and associations ingrafted on their minds, favourable to the establishment
of it, or even to its permanence, if established.   A people vain,
thoughtless, and easily excited ; in their disposition essentially
military ; nay, more, a people among whom such men of education and intelligence as were to be found, had been long exposed
to the influence of such writings and opinions, as were fitted to
loosen all the principles by which society is held together. Under
these circumstances, all perfectly known and acknowledged at
the time, it certainly now appears somewhat wonderful, that

such hopes could have been entertained of an experiment, so truly fearful and uncertain. Never, perhaps, was an instance where wishes were so mistaken for realities, where the influence of the feelings had such an effect on the understanding. To such an extent was this carried, that the truth is, that it was at first, and that it long remained, a mark of prejudice in those who lived at the time, of old age, of want of intelligence, or an indication of some attachment to arbitrary principles of government, to want sympathy in the proceedings or confidence in the intelligence of the patriots of the Constituent Assembly; it was a sort of mental phenomenon, in any wise and good man, to be explained and accounted for: no doubt some exceptions are to be found. Mr. Burke in this country is an obvious one, and M. Mallet du Pan in France is another. So early as November, 1788, this last observer, far from looking forward with hope and delight to the scenes that were disclosing themselves to his view, could only express himself in the following manner :—

" This violence, this anarchy," he writes, " still continues. The authors of it suppose that they are in six months to bring a government to perfection, transform an absolute monarchy into a republic, and administer, according to M. Lacretelle, the most beautiful lessons to all free states. In the mean time there are no two schemes, ideas, or proposals alike : assemblies are held in the provinces with or without orders, or contrary to orders. Every brain is heated. We have reasonings and counter-reasonings ; and instead of showing the different orders in the States how their interests agree, men are only occupied in showing them the contrary, in setting them against each other, and in creating a schism between the Tiers État and the other two orders. They have succeeded. The excess of the abuse of power has brought on an actual crisis, and this crisis will produce no good, owing to the extravagance of what is required and demanded. France is on the eve of seeing the times of Henry III. renewed, where the king had to combat one-half of the nation with the other."

This was written by M. Mallet du Pan in November 1788, and bears a strong testimony to his sagacity and intelligence. Instances of this kind no doubt occurred, but in general little fear seems to have been entertained in France, and nothing but hope in England.

Yet what could be more ominous than the state of affairs at the period where we have just left them, even so early as the middle of October 1789, but six short months after the meeting of the States General ?—The king a prisoner ; the first wise and good men, that were leaders of the Assembly, Mounier and his friends, throwing up the cause of the Revolution in disgust; the court and the adherents of the old régime emigrating or preparing to emigrate, looking only to foreign powers for succour ; the sovereign people triumphant, and every chance for peace and a happy adjustment of the national difficulties left to depend upon the influence of La Fayette and his friends on the one side, and the prudence of the king and his ministers on the other.   Surely this was but a melancholy situation of things, and little fitted to encourage such expectations as seem to have been maintained for many, many months, after the period to which we are now alluding.—During all these months, the Constituent Assembly proceeded, and in the way I have already in general described.

I do not write the history of the Revolution, and can only represent generally what you must attentively read yourselves. Great reforms were made, great and lasting benefits procured for France : I have already mentioned them ; but these were accompanied by the most violent subversions of property, and of all established authority: I have already alluded to them. No terms were kept with the patrons of the old opinions; no proper attention paid to the common principles of justice and right. A certain looseness of principle was observable, a certain indifference to those notions which bind society together, and are necessary to its very existence ; and this more particularly out of the Assembly, in the clubs that ruled the Assembly : on the whole, no system of general conciliation, mutual sacrifices, and temperate adjustments between the supporters of the Revolution and those who were to suffer by it.   In vain were claims and rights to this effect insisted upon by some who still remained in the Assembly, and whom Mounier and his friends should not have parted from.   Nothing of the kind was either carried into execution, or was its necessity sufficiently admitted even in theory by the majority of the Constituent Assembly.

But I am now speaking of their conduct more particularly during a period which I consider as a distinct interval, from the 14th of July 1789, to the king's flight in June 1791.   I do not mean to say that the difficulties of the Assembly were not always great, even during this interval, supposing them to wish well to the king, and the monarchy, and the cause of order and of peace ; but after this interval, and from the unfortunate event of the king's flight, their difficulties became more and more embarrassing; and it would not have been very possible, whatever had been their wishes and opinions in favour of the monarchy, to have properly satisfied the public, or secured their Revolution, when the king had once fled, and been brought back to his prison; not possible, without trenching materially upon the prerogatives that are most obviously necessary to the existence of every monarchy. I speak not, therefore, at present, of this last interval between the return of the king and the close of the Constituent Assembly, but of the interval between the 14th of July 1789, and the king's flight in June 1791. And where the blame is really to reach the Assembly, and I think without much hesitation, is, not only at the first opening of the States, but from this 14th of July 1789, to the king's attempted escape in June 1791, the interval we have first mentioned. Be it admitted that the queen and the court could not bear the Revolution, and wished only the return of the old régime; be it admitted, that the king wanted character; still it was clear, that as far as benevolence and humanity went, he did *not* want character, and that he did not at all insist on the return of the old régime, if the new régime was but made agreeable to the interests of his people, and reconciled in any tolerable manner to his natural feelings and ideas of his prerogative. Even during the 14th of July itself, in 1789, the only reasonable, or indeed I must think, possible solution of all the phenomena was, that he could not be brought to order the troops to fire upon the people; that he would go the lengths of having the troops drawn out to awe the populace into what he conceived a proper obedience to his authority, but had never for a moment admitted the thought of subjecting them, even if necessary, to military execution.

In this situation of things there was no necessity for destroying all the national safeguards and defences of the monarchy. The plea of necessity is all that is urged by the most violent of the democratic writers: the necessity cannot be shown. The better experiment, the experiment more consonant to humanity, to justice, and to wisdom, would have been to have made good terms with the monarchy and with the privileged orders, particularly the clergy; to have had confidence in the known gentleness, probity, and patriotism of the king; and not to have hurried on, while they were busy securing, as they thought, their Revolution, till they left the king no fair hope of honour or comfort to be derived from the new order of things; till his friends and adherents, and the patrons of the old opinions, could turn their eyes nowhere, as they conceived, but to foreign powers; and till every chance was incurred of a civil war, accompanied, in all probability, by a foreign invasion.

I cannot but suppose observations of this kind occurred, not only to Mounier and his friends from the first, but to many members of the Constituent Assembly long after; but why they influenced not the majority of the Assembly, why they occurred not sufficiently to the understandings of La Fayette and his friends (for their feelings, I admit, were always well directed), why they had no effect on the clubs, why they did not even reach the majority of the French nation, the people of property in the provinces and in Paris (I say nothing of the mob in or out of the metropolis, or of wicked and ambitious men wherever they might be found), why they were, on the whole, everywhere so little regarded or respected: this, I think, must be accounted for by such considerations as we have mentioned, all included under the general term of the influence of the new opinions; an influence that arose, not only from the plausible nature of the opinions themselves, but from the disgraceful conduct of the old government, through many prior ages of licentiousness and guilt. And when these new opinions were again (as it was supposed) illustrated and enforced by the late revolution and existing prosperity of America, though the cases were entirely dissimilar, this influence became, even among the enlightened and good (among too many of them at least), particularly in Paris, totally ungovernable and irremediable.

I cannot, as I have said, give the history. I will allude, however, to a few particulars.

Observe the situation of the parties from this 6th of October to the flight of the king.

The leaders of the Constituent Assembly would not, and perhaps thought they could not, separate the king from the court, and trust the one while they could not trust the other; and they therefore continued to make their terms such, that the king, though he might submit, could not possibly approve them.

The court and followers of the old régime wished for nothing but a counter revolution, and they thought it their best policy, forsooth, to throw difficulties in the way of the Constituent Assembly, and contribute to the failure and confusion of every thing, that the folly of the Revolution itself, and the necessity of a return to the old régime, might be the more apparent; looking, however, in secret to foreign powers for assistance to improve any opportunity that might offer, and no longer supposing that any such opportunity could be derived from any proceedings of their countrymen at home; mistaking thus the best and most humane policy: for the Constituent Assembly was, with all its offences and faults, the best master they were likely to have, if they would but cheerfully and sincerely acquiesce in the new order of things; and to look abroad was only to look for a civil war. The people (the respectable part of them) found themselves already more free and more happy than they had been, and they continued to indulge in the warmest hopes and expectations of a freedom and a happiness more and more increasing. The mob and their orators, for it is lamentable to think that they are an important part of the general picture, had been gratified in all the furious and degrading passions of their nature, and considered themselves as the persons whose interests were to be alone attended to, and of these interests they thought themselves the best and only judges. They were, therefore, always ready to be unreasonable, and to destroy all hopes of the Revolution; while the king, in the mean time, sat silent in the prison of his palace, fixed and determined on two points at least, but apparently on two only—not to shed the blood of his people, and not to give up his religion: in every other respect, without effort or remonstrance, observing every thing, but preventing nothing, and only ready to receive any benefit or assistance that might reach him, from whatever quarter it might come.

Such was the general situation of all the parties concerned in the Revolution during the period we are now considering, the period that intervened between the 5th and 6th of October, 1789, and the king's flight in June, 1791.

You will observe the events that took place, the measures that were adopted by the Constituent Assembly; I cannot go into the detail of them. They may be generally described by saying, that though many were of a very useful kind, highly favourable to the rights and liberties of the community; still they were on the whole such, and such was the disposition shown by the Constituent Assembly, that the king at last lost all patience, and attempted to escape.

I cannot, I say, go into the detail, but I will mention a few particulars. In the first place, they did not sufficiently secure themselves from the influence of the popular clubs and mobs of Paris. They made a Riot Act, to which I shall allude, and no more.

The great difficulty which the Constituent Assembly had

always to struggle with, was the mobs in the galleries, the mobs in the streets, inflamed by their orators, and, above all, as the Revolution rolled on, the clubs, who often put the mobs in motion, and were a sort of permanent mob themselves. The difficulty is very candidly considered by the Marquis de Ferrieres.

"Nothing," says the Marquis de Ferrieres, "would have been so easy as to restrain the people and their agitators, but they who wished well to the constitution, always distrustful of the king's sincerity, feared, if they repressed the people with too strong a hand, that they should thus deprive themselves of their services when they might stand but too much in need of them; they broke not an arm which they might want to use. Yes, if they could but have counted on the sincerity of the king and queen, if they could but have seen them unite themselves to those who were really the friends, and separate themselves from those who were naturally the enemies, of the new constitution, and still more the enemies of the leading constitutionalists, those constitutionalists would, I am sure (says he), have been the first to repress those disorders and make the people submit to the law."

All this may be very true, as the Marquis de Ferrieres states it, but it is only an explanation of the conduct of the Assembly and of the court, not a justification of either the one or the other. Both were, according to this statement, in fault; and the blame falls heaviest on the Assembly, for of all legislatures and houses of legislature, the first and most indisputable duty and policy is, to put down mobs and all *rival* clubs and associations; there is no other safety for the public or for themselves.

This last is a very endless subject, and one most important through every part of the French Revolution. You must be already, even from what you have heard in these lectures, perfectly able to comprehend it; and you will, I think, agree with me, as you read the history, that the Constituent Assembly failed in their duty on this point most completely; more particularly after the 14th of July. It was the point, of all others, which they should have resolved to accomplish, whatever they might think of the insincerity of the court, as of all others, the one most necessary to their success.

The club of the Jacobins was at first but a collection of the Breton deputies, who met every day, while the Assembly sat at Versailles, for the sake of mutual discussion and co-operation. Afterwards this sort of party association became more numerous, and all that were of the popular side were admitted. When the

Assembly got to Paris, the club met in the hall of the Jacobins, under the name of the Friends of the Constitution. Hitherto it had been only composed of the deputies; but members were now received from the commune and the districts: the club soon swelled to twelve hundred, was the rallying point of all the more violent promoters of the Revolution from time to time, had its affiliated societies all over France, soon began to exercise a sort of domination over the Assembly, and at length became the scourge of France and the terror of Europe.

The club of 1789, so called from the year of its formation, was the club of the constitutionalists, La Fayette, Bailly, le Duc de Rochefoucault, &c. These were more moderate from the first, and more reasonable, but like the Jacobins, they had to sacrifice to popularity, and being men of more principle and more sense, they were outstripped in the race, and exercised a far less important influence on the fortunes of the Revolution.

To the mobs in the galleries, the mobs in the Palais Royal, and the mobs in the clubs, were to be added the mobs of the press, the journalists, libellers, and political writers of every description. With such materials in existence, a commotion, an insurrection, was always ready. A desperate and bad man in the Jacobin club, or in the Palais Royal, if but gifted with popular eloquence, had no difficulty. Rumours, suspicions, falsehoods of whatever kind, were first whispered, and then openly circulated. The demagogues, the journalists, were in motion, speeches made, and pamphlets read, groups collected; these were united into a crowd, and the business was then done. But surely all this time, the want of all regular ideas of propriety, of justice, of humanity, and sense, of all moral feelings on the subjects of property and law, were most deplorably visible in all the members of the community taken together; in the people (of the second and middle ranks more particularly), who must have constituted the national guard; in the members of the clubs, and in those who were connected with the press, and who surely might altogether have furnished, it might have been supposed in every capital of a civilized country, a sufficient majority, a sufficient physical strength, for the purposes of the National Assembly, while it was only endeavouring to repress disorder, outrages, and crimes, and supporting and defending its own rights and authority; being, as it was, the only image of regular government then existing; and employed, as it would then have been, in asserting and protecting the most obvious interests of every society of human beings.

Some efforts, however, were made by the assembly, as I have announced to you, and I will now allude to them.   Soon after the king and queen had been brought to the Tuilleries, Mirabeau, who, though a tribune of the people, was still a man of sense, and well aware of the necessity of order and law, brought in a decree, imitated, he said, but not copied from the Riot Act of England.   This is the Riot Act I have just alluded to.

The decree is well expressed, in strong and just terms ; it has the same fault with our own act, that of requiring the magistrate, in the presence of a furious mob, to read it (at the peril, no doubt, often of his life); but it is extremely superior in one material respect, for it allows the rioters to come forward, to the number of six, and state their grievances to the magistrates, the rest withdrawing.

This decree was proposed on the 14th of October, 1789, and Mirabeau seems very properly to have received the applauses of the Assembly ; the business, however, was adjourned.   But it happened a few days after, that a baker was seized by the populace, and with every circumstance of the most ferocious injustice and cruelty, was murdered in the presence of the representatives of the commune. They came, therefore, to the Assembly, and implored them to pass the law immediately.   The subject of the decree was therefore resumed, and the law made and passed.   But a very great improvement was introduced, for the decree (or Riot Act), after a short and sensible preamble, stating, that liberty only could exist on the supposition of obedience to the laws, went on thus : first, the municipal officers, if the public peace is endangered, shall be bound to declare that military force must be produced ; and of this declaration, secondly, the signal shall be, the hanging out of the windows of the Town House, a red flag, and their carrying before them a red flag through the streets, wherever they, with their armed force, go ; and thirdly, on the appearance of this red flag, all crowds and collections of men shall from that moment be held criminal, and liable to be dispersed by force.

The former reasonable provision is then renewed, that six may be named to state grievances, the rest dispersing ; and after three notices given aloud by the magistrate, he may take what measures he pleases to put down the riot.   Proper distinctions are afterwards made, and different punishments enacted.

This Riot Act appears to me a great improvement on the Riot Act and law of England.   With us, a meeting or concourse of the people only becomes illegal, when it has become a just cause of terror to the peaceful inhabitants of the town or community, so that it is often impossible for the people to know whether they are obnoxious to the law or not; and they ought to have counsel and take their opinion every five minutes, as the case may alter in the eye of the law, from their increasing numbers, or the nature of their conduct. They may be fired upon if they are committing violence, but the custom having always been, for the last half century, for the magistrate *first* to read the Riot Act, the people ignorantly suppose that they are safe till the Riot Act has been read; and it then often becomes a question of fact, whether the Act has, or has not, been read; at all events, it cannot have been heard by rioters at any distance. Now, a red flag on a town house, or carried along by an officer, can always be seen; and there is also a justice and a humanity in allowing the people to send six to state their grievances, the rest dispersing, perfectly worthy of the imitation of an English legislature.

You will see the decree, as brought in by the lawyer Target and Mirabeau, and as afterwards left to stand, in the third volume of Bailly.

In the fifth book of the Marquis de Ferrieres, you may observe the conduct of Robespierre, the only deputy that resisted the enactment of this law; and that, in a regular speech, affirming that the magistrates, and not the people, were in fault. He probably hoped to be considered by the populace, as the only person who supported their rights and their sovereignty. Robespierre was always from the first the principle of evil.

The murderers of the innocent man who had perished were then punished. But in the event, the ferocious populace of Paris were never kept in any proper obedience to the laws, even when all that was required from them was, an observance of the common duties of humanity and justice; and the reproaches you have just heard from me must, I think, be considered as perfectly deserved both by the Constituent Assembly and the whole community.

This Riot Act, the Law Martial as it was called, was afterwards acted upon by La Fayette and Bailly, on an occasion of a riot clearly treasonable; people were killed. But some time after, this performance of his duty was made an accusation against Bailly, and he was on that account dragged from his retirement, and perished under the guillotine.

I stop to observe, that science had on this occasion not to be ashamed of her son. " You are afraid, Bailly," said one of the ruffians who surrounded him; "you turn pale and tremble." "'Tis the cold," said the philosopher, and calmly submitted to his fate.

Mirabeau seems to have become aware that the monarchy was in danger, for after procuring this Law Martial, he had again the merit of carrying (not a little by his own personal exertions and commanding eloquence) the decree, which threw the decision of peace and war considerably into the hands of the king. He had met, however, every opposition in and out of the Assembly, his name being hawked about the streets as that of a traitor; and he had been made to see how shifting was the breath of popular applause. "I know," said he, "that from the Capitol to the Tarpeian rock is but one step."

Such were the chief points that were carried in favour of the crown. What further particulars I have to allude to were of a different kind; for instance, the violent party, though overpowered by Mirabeau, on this last occasion had obtained a terrible advantage in the publication of what was called the Red Book, the register of the depredations and foolish and criminal expenses of the court: those of the former reign, out of respect to the present king's wishes, were not examined; and those of the present were less than might have been expected. They are considered at full length by Bertrand de Moleville. Still the publication of the Red Book was unfavourable to the royal authority.

The new opinions had always set strongly in the direction of republicanism; the expense of a monarchy is the best topic, whether of reasoning or abuse, which democratic speakers or writers can avail themselves of, and the disclosures of the Red Book (misrepresented and exaggerated as the facts it contained were sure to be), was a fatal event, when the Assembly, that is, the public, were determining what was the quantity of republicanism that was to be mixed up with the monarchy, for the better advancement and security of the public happiness. Decrees and opinions, and a language was adopted, as the language of the constitution, all highly unfavourable to the royal power. The domains of the crown were considered as belonging to the nation only: far from remembering that these domains were originally the property of the family of the Bourbons, the people considered themselves as highly munificent, when in exchange for these they established the Civil List. The bargain was but an injurious one to the crown, and the fact was, that far from being generous, they were not even just. But this was then of

little consequence; and this was not all. The king was thus
made to assume the appearance of a tax upon the country, of a
useless excrescence, the amputation of which would be the rid-
dance of an expense : he was now looked upon as salaried and
paid, an idea little consonant to the dignity that had been attached for fourteen centuries to the name of king. The titles of
the first French citizen, of the first public functionary, totally
altered the very nature and essence of all monarchy in the eyes
of the people. Instead of a prince invested, in right of his very
birth, with an authority that seemed to derive its source from
the very will and appointment of the Deity himself, the people
were now to see in their king but a delegate from themselves,
obliged to act, not in conformity to his own will, but theirs;
not strong in his own strength, but in theirs; not rich in his
own possessions, but in theirs; not illustrious on his own account, but on theirs; owing everything he possessed, inherited,
or enjoyed, to their liberality alone; their mandatary, officer
and servant, accountable, and referring for everything he was to
think and do, to their tribunal and their directions.

These new notions of the nature and situation of a king of
France, the result among the more violent and among the people
themselves, of the prevalence of the new opinions, might accord
with the feelings or befit the dignity of the president of a republic, or might satisfy the mind of a private citizen, raised by
his military merit to a throne amid the storm of a revolution;
but were fatal to Louis XVI., who was to fall through all these
immeasurable degradations, and yet to retain the respect of the
public, and still more, was often to be called upon to exercise
the unpopular offices of executive authority. No success could
possibly attend a disposition of things like this; no such change
of situation could possibly be supposed voluntary on the part of
·the king; and a wide field was thus opened for every description
of fear, distrust, and insinuation, complaint and accusation, on
the part of the more violent leaders of the Assembly, and the
demagogues of the Palais Royal. In all this there was no wisdom.

The question is not, what a king may or may not be in the
eye of philosophy and reason ; the question is whether the existing king was to be stripped of all the associations that belonged
to this character, as king of the French people. But even in
the eye of philosophy and reason, it is quite idle to talk of a king
as a mere man : he may be so to his medical attendant, or an
anatomist, but not so to others. He is a being who is to discharge high duties to the community, to save them from con-

tending for pre-eminence among themselves, and to be assisted by every possible association of honour and respect; and the question is, in the case before us, during the progress of a revolution, whether the leading men in the assembly, or popular men in the clubs and streets, *could be so ill* employed, as in tearing away from the monarch, or first magistrate if you please, all the long transmitted and inherited love and respect that belonged to the office, and during such a revolutionary period of violence and disorder, totally destroying all the supports and defences that had hitherto surrounded the throne as with a rampart; in short, all " the divinity that had before so hedged in the king, that treason durst not look at it." But considerations of this kind (the result, I venture to conceive, of a far sounder philosophy than that which leaves the most important interests of society to depend upon the mere abstract notions of utility, and the mere unassisted conclusions of the understanding, utility ill understood, and the understanding most superficially exercised), reasonings of this apparently humble nature were not likely to be relished by the heated men who were now conducting the Revolution, and not likely to oppose any proper obstacles to the current that was setting in, so clearly to the destruction of the monarchy. The right of peace and war had been determined favourably to the crown, but every other question much to the contrary. The Assembly had decreed, that justice should be administered in the name indeed of the king, but the magistrates of the police were to be elected by the people, and so were the higher judges. Again, the entire destruction of the nobility was now to follow; and this was accomplished while the grand measure of the federation was preparing. It is an important part of the Revolution, and I dwell upon it for a moment.

The middle of June had arrived, the 14th of June, 1790; the anniversary of the taking of the Bastile was approaching, and the general fermentation became greater than ever.

And two measures were now to be accomplished—the abolition of the titles of the nobility, and a grand federation : and now observe a particular circumstance by which they were prefaced, that was a part of the plan of attack, and was strongly indicative of the state of the public mind at this period, the middle of the year 1790 ; a circumstance that is quite a specimen of this fermentation which I have just spoken of, and of the French nation itself (how little fitted at the time to undertake such an enterprise as a revolution). The scene I allude to took place about this time in the Assembly ; you will find it regularly described and recorded in the histories; but it is a scene which you yourselves, in your own sound state of mind, will be unable to figure to your imagination without contempt and laughter.   Before then the titles were to be taken from the no-bility, and the federation exhibited, conceive, as a sort of pre-paratory measure, conceive a man presenting himself to a Na-tional Assembly, as the orator of the human race; bringing after him a hired mob of creatures, who were, each in his proper dress, to represent the various nations under heaven, English, Russians, and Spaniards, Turks, Africans, Indians, and Arabians, and in a solemn speech, addressed to the president, who was to keep his countenance all the time, and who actually did so, requesting to be placed in the middle of the Champ de Mars on the day of the ensuing federation.   " This civic solemnity," the orator ob-served, " will not be the festival of the French only, but also the festival of mankind ; the trumpet that sounds the resurrec-tion of a great nation has echoed through the four quarters of the world, and the notes of joy, of a chorus of twenty-five mil-lions of free men, have awakened nations, long buried in slavery; our mission is written in indelible characters upon the heart of every man.   You have proved beyond a doubt that the sove-reignty resides in the people ; now the people are every where under the yoke of dictators, who call themselves sovereigns, in spite of your principles.   The *ambassadors* of tyrants could not do so much honour to your august festival as most of us, whose mission is tacitly acknowledged by our countrymen, that is to say, by oppressed sovereigns," meaning thereby the people, the aforesaid English, Russians, Spaniards, Turks, Africans, Indians, and Arabians.

The president assented with due form and dignity to this uni-versal request of the habitable globe.   The Deputy Fermont voted that this request should be granted by acclamation, a request which came from citizens assembled, as it appeared, from all parts of the world : the motion was seconded in favour of these generous strangers, as they were called (who were hired in and about Paris to come from all quarters of the world); it was se-conded, strange to say, by one of the Lameths (distinguished members of the Assembly at the time), but he had another idea, he said, to lay before the Assembly : "The figures representing four provinces, which are chained as images of tributary nations at the feet of the statue of Louis XIV., are a sight not to be borne by free men.   These monuments of pride are not to stand in the reign of equality."   And after this sortie on the fine arts, for these unfortunate images were beautiful specimens of sculpture, at length and at last came the grand attack of all, to which all this degrading mummery was but an introduction. " This day," said the Deputy Lumbel, " we dig the grave of vanity. 1 move that all persons be prohibited from taking the titles of peer, duke, count, marquis, &c., and that nobility be no longer heredi- tary."

" Hereditary nobility," said Charles de Lameth, while he supported this motion, " shocks reason, and is repugnant to true liberty ;" another thought the same of the term " My Lord ;" M. de Noailles, of liveries ; M. de St. Fargeau, of all names but family names ; Mathew de Montmorenci, of armorial bearings. It was in vain that M. de Virieu exclaimed, " Urge not on this popular fury, which has already so dishonoured our Revolution;" it was in vain that the poor Abbé Maury observed, " that the very Romans themselves had orders of knighthood, and yet were free, and that in France to destroy the nobility was to destroy the monarchy." It was not till the conclusion of the debate that the coté droit began to perceive that it was seriously pro- posed to pass these decrees; and then indeed several deputies of the nobility sprang towards the tribune, and demanded with warmth to be heard ; but their remonstrances and their indigna- tion were lost and overpowered amid the general shouts of the coté gauche and the galleries. In a fortunate moment of silence, the Comte de Lansberg, the deputy from the noblesse of Alsace, was just able to observe, " My constituents will disavow me, and will hold me unworthy to appear before them, if I sanction by my presence a deliberation so injurious to their honour. I retire then, but it is in the grief of my heart. Submit your- selves (I shall say to them), yes, submit to the laws of the As- sembly. They will so submit, but they will know, at the same time, that gentlemen they were born, and that gentlemen they must live, and they must die; and that this nothing can pre- vent." Such was the scene, and such the conclusion of it.

The decree was considered by the Marquis de Ferrieres as but impolitic; it set the feeling of honour in opposition to the na- tional interest, amid a numerous body of men, who possessed a large part of the wealth of France at the time. Hitherto the nobles had suffered patiently enough the hostile measures of the Assembly, but they now became irreconcilable enemies to the Revolution, and a league was formed between the nobility, clergy, and the parliaments ; and they laboured with equal spirit and activity against a new order of things, which they could no longer tolerate for a moment, as it left them without name or place, the mere images and spectres of their former greatness. Indeed, on every account the decree was impolitic. The nobility had in reality been already put down, when they were refused their separate constitutional existence at the opening of the States, and had been mingled among the Tiers Etat in the National Assembly; and again, when on the night of the 4th of August their feudal prerogatives, distinctions, and properties were, without the slightest discrimination or reservation, all swept away and abolished; lastly, when they were to vote, like other citizens of the Electoral Assemblies. The influence, therefore, of their mere titles would have been gradually lost; and there was no need of outraging them in the tenderest point, by depriving them of this last illusion of their feelings, and the sole surviving pride and treasure of their hearts.

But a democratic feeling was to be indulged by the leading members of the Assembly, a democratic spirit was to be diffused among the people: every badge of inequality was therefore to be destroyed, and it was thought necessary to the Revolution, that the whole character of the government, and therefore of the country, should be altered; that every thing should emanate from the sovereignty of the people. Now, it is to this notion and spirit, acted upon more or less from the first opening of the States, that we object, as violent and unnecessary, as leading directly to confusion and a civil war, as rendering it totally impossible that the Revolution should be conducted by men of any peaceful feelings or sober sense. All might have been well, if the more violent friends of freedom could but have seen the real wisdom of the case as it stood before them, and been properly doubtful of themselves and of the public, and duly impressed with the uncertain issue of every thing human.

This is the sort of sentiment that I mean to pervade every part and portion of the lectures I am now delivering. I repeat my sentiment again and again, totally regardless of what may be the rules of taste or propriety of composition. It is the great impression that I wish you to bear away, accompanied, however, as it is in my own mind, and as I must expect it to be in yours, with a due sense of the indispensable necessity of civil and religious liberty to the regular and proper happiness and prosperity of every community, and in no respect withdrawing from your view the faults of the supporters of the old opinions.

The Assembly, for I must now return to their history, immediately after the abolition of the titles of the nobility, proceeded to support their Revolution by the measure I have already announced to you, the federation; a measure in itself more harmless and more adapted to the national character. The truth was, they were not quite at ease on the subject of the military force of the country; at least, they thought it advisable to pledge to the Revolution the national guards, everywhere dispersed over France, and the troops of the line. They therefore formed the project of an immense federation, to take place on the 14th of July, the anniversary of the taking of the Bastile; and deputations were to be sent from all the armed bodies by land and by sea, from all the different departments of the kingdom and constituted authorities of the capital. These were all to assist at the fête, in the presence of the National Assembly, the king, the queen, and the court: they were to be surrounded by the greatest possible number of spectators, three or four hundred thousand people. An immense plain, the Champ de Mars, was to be hollowed out into an amphitheatre; a superb altar to be erected; three hundred priests to assemble, and twelve hundred musicians; and an oath to be taken by these deputies, by the nation, and the king, of fidelity to the constitution, the great leading principles of which had been already sufficiently promulgated, though the constitution itself had not as yet been finally prepared and delivered.

The Histories and the Memoirs, particularly those of the Marquis de Ferrieres, will give you a sufficient description of this celebrated federation, so characteristic of the Revolution and the nation.

But the leading observation resulting from the whole is, that the Revolution and the National Assembly must now have been most clearly and universally approved and acceptable to the French people, or such a fête could neither have been attempted nor executed. This popularity of the Revolution, and therefore of the fête in honour of it, was in different stages of it severely tried and abundantly shown. It was intended, for instance, as I have mentioned, that three hundred thousand spectators should be accommodated with seats. Twelve thousand, some say twenty-five thousand, workmen were employed; but it was reported that the necessary preparations could not thus be finished by the day appointed. This would have been a serious difficulty anywhere but in France, and even in France must have been fatal to the success of the fête, if the Revolution had not been popular. But in an instant all Paris was in motion, and citizens of every age, sex, and condition, appeared with the spade, the pickaxe, and the wheelbarrow, all mixed and mingled together, to carry on the work. The women of fashion and the poissardes, those of good repute and those of ill, courtiers and butchers, players and monks, old men and children, capuchins, academicians, chevaliers of St. Louis, and workmen from the villages, headed by their mayors and curés,—all this assemblage of voluntary labourers was fed and accommodated by people travelling with taverns and portable shops, and enlivened by songs, and shouts of joy, and the national air of "Ca ira;" and the result was, that all the preparations for the fête were ready before the time appointed; and the triumph of these apparently curious and comical groups, but in reality these striking representatives of an overwhelming and therefore very serious and almost frightful patriotic enthusiasm, was quite complete.

It was in vain, in like manner, that the rain poured down in torrents on the day of the federation; the fête still went on. Nothing could oppose resistance to the universal joy. The dances were formed, and the processions moved forwards, and the music sounded; and neither earth below, nor sky above, the wet Champ de Mars, nor the drenching coldness of the descending clouds, had been or were of the slightest avail to repress the vivacity of the multitude, excited as they were by what was to them the dearest of all objects, a magnificent spectacle; fired, too, with exultation at the visible departure of the old régime, and gazing with delight on the approach and promises of the new.

And certainly, if we could forget for a moment all subsequent events, and the stain that has been brought on the great cause of liberty by this giddy people, by many of the very individuals here assembled, certainly there was something in this spectacle, this universal expression of interchanged happiness and affection, this apparent dedication of a whole nation to the leading principles of liberty, this resounding exultation of the people at their emancipation from the blighting and degrading influence of a government that had so long ceased to be respected, this union and amalgamation of the interests and wishes of the king and of the people well fitted to overpower the imagination and awaken the sympathies of the benevolent, wherever they might be found, in France or in England, in Europe or in America. It seemed no time now to hesitate or to examine, no time to consider what had preceded or what was to follow this glittering and magnificent show. Altars and arches were to be seen; the inscriptions that everywhere appeared were testimonies to liberty and to law. "The country and the law: let us die to defend them," was one, for instance. "The king of a free people, he is alone the king of power," was another. "Cherish liberty; you possess it, be worthy of it." "It is not birth that makes the difference between men, it is virtue only." "It is the law that should be everywhere; before it, all are equal." These were among the mottoes and inscriptions; and where the Bastile had once stood was an esplanade, and over every entrance to it was written, in a manner, affecting no doubt, yet truly characteristic of the nation, "Here we now dance."

But it was fêtes and festivals in honour of liberty that this sensitive, theatric people far better understood than the nature of liberty itself; and the scene before us has been thought the most awful and extensive exhibition of perjury that the world ever saw; for it must be observed that the same scene was acted at one and the same moment in every department of France. The perjury was that of millions of human beings swearing to a constitution which the next moment they destroyed; and it will be a warning, it is to be hoped, to mankind, never again to have recourse to such idle expedients, or rather to such impious mockeries. No legislation is so immoral as that which has recourse to oaths; none so unwise, as that which depends upon them. I speak not of the point of duty in those who take them. In the coarse legislation of commerce, custom-house oaths have become a proverb; and, even in the instance before us, Louis XVI. was a man of piety, and would not have bound himself by an oath which he did not mean to keep; but observe the temptation to which the integrity of his mind was on this occasion exposed. How could he resist the measure? How could he decline taking the oath? He was to all intents and purposes a prisoner, and had been so since the 5th and 6th of October. He had no force to oppose to that of the National Assembly; and not to assent to the oath in the general manner in which it was worded, would have been to say that he was determined to restore the old régime, that he would have no further concern with the Revolution, and in short to leave the patriotic party no measure but to dethrone him, or himself no measure but to resign his crown. He stood, therefore, at the federation, under the strictest political necessity to conform to the wishes of the Assembly, and to act the part allotted to him in this grand national performance. It is, indeed, sufficiently clear that the king, as far as the oath went, was perfectly sincere. No doubt the Revolution had rolled on, and far overflowed the boundaries within which he would have thought its course ought to be confined; still, he was desirous of the happiness of his people,

he had confidence in his own good intentions, he had no wish
for any authority inconsistent with the public good, and as yet
he did not despair either of the affection or the loyalty of his
subjects ; as yet he conceived that, if he could but weather
the storm, the storm would gradually subside, and that he and
his people might hereafter see happier days, and enjoy the calm
of mutual confidence and an improved constitution of the government.   It is sufficiently probable, therefore, that the king was
sincere when he promised to uphold the constitution by all the
means that were put in his power, and that he conformed, if
not with a cheerful, yet with a general acquiescence, to what
was required of him during the fête and ceremonials of the
federation.   Still, the oath was imposed upon him.   But he
was not entirely without his gratifications.   He seems to have
been much and very naturally affected by the general testimonies of loyalty and respect which, amidst all the fervour of
revolutionary feelings, were still paid him by many of those
who came deputed from the different provinces.   But when the
tumult and excitement of the fête were passed away, when the
National Assembly resumed its wonted course of procedure, and
when various circumstances continued to dispel the hopes and
illusions with which the king had soothed the benevolence of
his nature, different views of his situation seem gradually to
have opened upon his mind, and before the end of the year he
had begun to entertain thoughts of escaping from his prison,
and of neither acquiescing, nor appearing to acquiesce, in the
constitution, such as it was likely to become, or as it was even
then administered and understood, at the close of the year 1790.
The entire destruction of the ancient clergy of France was accomplished even before the federation of July 1790; their
property had been voted to be at the disposal of the nation.   In
the November afterwards they were to receive their stipends
only on their acquiescing in the new tenure that was prepared
for them : this they could not do.   I have already alluded to
this part of the general subject; and the unhappy monarch
found himself obliged to assent to the decree of the Assembly,
and appear to himself and to the world the approver and accomplice of all this intolerance and injustice.

His feelings, too, were violated to a degree that, patient as
he was, seems to have thrown him into a state of real illness
and fever, by an unfortunate occurrence that took place at the
Tuilleries (you will see the detail in the histories).   A body of
gentlemen, who thought his life in danger, and had rushed to

his assistance, were disarmed, and turned out of the palace by La Fayette and the national guard. La Fayette was not a man likely to have wantonly distressed the king, or needlessly to have treated his adherents with violence and disrespect; but, on some account or other, the impression left by this affair on the feelings of the monarch was of the most painful kind, and rendered the situation in which he was placed more than ever, in his eyes, a situation of humiliation and disgrace.

Another circumstance occurred (you will again see the detail in the histories), which still further outraged his feelings. He and the family wished probably to escape from the priests of the Constituent Assembly, and go to St. Cloud, during the Easter week of 1791, where a regular priest might assist them in their devotions; but the populace of Paris had got a notion that this expedition to St. Cloud was only a pretence; that the royal family intended to fly the kingdom and create a civil war. The same notion got possession of the national guards. The king's carriages were, therefore, stopped at the gate of the Tuilleries, and no entreaties, no efforts that La Fayette could make, whether of persuasion or force, were of the slightest avail, and the helpless monarch and his queen were obliged to submit and to return to their palace, which was not now nominally, but avowedly a prison.

It was impossible that an insult of this kind, at the gate of the Tuilleries, in the midst of the metropolis, in open day, and in the face of all Europe, could be tolerated; and events of this kind were well fitted to desolate the heart of the unfortunate monarch, and to show him that he was indeed fallen from his high estate, and at the mercy of the populace.

In addition to these circumstances, a negotiation with Mirabeau had been rendered fruitless by the death of that extraordinary man. You are not to suppose that the object of this negotiation was to restore the old régime, and that either the king meant to be an arbitrary monarch, or that Mirabeau was ready to be a traitor to the liberties of his country. The intention of both was to call a new Constituent Assembly, for the purpose of procuring better terms for the monarch than the existing Assembly offered. Any such plan (doubtful from the first) was, however, entirely at an end when Mirabeau expired; and the king conceived that he had no measure left but to try to escape from the Assembly and the populace of Paris, establish himself in some frontier town, collect around him that part of the army, the nobility, and the people that were still faithful to him, and (if necessary) with the assistance of foreign powers, in some mixed way, as he hoped, partly of persuasion and partly of force, by the combined operation of the hopes and fears, the good and bad feelings of his subjects, procure more honourable terms for *himself*, and a more stable and rational system of liberty for *them*. The only question was, whether the escape from the Tuilleries was practicable? and the king having at length persuaded himself that it was, he drew up a memorial to be presented to the Assembly, a manifesto that was to explain and justify to the people of France the motives of his conduct, and then he fled.

LECTURE XXII.

FLIGHT TO VARENNES.

IN my last lecture I have endeavoured to describe to you the situation of the king, and the circumstances which led him at last to conceive that he had no measure left but to try to escape from the Assembly and the populace of Paris. His project seems to have been to establish himself in some frontier town, as I have already mentioned, and to have called the well-disposed around him, to procure better terms from the National Assembly.

In the manifesto which he drew up and left to be presented to the Assembly, he observed, " that while the king could hope to see the order and happiness of the kingdom revived by the measures of the National Assembly, and by his residence near that Assembly, in the capital, he regretted no personal sacrifice; nor should he have objected to the nullity with which an absolute privation of freedom has infected all his proceedings, since the month of October 1789, if that hope had been fulfilled; but now that his only recompense for so many sacrifices is to behold the destruction of royalty, to see all the powers of government dissolved, all property violated, personal safety everywhere endangered, crimes remaining unpunished, and perfect anarchy domineering over the laws, while that semblance of authority given him by the new constitution is insufficient for repairing any one of those evils with which the kingdom is afflicted, the king, after having solemnly protested against all the acts which emanated from him during his captivity, believes that he ought to submit to the view of France, and of the whole world, a

detail of his own conduct, and of that of the government which
has established itself in the kingdom."

Such is the first paragraph of the memorial, and it is in itself
a justification of his flight.　The only point remaining is the
prudence of the measure; and the prudence of the measure
must have been thought to consist in the absence of every other
alternative.　To the king and his adviser, the queen, who was
long indisposed to the attempt, it must at last have appeared
that he was every day journeying on to his dethronement; that
this event might be accelerated by the failure of this expedition, but could only be prevented by its success.

The king, therefore, attempted to escape, but failed; and this
failure led immediately to the loss of all his consequence and
respect with the public, gave every facility to the violent promoters of the Revolution, and enabled the republican party
first to dethrone him, and then put him to death.　What might
have followed, if he had succeeded in the attempt, it may be
difficult to say; but these results at least, and they were inevitable results, are surely for ever to be deplored; and it is impossible for us not to turn with the greatest interest to inquire,
what can now be known of the history of this most unfortunate
expedition.

It appears to me that everything relating to it may be found
that can well be required.　In the collection of Memoirs now
publishing by the "Baudouin Freres" at Paris, you will find a
memoir, or an account of some kind or other, furnished by almost
every person that was concerned in it.　I will refer you to proper authorities, and mention a few particulars.　In the Memoirs
of Weber you will see an account (of itself sufficiently minute
and satisfactory) drawn up by the Archbishop of Toulouse, from
conversations that he himself had with the queen, with the Marquis de Bouillé, and with other individuals well informed of all
that passed.

Through all the years of 1789 and 1790, the king had, it
seems, turned away from every project of the kind, though
reasons were urged to him by his most devoted adherents, and
sufficient facilities afforded him during his stay at St. Cloud.

"In the summer of 1790 I spoke to the queen, and reasoned
with her," says the archbishop.　"'What would you have the
king do,' replied the queen; 'at a distance from Paris, without
money, without those personal qualities which might recall the
army to its allegiance, without any proper power of seeing his
own way, without any counsellor to show it to him and supply

his deficiencies, above all, with his horror of a civil war? Let us quit the subject.'"

From these few words may, I think, be collected the whole of the case, as it long appeared to the court, the queen, and the king; the different sentiments of each are here, however briefly, fully displayed. But towards the close of the year 1790, as appears from the Memoirs of the Marquis de Bouillé, the king had begun seriously to consider whether he could not withdraw himself from the domination of the Assembly. He saw, as he thought, that it was they who were to exercise all executive authority, even in its most minute details; his ancient ministers were dismissed, and more revolutionary ministers were substituted; and, above all, the persecution of the clergy, in which the king had himself been made to appear an accomplice, rendered his situation totally intolerable to him. He opened his mind to the queen, but she saw the difficulties and the consequences, and for a long time would not hear of any project of escape.

The very first point to be accomplished, that of quitting the Tuilleries, seemed quite impracticable; everywhere they were surrounded by guards and spies, within and without their prison: two or three valets and ladies of the chamber, were all that either king or queen could depend upon. When escaped, too, from Paris, some armed force would be necessary to clear the way for them to the frontiers. The project appeared totally hazardous and unadvisable. But at last the king was quite determined on some attempt of the kind, and the queen from that time bent her whole thoughts to the providing of the proper means for its success.

The first part of the enterprise, the escape from the Tuilleries, she resolved, in concert with the king, to undertake herself; and for the management of the second part, the king and queen looked round, and the Marquis de Bouillé was fixed upon. You will see in the memoir drawn up by the archbishop, and the memoir of the marquis himself, the communications that were interchanged and the arrangements finally made.

The whole project was for a time suspended by the negotiation with Mirabeau, but was on his death renewed; and the plan of the enterprise was this:—The queen was, as I have intimated, to provide for the success of the expedition till the royal family reached Chalons, and afterwards the marquis. He was to have military detachments in motion, on the plea of watching the movements of the Austrians, and some of them fixed at each post, under pretence of escorting a treasure, and then to receive and transmit the royal fugitives from place to place, peaceably and unobserved if possible, but if not, by force.

Now here it will be immediately seen, that as the Revolution was popular, the minds of the people everywhere excited and alive to every circumstance that occurred, and as any escape of the king and queen would necessarily be considered by them as the signal of a civil war, accuracy in point of time was everything. Detachments of troops, however stationed, and under whatever pretence, could not but be subjects of suspicion and alarm; and the longer they stayed at any post, without any known object, the more violent and ungovernable would these suspicions and alarms become.

You will be prepared by this consideration to sympathize with all the cruel accidents that from the first occurred to delay the royal family. The king and queen had fixed their departure for the night of the 19th. One of the ladies who was to be in attendance on the dauphin on that night fell sick; her friend therefore had to remain in service a night longer than was expected; but she was a suspected person, and this night was the very one appointed for the flight: and the queen had no resource but to put off the expedition for twenty-four hours, and to fix it for the succeeding night of the 20th. The Marquis de Bouillé was indeed apprized of the change on the 15th, but it was a change, he says, most inconvenient and untoward; and one of the officers, ignorant of the importance of what he was doing, neglected to observe the alteration in his orders, and to fix his relay at Varennes on the evening of the 19th instead of the 20th, giving thus a more prolonged and unnecessary alarm to the inhabitants. The next misfortune was, that more than half an hour was lost while the queen was finding the carriage that waited for her, after she had left the Tuilleries; neither she nor the gentleman (one of the body guards) who accompanied her, seem to have known properly the streets of Paris; a most unexpected difficulty: the point had not been thought of. No doubt this part of the archbishop's narrative is very improbable; but he had conversed with the queen, he says, and this was one of those particulars which the queen was most likely to have dwelt upon.

Afterwards, the Count de Fersin, who was coachman on this occasion, appeared to make a détour through many streets, but he did so probably to ascertain whether the carriages were gone, according to his orders, to the place where he was to meet them;

but on whatever account, another fatal half hour was thus expended before the travelling-carriages were reached, that stood
waiting at the place appointed.   Everything else was managed
by the queen and the count with great good fortune and address.
The escape, through an unsuspected room and door of the Tuilleries ; the passports, and the choice, as far as their fidelity went,
of the body guard, who were to act as couriers and attendants ;
but alas ! for the etiquette of an ancient court !   M. de Bouillé
had very properly required that M. D'Agoult, a man of presence
of mind and experience, should be one of the party, to take the
direction of it, and leave it unnecessary for any of the royal family to appear ; but M⁰. de Tourzel, who had the care of the
royal infants, could by no consideration on earth be persuaded
to give up her place and what she thought her official station ;
and the marquis was therefore left behind.   The result was,
that when difficulties occurred, as they were sure to do, the king
was sometimes uneasy and impatient, put himself forward too
often out of the carriage, was observed ; and this, and the want
of a man like the marquis at every turn of the expedition, contributed not a little to its failure.   But what turns occurred !
The queen, as she was leaving the Tuilleries, was certainly
passed by La Fayette in his carriage ; she was obscured by the
night and a large hat, but was close upon it ; so were also M⁰.
Elizabeth and M⁰. Royale ; they passed, too, one of the sentinels, as his back happened to be turned ; the king had to adjust
the buckle of his shoe almost under the eye of another sentinel ;
and the queen and the body guard, when they lost their way,
had to inquire it from a third, stationed at the Pont Royal, had
to return on their footsteps, and to traverse once more the courts
of the Tuilleries before they could arrive at the place appointed.
The queen, too, by a very silly and unworthy fancy for some sort
of dressing-case, without which she could neither travel nor exist
(you will see the story in M⁰. Campan), had awakened the suspicions of one of the ladies about her, who probably made out
all that was going on, and who had a lover in La Fayette's aide-
de-camp, M. de Gouvion ; and how this did not lead to a discovery of the whole scheme is inconceivable, more especially, as
Gouvion asserts, that he watched all the night the very door out
of which the royal family issued, in consequence of information
he had received.

Conceive, too, what must have been the sufferings of the royal
party when, within a few leagues from Paris, fresh delay was
to be occasioned, while the carriage was to be repaired, in consequence of an accident it had met with.

The fugitives, however, reached Chalons : there, one of the people of the town, as they changed horses, thought he recognised the king in the carriage. He went to the mayor, and was for stopping the party immediately, but luckily the mayor was not as much disposed to discover the king as himself, and contrived by a proper mixture of wise and prudential considerations to pacify the man, and the carriage passed on. It had not passed far, but stopping a moment, a person dressed like an inhabitant of the town came to the side of it : " You have not managed well," he said ; " you will be stopped ;" and he then disappeared ; probably some one who had also recognised the king or queen, but did not choose to interfere. This was but an uncomfortable incident to precede the next disappointment that occurred. At the Pont de Sommeville the king was to have found M. de Choiseul and M. de Goguelat with a detachment, but no one appeared. This detachment was to have received the king, and then given its impulse to all the other detachments, taking care itself to stop all couriers and communications from Paris. The king was extremely affected by this strange disappointment. " All is lost," said the queen to M⁰. Elizabeth ; " we shall certainly be stopped."

When the Marquis de Bouillé came to publish his memoirs, it was impossible for him not to express the disapprobation he felt at the conduct of the young Duc de Choiseul, who was placed by him at this Pont de Sommeville, and to whose disobedience of his orders he ascribed the failure of the whole scheme.

M. de Choiseul was obliged to publish a memoir on the subject. He gives, in this publication, his remonstrance to the marquis, and the marquis's reply, both excellent in their way. " The king may excuse and pardon you," said the veteran ; " but myself, I, who am your general, and who was responsible for the whole affair, it is for me to tell you your faults." The duke then proceeds to make his own statements ; and the memoir is explanatory not only of his own case, but descriptive of the whole and every part of the expedition, and nothing can be more interesting. I have hitherto chiefly followed the archbishop's account, given by Weber.

I shall now return to this Memoir of the young Duc de Choiseul, the nephew of the celebrated minister. What relates to his own justification may be told in a few words. He and M. de Goguelat were at their post at the time appointed, they and their hussars ; but they expected a courier to precede the king by an hour at least, and the king was to arrive at three : but two, three, four o'clock sounded, and neither king nor courier arrived. In the meantime, most unfortunately, from particular circumstances, which the duke states, the hussars placed at the bridge, and remaining there, hour after hour, had entirely disturbed and alarmed the town of Chalons and the neighbourhood: it was impossible to remain there any longer, and it was not easy either to stay or to move away, without causing the most dangerous suspicions. The people murmured aloud, and declared to the officers that they and their hussars were waiting for the queen; and, in short, a regular deputation came from the town to know why the hussars were posted there: the most intolerable remarks of every kind were made; and in this situation of things, to have had the king and his carriages making their appearance would have been fatal. It struck the duke and M. de Goguelat that as the expedition had been already put off twenty-four hours, some new adjournment of it might possibly have been thought again necessary; it was now half-past five, and in the midst of these cruel perplexities and most untoward circumstances, the duke was well pleased to profit by an incident that occurred; for in the midst of the crowd of people and national guards that surrounded him and his troop, he saw the master of the post, and he took the opportunity of questioning him what escorts of money had lately passed that way. "One this morning," said the master. "Indeed!" "I was myself one of the escort," added one of the national guards, who was standing by. "This must have been, then," said the duke to his brother-officer, M. de Goguelat, "this must have been the money we are waiting for; we need stay no longer:" so giving the necessary orders, and putting his troop in motion, with an air of tranquillity and indifference, as a thing of course, he quitted the place, and took the road to St. Menehould. The town and neighbourhood he left were pacified in an instant, and when the king arrived in about an hour after, all was calm and silent; the relays were found, and the carriages proceeded without remark or molestation. In the meantime the duke and M. de Goguelat, with their troop, had moved slowly on, but M. de Goguelat and the lieutenant of the troop, M. Boudet, both agreed, from what they had observed as they came up from Varennes, in the contrary direction, in the morning, that St. Menehould, which they had passed through, must not now be approached, nor Clermont; and so, on the whole, the duke and his party, turning aside from these towns, made for Varennes by by-roads; but difficulties, and an unfortunate accident having occurred to some of the troop, from the almost impassable nature of these roads, they reached not Varennes till more than an hour after the king had been stopped; a most unhappy circumstance, as will be seen hereafter. I now quit the duke's memoir, though I shall return to it.

The royal party, in the mean time, proceeded to St. Menehould, but the courier, M. de Vallory, was never sufficiently in advance, and was only five minutes before the carriage. It happened that he knew not exactly where to find the post-houses; he had to make enquiries; he excited attention, and thus drew together a crowd in a town already disgusted by the appearance and stay of the detachments that had been placed there under M. Dandoins; not to mention that the town was of itself extremely ill disposed to the royal cause. The king, instead of keeping himself concealed in the carriage, sat with his head at the window, uneasy at the delay, and this gave opportunity to Drouet, the master of the posthouse (who knew the queen), to compare at leisure his countenance and appearance with the picture on some assignats which he had that morning received, and to satisfy himself that certainly it was the king himself, however disguised, who was seated in the carriage before him. He communicated with a friend; but the dragoons, many of them, were walking with their officer in the street, and while he hesitated what to do, the carriage drove away. The courier had unfortunately, before they set out, inquired about the road from Claremont to Varennes, so the postmaster and his friend Guillaume had nothing more to learn. Varennes they saw clearly was their point, and mounting each a horse, they pursued the fugitives. They knew that there were dragoons stationed also at Clermont, and they thought it not advisable to make their effort there; so they took a cross road, and pushed on for Varennes.

We have next the relation of what happened at the next post, Clermont, given by the officer who was stationed there, the Comte de Damas. He makes a very unaffected representation of his difficulties and anxieties; the inquietude of the place and neighbourhood on the subject of the troops; his doubt about their fidelity; his uncertainty and misery when the king did not appear; hour after hour succeeding, and every hour increasing the impossibility of keeping either the troops or the inhabitants of the town in the frame of mind he wished. A valet, who dressed the queen's hair, of the name of Leonard, at last passed him, bringing him a billet to say that the Duc de Choiseul

thought the treasure would scarcely arrive, as was expected—
a fresh cause of uneasiness this. Verdun, where the garrison
was unfavourable, was near; if a tocsin sounded, all would
probably be lost. Nine o'clock came, but no appearance of the
king; and so, having no other measure to take, M. de Damas
ordered his men to dismount and go to quarters; and the town
being thus rendered tranquil, he quitted his dragoons, and employed himself in keeping watch on the road from Paris. At
last he saw the king's carriages approach: a few remarks were
interchanged with M. de Vallory, one of the body guards, and
again with M^e. de Tourzel, who talked (characteristically enough)
of the weariness of the children; and he was rewarded for his
sufferings by a few stolen glances of acknowledgment from his
royal master and the queen. At last he saw the carriages duly
forwarded on their journey, and his heart was set at ease. But
the courier on the box unfortunately gave the word to the postilions to go to Varennes; unfortunately, for the postilions,
when they had thus brought the carriage to Clermont, and were
afterwards returning to Menehould, were able to satisfy Drouet,
whom they met, that the carriages had been ordered to Varennes, and were certainly not gone to Verdun, to which place
the road, at a particular point, branched off. The postmaster,
therefore, made for the right place, for Varennes; and not only
this, but he avoided Clermont, where M. de Damas would have
stopped him, or, at all events, would have delayed him: but
everything was unfortunate. M. Lagache soon after reached M.
de Damas from Menehould, and told him that he had followed
two persons who had made pursuit after the king, but that he
had lost them at a cross turn in the road; that the dragoons were
prevented by the people at Menehould from coming up, and that
everything there was in confusion. M. de Damas was, however,
comforted, on the whole, by supposing that the king's carriages
were sufficiently in advance, and that if they once reached Varennes, where there was a relay and dragoons waiting, all would
be safe. He, however, ordered M. de Remy, a faithful and
active officer, with four dragoons and two fourriers, to follow
with all possible speed; they did so, but missed their way,
taking the road to Verdun: they were thus prevented from entering Varennes with the king's carriages, which, if they had
done, they would most probably have cleared away all difficulties, and got the king away, before Drouet could have collected
and arranged the means of stopping him. One mishap more.
But in the mean time, at Clermont, in the town where M. de

Damas and his dragoons still were, matters soon began to assume a very ominous appearance : in the result he was deserted by his troop, the people had surrounded him, called his officers traitors, and M. de Damas, with M. de Floir and a few others, had to fly and provide for their own safety as speedily as they could. M. de Damas and his companions thought it best to take the road to Varennes, expecting to come up with the king some leagues beyond, between Dun and Stenay.

The narrative of M. de Damas is extremely distinct, and has all the appearance of being entitled to perfect confidence. It is entirely simple and unaffected, but it is too short and too rapid a statement (after the manner of a soldier) of the more prominent facts ; still it is something more ; and it at least touches, however briefly, upon all the points that are interesting.

But now observe the singular state of everything at Varennes. The king arrives there ; stops opposite the house, which had been so described to him that he knew it instantly ; knocks and inquires for his horses, but no tidings of them ; the king and the queen get out ; M. D'Agoult is unhappily not with them, as the Marquis de Bouillé had intended ; they wander about to see what intelligence can be got ; M. de Vallory, one of the body guards, who acted as courier, does the same ; all in vain : they return to the postboys, once more desiring them to pass on over the bridge, and take them to the further part of the town ; the postboys refuse, for the horses, they said, were tired ; they were ordered to go no further ; they must wait, &c. &c. Now, while the king and queen are in this perplexity, and everything at a stand, consider for a moment what are the facts of the case, and what is going on elsewhere. The horses are all this time waiting for the king at an inn at the further end of the town, where the postboys will not carry the king, under the care of one of the. Marquis de Bouillé's sons, and of M. de Raigecourt, young officers who are expecting a summons from M. de Goguelat, or some courier ; near them are sixty hussars in their quarters ; in the *further* end of the town, also, under the command of a young officer stationed there by the marquis, and in attendance, though not in the secret of the expedition. But, in the mean time, Drouet and his friend Guillaume are approaching the town from the Paris side, for the purpose of stopping the king's carriages, and every moment brings them nearer and nearer ; and you will now recollect that the young Duc de Choiseul and M. de Gogue-lat are also coming up and making their way with their troop through by roads, as fast as they can, from the Pont de Sommeville to Varennes. M. de Goguelat, you will observe, knew everything about the relay and about the dragoons, at the further end of the town, and if he reached the place before Drouet, all was safe. Again, M. de Damas and his friends were also coming up from Clermont, while, in the mean time, M. de Vallory, who acted as courier, was looking about in the town, and making what enquiries he could. All this was at half-past eleven at night: the town itself quiet, and the people in bed; and still more to increase the critical nature of all these circumstances, the young de Bouillé and M. de Raigecourt are at this moment sitting at their inn at the other end of the town, with the window open, wondering why no courier reaches them, and listening to every sound in the hope every instant of his approach. And now it is to be remembered, that on the turn that these various circumstances might take, depended, on the one hand, the life of the king and queen, the existence of the monarchy of France, the events of the Revolution, dreadful as we have seen them, year after year; or, on the other, the chance perhaps of an adjustment between the king and the Constituent Assembly; or if that failed, the events of a civil war. Such was the importance of what was now passing in and about an obscure town of France in the middle of the night of the 21st of June, 1791. I doubt whether the historian can show such another half-hour in the annals of civilized Europe. Further, it is to be observed, that beyond the town of Varennes, a few leagues onward, was M. Deslon stationed with one hundred hussars; two leagues further, at Mouza, fifty horsemen of the royal German, and beyond, at Stenay, the marquis himself with a regiment of royal German, of undoubted fidelity; so that it was not only uncertain whether the carriages would be stopped at all, but whether, if stopped, a rescue might not be accomplished either by the officers and troops coming up on the Paris side of the town, or by the officers and troops stationed at the other.

But to return to the king. After much time lost in contending with the postilions, they at last agreed to take him over the bridge to the further town: but at an arch before the bridge was already stationed, waiting for his prey, Drouet with a few others; among them Billaud, so distinguished afterwards in the Revolution; and they found no difficulty in here stopping the carriage, calling for the passports, and insisting that the whole party should immediately go before the procureur of the commune.

The fact was, that Drouet had reached Varennes not long after the king did; had immediately alarmed Sausse, the procureur, who was a sort of fanatic in the cause of the Revolution, and orders had been given to call out the national guard of Varennes, to surround the quarters of the sixty hussars, and cut off their communication with the town, and to apply for instant assistance from all the neighbouring towns and villages, particularly from the garrison at Verdun and at Sedan. The bridge had been in the meantime blocked up by Drouet, a waggon overturned in the middle of it, and rendered as much as possible impassable, if the king should attempt to escape.

The royal family were received by Sausse with all possible courtesy; the passports were found right, but at the same time the king was told, that he could not possibly continue his journey at present, that the horses must be refreshed, and that the party would be better in his house than in the carriage and in the street. Into the house therefore they were obliged to enter. The queen soon saw the crowd gradually assembling round the door: she was not to be deceived by the apparent civilities of their hosts; she perceived too plainly that they were stopped, and that all was lost. The magistrate kept going out and returning, on pretence of hastening the horses—in fact, to make every disposition for the detention of his royal guests. And here again, therefore, every thing depended on the point of time, whether the officers could come up, for instance from the Paris side, soon enough to attempt a rescue, and before a sufficient force had been collected to render the attempt hopeless.

At last, it was supposed by Sausse and Drouet that all was secure, and the tocsin was then sounded in Varennes and the neighbouring villages: and in less than two hours some thousands of the national guard had assembled in the town.

But the noise of the tocsin and the general tumult had at last roused from their inaction the young de Bouillé and M. de Raigecourt, who had been waiting in the inn with the relay of horses. M. de Rodock too, the commander of the hussars stationed in the further town, had discovered that the king was stopped; and first this officer, and some time after the other two, having no other measures, as they thought, to take, all, and the two last with great difficulty and after being fired at, got out of the town as fast as they could, and pushed on to Stenay, to apprise the marquis, as soon as possible, of the disastrous events that had just occurred. They reached him about four in the morning, almost five hours after the arrest.

But the Duc de Choiseul, with his troop, at last got to Varennes, about an hour after the king had been stopped. He
found the town, he says, in confusion and lighted up, the inhabitants armed and in the streets, and the national guard disputing his entrance; but he insisted on seeing the hussars, (part
of his own troop) stationed in the town ; and he seems to have
overcome all difficulties, and to have faced all dangers with the
most consummate courage and address. He found, when he got
to the quarters of the sixty hussars, that they were now dispersed
and drinking in the town, and that officers there were none ; his
own part, therefore, of the troop, his own forty hussars, which
he had brought with him, were all he had to depend upon. These
therefore he harangued, told them the situation of the king and
royal family, trotted them up to the house which he had observed
to be surrounded by the national guard, cleared away this national guard, drew up his men before the door in order of battle,
and rushed in through the two national guards who were stationed there, to obtain an interview with the king and to take
his commands. He had also to thrust away some peasants that,
armed with pitchforks, stood as sentinels at the chamber door,
and with his drawn sword in his hand he presented himself
before his unfortunate master. M. de Damas and Goguelat had
followed him, for just as he had dismounted, it is to be observed,
and was making his way to the king, M. de Damas had come up.
" Are you in any force?" said the duke. " No," replied M.
de Damas, " I am alone ; my regiment has mutinied." So there
was evidently, whatever might be done or attempted, not an
instant to be lost.

" What is to be done?" said the king. " Save you," returned M. de Damas. " Give your orders, I replied," says
the duke in his Memoir. " Sire ; I have here forty hussars,
they will go as far as Dun perfectly well ; something must be
done. I will dismount seven of my hussars, place you and the
dauphin on one, the queen and the family on the rest. We will
surround you with the three and thirty that remain, charge
those that oppose us, cut our way through ; but there is not a
moment to be lost ; an hour, and all my hussars will be gained
over." " Can you answer for it," replied the king immediately,
" that in this unequal scuffle of thirty against seven or eight
hundred, a shot might not kill the queen, one of the children,
or my sister ?"

" A misfortune like this," I cried, " and I would shoot myself and die at your feet." " Ah ! come," said the king, " let us

reason coolly. The municipality does not refuse my passing on,
but says I must wait till break of day. Young Bouillé set off,
just as I got here, to apprize his father, to put the troops in motion ; they, no doubt, are ready. Were I here alone, I would do
what you advise, and make my way through ; but the queen,
the two children, my sister, their ladies, it is impossible to venture so many with a party so small as yours, a party that must
be made still less, for I cannot leave behind me these three gentlemen of the body guard. It is now almost one : Bouillé went
at half-past eleven ; you, too, dispatched a person when you
came. M. de Bouillé has no doubt placed his troops at different
distances ; those nearest will be first informed of what has happened by his son : they will be here one after another; it is not
eight leagues to Stenay, a distance that a man and horse will go
in two hours and a half : detachments will be coming up all
the night; M. de Bouillé himself will be here by four or five,
and then, without the family's running any risk, and without
any violence to any one, we shall get away in safety."

The narrative of the duke is at this particular point very important to the character of the king. You will observe how
natural, how forcible, were the considerations by which the conduct of the unhappy monarch seems to have been determined at
this crisis of his fate. He has been variously censured. He has
been accused of causing the failure of the expedition, by getting
out and losing time while he was eating : this is mere calumny.
Again, by wanting decision, and not ordering a passage to be
forced. No doubt he always wanted decision, when the consequence was to be the shedding of blood. He was not fitted to
rule a disordered kingdom, but I am not aware that this fault in
his character can be shown to have operated at any distinct
point or place, fatally to the success of the enterprise we are
now considering.

" The reasoning of the king," continues the duke in his Memoir, " appeared to me perfectly just ; I could urge nothing in
reply. How often have the king and queen recalled it to memory ! I appeal to those who have had the happiness to be
near them. Our conversation ended, M. Sausse, who had stood
at a distance, left us, as he said, to go to the commune to have
the horses ready by daybreak, that the king should then go to
Montmedy with an escort of the national guard, and that the
tocsin should be stopped."

" It was then about two in the morning, the number of
people about five thousand ; there were ten thousand the next

day.. The king consulted with me what was to be done. I acquainted him with every thing I knew. I had sent M. Aubriot to tell the marquis that all hope for the king rested on him. M. Aubriot went the four leagues to Dun in so short a time, that his horse could go no further. M. Deslon, who was in command there, gave him another, and instantly put his one hundred hussars into motion to come himself to the king's assistance at Varennes.

"M. de Damas and I calculated that the marquis would be there between five and six; but my forty hussars having seen their sixty comrades join the people, I expected they would soon do the same; and as M. de Damas and I perceived that the trying moment would be when the general and his troops arrived, we made our calculations and dispositions, as well as we could, to defend the house, and more particularly the staircase, and to contrive that the troops should get possession of the town before we could be all cut down. In this manner we passed the time till it struck five, but with an anxiety that was intolerable. We went out from time to time to observe what the disposition of the people was. On one of these occasions, M. de Goguelat was engaged in a scuffle with some of the national guards, and was severely wounded; but he got dressed, and appeared again (through suffering extremely) before the royal family. M. Deslon, from Dun, reached Varennes with his one hundred hussars, but found the town so barricaded and guarded, that all he could do was, to obtain permission for himself to see the king. An unfortunate prejudice had been entertained against him by the general, and had been communicated to M. de Goguelat and the king, who was somewhat reserved to him: a gallant and loyal officer, that would have saved every thing if he had but been in command at Varennes. 'I can give you no orders,' said the king; 'you see I am a prisoner. You must wait for the marquis; tell him how we are situated: he cannot be long.' M. Deslon retired.

"But hour after hour had passed away; our astonishment, our wretchedness had increased with every moment. No news of the marquis or of the troops in the neighbouring cantonments; the tocsin still sounded; the crowds of people increased; and at last, about five, M. Baillon and M. de Romeuf, La Fayette's aide-de-camp, arrived from the National Assembly. The scene was then changed."

Such is in the main the account of the young Duc de Choiseul, whose fate was truly hard: to have made all these exertions, to have confronted all these dangers, afterwards to be severely wounded, to be thrown into prison, and there left to expect his death as a traitor to his country, and in the meantime to be blamed by his illustrious general, the Marquis de Bouillé, as one of the main causes of the failure of the expedition.

One of the most cruel moments that the king and queen had to undergo was the moment when they were to set off for Paris, and to see this Duc de Choiseul, and M. de Damas, and the Baron Goguelat, left behind them. "Do not quit us," said the queen, with horror painted in her countenance. She knew too well the brutal nature of a French mob. The carriage drove away, and these gallant men were soon after abandoned, as it was thought by the royal family, to immediate assassination; and this must have been assuredly their fate, had it not been for the incredible exertions of the young aide-de-camp of La Fayette, M. de Romeuf, whom indeed the queen had engaged in their protection. They were bruised and wounded in every way. The people, like wild and hungry animals, were rushing upon them to tear them to pieces. They were at last, and with the greatest difficulty, saved, and lodged in confinement. Their prisons were then assaulted; the enraged and disappointed populace tried to fire at them through the air-hole. They were afterwards passed from prison to prison, expecting their trial, and of course their condemnation and death.

But the king did not forget the faithful and suffering friends of his misfortunes, the brave and loyal men who would have died to save him; and he made it his bargain with the National Assembly, when he afterwards accepted the constitution, and declared it to be one of his reasons for accepting it, that a decree should be passed in favour of all who had been concerned in the expedition, a decree of general pardon and oblivion.

We will now advert to other accounts that have been drawn up by those who were engaged in this unfortunate enterprise. You will already have seen that the cause, above all others, that prevented the escape of the king, was his not finding his relay of horses when he reached Varennes. He was five-and-thirty minutes by his watch, while inquiries were in vain made for them by himself and his gentlemen of the body guard, and during that interval Drouet had time to reach the town, and prepare measures for his arrest. We naturally wish to know how this could possibly have happened.

The fault, as far as there was any, seems to have lain with

the Baron de Goguelat. It may be described in a few words. It was he who was intrusted by the Marquis de Bouillé with the disposition and management of the relays. He was to leave Montmedy and to pass along through the different posts, take the forty hussars to the Duc de Choiseul at the Pont de Sommeville, and then to return when the king arrived there, apprizing, as he returned, all the different posts and relays of the king's approach.

But the Duc de Choiseul and he were not able to remain at the Pont de Sommeville, as you have seen, till the king arrived; nor durst they return through the different posts, St. Menehould and Clermont: they were obliged to make for Varennes by cross roads, and the baron had it not in his power, or forgot to contrive some means of informing the king's carriages where the relays were to be found; particularly at Varennes, where an alteration had been made, and the horses were no longer, as the king expected, at the Paris side of the town, but had been placed by the baron himself, or certainly with his knowledge, at the other end of the town.

I cannot but think that this is the real state of the case, though the baron does not acknowledge it, nor is he any where distinctly accused to the extent or in the manner I have thus presumed to censure him.

The young Marquis de Bouillé, in his Memoir, says precisely that the baron had placed the relays, two days before, at the inn in the lower town, and he thinks with good reason, but that he ought to have apprized the royal party of the alteration he had made in the first arrangement.

The baron has himself written a Memoir on the subject of this expedition to Varennes, and in one of the notes he alludes to this particular question before us, though in too general a manner. "The relay of the king," he says, "was at Varennes on the 19th. It was placed in one of the inns of the town, it mattered not where. There should have been officers to take care of it: there were none arrived on the morning of the 20th, when I passed. I had not been charged with the care of this relay, nor could I be, my mission taking me away fifteen leagues off, to the Pont de Sommeville."

This is all but loose and inaccurate; and though it were all true, still the question is, whether the baron, though he was to go to the Pont de Sommeville, was not to have returned, and preceded the king's carriage as a sort of courier, clearing away every difficulty, and preparing the relays for them as they ad-

vanced.   This is certainly the conclusion to be drawn from all
the memoir, and from the Memoir of the young Marquis de
Bouillé, and from what falls from the father; and though both
are so employed in censuring the young Duc de Choiseul that
they think not of the baron, it is the baron that I conceive must
be censured, as far as this relay is concerned, by any indifferent
person.

Either the baron depended on reaching Varennes, by the cross-
roads, before the king could arrive there ; or the importance of
this relay, and more particularly of the alteration of the place,
was, amid the agitations and disappointments of the hour, forgotten ; or he was unable to leave any one behind him at the
Pont de Sommeville to apprize the royal party where the horses
were *now* stationed.   Some of these suppositions must, I apprehend, be the true one ; and were the baron before us, and the
question put to him, according to his answers must be the regret
or the censure with which we should at last, very unwillingly,
visit the conduct of a faithful and gallant man like this, who had
risked his life in the service of his unfortunate master.

When we turn to the account that is given of their proceedings by the two young officers that were stationed with the relay
at Varennes, at the lower part of the town, nothing can be more
uncomfortable than the sensations with which we peruse it.
They arrive at an inn ; they appear to be highly circumspect
and prudent ; are made anxious in the extreme when they find
no courier appear ; at the same time, they had learned from the
queen's valet, Leonard, as he passed through, that the king had
certainly left Paris, though it was thought there was little prospect of his making his appearance, as expected.   The two young
officers, however, order their supper, go to bed, as the people of
the house were left to suppose, and sit in their room in the dark,
with the window open, listening ; but they seem always to have
supposed that the relays would be expected by the king and his
suite at *their* end of the town, and it never occurred to either of
them, at all events, that one of them should be on the look-out
on the road to see whether any carriage approached : they contented themselves with sitting, listening for the courier ; and it
actually appears, that while in this situation, they really did hear
(as the rest of the town was silent and asleep) they *did* hear
people walking about and talking, but they were unable to make
out what was said.   Soon after they heard noises in the town,
and at last the tocsin ; and after staying twenty minutes with
the horses ready for the king, if he got disengaged from what

they perceived must be his arrest, they found they could do nothing for the king's service more, but only endeavour to reach
their general as soon as possible, and tell him that every thing
was lost at Varennes, and that succour must be brought up immediately; that this was all they could now attempt; and this
they did attempt; they were fired upon, and with difficulty
escaped.   So unfortunate was every turn of this ill-fated expedition, and the more this exposé of one of these young officers is
examined, the more will this appear.   They found the relays at
the inn, placed there by M. de Goguelat; they considered him
as the pivot on which their own movements were all to turn;
they expected the king at eleven at the latest, the baron an hour
before.   About half-past nine, Leonard, the queen's valet, came
to the inn to get a horse for himself; he came there as a thing
of course, which prevented them from ever supposing that the
station of the relays was not known.   The baron not coming at
ten as expected, M. de Raigecourt went to the lodgings of the
officer who commanded the sixty hussars posted in the town (the
lodgings were actually in that part of the town where the king
first arrived), told him to be on the alert, him and his men;
that the treasure was coming.   The officer went to quarters to
get the hussars ready, M. de Raigecourt returned to his inn; it
might then be a quarter after eleven : he saw that the relays
were ready; all was quiet in the town; but in a quarter of an
hour after, all was tumult and uproar, and the king, they were
told, had been stopped.

It remains now to be considered, where was the general himself all the time that the king was expecting him at Varennes.

"I found the marquis," says M. de Raigecourt, the young
officer we have just been talking of, "about a quarter of a league
beyond Stenay ; my horse had dropped down under me, which
had delayed me a little, but I had got another, and the general
dispatched me to Montmedy, to order the regiment of Nassau to
make immediately a forced march to Varennes.   On my return
to Stenay, the general had gone with the regiment of the royal
German to the king's assistance, and I could not overtake him
till within a quarter of a league of Varennes, at half-past nine; so
that in nine hours, from half-past twelve, when I left Varennes,
the marquis had been apprized of the king's danger, and had
brought up a regiment, all mounted and equipped, to his succour,
a distance, backward and forward, of twenty leagues, the roads
extremely bad, and the night dark."

Such is in brief the account of M. de Raigecourt; but you

may remember, that a young officer, who had commanded the hussars at Varennes, left also the place to repair to the general, when the king was first arrested : apparently he should have already reached the marquis; but on adverting to the Memoir of the marquis's son, this does not turn out to have been the case. The account that M. de Bouille gives is, that he with his father (the marquis) and a few others, passed most of the night waiting on the road between Stenay and Dun, oppressed and overpowered with anxiety, catching every sound, and exposed to every vicissitude of hope and fear. As the morning advanced, the latter sensation but too much prevailed; and the general thought, when the day began to break, that it was for him to fall back on Stenay, and to be ready at his post. "Within a quarter of a league of the town we heard people," says his son in his Memoir, "following us at full gallop. The couriers from the king! Alas! no; my brother, with the Comte de Raige-court, and what was still more astonishing, the officer who was in command at Varennes. This was at half-past four; the king had been stopped at half-past eleven."

The young marquis then gives an account of the exertions made by his father and himself, to get the regiment of royal German drawn out for the king's rescue. The sufferings of both were great. The colonel seems not to have been sufficiently on the alert; at least, on some account or other, he and the soldiers, instead of all being ready to mount, with their horses saddled, as the marquis expected, were all in bed, and in short, the regi-ment was three quarters of an hour, instead of ten or fifteen minutes, before they were in motion; they were found, however, sufficiently loyal when they were harangued by their general. All possible dispatch was used, but just as they came in sight of Varennes, they were met by M. Deslon, who had commanded at Dun, and who told us, says M. de Bouillé, all that had hap-pened at Varennes, and added, that he and his troop had con-trived to swim the river, with the intention of falling upon the escort that was carrying away the king, but was stopped by a canal which they had in vain endeavoured to get across. This was at eight o'clock; it was now nine. The garrison of Verdun was in motion with artillery to support the people of Varennes; and it was impossible, after a nine leagues' march, to overtake the escort, or to succeed if we did, in any forcible attempt at rescue; and this even if we could have found any fords in the river before us, which we could not. All was evidently lost; we could only return as we came. I shall never forget," continues the young marquis, "the affliction painted in my father's countenance; I shall never forget the heart-breaking tone (I had often talked to him of his successful life), the accents of complaint and wretchedness, with which he broke the silence, and the grief in which he rode along. 'Well now,' he said to me, 'will you still talk to me of my good fortune?'"

Such appear to me the leading facts connected with this unfortunate expedition. It failed from the loss of time at Paris; from the want of M. d'Agoult to superintend and overcome the difficulties of the expedition; from the Duc de Choiseul's not being able to maintain his post at the Pont de Sommeville; from M. de Reney and his six dragoons missing their way, and taking the road to Verdun instead of Varennes; from the king's being recognized by Drouet; above all, from M. de Goguelat's forgetting, or being unable, to apprize the king's carriages where the relay was to be found at Varennes; from the desertion of the troops; and from the general popularity of the National Assembly and the cause of the Revolution, which made every accident that occurred irremediable and fatal to the royal fugitives.

I will now make two observations, and conclude. In the Edinburgh Review for October, 1823, there is a critique on the narrative given of this flight from the Tuilleries by the Duchess of Angoulême, one of the royal children at the time. Observe the loose manner in which the reviewer speaks of our present subject. "The principal misfortunes and blunders were," says the reviewer, "the arriving at Varennes, where relays of horses were provided for them, but not taking care to ascertain where those relays were to be found. Even this, however, would not have proved fatal, had their zealous and devoted adherents been able to travel on swift horses and a good road, as much as six miles an hour during that one night, and to get more help, supposing them to have no right to attempt a defence or a rescue with sixty hussars, and nothing but a mob to oppose; for, without ever dreaming that such a thing was practicable, three gallant and chivalrous spirits rode off, between ten and twelve o'clock, to the Marquis de Bouillé's head quarters, twenty-four miles distant, and brought back a regiment of cavalry, which did not arrive before nine, when the royal prisoners had been gone an hour and a half, and no attempt was made to overtake them." Such is the paragraph in the Edinburgh Review. It is thus, that in this world of ours, "this busy world, where praise and censure are at random hurled;" it is thus that the characters of generous and gallant officers are disposed of by lively and able men, like the Edinburgh Reviewer, in their closets or over their wine, in writings or conversation : and it is in this manner, that by a wave of the pen, or a glance of the thought, subjects are often adjusted and settled in any coarse and sweeping way that may occur; subjects which it would require the most patient examination, and even a lengthened report, to appreciate with the precision and delicacy that they deserve.

I know of no greater intellectual cruelty or injustice that men can exercise upon each other than this ; nor know I any more common source of erroneous judgments on the most important questions that may come before us.   Extremes are said to meet ; and certainly men of the most improved minds and brilliant understandings often assimilate themselves to the mere vulgar, by the rapidity with which they jump at their conclusions, the carelessness with which they depart from all candour and good feeling, and the violence and presumption with which they decide.   A few lively sentences, a smart sarcasm, and some general authoritative position ; these once produced and laid down, and they seem often to suppose that nothing more is necessary : they have shown the vivacity and vigour of their talents and understandings, and they are satisfied.

My next observation is of a still more serious nature, and connected with the evidences of our religion : for instance, the discrepancies that appear in the Gospels have sometimes been a stumbling-block to men of thoughtful and inquiring minds ; they have insisted that those narratives cannot be true, which sometimes differ with each other, and in a manner that cannot be reconciled.   In reply to this objection, Dr. Paley has remarked, " that he knows of no more rash and unphilosophical conduct of the understanding, than to reject the substance of a story by reason of some diversity in the circumstances with which it is related.   The usual character of human testimony," he says, " is substantial truth under circumstantial variety : this is what the daily experience of courts of justice teaches : when accounts of a transaction come from the mouths of different witnesses, it is seldom that it is not possible," he says, " to pick out apparent or real inconsistencies between them.   A great deal of the discrepancy observable in the Gospels," he adds, " arises from omission."   This is at all times a very uncertain ground of objection.   " These discrepancies," he continues, " will be still more numerous when men do not write histories, but memoirs, which is, perhaps the true name and proper description of our Gospels; when they mean to give such passages, or such actions and discourses, as offered themselves more immediately to their attention, came in the way of their inquiries, occurred to their recollection, or were suggested by their particular design at the time of writing."

Now what I have to observe is this, that I conceive, these remarks of this admirable writer, which, when applied with any fair discretion to any case of narrative, are perfectly sound, might be abundantly illustrated and confirmed by the accounts and memoirs to which I have been alluding, and from which I have been piecing out my narrative, such as it is, during the whole of the present lecture. The discrepancies are many, so are the omissions; the inconsistencies, the opposite statements, not a few; but who doubts of all that is important in the story? or who questions the veracity of the honourable and respectable men that present us with their narratives? And did it fall within my province, I should think no task with which I could be occupied, more interesting or more important, than to show, by reference to these memoirs, the propriety and justice of the different observations which I have just quoted from Dr. Paley. The queen, for instance, comes from the Tuilleries, some say leaning on the arm of M. de Moustier, others of M. de Malden; but is the conclusion from this that she did not come out at all? Circumstances are mentioned by some, and omitted by others, with respect, for instance, to her seeing La Fayette's carriage.

Again. From some memoirs we should suppose it was Drouet, the postmaster at Menehould, who stopped the carriages at Varennes; from others, that it was Drouet's son; from La Gache's own account, that he had galloped after a person, when he left St. Menehould, who, he thought, was pursuing the carriages; but it is clear from other accounts, that Drouet was in company with Guillaume, and that this person therefore could not have been Drouet, La Gache speaking only of one person; and yet M. de Damas says, that La Gache told him that he had galloped after two persons soon after he left Menehould; so that apparently it was, after all, Drouet.

Again. From some accounts it might be thought that Drouet entered the town of Clermont; from others, and from his own, that he passed near it, and avoided it. There are differences in the detail of what took place with respect to the king and queen; their getting out, their conversation, &c. &c., when the carriages first stopped at Varennes, opposite the house of M. Prefontaine. The Duc de Choiseul speaks of M. de Goguelat's being wounded in the shoulder: M. de Goguelat himself of receiving one wound in the breast, another in the head; yet was M. de Choiseul by the side of him afterwards for hours. The Duc de Choiseul relates his conversation with the king, while M. de Damas was in conference with him also: it is very important, extremely so, to the king's character in all its particulars. M. de Damas, when he comes to the corresponding place in his own narrative, takes no notice of it, mentioning only the important point, that after they had made their representations to the king, they saw that he had made up his mind to wait, and not to try force. M. de Vallory mentions, that M. de Damas reached the king after seven in the morning, soon after M. Deslon, whose conversation with his majesty he reports at length; and he then says, that between eight and nine in the morning, M. de Choiseul and M. de Goguelat appeared; that they had forced their way to the house, and that M. de Goguelat was wounded in the arm. All this is inaccurate. And he then says, that about ten o'clock the two aides-de-camp of La Fayette arrived. In his agitation M. de Vallory seems to have been totally insensible to hours and points of time; but is the conclusion, I must repeat, from the whole of these discrepancies, omissions, and contradictions, to be, that the main facts of the story did not take place, or that the gallant men concerned are not men of veracity? In this manner might I go on to a considerable length, though in any dissertation on the subject I must proceed with more regularity and more circumstantial detail; but you will already see sufficiently what I am endeavouring to exhibit to your reflection. I feel, indeed, that I am on ground where I have no allotted place or regular position.

The justice, however, of Paley's observation on the character of testimony, " substantial truth under circumstantial variety," having occurred to me again and again while reading these memoirs, and on this occasion by no means for the first time, I thought I might be allowed to mention the circumstance, though the subject itself, I am well aware, is too important to be properly considered by me, or by any one, but in a far more direct and regular manner.

LECTURE XXIII.

FROM THE FLIGHT TO VARENNES, TO THE CLOSE OF THE CONSTITUENT ASSEMBLY, Sept. 30, 1791.

I have omitted several particulars that occurred at Varennes, and during the return of the royal family to Paris; because I do not write the history of the French Revolution; but they will, I think, be interesting to you (who are to read it), and I may even now mention a few of them.

There can be no doubt of the king's intentions in this attempt to escape; that he meant no civil war, that he had no design but what he could fully and fairly avow. When he found that all efforts at concealment were in vain, he addressed himself to Sausse, the room was full of people, and expressed himself with a fluency and a frankness, that were, in a character like his, quite impossible, upon any supposition, but that of his entire sincerity. What his motives had been in leaving the Tuilleries, the nature of his captivity, his wishes and his hopes, all these he laid before his hearers, and he only begged to be taken any where but to Paris; to any town or place where he might assure himself of the real opinions of his people, and freely concur in whatever could contribute to their happiness; that he had no other desire; and that to accomplish such an end, he would make any necessary sacrifices of the rights of his birth and prerogative, or the claims of his own personal interests. The king expressed himself, according to the account of the historians, with a dignity, a goodness of heart, a simplicity, and with a warmth and an eloquence so far beyond what was expected from him, that the greatest impression was made on the bystanders; and even Sausse himself was so struck and affected by it, that he said in an under tone, "Nothing can be more reasonable than what he proposes, but it is now too late; and my head would answer it, if he was not sent back to Paris."

The different characters of the king and queen were marked when the decree of the National Assembly was brought them. La Fayette's aide-de-camp, M. de Romeuf, was known to them, and they had not expected that he at least would have been the bearer of it. The king took it hastily from his hand and read it. "There is no longer a king in France," he said, and threw it on the bed where the dauphin and the princess were lying. "It shall not soil my children," said the queen, snatching it up and throwing it on the ground. "And is it you?" she said, turning to the aide-de-camp. "Better I than another," replied M. de Romeuf: "I who know how to respect you, madam, as does my general, who is anything but an enemy." "Oh, *he*," said the queen, "*he* has nothing in his head but his United States and his American republic; he will see what a French republic is. Where is your decree? the insolents!" M. de Romeuf soothed her at last, and overcame her by the genuine sympathy which he exhibited, and by the tears (he was still young) that started to his eyes. "Well, save then," said the queen, "save those gentlemen there, when we are gone,—M. de Damas, the Duc de Choiseul, and the rest."

Her words were not in vain: their lives were saved, as I have already mentioned, and saved by M. de Romeuf at the hazard of his own. It was a miserable night that the royal family had to pass at Varennes, as if a man whose life was at issue, was to wait for the verdict of his judges, not for a few minutes, but for many, many hours. It was a miserable night; and it must have been again a miserable eight days, that they had to undergo, while they were returning to their prison, for it was a journey of eight days, as the national guards had to march on foot before them—the queen's hair turned grey in the course of it.

Being now the middle of June, the heat and dust were intolerable; but what were these? "Where the greater malady is fixed," as Lear said to the storm, "the lesser is scarce felt." Near St. Menehould, they had to see the Count de Dampierre rush to their carriage door to offer them, what testimony he yet could, of his loyalty and affliction; and they had scarcely heard the few words he could pronounce, amid his sighs and his tears, when they had to witness the sad consequences of his generous devotion to them, to see the people falling upon him and tearing him from his hold, and as the carriage went on, to hear his parting cries, and to leave him to be massacred behind them.

The same horror, the same agony, would have been again experienced near Meaux, but at Chalons they had been joined by the three commissioners from the National Assembly. A poor priest was in like manner endeavouring to make his way to the carriage, when he was seized by the national guards and by the multitude, who were evidently in the act of dragging him away to the same barbarous fate. "Save him! save him!" cried the queen to Barnave, who instantly rushed from the carriage, and by the generous fury and indignation of his cries and expostulations, rescued the unhappy man, and shamed the monsters by whom he was surrounded.

The conversation in the carriage between the deputies and the royal family had at length become free and unembarrassed, and turned upon all the important subjects that alone could occupy their minds. The king, the queen, and M*. Elizabeth, displayed each the particular graces and amiable qualities which belonged to their respective characters. The spectacle thus presented, of misfortune at least and the instability of everything human, was lost upon the hard republican nature of the vulgar Pétion ; but not so on the mind of Barnave, a man of genius and of eloquence, and who could not be unmoved by all that was so fitted to interest his taste and melt his heart. He was never wanting during the journey in every mark of respect that he could pay. When they arrived at the Tuilleries he fulfilled his promise to the queen, and by his personal exertions saved the lives of the gentlemen of the body guard who were on the carriage, and who would otherwise have been butchered on the spot; and he ever after rendered the king and the royal family every kind office of assistance and advice, which, as a member of the other side of the National Assembly, and a distinguished leader at the time, it was in his power to afford.

When you come to read the history, you will perceive that the conduct of the National Assembly, when the first intelligence was brought them of the king's escape, was calm and dignified ; they gave the necessary orders, made the natural inquiries, sent their communications to foreign courts, drew up a new form of oath for the national guards and troops of the line, and showing no alarm themselves, the public recovered from their first consternation, and the general effect of the whole was very unfavourable to the king and to the cause of royalty.

The feeling of the people was that of indignation ; that the king having sworn to maintain the constitution, had deceived and betrayed them, and the Assembly having put itself into possession of the executive power, and everything in Paris going on, just as before, a general impression arose, that a government could do as well without a king as with one. One thing, however, was necessary to the Assembly. The king had left behind him, when he fled, a memorial, a justification of his conduct, and this had been publicly read ; it was, in fact, his appeal to the people : and as the people were admitted by the Assembly to be their sovereign, it was impossible for them not to submit themselves to the same tribunal; and this they therefore did, and immediately published their reply.

These two state papers you will of course read attentively, for they in fact contain the question between the king and the popular party, from the opening of the States to the king's flight. Judging from what the king's brother says in the account he gives of his own flight, the conclusion is, that the king's memorial is, in the main, his own composition; and if so, it is quite of itself a sufficient evidence of the good sense that it has been lightly thought he did not possess, because he was wanting in decision of character, and unfit for action, which is not at all a necessary inference. The flight was kept a secret, and it is not easy to say who could have assisted him, except the queen, who was of too ardent a temper to have been useful to him on such an occasion, or his minister, M. de Montmorin, apparently the most sensible man near him, but who was very humanely kept in total ignorance of the whole affair, as he afterwards had it in his power to state to the Assembly, and thus saved his life.

"The queen," says Monsieur, "showed me the declaration which the king projected; we read it together. I observed some inaccuracies in the style, and it was too long; and there was an essential omission, that of a protestation against all acts during his captivity. The king told me to take the paper with me, and the next morning I set about correcting it, a disagreeable office at any time." And afterwards resuming the subjects, he says, "After all I have said, it may be supposed that I was the author of the Declaration of the 20th of June, but not so; I was but the corrector; many of my corrections were not adopted; all the close was added, after I had done with it, and such as it now stands, I never saw it till I reached Brussels."

The memorial, I must repeat, is, on the whole, very creditable to the king; any assistance that he could have received not having been in all probability very material. There are no sentiments of violence in it, and no expression of arbitrary feelings; no unmeasured accusations of the friends of liberty, no unlimited panegyrics of the supporters of the old regimé. These are all evidences of its being the king's own composition. The factious, and such men there surely were, are alone reprobated. Nothing that is inconsistent with an intention to be guided, if he was ever free to act, by a wish for the public good; understood, no doubt, in a manner different from what it was understood by the Assembly, and by men unfavourable to the rights and dignity of his crown, but not understood in any manner that

would not have been a sufficiently fair and honourable ground
for a mutual adjustment of the great interests of the community.

The king complains that the States General took upon themselves the name of National Assembly ; that they put the king
altogether out of the constitution ; that they refused him the
right of granting or denying his assent to such articles as the
Assembly should deem constitutional, reserving to themselves
the right of ranging in that class all such as they thought proper, and with respect to those that are purely legislative, re-
straining the royal prerogative to a right of suspension to the
third legislature, a right wholly illusive, as indeed it was.   He
complains of being held in a state of captivity ; that the interior
administration is altogether in the hands of the departments, the
districts, the municipalities ; that these bodies are elected by the
people ; that the king has, in like manner, no influence over
the army or the marine, over negotiations, or, in fact, over the
issues of peace and war, or lastly, over the finances.   He then
complains of the societies everywhere established, that these societies, without any authority for the purpose, deliberate on all
points of government ; correspond among themselves on all subjects ; make and receive denunciations ; post up their resolutions about the streets ; and have acquired such a preponderance,
that all the administration of judiciary bodies, not excepting the
National Assembly itself, is in a state of general obedience to
their orders.   "People of France," says the king, "was this
what you intended by sending representatives to the National
Assembly ?   Did you desire that anarchy and the despotism of
clubs should replace that monarchical government, under which
the nation has prospered during fourteen hundred years ?   Did
you desire to see your king overwhelmed with outrages, and
deprived of *his* liberty, at the moment he was employed in establishing *yours ?*"

"The more the king sacrificed," says the memorial, "for the
good of his people, the more the factious laboured to lessen the
value of those sacrifices, and to represent royalty under the falsest
and most odious colours.

"The calling together the States General; the doubling of
the deputies of the Third Estate ; the pains which the king had
taken to smooth the difficulties which might retard the assembling of the States General, and those which arose after their
opening ; all the retrenchments which the king had made in his
personal expenses ; all the sacrifices he offered to his people in
the session of the 23rd of June ; in fine, the union of the orders

effected by the manifestation of the king's desire, a measure
which his majesty then deemed indispensable for putting the
States General into motion; all his cares, all his labour, all his
generosity, all his devotion to his people—all has been miscon-
strued, all has been perverted."

After referring to the affair of St. Cloud and others, "What
pleasure will the king have," says the memorial, in conclusion,
"in forgetting all his personal injuries, and seeing himself again
in the midst of you, addressing himself to all Frenchmen, and
above all, the Parisians, when a constitution, which he shall
have accepted freely, has made our holy religion respected, when
government shall be established on a footing steady, yet allowing useful action, when the property or condition of no man shall
be troubled, when the laws shall be no more infringed with impunity, and in fine, when liberty shall be settled on a firm and
immovable foundation."

Such is the general tenor of the king's memorial; the doubtful
part of his case is handled thus : "In the month of July, 1789,
his majesty, in order to remove all cause of jealousy, sent away
the troops which he had not called about his person, until the
spirit of revolt had manifested itself in Paris, and even in the
regiments of his own guards; the king, relying on his conscience
and the rectitude of his own intentions, was not afraid to come
alone amongst the armed citizens of the capital."

This representation of the proceedings of the 14th of July will
scarcely be thought satisfactory now.   That the king's own intentions were good, may be true; but the question is, what were
those of his court and of his advisers, under whose influence, till
the very last turn, he seemed to act?

To this memorial of the king, the reply of the Assembly could
only be, that there were no rights in the king, or any one else
that were not merged in the rights of the public to freedom and
happiness; but they added, that the chief of the executive
power, or the first public functionary, had dared, on the 23rd of
June, to dictate his absolute will to the representatives of the
nation; that the army had menaced the National Assembly in
the month of July; that the people were not made for kings,
and that clemency is the only duty of those kings; that some
disorders had attended the Revolution; but ought the ancient
despotism to complain of the evils which it has itself produced?
—that it was not decent in that despotism to express astonishment that the people should not always have kept within bounds
in dispersing that mass of corruption formed in a series of ages

by the crimes of absolute power; that it was necessary that all the powers should be reconstituted, because all were corrupted.

This is the strain in which the Assembly naturally drew up their reply; and the two papers together, in fact, exhibit the whole question of the Revolution during this earlier and more important period of its progress—the question between Mr. Burke and his opponents—or nearly so.

The creditable part of the state paper of the Assembly is that which contains conciliatory expressions towards the king; the Assembly assumes the fiction of the king's being carried away by enemies to the country, and does not consider him as having voluntarily fled. "We shall bewail," says the reply, "the misfortunes of our king; we shall call down the vengeance of the laws on those who have drawn him from his post; but the empire shall not be shaken, the activity of the administration of justice shall not relax."

On the whole, this reply, considering the circumstances of the case, is not unworthy of the Assembly of a great people. It could take no ground, situated as it was, but this, that usurpations, as they were thought by the king, were in fact necessary, first to the acquiring, next to the securing, the liberties of the country, and that the whole of the old régime was, from beginning to end, founded on false principles.

At the same time, by the fiction that was adopted of the king's being carried away by force, a door was left open for conciliation with the king, and for his return to power; to such power, at least, as the constitution had provided for him. All this must have been owing to the influence of La Fayette and the Constitutionalists.

We must now return to consider what were the effects of this flight of the king on all the parties and authorities then existing in the state.

To the king one thing had now become clear, that the Revolution was popular; and more than this, it was now clear both to the king and the Assembly, that there was a republican party as well as the party of the Constitutionalists; that the Revolution had descended one step lower, and from a question between Mounier with his friends and the Constitutionalists, had got down to a question between La Fayette with his friends and the Republicans, or at least those who were disposed to sweep away the authority and rule of Louis XVI., and were or would have become Republicans.

This was the first unhappy effect of the failure of the flight, an effect still further confirmed and extended by the despair of the royal party and their general emigration. This is called their *second* emigration.

Where could they emigrate to, it was asked, but to the enemies of the country ; and for what purpose, but to return with them, if possible, to destroy the popular party, put an end to the Revolution, and restore the old régime? And what, in the meantime, what could the king be considered, it was again asked by the violent party, disposed to republicanism, what, but as an incumbrance, and it was added, an enemy also to the liberties of the country ? the king who must necessarily wish these invaders success, and who had now, as flight had failed, no other hope for the recovery of what he thought the just rights and prerogatives of his crown.

These were reasonings but too natural, when the nobles and patrons of the old system betook themselves to the totally unjustifiable measures of repairing to foreign courts, instituting a system of negotiations and intrigue, and appearing in a menacing attitude, while the clear majority of their countrymen was evidently against them, and the king and royal family in the possession and at the mercy of the Assembly, or rather of the people of Paris.

" What do I hear," cried the furious Danton, " Louis XVI. not forfeited his crown? What! has he not himself declared that he was hunting after the means of destroying the constitution ? Is he weak or is he criminal ?"

Placards were placed in every street in Paris by the club of the Cordeliers. " France," they said, " was a slave in 1789, supposed herself free in 1790, and really is so now, at the end of 1791. Louis XVI. has abdicated ; Louis, therefore, is henceforward nothing to us, unless, indeed, he becomes our enemy. We are, then, in the same state that we were placed by the taking of the Bastile. The only question is, whether we should name another king or not."

Not only were the demagogues and the clubs, but the journals and the press, in a state of the greatest fury and activity. " O day of triumph !" said one of the popular pamphlets then current, " O day of triumph ! happy Frenchmen ! the perjured is arrested. The traitor Louis ought to suffer his chastisement ; it is not death that he deserves. He has sworn to maintain the constitution ; he is perjured ; he is no longer worthy to bear the sublime title of king of the French. No, no : suppose not, Frenchmen, that he will be faithful if you pardon him."

Both the Orleanists and the Republicans were endeavouring

(the better to accomplish each their different purposes) to prepare the public opinion for the dethroning of the king.   On all
the walls in Paris, on the corridors of the Assembly, were pasted
an address to the people of France, signed by one of the aides-de-
camp of La Fayette, but really written by Paine.   " Friends
and citizens," said the address, " the perfect tranquillity, the
mutual confidence, which reigned amongst us during the flight
of the ci-devant king, the profound indifference with which we
saw him brought back, are unequivocal signs that the absence
of a king is better than his presence ; that he is not only a su-
perfluity, but a weight that presses heavy on the nation.

" Let us not deceive ourselves.   All that concerns this man
may be reduced to four points :—1st. He has abdicated ; he has
deserted his post in the government.   2ndly. The nation can
never again restore its confidence to a man, who, faithless and
perjured, clandestinely fled, and evidently intended not to return,
but with a force sufficient to dictate laws to us.   3rdly. Was
this his own doings, or that of others ?   Of what consequence is
it to us whether he is weak or hypocritical, an idiot or a tyrant ?
He is equally unworthy of the functions of royalty.   4thly. He,
therefore, is free from us, as we from him.   He has no more authority, and we owe him no more obedience.   We know him
no more, but as an individual ; one among others, as Louis de
Bourbon."

The address then finished with referring all the evils which
France, in the long pages of history, appeared to have endured,
to its kings, the worthlessness of the office, its expensiveness,
&c. &c. ; and it finished by observing, somewhat humanely,
" that France was not to dishonour itself by showing any resentment against a man that had dishonoured himself."

These different specimens of the speeches, placards, and pamphlets will show you that the violence and the activity of the Republican party in and out of the Assembly were very great.
The king was provisionally suspended, and he and the royal
family were kept strictly confined and constantly and offensively
watched in the Tuilleries.

All this was to be expected ; and you are now to *continue* to
observe what was the conduct of the three great leading divisions
of opinion in Paris and in the Assembly at the time.   The tone
of the Republican party has just been described to you; and
with respect to the others, we will first turn to La Fayette and
the constitutional party.   They had never wished to destroy the
monarchy, and their part was clear if they were men of cou-

rage and of principle : they were now to support their constitution; and this they certainly did, with great spirit and integrity.

Barnave had been much struck, while coming from Chalons, in all that he had observed in the carriage; the good sense and good intentions of the monarch, the spirit and graces of the queen, and the unaffected piety, quiet reasonableness, and amiable qualities of the Princess Elizabeth. All these merits he probably now thought worthy of a better fate. He had been originally and long one of the most eloquent and distinguished opposers of the court and a powerful enemy to the monarchy, but he probably now saw his mistake, and he dedicated himself entirely to the preservation of the royal family and to the maintenance of the peace and order of the community. He, and La Fayette, and the Lameths, and all the more intelligent friends of liberty, perceived clearly that the new constitution was the only chance ; that it must at all events be tried and supported ; that on the one side they had to resist the old régime and the interference of foreign powers, for in this direction they could see no liberty, and certainly a civil war ; that on the other side, they had to resist the clubs and their republic, since a republic could only be introduced by the dethroning and probably the trial and execution of the king ; while here, too, it was not liberty that was to be found, but a civil war and the power of the sword. On every account the constitution, the experiment of a limited monarchy, limited as little as was now possible, was the only chance.

I have from the first contended, during all these lectures, that the friends of liberty should have rallied round the king and the monarchy long before, and so early as in the session of the 23rd of June 1789 ; but this chance was lost, and this mistake, if it be one, having been committed, all that was yet possible, they now attempted with great spirit and ability. Barnave drew up a very judicious answer for the king, when commissioners were sent by the Assembly to receive his declaration. It was exculpatory, yet with proper dignity and temper, and not, in what it affirmed, inconsistent with the truth, "that he had never meant to leave the kingdom ; that he had formed no project with strangers or emigrants to that effect ; that in the memoir he had left to be transmitted to the Assembly, he had not so much objected to the principles of the constitution, as to the inadequacy of the means allowed him to carry it into execution and to the little liberty that was left him either to judge of or to assent to it ; that he had discovered on his journey, which he could not do at Paris, how much the general opinion was in favour of the constitution; that he had no wish inconsistent with it, and would make every sacrifice to it, as he had been always ready to do; and that he would forget everything that had disturbed and disgusted him, if he could but accomplish the peace and happiness of the nation."

This declaration, though not entirely satisfactory (for, after the flight, what could be?), was on the whole fitted to produce a good effect; and with this the Constitutionalists were to go to the Assembly, and, assisting it with every reasonable consideration that they could offer, procure from the Assembly and from the people of Paris the establishment of the constitution, that is, the establishment of a limited monarchy.

So much for La Fayette and the Constitutionalists. We will now turn to the Royalists.

At this crisis, then, of the fate of Louis and the monarchy, what was the conduct observed by the third remaining party, by the coté droit, by the determined supporters, as they thought, of both?

The Abbé de Meaux and D'Espremenil drew up a paper and got it signed by two hundred and ninety of the deputies, the object of which was to protest against the Constitutionalists, their constitution, and all their projects and designs; and at the very moment that the king and the monarchy wanted every assistance to enable them to maintain their existence *at all*, this was the very moment chosen by the warmest friends of both, as they thought themselves, to show to the people of France and the Assembly that nothing could serve or satisfy them but the restoration of the old régime. They were determined, they said, to stand aloof, to take no part; and instead of assisting Barnave, La Fayette, and the Constitutionalists, against the Republicans, in and out of the Assembly, to leave them to manage as well as they could; that was in other words, to leave the king no hope but from the interference of foreign powers, and the chance of a civil war: the very expedients of which (of the last at least) he had always, both in words and in practice, shown a perfect horror.

This declaration or protest is given by Bertrand de Moleville. "It is the part of history," he says, "to collect these honourable acts, as so many monuments of courage and fidelity."

"In the midst of the insults," says the protest, "offered to the monarch and to his august family, and, in their persons, to the nation at large, what is the monarchy become? The decrees of the National Assembly have concentrated in themselves the whole regal authority; even the appearance of royalty no longer exists; a republican interregnum is substituted in its stead." Now, surely it might here be asked these protesters, Is all this to be wondered at, after the failure of such a measure on the part of the king as an endeavour to escape?

" Before the disastrous period at which we are arrived," continue the protesters, " we could at least embrace the phantom of the monarchy. We combated for its wrecks, and the hope of preserving it justified our endeavours. Now, the last blow has been given to the monarchy; but, deprived of this great motive, duties of another kind present themselves: the monarch exists; he is a captive; it is for the interest of the king we must rally; it is for him, for his family, it is for the loved blood of the Bourbons, that we should remain at a post where we may watch over so precious a deposit.

" But while we perform this urgent duty, let not our constituents expect that we shall interfere in any subject foreign to it. When a single interest can force us to sit with those who have erected an irregular republic upon the ruins of the monarchy, it is to that single interest we devote ourselves entirely. From this moment a profound silence on whatever is not relative to it will mark our sorrow, and be at the same time the only expression of our constant opposition to all the decrees. We shall henceforth take no part in deliberations which do not relate solely to those interests which remain for us to defend."

Such are the leading paragraphs of this declaration of the coté droit.

I must confess, that it appears to me a more striking instance cannot be produced of the impracticable conduct of which men the most respectable may be guilty, and of the manner in which they may deceive themselves, while they are engaged in political struggles, acting under the influence of their own personal resentments and irritations, while they give out and suppose themselves to be influenced by a regard to others, and by interests of a higher and very different nature.

Were such men as the Abbé de Maury and D'Espremenil to be told that the king, after his flight, could not be in the same situation as before? Was it not evident through the whole of that flight that the Revolution was popular? Was it not plain that a republican party was appearing, and was already in great force in Paris? Was not the dethronement of the king and a republic the obvious consequence that might have been expected of the king's being brought back a prisoner from Varennes? Suppose the emigrants and foreign powers appeared in force on the frontiers, suppose them marching to Paris, had they not already seen enough of the violent demagogues and mobs that it contained, to satisfy themselves that the first effect of any such crisis would be the massacre of the king and all the royal family together?

How was it possible at this period to attempt a restoration of the old régime but by a civil war? How could it possibly be carried on while the king was made prisoner by the people of Paris? What hope for him? Was it his wish; had it not been his constant effort to avoid all shedding of blood; and was there, after all, no difference between the constitution proposed by La Fayette and his friends, and a dethronement?

Under all the unhappy circumstances of the case, was it not the duty and best policy of the friends of the king to adhere to what appeared to be thought even by the king himself his own best duty and policy, not to drive things to extremities; to procure the best terms he could; to take the chance, whatever it might be, of giving the public time and opportunity, if possible, to cool down in the absence of opposition, and to subside into sentiments of greater moderation and reasonableness? The necessity might be hard, but it was not one to which their royal master thought it advisable to submit? Were they not to do the same, if on any other supposition, they must evidently sacrifice his life and crown? What conduct could the Republicans and his enemies wish them to pursue but the conduct they were pursuing? From the first, had not their unhappy king, meaning only the good of all, but unable to shed the blood of any, stood in the midst, between the court party on the one side, and the popular party on the other, to be sacrificed to the fury and contentions of both; and was this warfare to be persevered in even now, and to be continued, till he was to be dragged from the prison where he then was, to perish on a scaffold, or to be massacred in some insurrection of the people? Men may be in their characters respectable, and in their principles respectable, and in their intentions respectable; but if they will take no account of the circumstances in which they are placed; if they will listen to no suggestions of prudence and common sense; if sentiment or inherited opinion is to be everything with them, and reason nothing; if the world is to dissolve in ruins around them because they, it seems, can stand fearless amid the general wreck; if such are to be the rulers of the world, and the statesmen of the world, to such men the world will be seldom found to owe much obligation. However they may gratify their own notions of right and duty, they will be the enemies rather than the friends of mankind, and they will be the very persons whom of all others one should wish, for the sake of the peace and improvement and happiness of society, to banish as much as possible from all interference in public concerns; for to what end will they interfere, but to render all the efforts of sober and reasonable men idle and impossible?

The chapters of Bertrand de Moleville, that refer to this period of the history, are, I conceive, particularly instructive. Nothing can be so unfair as they are to the Constitutionalists, and so irrational in every point of view.

It is, as if the king were to have the chance of an escape from the Tuilleries, and then be in the same situation as before; as if men were to have the benefit of two opposite alternatives of conduct. He quotes a part of a speech from Pétion (p. 241), and then says, "Pétion concluded by moving that the king should be arraigned and tried by the National Assembly, or by a convention appointed expressly for that purpose.

" This motion," he adds, " with which the sitting concluded, obtained some applauses from the members of the coté gauche, but too few to alarm the coté droit, who, true to the resolution they had taken, kept a profound silence. This debate was continued in the two following sittings."

And then he goes on to observe, that " the Republican party, enraged at finding themselves in a minority in the Assembly, were extremely active in stirring up the people against the majority.

" The most violent placards and pamphlets deluged the capital: the revolutionary clubs entered into the most seditious resolutions; that of the Jacobins voted an address of censure and abuse to the National Assembly, because they had sent commissioners to meet the king, instead of ordering him to the bar. Brissot read a discourse to the Jacobin club," he says, " to show that the king might, and ought to be tried: the composition was ordered to be printed. The proposition with which it concluded was repeated," he says, " in the vociferations of the popular groups."

These are the representations of Bertrand de Moleville; and in this state of things, two hundred and ninety of the friends of the king and monarchy are, forsooth, true to their resolution, to sit silent and leave the battle to be fought by the Constitutionalists. They are to offer no assistance to the king and his

family; he is to appear left to exist or perish, according to the
issue of the contest, and all this because the Constitutionalists
had originally, in the general fermentation of public opinion,
and indeed of the world itself, allowed their imaginations to be
too much inflamed, and had not rallied round the king and the
monarchy early in the Revolution, though they were risking
their lives, certainly their popularity, to do so *now*. They had
at first gone too far, it might be admitted, had made mistakes
in the cause of liberty, but they were now labouring to repair
them; they had never meant injury either to the king or to the
monarchy, however the ardour of their prior proceedings might,
with the assistance of the faults of the court itself, have endangered both; and they were now, at least, the only chance of
protection that the king and monarchy really had. This might
surely have been acknowledged by Bertrand de Moleville; but
not so; and the members of the coté droit, as the Marquis de
Ferrieres observes (vol. ii. p. 407), consulted more their wish
to injure the Constitutionalists, whom they hated, than the use
they might be of to the king and royal family.

If we turn to the Memoirs of the Marquis de Ferrieres, he
will be found, as usual, more reasonable and candid than Bertrand de Moleville.

"The Constitutionalists," says he, "wished for a re-union
with the coté droit; the nobles of the Constitutional party
wished it evidently; but the great lords," he continues, "the
high clergy, the members of the parliament, the financiers,
wished for no new constitution, under whatever modifications
or concessions; it was the old régime, the whole of it, that they
wanted; that, and nothing else. To the constitution therefore,
though it might have brought with it peace, they preferred the
chance of the ruin of the monarch, and the chance of the ruin of
themselves, provided there remained to them the hope of the old
régime."

Such is the description given of the conduct of the coté droit,
not only by Bertrand de Moleville, but by the Marquis de Ferrieres himself, one of the order of nobles; and it is melancholy
to dwell on such passages in history.

As the marquis proceeds, in his tenth book, if you accompany
him, you will see a very animated account of what passed in the
Assembly, while the Constitutionalists were struggling for the
defence of the king and the monarchy, against Pétion and the
Republican party. This speech of Barnave was very striking,
and was instinct with a wisdom that was quite prophetic. And

that the Republican party did not attend to it, is one, I conceive, of the lessons of the Revolution; on this account I will call your attention to it for a moment.

Barnave, then, showed how different were the cases of America and France; the necessity of a monarchy to France, the nature of a limited monarchy; the principles of a government, representative and monarchical; the inviolability of the monarch; the nature of his responsibility; where responsibility was to exist, and might be suffered to exist. He alluded to the case of England; made at every turn of the great subject before him, the most sound and reasonable distinctions; exhibited in truth the mistakes of those who differed from him, but in the most calm and inoffensive manner, and then concluded with the following remarks, which surely ought to have impressed the Republican party, at least all those of them who meant well.

"But all further change," said Barnave, "is now fatal; every prolongation of the Revolution must be disastrous. Are we to put an end to the Revolution? are we to begin it again? If you once distrust the present constitution, where are you to stop? Above all, where are you to stop those who are to succeed to you? You have done everything for liberty, for equality: no arbitrary power has been allowed to escape; no usurpation, whether arising from selfishness or from property, has been spared; every man has been rendered equal in the eye of the law, whether civil or political. You have recovered and restored to the state whatever had been at any time taken from it, and hence results this great truth, that if the Revolution advance a step further, it cannot do it without danger: that as far as civil liberty is concerned, the first consequence would be the destruction of royalty; that, as far as equality is concerned, the destruction of property.

"You all of you know, that the night of the 4th of August gave more force to the Revolution than all the constitutional decrees: but for those who would now go further, what other night of the 4th of August remains, unless you will have laws against all property whatever? There is none of us that ought not to feel, that it is the common interest that the Revolution should now stop: those who are losers should perceive that it is impossible now to make it retrograde, that there is nothing now to be done but to make it settle and fix; they who have been the authors of it, and its assistants, should perceive, that it has reached its appointed term; that the welfare of their country and their own glory require that it should continue no longer:

even kings themselves, if truths so fundamental could obtain entrance into their counsels, ought to perceive, that even as far as *they* are concerned, there is a wide difference between a grand reform, and the abolition of royalty, and that if we do but stop here, they are still kings.

" Regenerators of the empire! Representatives of the French nation! follow on and persevere in your course. You have shown that you have courage to destroy the abuses of power, that you are competent to supply their place with wise and salutary institutions; prove, then, that you have also the force and the wisdom to protect and to maintain them. The nation has just given a sufficient proof of its energy and its courage : it has produced, and it has solemnly exhibited its full opposition to the attacks with which it was menaced. Continue the same precautions : let our functions be powerfully defended, but at the same time with our power, let us prove our moderation; let us offer peace to the world, disquieted, as it is, by all the events that have taken place amongst us; let us offer an opportunity of triumph, a genuine satisfaction, to all those who in foreign countries have taken an interest in our Revolution. From every land they cry to us, ' You are powerful, but be wise, but be moderate.' It is here that you will find the last finishing point of your glory; it is thus that you will show, that as the circumstances vary, you have the different talents, means, and virtues, all ready for their occasion, and that you can show and employ them as the exigency may require."

It is very honourable to Barnave, that these were the sentiments with which he endeavoured to impress the minds of his countrymen on the present occasion, but it was in vain; he could produce no effect upon the violent party on either side, neither on the court nor the Jacobin club; and his speech becomes one of the lessons of the Revolution.

The Republican party, when they found the Constitutionalists too strong for them within the Assembly, immediately turned to their followers *without*. They got up a petition, as they called it, requiring the National Assembly to receive the abdication made by Louis : a petition declaring that he was a perjured and fugitive traitor, and that they would never acknowledge him for king unless the majority of the nation differed from them : and they finished by an insurrection against the Constitutionalists in the Champ de Mars. La Fayette and Bailly called out the powers intrusted to them to preserve the laws and the peace of their country : they acted upon the provisions, as we have described them, of their new Riot Act : several people were unhappily killed, but nothing could be more regular and justifiable than the behaviour of these magistrates. This was, however, the occasion on which, as I have mentioned, Bailly lost all his popularity, and the populace and the Republican party were so enraged, that he was afterwards dragged from his retirement, and for the discharge of his duty, publicly executed.

The Republican party could not, in this first effort to dethrone the monarch, succeed; they were prevented by La Fayette and Bailly; but on the 10th of August in the subsequent year of 1792, as is well known, they did.   The allied powers had then openly interfered, and their victory was thus rendered easy. The great question that now, however, in the middle of 1791 remained, was the king's acceptance of the Constitution.

It can scarcely be believed possible, but the fact was, that every effort was made by the Royalists to prevent this acceptance, though it was quite clear that the king must immediately adopt this measure or descend from his throne.

Duport and Barnave were at last so alarmed themselves, and so alarmed the ministers, that Louis was prevailed upon to accept the Constitutional Act, purely and unconditionally.   He sent a letter to the president to announce his intentions; it was judicious and dignified.

After stating his case to a certain degree and his reasons, "he accepted the Constitution," he said, "and engaged to maintain it at home, and to defend it from all attacks abroad, and to cause it to be executed by all the means which it placed in his power."

He observed, "that he did not indeed perceive in those means so intrusted to him, all the strength that would be necessary to give motion and preserve unity in all the parts of a vast empire; but as opinions were divided on these subjects, he consented to their being left to the determination of experience ; that if he faithfully used all the powers which had been placed in his hands, no blame could be thrown upon him ; and the nation, whose interest alone ought to serve as a rule, might hereafter explain itself in the manner which the Constitution had provided.

"That the Constitution being finally decreed, Frenchmen living under the same laws ought to know no other enemies but those who infringe them.

"Let us consent," said the king, as he concluded, "to an oblivion of the past, and let the accusations and the prosecutions, which have arisen from the events of the Revolution, be abandoned in a general reconciliation."

The Assembly sent a deputation to acquaint his majesty " that the reading of his letter had been interrupted by repeated applauses ; that the Assembly partook of his majesty's desire to extinguish all animosities, and had hastened to pass, and now transmitted, a decree which obliterated every trace of a Revolution now concluded."

The king was greatly affected by the message ; said, " the day would be memorable in history ; that he wished it might put an end to discord, that it might unite all : I wish," said he, " that we may be but one."

Now, I must confess, that in these short state papers was traced, as far as I can judge, the good sense of the whole case, as it then stood at the close of the sitting of the Constituent Assembly ; the case, that had at last resulted from all the mistakes, and follies, and faults, of all concerned. It was in vain now for any party to endeavour to punish the other for its offences ; right or wrong, the Constitution was the issue at which they had all arrived,—it was the only chance left for law, order, peace, or the present or future establishment of civil liberty. The high party might turn to foreign powers and call for their interference ; the low party might be more and more determined on a republic, or a government that could not be distinguished from one ; these parties might act and re-act upon each other : but this was for each to gratify their passions, not consult the interests of their country, or the interests of mankind ; it was not to do credit either to the cause of right and order on the one side, as would be pretended by the high party, nor of liberty on the other, as would be pretended by the low ; but to degrade and stain the sacred cause which each affected to regard,—to ruin and to destroy it by fury and violence, and anarchy and bloodshed.   But it is too often thus : and the mortifications of any observer of the conduct of men, when acting in parties and bodies, are unceasing.

The Constituent Assembly was now dissolved. The scenes that took place in Paris, illuminations, rejoicings, &c. &c., you will read in the historians, and may easily conceive.

The observation with which Bertrand de Moleville concludes his account is this.   " Thus terminated," says he, " this guilty Assembly, whose vanity, ambition, cupidity, ingratitude, ignorance, and audacity, have overturned the most ancient and the noblest monarchy of Europe, and rendered France the theatre of

every crime, of every calamity, and of the most horrible catastrophe. Can these treacherous representatives ever justify themselves in the eyes of the nation for having so unworthily abused
their confidence and their powers?" This is the representation
on one side.

"Spite of the faults," on the contrary, say the historians, the
Two Friends of Liberty, "spite of the faults which the Constituent Assembly may be reproached with, and which were, in a
great measure, the result of the circumstances in which they
were placed, rather than their own, history has no period to
show us in which so much and such great things have been done
in so short a space of time. The Constitution of 1791, with all
its faults, for ever deserves the gratitude of the French people,—
because it has destroyed, never to return, every trace of feudal-
ism ; imposts the most fatal to agriculture ; the privileges of particular persons ; the usurpations of the priesthood over the civil
power, and the proud pretensions of ancient corporations ; because it has realized what philosophy for ages has in vain wished,
and what monarchs the most absolute have never dared to undertake ; and because it has established that uniformity, which no
one could have ever hoped for, in an empire formed by gradual
accretions from time to time, and with which, under a good government, there is no prosperity which France may not realize."

This is a representation very different from that of Bertrand,
which you have just heard, and one far more reasonable. You
will find a very strong indictment against the Constituent Assembly in Mounier : he reproaches them with many and great
faults, and seems to see none of their merits. By Necker, the
objections to their conduct are stated very fully but very calmly,
and I think reasonably. "History," says his daughter, M⁰. de
Stael, "ought to consider the Constituent Assembly under two
points of view,—the abuses destroyed, the institutions created.
Seen under the first point of view, the Constituent Assembly has
very great claims to the gratitude of mankind ; under the second,
the most serious faults may be objected to the Assembly."

This last may be considered, I conceive, as a fair précis of the
whole subject, but it is in general terms ; and it is for you to
consider the detail, and investigate the particulars on which
these general positions can be rested.

The later writers on the French Revolution, M. de Mignet and
others, indulge themselves in these general positions, after the
manner of M⁰. de Stael ; but, very differently from that affecting writer, they resolve everything into a sort of fatalism, which

seems to absolve at once all the parties concerned in the Revolution from all charge of either folly or crime. Great general causes they hold must necessarily produce their effects; and all further inquiry, all praise or censure, it may hence be inferred (though they do not dare openly to infer it), are but a waste of time, and out of the question. This they do not exactly say, but this is the conclusion.

" We must require," says M. de Thiers (and Mignet is entirely of the same school of fatalism), "we must require from men, and from the talents of men, at every epoch, that only which they have it in their power to do. In the moment of a revolt against the injustice of ranks, how are men to acknowledge their necessity; how constitute an aristocracy, when it is against aristocracy that the war is raised? To constitute royalty, indeed, would have been more possible, because it is placed at a greater distance from the people, has been less oppressive, and discharges functions that appear more necessary.

" But I repeat it," says M. de Thiers, "if these errors had not been in the Assembly, they would have been in the nation; and the course of events will show, that if the Assembly had left to the king and to the aristocracy all those powers which it did not leave them, the Revolution could not less have taken place, and that in all its excesses." Indeed!

This is surely a most unexpected, most unreasonable, and, at the same time, most comfortless position for the historian to lay down.

" To convince ourselves of the truth of this," says he, " we must distinguish between revolutions that arise among a people long enslaved, and those who are free: no doubt there will be more difficulty in the one case than the other. At Rome, Athens, and elsewhere," he continues, "one sees the nations and their rulers contend with each other for more or less of authority. But in modern times, when the people have been quite despoiled, the case is different: thoroughly enslaved, they are for a long time torpid: the upper and more enlightened classes are roused at last; they start up, and recover a part of the power. This awakening, that has thus taken place, gradually descends, and so does the wish for power; it at last reaches the lower classes, till the whole mass is in movement. Soon satisfied with what they have obtained, the most enlightened classes wish to stop, but it is no longer in their power; they are incessantly trampled upon and pushed forward by those who follow them. Those who stop, though already almost the last, if they oppose the last, become in the eyes of the last an aristocracy, and are immediately so denominated ; the bourgeois is called aristocrat by the artisan, and as such is persecuted and pursued.

"It is thus," he continues, "that in the Constituent Assembly we may observe those who are first enlightened, and who first exclaim against the power that is absolute over all ; we may observe them wise enough to see what is due to those who have everything, and those who have nothing : to the first, the Assembly would have left a part of what they had, because they had possessed it always ; and for the second, it would have procured the instruction and the benefits that in consequence of this instruction belonged to them. But with the one there is no sentiment but regret, nor with the other but ambition ; the one would recover everything, the other would require everything ; and a war of extermination is the result."

Such is the description given by the historian (not that I admit the description to be at any one moment exact), and no doubt he afterwards remonstrates with each party on the unreasonableness of their particular views ; but the general effect of the whole representation is, that every thing in the way of folly, and fault, and crime, is the result of the operation of general principles, linked together by a sort of invincible necessity, which one may deplore indeed, but which we should in vain endeavour to burst through or prevent.

Now to all remarks of this kind in M. de Thiers, or M. de Mignet, or M. de Bailleul, or any other reasoner of their school (it is a revolutionary school, as far as we are now considering it), it may be surely replied, that what is said in the way of explanation is one thing, but to introduce the doctrine of necessity into the affairs of the world is quite another.

Men may be shown the motives that have operated on others, or that may hereafter be likely to operate upon themselves ; this may be the philosophy of history ; they may be told the nature of their temptations. All this is the proper office of the commentator on the past ; but it is quite another thing to represent these temptations as irresistible, or to speak any language that can admit of any such interpretation. Let the historian explain the past ; but could he not have equally explained it, whatever the past had been? Let him, then, do no more than explain ; let him not thus talk of events as if they had been inevitable. Reason, and wisdom, and virtue, and everything, human and divine, is at an end upon any such supposition.

We have nothing but fate, necessity, and irresistible connexion—

> "And helpless man, in ignorance sedate,
> Rolls darkling down the torrent of his fate."

The discussions of the schools need surely not be introduced
into the ordinary affairs of mankind, and the politics of the
world.

I would wish to recall you, therefore, to the facts of the case,
as I have endeavoured to exhibit them to you in the course of
these lectures.   Lose not yourselves in generalities like those,
of these historians and commentators, but consider at each point
the circumstances before you, and give your praise and your
censure, and draw your lessons of instruction, as you are bound
to do upon this occasion as on every other, on the supposition
that all men, and more particularly patriots and rulers, are to
resist the temptations of their situation; that they are to
respect the rights and reasonable expectations of each other;
that they are to do justice and love mercy, and not resolve every
thing into a question of violence and force, and into a submission to what they call the irresistible influence of general causes
and principles, till they wrap themselves and others in a deso-
lating storm of anarchy and blood.

I have at every point of this fearful story stopped to compare
and consider, to the best of my power, the mistakes and faults
of every party in their turn ; and you must do the same.

You must proceed on the supposition of mistakes and faults,
of temptation and resistance, of wisdom and folly, of vice and
virtue, as in private life so in public, as on a smaller scale so on
a larger; men must never be suffered to suppose, that they are
not to proceed according to the ordinary moral interpretation of
human actions, and when they have been guilty of faults or
crimes, to talk of necessary motives, of the uncontrollable influence of the great principles, which after their faults and crimes
have been committed, they say have been operating on the
fortunes of the world, and therefore on their own particular
conduct, as engaged in the affairs of the world.   These are
ready excuses for any enormity ; and as they are refused to the
criminal by the judge, so are they refused to the criminal by the
historian.

And now that we have reached the period when the Constituent Assembly was dissolved, you must endeavour to estimate
the conduct first of the Assembly, by placing before your view
the facts, favourable and unfavourable; and next, in like

manner, that of the king, the court, and the public; finding explanations, if you please, of the conduct of both the one and the other, in such general principles as you may have observed to influence them, but not therefore excuses, still less justifications, least of all, reasons for supposing that all wisdom and counsel in the concerns of mankind are vain.   And to proceed, then, upon the usual principles of human conduct, and after the usual manner of history, we may remark, that the Constituent Assembly procured for France many benefits that were most important, and that were permanent.   Torture and judicial barbarisms were abolished; the commercial jurisprudence reformed; the principles of religious liberty acknowledged; monastic vows discountenanced and suppressed; *lettres de cachet* put an end to, and personal liberty rendered sacred; equality of taxation introduced; no interior customs allowed; provincial jealousies and animosities swept away, and an uniformity of administration everywhere established.   Feudal rights were all annulled; all sorts of exclusions; and every shackle laid on industry removed; and a national force of an admirable nature instituted—the national guards; and it would be unjust to deny that this Assembly proclaimed the first principles of a free government.   The Assembly may not have skilfully either interpreted or applied, but they constantly acknowledged them; and these eternal principles of truth, thus exhibited, can never be without their effect in calling the attention of the people of France, of Europe, and of the world itself, to the real end and meaning of all good government, the happiness of the people. Merits of this kind the Assembly may certainly claim for themselves, and they are great and lasting.   Their mistakes and faults I have from time to time endeavoured to impress on your minds, for they were those of the leading members of the Assembly, who must be considered on the whole, as the friends of freedom; and of such men the mistakes and faults (as I must for ever repeat) are above measure important.

They began too much from the first on a system of usurpation; they should have closed with the king and the court on the terms he proposed to them in the sitting of the 23rd. Again, when their victory was complete, after the 14th of July, they should have had the magnanimity to have trusted the king, and made their terms good; given the executive power full strength, and rested on the force of public opinion, which was everywhere so clearly in their favour, so powerful, and if they had but reflected, so truly formidable: they were always too sweeping in their views, and too experimental in their measures.

There is no difficulty in exposing the faults and inconveniences of any existing system, or the superior advantages that may be expected from a new one; the difficulty always is, how to introduce a new one, without inflicting misery and ruin, and throwing into a state of hostility those who have been brought up, or are benefited by the old one; even endangering in the course of the experiment, perhaps destroying, the happiness of the community. The proper management of this difficulty is, in truth, the great question at issue between Mr. Burke and the leaders of the Constituent Assembly; and Mr. Burke must be considered, I conceive, as having reason on his side, when he accuses them of not building sufficiently on old foundations; of being sanguine, rash, and presumptuous; of not proceeding after the manner of wise and regular statesmen; destroying the nobility and the right of primogeniture, and thus rendering monarchy impossible.

Even they who do not agree with me, while I thus far agree with Mr. Burke, will at least allow that they disregarded, in a manner totally unpardonable, the rights of property; that to the clergy they were cruel, unjust, and ungrateful; that they rested everything too much and too long on the will of the people; that they debauched them by flattery and submission; and that they took no proper care to have the laws respected. Thus far the most popular reasoners must, I conceive, agree with me. The Assembly had a national force at their command, consisting very much of the middle ranks of society, and they ought to have taken care that the common feelings of mercy and justice were observed, and the brutal leaders of mobs punished, or they should have retired at once from the scene, and broken up their sittings in despair; or rather they should have done their duty, be the consequences what they might; and no duty was evidently more imperative upon them, than not to suffer themselves to be bullied and overpowered by tumultuous galleries and legislative clubs.

At the close of their sittings they made a vain effort against these clubs, which should have been made a year and a half before; and though they saw the Republican party drawn up before them, rising in strength, and powerful in popularity, though they had only just put them down by force, they assented to the motion of Robespierre, voted themselves not eligible to the next Assembly, and left the king, whom they had not ceased to love, and the constitution which they had themselves made, to their fate. What mistake could be so obvious, or likely to be so fatal?

That the assembly exerted themselves in the most laudable manner to protect the king and the monarchy, after the return from Varennes, is very true; but at periods before that return, I cannot see in the leaders of the Constituent Assembly that caution, wisdom, and forbearance, and that virtuous adherence to the great principles of human society which should distinguish the conduct of the friends of freedom; for without these, their efforts can never be successful.

For the court party, indeed, no defence whatever, can be made. In every attempt to ameliorate the situation of their country, they resisted from the first the king, and every minister in his turn; they were always opposed to M. Necker; they fatally interfered in his conciliatory plan, produced by the king on the 23rd of June (the last chance of France); they brought forward the troops to dissolve or control the Assembly, though they knew the king would not suffer the troops to fire on the people; they then parted off from the king, and brought his cause into suspicion by tampering with foreign powers; they next turned away from the Constitutionalists even after the unsuccessful flight to Varennes; and they then made every effort to convert these foreign powers into invaders of their country, a measure scarcely in any conceivable case defensible, certainly not defensible in the existing situation of their country and of their king.

The king, in the mean time, was to have accumulated on his head the faults and mistakes of every party and his own. Whoever was wrong, whether himself or others, it was he who had to suffer; and of all the mortals that were ever called upon to rule among mankind, Louis XVI. must be considered as the most unfortunate.

LECTURE XXIV.

WAR WITH AUSTRIA, 20 APRIL, 1792.

WE now proceed to the history of the second Legislative Assembly.

The story of the French Revolution is afflicting in the extreme; the changes are rapid, and every change is for the worse. The vista darkens as we advance, and it seems to lead we know not whither.

The Legislative Assembly had no sooner met than it was quite clear that the Revolution had descended one step lower. Where before the court party had sat, were now found the Constitutionalists and the friends of La Fayette; and their former places on the left of the Assembly were now filled by men who considered themselves as the supporters of the cause of freedom, but who were far more violent in their expressions, and more republican in their tone, and who appeared many of them ready to urge the new opinions to far greater lengths than had been done by their former assertors; indeed, to any democratic lengths that could well be conceived possible.

These men were afterwards distinguished by the general names of Girondists and Jacobins.

The two fatal mistakes of the Constituent Assembly soon began to produce their full effect,—first, the mistake of rendering themselves ineligible to the Legislative Assembly; and again, the mistake of not making more early and more decisive efforts to put down the Jacobin clubs. Little or no attempt seems to have been made on the subject of the elections; the democratic clubs seem to have every where influenced the choice of the electors, and this should only have rendered the king and the court aware how difficult and perilous was their situation.

When the Assembly met, there was little disposition shown to pay proper respect to the king or his high office. It had been even intended to assimilate him to their president, by placing both on the same sort of chair; and though this was not done, the manner and reception of the Assembly were, on the whole, so humiliating in the apprehension of the king, that the unfortunate monarch was quite overcome by his feelings of mortification and despair; and on his return to the palace, burst into tears, lamenting to the queen that she should ever have come to France thus to see the degradation of its sovereign. Madame de Campan, who tells the story, says that the queen was obliged to desire her, as she stood motionless before them, to leave them, that she might no longer be a witness of her own confusion and distress, and the agony of the king.

You will now have to read the history of the Legislative Assembly: it continued sitting for ten months. It is, in truth, still the history of the conflict of the old and new opinions. For ten months you are to see the dreadful struggle that ensued.

The king and the Constitutionalists, the intermediate parties, in vain endeavouring, the king to prevent the shedding of blood and a civil war, and the Constitutionalists to save their country from the influence of foreign powers, and, at the same time, to repress the violence of the popular party, which was hastening to the dethronement of the king.

These efforts were vain. The faults of each and of all, you will have opportunity enough to observe. This struggle, then, between the supporters of the old régime, aided by the Constitutionalists, between these on the one side, and the Girondists and the Jacobins on the other, produced, first, the war with Austria, and, at length, the insurrection of the 10th of August, and the dethronement of the king.

The war with Austria was the great turn of the whole revolutionary history; and you cannot reflect upon the conduct of all the parties concerned too attentively: it must be the main subject of this lecture. Be not repelled by any tediousness in the discussion; this must be submitted to. I must again repeat that this war with Austria was the great turn of the whole revolutionary history. The only chance of the king and the constitution, as it then stood, was peace.

You will easily comprehend that political reasoners will differ widely, and consider the war with Austria as defensive on the part of France, or not, very much as they think the cause of the Revolution was at the time favourable to the great and permanent interests of mankind, or not; the cause of freedom or of licentiousness.

You may see a debate in our own House of Commons, in February, 1800, where Mr. Pitt considers the war as unjust and unnecessary on the part of France; and Mr. Fox, on the contrary, as perfectly called for and unavoidable, from the menacing conduct of the German powers. Real grounds of difference no doubt existed, in consequence of the revolutionary proceedings of the Constituent Assembly with respect to the fiefs in Alsace, and on the subject of Avignon; but besides these causes of difference, there were others of a nature still more animating and important.

The followers of the court, and the supporters of the old régime, were continually flying to Germany, and were there received and patronized. While this was the case, it was impossible to pacify the Girondists and the Jacobins on the one side; and, in the mean time, the Jacobins and Girondists were themselves making furious speeches, and carrying measures hostile to the king, to the monarchy, and the clergy: it was therefore equally impossible, on the other side, to calm the continental powers, or prevent them from thinking that in the Jacobins they saw only the enemies of the human race destroying their own country, in the first place, and preparing also to destroy, if successful, every civilized government in Europe. Whatever, therefore, had been the real grounds of difference between the two, they would have been lost and overwhelmed in the contention of such powerful motives of action as these. The great misery was, that there was no common ground for the two more extreme parties. The court, for instance, the patrons of the old opinions, with the German powers, could not bear the Revolution under any possible modification or aspect ; it was from the beginning, and through all its stages, insolence, injustice, and absurdity ; and they never would give their assistance to the Constitutionalists, the intermediate party. On the contrary, the more violent friends of freedom were determined that the Revolution should not be put down : that neither the court within, nor the foreign powers without, should restore the empire of what they considered tyranny and priestcraft, and in different ways " the enormous faith of many made for one." This at least is the plea, and the case of the Girondists and Jacobins, stated as they would themselves state it ; and rather than suffer this, as they would have said, they were evidently ready to dethrone the king, erect a republic, or face any situation of anarchy and bloodshed that could be necessary. Political enthusiasm may reach the fury of religious enthusiasm, as it was shown in the present instance of France ; and as the year 1792 rolled on, the general inflammation (whether with or without reason) of the revolutionary leaders, and of the people of France, and particularly of Paris, became totally desperate and ungovernable.

The king and his ministers were in the meantime placed in a situation singularly embarrassing.

The king had accepted the constitution, though he thought but ill of it ; still he had publicly accepted it, and he had declared to his ministers, when confidentially questioned upon the point, that he meant faithfully to adhere to it. They were, therefore, to do the same ; but they themselves thought worse of it than did their master ; and both the one and the other conceived, that, by a regular administration of it, its total inefficiency for all the proper purposes of government would be shown ; that material alterations must be the consequence ; and that these must be made in favour of the royal power. Nor were they at all unwilling to receive, for any purpose of this kind, the assistance of the German powers : the king, as far as this was possible, without bloodshed and a civil war ; his ministers and the court, at any risk, and expense of violence and commo-

tion; and both the one and the other contented themselves
rather with a formal and exact administration of the power of
the constitution according to the letter than according to the
spirit of it. There were exceptions to this description of the
king's ministers, Delessart Narbonne, Duport du Tertre; but I
allude to the king's confidential ministers and advisers, Bertrand
de Moleville and others. The king studied the constitution minutely; but, under these circumstances, the jealousy and ill-
humour of the patriotic party were incessant. It was easy to
find subjects of complaint and grounds of distrust, particularly
while the assembling of the French princes and emigrant nobility
at Coblentz and other places, and the late flight of the king to
Varennes, were facts so notorious, and appeared to speak their
own lessons so distinctly. Whatever the king or the ministers
might openly say in the way of remonstrance to the German
powers, all, it was supposed, would be considered by them as
null and void, and be perfectly understood; the king and his
ministers were, therefore, held to be silently and insensibly betraying the cause of the Revolution, and preparing the country
for subjugation by its enemies. And all this time the speeches
of the Jacobins and members of the Legislative Assembly, accusing and vilifying the court and the ministers, only served to
justify the king and his ministers in their unfavourable opinion
of the constitution, and to confirm the French emigrants and
German princes and sovereigns in their total abhorrence of it.
Fear and jealousy are principles inaccessible to all reasoning and
all evidence: and it was scarcely to be expected under circumstances like these, amid the conflict of the new and old opinions,
that a rupture between France and Germany should be avoided,
or that the rupture should not be followed by calamities of the
most afflicting nature.

I have made these preliminary observations that you may see
the importance of the subject, and be therefore the better disposed to read the many debates in the Assembly, and the many
memoirs and state papers that now present themselves to your
perusal: many more than I can here consider, than I can even
describe, than I could almost enumerate.

Indeed, there is no portion of the general subject at which we
have yet arrived, so fitted to perplex and overwhelm the mind
of the student, as the one now before us, from the multiplicity
of the documents that exist, the delicate nature of the points to
be considered, the difficulty with which a judgment can be
formed, sometimes of the facts, sometimes of the principles con-

cerned; and yet a rational student will summon all his powers
and attention to the task before him, for never was a subject
presented to him more worthy of their exertion. These facts
and these principles led immediately to the Austrian war, afterwards to the dethronement of the king, the invasion of France,
the summoning of a convention, and the trial and execution of
the sovereign. These are awful events, and even these are not
all; they were followed by others but too well known and remembered: and some attempt to form a rational estimate of the
subject before us must be made.

The circumstances, then, that led to the Austrian war, were,
—1st, the differences that existed on account of the fiefs in
Alsace, and the treatment of Avignon: and 2ndly, the assembling of the emigrant princes and nobles, and the menaces, on
the part of the German powers, of an interference in the affairs
of France. We will advert to each in their order.

There is a very full account of these first differences between
the German powers and the leaders of the French Revolution,
on the subject of these fiefs, in Dodsley's Annual Register for
1790, in the beginning of the seventh chapter.

The Duke of Würtemburg with many other princes, both
secular and ecclesiastical, held great possessions in Alsace and
other provinces, which countries France had at different times
wrenched from the empire; and though the paramount dominion
had thus been transferred to France, these several districts, with
all the ancient rights appertaining to them, had been secured,
confirmed, and guaranteed to their proper and original possessors by the celebrated treaty of Westphalia, to which France
was herself a party, and from which alone she could derive any
legal title or claim to the provinces in question, of which those
lesser fiefs composed a considerable part. But, alas! what were
feudal rights and treaties of Westphalia to the Constituent Assembly on the night of the 4th of August, 1789? and how vain
were any reasonable expectations that might be entertained by
those who professed the old opinions, amidst the storm and
uproar of the new. What were such rights, and treaties, and
expectations, on that celebrated night? what could they ever be
afterwards? The Assembly, indeed, so far recovered at last
its sense of propriety as to vote an indemnity to the German
princes; but the princes had made regular appeals, after the
ancient manner, to the Diet of the empire, had early become
angry and inflamed, were not disposed to sell or barter their
birthright, and professed not to understand the manner in which

the French revolutionists were accustomed to turn all matters, however serious, to ridicule, which did not correspond with their own new ideas; and while the Assemblies, both Constituent and Legislative, only showed a sort of arrogant indifference, and only ordered the offer of indemnification to be repeated, the seeds were sown deep of severe and bitter animosity on the part of the powers of Germany, and they were made to hate the Revolution and all its abettors.

Again: you will see a good and shorter account given of the same subject by Coxe, in the fifty-fifth chapter of his "House of Austria."

You will find, also in the Annual Register for 1790, and in a note of Coxe, the case of Avignon, which became another source of dissension. This town was the capital of countries that formed part of Provence, and they had been sold, in the fourteenth century, by Joanna, Countess of Provence, to the popes. Avignon had been once the residence of popes, and was an integral part of the papal dominions. The whole district, however, had been originally comprised in the kingdom of Arles, and was still considered as a fief of the German empire. The emperors, as liege lords, had ratified the cession made by Joanna. But what an insult to the Abbé Sieyes and his eighty-three departments, and to all the new notions and the dignity of France, was the residence of a pope in one of her provinces! and who could venture to mention such a personage as Joanna, or the fourteenth century, or the ratification of a liege lord of the German empire, at a sitting of the Jacobin club? The result of the whole was, that the German States were convinced, from the treatment of their fiefs and the seizure of Avignon, that the new rulers of France were animated with a spirit of hostility and encroachment more than had ever inspired either Richelieu or Mazarin, or, even in the person of Louis XIV., had ever threatened the independence of the empire and of Europe.

These were the real differences that I alluded to as existing between France and the German powers, and these differences, in any common state of things, might have been adjusted by indemnifications and concessions on the one side and on the other. But these grounds of dissension or any grounds of dissension became far more deep and important amid the irreconcilable opposition of the old and new opinions that had now unfortunately taken place.

So much for the first part of the subject, the real differences to which we have referred on the subject of the fiefs and of Avignon.

But with respect to the second, the interference of Austria in the affairs of France, to form a judgment upon this also, is a task far more difficult in the accomplishment.

Nothing can be so easy as with Mr. Burke to look at the conduct and debates of the Legislative Assembly, and to see there nothing but fury and violence; to vote the Girondists, anarchists, the Jacobins, ruffians, and to call the war, on the part of France, a mere war of revolutionary injustice and rage. In like manner, nothing can be more easy, on the other side, than to say that the cause of the court of Austria was the cause of kings from the first, and of kings against their people; and that the Girondists and Legislative Assembly had no alternative but to make Austria unmask herself as soon as possible, and defend their Revolution by open war against the attack she was meditating. Nothing can be more easy than these two opposite views of the question. The materials for the support of *each* are abundant, and the difficulty is immense for those who would wish to form a reasonable estimate of the conduct of all parties. I have found it so; and it was wearisome and disheartening in the extreme to go on for weeks and months assenting to opposite views and reasonings, each in their turn, first to the one and then to the other.

But from a fatigue and a misery of this kind I must now make what effort I can to protect you, who hear me. Without, therefore, dispersing our attention and losing our subject among the debates and memoirs that present themselves, I shall propose to you to look patiently at the state papers, and see what all these conflicting views and opinions really come to, and what are the practical results from time to time. I conceive this is a clue that will lead you through the labyrinth tolerably well, if you will follow the thread calmly and with proper perseverance.

These state papers you will find, sufficiently for your purpose, in the Annual Register for 1792, part ii.; but they are not placed in their proper order, and you must follow the dates, beginning with the earliest.

In my first rough draught of the lecture I am now giving, I had here proceeded to give extracts from these state papers at some lengths, which I had meant to read to you, and which I thought would have put you in immediate possession of the merits of the case, and have, at the same time, justified the view of it which I intended ultimately to propose to your consideration.

But the style of state papers, even when they are sincere and honest, is so formal, so many words are employed to limit, and guard, and properly express what is meant, that extracts from them, however curious and important, produced in the way I have mentioned, would, I afterwards thought, be wearisome to you, and even somewhat difficult at the moment, exactly and entirely to comprehend. I have therefore thought it best to give you some general notion of these state papers, in some more broken and irregular manner, using the words of them whenever I could, and exhibiting to you what I conceive to have been, on the whole, the drift and purport of them. My appreciation of them you must therefore for the present suppose to be just, and take for granted; but only for the present. I must depend on your reading them. They are not many in number. When read, though not perhaps when only heard, they can be sufficiently comprehended. They led to such important results, that they must be considered.

To advert then to these state papers. They begin with a manifesto from the French nation, sent to all the courts of Europe, professing a love of peace, but declaring that France could not consider that as a friendly territory, in which existed an army waiting only the prospect of success for the moment of attack.

All this, you will see, was directed against the German powers, for protecting the emigrants, allowing them to assemble at Coblentz, &c. &c.

The Elector of Treves was more particularly alluded to. Some official notes are interchanged; but at last, on the 16th of January, 1792, the French king informs the Legislative Assembly, that his minister at Treves declares, "that the dispersion of the emigrants is as real and as complete, as the nation had desired and the king directed."

On the whole, you will see, that on this particular point concessions were made by the Elector of Treves and the Emperor Leopold.

But soon after, on the 25th of January, 1792, the Legislative Assembly renew their accusations and complaints against the emperor, whom they consider as having formed a concert injurious to the sovereignty and safety of the French nation. They state their reasons for thinking so, and the French ambassador is ordered to require proper explanations from the imperial court.

"It is apprehended (the ambassador in consequence declared to that court) that there does indeed exist a combination be-

tween the principal powers of Europe, for the purpose of producing some change in the French constitution; that a congress
is to be established; that uniting their powers and their means,
they will endeavour to force the king and the nation to accept
those laws which they may make."

Allusions were made in this state paper to various steps that
had been taken by Leopold to combine the German powers into
a sort of union, to protect the king and the monarchy of France
from the outrages and machinations of the democratic leaders,
and more particularly the Jacobin clubs and popular societies.

Such was the real purport of the French remonstrance to the
Court of Vienna in January 1792. When you look at it, you
will see that the whole matter was brought to an issue. "Do
you," it said to the emperor, " and will you, interfere against
the French Revolution, or not?" This was the real meaning
of the whole; and it now becomes an object of great curiosity
to see, when thus pressed, what was the answer which the
Austrian cabinet returned.

The explanation then that was returned, as you will find,
came to this:—That there had originally existed a necessity for
the concert of the sovereign powers, and that it had therefore
been formed—this was not at all denied—but that since the
king had accepted the Constitution, it had been suspended.

I will quote a paragraph or two from the reply of the Austrian
court.

"When France gave to Europe," says the reply, "the spectacle of a lawful king, forced by atrocious violence to fly; pro-
testing solemnly against the acquiescence which they had extorted from him, and a little afterwards stopped and detained
prisoner by his subjects: yes, it then *did* concern the brother-
in-law and the ally of the king, to invite the other powers of
Europe to join with him in a declaration to France, that they
all view the cause of his most Christian Majesty as their own;
that they demand that this prince and his family be set at liberty
and have the power to go where they please; and they require
for these royal personages inviolability and due respect, which,
by the laws of nature and of nations, are due from subjects to
their princes; that they will unite to avenge, in the most signal
manner, every further attempt that may be committed, or may
be suffered to be committed, against the liberty, the honour, and
the safety of the king, the queen, and the royal family; and
that finally, they will not acknowledge as constitutional, and
legally established in France, any laws but those which shall

have the voluntary acquiescence of the king, enjoying perfect liberty.

" But if, on the other hand, these demands are not complied with, they will in concert employ all the means in their reach to put a stop to the scandalous usurpation of power which bears the appearance of an open rebellion, and which, from the danger of the example, it concerns all the governments of Europe to repress.

" These," says the reply, " are the terms of the declaration which the emperor proposed, in the month of July, 1791, to the principal sovereigns of Europe to be made to France, and to be adopted as the basis of a general concert. He defies a word to be found which is not sanctioned by all the principles most sacred in the law of nations ; and is it pretended that the French nation has raised itself, by its new constitution, above the universal law of all countries in all ages ?"

Such is the language of the reply, not very unnatural, it must be allowed, from the Austrian court, on the subject of the concert of the allied powers that had been formed against the violent proceedings in France. But this concert was declared to be *suspended*. What, then, was the language of the same court on this most important point of the suspension ?

The words of the Austrian reply are these :—" This suspension," it says, " was caused by the king's acceptance of the constitution, and by the appearance that he had done it freely, and in hopes that the dangers which threatened the liberty, the honour, and the safety of the king and royal family, as also the existence of the monarchy of France, would cease in future. It is only in case these dangers shall be reproduced that the concert will again resume its activity."

Such was the reply and explanation of the emperor on the original concert of the sovereigns, and its subsequent suspension ; nor can it be denied that it was sufficiently explicit. The celebrated letter from Padua, and the treaty at Pilnitz, &c. &c. were, it seems, all to be considered as no longer in operation, the king being now at liberty, and having accepted the constitution. But then it was to be observed that they were suspended—no more. The right of interfering in the affairs of France was, therefore, maintained. The concert of the sovereigns was only suspended while the king and royal family were well treated ; and what was more, while the form of government was monarchical. Such was the explanation and the answer of the Austrian court.

Now these, it must be observed, were conditions, as it were, prescribed to the French nation by the allied powers; and to make conditions of this kind cannot but be considered as trenching upon the independence and sovereignty of a great people. It was impossible that they should not be so considered in France.

I do not at all deny that it was very natural for the emperor, and even the German powers, to feel as they did. Though we may ourselves have far different notions of civil liberty and the rights of the community from any that can have been supposed to be entertained by the sovereign and princes of Germany, still it is not very possible for us, ourselves, to behold, without indignation as well as regret, the lengths to which the patrons of the new opinions proceeded, even while the Constituent Assembly was sitting; and we neither wonder at the flight of the king, nor refuse our sympathy with the feelings he expressed in his parting manifesto addressed to the Assembly. Even on the present occasion, I am far from saying that we can refuse to acknowledge as generous and just the sentiment at least, that pervades the extracts I have quoted from the Austrian reply, the sentiment of resentment excited by the injustice and wrong committed by the French nation against a monarch that surely had deserved a kinder treatment from a civilized people. But the question is, how this sentiment was to be exhibited; what direction, without justly offending an independent people, this sentiment was to take; what conduct, what measures were to result from it; how it was to be made useful to the unfortunate king and his family; how best it could support the monarchy of France; how it was to be made subservient to the cause of order, of peace, and good government upon earth. This was indeed a question, the delicacy and difficulty of which the German courts seem little to have comprehended at the time, and still less the emigrant French princes and nobility. These observations on the one side and on the other I must leave to your consideration.

We give the German powers full credit for the sincerity of their professions; I see not, at this particular period, why it should be refused them. Subsequently, indeed, their manifestoes were of a different nature, but I am addressing myself to those which are now before us; and the first are always, in a moral point of view, the most important.

To return, however, to our subject. Whatever we may think of the reply of the Austrian court, and even we ourselves have been compelled to protest against the sort of menacing interference and superintendence which it intimated over the interior concerns of an independent people ; whatever may be our own sentiments on this occasion, it will easily be supposed that this sort of reply, that we have quoted, could not but fortify the democratic writers and speakers of the Assembly and Jacobin club in their representations, that the allied powers meant only to assert the cause of kings, meant only to produce a counter-revolution.

But the Austrian reply did not stop where we have stopped, for it proceeded to make other observations, which, though but too much founded in truth, went still further to exemplify an interference in the affairs of France, and to push that system of interference still further beyond the limits which the honour and sovereignty of an independent nation can admit. The reply, in short, went on to comment on the practices of the Jacobins, and the more violent leaders of the Revolution.

" No," says the reply, " the true cause of this ferment is the influence and violence of the Republican party, condemned by the principles of the constitution, and proscribed by the Constituent Assembly ; a party, whose ascendance in the present legislature has been viewed with dread by all those who have the good of France at heart.

" It is the violence of this party which produced those crimes and scenes of horror which disgraced the commencement of the reformation of the French constitution, called for and secured by the king himself, and the consummation of which Europe would have seen with unconcern, had not attempts, forbidden by all laws, human and divine, forced foreign powers to unite for the preservation of the public tranquillity, and for the safety and honour of crowns.

" It is the agitations of this party, who, since the new constitution has declared the inviolability of the monarchy, invariably seek to overthrow and sap its principles," &c. &c.

" As they well know," continues the reply, " that the majority of the nation is unwilling to adopt their system of a republic, or more properly, of anarchy, and as they despair of succeeding to bring it about, if tranquillity should be established in the interior of the nation, and peace preserved with the surrounding powers, they direct all their efforts to foster the internal troubles, and bring on a foreign war."

The reply then proceeds still further to describe and to reprobate the practices of this particular party in France against their own country, and against foreign powers, and then observes,

" that notwithstanding these offensive proceedings, the emperor will give to France the clearest proof of the constant sincerity of his attachment by preserving, on his part, that quiet and moderation which his friendly concern for the situation of the kingdom inspires. He does justice to the personal sentiments of the king, his brother-in-law. He is far from ascribing such measures to the majority of the nation, who either groan under the evils produced by a frantic party, or involuntarily take a part in the errors and prejudices which are instilled into them against the conduct of his imperial majesty."

" Finally," says the reply, " it is with the same amicable view that the emperor opposes truth to malevolence, being persuaded that his Most Christian majesty and the sound and major part of the nation will plainly see the professions and actions of a sincere friendship, and be much obliged to him for dissipating freely and without management the illusions to which it is intended they should fall victims."

Now certainly this reference to a frantic faction, this distinction made between this party and the sound and major part of the nation, was not to be justified on any principles of international law, nor likely to lead to any system of amity and peace between the two nations; nor, finally, at all fitted to serve the cause of the king, or the cause of order and good government in France.

This may, I think, be said, supposing the intentions of the emperor to have been everything that they pretended to be. But you must judge for yourselves. I have quoted from this state paper at greater length than I had at first intended, that you may be able, as immediately as possible, to form some judgment of the subject before you. You see evidently here displayed the conflict of the new opinions and the old.

You will perceive it still more in the debates of the Legislative Assembly and the proceedings of the Jacobin club. By one unhappy circumstance and another, mankind had got elevated into a most frightful state of excitation, and this so early as the beginning of 1792; and on every account the prospect both to France and Europe was tremendous.

This reply of the court of Austria was sent to the French ambassador, accompanied by a note from the Austrian minister, Prince de Kaunitz, stating still further the opinion of the emperor, on the character and practices of the Jacobins, " as a pernicious sect, the enemies of the Most Christian king, and of the fundamental principles of the present constitution, and the dis-

turbers of peace and public repose;" and the envoy of the king
of Prussia informed the French minister at Paris, that the
Austrian dispatch contained the principles on which the courts
of Berlin and Vienna were perfectly in concert.

The question now is, what was the conduct of France ? Was
the matter suffered here to rest ? That could scarcely be expected ; but certainly, in the event, a very dignified forbearance
was shown in the next French dispatch on the subject of the
Jacobins and all that was so justly offensive in the Austrian
note. " The king," replies the next French note, " thinks that
it neither becomes the dignity nor the independence of the nation to discuss objects which he is of opinion relate to the internal concerns of the kingdom ; but his majesty observes the
assurances given in the name of the emperor, that far from supporting the projects and pretensions of the emigrants, he was
desirous to convince the French nation of the falsehood of those
reports which had been propagated against his imperial majesty,
and which impute to him designs against the safety and independence of France, by plans and alliances tending to interfere
in the government and overturn the constitution.

" His majesty," the note goes on to say, " has found in the
answer of the deceased emperor (Leopold had just died) some
amicable and pacific overtures, and he has received them with
pleasure."

The note is calm and decorous, and respectful ; but it declares, that the king cannot behold without uneasiness a confederacy, the object of which appears to give just cause of alarm,
and that in consequence, he demands of his ally, the emperor,
to abandon that confederacy, and to renew his assurances of peace
and union.

The great point therefore, you observe, was still at issue between the two courts. The confederacy, however its original
intentions might be resigned, or rather suspended, was still existing, and its very existence was thought by France a measure
of hostility : the new emperor was therefore required to abandon it, and return to his former state of amity and alliance with
the French nation. The note afterwards went on to observe,
that the French king charged his ambassador to promise, that as
soon as his imperial majesty shall have engaged to discontinue
all preparations for war in his dominions, and to reduce his military force in the Low Countries to the footing they were on, at
the 1st of August, 1791, his majesty will also discontinue all
preparations, and will reduce the French troops in the frontier
departments to the ordinary state of the garrisons.

The whole affair then, you may remark, was reduced to these two points; first, of the confederacy; and secondly, the troops in the Low Countries; distinctly; but without any intemperate observation, in reply to the Austrian remarks on the state of the French government and the parties of the state : and this forbearance must be considered as conciliatory on the part of France, as becoming, and as very creditable, to the French minister,. Delessart.

What was now, then, the language of Austria ? Was the great point of the confederacy given up, or at all modified ; or any new assurance or promise on the subject of interference made ? The answer was this, and you will observe it, as it turned out to be the ultimatum of the Austrian court, this answer of the 18th of March.

" The king of Hungary and Bohemia (afterwards the Emperor Francis) knows not of any armament, or any measures in the Austrian states, which can be denominated preparations for war. The defensive measures ordered by his late imperial majesty, are not to be compared with the hostile measures of France ; and as to those which his apostolic majesty shall judge necessary for the security and tranquillity of his own territories, and above all, for stifling the troubles which the example of France, and the criminal proceedings of the Jacobin party, foment in the Belgic provinces, he neither can, nor ever will, consent previously to tie up his hands with any one whomsoever, nor has any one a right to prescribe limits to his conduct."

Such was the Austrian reply with respect to *one* of the points at issue, that of the troops ; and the propriety of it depends evidently on the state of the facts. The enthusiasm, however, of the new opinions in Paris was so violent, and those who professed them were so animated with a spirit of proselytism, that there can be no doubt that this Austrian reply was, so far as their Belgic provinces were concerned, very reasonable, and perfectly justified, by all the existing circumstances of the case, though this was loudly denied by the French patriots. But on the second and main point the answer was this :—

" With respect to the concert in which his late imperial majesty engaged with the most respectable powers of Europe, the king of Hungary and Bohemia cannot anticipate their common opinions and determinations ; but he does not believe that they will judge it expedient to dissolve the concert until France shall have removed the causes which provoked or necessitated the opening of it. His majesty on his part expects this the more, as he presumes too much on the justice and reason of a nation, distinguished by its mildness and wisdom, to abandon the hope, that it will not be slow to withdraw its dignity, independence, and repose, from the attempts of a sanguinary and furious faction which promotes anarchy, in order to destroy, by insurrection and popular violence, all exercise of all sorts of authority, laws, and principles, and by an illusive mockery of words, is attempting to rob the Most Christian king of his liberty, to destroy every constitution and all regular governments, and to violate the faith of the most solemn treaties, and the duties of the most sacred public rights.

"But should their designs and their artifices prevail, his majesty (the king of Hungary and Bohemia) flatters himself that at least the sound and principal part of the nation will then behold, as a prospect of consolation and support, the existence of a concert, whose intentions are worthy of their confidence, in the most important crisis which has ever affected the common interests of Europe."

Such was the reply, the ultimatum in fact of the Austrian court.

Now this was certainly not at all to withdraw or modify the confederacy, but to say clearly that it existed, and that however it might tolerate the Constitutionalists, that it could not tolerate what it called a sanguinary and furious faction, and that it expected the sound and principal part of the nation would have recourse to the confederacy for support against this faction, if it prevailed ; and under this term faction, the Girondists, as well as the Jacobins, that is, the main rulers of France at the time, must have considered themselves as included.

The question then is, was this an interference in the internal affairs of France, that justified a declaration of war on the part of France, or not ?

This is a point on which, under the extraordinary circumstances of the case, reasoners may differ, but I conceive that it was. The rulers of France at the time saw themselves menaced, stigmatized, and as nearly as possible proscribed, by a foreign power, on account of their conduct to their own king, in their own country.

They could expect nothing but exile, imprisonment, and death, if these foreign powers invaded their country in defence of the monarchy and succeeded; and not only this, but in that case a counter revolution was inevitable ; and finally, whether the allied powers were likely to invade their country or not, depended merely on their own views of their chances of success.

As men, therefore, and as patriots, the question of war was to them merely a matter of prudence. They were menaced, and they were to anticipate the designs of the allied powers by an open rupture, or they were to remain at peace, and take the chance of some favourable alteration in their councils, just as they thought the safety of their lives and the interests of their Revolution required.

The law of nations, I apprehend, was with them; and the only points they had to consider were those I have mentioned.

The violent party in Paris took little time to decide. Delessart, the minister for foreign affairs, was dismissed and disgraced as too spiritless and temporizing. Dumourier, then a sort of Girondist, was called in to conduct the negotiations, in what was called a less feeble manner. This produced an animated dispatch, the purport of which was to show the court of Austria, that they were mistaking their true interests in going to war. This was followed by another, in which Dumourier set himself to refute all the reasonings of the Austrian court; "that it was impossible to believe that troops were sent into the Brisgau, those in the Milanois reinforced, and an army forming, attended with a train of besieging artillery and immense magazines, for the purpose of maintaining tranquillity in the Netherlands; that there was no reason why the concert of the different courts should continue on the same ground as before, that is depending on events; that the French government possessed strength, and rested on a firm basis; that it had nothing to do with a republican system; that a league formed against France, must be for the purpose of dividing her spoils; that if the successor of Leopold was willing to observe his treaties with France, he must, without hesitation, break off those which he had made unknown to her, and with hostile intentions against her, and he must withdraw those troops by which she was threatened."

"Endeavour, sir," said Dumourier to his ambassador, "to finish this negotiation some way or other before the 15th of April. If from this moment to that epoch, we should be informed that the troops remain on the frontiers and receive reinforcements, it will no longer be possible to restrain the just indignation of a spirited and free nation, which it is attempted to debase, to intimidate, or to impose upon, until all preparations be ready to attack it."

The ambassador, in his answer to Dumourier, describes a conference which he, in consequence of his dispatch, had held with the Austrian minister; and the result of the whole was, a declaration from Austria, that the note of the 18th of March, to which I have already so particularly directed your attention, contained their answer to the demands that had been renewed by France, and that the disposition expressed in that note, it was observed, could be the less altered, since it contained also the opinion of the king of Prussia upon the affairs of France, an opinion agreeing in all respects with that of the king of Hungary.

The consequence was, a declaration of war on the part of France, against the king of Hungary and Bohemia.

You will see in the Annual Register the report read to the Assembly, as an exhibition of the case of France, by Dumourier, and afterwards on the other side, the proclamation of the government of Brussels: this last state paper, though no doubt but too descriptive of the unjustifiable proceedings of the French enthusiasts, must be considered rather as a manifesto against approaching invaders, than a calm statement of a case. You must afterwards read the counter declaration of the court of Vienna against France, which is the most regular and decorous of the three.

None of these papers place this great subject in any new light; the main point at issue is evidently that of the interference. " It merely depended," says this final declaration from Austria, " it merely depended on those who at present reign over France, to make this concert cease immediately, by respecting the tranquillity and the rights of other powers, and to guarantee the essential basis of the French monarchical form of government against the infringements of violence and anarchy.

" Every cause of uneasiness would have ceased, if such dispositions had prevailed in France, and the whole court of Vienna, far from justifying any blame of its views, would have evinced its ingenuousness and moderation.

" Those who reign in France," says this counter declaration in conclusion, " pretend that the sovereignty of the French nation is injured by the establishment of a concert, whose first view has been to save the only lawful sovereign of France, while they, in the mean time, daily attack and provoke all the sovereigns of Europe in the most inconsiderate manner and with the bitterest invective. In short, they dispute with the crowns the participation and the right of interfering in or being concerned about the consequences of their new constitution, whilst they, with all their might, endeavour to subvert all governments, by spreading all over Europe the bane of seduction and insurrection."

These are the points insisted upon in the Austrian defence, and they are the real points of the case, no doubt. You see here distinctly the conflict of the new and old opinions. Their supporters could no longer keep any terms with each other.

And again, you will perceive, on the other hand, that these points are also properly stated on their part by the Legislative Assembly, in their decree of war, on the 20th of April.

But the Assembly very judiciously commissioned the celebrated Condorcet to exhibit their case in a distinct exposition of their motives, and this he has done, and with great ability; and you will find the paper in the notes of the History of Thiers, vol. ii.; nor can you be said to have finished the consideration of the subject, till you have weighed the argument he employs. He addresses himself more particularly to the real and main point—the interference of the foreign powers.

" The French people," says he, " free to fix the form of their government, can in no respect have injured, while using this power, either the safety or the honour of foreign crowns. Are the rulers of other countries, are they to include in the number of their prerogatives a right to oblige the French nation to give to the head of their government the same power, which they themselves exercise in their own dominions? Because they have subjects, do they mean to prevent the existence of free men elsewhere? How is it that they do not see that in allowing themselves to do everything for what they call the safety of crowns, they declare lawful everything that a nation can in like manner do for the liberty of another people?"

" If violence and if crimes," he says, " have accompanied particular seasons of the French Revolution, it was to the depositaries of the national will that alone belonged the power of punishing them, or of burying them in oblivion. Citizen or magistrate, whatever be his title, no one can demand justice, but from the laws of his own country; he can expect it from no other. Foreign powers, while their subjects have not suffered from these events, can have no just reason either to complain of them, or to take hostile measures to prevent their repetition.

" These pretended motives, therefore, of a league against France," he continues, " are but a new outrage to its independence. France has a right to require a renunciation of such offensive preparations, and to consider a refusal as an act of hostility. It is to make changes in her constitution; it is to violate that equality which she has made the basis of her system. It is these that are alone the object of the enemies of France. They wish to punish her for having acknowledged in all their extent the rights that are common to all men."

Paragraphs like these will give you for the present a sufficient idea of this exposition, by Condorcet, which at last becomes a very animated and eloquent appeal to the French people, calling upon them to resist their enemies, and to conquer or perish with their constitution and their laws.

Such is, I think, a fair exhibition of this subject of the war with Austria. You may now look at the memoirs and the histories; and if you have already done so, you may look at them again. No doubt there is a sort of esoteric history and exoteric history of everything, and these memoirs and histories may explain to you how these state papers came to be what you see them; but I have been myself, as I have already told you, lost, and perplexed, and overpowered to weariness and despair, amidst these memoirs and histories, amidst their conflicting views and opinions, statements, and facts. I have found, as I thought, relief, by attending to these state papers, by following where they led me. It is by their state papers that nations and parties must be tried; it is by these that they are content to be tried.

It is in these that they appear to posterity and the world; and the only question always is, how far they are sincere.

In the case before us I see no sufficient reason to doubt the sincerity of either party. The leaders of the French Revolution had gone such lengths that the Austrian court and the supporters of the old opinions may have truly felt, and perfectly thought, every thing that these state papers express, and not at all meant the division of France or the sharing of her spoils; and the conduct of the emigrants, and the electors of Germany, and the emperor and king of Prussia had been such, and such was also the situation in which these French leaders were placed, that they might on their part very thoroughly believe that they should be sooner or later invaded; that at all events they were menaced; that the concert openly avowed in the face of Europe, was an affront to the independence and sovereignty of their country; that it was in itself a justification of war; and finally, if this concert was not resisted, while the enthusiasm of the French people was fresh and warm, that a counter revolution might ultimately be the consequence. I must confess, that with all my horror of war, of counsels of violence of enthusiastic and furious men like these Girondists, and of dreadful and guilty men like these Jacobins, I must confess that on this particular point of the Austrian war, I am, on the whole, compelled to agree with them. It was reduced to a question of prudence; they had a right to wage it, if they thought fit; whether prudent or not is a subsequent question. I see not how, upon any other principle, the peace of the world can be maintained, or the proper sovereignty and independence of nations be preserved, nor finally, upon any other principle, what chance there can ever be for the general cause of the freedom of mankind.

LECTURE XXV.

GIRONDISTS, ETC.—ROLAND—DUMOURIER.

AUSTRIA might have no right to complain if France declared war against her, but whether France was wise in doing so is quite another question. Nations are to maintain the character of their independence. It can never be their wisdom to be otherwise than perfectly alive to such considerations; but the circumstances in which the country was placed were quite unexampled, and the leaders of the Legislative Assembly, and under their influence, Dumourier and the last Girondist ministry so conducted themselves, that the war seemed at length defensive rather on the part of Austria than of France.

Men are always so eager to go to war, war is always so dreadful a calamity, that through the whole of these lectures I have never lost any opportunity of exhibiting to you, what I conceive to be the folly of mankind on this tremendous subject. It is the great instruction of history; and because after a war, as after the eruption of a volcano, a country does not disappear, or a community does not cease to exist—because our planet rolls on as before, men seem insensible to its nature, to the crimes and cruelties that it produces, and the afflictions and agonies by which it is attended. Observe on this occasion the Legislative Assembly.

It was in vain that the deputy, Hua, insisted, "that the question was far too important to be treated in an evening sitting, at a moment when the passions, agitated on so many accounts, might hurry France down an abyss of unexampled calamities." (From the Two Historians.) He was refuted by murmurs. "No doubt," said the deputy Pastoret on the other side, "we must not be carried away by enthusiasm; we, above all others, the legislators of a great empire; but are our provocations only an affair of yesterday? Is not our patience yet suffi-

ciently clear? Are we, even *now*, to be accused of enthusiasm?
. . . . . It is surely time to break away from this long state of
uncertainty; it is time that we should see a great nation display all its courage, and all the force of its will, in defending
the cause of its liberty, and in that, the universal cause of every
people. Yes, liberty is now to triumph, or despotism to destroy
us; never have the French people been called to higher destinies. Knowing, as we do, the courage of the national guards,
the zeal they have shown in defence of their country, can we
doubt the success of a war undertaken under such auspices?
Victory will be faithful, nor desert the cause of freedom; and
soldier citizens, and citizen soldiers, will rush forward with
equal emotion to defend her and to secure her by their triumphs.
Never has the French nation better felt the necessity at once of
glory and of independence."

·. To sentiments like these, so elevated and imposing, it was
not possible to offer resistance; one voice, however, was heard
above the storm. Observe how reasonable, as France was then
situated, were the remarks that follow.

"If ever," said the Deputy Becquer, "there is a moment
when a nation requires a calm, it is immediately after the concussions of a great Revolution. The violent movements that
accompany the destruction of ancient abuses, cause inevitably a
number of individual calamities, that can only be repaired in the
bosom of peace. To call for war under circumstances like these,
is to call for the prolongation of every affliction and distress, and
to retard the return of the national prosperity. New institutions
can only have a trial in seasons of tranquillity and repose; war,
on the contrary, is a state of crisis that unceasingly, while it
lasts, opposes itself to every regular movement of the body politic; and every nation therefore that wishes to regenerate its institutions, must carefully avoid war. But never was the general
principle so applicable as to us. Our constitution is not yet
firmly established; our constituted authorities, as yet, are uncertain in their march, and the law obtains not, as yet, the obedience which doubtless it will at length obtain, when it has become to us a habit and a duty; intestine dissensions agitate our
departments. If our armies are fighting abroad, who shall restrain the seditious at home? And there is another point to be
considered, that of the finances: our finances require some years
of repose to re-establish them in any order. I know the prodigies that are to be expected from the valour of Frenchmen fight-

ing for their liberty; but what, if the war is to become general, and we are to sustain it?"

The deputy then went on to show (observe the reasonableness of his views), that the first hostilities must take place in Brabant; that England would necessarily interfere, still more, if Holland was to be endangered; and that in short, everything which turned the scale in favour of France, would necessarily be to England an occasion of inquietude and of arms. "And why," he cried, "why thus rush into a war? Why call down this most cruel of calamities? Above all, why say that it is inevitable, while all the powers have an interest opposed to it, and declare that they wish not to attack us?

"A concert between Austria and Prussia is supposed. No doubt the nation has very just reason to complain of this coalition of kings; no doubt the court of Vienna has been wrong, and we ought not to suffer her to usurp a sovereignty over us by an interference in our internal administration. But supposing that these powers refuse to renounce this concert, would this be a sufficient reason for declaring war against them? Are we to declare it for a mere suspicion, for a mere menace that has no real meaning? This concert is but a system defensive on their parts, and one which they have adopted out of regard to themselves, *not* hostility to us."

These last few sentences of the deputy are, I think, decisive of the question, as to the necessity of the war on the part of France. I do not say the exact right, but the prudence, the expediency of it, and the immediate necessity of it. I must confess, too, my reverence for the great maxim—"justa bella, quibus necessaria."

"Can we possibly require them," continues the deputy, "in the midst of the general effervescence everywhere visible in France, when the sounds of war have been heard within these walls, can we possibly require foreign powers to repose upon our declaration, that we will renounce all schemes of conquest; require them to take no defensive measures, while the ardour and impetuosity of our national guards is eternally menacing them with invasion? The truth is, that if after all this we attack Austria, we shall force all the sovereigns of the world to unite in a league against us; for they will feel that their thrones are shaking under them, and that they have a common cause to maintain in this struggle between liberty and despotism. A free nation, shall it be guilty of such a breach of neutrality, as to call down upon neighbouring nations all the calamities of war, to revenge itself for insult offered it by a mere minister? False would be the glory that could arise from avenging any outrages of a nature like this. Let us renounce then an enterprise which has no reasonable object; let us defend ourselves if any power should dare to attack us; this, and no more. If with this we are content, we shall, in all probability, have no war, for it will be the interest of none of them to wage it against us: on the contrary, by provoking them to war, we shall prejudice our own cause in the eyes of all neighbouring nations; they will consider us as aggressors; they will represent us as a restless people, that disturb the peace of Europe, in contempt of treaties, and even of our own laws. You will then have to combat, not only the despots, but the people themselves, armed against you by the hatred which you will so naturally inspire, as the disturbers of their country's repose."

But observations of this calm and very reasonable nature, often, as you will have remarked, quite prophetic, were in vain submitted to the consideration of the Assembly. It is ever thus: and it was the deputy who rose to reply, and others on the same side the question, who found, as usual, an audience disposed to listen and applaud. The violent party entirely prevailed, though at this period peace and repose might have been the preservation of France and her liberties; certainly was her only chance.

And now I stop for a moment to observe, as I have before observed, and shall have for ever to observe, that the French Assemblies and French people rushed into all sorts of mistakes and crimes, not from want of able and virtuous men to counsel them aright—far from it—such men were always found; and were you to commit the error of supposing otherwise, you would not sufficiently estimate the warning that this French Revolution holds up, in every part and portion of it, to all men of ardent minds, if they mean well. Able and virtuous counsellors, who spoke the words of caution and moderation, and justice, and humanity, were by such men not regarded; and this is the great lesson.

On the whole of the case before us it may be observed, that it is truly melancholy to see a great question like this, in the affairs of mankind, brought to an issue so tremendous as that of war; to see that the parties concerned, all of them, committed the faults to which they were exposed.

It was the business, for instance, of the Girondists and Jacobins, to have left the German powers no excuse for assisting the emigrants; to have observed minutely all the relations of peace and amity between France and other independent powers; to have violated no feudal claims and no ancient treaties : and not to have supposed, that the world was to be submitted on a sudden. to the particular system of their *new* opinions. But their conduct was very different. And in like manner, it was the business of the German powers to be entirely on the defensive ; to have avowed this distinctly ; to have abstained from all menace ; to be ready to repel acts of aggression on their possessions, on their constitutions of government, but not to mingle themselves in the affairs of France ; not to suppose that they could separate a particular knot of individuals, the Jacobins for instance, from the rest of the people, and conceive they could wage war against one of their clubs, however abominable, without waging war against the kingdom.

But very different were their views and systems ; and France and Europe were long the victims, and the most unhappy victims, of these deplorable and somewhat obvious faults in both parties, on the one side and on the other.

This Austrian war was the first great turn of the whole contest between the monarchical and popular party, after the meeting of the Legislative Assembly. I have therefore called your attention to it very particularly ; it must be well considered. My opinion, such as it is, I have stated to you. It was left too much by the language of Austria, to be, to the rulers of France, a question of prudence ; but it was not decided by the Girondists as prudence would have dictated ; not, as I conceive, it ought to have been : not with a due attention to the interests of France, or the cause of their Revolution. The best chance for those interests was, at the time, the constitution of La Fayette. It was not likely to stand in case of a war ; and if it did not stand, a wide field was opened for every species of anarchy and disorder.

This is a very serious accusation to make against the popular party (by which words I shall hereafter always mean the Girondists and Jacobins), but it is an accusation that I conceive is just.

We have now considered the first great subject that was before us, the Austrian war.

I mentioned, in my last lecture, that the struggle between the new and old opinions produced also, at last, the insurrection of the 10th of August, and the dethronement of the king.

This was the work of the Girondists and the Jacobins, and the Girondists are chiefly responsible for it.

The conduct and character of the Girondists will, therefore, for some time, directly or indirectly, be the great subject of our consideration.

Their great measures were—

1st. The war with Austria. This we have already noticed.

2ndly. Their two decrees: one for a camp of twenty thousand men, near Paris; and one for the proscription of the priests.

3rdly. The irruption into the palace on the 20th of June, 1792.

And, finally, their attack of the palace on the 10th of August, 1792, and dethronement of the king.

These measures must be all considered, and they will occupy us long.

But if such were their measures, it will be said, what doubt can there be of the unpardonable nature of their conduct?—how can this be made a question?

The difficulty is this. The conduct that is blamed in the Girondists, from the opening of the Legislative Assembly to its conclusion, was always explained and justified by them on this principle, that a counter-revolution was intended by the court, and that they had no alternative but to act as they did.

Now this intention of the court cannot be denied; and here lies the difficulty.

It is very true that the king had no horror like that of a civil war, and would have perished on a scaffold rather than the blood of his subjects should be shed; but sentiments of this humane and benevolent character could not be supposed for a moment to have been entertained either by the queen or the great body of the king's more immediate ministers, friends, and counsellors; and the return of the old régime was supposed to be, in their apprehension, the great object to be attained, and at any risk or expense. It was impossible for the popular party not to conclude that the king and the court were intriguing with foreign powers; and though some of them might duly estimate the amiable disposition of the king, it was natural, it was not unreasonable for them to believe, that his mild counsels, and even his authority, would be lost amid the tumult and temptation of any successful invasion from foreign powers, and that the liberties of France would be gone for ever.

Here, then, is the difficulty of the case. We may say, and, as I conceive, with perfect justice, to the Legislative Assembly, to the Girondists, and more especially to the Jacobins, "You over-rate the danger; neither the court nor the foreign powers are so willing or so able to attack your liberties as you suppose.

You yourselves, by your fury and outrageous behaviour of every
kind, increase the danger, and in fact provoke these' foreign
powers, and, as they will think, oblige them to attack you.   It
is not in this manner that you can best defend your liberties."
All this, and much more than all this, I contend, might have
been truly said to the popular party, of whatever description;
but it is impossible to deny the danger; it is impossible to say
that a counter-revolution was not intended, by the court at least:
this was supposed by the popular party, and acted upon, and
sufficient evidences of it, though of a general nature, now exist;
and being right in this point, they cannot be dismissed from our
thoughts, certainly not the higher Girondists at least, as without any claim to be heard, and as mere furious revolutionists and
unprincipled men of blood.   Their views, opinions, and feelings
must be considered; and as this can only be done amid histories
and memoirs of the most contradictory nature, and amid crimes,
and cruelties, and horrors of the most revolting kind, very great
must be the perplexity and the hesitation of any man who would
show a proper repugnance to violence, bloodshed, and anarchy,
and yet evince a due respect for the cause of liberty, however
obscured; and, finally, who would endeavour to do justice to
characters of every description: a duty this last, not only more
particularly incumbent upon those who read or write history,
but incumbent upon men at all times and on every occasion, however difficult and painful the task may often be.

Such is, I conceive, a fair statement of the case of the Girondists; and having made this statement, I have now to represent
to you that what is thus urged in their favour, though not without its weight, is, after all, not, I think, a sufficient defence,
when all the various circumstances of the case are regularly and
fairly estimated.

The following observations may, I conceive, be made; and
you will, I hope, remember their general import, when you come
to read the history, and judge for yourselves how far they are
reasonable, and borne out by the facts and the general principles
of all political science.

La Fayette and his friends had endeavoured, as I have formerly said, to repair their mistakes, when thy saw, after the
flight to Varennes, that the king's throne and life were in danger, and they had appeared to succeed: a republic was not proclaimed; the violent party was put down (put down by *them*),
and the constitution was proposed to the king and accepted;
but the false steps these Constitutionalists had made during the

Constituent Assembly could never afterwards be recovered. The king had shown, by his flight, that he could not reconcile himself to their notions of liberty, at least, to their practical exposition of them ; and when the Legislative Assembly met, the more popular party in and out of the Assembly would never place any confidence in him, whatever might be either his professions or his measures ; and their only concern and only duty, as they thought, was to prevent him and the court, between whom they would see no difference, from making a counter-revolution. This could best be done, as they unhappily imagined, by vilifying his office and diminishing his power, by questioning the expediency and resisting the operation even of the prerogatives intrusted to him by the constitution. And, most unfortunately, not only may these remarks be applied to the Girondists, and even to the Legislative Assembly in general, but still more may they be applied to another party, the Jacobins, who were ranged beyond the Girondists, and who seemed to have no wish but to bring matters to an issue as soon as possible, dethrone the king, probably erect a republic, at all events dissolve the monarchy first, and take the chances, whatever they might be, that were to result from it. Such was the afflicting situation of things from the moment the Legislative Assembly met. With every hour they grew worse. The great and only hope for France, for its peace, and the best interests of its freeedom, was, *then* at least, the maintenance of the constitution of La Fayette ; but it was too popular for the court, and not sufficiently so for the patriotic party ; and, lastly, the king himself never approved it ; it afforded him no adequate protection : still, having publicly accepted it, he told his ministers, as I have already mentioned to you, at the opening of this second Assembly, when questioned by them confidentially on the subject, that he meant faithfully to adhere to it ; and at that time he was sincere ; but the eternal distrust and continually increasing violence of the Assembly and of the clubs made him lose all hope of any comfortable exercise of his authority to be derived from the popular party, all hope of the constitution, and all good opinion of the patriots, of whatever description. All the pleasures of existence itself were at an end. He feared for the lives of his queen and family ; he had no expectation of long preserving his own. With every hour his difficulties and dangers increased. Did he strive to sacrifice to popularity, he could only do so by weakening what power was left him ; did he attempt to assert his prerogative, he only provoked resistance, and in no struggle could possibly suc-

ceed. He was in so unhappy a situation, that reasonable measures appeared of no use, and mistakes were fatal.

Such was the state of things during the latter part of 1791
and early part of 1792; and when you come to read the history,
you will see the king at last obliged to propitiate the Girondists
and the violent party by choosing a new set of ministers from
among themselves, Dumourier, Roland, and others, who had
their confidence, not his; and you have then war declared with
the king of Hungary and Bohemia, which was their measure,
not his. The king was visibly affected, when he came to announce it to the Assembly. The war, as he must have seen,
only multiplied the chances of his dethronement; it had, on that
very account, been urged on by the Girondist Brissot, as he
himself afterwards proclaimed.

The war was declared; and you have next to observe the two
famous decrees which I have mentioned. These were presented
to the king: the one for the formation of a camp with a large
body of men near Paris; the other for the purpose of sending the
nonjuring priests out of the kingdom. This was to be done upon
the slightest grounds; it was sufficient (e. g.) that a representation
was made to the municipality from twenty people of the district.
The first (the decree of the camp) appeared to the king a scheme
to collect an armed force for his destruction; the other, to violate every feeling of religion or justice that he could be supposed
to entertain. He refused his sanction; and there was at last an
insurrection and an attack made upon him on the 20th of June,
in his palace, to oblige him to give this sanction, or, in case he
continued to refuse it, to take the chances, in the confusion and
the tumult, of at least dethroning him. Finally, as the insurrection answered neither of these purposes, we at last see the
palace actually stormed on the 10th of August, the king obliged
to fly to the Legislative Assembly, his powers and office suspended, a new Assembly called, and the king then, immediately
on its meeting, dethroned and imprisoned. These are, in a few
words, the main events that we are now to consider; and, though
nothing can be more interesting than the different accounts we
have to peruse, any real friend to liberty will find his mind, I
think, not a little perplexed on account of the difficulty I have
described to you, and even wearied, amid the opposite sentiments
and representations by which he will see himself surrounded, each
plausible in its turn, and each well fitted to attract his sympathy;
if on the one side he is unable, as a friend to freedom, to wish
for a counter-revolution, and again on the other, not satisfied

that the Revolution should proceed on a system of violence and tumult. It is now, however, again incumbent on me to offer you my opinion, which, on the whole of the case, is entirely against the Girondists.

For it is not too much to say, that their conduct altogether, from the first meeting of the Legislative Assembly, was marked by violence and unreasonableness; that they always acted, as if both the king and the constitution, sooner or later, were to be disposed of and set aside. While their cry was continually in favour of the constitution, they never suffered it to be fairly tried; and when they availed themselves of what they thought their right, to go to war with Austria, the most fatal measure, as they knew, both to the king and the constitution, they never properly joined La Fayette and the Constitutionalists, though the majority at this time both in and out of the Assembly. Those Constitutionalists were as determined as they could be, to beat off all foreign invaders; and this was a bond of union sufficient, if they had taken reasonable views of the best interests of France.

Men having the independence and freedom of France at heart, and seeing both menaced by the court and the foreign powers (and this is the case of the Girondists), should have made every sacrifice to secure the confidence and co-operation of those who had the same objects in view, and particularly of the Constitutionalists, who had actually framed the constitution, and had no hope, nor wish, nor system, but to defend it. Instead of thus uniting their strength with La Fayette and his friends, and instead of exhibiting this regular, reasonable, lawful defence of the independence and liberties of their country, they could see no better mode to adopt, than violent speeches against the king, than menacing his life if he did not assent to their decrees, calling out the people to assault his palace, and, amid the horror of an insurrection, proceeding to dethrone him.

This is not, I think, an unfair view of their conduct, and I do not see the circumstances in their situation by which it can be justified. There are no circumstances, perhaps, that could justify a resort to such counsels of anarchy and blood; but even at the last, when they might say they were proscribed by the allied powers, and were only standing on their defence, still their proper answer and defence was joining, with all their strength and influence, the Constitutionalists in the Assembly; and joining with all their spirit and their courage, La Fayette and the regular armies of their country, who were opposed to those allied powers in the field.

Even amid the king's ministers and friends, they must have been well aware, that there were many who wished well to the constitution and the liberties of France. Malouet and others, who were even in the king's counsels, had no desire to see a return of the old régime; and if at last such men appeared to be driven to favour any counsels that could save them from mobs and insurrections, and from the Revolution (such as the Revolution seemed likely to become), this was owing (the Girondists should have seen) to their own original violence and unreasonableness; in a word, to their own republican tone and manner from the first opening of the Legislative Assembly.

Such is, I confess, my own particular view of the case, even of the Girondists, the more respectable portion of the popular party of the Legislative Assembly (I say nothing of the Jacobins, it is unnecessary); and these are my accusations, serious indeed if they are just, and well fitted to be a warning to men of daring and ardent minds, such as naturally engage in revolutions; and who, as we may judge from the instances before us, are exposed to the chance of being mixed with, or soon insensibly becoming, from the supposed necessities of their situation, men of anarchy and blood.

I have now stated, as I conceive, the case of the Girondists, and offered you an opinion upon it. We will now proceed.

The opinion I have offered you will continually make its appearance in the general description I shall give of the great scenes of the history. This sort of repetition you must excuse, for it is not very possible to avoid it; and the better to enable you to consider the subject, I will now immediately mention the books and memoirs which in my opinion, you can consult with the best advantage.

It is at this point of your progress that you must turn, first to the Memoirs of Mᵉ. Roland, and afterwards of Dumourier. Mᵉ. Roland was one of the most extraordinary women of these extraordinary times, and Dumourier was a man of great ability, who acted a very conspicuous part in them. The character of the first is easily estimated. She was a person of very strong sensibility, of great talents, and a passionate admirer of liberty, but on the republican model. It is, however, not so easy to judge of the minister Dumourier: his talents are clear and undoubted, but not so his virtues. I conceive, however, that he meant well to the king and to his country; it is difficult to those who read his Memoirs to suppose otherwise. You must also turn to the Memoirs of Barbaroux. And, in opposition to all these works, you must consider the representations of Bertrand de Moleville, the king's confidential minister and friend As an estimate of the whole, you may refer to the second volume of Thiers, which, though I need not subscribe to all its opinions, I may still think very able and deserving of your attention. You will, of course, continue your perusal of the Memoirs of the Marquis de Ferrieres, and the History by the Two Friends of Liberty. Other writers and memoirs will present themselves, but to these I refer you in the first place.

The part of the work of M⁰. Roland that is to our present purpose, is her account of the first ministry of Roland and her portraits, where the leaders of the Gironde party find their place. Every word is to be observed, for the whole is the best and most favourable representation we can possibly have, of the views and conduct of the Girondists. It is not too much to say, that M⁰. Roland was the most pure in principle, and the most powerful in talents of all the party; and her statements and opinions must therefore be attended to. It is in vain to attempt (I must repeat) to derive instruction from history, unless we enter into the feelings of the different actors in the scene, and weigh and examine what they consider the proper state of their case.

M⁰. Roland and her husband had been brought to Paris, had become acquainted with the leading men during the earlier seven months of 1791, had retired in September, and returned in December.

About the middle of the March of the next year (of March 1792), they were told, she says, by one of their friends, that the court thought it necessary to make an effort for popularity, and was ready to take Jacobin ministers; that the court probably wished to receive the worst, and the patriotic party to provide the best; that Roland was fixed upon as one. Brissot and Dumourier waited upon him, and the arrangement was made. She disliked and distrusted Dumourier from the first; represents what passed at the cabinet councils of the king, as more like the chit-chat conversation of a drawing-room than the deliberations of a set of statesmen; but describes the king as having quite made a conquest of Roland and Clavière. " 'Good God !' I often cried to them," she says, " when I saw them going to council, 'you seem to me always ready to do some foolish thing or other.' For my part," she continues, "I could never have any faith in a constitutional king, made out of one born under despotism, educated for it, and accustomed to the exercise of it. Louis

XVI. must have been a man far above the vulgar, to have sincerely wished a constitution that restrained his power; and had he been such a man, he would never have suffered the events to take place which led to the formation of such a constitution." In another part of her work she says, " that she always appealed to the king's flight to Varennes as decisive of the point."

Now here, I think, we have the whole of the case. However her husband and his friends might appear to Me. Roland to be thrown off their guard by the agreeable manner and apparent patriotism of the king, neither they nor any of the party, nor even the majority of the Legislative Assembly itself, ever acted on any other principles but those which she has here herself expressed and described as her own,—those of total distrust and suspicion. And this was, I conceive, their fault, though a natural one: they never gave either the king or the constitution a fair trial. To hope nothing, to believe nothing, and to risk nothing, was not to give either a fair trial; it was not to reconcile the king to his fate, but the contrary—it was to expose him to the temptation, it was almost to lay him under the necessity of turning to foreign powers for assistance; it was to dispose and oblige those powers, in like manner, to come to his relief; it was to pursue counsels, that while they appeared to defend the Revolution, could only lead to some dreadful termination of it, some disgraceful or appalling crisis, some attempt to dethrone the king, a civil war, perhaps a return to the old despotism.

The two points on which you are now to fix your attention are the two celebrated decrees. I have already mentioned them: that, for the formation of a camp of twenty thousand men near Paris, and that of the proscription of the priests. These were the great measures of the Girondists.

The king could not be brought to sanction them. The first he thought inconsistent with his existence as a king of France; the other, with his principles of justice and religion, as a man and a Christian: while, on the contrary, the popular party held these measures to be necessary to the safety of the country and the success of the Revolution; and the king's resistance to them, as a sufficient proof of his intentions to produce a counter-revolution by means of the allied powers, whose armies were now approaching.

This was a dreadful crisis to which matters were reduced; nor will the student, even now, at the distance of time and place, be without his perplexity, when he has the two following great leading facts, on the one side and on the other, held up to his consideration; for instance, that, first, the popular party were *ready* (all of them), were desirous (many of them) to dethrone the king; and again, on the other side, that the court was intending a counter-revolution, and the forces of the allied powers actually on their march to Paris. He will not, I say, be without his perplexity.

Each party might now be perfectly sincere in their opposite representations of the nature of these decrees, and their particular views be now but too irreconcilable. But what we contend for is, that the violence of the Legislative Assembly and of the Girondists, from the first of their sitting, brought matters to this deplorable crisis; that such violence is, therefore, the proper subject of our censure: but, after this censure has been pronounced, the nature of their conduct now, at *this* particular moment, and on this particular subject of the camp, is much more doubtful.

With M⁰. Roland and with the party these decrees were everything; they are the great subject of all the very interesting portion of her memoirs now before us; they gave occasion to her two very celebrated letters to the king; they caused the dismissal of Roland and his friends from the ministry; and they were the cause, they were the justification produced, of the insurrection of the 20th of June, and (with the assistance of the approach of the combined armies) of the attack on the Tuilleries, and the dethronement of the king. Observe the views and language of M⁰. Roland.

"Troubles," she says, "on the subject of religion and the dispositions of the enemy, rendered some decisive decrees necessary; the king's refusal to sanction them unmasked him completely: his good faith had already become suspected by those of his ministers who had before been led to suppose it real." She then gives an accout of the celebrated letter to the king which she herself drew up, and of all that passed on the occasion. There were originally two letters; you will see them both in the notes of her Memoirs: the second was presented to the king. What I wish you to remark is the sincerity with which M⁰. Roland seems to have drawn up the letter. "It is a very bold measure," said Pache to her. "Bold," she replied, "no doubt, but it is just and necessary; what signifies anything else?" "I am convinced," she says afterwards, "and I conceive the event has proved it, that this letter has contributed extremely to enlighten France; it proposed to the king, with so much force and good sense, what the king's own interest should have taught him to do, that one may see clearly that he would have acceded to it had he not been determined against the constitution, determined not to maintain it."

The letter was sent on the 11th of June : Roland was dismissed. But on the 20th of June, the mob broke into the palace to oblige the king to sanction the two decrees. The king appears now to have been quite at the mercy of the popular party ; even his body guard of one thousand eight hundred men, which the constitution allowed him, had been, under proper pretences (the king unable to resist), disbanded : there seem to have been no means left him to support his authority ; yet M⁰. Roland during all this time almost despaired of the patriotic cause, and writes thus : "and this is a sort of proof, by the way, of the sincerity with which she and the *leading Girondists*, at least proposed and urged on these decrees."

"It was in the course of the month of July," she says, "that seeing affairs get worse from the perfidy of the court, the advance of the foreign forces, and the feebleness of the Assembly, we set ourselves to consider where Liberty might fly to, menaced as she was. We often talked with Barbaroux and Servan of the excellent disposition of the south, of the energy of the departments in that part of France, and of the facilities there afforded for founding a republic if the court should triumph and subdue the north and Paris. We took the maps, studied the military positions, &c. &c., and we all agreed, that after a Revolution that has afforded us such vast hopes and expectations, it was impossible for us to fall back into slavery ; that everything must be attempted to establish, somewhere or other, a government that was free. 'That must be our resource,' replied Barbaroux, 'if the Marsellois, that I have accompanied here, are not sufficiently seconded by the Parisians to overpower the court : this, however, I hope will not be the case, and that we shall have a convention that will give us a republic for the whole of France."

"We could see," continues M⁰. Roland, "without any further explanation, that an insurrection was intended ; indeed it appeared inevitable, as the court was making preparations which indicated a design of overpowering us by force. It will be said, indeed," she subjoins, "that the court was acting in self-defence ; but the idea of any attack upon the court would either never have occurred to any one, or at least would never have been taken up by the people, if the king and his ministers had executed the constitution faithfully. The firmest Republicans, however aware of its faults, wished only for the constitution for the time, and would have waited for ameliorations in it from time and experience."

A corresponding passage occurs in the Memoirs of Barbaroux. "Roland asked me," says he, "what I thought of France, and of the means of saving her. I opened my heart to him, and in return he said to me, 'Liberty is lost if we do not instantly counteract these plots of the court. La Fayette is meditating treason in the north; the army of the centre is disorganized; there is nothing to hinder the Austrians from being here in six weeks. And have we been labouring,' he continued, 'for three years together at this noble Revolution, only to see it overturned in a day? If liberty perish in France, it is for ever lost for all the rest of the world; all the hopes of the philosophers are deceived; a tyranny the most cruel will fall heavy upon the earth. Let us prevent a calamity like this; let us arm Paris and the departments of the north; and if they fall, let us carry away to the south the image of Liberty, and somewhere or other let us found there a colony of men that are free.' At these words the tears rolled down his cheeks, and so did those of Mᵉ. Roland, affected by the same sentiment, and mine also. What consolation in these effusions of confidence when the heart is in affliction!

"I drew a picture therefore," says Barbaroux, "of the resources of the departments, and of our hopes," &c.

These I consider as very striking paragraphs, as showing very clearly what the feelings and opinions of the Girondists were, giving them every credit they could desire, and as exhibiting, therefore, a memorable and edifying picture of the enthusiasm with which those who engage in political concerns may be animated. The Girondists, instead of making it their study, from the first of their meeting in October, 1791, to reconcile the king to the constitution, by every possible attention, on their part, to what they knew must naturally be his prejudices, if such they chose to call them, began with very offensive behaviour, and never ceased their opposition till they at last arrived at the pitch of excitement here displayed, and were ready for any enterprise of violence and blood, if necessary to secure their objects: an awful lesson this. Mᵉ. Roland sees a young man, Barbaroux, just come up from the south, actually preparing an insurrection without the slightest emotion or remark addressed to him on the subject. Her husband votes that La Fayette is meditating treason, though the very constitution, they both talk of maintaining, was his work, and though he was the most dis-

tinguished friend of freedom then in existence. I do not say
that the king was not, from the first meeting of the Legislative
Assembly, a proper object of suspicion, and for the reasons M⁰.
Roland mentions; I do not say that a counter-revolution was
not always to be dreaded, that the invading armies were not, at
all events, to be resisted; but I say that the Girondists, from
the first, contributed to increase and produce the very difficulties
and dangers by which they can alone attempt to defend their
conduct; that they never were the friends of the constitution of
1791; that they, on the contrary, insensibly, and at last visibly,
brought about its overthrow, and were, therefore, the real enemies of the liberties of France, as matters then stood; that they
so conducted themselves, that they have generally been considered as Republicans, as even disposed to introduce a republic
into France from the first : however this may be, I contend that
to conduct themselves in such a manner as to be so considered,
to be insensible to the very popular nature of the constitution,
as it was left by the Constituent Assembly, to the very great
importance of some return to peace and order, to be so indifferent
to the dangers and calamities that were to be expected from the
violence and disposition to anarchy which they saw in the Jacobin party, all this, I contend, was a blindness and a rage of enthusiasm, to say the best of it, which should for ever operate as
a warning to all who engage in political concerns, more particularly when any alterations in the constitution of their country
are intended.

I will now, before I conclude, remind you of the Memoirs of
Dumourier. You may begin with the fifth chapter. I will
give you an extract from his work, which will show you but too
plainly the dreadful perplexities and even agonies of mind that
must have belonged to these unhappy times.

Dumourier was called into power, with Roland and the
Girondists, with what was called the Jacobin or Sans-culotte
ministry; and I see not how we are to deny him the praise of
having first made every effort to save the monarch, and this
being, as he thought, impossible, of having then endeavoured,
by joining the army, to save his country from her invaders.

He became a minister on the 15th of March. The king and
court were prepossessed against him. He declared to Louis
from the first, " that he was the zealous servant of his majesty,
but that he belonged to the nation; that he would speak no
language but of liberty and the constitution." " I like your
frankness," replied the king; " I, too, wish only for the con-

stitution." The queen next chose to see him. He found her alone, extremely agitated, her colour high; and he represents himself as deeply affected by what were evidently the sufferings of the unfortunate princess.

"You are all-powerful," she said, in a majestic and irritated tone, "but it is by favour of the people, who soon demolish their idols. Your existence depends on your behaviour. They tell me you have good talents. You must be aware that neither the king nor I can bear these novelties nor the constitution; I tell you so frankly: take your side." The queen must have here supposed that the allied powers were to interfere and to be successful. "I stand," replied Dumourier, "before the king and the nation, but I belong to my country. Your safety depends on the constitution. Far from being a calamity, it will be a happiness to the king and his glory." "It will not stand," said the irritated queen; "take care of yourself." "I am more than fifty years old," replied the minister; "my responsibility as such is, I know, not the greatest of my dangers." "What can you say worse of me?" cried the queen: "do you think me capable of having you assassinated?" and the tears started to her eyes.

"God forbid," replied the minister, agitated as much as the queen herself, "that I should do you such cruel wrong. The character of your majesty is grand and noble; you have given heroic proofs of it, and they have bound me to you." The queen grew calm. This was in the main the conversation that passed, at least as Dumourier has related it; and the minister had then an opportunity of explaining what he thought was the situation of herself and the king; that there was no separating their interests from those of the nation: in other words, that the constitution must be made to stand, and that there must be no counter-revolution. The queen seemed at last to be convinced of the truth of what the minister said; but the horrible publications of Marat and the Jacobins soon revived all her unfortunate opinions.

They were but too natural. "I am quite overcome," said the queen to the minister one day in the presence of the king; "I cannot even show myself at the window. It was but yesterday I did so, and to get a little air, when one of the cannoniers, after a gross insult, told me, it would be a pleasure to him to have my head on the point of his bayonet. That terrible garden there: on one side I see a man mounted in a chair, reading aloud all sort of terrible things against us; on the other, some officer or abbé dragged into one of the basins in the midst of abuse and blows; and all this time you see others playing at football, quite unconcerned. What a residence to be placed in! and what a people!" Dumourier had nothing to answer; what could he answer?" but still he returned always to the same point, and advised that a common cause should be made with the Assembly, always looking upon a counter revolution as impossible. Now for Dumourier to think thus, and to act upon his opinions so early as the spring of 1792, was to show great sagacity and firmness.

The great question was, as you have already seen, what was the king to do on the subject of the two decrees; and Dumourier seems to have fought the battle of his unhappy master with great spirit and ability at the council board. He reproached the minister Servan for having proposed the decree of the camp, without having first taken the pleasure of the king, without having received even the sanction of his own colleagues; and he startled even the Girondists themselves, by remonstrating with them on their folly in attempting to bring twenty thousand federés to form a camp near Paris, nineteen thousand of whom would be Jacobins, of whom the first daring, ambitious man would be able to avail himself, and probably destroy the authors of the decree themselves; and this troop, too, to be brought to Paris, while the armies were weak and the frontiers bare.

Such were the terms in which Dumourier expressed himself at the council-board; and the result at last was, that Dumourier was summoned to the palace, and requested, both by the king and queen, to rid them, if possible, of their three insolent and factious ministers, Roland, Servan, and Clavière. Dumourier had not been on good terms with them for some time before, and they were now dismissed.

But Dumourier, as well as the ministers that succeeded, thought the sanction of the two decrees necessary, not only to the king's safety, but to their own, and indeed to their character, that they might not appear to have sacrificed their principles to their elevation.

But the king afterwards, though he would have sanctioned the decree for the camp, could not reconcile his conscience to the decree against the priests. Dumourier had to resign, and at length to render in his accounts to the king and take his leave. ",You go then to join the army of Luckner?" said the king. "Yes, sire," replied Dumourier, "I am delighted to quit this frightful city. I have but one regret; you are in danger."

"Yes," replied Louis with a sigh, "I certainly am." "Ah, sire!" returned the minister, "you can no longer suppose that I speak from any interested motive; let me implore you not to persist in your fatal resolution." "Speak no more of it," said the king; "my part is taken." "Ah, sire! you said the same, when in this very chamber, in presence of the queen, you gave me your word." "I was wrong then," said the king, "and I repent that I did so." "It is now, sire, that you are wrong, not then. I shall see you no more. They abuse your religious scruples; they are leading you on to a civil war; you are without force, and you will be overpowered. History will accuse you of having caused the calamities of France : observe the ridicule attached to the character of James II." "God is my witness," said Louis, putting his hands on those of Dumourier, and in a tone of the deepest affliction, "God is my witness, that I wish the happiness of France." "I doubt it not, sire," said Dumourier, the tears in his eyes, and overcome with his feelings; "but you are answerable to God, not only for the purity, but for the enlightened direction of your intentions. You think you are protecting religion, and you are destroying it. The priests will be massacred; you will lose your crown, perhaps your wife, your children." A short silence for a moment ensued; the king pressed his hand. "Sire, if all the French knew you, as I know you, our calamities would soon be at an end. You wish the happiness of France; it requires then the sacrifice of your scruples. You have been sacrificing yourself to the nation ever since 1789; continue to do so, and our troubles will at length cease; the Constitution be accomplished, the French return to their natural character, and the rest of your reign be happy."

"I expect my death," said the king, with a mournful air, "and I already forgive them. You I thank for the sensibility you have shown. You have served me well, and you have my esteem. If I am ever to see a better day, you shall have proofs of it." The king then rose hastily, and went to a window. Dumourier gathered up his papers slowly, that he might have time to compose himself before he left the room, and as he opened the door, the king made an approach to it, and addressing him with great feeling, "Adieu," he said, "all happiness attend you!"

LECTURE XXVI.

KING'S MISSION BY MALLET DU PAN.

The king might be sensibly affected by the generous devotion of Dumourier to his cause, but it was no longer in his power to adopt his counsels. He had taken other views of his own situation, and had of late hoped for relief under his misfortunes from another source. He had been led to consider what assistance could be derived from without. The armies of the German courts were in motion ; war had been declared ; every calamity was impending over himself and his country; and though Dumourier could see no alternative but resistance to all invaders, the king had entertained other hopes, and had thought, by a communication to the emperor and the king of Prussia, not only to prevent the horrors of war, but procure a situation of more dignity and repose for himself.   But this was a strong measure, and one of doubtful policy ; and the question that we have now therefore arrived at, is the conduct of the king with respect to foreign powers.

There can be no doubt, that the court and its adherents never could endure the Revolution from the first; and that they were always looking for assistance from the emperor and the German princes.   But we have all through these lectures made a distinction between the king and his court, and we have continued this distinction down to the period before us.   The Girondists, indeed, made no such distinction, at least never acted upon it ; and the Convention afterwards put the king to death, on the plea, that he had intrigued with foreign powers, and been a traitor to the liberties of his country.

It is therefore a point of great curiosity and importance to determine, what were really the views and the conduct of this unfortunate monarch at this particular period, the first half of the year 1792.

I consider Bertrand de Moleville as sufficient authority on a subject of this nature.   He held the Revolution, and all its abettors, in such abhorrence, that he thought he could not do greater honour to any man, than by representing him as unfavourable to it ; as endeavouring to stay its progress ; as ready to restore the old régime by any means in his power ; by force, if necessary, or even by calling for the invasion of foreign powers. He seems to me to disguise no project of this sort, that we can

suppose to have been formed; and we need look no further than
the account he gives for information of this kind. All through
his work you will see the distinction exist which we have set
up between the king and those around him. It was evidently
a subject of much secret lamentation, that the king had such a
horror of a civil war, and of shedding the blood of his subjects;
and Bertrand de Moleville would have considered himself as
adding to the respectability of the character of his royal master,
if he could have described him as more indignant, than he appeared to be, with the patriots, as more shocked with the diminutions of his prerogatives, as more ready to call for assistance
from whatever quarter it could be procured.

He says, however, positively, that the king, on being confidentially asked, gave his ministers to understand on the opening of
the Legislative Assembly, that he had adopted and meant to be
faithful to the constitution ; and in this frame of mind we must
have supposed him to have remained at any period of time, during which Bertrand de Moleville says nothing to the contrary.

I hasten therefore to the period now more immediately before
us.

Writing the history of March 1792, "The king," says Bertrand de Moleville, "reduced to the fatal necessity of forming a
new ministry (the Girondist ministry) at a moment, when it was
impossible for him to call upon a single individual on whose attachment he could depend, appeared more affected and uneasy
than ever, at the danger of his situation. Instead of the air of
contempt and indifference with which he had till then borne the
insults and outrages he had been exposed to, by the audacity of
the Assembly and the rage of the Jacobins, consternation and
dejection were marked in his countenance during the melancholy
council of the 10th of March, the last I ever attended."

" In the subsequent month of April," he says, " the answer
of the Austrian court (referring to the note of the 18th of
March), which the Assembly had indecently treated as evasive
and insignificant, completely seconded the views of the factious,
and concealed under the veil of public interests, and of the
honour and dignity of the nation, the guilty motives of their
wishing for war. They provoked it so eagerly, only that they
might have more opportunities and means of attacking the
king, and rendering him odious to the people, by accusing him
from time to time of treachery, and of holding intelligence with
the foreign powers. The scrupulous accuracy," he says, " with
which his majesty, true to his oath, carried the constitution

into execution, had hitherto disconcerted all the manœuvres of the Jacobins; and the charges they were continually making against him, of not liking it, and of wishing to overthrow it, in order to restore the old system, were no longer considered, but as calumnies too vague and worn out to produce any effect.

" War opened a vast field of new impostures, much more serious, and doubly dangerous, as the eager credulity of the people in tales of plots, treachery, and correspondence with the enemy, made it unnecessary for those who circulated such impostures, to adduce any proof of them, or even to support them by the least reference.

" The king," he continues, " was aware of these dangers, which alarmed him much more for his family than for himself. But his mind was affected in a still greater degree, at the melancholy prospect of any species of calamity which war would bring upon France, and he saw with the deepest sorrow that it was now become inevitable.

" All that the king could do, was to delay and impede, by every means in his power, the fatal decision of the council on M. de Noailles' last dispatches ; nor did his majesty consent to propose to the Assembly to declare war against the emperor, till he had obliged all the ministers separately to give him their opinions written and signed."

From these extracts, and from all the particulars of the case, it is very clear, that the king gave no assent to this war ; no assent, addressed either to the one party or the other. He saw in it no peace for himself, and no happiness for his people.

But information still more curious and important is soon after imparted to his readers by Bertrand de Moleville.

In the opening of the campaign, it appears that the Austrians had the advantage. The number of those who emigrated became daily more considerable; whole regiments went over to the enemy.

" They are only traitors who have deserted," said the war minister, Servan, in the sitting of May 14 ; " it is, perhaps, a blessing we ought to look for : nothing can be more fortunate for the troops than to see the filth, that may be among them, drained off."

" But the king," says Bertrand de Moleville, " far from yielding to this patriotic security, saw, with the deepest sorrow, France engaged in an unjust and bloody war, which the general disorganization seemed to render it impossible to carry on, and which more than ever exposed our frontier provinces to inva-

sion. His majesty, above all, dreaded a civil war, and did not
doubt that it would break out on the news of the first advantage
gained over the French troops by the emigrant corps, which
formed a part of the Austrian army. It was, indeed, but too
much to be feared, that the Jacobins and the people, in their
fury, would make bloody reprisals, on the priests and nobles
remaining in France. These fears," says Bertrand de Moleville,
" which he expressed in a letter to me, were the occasion of
my proposing to him (and you will observe this statement which
Bertrand de Moleville is now making) to send a person of confidence to the emperor and king of Prussia, to endeavour to
prevail on them not to allow their armies to act offensively
against France, until they should be under the inevitable necessity of so doing; and even in that case, to let the entrance of
their armies into France be preceded by a manifesto, in which
they should declare, ' That forced to take arms by an unjust
attack, they did not impute that aggression either to the king
or to the French nation, but to a criminal faction, which oppressed both; that, consequently, far from departing from
the sentiments of amity which united them to France, their intention, on the contrary, was to deliver that nation from tyranny,
and restore it to legal order and tranquillity; that they had no
view of interfering with the form of government, but merely
secure to the nation the right of adopting that, which suited it
best; that all idea of conquest was foreign to their thoughts;
that private property should be by them equally respected as
national property; that their majesties took all peaceable and
faithful subjects under their protection; that they considered as
their enemies those only who were the enemies of France, viz.
the faction of the Jacobins, and all its adherents,' " &c. &c.

Such is the very remarkable account given by Bertrand de
Moleville; and these must be considered as at that time (May
1792) the sentiments of the king, since they were these which
the minister proposed to him to adopt, in consequence of what
he had observed to be passing in the king's mind; and they must
be considered as benevolent and moderate, and on the whole as
patriotic, in the king and his advisers, if it be remembered, as
it must always be, that no one ever supposed (*they* at least did
not) that any effective resistance could be made to the progress
of the allied forces. All this is true; but, at the same time,
you will immediately see, that there was here a distinct communication between the king and the allied powers, and you must
be aware, that *this* was in itself a very objectionable measure.

" In consequence," continues Bertrand de Moleville, " of the manner in which I had often heard M. Malouet speak of Mallet du Pan, I advised the king to employ him on this occasion. The talents and probity of Mallet du Pan were not unknown to the king, who immediately agreed to my proposal."

After some other particulars, Bertrand de Moleville goes on to mention, that the instructions which related to this mission were drawn up by Mallet du Pan according to the king's directions; that they were composed, in the main, of seven articles, and were of the following tenor:—

" 1. The king not only exhorts but beseeches the princes and the French emigrants to give no grounds, by a hostile and offensive concurrence on their part, for divesting the present war of the character of a foreign one waged between different powers.

" 2. He expressly recommends to them to leave to him and the interfering courts the consideration and care of their interests when the time for treating them arrives.

" 3. They must appear only parties, and not arbiters in the dispute; as the arbitration should be reserved for his majesty, when restored to liberty, and for the powers requiring it.

" 4. Any other conduct would produce a civil war; endanger the lives of the king and his family; overturn the throne; cause a massacre of the royalists; secure to the Jacobins all the revolutionists who have abandoned, and who are daily abandoning them; rekindle a fire that seems dying away; and give great force to a resistance, which will yield at the first successes, if the fate of the Revolution shall appear exclusively intrusted to those (the royal family) against whom it was directed, and who have been the victims of it.

" 5. To represent to the courts of Vienna and Berlin the propriety of a manifesto, in common for them and the other states who have entered into the confederation; the importance of drawing up this manifesto in such a manner as to distinguish the Jacobins from the rest of the nation; to encourage all those who may return from their error; or, who, not wishing for the present constitution, desire a suppression of abuses, and a rational liberty, under a monarchy limited by law.

" 6. To state in the manifesto the fundamental truth, that the war is directed against a faction destructive of society, and not against the French nation; that it is the defence of legal governments and nations against a furious anarchy, &c. to remove all fear of dismemberment; to impose no laws, but to declare with energy to the Assembly, administrative bodies, &c. that they should be held individually responsible, in their persons and property, for all outrages committed against the sacred person of the king, or those of the queen and their family, and against the persons and property of any citizen whatever.

" 7. To express the king's wish, that in entering the kingdom the powers should declare that they are ready to agree to a peace, but that they neither can nor will treat but with the king; that in consequence they require that he should be restored to full liberty ; and then, that a congress be assembled, in which the different interests shall be discussed on the grounds already settled, the emigrants be admitted as parties complaining, and the general plan of reform negotiated under the auspices and guarantee of the powers."

Such were the instructions, according to the account of Bertrand de Moleville ; and the king, he afterwards says, explained them in a most ample manner, and these explanations were communicated to Mallet du Pan; and Bertrand de Moleville disclaims on the part of his majesty all jealousy of the emigrants and princes, such as had been imputed to him; that he observed always, he says, in the king the most affectionate friendship for the princes; but, above all, an extreme horror at the least idea of a civil war.

Afterwards it appears, that Bertrand de Moleville sent Mallet du Pan (who had proceeded on his mission) a detail of the occurrences on the 20th of June ; and observed to him, that it was very much to be feared, that similar scenes would be repeated, and with consequences still more disastrous, unless the factious were restrained by the dread of a striking and speedy vengeance. " I dwelt consequently," says he, " with the greater force on the necessity of hastening as much as possible the publication of the manifesto, without which, I said, all was lost."

Bertrand de Moleville, in his history of July, observes : " The manifesto of the powers (the Duke of Brunswick's manifesto) at length appeared, and for a moment gave a pause to the manœuvres which agitated the capital.   The manifesto so much expected, was not that, the plan of which had been proposed by Mallet du Pan and agreed to, but one drawn up by Dulimon, as dictated by the ministers of the emperor and king of Prussia; and the Duke of Brunswick, who signed it, as commander-in-chief, had not even been consulted upon it.   The publication of it produced an effect the very reverse of what had been expected."

Such are the representations of Bertrand de Moleville, and

these must now be considered as the facts of history; they are
intended to be such by this confidential minister, and for the
reasons I have mentioned, may as such be received.

Now, on the whole of this case it may be observed, that there
is a great distinction to be made between originally exciting and
calling upon foreign powers for assistance, and afterwards endeavouring to influence their conduct, when they had already
been placed in a hostile attitude; when war had been already
declared; when they were already approaching as enemies and
invaders; when they were approaching, whether the king interfered and offered his own counsels and requests, or not. The
king is entitled to the full benefit of all the observations that
can be made, founded on this distinction.

The king, it must be again observed, meant not a civil war;
he thought he could, by proper demonstrations of the strength
and wishes of the foreign powers united to his own, awe the
factious, and enable the well-disposed to support his cause, and
in *that*, as he believed, the cause of the best interests of France.

But, on the other hand, it is clear that a counter-revolution
was intended. There is nothing said by Bertrand de Moleville
of La Fayette's constitution or the liberties of France; and the
king, by sending a confidential agent to these allied sovereigns,
showed that in his existing situation he was ready to receive
assistance from them, and that he did not think their interference in itself unlawful, if they would take his advice; at
least, there does not appear to have been any thing said of this
nature to the allied powers, though there is to the emigrants:
they, it seems, are not to press forward, lest a civil war should
be the consequence; but with regard to the allied powers,
though they are not to impose any law on France, or proceed at
all, but with the approbation and sanction of the king, still, on
these suppositions and with these reservations, the national dignity is considered as uninjured, and the interests of France sufficiently consulted.

The character of the king must, I think, be submitted to any
censure that is fairly deducible from these last statements. We
do not say with the king's accusers, and even the historian
Thiers, that he invited the allied powers into France, but that
he communicated with them, when coming. He did not indeed
prevent their coming; but invite them, or cause their coming,
he did *not*.

But we will return to considerations of this kind hereafter;
for I have now to mention to you, that though I think these are

ample materials for the reflection of the student, thus furnished
by Bertrand de Moleville, still, that materials even more ample
than these exist; and I will now proceed to exhibit them to
your consideration.

It has happened that the son of Mallet du Pan found, among
his father's papers, a copy of the memorial which was actually
presented to the allied sovereigns. This is the gentleman to
whom I expressed my obligations in so strong a manner at the
opening of these lectures, and he has kindly furnished me with
this memorial, and allowed me to endeavour to turn it to the
purposes of your information and instruction in any manner I
can. This is the memorial to which Bertrand de Moleville alludes, and of which he means to give his reader a general representation by the seven articles I have quoted from him; but the
memorial itself, though the main purport of it is very fairly
given (a testimony this to the good faith of Bertrand de Moleville, as an historian) is far more full and circumstantial, and
affords, as it appears to me, a very complete and distinct view
of all the opinions, hopes, and fears that were entertained by
the king at this critical period, not only with regard to his own
situation, but to, the characters and intentions of all the parties
around him. I shall, therefore, give you the best notion of it I
can, immediately, and I shall leave it on the table for the inspection of any one who would wish to consider it for himself.

In the first place, it is clear, from this memorial, that a
counter-revolution was intended. The very first words are
these (I translate from the original):—"Two inseparable objects present themselves in the management and aim of the approaching counter-revolution; first, the means of effecting it;
and, secondly, those of maintaining it." '

And again :—"The means of success," says the memorial,
"exist in foreign combination and forces; but we must not here
confine ourselves solely to the consideration of the first resistance
which will be offered by the armies of the Revolution." These
are the words; so that a counter-revolution was the object, the
allied armies the means, and the armies of the Revolution the
difficulty—the enemy to be overcome.

And with respect to the new order of things that was to be
introduced, it was not the constitution of La Fayette, or any
modification of it, but a limited monarchy : on the whole, the
old régime cleared of its abuses; but the views of the king on
this part of the subject will best be seen by attending to the
various observations that are made by him on the parties then
existing in the state.

"At the present moment," says the memorial, "the capital is almost entirely in the hands of the Jacobins, who possess the majority in the National Assembly, all important places, and the municipalities. His majesty's council cannot support itself another month."

You see here that no great distinction was made by the king between the Girondists and the Jacobins. Thus again :—

"The Jacobins," says the memorial, "are divided into two sections, which pursue the same ends by different measures, and which, often at variance, are always ready to re-unite when a fresh blow is to be struck at the royal prerogative, or some attempt made against the superior classes.

"The section now in power has for its chief president the Abbé Sieyes, who governs it along with Brissot, Condorcet, Pétion, Gensonné, Vergniaud, Guadet, and Manuel." These, as the student is aware, were the leaders of the Girondists.

"This cabal," says the memorial, "had formed the late ministry. Besides its *own* adherents, it generally rallies to its side the great majority of two hundred and fifty political or cowardly knaves, who have classed themselves in the National Assembly under the appellation of Independents. The project of this cabal is to form a republic, not in name, but in fact ; by a reduction of the civil list to five millions, by the retrenchment of most of the powers left to the king, and by a change of dynasty, in which the new chief should be a kind of honorary president of the republic, to whom they would give an executive council, appointed by the Assembly, that is, by their committee."

The description here given, by the king, of the Girondist party, as it stood at this period, cannot, I think, be considered as incorrect. The *motives* of their conduct would be the only point to be disputed. With some, they would be found in a lust of power and a taste for violent counsels ; with others, in a proper distrust of the king, and a patriotic determination to maintain their Revolution.

There will be no difference of opinion with the king on the subject of the lower section, the Jacobins.

"The second party," says the memorial, "which divides the Jacobins, is composed of rude agitators, of impatient Republicans, of wretches who, not being able to endure any government, desire eternal anarchy.

"By the help of their charter of the Rights of Man, they would extend their levelling principle over all legal pre-eminence, and over all property ; they will have no king ; and the only government they desire is the democracy of a deliberating mob. Robespierre, Danton, Chabot, Merlin, Bazire, Thuriot, and a hundred others of the same species, supported by the club of the Cordeliers and by the fraternal societies, manage this disorderly faction, which retains a very numerous party in the club of the Jacobins, which has the disposal of most of the popular libellers, of the pike-men, and of the scum of the capital."

I do not, I say, think that much objection can be made to this description of the dreadful men who are commonly meant when we speak of the Jacobins; nor, again, to what follows:—

" Both these parties," the memorial goes on to observe, " work by the same means, but the first (that of the Girondists) acts less openly, carries on its crimes with less impetuosity, has the advantage over the other of cunning, of some ability, of being directed by the Abbé Sieyes; but the vilest agents, rioters by profession, brigands, regicides, fanatics, villains of every kind, form the army, common to both, and they do not leave it a single day unemployed."

This statement, too, of the memorial, must, I conceive be allowed. You will observe hereafter, if you read her Memoirs, an admission to this effect by Me. Roland. " The pack," she talks of, whose excesses, as she calls them, " were not at all what she could approve, or what should go unpunished."

After observing that the Duke of Orleans is connected with the lower Jacobins, the memorial proceeds to consider the party of the Constitutionalists and the Feuillans. And here I must remark, that on no occasion does the court or even the king appear to such disadvantage, as whenever this intermediate party of La Fayette and his friends are concerned. As it strikes me, all reasonableness and candour are then at an end. That these patriots made mistakes, may be admitted; I have exhibited what I think they were, through the whole of these lectures: but that they were patriots, and did not mean ill to the monarchy, must surely be allowed. But no merit of this kind was sufficient; nothing could atone for the original crime of having been the first and great movers of the Revolution, and the antipathy of the queen and the court to La Fayette may be shown, in more instances than one, to have not a little contributed to their own destruction.

The conclusion (and it is a very mortifying one) is, that no principles of civil liberty can be endured by those rulers of the earth, who have been bred up under arbitrary governments; and if this was not also the case with Louis XVI., though it was with the queen and in general with the higher orders of France, it is a merit in him which should never be forgotten.

But to return to the memorial. " It is not easy," says the memorial, " to class the Constitutionalists and the Feuillans. They form a heterogeneous compound of motley characters ; men of various inconsistencies, of dissimilar sentiments, of contradictory plans, of enthusiastic metaphysics, and of a disappointed ambition which seeks only to rise again."

The memorial then goes on to describe these men, and the different projects that they had attempted, but in a manner too detailed to admit of quotation, and, I must add, in a manner that appears to me unfair and unjust.

These men (La Fayette and his friends) rallied round the king on his return from Varennes ; they saved him from the dethronement that would have been *then* the immediate measure of the violent party, of Pétion and others; they produced, and upheld and insisted on the constitution ; they thus gave the monarchy of France its last and only chance. It was impossible to do more, after the king and court had tried their own measure, and had failed, an attempt to escape ; and, under these circumstances, it is not very agreeable to read the following paragraph, which appears in the memorial :—

" Next to these come the idolaters of the constitution, a species of maniacs, whom the factious enthusiasm or political affectation (bel esprit) attach to their superstition. They have persuaded themselves, that if it were not for the Jacobins, the constitution would prosper ; and it has hitherto been impossible to persuade them that the constitution itself is the origin and support of the Jacobins, and that if those of St. Honoré were destroyed, it would produce others in the course of six months."

This, I must repeat, is not the paragraph that might have been expected in a memoir drawn up under the eye and direction of the king.

So much for what is said, in this memorial, of the Jacobins, the Girondists, and the Constitutionalists. It is, in the last place, curious to inquire what is said of the remaining party that first appeared in this Revolution,—the party of Mounier, Lally Tollendal and his friends. These fare better ; and the paragraph is indicative of the opinions of the king from the first breaking out of the Revolution to the period before us.

" We shall not speak here," says the memorial " of that particular section, which previous to the crimes of Versailles had placed itself between the first two classes and the authors of the present constitution; that is to say, the partisans of a legislative body in two divisions, of which one was the Chamber of Peers. *They* are all agreed as to the necessity of re-establishing the royal authority in all the power and dignity, which are compatible with that degree of public liberty which the government of a great empire can admit of; they are unanimous in recalling the clergy, the national religion, the nobility, and the great tribunals. There is no fear of any kind of opposition from *them*, because there is not one of them who would not prefer an absolute monarchy to the monstrous laws of the present time, and to the authority of the men who have established them." This is just.

Such is the description furnished by the memorial of the parties by which the king was surrounded. Nothing is said by the king of the Royalists or his well-wishers, their numbers, or their influence; and this is creditable to the memorial. The memorial then proceeds in the following manner :—

"The political chart which we have just marked out should teach us to foresee the different effects which will be produced upon the minds of men; the progress and the existence of the counter-revolution, according to the forms and measures by which it may be effected.

" Policy, therefore, prescribes to us a regard to such of these interests, as can be reconciled with the fundamental object of the counter-revolution, and the neglect of which might unite the whole mass of revolutionists in the wish and endeavour to carry on a prolonged opposition.

" Whatever serves to disarm resistance and to facilitate submission ought to be employed; but nothing would more effectually tend to prolong the one, and retard the other, than the furnishing all parties with equal motives for persevering in rebellion."

And now, it is at this point that I must request the student to recollect what the style and manner of the Duke of Brunswick's manifesto turned out to be—the manifesto which the memorial was sent to influence. He is to recollect the fury and violence of its language, its effects upon Paris and upon France, and indeed upon all the friends of liberty all over the world. It is of great importance to the character of the king and his advisers, to observe, how far this memorial, now before us, went to suggest or to countenance the expressions made use of in this manifesto of the duke. Hitherto the memorial takes good ground; it goes on thus :—

" These considerations (considerations of policy, as just described) are inapplicable to *some* of the Jacobins and to their leaders. *These* men can be conquered by fear alone. Their maxims, their plans, and their practice, forbid any species of confidence. Crime is their only interest, their only resource, their only thought. Any conciliating measure would appear to *them* an avowal of timidity, and would embolden their assurances. With respect to *them*, therefore, power should show itself under its most formidable appearance. The manifesto should consider these corporations, which are the scandal and the horror of three-fourths of the nation, as excommunicated societies, for the members of which there remains no hope of escape, no toleration for their doctrines. The preservation of their lives is the only favour which can be promised to such among them as have not been led by fanaticism and error into the commission of crimes, and are resolved to leave the standard of their unworthy chiefs. They alone have provoked the war, and it is fit that upon them should fall the punishment."

Now it might be very fit, as the memorial here declares, that the lower Jacobins should be punished; but the question is, how far it was prudent thus to denounce them. The Jacobins might be very proper objects of moral indignation, and not unfairly represented in the paragraph we have just read; but were they in force? were they formidable? Though three-fourths of the nation might regard them with horror, were they not likely to compensate for their want of numbers by their activity and energy? Were they, or were they not, in possession of the capital, where the king and royal family were imprisoned and in their power? What were likely to be the consequences of making those men desperate, of whom it was just before said, that crime was their only interest, resource, and thought? Would not silence with respect to such men have been the best line of policy for the memorial to take? The great fault, or mistake of this memorial, as of the manifesto of the Duke of Brunswick, and of the reasonings of the allied powers from the first, seems to have been, to suppose, that they could set off a part from the whole; that they could punish the Jacobins, without interfering with the feelings or violating the dignity and independence of the *rest* of the nation: a vain hope, which the general principles of human nature and the phenomena of the Revolution, as they saw them every day exhibited in the capital, should have for ever prevented them from indulging for a moment.

What the king and his advisers attempted to do, was to excite terror in the evil-doer, and confidence in the well-disposed.

These were the somewhat inconsistent objects that they endeavoured to accomplish ; and therefore the memorial went on in the following manner (but certainly not at all in the manner of the Duke of Brunswick's manifesto) :—

" But this just severity, which cannot be announced in too threatening a manner, should leave an opening for the far more numerous body of milder Revolutionists. It would be unjust and dangerous to confound them with the factious demagogues who domineer over the kingdom.

" Towards the majority, wisdom counsels us to employ at the same time, terror and confidence.

" Terror, because nothing else can destroy the illusions with which many persist in blinding themselves ; nothing else inspire with some degree of courage those weak characters, who might be led by habit, or by a fear of the Jacobins, to rejoin the ruling party, if they did not see it on the eve of perishing ; nothing else make a deep impression upon such as are in doubt, or still misled by errors, by showing them that such chimeras are passing away ; nothing else overcome in others the false point of honour which leads them still to defend the constitution, and, above all, take away from the different leaders of the Feuillans the hope which has been the grand object of their attention during the last six months, that of placing themselves in a situation which should enable them to treat with arms in their hands, and to finish by a capitulation.

" Confidence will strengthen the effect of terror, and lead it to the desirable result of confining all resistance to the Jacobins exclusively, and of counterbalancing their influence in the interior, which might lead to new catastrophes during the final struggles.

" This confidence is nothing else than security for the future. It will arise from the assurance, that there is no intention to class the factious, by whom nothing has been held sacred, with men who have been deluded, and to confound mistakes of the understanding with perverseness ; errors of opinion, with a code of crime, immorality, and anarchy.

" This distinction," the memorial goes on to say, " will not flatter the self-love of the Constitutionalists, but will appear to them a proof of equity, and hold forth to them a safeguard ; and we cannot suppose them foolish enough to partake in the resistance of the Jacobins, when they will no longer have to fear the same danger.

" Confidence will arise from the care that shall be taken to destroy the apprehensions which have been created of intended vengeance, of implacable resentment, and of an oppression which would fall equally upon the mistaken and the criminal. It will finally and especially arise from the belief, that the king will be the only arbiter of the fate of the different parties, and the pacificator of the kingdom; that to him alone will be intrusted the destiny of the laws, as well as of individuals; in a word, that neither the one nor the other will be given up at discretion and exclusively to the emigrants and foreign powers.

" The tyranny of the Jacobins has compelled the Feuillans, and the greater part of the Revolutionists, who are ashamed or half converted, to look at the royal authority as their anchor of mercy. If they were to-morrow to triumph over their adversaries, there is no doubt that they would immediately strengthen the power of the king. For the last three months, the greater part would have arranged themselves around his majesty, if they had had as much courage as good will; and if the Jacobins, by their indefatigable activity, had not held the poignards of their assassins, and the torches of their incendiaries, over all who dared to avow any attachment to their monarch.

" The preceding arrangements depend upon the belligerent powers, and upon the French princes and emigrants; they agree with the wishes of the king, and with the opinion which positive information and the general interest have led him to form. His majesty attaches the highest importance to the careful consideration of his representations. He adds his prayers to his entreaties, that they may obtain the attention which he solicits. He solicits it in the full independence of his reflection and of his will. No foreign influence has prepared or produced his representations on this subject; they result from exact acquaintance which his majesty has, of the disposition of the public, by means of the daily accounts which are faithfully presented to him, of the capital and of the departments; so that no one within or without the kingdom possesses so much certain information, whereby to state and know, what is to be feared or hoped in the interior, according to the nature of the ways and means by which the exterior power will act.

" All will become easy for the present and for the future, if the king's views are adopted; if not, all will probably become involved in peril, uncertainty, and difficulty. Force must again raise up the monarchy, but opinion must sustain it; it is in the hearts of the people that the roots of stability must be planted. The powers employed to produce a physical submission should also be directed to the attainment of a moral submission; and to the same point should be directed the efforts of all who wish to prevent any new shipwreck of the state."

These are the terms of the memorial; and they must be considered as creditable to the magnanimity of the king, and as indicative of benevolence and patriotism. This must surely be the conclusion, if it be considered, that the general belief was, that the allied powers could not be resisted; and again, if the unhappy circumstances in which the king was placed be also considered; the company and the conversation by which he was always surrounded; the opinions in which he had been educated; the disappointments he had sustained; the state of insignificance to which he had been gradually reduced; the outrages he had been exposed to, himself, his queen, and his family; the cries of fury, the menaces, the insults, that resounded loud around him, wherever he turned; the dreadful men that were rushing forward to pull him from his throne, to massacre him by their assassins, or tear him to pieces by their mobs. These lamentable circumstances and exigencies of his case must be considered, and placed not only to the credit of the king, but of his advisers, and particularly of Mallet du Pan, who appears to have been on this occasion his chief adviser, and who had to rise superior to many personal irritations and resentments of his own, being at the moment all but denounced by the popular party (and at last he was denounced in the Assembly by one of its members), on account of a journal which he edited, and which they would have done better to have listened to, than to have proscribed.

Allowance, I say, must be made for all the circumstances of the case as it at last existed; and it will then I think be admitted, that the good intentions and good feelings of the king and his advisers are seen in this memorial: and the only question remaining is, whether on account of the same deplorable and irremediable circumstances of the case, the propriety and the wisdom of the whole measure may be also admitted, as well as the good intentions and good feelings. This is indeed a very different question; and it cannot be denied, that all general principles seem unfavourable. No maxim so undoubted, as that foreigners are never to be called in; and nothing could in itself be so imprudent, as to tamper with foreign powers: nothing so impossible, as to suppose, that the leaders of any revolution would allow for a moment their interference; would think for a moment, that any king and court could afterwards be either able or willing to control the foreigners they had once admitted to their assistance. Such are the general views and maxims that belong to any case like this in the politics of a country; and it remains for the student to consider, how far on this present occasion the king and his advisers were, or were not, justified in violating such general rules or maxims; or how far they did, or did not, persuade themselves, that such consequences, as are always apprehended by such general rules and maxims, were in their instance likely to ensue.

The distinction which the king took was this: that the allied powers were advancing in the usual form and manner of those who were waging war; that this war he had done everything to prevent, but being unable to prevent it, he might fairly attempt to be a mediator between these powers and his subjects, a general pacificator; might save his country from anarchy and crimes; and putting down the Jacobins, make terms with the rest of the Revolutionists, and re-establish his former dignity and power, with such limitations as he thought the general happiness of his people required.

Reasoning in this way, he made a distinction between the allied powers and the emigrants. Any separate attack, any separate success on the part of the latter, he conceived could only be followed by a civil war,—the great subject of his horror at all times; and the mistake, the illusion, whatever it may be called, of the king, was, his supposing that any such distinction would be made by the patriots or people of France, or that every thing he was addressing in the memorial to these princes and emigrants would not be by those patriots and that people, considered as applicable to invaders of every description, whether emigrants or not, whatever might be their manifestoes and declarations, under whatever palliatives and assurances they came forward, after first denouncing particular clubs and bodies of men, and marching on at all events to interfere in their Revolution, and to assail their country by arms.

It is, indeed, quite curious to observe, how little the king and his advisers took into their account (or at least the king) the general effect that would be produced on the country by any hos-

tile aggression from Prussians and Austrians; how little they
seem to have been aware, that what they thought the necessary
effects of the hostile attack of the emigrants, would be equally
so of the hostile attack of *all* foreigners whatever.

In the memorial appear (though I have not time to quote them)
many other very remarkable paragraphs. Suppose them to refer
not to the emigrants but to be addressed to the king himself, as
reasons why he should not approach those allied powers with
any advice and interference whatever,—as reasons why he could
only implore them not to wage war against France at all,
under whatever plea, whether just or not: supposing them *thus*
to be addressed, and they are quite prophetic, they exhibit distinctly the effects that were afterwards produced by the hostile
appearance of the foreign armies on the frontiers and in the kingdom; and they are the very considerations that, from the first,
should have been urged at the courts of Berlin and Vienna, to
have prevented, on their parts, all mention of clubs and Jacobins
by name, and all war against their proceedings, if the future
peace of France, if any tolerable adjustment of the Revolution,
if the safety of any Royalists and priests yet remaining in the
kingdom, if the lives of the king, the queen, and the royal family,
were considered as objects of any importance.

No doubt the Duke of Brunswick's manifesto added new fuel
to the flame that would naturally have been excited, and turned
the flame into a conflagration that became furious and irresistible; but I look upon the denouncement of the Jacobins by
name, and the apparent unconsciousness of the effects that could
not but be produced by the invasion not only of emigrants but of
foreign armies, under whatever plea or modification, as the important, though very natural, mistake of this very respectable
and (all circumstances considered) patriotic memorial.

Such, then, as appears from this memorial, such were the
sentiments entertained by the king, and perhaps by most of his
advisers, of the different parties of the state, and the treatment
they were to receive from the allied powers. The war was to
be a foreign war; was not to be distinguished from any other
foreign war; was not to be suffered to assume any other character; the king was to be a mediator and pacificator between
the foreign armies and his own subjects; the Jacobins were to
be put down, as men with whom no terms could be kept; any
other description of patriot was to be conciliated and protected;
the ancient orders were to be revived; the king restored to his

former dignity and power, with proper limitations; and equal laws were to be introduced for the protection of property; on the whole, a counter-revolution to be effected, but *not* one that Mounier and his friends (the first most respectable patriots of the Revolution) would have been unwilling to accede to.

The memorial was presented to the King of Prussia on the 14th of July; the day following, to the Emperor of Austria and the proper ministers. Mallet du Pan had before informed Bertrand de Moleville, that when he was properly accredited, the ministers of Vienna and Berlin conversed freely with him, and manifested to him intentions from which he conceived great hopes.

On the 20th of July it appears, from Bertrand de Moleville's account, that Mallet du Pan left Frankfort, considering his mission entirely at an end, by the acquiescence of the powers in all the king's views, and by their adoption of the manifesto he had been charged to propose to them. " He had so fully justified," continues Bertrand de Moleville, " the king's confidence in him, by the wisdom and success of his negotiation, that his majesty authorized me to testify to him, how much he was satisfied with it, and to tell him that he wished to have no other negotiator with the powers."

He was then recommended to return to Frankfort, but the minister's letter was received by Mallet du Pan, at Geneva, at the moment when the Austrian and Prussian armies were on their march, and just when the Duke of Brunswick's manifesto, so different, it is added, from that proposed by him, was published; and these circumstances induced him to consider his return into Germany as useless.

To this manifesto of the duke I need not now allude. It is sufficient, at present, to observe, that the king is not responsible for it, nor even the court; it has seldom been mentioned, but to be lamented or reprobated.

We must rather turn now, finally, to enumerate what estimates we have made, what conclusions we have drawn, while we have been detailing the various particulars that have been exhibited to the student in the course of these three last lectures. The general principles that are applicable to political situations are, for the most part, sufficiently acknowledged, but the situations we are here concerned with are matters of great debate, and it is not easy to understand the characters and views of the different actors in the scene. No subject, how-

ever, can be so important, so singularly, so tremendously
interesting.

From the nature of human beings and human affairs, questions
like these are necessarily mingled and mixed questions; but it is
our duty to endeavour to arrive at what decisions we can, proceeding with proper modesty and care, and at all events endeavouring to comprehend the feelings and the views of all who
took a part in these memorable transactions.

Our first and main position is, that the king, and still more
the court, were natural objects of suspicion and distrust, not
only after the flight to Varennes, but before; still that the
Girondists were wanting in proper confidence in the goodness
of the king's intentions; that they continually made the Revolution more hateful and oppressive to him; and that they
themselves created the evils against which they professed to
provide.

That with respect to the great subject of the Austrian war,
the points seem to be, that though the allied powers meant only
to act on the defensive, they expressed themselves in a manner
so offensive to the national dignity of France, and assumed to
themselves such a power of interfering in the government of the
country, that they left the popular party in France a right to
declare war if they thought it necessary to the interests of their
country; and yet we afterwards contended that, under the circumstances of the case, the Girondists ought not to have made
war, and that by doing so they could not but bring their Revolution into the greatest difficulties, reducing everything to the
chance of despotism on the one side, and anarchy on the other.

We next held, that the king did everything in his power to
prevent the war, and was deeply affected by the calamities to
which he saw France thus exposed, as well as clearly aware of
the dangers that were thus made to threaten himself; that he
was not wanting to the constitution, or indisposed to give it a
fair trial, till the Jacobin ministry, as it was called, was forced
upon him, and war declared against Austria; that from that
time he turned to other counsels, as we have seen in the lecture
I have now delivered; that not having called the allied powers
into France, he thought he might be a mediator between them
and his subjects; that a counter-revolution was now his object,
but not arbitrary power; that his intentions were still benevolent and patriotic, but that his interference, or any interference
with the combined powers, was exposed to the objection, that no

foreign armies are ever to be suffered to intermingle themselves in the concerns of a country. We contended, however, that allowance must be made for the unhappy monarch: his country, he must have thought, had no other chance of escape from calamity, or himself from a scaffold; his family from assassination, or his friends from massacre.

On the whole, the great mistake seems to have been, on the one side and on the other, that the supporters of the old régime thought they could set the Jacobins apart, and make war upon the clubs and more violent Revolutionists, and not on the rest of the nation,—this seems to have been their mistake from the first; and that, on the other hand, the supporters of the Revolution kept no bounds in their spirit of proselytism, and justly alarmed every neighbouring country, after first violating the feelings of every one who differed from them in their own. And thus far, indeed, I see no reason to congratulate either of the parties on the wisdom or virtue of their proceedings.

In conclusion, it is truly melancholy to observe in mankind such a total want of all moderation, of all reasonable attention to the feelings and opinions of each other. The patrons of the old opinions, for instance, and the German courts, would have disliked the Revolution under any circumstances, and under any possible modifications; and the complaints and representations of the emigrants, and the sufferings of the royal family, when the Revolution turned out to be so very destructive of all established authorities and opinions, excited the strongest sympathy in all the governing classes. All this was very natural, particularly the sentiment of moral indignation by which they were animated; still, when every allowance has been made for their situation, the best *manner* of interference was evidently a question of the greatest difficulty; and some more prudence and discretion might have been expected, and some more attention than was, in fact, shown to the acknowledged rights of independent nations, to those especially of a great kingdom like France, under an acknowledged state of revolutionary excitement at the time.

And again, with respect to the patrons of the new opinions, they might look down with contempt on the old governments and the prejudices that supported them: they were free, no doubt, to follow where their reasoning seemed to lead them, in making up their *own* opinions; but why were they to be animated with such a restless, offensive, revolutionary spirit of proselytism?

Their principles and notions went certainly to the disturbance and even the subversion of the other feudal governments of Europe. Why were they to proclaim them everywhere, disseminate their revolutionary writings, and establish their clubs?

It afterwards appeared, that wherever the French armies went, the ground was prepared for them; the friends of the new opinions were found organized, the clubs in activity, and the foundations of society, as it had hitherto existed, subverted. But why all this aggression, this invasion, this war, this exterminating war, to be waged against all constituted authorities in the dominions of independent nations? The great truths of civil liberty, it will be said, as of religious liberty at the time of the Reformation, are everywhere to be propagated, that others may participate of the benefits we ourselves enjoy, and that the happiness of mankind may be made progressive.

This is a principle (the dissemination of truth), no doubt, of the most sacred nature, one to which we owe everything that has improved or dignified our nature; but it is a principle which, when opposed to established opinions, must always be exercised with circumspection and care. It can be exercised by no man, and by no description of men, without incurring the most awful responsibility, and a far greater responsibility than is generally supposed: certainly it must never be exercised without an examination of the new opinions, which are to be propagated, and the old opinions that are to be overthrown, far more grave and anxious than has been often exercised; without an attention to the particular circumstances of the case, far more provident and patient than has been often shown.

On this great occasion of the French Revolution, on this great crisis in the affairs of the world, the enthusiasm, the spirit of proselytism of the patrons of the new opinions, was totally ungovernable and unpardonable. They had neither sense nor patience in comparing the value of their own new opinions with the old, nor mercy nor forbearance in their conduct to those who differed from them.

With regard to the king, his case is exhibited in the memorial I have produced. What he hoped, and feared, and wished, and attempted, are all here. This document I consider as the very image and identification of his mind and nature. No doubt the general principle was against him; no communication whatever is to be held with foreign powers for the purpose of influencing the internal concerns of our own country. We dispute not a principle so universally salutary and important, so supported by experience as well as by theory. But what is to be our censure, if we consider that he had made every effort to prevent the war; that these foreign powers were approaching as enemies, whether he interfered with them or not; that the popular party in the capital were pressing forward upon him to trample him down into the dust; that he had no other hope, no other chance for his crown and dignity, but what he could derive from the assistance of the allies; that he not only saw them approaching, but had no doubts of their success? What is to be our censure, I say? Is it to be expected from human wisdom, from human feelings, that the king should, in this situation, adhere to a general principle in political science, when, by deviating from it, he only attempted to be a pacificator between his subjects and their invaders, turn his influence with the one to the best interests and purposes of the other, and endeavour to put an end to the calamities of his country, and, if possible, his own.

MEMOIR.

PRESENTED BY MALLET DU PAN TO THE ALLIED SOVEREIGNS ON THE PART OF LOUIS XVI. ON THE 14TH OF JULY 1792.

DEUX objets inséparables se présentent dans la conduite et dans le but de la prochaine contre-révolution : d'abord les moyens de l'opérer ; ensuite ceux de la maintenir. Sans leur connection mutuelle, les moyens de succès pourraient contrarier ceux de stabilité, et les victoires ne feraient que préparer bientôt de nouveaux dangers, ainsi que de nouveaux troubles.

Les moyens de succès existent dans les combinaisons et dans les forces étrangères ; mais on ne doit pas se borner à considérer ici, et uniquement, la première résistance qu'opposeront les armées de la Révolution.

Il faut craindre les suites de leurs défaites ; de leur dispersion au moment où elles se replieront dans l'intérieur : l'appui que ces masses indisciplinées promettent aux chefs des factieux, qui tenteront de les réunir dans les Provinces Méridionales ; le passage de la présomption à la férocité ; l'habitude des violences subites qu'on a fait contracter au peuple à chaque moment de crise ; le deuil qu'un jour de frénésie ou l'ordre des démagogues, peut étendre sur a famille royale, et toutes celles dont les sentimens sont notés d'aristocratie ou seulement suspectes. Il faut prévenir encore une réunion des Révolutionnaires divisés, sans détruire les motifs de ralliement ; et réduire les résistances au moindre terme possible. On doit même tendre à leur donner pour adversaires, et à se ménager comme auxiliaires de la sûreté intérieure, ceux des Révolutionnaires que l'anarchie, la réflection, les désappointemens personnels et la tyrannie des Jacobins ont soulevés..

Pour y parvenir, il paraît indispensable d'employer simultanément la terreur et la confiance ; ou en d'autres termes, d'ôter aux uns l'espoir d'éviter les suites de la guerre qu'ils ont provoquée, de conserver aux autres l'espérance que ses suites leur seront moins funestes que l'oppression sous laquelle ils gémissent, et qu'une constitution qui ne peut pas même les défendre contre la puissance des clubs.

On ne comprendrait qu' imparfaitement l'importance de cette séparation des intérêts, dont peut dépendre la sauvegarde de l'intérieur ; et dont dépendra sûrement la facilité à faire rentrer le royaume entier dans l'obéissance, si l'on ne se forme une idée juste des différens partis qui agitent la capitale et s'y disputent l'autorité.

Presque toute entière elle est dans ce moment entre les mains des Jacobins ; majorité de l'Assemblée Nationale, places importantes, municipalités : le ministère vient de leur échapper ; aussitôt ils ont armé la multitude contre le roi : il est moralement impossible que le conseil actuel de sa majesté puisse se soutenir un mois entier.

Les Jacobins se divisent en deux sections, qui vont à peu près aux mêmes fins par des mesures différentes, et qui souvent brouillées par des *dissentimens* personnels, d'ambition ou de défiance, sont toujours prêtes à se réunir toutes les fois qu'il faut porter un nouveau coup à la prérogative royale, ou exécuter quelqu' attentat contre les classes supérieures.

La section actuellement dominante est présidée en chef par l'Abbé Sieyès, qui la gouverne avec Brissot, Condorcet, Péthion, Gensonné, Vergniaud, Gaudet, Manuel. Cette cabale avait formé le dernier ministère. Outre ses propres adhérents, elle rallie assez ordinairement à ses décisions la majorité des 250 fourbes, politiques ou poltrons, qui se sont classés dans l'Assemblée sous le sobriquet d'*Indépendans.*

Le projet de cette cabale n'est pas la république, nominativement, mais la république de fait ; par une réduction de la liste civile à cinq millions ; par le retranchement de la plûpart des attributs laissés au roi par un changement de dynastie dont le nouveau chef serait une espèce de président honoraire de la république ; auquel ils donneraient un conseil exécutif nommé par l'Assemblée ; c'est à dire par leur comité.

La seconde ligue qui partage les Jacobins, est composée des agitateurs grossiers, des républicains impatiens, des misérables qui ne pouvant supporter aucun gouvernement, désirent l'eternité de l'anarchie.

On ne leur découvre d'autre principe que celui d'une application immodérée et à rigueur, des *droits de l'homme*. A l'aide de cette charte ils aspirent à changer les loix et les officiers publics chaque semestre, à étendre leur nivellement sur toute autorité régulière, sur les éminences légales, sur les propriétés. Ils ne veulent point de roi : le seul régime qu'ils ambitionnent est la démocracie de la canaille délibérante.

Robespierre, Danton, Chabot, Merlin, Bazire, Thuriot, et cent autres de cette trempe, soutenus par le club des Cordeliers, et par les sociétés fraternelles, administrent cette faction désordonnée ; conservent un parti très nombreux dans le club des Jacobins, qui dispose de la plupart des libellistes populaires, des gens à piques, et de l'écume de la capitale.

La jalousie, une différence d'opinion au sujet de la guerre, jetèrent quelque désordre entre ces deux cabales : on vit le moment où elles allaient se séparer. La haine du gouvernement monarchique et la nécessité de tenir tête aux Feuillans ne tardèrent pas à les rapprocher.

L'une et l'autre opèrent par les mêmes moyens ; avec cette différence, que la première marche moins à découvert, ménage quelques bienséances, et conduit ses crimes avec moins d'impétuosité. Elle a sur l'autre l'avantage des raffinemens, des talens, et d'un plan dont les principaux fils sont tendus par l'Abbé Sieyès. Les plus vils agens, les perturbateurs de profession, les brigands, les fanatiques, les scélérats de tout ordre, voilà leur armée commune : ils ne la laissent pas un jour dans l'inaction.

Le Duc d'Orléans a des rapports avec la seconde de ces deux ligues : la seule dont il lui reste quelque chose à espérer par un bouleversement complet.

Il est moins facile de classer les Constitutionnels ou Feuillans. Ils forment une complication hétérogène de vues croisées ; d'inconséquences différentes ; de ressentimens sans analogie, de plans contradictoires ; d'une métaphysique enthousiaste ; d'ambitions deçues, qui cherchent à se relever.

Faute de pouvoir et de force réelle, les plus apparens de ce parti ont eu recours à l'intrigue. Ils manœuvrèrent au château des Tuileries, dans l'Assemblée, dans les départemens, et cherchèrent à s'emparer du gouvernement et du corps législatif, avec l'argent du roi. Leur principal objet était d'écraser les Jacobins, de faire chasser les membres actuels par les départemens et par le peuple ; de leur substituer une nouvelle assemblée à laquelle le roi eût appellé une partie des constituans ; et de modifier alors la constitution en renforçant la prérogative royale, et en instituant une seconde chambre élective par le peuple, sous de certaines conditions.

Cette entreprise, dont quelques alentours de LL. MM. ont cru trop facilement l'exécution, en la regardant comme un port de sûreté momentanée a été bientôt connue et culbutée. Le seul effet de ces intrigues a été d'enfermer M. Delessart à Orléans, de créer au roi de nouveaux dangers, de fournir des armes aux Jacobins, et d'allumer entr'eux et les Feuillans une haine implacable.

Les deux Lameth, Beaumetz, Barnave, Duport, D'André, dirigaient ce projet. Ils tentèrent de rassembler aux Feuillans tout ce qui voulait la constitution avec un roi, ou plutôt tout ce qui voulait la constitution sans être Jacobins.

MM. de la Fayette, de Narbonne, et une autre société de manipulateurs, suivaient des vues analogues, mais par d'autres moyens, principalement tirés de l'armée. En conséquence, M. de Narbonne appuya la guerre dans les conseils. Ces mesures, conformes au génie de leurs auteurs, et conduites avec la dernière étourderie, n'ont pas eu plus de succès que les précédentes.

Sous ces deux ordres de chefs divers se range la masse des Feuillans de l'Assemblée, da la capitale, et des provinces ; mais sans former un véritable parti ; car on n'y distingue ni doctrine, ni plan commun, ni système de moyens, ni ressources calculées. Le penchant qui a toujours entraîné une partie de ces Constitutionnels aux démarches les moins périlleuses, lui a préscrit guerre offensive aux aristocrates, sans force, et guerre défensive aux Jacobins, puissants. Une foule considérable a arboré ce pavillon par politique, afin d'échapper aux fureurs qui poursuivent les désapprobateurs trop déclarés de la constitution. Beaucoup d'administrateurs, de nouveaux juges, de bourgeois, de propriétaires des villes et des campagnes, et environ 100 membres de l'Assemblée, sont dans cette première catégorie. Elle comprend, en général, les honnêtes gens du parti, et ceux qui, de bonne foi, s'avouent l'impossibilité de soutenir le nouveau régime.

Après eux viennent les idolâtres de la constitution ; espèce de maniaques qu'un enthousiasme factice ou le bel esprit politique attachent à cette superstition. Ils se sont persuadés que sans les Jacobins, la constitution chéminerait ; et il n'a pas été possible de leur faire apercevoir encore, que la constitution seul enfantait, soutenait des Jacobins ; et que ceux de la Rue St. Honoré détruits, elle en ferait reparaître d'autres dans six mois.

Une troisième classe de Constitutionnels est inspirée par l'intérêt et par la vanité ; par intérêt pour ceux à qui le régime actuel a procuré des places et des avantages ; par la vanité, pour ceux à qui il a procuré quelque distinction. Une grande partie de la garde nationale non soldée, est dirigée par l'un ou l'autre de ces deux mobiles.

Presque généralement, on découvre dans ces trois catégories un mécontentement prononcé ; une incertitude complette sur la durée de la constitution ; un penchant d'instinct et de raison à se rallier au roi, et encore plus de haine contre les Jacobins que contre les aristocrates.

En avant d'eux, ainsi que nous l'avons dit, sont les esprits plus

déliés, qui, avec l'ambition d'être chefs, n'ont jamais pu y parvenir
du moment où ils ont délaissé les moyens pervers par lesquels ils
ont concouru à opérer et à soutenir la Révolution.

Il est douteux qu'on rassemblât dix de ces démagogues détrônés
concordans dans leurs vues, et dans leurs motifs de conduite.

Quelques-uns ont horreur des crimes, et veulent sincèrement
sauver le roi et la monarchie.　D'autres n'aspirent qu'à la domination, qu'à élever leur faction sur celle des Jacobins, et à se rendre
maîtres de l'autorité.　De troisièmes s'accommoderaient d'une
contre-révolution qui leur laisserait une grande influence, ou qui,
du moins, ne les replongerait pas dans l'humiliation et l'obscurité.

A côté de ceux-ci se trouvent des hommes, auxquels une conduite
odieuse, pendant deux ans et demi, inspire, sinon des remords, du
moins des craintes ; qui sans défendre leurs torts, appréhendent
d'en être punis, qui frémissent à la vue du triomphe des classes
envers lesquelles ils n'ont eu aucun ménagement ; et dont la contre-
révolution, sans beaucop offenser peut-être leurs opinions actuelles,
mortifierait toutes leurs passions.

Ces constitutionnaires, réels ou prétendus, embrassent la très
grande majorité des citoyens de tout ordre qui ont voulu et adopté
la Revolution : mais avec des opinions chancelantes ; avec des
idées irréconciliables entr'elles ; avec la sottise de gémir des effets
en jurant de maintenir les causes ; avec un défaut total de caractère,
d'union, de hardiesse, et ainsi mélangés de romanciers politiques,
d'écrivains à système, de phrasiers, d'intriguans, de Machiavelistes
sans vue et sans nerf, ce parti constitutionel n'a jamais eu qu'une
consistance artificielle et passagère.

On ne parlera point ici de la section particulière, qui, avant les
forfaits de Versailles, s'était placée entre les deux premiers ordres
et les feseurs de la constitution actuelle ; c'est à dire, des partisans
d'un corps législatif en deux divisions, dont l'une de chambre de
pairs, sur la formation de laquelle les adhérens de ce système
réprésentatif ne présentèrent jamais d'idée distincte.　Quoique
persévérant dans leurs opinions, presque toujours aussi mal enten-
dues que mal jugées ; mais aujourd'hui modifiées par une funeste
expérience qui leur manquait, ils sont tout réunis à la nécessité de
rétablir l'autorité royale dans la force et la dignité compatible avec
le dégré de liberté publique que peut supporter le gouvernement
d'un grand empire.　Ils sont unanimes à redemander le clergé, la
religion nationale, la noblesse, les grands tribunaux.　On n'a à
craindre de leur part aucune espèce d'opposition, parcequ'il n'en
est pas un qui ne préférât pas même la monarchie absolue aux lois
monstrueuses du moment, et à l'autorité des hommes qui les ont
instituées.

II.

La carte politique qui vient d'être crayonnée doit faire pressentir
les effets divers que produiront sur les esprits, l'approche, les pro-

grès, l'existence de la contre-révolution, suivant les formes et les
mesures par lesquelles elle s'opérera.

Evidemment, elle frappera dans des sens différens ces tribus
désunies, dont les passions, les principes, les intérêts, se rencon-
trent sur certains points et se divisent sur tous les autres.

La politique prescrit donc de ménager ceux de ces intérêts qui
peuvent se concilier avec l'objet fundamental de la contre-révolution ; et dont la négligence rendrait commun à la masse entière de
révolutionnaires, le désir et le dessein d'une opposition prolongée.

Tout ce qui sert à désarmer les résistances et à faciliter la soumission doit être employé ; hors, le vrai moyen de généraliser celles-
là, et de retarder celle-ci, serait de fournir aux uns et aux autres
des motifs égaux de persévérer dans la rebellion.

Ces considérations ne peuvent s'appliquer à la tête, et à une
partie des Jacobins.   On ne les subjuguera que par l'effroi.
Leurs maximes, leur plan, leur example, ne permettent aucun pro-
cédé de confiance.   Ils n'ont d'intérêt que celui du crime ; d'autres
ressources que le crime.   Les ménagemens leur paraîtraient des
aveux de timidité, et les enhardiraient.   Le force se montrera donc
à leur égard dans l'appareil le plus menaçant ; le manifeste considérera ces corporations, qui font le scandale et l'horreur des trois
quarts de la nation, comme des sociétés excommuniées, auxquelles
on ne laisse aucune espérance d'échapper, ni de grâce pour leur
doctrine.   La vie sauvée est le seul prix qu'on puisse promettre à
ceux d'entr'eux dont l'égarement ou le fanatisme n'ont pas com-
mandé des forfaits ; et qui quitteront les drapeaux de leurs indignes
chefs.

Eux seuls ont provoqué la guerre : sur eux doit en tomber le
châtiment.   Mais cette grande vérité qu'on ne saurait annoncer
d'une manière trop comminatoire, doit ouvrir une issue au reste
beaucoup plus nombreux des révolutionnaires mitigés.   Il serait
injuste et dangereux de les confondre avec les factieux effrénés qui
maîtrisent le royaume ; car alors, par nécessité ou par faiblesse, ils
se rejetteraient dans leurs bras, et se rendraient vraisemblablement,
ne fusse que par inertie, les complices de leur opposition et de leurs
enterprises ultérieures.   Envers cette majorité, la sagesse conseille
l'emploi simultané de la terreur et de la confiance.

De la *terreur*, car elle seule peut détruire les illusions dont
beaucoup d'entr'eux persistent à s'étourdir ; inspirer quelque courage aux âmes faibles que le peur des Jacobins, ou l'habitude,
redonneraient à la faction dominante, s'ils ne la voyaient pas à la
veille de périr : faire une impression profonde sur des esprits
flottans, ou séduits par des erreurs en leur montrant le dernier jour
des chimères : balancer chez d'autres le faux point d'honneur qui
les entraîne encore à la défense de la constitution ; et surtout
enlever aux chefs des Feuillans l'espoir sur lequel ils ont porté
toutes leurs vues depuis six mois ; celui de se mettre en état, de

faire accommodement les armes à la main, et de finir par une capitulation.

La *confiance* soutiendra l'effet de la terreur, le conduira au résultat désirable, de réduire les résistances exclusivement à celle des Jacobins, et de contrebalancer dans l'intérieur, durant les dernières crises, leur influence, qui peut amener encore de nouvelles catastrophes.

Cette confiance n'est autre chose que la sécurité pour l'avenir. Elle naîtra de l'assurance qu'on ne prétend pas confondre des factieux, pour qui rien n'a été sacré avec des hommes abusés ; les égaremens d'esprit, avec la perversité ; des opinions erronées, avec un code de crimes, d'immoralité, d'anarchie. Non seulement cette distinction flattera l'amour propre des constitutionnaires ; elle leur paraîtra, de plus, une preuve d'équité ; elle leur montrera une sauvegarde ; et on ne peut les supposer assez insensés pour partager la résistance des Jacobins, lorsqu'ils n'auront pas les mêmes dangers à craindre.

Elle naîtra du soin que l'on prendra de détruire les appréhensions, répandues, de vengeances méditées, d'implacables ressentimens, d'oppression, qui envelopperait également les torts et les délits.

Elle naîtra enfin, et plus particulièrement, de l'opinion, que le roi seul sera l'arbitre du sort des différens partis, et le pacificateur du royaume ; qu'on réserve à lui seul la destinée des lois ainsi que celles des personnes ; en un mot, que les unes et les autres ne seront pas livrées à discrétion et exclusivement aux émigrés, ni aux puissances étrangères.

La tyrannie des Jacobins a forcé les Feuillans et la plus grande partie des révolutionnaires honteux, ou à-demi convertis, de considérer enfin l'autorité royale comme leur ancre de miséricorde. Si demain, ils triomphaient de leurs adversaires, nul doute qu'ils ne fortifiassent sans délai la puissance du roi. Depuis trois mois la plupart se fussent rangés autour de sa majesté s'ils avaient eu autant de courage que de bonne volonté ; et si les Jacobins, par leur infatigable activité, n'eussent suspendu les poignards de leurs assassins, et les torches de leurs incendiaires, sur quiconque osait avouer son attachmement pour le monarque.

III.

Les dispositions précédentes dépendent des puissances belligérantes et des princes et émigrés Français. Elles sont le vœu du roi, le conseil que lui dictent des lumières positives, et l'intérêt de tous. Sa majesté attache la plus haute importance à ce que ses representations soyent méditées. Elle va jusqu'à joindre ses prières aux instances pour obtenir la déférence qu'elle sollicite. Elle la sollicite dans la pleine indépendance de sa réflection et de sa volonté ; nulle impulsion étrangère n'a préparé ni produit ses recommandations à cet égard : elles résultent de la connaissance

exacte qu'a sa majesté des dispositions publiques, par les comptes
journaliers qui lui sont fidèlement rendus de la capitale et des
départemens ; ensorte que personne dans le royaume on au dehors,
ne réunit autant d'informations certaines, pour constater ce qu'il
faut craindre ou espérer de l'intérieur, suivant la nature des formes
et des mesures par lesquelles on développera la force extérieure.
Tout deviendra facile dans le présent et l'avenir si l'on concourt
aux vues du roi : tout se compliquera, peut-être, de périls, d'incertitudes, de difficultés, si l'on s'en écarte.

La force doit remettre la monarchie debout ; mais c'est à l'opinion
à l'affermir : c'est dans les cœurs qu'il faut planter les racines de
stabilité ; c'est à féconder une soumission morale que doivent se
diriger les moyens de soumission forcée, et les efforts de quiconque
veut prévenir de nouveaux naufrages. On ne considérera dans
cette note que les motifs de persuasion qui concernent les royalistes expatriés ; sa majesté attend leur condescendance à ses
intentions éclairées, de la magnanimité et de l'attachement des
princes de son sang, ainsi que des sentimens de la valeureuse
noblesse qui a tout sacrifié au désir de sauver la monarchie, et des
citoyens de tous ordres qui ont partagé ses souffrances et son exil.

Le roi desire que par un concours offensif et trop distinct, leur
participation à la guerre actuelle ne lui fasse point perdre le caractère de guerre étrangère, faite de puissance à puissance. Sa
majesté n'a jamais mis en doute une résolution unanime de leur
part de lui confier le soin des intérêts compromis, ne que les
princes se considéreraient comme parties lésées dans un différent
dont l'arbitrage sera exercé par sa majesté lorsque le sort des armes
aura fait rendre la liberté nécessaire à l'exercice de la puissance
royale.

Sans doute de trop justes ressentimens appelleraient les princes
et la noblesse à venger trois ans d'outrages et à attaquer, eux-
mêmes, d'aussi criminels usurpateurs : sans doute il fut un moment où la guerre civile n'eût été de la part des opprimés que
l'exercice du droit de repousser la force par la force. Les calamités publiques et particulières auraient peut-être été moins
longues sans être plus affreuses.

Mais la guerre extérieure, dont la Providence inspira la déclaration aux factieux, est destinée à faire, maintenant, avec moins
de périls, de malheurs, et d'incertitudes, ce qu'on pourrait espérer
de la guerre civile.

Détournons de dessus la France la cumulation de ces deux fléaux.
Ils s'étendraient de la manière la plus affreuse sur trois cent mille
familles dispersées au milieu d'un peuple frénétique : ils mettraient
en danger les jours du roi, ceux de la reine et de la famille royale :
ils feraient renverser le trône, livrer la propriété au pillage, égorger
les royalistes, les prêtres restés dans le royaume et menacés : ils
rallieraient aux Jacobins les révolutionnaires moins forcenés : ils
ranimeraient une exaltation qui tend à s'éteindre, et rendrait plus

opiniâtre une résistance qui fléchira devant les premiers succés décisifs ; lorsqu'on verra des intermédiaires entre les émigrés armés et la partie de la nation à réduire.

Le cœur humain ne change point. On craint de ceux qu'on a cruellement offensés : on n'espère de pardon de ceux envers qui on fut impitoyable. Le peuple est incapable de s'élever à l'espoir d'une générosité dont il n'a pas le sentiment.

Les différentes factions qui ont bouleversé l'empire redoutent, en conséquence, de rencontrer dans les princes et les émigrés, des ennemis, dont ils ne doivent attendre aucun ménagement. Ils ne les entrevoyent qu'entourés de chaînes, de bourreaux, de flétrissures, d'instrumens d'oppression.

Ce préjugé a été fomenté sans relâche par les libellistes de la Révolution, par les harangueurs à la tribune, par les efforts des assemblées et des clubs ; et s'il faut le dire, la légèreté des discours de quelques têtes jeunes et ardentes, la virulence maladroite et toujours menaçante de quelques écrivains royalistes, qui ne parlent que potences ; enfin le silence de longanimité que les princes ont cru devoir à leur dignité, au milieu des imputations renaissantes et des proscriptions de l'Assemblée, ont envenimé, enraciné cette prévention. Il est aisé d'en apercevoir les suites, dans le cas, où les émigrés, réunis en corps, dirigeraient des opérations offensives contre les frontières du royaume.

La fureur, la résistance, la soif du carnage, se porteraient contr'eux : on laisserait les autres points à découvert ; on abandonnerait la France aux étrangers afin de la fermer aux émigrés. Si l'on n'égorgeait pas les prisonniers, il n'est aucun genre de violence dont ils ne devinssent les victimes. Le stoicisme des braves militaires qui marcheront sous les étendards des princes serait à pure perte contre des hommes qui ne respectent ni les lois de la guerre, ni celles de l'honneur. Qu'on n'allègue pas la crainte des représailles. A-t-elle prévenu le meurtre des Tyroliens ? La férocité populaire ; celle des soldats licencieux qui ont brisé tous les freins, furent-elles jamais subordonnées au calcul de la prévoyance ?

La première nouvelle d'une action entre les royalistes et les troupes de l'Assemblée Nationale, deviendraient le prétexte de nouveaux forfaits et le signal d'une boucherie dans tous les lieux où les clubs dominent les autorités administratives.

En attirant eux-mêmes les armées étrangères sur le royaume, les Jacobins ont affaibli l'opinion que cette invasion résultait des efforts des émigrés. Contre leur intention, cette extravagante démarche a procuré quelque sauvegarde aux royalistes de l'intérieur. Le peuple des départemens a cessé de menacer de massacrer et de piller les adhérens de ceux que les siens allaient combattre sur la frontière. L'approche prématurée des royalistes du dehors, et leur réunion distincte pour s'ouvrir, séparèment des forces étrangères, un passage dans le royaume, redonnerait à ces dispositions populaires toute leur énergie.

Il ne faut pas s'exagérer les effets de la terreur. Certainement si le peuple est affrayé, ses excès ne sont pas aussi probables ; mais ce n'est chose ni aussi prompte, ni aussi facile qu'on se l'imagine d'inspirer une crainte salutaire à des chefs dont tout atteste l'ignorance et la présomption ; qui sont eux-mêmes dupes des illusions qu'ils ont créés ; qui se croyent invincibles derrière leurs énumérations civiques ; et qui calculent la guerre comme ils ont calculé la législation, par l argumentation des nombres. Sans doute la réflexion et la raison peuvent les désabuser ; mais s'ils étaient raisonnables et réfléchissans, leur conduite offrirait-elle depuis six mois une suite d'actes de fureur ?

On ne réussira pas plus facilement à pénétrer le peuple d'une épouvante efficace. En général, il n'existe pour la multitude d'autres dangers que ceux dont elle touche les instrumens et la présence matérielle. Plus spécialement encore, ce caractère appartient au peuple de Paris, dont l'ignorance et l'inconcevable crédulité sont le jouet des prestiges les plus grossiers : qui, journellement, est obsédé d'écrits, de fables, de discoureurs publiques, de présidens d'attroupemens, de lecteurs de cabarets et d'atteliers, associés pour l'entretenir de ses victoires, de ses conquêtes, de la détresse de ses ennemis ; de l'immensité de sa puissance, des talens de ses chefs, de l'enthousiasme que la liberté Française inspire à tous les peuples et à toutes les armées. Quiconque n'a pas suivi ces rendezvous d'instruction où l'on aiguillonne sans cesse les préjugés populaires : quiconque n'a pas questionné les divers états ; à commencer par ce qui s'appelle la bonne bourgeoisie de Paris, et à finir par la populace, n'aura qu'une imparfaite idée des succès de la démagogie en ce genre, comme dans tous les autres.

Ces réflexions, fondées sur des observations suivies, commanderont peut-être aux augustes frères de sa majesté, à leur conseil, et aux royalistes, de subordonner leur courage impatient à la prudence ; et une fois armés, de n'agir qu'avec les précautions, à l'époque, et par des mesures , qui puissent prévenir les malheurs inséparables d'un plan différent.

Par les mêmes motifs, il paraîtra sans doute convenable que dans le cas où les princes feraient précéder leur mouvemens d'une déclaration, ce manifeste soit calculé sur celui des puissances ; qu'on s'y renferme dans des assurances générales, en évitant tout ce qui prêterait aux commentaires perfides des factieux ; qu'on y présente les princes comme les libérateurs du peuple ; qu'on promette paix, sûreté liberté légitime ; qu'enfin l'on écarte tout ce qui manifesterait une volonté de faire prévaloir telle ou telle forme de gouvernement ; et qu'on se borne à déclarer que l'on agit pour faire rendre au roi sa liberté ; et pour rétablir le governement monarchique, tel que sa majesté a entendu le circonscrire.

Sa majesté très chrétienne, pleine de confiance dans les sentimens généreux et dans la sagesse des cours de Vienne et de Berlin,
se plaît à espérer qu'elles considèrent du même œil sa situation,
celle de la monarchie Française, et les moyens de terminer la
guerre actuelle, sans exposer l'intérieur du royaume à de nouvelles
catastrophes.

Elle désire, elle sollicite, que le manifeste qui précédera les opérations, soit établi sur des bases analogues à celles dont on vient
d'exposer l'importance ; et que la promptitude de sa publication
prévienne des calamités imminentes.

Elle se persuade que les effets à attendre des craintes à inspirer
résulteront d'abord de la certitude qu'acquerront les factieux, qu'en
déclarant la guerre à sa majesté apostolique, ils l'ont, par le fait,
déclarée à l'Europe même ; et que le manifeste des cours de Vienne
et de Berlin exprime des sentimens ainsi que des projets communs
aux différentes puissances qui ont formé le concert.

Le peuple mesure toujours ses dangers sur le nombre de ses
ennemis : ses chefs perdront la ressource de le tromper, comme ils
l'ont fait jusqu'à ce jour, par l'assurance qui ni le corps Germanique,
ni les puissances du Nord, ni celles du Midi, n'épouseraient les
intérêts de la querelle actuelle; une réunion si menaçante déchirera
le bandeau des illusions ; et en imposera avec d'autant plus d'efficace, que ni l'Assemblée, ni le peuple, n'y sont préparés.

Dans le même but, il paraît essentiel que le manifeste ne laisse
aucun espoir de voir poser les armes avant que le roi soit mis en
liberté, et son autorité légitime rétablie.

Tout ce qui laisserait entrevoir la possibilité de se soustraire au
sort de la guerre, par des négociations dilatoires, ou par des ac-
commodemens imparfaits, retarderait la soumission et préparerait
au roi de nouveaux dangers ; car on ferait servir de nouvelles violences, auxquelles il succomberait probablement, à le forcer de
rallentir l'activité des puissances belligérantes.

L'impression de terreur résultera encore, et principalement,
d'une déclaration énergique à l'Assemblée Nationale, à la capitale,
aux corps administratifs, aux municipalités, aux individus, qu'on
les rend personnellement garants, dans leurs corps et biens, du
moindre préjudice apporté à la personne de leurs majestés, de leurs
familles, et aux citoyens quelconques.

Cette déclaration doit frapper encore plus particulièrement sur
la ville de Paris.

On soutiendra la terreur par la confiance, en déclarant qu'on est
armé contre les factieux, non contre le roi et la nation ; qu'on
prend la défense des gouvernemens légitimes et des peuples, contre
une anarchie féroce, qui menace la tranquillité de l'Europe entière,
prépare les plus horribles calamités, et brise, entre les hommes, les
liens sociaux.

Cette forme enlevera aux factions un argument dont elles ont
tiré et dont elles chercheront encore à tirer le plus grand avantage ;
savoir que c'est ici la guerre *des rois contre les peuples*.

La confiance, ainsi fondée sur cette distinction entre les factieux, maîtres du royaume, et la reste de la nation, serait fortifiée encore par l'attention à ne proposer, à n'imposer aucune forme de gouvernement; et à déclarer qu'on s'arme pour le rétablissement de la monarchie; pour la liberté du monarque; pour la réstauration de la paix.

Cette mesure fléchira la plupart des révolutionnaires lassés ou incertains, qui, sans vouloir la constitution actuelle, craignent le retour des grands abus, les vengeances, l'oppression, et qui savent que S. M. T. C. sera leur plus sûr protecteur contre ces dangers; et desquels on peut attendre la soumission dès qu'on leur présentera une issue sans ignominie, une monarchie sans arbitraire, des loix protectrices des personnes et des propriétés.

La profonde sagacité de LL. MM. I. et R. leur aura sans doute fait déjà pressentir ces observations : la destinée du roi, de la reine, de la famille royale, du trône, de tous les propriétaires et du royaume en général, peuvent en dépendre.

Mais l'accélération du manifeste est en ce moment l'objet principal de la sollicitude de S. M. T. C. Elle l'invoque avec des instances redoublées : tout ce qui l'entoure, tout ce qui juge sainement les mouvemens de Paris, est unanime dans cette invocation.

La guerre est en ce moment oubliée à Paris et dans les provinces : on ne s'en occupe, on ne s'en intimide pas plus que des batailles des Anglais dans l'Hindostan. Les Gazettes ont beau annoncer la marche des troupes étrangères : cent libelles populaires rassurent chaque jour les Parisiens. Le silence absolu des puissances depuis la déclaration hostile de l'Assemblée; la guerre défensive du Brabant, des revers sans conséquence, des affronts qu'on ne sent point; la formation nécessairement lente des armées; le délabrement, la dispersion, la détresse où l'on a vu rester les émigrés Français; tout a concouru, à accroître l'étourdissement. Les appréhensions des plus timides ne vont pas au-delà de l'idée, qu'avant d'oser les combattre, on leur proposera un accommodement dont ils se moquent, ainsi que du danger que paraît courir leurs frontières.

C'est à ces différentes causes de sécurité qu'on doit les progrès de l'autorité des Jacobins, leurs dernières entreprises, et l'affreux attentat du 20 Juin. On leur a laissé le tems de mûrir la combinaison de nouvelles catastrophes : le moindre délai leur donnera celui de les exécuter.

On ne doit pas s'y méprendre. Si cette épouvantable journée du 20 Juin; cette inouïe scène au milieu des forfaits de la Révolution, où l'on a vu LL. MM. livrées à des outrages, exposées à des périls qui font frémir l'imagination : si ce jour de deuil et d'opprobre ne s'est pas terminé par deux régicides, il faut en rendre grâce à une seule circonstance.

LL. MM. ont été uniquement sauvées par une de ces impressions populaires que l'habileté des démagogues ne peut prévenir.

Ils n'étaient pas maîtres de tenir en garde cette populace contre l'ascendant de la majesté royale, de la présence de ses souverains, de l'effroi involontaire qui enchaînait leurs bras régicides, à la voix des augustes personnes dont l'héroïque fermeté désarma ces âmes sanguinaires.

Dans l'alternative de consommer leur crime en rallumant la fureur de la multitude, ou de la réserver à de nouveaux attentats, la politique dicta aux chefs, de ne pas se découvrir aussi manifestement ; de ne pas prendre sur eux la responsabilité exclusive du dernier forfait à commettre, et de ne pas s'enlever la ressource de la rejetter sur l'égarement du peuple.

Depuis cette époque les mêmes périls demeurent suspendus sur la tête de LL. MM. Ce n'est qu'à force d'artifices et de moyens précaires qu'on défend encore leur existence. D'un jour à l'autre la France et l'Europe peuvent être dans le deuil. LL. MM. comptent les minutes jusqu'à la publication du manifeste : leur vie est une affreuse agonie.

Dans le courant de ce mois, les factieux rassemblent à Paris une nouvelle fédération de leurs satellites. Si les dispositions extérieures ne contrabalancent pas la hardiesse de leurs complots ; si le courage du roi dans cette fatale extrémité n'est pas secondé par la déclaration des puissances, et par la rapidité d'opérations actives, il faut s'envelopper la tête et se soumettre à la Providence.

L'assassinat de LL. MM. serait le signal d'un massacre général : les ressorts qui supportent encore en France la société ne tiennent plus qu'à un fil : un bouleversement effroyable la menace, et dans moins de cinq semaines elle sera peut-être dans un état pire que St. Domingue.

Quelle réstauration opérer alors sur un pareil entassement de calamités ! La guerre, son but, ses effets, tout changerait de nature. Mais il suffit d'avoir présenté ce tableau avec la franchise d'une rigoureuse vérité, pour placer une confiance entière dans l'humanité, et dans les lumières des cours de Vienne et de Berlin.

Présenté au Roi de Prusse le 14 Juillet 1792 ; et le lendemain à Sa Majesté Impériale et Royale, ainsi qu'à Mons. le Vice Chancelier d'Etat, Comte de Cobentzel, et au Baron de Spielman, Premier Référendaire de la Chancellerie d'Etat.